ADENAUER

ADENAUER

The Father of the New Germany

Charles Williams

JOHN WILEY & SONS, INC.
NEW YORK • CHICHESTER • WEINHEIM • BRISBANE • SINGAPORE • TORONTO

For Jane

No part of this publication may be reproduced, stored in a retrieval system, or transmitted in any form or by any means, electronic, mechanical, photocopying, recording,
scanning, or otherwise, except as permitted under Section 107 or 108 of the 1976
United States Copyright Act, without either the prior written permission of the
Publisher, or authorization through payment of the appropriate per-copy fee to the
Copyright Clearance Center, 222 Rosewood Drive, Danvers, MA 01923, (978)750-
8400, fax (978)750-4744. Requests to the Publisher for permission should be addressed
to the Permissions Department, John Wiley & Sons, Inc., 605 Third Avenue, New York,
NY 10158-0012, (212)850-6011, fax (212)850-6008, email:
PERMREQ@WILEY.COM.

This publication is designed to provide accurate and authoritative information in regard
to the subject matter covered. It is sold with the understanding that the publisher is not
engaged in rendering professional services. If professional advice or other expert assistance is required, the services of a competent professional person should be sought.

Library of Congress Cataloging-in-Publication Data

Williams, Charles
Adenauer : the father of the new Germany / Charles Williams.
p. cm.
Includes bibliographical references and index.
ISBN 0-471-40737-2 (alk. paper)
1. Adenauer, Konrad, 1876–1967.   2. Heads of state—Germany (West)—Biography.
3. Germany (West)—Politics and government.   I. Title.

DD259.2.W518 2001
943.087'092—dc21
[B]
00-047312

Printed in the United States of America

10 9 8 7 6 5 4 3 2 1

CONTENTS

CONTENTS

Contents

LIST OF ILLUSTRATIONS

PIBB: Presse- und Informationsamt der Bundesregierung, Bundesbildstelle, Bonn
StBKAH: Stiftung Bundeskanzler-Adenauer-Haus, Bad Honnef

PREFACE

The story of Adenauer's life can best be seen as three stories in one. The first is the story of a homeland: the land of the Rhine, that ambiguous and mythic river which — like Adenauer's own life — rises in obscurity, gains strength and momentum in its course, but ends in doubt and confusion. The second is the story of the emergence of a fourth Germany out of the shipwreck of the three earlier Germanies through which he lived. The third is the story of a man who lived a full and occasionally dangerous life, who was disliked by many for his complex and difficult character but who, at the end of his biblical span, summoned the energy and ambition to bring his country back into the civilised world from what seemed to be permanent ostracism and into a new Europe based on the recognition of individual freedom, tolerance and, above all, democracy.

The passage of years and the onward march of events provide another peg on which to hang the triple story. The collapse of the Berlin Wall in 1989 and the subsequent reunification of Germany have brought to light new sources of information from the former Soviet Union and its satellites. Moreover, distance lends its own perspective. It may now be possible to put Adenauer's whole life, with its three stories merging into one, into the context of history. That he can legitimately be called a great leader is no longer in doubt; but who this difficult man was and why the accolade of greatness seems appropriate needs to be explored and examined. This I have attempted to do in this book.

Pant-y-Rhiw
April 2000

PART ONE

The Kaiser's Germany

I

COLOGNE: 1876

*'Die Eindrücke im Elternhaus sind bestimmend für das
Leben eines Menschen'**

KONRAD HERMANN JOSEPH Adenauer was born in 1876, at half-past three in the morning of Thursday the fifth of January, the eve of the Epiphany, as he himself might have put it, of Our Lord Jesus Christ. The birth took place at his parents' home in Cologne – Balduinstrasse 6, the birth certificate records – and, although occurring at an obviously inconvenient hour, seems to have passed without unusual incident. The future Chancellor of the Federal Republic of Germany, his parents' third son, accordingly arrived into this world, admittedly by the light of an oil-lamp and on a cold winter night, in good health and apparently lusty spirits.

It was not until the following day, the feast of the Epiphany itself, that the baby's father, Johann Konrad, made his visit to the official registrar to record the birth. No doubt he took time, after absorbing the emotion of the safe delivery of a third son, to go to Mass to celebrate both the event and the feast in the appropriate manner. Given his intense and unremitting piety, it

---

* 'A man's life is determined by the first impressions received in the home of his parents': Adenauer, quoted in P. Weymar, *Konrad Adenauer: Die autorisierte Biographie* (Munich, Kindler Verlag, 1955), p. 13.

3

would have been the natural thing to do. Furthermore, it would not have given any offence to the registrar. Catholic feast days, however important in the Church's calendar, were not recognised as public holidays by the Prussian administration of the Rhine Province, and the rich ceremony of the Church could be conveniently followed by the more prosaic – but equally laborious – dealings with the civil authority. It was accepted, with understanding courtesy, that the two cultures had to live side by side.

The birth certificate was duly inscribed by the registrar in the Prussian script, read out to the father, and countersigned by him as a true record, with the child's names properly spelled out. Konrad Adenauer was by that act formally registered as a citizen of Prussia, born of parents of the Catholic 'religion' – as the certificate has it – and resident in Cologne. Thus was illustrated, even at his birth, one of the paradoxes of Adenauer's long life: a profound attachment to his birthplace of Cologne and to its Roman Catholicism coupled with, and on occasions conflicting with, an equally profound loyalty to a Germany which included a largely Protestant Prussia.

In fact, the origin of that paradox lies even further back in time. The truth is that, whatever their, or his, subsequent pretensions, Adenauer's parents were themselves of what was known, then as now, as 'mixed stock'. His father, for instance, Johann Konrad Adenauer, the son of a baker from Bonn – who had moved to Messdorf (at that time on the outskirts of but now a suburb of Bonn) when the bakery in Bonn failed financially – was by birth a Catholic Rhinelander. Yet at the age of eighteen he had volunteered to fight, with apparently every intention of pursuing a military career, for the King of Prussia. Adenauer's mother, Helena Scharfenberg, although claimed later to be 'pure Cologne' (and indeed she had been born there), was the granddaughter of an oboist in a regimental band from Bad Sachsa, in the Harz region of Saxony, who had settled in Cologne almost by accident. Furthermore, her father, August Scharfenberg, was a Protestant, and although he married a good Catholic shopkeeper's daughter from Bonn there was no disguising the fact that their daughter was the product of a mixed religious marriage – not at all the 'native of the Rhineland' that her son later claimed.[1]

True, Johann Konrad's progress in the Prussian Army was far from remarkable. He spent fifteen years in relatively undistinguished service, rising to the rank of Warrant Officer in the 7th Westphalian Infantry Regiment at the time of the Austro-Prussian War of 1866. The high point was at the

dreadful battle of Königgrätz, where he took part in the storming of the heavily defended village of Problus and was, like many others on that day, badly wounded. As such, however, his story is probably no more than typical of the ordinary Prussian soldier of the times.

There were, of course, later elaborations of Johann Konrad's heroism at Königgrätz, revealed when his third son had risen to eminence. But the assertions that he was 'finally rescued from under a pile of dead and wounded . . . clutching a captured Austrian flag',[2] or that 'he had been promoted to Second Lieutenant . . . for bravery in the face of the enemy',[3] both of them Adenauer's own description of the event – although at different times – are, to say the least, not supported by the surviving military records. The truth seems to be that Johann Konrad was awarded a Military Medal (2nd Class) for bravery on the day and was subsequently invalided out of the army, with promotion to the rank of Second Lieutenant 'as a full invalid temporarily incapable of fulfilling an occupation'.[4] Having rendered his undoubtedly courageous service to the King of Prussia, he deserved an honourable retirement. He was nonetheless recalled to the Prussian colours to serve as a non-combatant quartermaster in the Franco-Prussian War of 1870–71. At the end of that brief war he was finally discharged, with a modest war service medal and with what was certainly no more than a modest military pension.

Now returned to civilian life, and without any possibility of recall to military service, Johann Konrad had to face up to the future. He had no educational qualifications beyond attendance at primary school. He had been badly wounded, and both physically and mentally was a product, after all those years, of the Prussian Army. The prospect of a profitable job in the new Cologne of the triumphant German Empire was, under those circumstances, far from promising. Nevertheless, he managed to secure a clerical post in the Prussian judicial system, working in the administration of the courts for some thirty unspectacular years, starting his career as secretary to the Court of Appeals and ending it as Chief Secretary to the most senior court in Cologne, gaining in the process the proud title of *Kanzleirat*, or senior clerk.

In fact, it was as high a position as he could have hoped for without a university degree or diploma of any sort, and he only reached it by dogged application to the work in hand, boring as it undoubtedly was. 'He was a stern man,' wrote one of his contemporaries, 'not particularly likeable, but

highly responsible and conscientious.'[5] As a reward for conscientiousness he was in 1891 awarded the Order of the Red Eagle (4th Class). Although an apparently modest decoration, it was unusual for someone who had held no more than clerical office, and Johann Konrad must have been suitably proud. Indeed, in 1905 he was awarded an even higher honour, the *Kronenorden* (3rd Class), which was significant enough for it to be engraved on his gravestone. All in all, his second career was perhaps as good as he could have hoped for.

Johann Konrad Adenauer may not have been particularly likeable but he left a profound impression on his third son. At home he was a humourless and unrelenting father, always correctly dressed, his military moustache and pointed beard properly clipped, his high collar reaching up to his chin, which in turn was set below an unsmiling mouth. Only his eyes betrayed the restrained disappointment of a man who would have wished to remain a fighting soldier but was condemned to spend his life at a desk as a clerk. Indeed, it seems that there were only two compensations for the disappointments of his working life: his religion and his family.

Both responsibilities were taken with ponderous seriousness. Religious observance for himself and his family was at the centre of life. Every day there were prayers at home in the morning and in the evening. Every workday, it is said, he used to stop on his way home to visit and say a prayer to the Black Madonna in the Kupfergasse. No meal could start without Grace, and on Sundays Mass at the Apostelkirche in the morning, and a further visit for silent, contemplative prayers in the late afternoon, were obligatory not just for him but for the whole family. At home there were frequent homilies on the nature of sin; and eternal hellfire, as well as the long, wasted half-life of purgatory, figured extensively in his admonitions to his wife and offspring. For a young child, it could hardly have been more daunting.

Religious observance apart, with his family Johann Konrad was equally stern in setting rules of behaviour. There was no question about who was the master in the home. He could easily lose his temper, and was quick to reprove any fault or misdemeanour. On the other hand, although with his children he was a disciplinarian — and must have been terrifying in his rage — he seems to have been genuinely concerned for their welfare and to have commanded great filial devotion and respect. Love was perhaps another matter; but even up to Johann Konrad's death his third son, at the age of thirty, would visit his father on his way back from work, and had his father's

photograph hung in his own bedroom at Rhöndorf throughout the long years that he lived there.

Johann Konrad was determined that his sons should have the educational advantages which he had never had. Access to higher education would, he believed, allow them to break through the class rigidities of the Cologne of the day. The gate once opened, they would march on through to a more ful-filling life than he himself had been able to live; and he scrimped and saved to that end. Admittedly, he was never known for his generosity with money, but in this case it was saving for good purpose. Education was the key to advancement, and Johann Konrad was set on providing the means for his sons to have it. Nor, to be fair, was it just a matter of money. When it came to it, he taught all his children himself between the ages of five and six, in the year before they went to school, to make sure that they were ahead of their contemporaries.

It was most likely in 1864, while his regiment was stationed in Cologne, that Johann Konrad, at the age of thirty-one, met his future wife Helena, then aged fifteen (even at that age, apparently, a devout Catholic). On his return from the Franco-Prussian War in 1871 he sought her hand in mar-riage. A match between two such children of the Church was, presumably after appropriate investigation by both sides, considered suitable. It was equally convenient that they were from the same social class – he a judicial clerk, she the daughter of a bank employee. Regrettably, however, there was to be little in the way of dowry that the bride could bring to her new hus-band.

So far, the account of the engagement and subsequent marriage seems simple and natural, and in keeping with the times. In later life, however, Konrad Adenauer promoted the unlikely story that his father would have pursued a military career had it not been for his meeting Helena. 'It was out of the question,' he is recorded as saying, 'for Scharfenberg, the small bank clerk, to provide the dowry then required for the bride of an officer. Lieutenant Adenauer would have been refused permission to marry. He decided to leave the army and become a court clerk . . . I know this from my mother.'[6] This version, to put it in the mildest manner, is hardly consistent with the recorded facts; but, if nothing else, it serves to demonstrate the abil-ity of Johann Konrad's third son in later years to modify the truth to what he perceived to be his advantage when it was required.

Although the Adenauer–Scharfenberg marriage was eminently suitable by the usual social standards, in the event the going was far from smooth. To start with, Helena was only twenty-two years old when she married, and had lived a secluded and conventional childhood and adolescence. Johann Konrad, on the other hand, was thirty-eight and had lived something of a colourful life already. In those circumstances, marital adjustment was bound to be difficult. Moreover, Helena was lively – not beautiful, with her square Saxon face and wide nose, but her eyes and mouth were ready to light up with laughter and a sense of fun. ('She used to sing all day long,' Adenauer's recollection runs, 'while doing her housework.'[7]) Johann Konrad, by contrast, was full of discipline and gloom.

Nevertheless, the couple seem to have settled down with no more than the usual early marital disputes. Johann Konrad rented a house in the Balduinstrasse. The house itself was small, as indeed were all the houses in what was, after all, a narrow alleyway in the centre of old Cologne. The outlook was no better than dismal. Three windows looked on to a feverish and insanitary street, along which the world seem to come and go the whole day long, the ladies picking up their skirts to avoid the dirt and the men protecting their hats from any bits of rubbish which were from time to time thrown out of the windows. The Adenauers' house had only two storeys, and the rooms were no more than 'nine or ten square feet'.[8] One, possibly the only, redeeming feature was a small garden at the back, with a tree, two vines, a vegetable patch and a small area of grass which was used for bleaching linen and which, with some imagination, might be considered to be a lawn. The young Konrad was allowed two small plots of his own, one for flowers and the other for radishes. 'This was the first lesson the earth taught,' Adenauer was later to say.[9]

As such, for a lower-middle-class family in Cologne at that time, the house was reasonable enough. But such was the parsimony of the father – perhaps, as it turned out, in a good cause – that the whole of the second floor, and part of the first, were let to paying guests. The ground floor was, as a result, very crowded. New babies had to sleep in their parents' bedroom; brothers had to share a room and even a bed. Furthermore, Helena not only had to look after the 'various tenants'[10] but also wanted to make some extra money for the household by taking in needlework and sewing. It is little wonder that the children, as and when they were born and started to grow, caused the disruption that is inevitable in the confined space of any small house, even if they were able to go out on fine days to play in the little garden. Each, in its turn, demanded attention, and would cry, scream or fight for it depending on age, relative strength and seniority. In this matter, the third son was doubtless no different from the rest.

By the standards of the day the baptism of the new baby seems to have taken some time to organise. In the event, it was three weeks before the ceremony took place. Presumably relatives had to be advised but, above all, godparents had to be selected. None of this was easy, not least the choice of godparents. In truth, there seem to have been few volunteers, and the one whose name has survived – Konrad Tonger – could hardly be described as of great distinction. In fact, he seems to have been something of an odd fish. He was a dealer in bits and pieces, and had accumulated a modest fortune – although nobody knows quite how. He never married, and ended up as a bachelor lodger in Balduinstrasse 6, making friends with his landlady and the rest of the family. He was an obvious candidate for recruitment as godfather to the new Adenauer son, and seems to have readily assented. In return, he presented his godson with a gold watch and left to the parents a legacy of his entire fortune of 30,000 marks, designed to provide for the proper education of his landlady's three sons. Sadly, his generosity, at least as far as the third son was concerned, was in vain. The legacy was invested unwisely and dribbled away (Tonger himself having died when his godson was only three years old, cared for until his death, as it happened, by Helena Adenauer). Only the gold watch survived, treasured by his godson and carefully preserved throughout the long years at Rhöndorf.

The baptism duly took place on Thursday, 25 January 1876 at the nearby Mauritiuskirche. As a piece of architecture, the church was not particularly striking. It suffered from the wave of mid-century modernisation that overtook many attractive Romanesque churches during those materialistic years. In December 1859 the old church had been demolished – apparently to nobody's particular regret – and replaced with a new construction designed in what became known as the 'Cologne Historical' style by the then diocesan architect Vinzenz Statz. The style, if it can be called that, was in practice little more than a pastiche, but the church had a certain cavernous grandeur about it (and, indeed, survived the Second World War reasonably intact until pulled down in its turn in the 1950s to give way to a more modern building – to which Adenauer presented a bronze bell in 1959).

The ceremony was certainly simple, and in the lowest possible key. It was not the time in the Adenauer house for expensive fripperies, and it is certain that after the christening 'no party was given'.[11] The business properly done, life could return to normal. Not that normal life was easy. Apart from the new baby, the two elder sons, August and Hans, also needed looking after, and as Konrad grew in years the mouths that needed feeding became more difficult to satisfy. Money was scarce – one Christmastide the children agreed to go without meat for several Sundays in succession so that their parents could afford to buy a tree and candles for the feast itself. The children had to help, too, in the house, and each brother passed on his clothes to the next brother down. Even the young Konrad had to earn his keep: at the age of five, he recalled, 'I helped [my mother] by pulling out the tacking threads [of the aprons she was sewing] . . . I was paid one pfennig for each apron.'[12] Only from time to time were there holidays, during which they would all leave Cologne to stay at harvest time in a *Gasthaus* near Messdorf owned by an old friend of Johann Konrad's family.

Such was Adenauer family life. It may have been hard, but there is no reason to suppose that it was unusually harsh. Certainly there were many families who could have told similar stories, a number of which would have told of very much greater hardship. Moreover, although the dangers inherent at the time in poverty were many – disease, malnutrition, and, above all, infant and child mortality – at least in these the Adenauer family were relatively lucky. A fourth child, a daughter, born in the spring of 1879 – baptised Emilie Helena Marie Louise, but always known as 'Lilli' – grew healthily to adulthood. Their misfortune was in the last child, Elizabeth, born in 1882, when Helena was no more than thirty-three years old. After only four months, the baby fell seriously ill. The doctor was summoned – always a solemn event. There were conversations with the parents in low tones. The sons, as might be imagined, were straining to hear every word. The doctor emerged with grim news, and, in 'the dark, narrow hall of our little house' told the father that the little girl was suffering from meningitis and that he was not sure 'that she would pull through'. Furthermore, the doctor went on, 'I'm not sure that one should wish for it, because it is most unlikely that she would ever recover mentally.'[13]

What followed was a family scene of the most intense pathos. After Johann Konrad had seen the doctor out of the door and to his carriage, he came back in, 'his face . . . as pale as death'. The family gathered round the table for supper in the usual manner. Grace was said, and the meal was eaten – again as usual, but in a manner much more subdued than was normal. At the end of the meal Johann Konrad said without notice: 'And now let us pray for our little Elizabeth.' He knelt down beside the table. Helena knelt beside him, and the children followed suit. 'O Lord God,' the father started, asking the others to repeat the words after him, 'take this child with you. Spare her the cruel fate of having to live in this world without mind or reason. Lord God, have mercy on her.' The children dutifully repeated the words after their father, but Helena suddenly understood that Johann Konrad was praying, and instructing his children to pray, not for Elizabeth's recovery but for her death. This was more than the mother could stand. Helena stood up, burst into tears and, with her face in her hands, ran from the room. She locked herself in, and cried all day and night; and when Elizabeth died, two days later, refused to go to the funeral.[14]

The effect of all this on a six-year-old boy can only be imagined. His father had openly prayed, and had asked him openly to pray, for the death of his baby sister. And he had done so. At the time, of course, he had not understood his mother's reaction. 'It only became clear to me much later,' Adenauer admitted, 'what she must have felt in those moments of prayer.'[15] It is a sad commentary on his upbringing that for a long time the boy, and then the man, was unable to understand, let alone sympathise with, a mother's feelings about the loss of a child or the shock which she must have felt when she heard her husband praying for their – his and her – daughter's death. It also demonstrates a total acceptance of the patriarchy of his family life. If the head of the family decided that it was the right thing to do, then there could be no argument; feminine sentiments, even if they were understood, which at that moment at least they clearly were not, should be ignored. In unemotional and rational terms, if such ever exist, there was of course a perfectly reasonable justification for Johann Konrad's position; and if Elizabeth had already lived a long and full life it would have been both sensible and loving to pray for a peaceful end to an existence which was becoming intolerable through suffering.

But the males of the family had quite failed to comprehend that the death of a baby is, particularly for the mother, on a quite different emotional plane. Given this incomprehension, and the unbending inhumanity of the father, it is only possible to guess at the subsequent relations between Johann Konrad and Helena. Certainly there were no more children. Later, the whole family moved from the house in Balduinstrasse to an apartment nearby – but with no garden, to young Konrad's displeasure. But whether or not there was any emotional reconciliation between the two after the trauma of the dreadful event is unknown. What *is* known is the lesson drawn by their third son: it taught him, he himself said, to understand the meaning of the words *Fiat voluntas tua* ('Thy will be done') in the Lord's Prayer; that this is all that the children of God should ask, and nothing else. It did not, apparently, teach him anything about women.

Adenauer family life, however inward-looking and absorbed in its own domestic strains, did not take place in a vacuum. It was part of the wider community of the city, and the city was full of life and change. In the late 1870s and early 1880s Cologne was starting to come awake. True, the Prussian administration had done its best to favour its new Rhineland acquisition in the years after 1815, but there were times during those years when their efforts were far from tactful. Large statues of Prussian kings, such as that of Friedrich Wilhelm III on an outsize horse or Friedrich Wilhelm IV cast in flamboyant bronze, were much mocked, particularly during the pre-Lenten Cologne carnival, when almost any anti-Prussian joke was given unofficial licence by the authorities. More to the point, however, was that, thanks to the Prussian municipal statute of 1856, Cologne was able to vote directly for a city council which then elected the city's mayor (although formality demanded that the mayor so elected was officially appointed by the King of Prussia). The mayor became in practice the city's chief executive, with responsibility for the shipyards and ports, construction, schools, social welfare, health and the arts.

It was after the proclamation of the German Empire in 1871 that Cologne had started to reap the benefit of independent mayoral rule combined with Prussian oversight and, indeed, financial support. The apogee of this new confident harmony was the consecration of Cologne Cathedral, left unfinished in the fifteenth century, whose construction had been resumed in 1842. It was in October 1880 (two years before the birth and death of the baby Elizabeth) that the Adenauer family was able to witness one of the most splendid ceremonies that the city had ever seen. The Kaiser himself, surrounded by an entourage of unparalleled magnificence, proceeded through the streets of Cologne, acknowledging the cheers of the grateful populace as he went, until he arrived at the steps of the now finished cathedral, from which were declared not only the official consecration but also an affirmation of the unity and strength of the German Empire. It was an event quite spectacular in its theatricality and, as might be expected, impressed itself indelibly on the mind of the four-year-old Konrad Adenauer.

But this was not the end of it. Cologne was declared a strategic military centre. In the early 1880s a ring of twelve large forts with communication trenches and walls surrounded the city, and some 12,000 Prussian troops were quartered in the city itself. Their fathers had been cheered on their way to war with the French ten years before ('for three-quarters of an hour the cheering never stopped; "*Wacht am Rhein*" could be heard all around the Cathedral'[16]) and the soldiers were part of the social and street life of the city. As if this was not exciting enough to a young boy, this was the era of the railway. Trains came and went from the great railway station by the cathedral, across the great Hohenzollern Bridge for the east and the unknown capital city of Berlin, or down the river to Bonn and Koblenz, or up-river to Düsseldorf and the factories of the Ruhr. These were places of magic and mystery to a city boy, and the trains which went there objects to excite the imagination.

The city, too, was in the late 1870s on the verge of, and almost preparing itself for, a transformation. The hectic expansion of the city outwards was yet to come. The trams were still horse-drawn and inefficient; the carriages crowded up against one another in the narrow streets; the markets were still chaotic; and petty criminals flourished. Yet the place had a bustling energy which only needed direction to turn the city from a provincial capital into one of the great centres of Germany and, indeed, Europe. It needed a mayor of power and decision. One such was to emerge in the following decade. For the moment it was a city in waiting.

'My father didn't talk very much about that time,' Adenauer's son Max has written, referring to the years in Balduinstrasse.[17] It is perhaps understandable. Recollections of early childhood are frequently dim and distorted. Yet on the evidence, such as it is, it is hard to believe that those years, formative as they are on the character, were easy for the young child. In later life, to be sure, Adenauer was at pains, when interviewed about the period and his parents, to emphasise their love and devotion (while admitting that his father's discipline was 'strict'[18]). Nevertheless, on such occasions his voice, while retaining the lilting accent of the Rhineland, takes on an even drier tone than usual. It is as though he felt diffidence, and possibly embarrassment, at discussing the intimacies of early family life. He did not believe, he is reported as saying on one occasion, that in his early childhood life in his parents' home differed from that of the average family, although he did admit that his parents would quarrel, both of them being 'rather short-tempered'.[19] That, however, was as far as he would go, apart from what sounds like a somewhat mechanical passage describing his father's virtues – sense of duty, honesty, industry and so on.

No doubt it was all true; indeed, his father's career bears it out. But those are public virtues. Much is said about parental rules; little is said about parental love. It is as though Adenauer wished to avoid the subject altogether. This, of course, may have been deliberate. Although his family lived in Cologne, it is a fair conclusion that it was the discipline of Prussia rather than the raucous jollity of the Rhineland which ruled in the parents' home, and Adenauer both felt himself, and wished to present himself, as a son of the Rhine. Be all that as it may, it certainly was true that his father had prepared him well for the next stage in the child's life, the point at which he entered the rigours of the Prussian education system. But the doubt remains whether the little boy had received from either parent in full measure the good cheer, the open expression of love or the gentle guidance which would allow him to develop easily to an untroubled maturity. The abiding impression of Balduinstrasse 6 is that laughter and gentle affection were at a definite premium.

2

'Gaudeamus Igitur Juvenes Dum Sumus'*

'Schlüter ist mein einziger, wirklicher Freund gewesen'†

A CHILD'S FIRST day at school carries its own particular kind of psychological shock. The family of hearth and home, whatever it may be, suddenly leaves the child alone. Even though the transition from loved – or unloved – child to lowly pupil might have been carefully prepared, there is no preparation, nor can there ever be, for the first day at the first school. The parents, of course, may lead the child by the hand, and guide him or her in the first steps into what is to be his or her new environment. But thereafter nothing is the same. There is a new world, a new set of social relationships, a new vocabulary, a new test of competitive strengths; in short, a new set of experiences quite different from anything the child has ever known before.

Johann Konrad had, in his own limited way, done what he could to prepare his third son for the event. There is no doubt that he meant well. But, in the circumstances, it was an odd form of preparation. In fact, it seems to have been no more than a strict instruction in what his son would have to

---

* 'Let us therefore rejoice while we are still young': German student song.
† 'Schlüter was my one and only real friend': Adenauer, quoted in P. Weymar, *Adenauer*, p. 32.

learn and how he would have to learn it. The object of the exercise was, by all accounts, quite simple: to ensure that the young Konrad would start the competitive race, such as it was, ahead of his contemporaries, and so to ensure that he would move on beyond the elementary school to the more promising educational environment of the *Gymnasium* (in modern English terms a grammar or high school), and from there to university. In all this, there was no question of what might be called psychological preparation for a different social environment. All that mattered was the ultimate end: that the boy should achieve what his father had never achieved – a university degree, and with it entry to a career pattern and social class to which, in the Cologne of the day, his father had been unable to aspire.

Johann Konrad therefore instructed his son, not in how to cope with any other problem – bullying at school, for instance – which he might meet, but in the minutiae of the first-year curriculum of the Prussian *Volksschule*. The instruction seems to have been pursued almost to the point of obsession. But, apart from simple intellectual tuition, Johann Konrad does seem at least to have pursued his own particular strategy. The main educational objective, of course, was that the third son, like his two elder brothers, should be equipped to pass the competitive examinations which would lead to the promised land. But there was a second: the matter of Christendom. Johann Konrad was determined that his son should not deviate from the true faith of Catholic Christianity, whatever other influences he might be subjected to in the course of his schooling, at elementary or at any future stage.

The first objective – of educational advancement – explains itself. In the Prussia of the early 1880s, the *cursus honorum*, such as it was, was carefully laid out. All male children were to attend school between the ages of six and fourteen. The compulsory nature of this obligation, enforced as it was by a conscientious school inspectorate, was admired by political radicals throughout the Western world. Nowhere else was education of the young given such a degree of priority. True, the system in practice did not live up to the high ideal. In rural areas, small boys were crammed into classes of eighty or more, since there was only one room for the school. In the towns, things were better, but there was still serious overcrowding and, in spite of the benevolent intentions of the Prussian authorities, neighbourhood – and hence class – distinctions between different schools. In such an uncertain educational environment, it is no surprise that a conscientious parent who had ambitions for his sons took at least part of their education into his own hands.

The second objective was more subtle but, in Johann Konrad's eyes, just as important. The distressing fact was that the system of education in Prussia had been at the centre of the *Kulturkampf* of the 1870s – Bismarck's political attack on the Catholic Church on the grounds that it had become a state within a state. Schools which had formerly been under the supervision of religious authorities had been abruptly secularised. Priests had been removed from supervising the education of children and even from the teaching of religion in schools; and it was not until the anti-Catholic movement lost momentum that a halt was called to the attack on the confessional base which had traditionally been the norm, particularly in the Catholic Rhineland. Even then, there had been no question of going back to the era before the Kulturkampf, of abandoning the 1872 School Supervision Law and the accompanying General Regulations, which had set the objectives and curriculum of the whole Volksschule system, or of reversing the Imperial Decree of 1876 which had determined that religious instruction in schools should be under the control of the state.

The whole controversy was deeply troubling to Johann Konrad. As a loyal servant of Prussia and the German Empire which Prussia had spawned, he would have felt bound to support the decisions of the Kaiser's ministers. On the other hand, he himself could not possibly approve of such a brutal assault on what, after all, were received truths, and he was certainly aware that the attack on the position of the Catholic Church had aroused the most intense hostility in the Rhineland. But there was a further problem, which made the father's position even more delicate. In spite of the Catholic hostility, the plain fact was that the secularisation of school supervision had led to an unexpected but decisive improvement in educational standards in the Rhine Province. Previously, under the supervision of the Church, the Volksschule had languished. It was more important, the Church authorities had felt, that pupils should be instructed in the eternal verities than in German grammar. That had all now been changed. What might be useful to the child in this life had replaced the emphasis on what might eventually be useful in the next.

None of these circles were easy for Johann Konrad to square. His only solution was to make sure that the young Konrad was aware of the eternal verities – which he did to the point of boredom – and to school him in the practical curriculum to which he was about to be subjected. This meant teaching him the basic elements of the first-year Volksschule programme as stipulated in the General Regulations of 1872: German grammar, simple arithmetic, the first steps in geography and history.

In all this, Johann Konrad would have emphasised the loyalty due to the Kaiser, although to the young boy the idea that the object of education was to create 'the basis of God-fearing behaviour, *Vaterlandsliebe*' ('patriotism' – although with a somewhat stronger flavour) 'and the acceptance of the state and current social conditions' must have been incomprehensible.[1] But, incomprehensible or not, ideas which are drummed into a six-year-old boy by his father, on the eve of his going to his first school, are likely to be engraved indelibly in the child's subconscious memory. And in Adenauer's case they undoubtedly were. Nevertheless, and concurrently, Johann Konrad insisted on proper respect for the teaching of the Catholic Church. The compromise between the two must have been, to say the least, uneasy.

At the end of the feast of Easter in 1882 Konrad Adenauer entered the Knabenschule an St Apostel. The school lay close to the Apostelkirche, and so within easy walking distance of his home in the Balduinstrasse. There was no uniform to dress up in – many of the boys were too poor to afford one, nor did the school require it. The classes were large, perhaps as many as fifty boys to a class, but young Konrad was at least fortunate in that, thanks to his father's tuition, he was able to miss the first-year class and pass – without any apparent objection – directly into the second.

There, from Monday to Saturday of every week, and with only six weeks' holiday in the whole year, he had to sit with the other boys for six hours each day, starting at eight o'clock in the morning, to learn from a teacher who stood at the front of the class speaking down, in every sense, to the massed ranks below him. Discipline was strict – the strap on the hand being the preferred form of punishment – and learning was almost entirely by rote. When he left school to go home for his meal, the boy was given homework to be completed by the following morning. It needs little imagination to guess that his homework was thoroughly checked and tested by his father on his return from work, and that only then would he be allowed to go out and play in the street or on the nearby city wall. All in all, for a six-year-old it was a hard enough day.

Given this schedule, it is hardly surprising that the young Adenauer's health suffered. During his three years at the Knabenschule, he survived a mild attack of tuberculosis (which left his lungs permanently prone to infection) as well as the customary childhood illnesses. There were problems with his bone structure as he grew in height. 'For six weeks,' it was reported about one occasion, 'he had to lie in plaster and later walk around with steel braces up to his hips.'[2] All these difficulties led to a degree of loneliness. He seemed to others to be rather eccentric, was painfully shy and apparently had no friends.

In short, there is little doubt that he did not enjoy those three years, so much so that in later life he was reluctant to refer to them. Nevertheless, the whole process, painful though it might have been, seems to have served its purpose. Besides becoming reasonably proficient in reading, writing and arithmetic, he learned enough history, geography, geometry, natural science and, of course, appreciation of the virtues of the Prussian fatherland to allow him to sit for the examination which would take him to his next educational stage, the Gymnasium.

It was far from easy. In the Prussia of the day fewer than one in ten boys succeeded in graduating from the humble Volksschule to the heights of a Gymnasium. The entry examination was set by the authorities rather than by the schools themselves, which made detailed and specific preparation almost impossible. Furthermore, since education at a Gymnasium opened the door to university and then to a profession – with consequent advantages in movement up the ladder of social class – the contest for entry was fiercely competitive.

The ladder of class was particularly marked. A Gymnasium was a wholly different type of institution from a Volksschule. Pupils wore uniforms, caps, proper collars and ties, and considered themselves more than a cut above their erstwhile colleagues, whom they had left behind to finish their education at the age of fourteen and consequently to settle for an altogether lower professional and social status. There was no greater divide in the adolescent world of the Cologne of the 1880s than that between the swells at the Gymnasium and the rest.

Thanks to his natural intelligence – and perhaps more to his father's bullying – Adenauer was successful in the examination. So it was that in 1885 (again at Easter, which was the beginning of the school year throughout Prussia) he took another upward step in his fledgling career: entry into the Apostelgymnasium. It was indeed an upward step, but it was also a cultural change, and his first day at the Gymnasium was no doubt as daunting as the day he entered the Knabenschule. It was a new world, peopled by a new set of characters and with new rules of behaviour.

For a start, the whole thing was much larger. The building itself was relatively recent. It had been constructed in the – impressively ugly – style best described as 'neo-romanesque', when the nearby Marzellén-Gymnasium had become too big to manage. A daughter school had been built in the Apostelplatz, originally with funds provided by a Catholic foundation. It was equipped with eight classrooms, each able to cope with up to fifty pupils, a science laboratory, and accommodation for the headmaster and the domestic staff. In short, the Apostelgymnasium had been considered to be a triumph of both modernity and the Prussian educational system (in those days, at least in Prussia, thought to be synonymous). As such, the school had been opened with great pomp and ceremony on the day of the King of Prussia's birthday in 1860.

Since that time, Cologne itself had undergone something of an architectural revolution. In 1886, the city council had elected – as it turned out, somewhat to their subsequent regret – the autocratic former Mayor of Düsseldorf, Wilhelm Becker, to be their own mayor. On assuming office, Becker marched forward with determination, using all the powers available to the mayor of the city and deploying very considerable skill in public relations.

He negotiated the absorption into the city of the industrial suburbs on the eastern bank of the Rhine, Deutz, Mülheim, Poll and Merheim. More than that, he forced through an extended building programme in the centre of the city itself. The old city wall by then demolished, Becker created parks, not least the largest, the Stadtwald, not as a luxury but as a necessity in an urban environment. Whole streets were torn down and reconstructed; the transport system was modernised. It was all very expensive, of course, and the city council made the inevitable clucking noises; but, having elected him and given him the powers, there was nothing they could do to stop him.

The effect of all this was that by the time the nine-year-old Adenauer arrived at the Apostelgymnasium the short walk from Balduinstrasse to the Apostelplatz was like walking through a modern building site. Indeed, throughout his stay at the school the noise of the work going on around it must have greatly distracted the process of teaching and learning. But the noise and disturbance of the surrounding streets were not the only problems that the school had to face. Certainly, between its opening and the day of

Adenauer's arrival, the school had been steadily accumulating pupils, and by 1885 could boast a total of more than 250; but the process had been far from smooth and the intervening period far from happy.

The fact was that the Apostelgymnasium, too, had been a casualty of the Kulturkampf. Its severely Catholic confessional identity had been curbed as the state took control of the school away from the Church. But the Catholic tradition – in the end and after a long and bitter struggle – had proved far too strong to be killed off by a government in Berlin, and as the counter-attack gained strength the tradition re-asserted itself. To be sure, pupils were no longer officially encouraged to take part in the annual Corpus Christi procession carrying large banners; but Mass was said on Thursdays and the priests at the Apostelkirche were very much in evidence. It was an admirable example, as the headmaster August Waldeyer pointed out in his inaugural address (putting the best face on it that he could), of the synthesis of Catholic humanism and German imperial patriotism.

That was all very well. But the synthesis was far from easy. The Catholic Church in the Rhineland, however fierce in its theological conservatism, had a developed social conscience. The curriculum of the Gymnasium, too, lent itself to greater freedom of thought, based as it was on the humanities, particularly the Latin and Greek languages, history and the teaching of the Christian religion. The Prussian authorities, on the other hand, and particularly the Kaiser himself, insisted that the aim of education was to convince young people that 'progressive' political notions, such as those of social democracy, were not only against the laws of God but also immoral and impractical, and consequently dangerous to the individual and society. These two differing views were not easily reconciled; indeed their reconciliation was only made possible by the Archdiocese of Cologne distancing itself, in terms of Church politics, from the Vatican. Loyalty was thus the preserve of the Prussian state and the German Empire, and the pupils were not allowed for one moment to forget it.

By all accounts, Konrad Adenauer was a diligent, if unremarkable, pupil. He learned Latin and Greek texts by heart, studied German grammar, read German and French history, experimented with physics, performed well in the gym, and was always in the top six in his class. He also – strange as it may now seem – had an excellent singing voice. But socially he was something of a loner. Although he seems to have been well liked by the other boys, he kept himself to himself. Throughout the whole nine years he only made one friend – Ildefons Herwegen – and when Herwegen left the school without completing the full course there was nobody who replaced him in Adenauer's affections. The young man – since that is what he was rapidly becoming – took to reading books, which he did voraciously and at great speed. Almost anything would do: Jules Verne was a particular favourite, but Dickens was also on his agenda – he told a classmate that he had read *David Copperfield* 'four times running'. It was at least something to occupy the attention of the shy and lonely adolescent.

Religious instruction was an altogether more serious matter. He was confirmed, and made his first communion, almost certainly in May 1890, at the age of fourteen. As always, it was a solemn moment. A photograph of him on the day shows an almost painfully thin teenager, tall for his age, his hair close-cropped in the Prussian style of the time, dressed in a dark, tightly-fitting suit with a high collar, a white flower and ribbon pinned on his chest, making what seems like an unsuccessful attempt to smile. He certainly seems to be far from happy.

If so, there was some justification for gloom, since he was being introduced to the full range of complex religious observances with which he would thereafter be bound to comply. The sacrament of confession was a case in point: the rigorous self-examination to be undertaken before confessing to a priest took three whole pages of small print in the prayer book then in use in the Archdiocese of Cologne. 'Have I sinned through impure thoughts? Or looks? Or speech or song? Have I sinned through impure deeds, either alone or with others?' It went on and on in the same vein.[3] Furthermore, the priest, when it came to it, would make quite certain that the self-examination had been properly performed.

If the priests were stern, the secular teachers were hardly less so. There were, apparently, some 'vicious teachers',[4] whose preferred method of punishment was to cuff boys around the ears, to the point where there was at least one known case of a severely damaged eardrum. Adenauer himself recalled in later life that the school was a 'shop of horrors'.[5] Particularly unpleasant were the two rooms in which boys who had committed serious offences were locked up for long periods. All in all, life for the pupils was harsh and unremitting, but – to put it in the context of the time – perhaps no more so than schools in other countries in those days, particularly in England, where some institutions appear to have been little more than excuses for licensed sadism. By contrast, too, pupils in the Gymnasium were

comparatively well – even if rather mechanically – taught (the serious deficiency, however, being that there was no instruction in any language other than German).

In fact, there were even some enlightened and sympathetic schoolmasters: Professor Ernst Petit, an acquaintance of Heinrich Schliemann, the discoverer of ancient Troy, used to invite a group of boys, including Adenauer, to his house on Sundays and show them photographs of the latest archaeological excavations. It seems to have been an innocent enough diversion – without the overtones that some might assume – and Adenauer, at least, appears to have profited from the Professor's attentions, claiming later that he had been encouraged to take an interest not just in the cultures of Greece and Rome but also in art generally. The claim, like much of what Adenauer said in his old age about his childhood, may or may not be true, but his Sundays with the Professor undoubtedly left their mark on the young man's cultural development. It was a useful supplement to the generally dull routine of learning Classical texts, or even German poetry, by rote.

In the early spring of 1894 Adenauer was due to take his *Abitur*, the final examination of secondary education. The episode, normally so worryingly serious, in this case had its comic side. One of the twenty-one pupils of the *Oberprima*, the class due to take the examination, had apparently stumbled across the papers setting the subjects for the German essay and giving in full the German text to be translated into Latin. His announcement of the coup caused a sensation among his colleagues. Immediately, a secret meeting of the class was called to discuss tactics, and it took place around a gas-lamp in the back room of a restaurant in Ehrenfeld. It was a dangerous affair, not only because of the danger of discovery but, even more alarming, because the students started lighting up cigarettes and pipes before the meeting started, adding to the already serious risk of fire.

It was certainly useful to have the subjects of the German essay beforehand – the students immediately agreed to set up 'committees to undertake research on a communal basis';[6] but it was the Latin prose which was to cause the most intense tactical disputes between the students. Obviously, if all twenty-one produced an immaculately correct Latin text on the day, suspicions would unavoidably be aroused. But now that they were all in the know, the question was how a solution to the problem could be found so as to avoid discovery while making maximum use of the information to hand.

It was Adenauer who came up with the solution. Each student was to

introduce a number of mistakes into the perfect Latin text, the number and nature of the errors to be determined by the standard of the student's previous work in the subject. The same principle, he went on, should apply to the German essay. By way of example, Adenauer considered that a student named Mauhs should make four mistakes in his Latin prose, while Mühlens should write an essay just good enough to be marked 'satisfactory' – but no more.

It was, of course, cheating; but it was organised cheating. All the candidates played a part, and the objective was not for one to gain a competitive advantage over another but for all to pass the examination. This, indeed, was what happened; the organisation in which Adenauer had assumed a leading role had operated smoothly. Furthermore, the Abitur class of 1894 at the Apostelgymnasium was generally agreed to have been the most accomplished of the decade. Adenauer himself wrote a rather sentimental essay on 'Tasso and the Two Female Characters in Goethe's play *Torquato Tasso*' for which he was awarded the 'satisfactory' mark. In fact, this was somewhat lower than his usual standard, since his overall Abitur grade in German was 'good'. But he had certainly shown an early talent for organisation, even if in a rather dubious cause. Needless to say, it is not known whether he confessed the whole story when seeking his next clerical absolution.

The young man had now achieved the necessary qualification for entry into university, where he wished to study law. But there was an immediate disappointment. The Tonger legacy having disappeared, and Adenauer's two elder brothers being at university already, there was simply no more money for the third son. His father explained this to him in solemn tones, and the decision was accepted without demur. He would have to take a job, and that was that. His father told him that there was a vacancy at the banking house of Seligmann – 'an old-established firm of high standing', he went on – and suggested that his son take it up.[7] Thus, on 1 April 1894, Adenauer joined Seligmann as an apprentice.

'I had a poor time of it,' runs his account in later life. 'I had to be first at the office in the morning, take the ledgers from the strong-box and place them on the desks, pour out the clerks' breakfast coffee, and run errands to the post office.'[8] In other words, it was a thoroughly boring job. There were, however, two features which, if not redeeming, were at least instructive: he learned, as he said himself, what it means for a young man to be compelled to take a job he does not want; and he had at least seen the inside of one of

the famous Jewish banking houses. The experience was to that extent useful for the future.

But it was still tedious, and Adenauer used to arrive home in the evening not only bored but depressed. It was more than his parents could stand, and after only two weeks Johann Konrad took him aside to tell him that they had decided to cut down even more on domestic expenses to allow him to continue his studies, and that, furthermore, he had made an application to the Krämer Foundation, a Cologne charitable organisation which gave bursaries to help with the education of deserving sons of middle-class parents. Adenauer was almost overwhelmed with gratitude to his father. 'I shall never cease to be grateful to my father,' he said in later life.[9]

The Adenauer who emerged from secondary education – and from his brief career as an apprentice in banking – was a young man quite uncertain about his future direction. There was not enough money for riotous living, even if he had been inclined to it. Physically, he was in much better shape than he had been at the Knabenschule, and, although still thin, particularly in his oval-shaped face – a feature accentuated by his close-cropped hair – he was tall and upright. But to judge from the end-of-term photograph of the Oberprima in March 1894 (marked on the back with his rather bizarre nickname 'Toni'), it seems to be a face which lacks self-confidence when compared with his classmates around him. In short, although he had been a good pupil and 'his conduct was always orderly and beyond reproach',[10] the abiding impression is of an eighteen-year-old halfway between boy and man. It would take a few more years at university and beyond, away from his family, for him to develop to the full stature of manhood. Without a doubt, it was time for him to move on, out of, and away from, Cologne.

The city of Freiburg im Breisgau lies in Baden, at the southern end of the Black Forest, where the Rhine, having emerged from Lake Constance to flow westwards along the Swiss frontier, curls round to the north on its long journey through Germany and Holland to the sea. In 1894, when Adenauer enrolled as a law student at Freiburg University, it was a pleasant and gracious place, nearer France than Prussia in spirit, as indeed it was in geography, and still bearing nostalgically the traces of its four centuries of Austrian rule. The city itself boasted a fine cathedral, its pointed spire standing proudly against the backdrop of the wooded slopes of the Schlossberg, a fitting symbolic presence for the Archbishopric of the Upper

25

Rhine. Furthermore, the surrounding countryside of the Black Forest itself, the Höllental and the Feldberg, was, and is, gentle and attractive.

For some time, it had been the custom for many boys, after passing their Abitur in Cologne, to start their university career in Freiburg. There was no particular reason for this, except the usual one: that at that age boys like to go where their friends go. To be sure, the university had a strong Catholic bias; the style of life was relaxed; and in those days a semester at Freiburg seemed to be regarded as a something of a holiday after the rigours of a Gymnasium. It was well known that the number of students enrolling for lectures exceeded by a wide margin the number who actually attended. Moreover, in Adenauer's own words, 'all things seemed to have their firm, appointed place on this earth; nobody could have imagined the turmoil the next decades were to bring'.[11] All this was attractive to the young Adenauer, and it is little wonder that he remembered his period at Freiburg with affection.

There was even a sign that he was starting to come out of his protective emotional carapace. He still kept up his 'invisible barrier', but he did join the Catholic student association, Brisgovia, whose drinking sessions were apparently 'kept within acceptable limits' – whatever that might have meant; and he went on outings to pubs or to 'Dattlers on the Schlossberg', and for long walks along the Höllental to the large lake of Titisee.[12] He even – such was the fashion of the times – grew a small moustache.

For all this – admittedly tentative – lowering of the wall between him and his student colleagues, it would be wrong to imagine that Adenauer neglected his studies. He had been disciplined by his father far too well for that. Besides, he knew that his parents were scrimping and saving for his education and although he seems to have had enough money to go out 'drinking . . . with the rest of us . . . he always managed to make ends meet',[13] he always turned up for the first lecture at eight o'clock sharp on Monday morning. To be sure, his industry and sense of duty could occasionally get on the nerves of his fellow students, 'but secretly we were all most impressed'.[14]

One of the reasons that Adenauer obviously felt at home in Freiburg lay in the fact that his contemporaries from Cologne were in general from his own background – sons of civil servants, court clerks, shopkeepers and the like – whose parents had, like his own, made a substantial financial sacrifice to send their sons to university. It was certainly not a group from the upper class, whether nobility or banker. Many of them were as short of money as

he was. Within that group, not only was Adenauer at home but he seems to
have acted, at least for one of them, as an unofficial accountant, being asked,
and accepting, the task of administering monthly allowances by those who
were too spendthrift to do it for themselves. Each day the allotted sum was
handed out to the trusting colleague. There was no right of appeal, nor was
there any supplementary top-up if the unfortunate went and spent his daily
allowance on the spot. It seems that financial discipline – not to say a certain
vicarious stinginess – was the only rule that Adenauer was prepared to entertain in the matter.

In all the turbulence of his first semester at university, Adenauer, by his
own account, made only one real friend: Raimund Schlüter. Schlüter had
arrived at Freiburg to study law at the same time as Adenauer and, like
Adenauer, he was something of a loner. The son of Westphalian peasant
parents, he had managed to work his way through the competitive educational system to achieve a place at university. As shy as Adenauer (whose face,
when anybody – particularly girls – spoke to him, 'always went red'[15]),
Schlüter hardly spoke to anybody. Pale in the face, wearing large, round
spectacles, he seems in photographs to be a strangely eccentric figure. If so,
it was understandable. His mother, as well as all his brothers and sisters, had
died of tuberculosis, whereupon his father had sold his house and moved, in
his loneliness, to Cologne. Shy and eccentric Schlüter may have been; but he
was upright and honest – and poor. In all ways he suited the young Adenauer
well.

After one semester – then, as now, there were two semesters in a year –
Adenauer, followed by the now faithful Schlüter, moved to Munich. Again,
it was something of a natural progression, following, as another student colleague put it, 'my friends from Cologne'.[16] This peripatetic arrangement was
by no means exceptional. On the contrary, it was unusual for students to
pledge their loyalty to one university for the full period of their undergraduate education. It was thought to be an important part of their development
to breathe the fresher air of a different establishment, and once enrolled in
one university the transition to another seemed to raise no difficulties.

In fact, in Adenauer's case the transition bore substantial fruit. There was
a short break, spent with his family in Cologne, before he was off for two
semesters to southern Bavaria, in common with 'friends from Cologne'.
The experience was undoubtedly beneficial. Munich was, and is, a capital
city, with its own heady charm; and, besides, to keep him company, there was

his friend Schlüter. There was the Alte Pinakothek, with its grand collection of paintings that the two had never seen. There was, too, the Residenz Theatre, the State Opera and, not least, the enthusiasm of King Ludwig for the revolutionary composer, Richard Wagner – only a decade or so dead but still the fashion of the day. Adenauer and Schlüter together found themselves in a different world.

Not only was it a different world, but – unlike today – life for a student in Munich was not expensive. From his monthly allowance of 90 marks, Adenauer would have had to allocate no more than 30 or so for his board and lodging. For the first time in his life, he was able to save for holidays. It was not just a matter of regular visits to the Alte Pinakothek, which were, indeed, made. Together with Schlüter, he made excursions to the lakes of Bavaria, to Switzerland and even as far afield as Italy and Austria. For their summer holiday they went as far as Venice, Ravenna, Assisi and Florence, mostly on foot and sleeping in haylofts or, when no friendly farmer could be found, in the waiting-rooms of railway stations. The trip took them no less than six weeks. It also exhausted their available funds.

It was this cultural odyssey which seems finally to have broken the back of Adenauer's father's patience. It was all very well, but Johann Konrad was certainly not prepared to deprive himself and his family simply to allow his son to gad about on the shores of the Adriatic. A stern missive was sent asking him for a full account of his expenses and requesting him not to continue wasting his time and his father's money in Bavarian frivolity. Many a son, of course, has received such a missive from many a parent in such circumstances, but the effect of Johann Konrad's intervention was little short of electric. The young man was to leave Munich at the end of his second term and return to the Rhineland and sobriety. There was to be no argument, and that was that.

As it happened, Johann Konrad's instruction came at just about the right time. In order to complete his university studies and to qualify as a lawyer able to practise in Prussia, Adenauer had to complete his examinations at a Prussian university. He therefore transferred, as was his right, to Bonn – followed, naturally, by his friend Raimund Schlüter. But there was serious work to be done, and both friends set about doing it. Adenauer promised his father that he would complete his studies in the minimum time possible, a total of six terms in all. And this he did.

From the autumn of 1895 to the spring of 1897, his final three terms in

Bonn were little more than unremitting drudgery. Admittedly, he joined the Catholic student association, Arminia, and there were occasional (seemingly rather formal) parties for the members each term, the occasional expeditions to restaurants in Bad Godesberg or walks in the Siebengebirge – and even the odd fancy dress ball for a bit of fun – but for the rest it was all work, discipline and no play.

Adenauer himself in later life took a somewhat masochistic pleasure in telling of the times when he worked by gas-lamp well into the night, or how he took off his shoes and socks and put his feet in a bucket of cold water to stop himself falling asleep (even to the point where his mother showed maternal anxiety for his health). But, although he was undoubtedly intelligent, all the effort and concentration which he devoted to his work could not make him a brilliant student, and although at the end of the appointed three years he emerged as a junior, permitted to practise law in the Prussian courts (without being allowed to receive fees), his grade in the final examination had been no more than 'good'.

For a young man just turned twenty-one it may not have been much to show for three years' hard work, even if the serious effort had only begun on his return to Bonn. Munich had certainly expanded his interests – particularly in the visual arts – and, to that extent, had broadened his character. But after his concentrated efforts at Bonn, Adenauer might have expected something better. The truth was that, in the end, his intellect was, among his peers, no better than average. Of course, the average itself should be seen in the educational circumstances of the time. The system was severely meritocratic, and even 'average' put Adenauer in the upper 2 per cent of his contemporaries. He had travelled along the familiar path of the Volksschule, had achieved the distinction of entry into a Gymnasium, and from there had won what was at least a reasonable outcome from his university career. It was not brilliant, but, like Bismarck before him, he might have reasonably been able to say that he was an honest product of the Prussian educational system of the time.

There remains, of course, the problem, if it is a problem, of Adenauer's sexuality as an adolescent and as a young man. Unsurprisingly, there is no evidence on the matter. When others were questioned about any affective relationships during his life as a student, the response was a somewhat bewildered 'no; nothing of that sort was in Konrad Adenauer at all'. When questioned himself in later life, his answer was a curt 'no'.[17]

Nevertheless, there must be questions about his relations with his great ('and only real') friend Raimund Schlüter. Since the young Adenauer blushed whenever addressed by 'girls', it would be easy to suppose that those relations were inherently homosexual. So they probably were, but – equally probably – they were not homo-erotic. Intense friendships between adolescent and post-adolescent males were far from uncommon at the time. German (and English) histories of the late nineteenth and early twentieth centuries are full of them. But the sexual nature of such relationships remained latent, or at least sublimated in religious fervour; and there is no reason to suppose that Adenauer and Schlüter were any different from the others. The matter of how the young Adenauer – or the young Schlüter, for that matter – relieved the physical desires of young manhood remains, as it no doubt always will, undiscovered.

The wheel was now about to come full circle. Konrad Adenauer had left his parents' home, first in part and then decisively, to go through the various stages of the educational process which his father had wished for him. There had been periods which he had enjoyed – his stay at Munich was probably the highlight. There had been periods which he had detested – the Knabenschule an St Apostel probably took that prize. In sum, he had emerged from the long process properly educated by the standards of the time, but emotionally constricted; in other words, he was not yet fully grown up. But now, ironically, he was to return to his parents' house, to live there continuously while he looked for, and then worked at, a job for which he was to earn no money.

For a 21-year-old to be wholly dependent on his father for his mere subsistence is galling enough, but it is made worse when the father's educational background and breadth of experience is so greatly inferior to the son's. It therefore comes as little surprise to find that on his return, as what might be called a permanent lodger in his parents' house, Adenauer had his first serious dispute with his father. But it was not just a family spat; it was much worse than that. Johann Konrad's third son was set to challenge the basis of his father's most cherished belief: the whole question of the legitimacy of what was, in the words of the Nicene Creed, one Holy, Catholic and Apostolic Church.

3

THE END OF YOUTH

*'So hilf mir Gott'**

'SOON AFTER MY examination to become a junior counsel I went through a religious crisis.'[1] Thus runs Adenauer's only recorded account of a somewhat mysterious episode in his early adult life. His account is not merely perfunctory; it is almost dismissive. When pressed in later life, he even tried to explain it away as no more than a mild and perfectly normal youthful rebellion against received parental views. But in truth it was rather more than that.

Adenauer's parents' Catholicism was not only strict but blindly orthodox. Along with their unrelenting – and at times suffocating – piety came the unswerving conviction that the teaching of their Church was the continuing revelation of God through the Holy Spirit. There could be no possible argument on the matter. Any deviation from that view was heretical, and, as the night follows the day, led inevitably to eternal damnation. That, of course, was all very well until the Vatican Council of 1871, which, in its declaration of papal infallibility *ex cathedra*, had split the Church, and had provoked doubts throughout northern Catholicism. The old certainties suddenly became suspect; doubt was in the air.

---

* 'So help me God': from the oath of allegiance and the marriage vows.

The Adenauers' third son, although he had followed the well-trodden route of Catholic universities and had dutifully joined the appropriate Catholic student associations, had by the very nature of his education – particularly in Munich – been exposed to the intellectual wind of the 1890s which, unlike the calm of previous decades, was suddenly turbulent. He shared the doubts of northern Catholicism. Furthermore, the religious faith of tradition, be it Protestant or Catholic, was confronted by the advance of science. The evolutionary theories of Charles Darwin had caught hold, and had been followed by an even more provocative assault from the German natural scientist Ernst Haeckel. This new – and perhaps unexpectedly violent – wind had led even the hitherto orthodox young Adenauer to question the basis of previously unchallenged beliefs.

Under those circumstances, the return to the parental home was more than usually difficult; indeed, there must have been, between the parents and the son, a deeply disturbing conflict. Adding fuel to an already lively fire was the coincidence of the impending ordination of Adenauer's elder brother Hans to the Catholic priesthood precisely at this time, with all the serious commitment from the ordinand and his family that this implied. It is little wonder that in his old age, when trying to put a favourable gloss on his relations with his parents, Adenauer was inclined to brush the whole episode aside.

Oddly enough, in this awkward situation it was a Zwinglian Protestant who came to the rescue: the Swiss theologian Carl Hilty. Hilty himself led a remarkable life in a number of quite different ways. Born in 1833 in the canton of St Gallen in Switzerland, he studied in Paris and London, became in turn a professor of law at Bern University, a member of the Swiss National Council (the Swiss parliament), chief auditor of the Swiss Army and, finally, Switzerland's first representative at the International Court of Arbitration in The Hague. In his spare time, as it were, he was a Protestant lay preacher; and, as such, found space to write a number of books devoted to the practical application of Christianity to a working life. As it happened, two of these books, entitled *Glück* ('Happiness') and *Was ist Glaube?* ('What is Faith?') were published during the period of Adenauer's greatest doubts; and they were read with particular attention by the troubled young man. Their effect was striking; indeed, so striking that the two books occupied a place in the shelves of his bedroom – with several passages heavily underlined in pencil – to the end of his life.

Admittedly, in today's terms Hilty's prescriptions for happiness sound on the edge of the bizarre. He praises what he described as 'the art of work'. Life was not there to be enjoyed but to be organised 'productively'. Work should be started promptly and punctually, and should last each day for 'a certain carefully measured amount of time'. The values of the Stoics – with a Christian slant – are given great prominence: the imitation of an ideal person; silence (or at least no more words than are strictly necessary); avoidance of anything which looks like luxury; abstention from sexual intercourse unless 'legally authorised'; and, bafflingly, 'if you wish to enter into conversation with someone . . . imagine how Socrates or Zeno would have conducted himself in such a situation'.[2] The ideas may have been powerful, but (admittedly with hindsight) it is far from easy to see how such prescriptions could reasonably have been put into practice at the turn of the twentieth century.

Nevertheless, bizarre or not, Hilty's prescriptions found a ready audience. Indeed, by 1910 his book on 'Happiness', in all its three volumes, had sold no fewer than 100,000 copies. Adenauer became one of his earliest readers, and one of his professed admirers. Particularly noted were some of Hilty's aphorisms: 'One should only hate things, not people'; 'It is wise to appear cool in front of people who wish to impress us'; 'Misfortune is a necessary part of human life'; 'Every form of self-education begins with the crucial decision to pursue a significant goal in life and to avoid anything that militates against it'; and, heavily underscored in Adenauer's pencil, 'A certain inclination to solitude is absolutely necessary for calm spiritual development and above all for happiness'.[3] Such aphorisms, chiming as they did with Adenauer's own inherited asceticism, helped, as he himself said, to allay his doubts about Christianity itself. But they were not specifically Catholic, and the compromise remained uneasy. To be sure, Adenauer continued to observe the outward manifestations of Catholicism, attending Mass regularly, fasting at the appropriate times, and going to confession regularly. But at the same time it became true to say, as did one of his government colleagues late in his life, that he remained 'inwardly Protestant'.[4]

If problems of religious difference caused unease in the family home, the unease was certainly aggravated in practical terms by Adenauer's continuing financial dependence his father. In May 1897 he began a period of just over four years' training to qualify for the higher position of Assessor, which would allow him to practise in the courts and give him entry, should he so wish, to the civil service – and hence to the administration of the courts. But even to start on the course, he had to present an affidavit from his father committing him to grant to his son 'the means of subsistence appropriate to his standing'.[5] The negotiations could not have been easy; such negotiations never are. Fortunately for both, the father's financial burdens of educating his elder sons had by then been lifted, and so high were Johann Konrad's social ambitions for his third son – and by extension for himself – that the affidavit was signed, presented and duly accepted by the authorities. Johann Konrad was by then, after all, a senior court clerk, and his signature was undoubted.

On 1 June 1897, Adenauer took the solemn oath of allegiance at a public meeting of the Cologne Civil Court, to 'be submissive, loyal and obedient to his Royal Majesty, King of Prussia'. The oath went on to commit him to carry out the duties of his office 'to the best of my ability and conscience' and to observe 'conscientiously' the constitution; it ended with the usual words 'so help me God'.[6] Whatever the feelings of Adenauer at that point about God, this was a decisive moment in the young man's life. It would be idle to suppose that the oath was made in any spirit of frivolity. Adenauer was not that sort of person; nor would he ever be. The compromise between his Catholicism – whatever doubts he may have had at the time – and his loyalty to Prussia was now formalised in the most binding manner. This was to be the base for his early life and career.

The career, whatever the future was to bring, started – as many careers do – with a period of some tedium. As a new trainee in the practice and administration of the law, Adenauer was assigned to the District Court in Bensberg, a small and undistinguished town (the only inn was named, in a flight of attempted touristic fantasy, after Grimm's imaginary children, Hänsel and Gretel) some fifteen kilometres to the east of Cologne in the woods of Königsforst. Every morning, except for Sundays, he would cross the river and make the journey through the suburbs of Deutz and Kalk until he arrived at the hill below which Bensberg sheltered. On arrival at the small District Court he went to his place by the presiding clerk and helped him in whatever menial way was required. When the court rose, Adenauer made his solitary way back across the Rhine to his parents' house. It was not an occupation of much amusement, but it had to be done, and done it was – for nine whole months.

But at least Bensberg had been a new place, and the court relatively small and friendly. After that, it was back to the city, and a transfer to the Cologne District Court. Here there was at least one advantage. Adenauer was able to make regular contact again with his old friend Schlüter, who was also going through the same process, and revive the companionship which they had known at university. For his first six weeks Adenauer was assigned the task of taking committee minutes. This was followed by one month of service in the 4th Criminal Court; five months in the 2nd Civil Court; two months in the 4th Civil Court; two months in the 1st Chamber for Commercial Affairs; four months in the State Prosecutor's office; six months in the office of a senior judicial councillor; a further six months in the office of the Royal Notary; then six months as a serving clerk in the Cologne Lower District Court, before he returned to the Upper District for the rest of his training. One can only imagine Adenauer's sense of relief when, on 30 May 1901, he asked the President of the Royal District Court in Cologne to approve his candidature for the final examination to become a fully-fledged Assessor.

The application was duly forwarded to the Prussian Ministry of Justice in Berlin, together with the regular — and favourable — assessments of Adenauer's progress which had been made as a matter of course. There was, however, one snag. The general assessments had certainly been good: 'The conduct of the candidate both at work and in private was entirely appropriate.'[7] But there was a small note, written in the hand of the President of the Court, which served to cast a cloud over the whole application. 'The candidate,' it ran, 'has been referred to the Home Reserve and has not served.'[8] In other words, Adenauer had been called up for full service in the Prussian Army, but because of his chronic bronchial weakness had been placed — like his brother August — in the Home Reserve. Unlike his brother, however, he had failed ever to turn up for service.

This was hardly a good recommendation to the Prussian authorities, and Adenauer was duly taken to task. Although he pleaded ill-health, and referred to doctor's certificates to justify his absences, nobody in Berlin seems to have been impressed. The result, whether due to this unfortunate lapse of attention to duty or for another reason (possibly his origins and religion told against him), was that when it came to the final grading in October 1901 in the Grosse Juristische Staatsprüfung, as it was known, Adenauer was marked no better than '*ausreichend*' ('satisfactory').

Potentially, it was a disaster. Certainly, he was now an Assessor, and fully qualified for remunerated employment in a Cologne court. But instead of being rewarded with a position in the Upper District Court, the best he could achieve – at the instigation of the Ministry of Justice in Berlin – was an unpaid job in the Lower District Court. This was far from what Adenauer had hoped for, or indeed expected. The only possible escape was to apply for a position in the State Prosecutor's office, where he had worked during his training. As it turned out, there was a temporary vacancy in the office, and in January 1902 he was accepted (earning a salary – albeit modest – for the first time at the age of twenty-six). Furthermore, by diligence and attention to detail he managed to earn the approval of the Senior Prosecutor, to the point where in May of that year he was licensed as a junior prosecutor. Hilty's prescriptions, of organised work as the foundation of a successful life, seemed to be bearing fruit.

Yet although it was exciting – and necessary – at last to be earning money, there was a note of sadness: it was time to say goodbye to Raimund Schlüter. Their close friendship had continued throughout the time of his tedious four years of court training. They had seen a great deal of one another, and had even at times worked as colleagues in the same Cologne courts. Schlüter, too, had applied at the same time as his friend for his final examination, and indeed had become an Assessor in the same autumn of 1901. But Schlüter had failed in his efforts to return to a post in Cologne, and had settled for a job in a small District Court in the little town of Gmünd. It was an attractive enough place, and suited Schlüter well – a community of no more than 5,000 souls in the wild beauty of the Eifel mountains. Nevertheless, it meant the end of the close friendship with Adenauer. Certainly, they would see each other from time to time, but nearly seven years of almost daily contact were now over. Their farewells bear the unmistakable mark of their deep friendship, all the more touching for being so restrained. 'Be careful about your health, Schlot' – Adenauer still used Schlüter's nickname from Freiburg days; 'And you, don't work too hard, Toni' – Schlüter the same; 'Write soon'; 'Of course, if there is something interesting to say'. A handshake, and then it was goodbye.[9]

But life had to move on. Indeed, at this point it was moving on rather fast. With his income now secure, if small, Adenauer felt able to spread himself a little. His natural shyness obviously inhibited him, but by the end of 1901 he had joined a tennis club in Cologne. Tennis, in fact, was one of the main social activities for young people of both sexes, to the point that rackets were frequently referred to as 'engagement paddles'. Of course, it was all very decorous: women wore long skirts and high-necked blouses and men only took off their jackets when they ventured on to the court itself. But none of this prevented a certain skittishness among the young things, and many marriages were planned, or dreamed about, at tennis parties. One such club was known as the 'soaking wets' from the insistence of the members in playing even in the wettest of weathers; and it was, in fact, the 'soaking wets' that Adenauer joined. It was eminently suitable, in that it had a predominantly Catholic membership; but it was also a way for Adenauer to meet girls, and furthermore girls of a higher social class than the mere son of a senior court clerk would normally meet. One such was Emma Weyer.

Emma was a true daughter of the Cologne *haute bourgeoisie*. On her father's side, the name of Weyer was much respected. Her grandfather had, as the appointed city architect, overseen the restoration of the great churches which had suffered under the Napoleonic occupation. Furthermore, he had planned and supervised the building of the stock exchange, the city hospital and a number of new schools. In the course of his career he had accumulated a fine collection of more than 300 paintings of the highest quality – Cranach, Dürer, Holbein, Memling, Van Dyck, Rembrandt and Rubens. To be sure, most of his collection had been sold off to meet his debts after a speculative investment in railways had gone badly wrong; but that regrettable adventure – not uncommon at the time, in fact – had not affected the general reputation of the Weyer family in Cologne.

Emma's mother came from an even more respectable background. Her own grandfather had been a Berghaus – a name to be treated with reverence in the Cologne of the day – and she herself was a Wallraf – equally a name of the highest standing. All in all, Emma could, and probably did, take pride in her parentage and upbringing. But, in spite of the privileged position which they enjoyed, family life had been far from satisfactory. Emma's father had been killed in an accident while hiking over what had proved to be unexpectedly rough terrain, and her mother had thereupon plunged into the deepest mourning. There was even talk of her taking the veil in an enclosed conventual order. Deterred from that course by her responsibilities to her two daughters, Emma and her sister Mia, she had had her emotional revenge, if that is what it was, by insisting that the family home should be one of impenetrable gloom.

Emma herself was not beautiful or indeed particularly elegant. But she was by nature cheerful and the atmosphere of her home was, to her, far from encouraging – hence the hours spent at the tennis club, the one activity of which her mother seemed to approve. Of course, it was understood between them that even the freer social ambience at the club was only acceptable within the context of the upbringing of a girl of a 'good' Cologne family of the day. Compared with their contemporaries in France, that upbringing, and their general position in what was very strictly a man's world, was hardly inspiring. One – admittedly somewhat radical – writer complained that her education had been directed to one purpose and one purpose only: 'that I might one day be able to provide my husband with *eine hübsche Häuslichkeit* ["a pretty home life"]'.[10] Under the circumstances it is not surprising to find that Emma was anxious to jump from what was to her a disagreeable, almost monastic, existence into what at least appeared to be the possibility of some degree of good cheer.

Not that Konrad Adenauer was ever a gloriously high example of good cheer; but, from the evidence of the photographs of the period, there was a certain glint in his eye which had not been there before. Besides, his moustache had taken on a more flamboyant – even something of an exotic – elongated shape. Somewhat surprisingly, and perhaps for the first time since his year in Munich, in the photographs of the time he has every appearance of enjoying himself. If this is so, there were two reasons for his new contentment: first, he had met a young lady (of a higher social class, which was to his and to his family's advantage) who was obviously attracted to him and to whom he was – with his customary reserve in personal relationships – equally attracted; second, he had decided that he had had enough of the State Prosecutor's office and was resolved to seek a different career. It is not difficult to believe that the two reasons were interlinked.

In mid-1902, Adenauer proposed marriage to Emma Weyer at a summer party for lawyers at the Rolandsbogen overlooking the Rhine. Emma, at her most cheerful and sporting a large hat decorated with cherries, immediately – perhaps to Adenauer's surprise – accepted his offer, and ran off to tell her brother. But there remained the necessary formalities, which were by no means easy. The daughter's hand in marriage had to be asked of her mother. So it was that on a dreary Sunday morning the young Assessor turned up, properly dressed in his high collar, at the Weyer home to ask for the mother's approbation for his engagement to her daughter Emma. As might be imagined, the interview was sticky. There was, of course, the matter of the difference in social class; the son of a clerk was asking in marriage the daughter of a Weyer and the granddaughter of a Wallraf. But even more important was the problem of how Adenauer intended to support his wife. He could not possibly do so on his salary of 200 marks from the office of the State Prosecutor. So what, the mother asked, did he propose to do?

At this point in the interview, Adenauer seems to have resorted to bluff. He talked up his prospects in the legal profession, and claimed that before long he would have an annual income of 6,000 marks. In truth this was little more than wishful thinking, to put it in the most charitable light. After his relatively poor examination result the prospect of acquiring a position in the higher ranks of his profession was remote. Nevertheless, the tactic seems to have worked. Adenauer succeeded in his suit – helped, no doubt, by encouraging and persuasive arguments put to her mother by Emma herself. Frau 'Direktor Weyer' gave her assent, and the engagement was duly announced. In order to redeem his dubious promises to his future mother-in-law, Adenauer then set about getting a better-paid job in order that the couple could be married in reasonable financial security – without depending on the beneficence of a mother-in-law who was certainly able to support them but on whose generosity neither of them would have wished to rely.

The engagement secure, much to the surprise of her family her new-found love released in Emma qualities which she probably never knew she possessed. She wrote love poems to Adenauer almost daily. This in turn gave colour and life to what was hitherto no more than a tolerably pretty face. She suddenly felt herself to be beautiful, and became so as a result. 'Radiant' was the word her clearly astonished brother used about her. In short, she was quite obviously and openly in love. Adenauer, on the other hand, was more restrained. Admittedly, his moustache became even more flamboyant – it now stretched on each side of his face almost as far as his ears. But there were times when he felt it necessary to dampen Emma's exuberance, which he used to do with his favourite weapon, the ironical sally. Where she wrote poems using the familiar '*du*' he wrote postcards using the more formal '*Sie*'.

As it turned out, it was to be eighteen months before they were in a position to marry. Adenauer kept looking for a better job, but without success. He even asked one of his old friends from the Bonn Arminia what might be his prospects of becoming a town councillor in Gelsenkirchen. Interestingly enough, it was the first time he had shown curiosity about local politics; but, his mind now sharpened, he went to the length of sketching out some preliminary ideas on his own views of society (which followed, unsurprisingly and almost too neatly, the then current social philosophy of the Catholic Church). But that did not work either. It came, in the end, to nothing. It was all very frustrating, and it is little wonder that Adenauer's health started to suffer yet again. Absences from work for reasons of sickness grew in number. He talked vaguely of becoming a country notary in an obscure small town. He had a love of nature, he said, which would occupy his attention; he was also fertile in inventing new ways of doing things; and that, together with his prospects as a country notary, would secure his future with an undoubtedly loving wife. Nevertheless, however genuinely meant, none of it sounded wholly convincing.

All that changed, however, in the autumn of 1903. Adenauer was granted a twelve-month leave of absence in October of that year from the office of the State Prosecutor to enable him to stand in for the lawyer Hermann Kausen. In fact, it was no more than a temporary appointment as a replacement for a senior — but far from the most senior — lawyer acting in the Cologne courts who happened to be ill at the time. But there were two things which made this opportunity different from any other: first, that Kausen, although bad-tempered and suspicious, was the leader in Cologne of the Centre Party, the exclusively Catholic party which controlled the then majority on the Cologne City Council; and, second, that it gave Adenauer an opportunity to develop his forensic skills, not just as a prosecutor, but as a professional and competent lawyer. This he did, and before long he had established a reputation, not for histrionics, but for an eloquence which 'worked on judges like a gentle and persistent country rain which washes away all opposing arguments'.[11]

'Gentle and persistent country rain' it may have been; but it was none the less effective, and Adenauer's reputation as a combative lawyer was beginning to be recognised among those who managed the law — and local politics — in Cologne. As a result, his wedding with Emma could now take place without provoking the accusation that he was marrying only for social advancement. On Tuesday, 26 January 1904, therefore, the appropriate witnesses were assembled for the civil ceremony at the Prussian register office in Köln-Lindenthal, the registered residential district of the bride. Bride, bridegroom and witnesses assembled in appropriately formal dress for the occasion; and the deed was done.

But the much more important event, certainly as far as both families were concerned, took place in the parish church of Lindenthal on the following Thursday: a Nuptial Mass, at which, it must be assumed, the bride appeared in the customary elaborate white dress with a long train and the groom in the customary frock-coat with high collar. Strangely enough, although there had been formal photographs of the couple at the time of their engagement in 1902, there are no surviving photographs either after the civil wedding or after the Nuptial Mass.

The Mass was followed by a lunchtime reception at the Hotel Grosser Kurfürst in Lindenthal, which in turn was followed by a formal dinner, with the bride and groom leading the after-dinner dancing. No doubt the grand relatives of the Weyers were invited and the Adenauers merely tolerated. Certainly Raimund Schlüter was not invited, and sent a somewhat formal telegram to his erstwhile friend. All in all, it must have been – as such occasions tend to be – an exhausting day, and it is little wonder that on their first honeymoon night the couple managed to get no further than Bonn – just a few miles down the road.

Now married, a rather different Adenauer started to appear. True, throughout his long honeymoon, almost obligatory for a middle-class couple at the time, he kept very careful accounts, noting each expenditure in exact handwriting in the evening of the day in which it was incurred. He was also anxious to restrain Emma when they arrived in Monte Carlo and she showed evidence of over-enthusiasm for the casino, leading her away from the tables after she had won and then lost an admittedly small sum of money – the amount duly recorded in his accounts. But all that, in a sense, was the Adenauer of his childhood, of his parents' influence, of his training as a lawyer and then as a clerk in the Prussian courts. What is quite new in his character comes out with sudden and striking force in the diary which Emma kept during their honeymoon.

Emma's honeymoon diary is not by any means a distinguished piece of German literature. But, whatever the stylistic shortcomings, it portrays her new husband's emotional release in ecstatic terms. The morning after the couple's arrival in Bonn, for instance, which in reality was foggy and bleak in the middle of a Rhineland winter, is described in idyllic terms: 'A fine mist lies over the Rhine . . . gulls fly restlessly over the river . . . not for a long time have we looked into the future in such a happy and carefree manner.' Into Switzerland and to Montreux, 'Flocks of white gulls hovering on the gusts of wind . . . we sledged down the slope over a snow-covered path . . . above us the blue sky, below us the wide expanse of Lake Geneva . . . can you imagine anything more wonderful? How our sledge raced and our cheeks reddened! What fun! Playful as children we enjoyed sledging over the snowy ground, happy as children as we gazed at the unending beauty.'

So it goes on. When they went on to Geneva, 'the rain still comes down in fine strands' (in other – more mundane – words, it had been pouring with rain for some days). 'Everything is covered by a gentle bright ray of light which seems to emanate from the ground' as they moved down the Rhône valley. In Marseilles, 'a mild spring air . . . has tempted us on to the main street . . . in late evening. We have entered another country.' There is a mild note of disapproval in that 'girls in native costume sit at the stands selling violets, a little bit dirty but exotic and unusual-looking', but that passes when the couple arrive at Monte Carlo and from there go on to the Italian Riviera.[12] Finally, it was Genoa and Milan – with a brief stop to peer at Leonardo's *Last Supper* – and then back through Switzerland to Cologne. By that time it is hard not to believe that cultural exhaustion, if nothing else, had started to set in.

Of course, it is easy today to poke fun at honeymoon diaries of the first decade of the twentieth century. But it is also easy to forget that that was the decade in which Europe, as a continent, was more open to uncomplicated travel than it has been since, and that the wonders which are now so easily taken for granted were then strange and, for that reason, the more beautiful. When Adenauer went on his honeymoon, at the age of twenty-eight, it was the first time he had been outside Germany since his student travels with Schlüter when they were at Munich together, and it was the first time he had spent any long period of time with a woman, particularly a woman who so obviously loved him.

The whole honeymoon period is revealing of Adenauer's character at the time. Disciplinarian he might be. Hard worker, and meticulous, he might be. Fierce and angry, on occasions, he might be. But towards his intimates, Emma's diary reveals an unsuspected tenderness. Honeymoons can end either in disaster or in increased love. There is little doubt how the honeymoon of the first three months of Adenauer's first marriage ended; and it was a happy couple that set up house in a small, but well furnished, apartment in Klosterstrasse in Lindenthal, at a convenient distance – but not too far – from Emma's parental home.

There was, however, one incident that had disturbed both of them during their honeymoon. In Montreux in Switzerland the couple had seen in their hotel a number of guests with obvious signs of tuberculosis. 'These poor people,' Emma's diary comments, 'they hope for a cure but many of them already have the mark of death upon them . . .'[13] It was a worrying sight, since it must have reminded Adenauer of his friend Schlüter and the decimation by the disease of Schlüter's family. Strangely enough, only just after another holiday which he and Emma had taken with his brother Hans in July 1904, Adenauer received in September another, this time excited, telegram from his friend in Gmünd. In it, Schlüter announced that he himself was to be married. His bride-to-be, the excited telegram went on, was the daughter of a local doctor. Congratulations were immediately returned, and Adenauer prepared himself for the journey into the Eifel to witness his friend's wedding. But the next news from Gmünd carried the simple and shocking message: Raimund Schlüter, suddenly and unexpectedly, had had an attack of tuberculosis. He was dead.

Adenauer left his wife and hurried to Gmünd to his friend's funeral with another of Schlüter's friends from the Brisgovia in Freiburg. There was nobody else in their compartment, and as the train rattled along up into the mountains, his companion tried to reminisce about 'Schlot' and their university days. Adenauer remained silent. Even when his companion asked him questions to try to cheer him up, Adenauer seemed not to hear. When the question was repeated, Adenauer gave an evasive or even monosyllabic reply and lapsed again into silence. When they arrived at Gmünd, the sky was slate-grey and it was raining. They were met by Schlüter's prospective father-in-law, the doctor, fighting back his tears.

On the way to the funeral he told them the story. Schlüter had been quite open with him, he said, about his family history of tuberculosis and of his own fears; and before his engagement had asked to be examined. The doctor had done so, had pronounced him clear and had laughingly told him not to worry. A few days later, a fortnight before the wedding itself, Schlüter had suffered a haemorrhage during the night and had been found dead in bed the following morning. On the table by his bed a prayer book lay open. He had been planning to go to a general confession – prior to his marriage – in Cologne the next day. During the telling of the tale and on arrival at the church, Adenauer was silent and perfectly controlled. At the grave, he stood stiff and erect, 'without a tear'.[14]

The death of Raimund Schlüter marks the end of Konrad Adenauer's youth. Until then, whatever his relations with his parents and however uncertain the pattern of his future career, he had not had to confront the issue of death. That had now been presented in its starkest form: the death of the 'only real and true friend' of his youth. He was now married, with all the emotional difficulties and reponsibilities which that entailed. He was an established lawyer in Cologne, under the protection, if such it was, of the leading member of the governing party in the city. Whatever the outcome of his endeavours in the future, the past – Schlüter's past – was now behind him. It was time for his life to move on.

4

THE LADDER OF AMBITION

'Ich bin bestimmt genau so gut wie der andere'*

NINETEEN HUNDRED AND six was the first watershed year in Adenauer's long life. In the course of that year he reached the age of thirty, started a new career, moved house, lost his father and gained a son. Admittedly, these events were spread over several months, but their cumulative impact on the direction of his life was none the less powerful for that. The end of his youth, such as it was, had been marked by Schlüter's death; his father had dominated his childhood and adolescence; his pursuit of a profession as a lawyer had been aimless and uninspiring; and his marriage had revealed, for the first time, a vein of genuine – if somewhat erratic – sentiment. The year of 1906 was to turn the youth into a man, and to point him to the new career which he was to follow for the rest of his life.

Running through it all, there was the recurring theme of Adenauer's health. It is in some respects a puzzling problem. Certainly he had been delicate as a child, except, apparently, at the Apostelgymnasium. There also were

---

* 'I am certainly quite as good as the other man': Adenauer, quoted in P. Weymar, *Adenauer*, p. 46.

moments in his university career when his health seemed to be in danger of breaking down. But apart from the usual difficulties of a growing child, it seems to be generally true that bouts of illness occurred when he was bored or under stress. Of course, there is no reason to be surprised at that; the phenomenon is well identified in modern psychology. Such illnesses can be exaggerated in the mind, or induced, or even, at times, imagined. On the evidence, it would certainly seem that Adenauer worried about his health, sometimes to the point of – perhaps mild – hypochondria.

An example occurred just before the beginning of the decisive year. Somewhere around the autumn of 1905, his doctor had discovered the presence of excessive amounts of glucose in his urine, and had promptly pronounced him diabetic. In the light of this diagnosis, Adenauer had requested, and obtained, a month's leave of absence from court duties to build up his strength. As there was at the time no known treatment for diabetes, his doctor put him on a stringent sugar-reduced diet. Adenauer managed to adhere to this for most of the time – thus increasing his reputation for Spartan asceticism – although in later life he confessed that at times 'he would eat heartily, and afterwards drink a glass of warm water and stick his finger down his throat'.[1]

But it is by no means certain that the doctor's diagnosis was correct. *Diabetes mellitus*, which is almost certainly what his doctor had in mind, if indeed he had any such precise definition in mind, is in clinical terms a disorder rather than an illness. It results from the inability of the body's metabolism to convert the necessary amount of glucose into energy and to absorb or eliminate the unwanted balance, thus causing damage to the kidneys which, if left unattended, can ultimately prove fatal. The condition was well known even in antiquity. The most graphic description was provided by Arateus of Cappadocia in the second century AD: 'Diabetes is an awkward affection,' he wrote, 'melting down the flesh and limbs into the urine . . . patients never stop making water . . . life is short and painful . . . they are affected with nausea, restlessness and a burning thirst and at no distant term they expire.'[2] Nowadays, of course, the disorder is normally corrected with the use of insulin, but in 1905 insulin had not been synthesised for medical usage, and dietary regulation was the only treatment possible. But, whatever the means of correcting the metabolic imbalance, the disorder itself is permanent.

In Adenauer's case, however, it is reported that after he had adhered to his diet for some fifteen years, the disorder then disappeared. Such a development is clinically impossible. Given this, it is difficult to resist the conclusion that the doctor was over-enthusiastic – to say the least – in his diagnosis. The excess glucose may well have been a purely temporary phenomenon (as a matter of medical fact quite easily induced) and, if so, would have disappeared quite normally with time. Adenauer's prolonged dieting, which gave him such a reputation for asceticism, may well have been unnecessary. The unanswered question, of course, is whether in truth he preferred asceticism, and was quite content to have a suitable excuse.

Certainly, even if the doctor was wrong, Adenauer himself was perfectly content to accept his diagnosis. Nor was this the only case where his illness seemed to give him some obscure form of satisfaction. Throughout his early life, Adenauer was repeatedly reported as suffering from ill-health in one form or another. At various times (and sometimes simultaneously) he is described as susceptible to bronchitis, as suffering from frequent and severe headaches, and as a victim of insomnia. At other times all sorts of other illnesses apparently crowded in on him. Nevertheless, although there is no doubt that in his childhood his health problems were real, there is equally no doubt that he lived to a great age, and that in old age he was fitter than men and women many years his junior. The suspicion certainly must be that at least some of his reported illnesses were – to put it politely – somewhat exaggerated in the telling, and perhaps even imagined.

Certainly, Adenauer himself was not shy in discussing with others, and later even with his children, the state of his health. In 1914, for example, he developed a small blood clot in his leg, whereupon he summoned his children, showed them his leg and said gloomily: 'When the clot in my leg moves, I will die quickly.'[3] His children were duly impressed, particularly as their nanny had continually told them of their father's 'tender health' and had related that Adenauer had been refused life insurance on grounds of health risk. (But, as his son rather tartly observed, 'Father's thrombosis was cured, but Mother died'; and Adenauer, of course, lived for another fifty-three years.[4])

Whether mis-diagnosed – and possibly exaggerated – or not, Adenauer had certainly convinced himself that he entered the crucial year of 1906 as a diabetic. After all, he had only just finished his leave of absence for 'diabetes'. But, as with many of his illnesses, this did not prevent him from settling down again to act as a temporary assistant judge in the Cologne

District Court. But it was while he was performing what turned out to be his last legal task that a quite unexpected opportunity arose. It so happened that a vacancy occurred for the job of *Beigeordneter* (perhaps translatable as 'Deputy to the Mayor' or 'Member of the city government') in the administration of the city of Cologne. The post was a senior one – there were only twelve of them, each running a department and answerable directly to the mayor – and, as such, was subject to direct election by the City Council. Equally, it was a post of great responsibility.

There was no reason to believe that Adenauer, who, after all, had only spent a few years in relatively junior positions in the administration of the courts, was remotely qualified for the job. Indeed, it was little more than cheek for Adenauer to think of putting himself forward. As for his motives for doing so, these were certainly mixed. There was no doubt a financial attraction for a thirty-year-old: the post carried an annual salary of 6,000 marks (probably, on a reasonable estimate, equivalent to about DM 60,000 or £20,000 in today's values). Furthermore, he was obviously rather bored with the law, and the prospect of another career must have been enticing. Most compelling of all, however, would have been the immediate lift in social status which the position would give him. A senior civil servant was someone to command respect in the social constellation of Cologne, and Adenauer was conscious both of his own and of his father's social ambitions.

Cheek it may have been, but, once decided, Adenauer chose his route well. The City Council was at the time divided between the Liberal Party and the Centre Party, and the leader of the Centre Party group on the Council was none other than Adenauer's former employer Hermann Kausen. Kausen was also a member of the commission designated under Cologne's constitution to put up candidates. It was to him that Adenauer went. The approach, as might be imagined, came as something of a surprise. At the time, Kausen was inclined to favour the candidature of a judge from Saarbrücken. 'Why don't you take me, Herr Justizrat?' asked his former protégé. 'I am certainly quite as good as the other man.' Kausen seems to have been impressed by this effrontery and, after consultation with the head official in the personnel department ('Tell me . . . whether we can make something of him'[5]), put Adenauer forward as the Centre Party candidate. It was at this point that Adenauer could play his second card: the Wallraf connection. Thanks to his marriage, the Wallrafs were now part of his extended family – and they had powerful connections in the Liberal Party. Emma's uncle, Max Wallraf, was approached; his endorsement was sought and granted. By now, it was clear that the young man had manoeuvred with great skill.

Supported by both the Centre Party and the Liberal Party (and approved by Mayor Becker), and helped by the general but unspoken view that it was the turn of the Centre Party to take the job, Adenauer was elected Beigeordneter on 7 March 1906 with no fewer than thirty-five votes out of thirty-seven, the two missing being spoilt ballots. This was without doubt the decisive moment. The law was now left behind; Adenauer's long political career had begun.

Adenauer's father was, of course, delighted. 'Konrad,' he said when he heard the news, 'now the target you must set yourself is to become the Mayor of Cologne.'[6] His delight, however, was short-lived. Three days later, at the age of seventy-three, he suffered a severe stroke while resting at his home. A message was sent to Adenauer at the court where he was sitting. He rushed home as quickly as he could, but arrived too late. His father was dead. The only consolation was that death had been peaceful and mercifully quick. It was even noted that on his deathbed, his eyes closed and his hands clasped, the old man seemed to be smiling.

The loss of a parent, particularly of the first parent to die, is inevitably a traumatic event. To be sure, there are practical arrangements which have to be made and which occupy the mind: the funeral has to be organised; relatives have to be informed; the deprived partner has to be succoured. But there has to be time to grieve. Everybody has their own way of grieving, but Adenauer's was, to say the least, unusual. Just as he had remained motionless and silent at Schlüter's grave, so he was at his father's funeral. Furthermore, as far as is known, he never discussed his feelings about his father's death until just before his own in 1967. They were kept to himself as securely as his father's body was kept in its grave. In fact, the same was to be true when his mother died in November 1919. Stoicism, as he had been taught in his childhood, was to be the governing force.

Two weeks later Adenauer started his new job. It was not easy. To start with, he was still living in the shadow of his father's death. Then, as the youngest of the twelve deputies, and the most recent arrival, he was the most junior in status. This position was aggravated by the terms of his appointment: the vacancy had occurred at the head of the department for civil engineering, but Mayor Becker decided to put Adenauer in charge of taxation and move the previous incumbent to civil engineering — certainly not a promotion. Then there was the matter of party affiliation, which could not be kept secret, and led to disputes in the committee of the twelve between the Centre Party members (of whom Adenauer was now one) and the Liberals. Finally, there was a clear difference of approach between the lawyers, who were in the majority, and the technical specialists – who thought the lawyers' approach to the city's problems to be crabby and unimaginative.

All in all, it was a difficult working environment. But the improvement in Adenauer's finances was compensation enough. Indeed, with his 6,000-mark salary now assured, he could afford to move out of the apartment in the Klosterstrasse, which was small and cramped, and rent a house, also in the suburb of Lindenthal but in the more elegant Friedrich-Schmitt-Strasse. Adenauer had already decided that it would be right for his widowed mother and his sister Lilli to join him there. Since his mother had difficulty with the stairs to the top floor (and could not possibly live on the ground floor, which looked directly on to the street) he and Emma took the ground floor and the top floor, and the first floor was reserved for his mother and sister.

Such arrangements, of course, are never easy; mothers-in-law often make uncomfortable lodgers, particularly when they are in deep mourning for their lost husband; and the house was divided inconveniently. But Emma put up with it without open complaint. She knew the loyalty Adenauer owed to his mother, and if this was what he wanted, so be it. She was far too fond of her husband to make any complaint which might hurt him. Besides, she knew her place; the husband's decisions were final. That was what she had been brought up to believe – and what she had accepted at her marriage.

But it was perhaps the more difficult in that Emma herself was by then pregnant. True, the family could afford servants appropriate to their position, a cook and two maids (of whom one was Emma's personal maid) and the domestic chores were left to them – with only the minimum of interference, by way of instructions, from the lady of the house. Nevertheless, the pregnancy was not easy nor, when it came in the autumn of the year – on 21 September 1906 – was the birth. Indeed, it was difficult and very painful, and although both parents were pleased that the baby was a boy – to be named Konrad – Emma took a long time to recover. She seemed to be in constant pain, but neither the midwife nor the doctor could detect the source of the pain.

At this point, and for the first time, Adenauer became seriously worried for his wife. It was quite clearly no longer a matter of the normal problems of recovery from a difficult birth; in spite of his inexperience, and possible masculine distaste in such matters, he realised that something more fundamental was wrong. It was time for the husband to intervene over the heads, if need be, of the females of the family. This Adenauer did. Once the matter was taken in hand, he acted with thoroughness and despatch. Different specialists were called in, and Emma was taken to hospital for observation over a period of days. Finally, after a good deal of argument among themselves, the experts arrived at an agreed diagnosis: Emma, it appeared, had a slight curvature of the spine which was impeding the proper functioning of her kidneys. The process of diagnosis had been difficult, but worse still – and distressingly for both Adenauer and Emma – there was not much that could be done about it. All that was prescribed was a strict diet and the avoidance of undue strain; in other words, the doctors had given up. What was clear, however, was that, although there were to be good periods, from then on her health had to be regarded as permanently suspect.

Emma's condition cast a long shadow over the family home. True, she bore the pain, when it came, with great fortitude, and seems to have kept to her diet. But it was no longer the cheerful and romantic Emma of two years back. Not that the home became as gloomy as her mother's had been. Emma had no trace of morbidity; furthermore, she had many friends, and an extended family. There were always visitors coming and going. There was also the baby, 'Koko', to provide amusement. But the atmosphere had undoubtedly changed. Moreover, since it was difficult for the couple to go out in the evenings, the hectic social life of middle-class Cologne was effectively barred to them (not that Adenauer minded much, social life of that sort not being particularly to his taste).

Adenauer's reaction to this new state of affairs was twofold, and to some extent contradictory. In part it was to immerse himself in his work; but in part it was to go out of his way as much as possible to be with Emma, taking her for long holidays in the Black Forest or the Swiss Alps and being particularly assiduous in the middle of his working day, taking a full two hours for lunch at home. This made for a curious timetable, but, although curious, it was, as might be imagined, always carefully organised. In his work, Adenauer was already gaining the reputation of a hard taskmaster, even before his new-found dedication. He took his responsibilities with the utmost seriousness and diligence – even to the point of irritating his subordinates by demanding that they produce records of business left incomplete after two weeks: 'I will take direct action against civil servants who take an excessive time to complete their work.'[7] He looked, and sounded, a distinctly fierce young man (indeed, he had by this time got rid of his rather engaging elongated moustache and was clean shaven; and the twinkle in his eye of 1906 had long since disappeared).

His office day started at nine in the morning and ended at about eight o'clock in the evening. Nevertheless, he would very often stay at his office longer, particularly when the City Council was in session, when he would sometimes remain at his desk as late as midnight. Once he arrived home, however, either at one-thirty for lunch or for supper in the evening, a different Adenauer appeared. He was affectionate to his mother and sister, and, as for Emma, 'he did everything for her'.[8] In truth, there was not much he could do but show gentleness and affection, but this he did in full measure. Emma, still loving but slightly in awe of her husband and his new determination in his work, responded to this treatment, and for a time it looked as though she might be getting better. Indeed, it seems certain that full marital relations, previously inhibited by Emma's condition, were at that point resumed.

But for Adenauer it was obviously a difficult and stressful life, both at work and at home, and it is little wonder that he complained of headaches. Photographs of the time, too, show him looking rather depressed. Yet, as often happens in times of depression, his career was even then not just progressing normally along an even path but was about to make a sharp upward move. The circumstances were admittedly complicated – to the point of the bizarre. In the autumn of 1906, around the time of baby Konrad's birth, the Upper Administrative Court in Berlin ruled that the elections to the Cologne council which had taken place in the previous year – on the hugely complicated Prussian three-class system – were invalid for the Second Class. Since the Liberals customarily won the First Class easily and the Centre Party customarily won the Third Class just as comfortably, the Second Class provided what would nowadays be called the 'swing vote'. In 1905 the Centre Party won that vote, and as a result achieved a slim majority on the council. The elections for the Second Class being now declared out of order, the Centre Party lost its majority to the Liberals, who at that point had the majority – of just one.

In itself, this can hardly be described as a matter of great moment. After all, a change in majority control of a Prussian city, however important, was not an event which would change the world. But from Adenauer's point of view, the fall-out from the event was of the greatest importance. The Liberals, quite naturally, wanted to see a Liberal mayor in office. Mayor Becker, by then seventy-one years old, was gently induced to retire with two years of his period of office still to run. In the subsequent election, the Liberals put up as their candidate Wilhelm Spiritus, the Mayor of Bonn; the Centre Party put up Wilhelm Farwick, the Erster Beigeordneter (First Deputy to the Mayor) of the day; and there were two independents. One of the independents, however, was no less than Emma's uncle, Max Wallraf.

The negotiations over who was the most suitable candidate were long and tortuous. Finally, Wallraf's father-in-law, Joseph Pauli, a landowner of considerable stature and, more important, a member of the Liberal group on the council, declared roundly that, whoever might be the Liberal candidate, it was in his view imperative that the next mayor should be a native of Cologne and that, furthermore, after two incumbents who had been Protestant it was time to elect a Catholic. He and his followers, he made clear, would not vote for Spiritus, be he or be he not the official candidate of their party. So Spiritus was out of the race. Nor, he went on, would he vote for any candidate put up by the Centre Party; and the other independent was quite obviously wasting his – and everybody else's – time. The obvious compromise candidate was Pauli's own son-in-law, Max Wallraf. It soon turned out that Wallraf was acceptable to the Liberals, simply because he was Joseph Pauli's son-in-law; he was acceptable to the Centre Party, because he was a Catholic; and he was generally acceptable because he came from one of Cologne's great families. In the end, therefore, it came as no surprise to anybody when, on 13 July 1907, Wallraf was unanimously elected Mayor of Cologne. Never, perhaps, had the exclusive and in-bred nature of local German politics been more blatantly displayed.

The result was pleasing to Adenauer in two different ways. Obviously, it was to his advantage that his wife's uncle – referred to within the Adenauer household as '*notre cher oncle*'[9] – was the new mayor, although Wallraf's wife disliked his nephew-in-law and their personal relations were never particularly cordial. More important was the fact that Mayor Becker had decided, once the Centre Party had lost its majority on the council, to change the political balance in the committee of deputies to the mayor to reflect the balance of the new council. In his new scheme of things, Adenauer was to be demoted from the tax department. Fortunately for him, the plan was late in appearing, and could be postponed until after the mayoral election. So it was, and after the election the whole plan was then quietly shelved by the newly elected Mayor Wallraf.

Max Wallraf himself was not in truth particularly impressive, either as a politician or as a man. In fact, he was something of a blusterer. To be sure, he had had a number of years' experience in the Prussian civil administration and was at the time of his election to the mayoralty of Cologne a senior official in the government of the Rhine Province in Koblenz. But none of that had amounted to much. In Cologne, he seems to have been reasonably popular, perhaps because of his connections, perhaps even because he had a way with words and spoke well in public; but more likely because he cut something of a dash, dressing his good, if plump, figure elegantly and wearing his top hat at a jaunty angle. True, he may have spent too much of his time out shooting, relying on his subordinates to run the city, but the city was none the worse run for that, and at least he hung the old flags of Cologne from the roof of the Gürzenich Hall. In short, he may have been rather lazy, self-satisfied and perhaps a little smug, but in the last, heady years of the Wilhelmine era before the First World War, that was more or less the average for the Cologne *haute bourgeoisie*; and Max Wallraf was no more, and certainly no less, than a man of his time.

Because of his frequent absences, and of his temperament, Wallraf was a master of the art of delegation. Further, since he had been a compromise candidate for mayor, he followed the route of compromise in his mayoralty. When the communities on the eastern, or right, bank of the Rhine were finally incorporated into Cologne it was to general approval. He may have been considered by some to be too flamboyant – one newspaper claimed that he had installed a lavatory of pure marble in the City Hall to welcome the Kaiser on one of his visits – but that was not necessarily thought to be such a bad thing. Thanks probably to Adenauer's management of the tax department, and to the gradual recovery from the economic stagnation from which Germany had suffered after the major recession of 1903, he could claim with some justification that he had gone a long way to balance the city budget – no mean feat, as future events were to show.

Adenauer's diligence and intelligent management was certainly valued by the mayor, but it was not until 1909 that his next piece of good fortune occurred. Farwick, the Centre Party's candidate for mayor in 1907 and the

First Deputy to the Mayor, had by then had enough of Wallraf's administration – in character he was almost the opposite to Wallraf, relatively
modest and socially conscious – and had decided to seek a job in the private
sector. It was not too difficult; he had, after all, virtually run Cologne for the
last few years, and it was not long before he was offered, and accepted, an
executive directorship of the Schaffhausen Bank. His departure left a vacancy
in the position of First Deputy to the Mayor.

Once more, those in the city with experience of previous similar negotiations girded themselves for action. The position was tantamount to that of
deputy mayor, and, given Wallraf's particular management style and the
constitutional provision that he was due to remain mayor for a further nine
years, was a matter – at least in their estimation – of the highest importance.
By this time, in fact, the political balance on the council had shifted yet
again. The Centre Party had once again achieved a majority (this time legitimately) and were determined to impose their own candidate in succession
to Farwick, who had been their man in the first place. The Liberals, on the
other hand, were anxious to frustrate the Centre Party, and claimed that since
the appointee would be an official it was quite wrong to make the decision
one of party politics. Wallraf himself abstained from participation in the
long negotiations, on the very reasonable grounds that his nephew-in-law
was clearly a possible candidate.

In the end there were only two possible candidates, Adenauer and one of
his senior colleagues, Bruno Matzerath. After a discussion of great length,
the Centre Party caucus decided on Adenauer. His election was, after that,
a foregone conclusion. Nevertheless, the Liberals, although they did not put
forward a candidate of their own, refused to vote for him. They simply muttered that Adenauer's nomination was 'not compelling, based on the needs
arising from the interests of the city'.[10] In other words, they thought that it
was a political stitch-up, which indeed it was. The unanimity which had been
achieved in 1906 had broken down. But it was enough, and on 22 July
1909, at the age of thirty-three, Adenauer was elected First Deputy to the
Mayor of Cologne, and thus became the second most powerful man in the
city.

The election provoked great resentment. It was not just the Liberal
establishment who objected. Adenauer was, after all, the youngest Deputy
to the Mayor in a city where tradition, age and experience counted
for much. Here, they said, was a young upstart infiltrating the city's

administration, relying on the family connections of his sick wife for the purpose. The great families of Cologne, not least the Pauli dynasty, felt that it was all going too far. Adenauer certainly received the message loud and clear – particularly since it came from his wife's aunt – that he should not be too presumptuous in his new position. He should remember that the mayor was the mayor, and even though he might be the mayor's senior representative the ultimate authority rested with the mayor himself. He would forget that message at his peril.

As it happened, Adenauer took office at a particularly fortunate time. His new salary of 15,000 marks per annum, increased to 18,000 marks (again, on a reasonable estimate equivalent to some DM 360,000 or £120,000 in today's values) once the controversy over his appointment had died down, put him in the highest bracket of the Cologne middle class – although some way below the richer members of the Cologne aristocracy. Nevertheless, land in Cologne was still relatively cheap after the recession, and Adenauer was able to afford to buy a plot in the Max-Bruch-Strasse – just next door to the city park and in one of the smartest areas of the city – and to borrow enough to build himself an impressively large house. By 1911 the thing was done, and the Adenauer family – mother, sister, Adenauer himself, Emma, 'Koko' and a more recent arrival, baby Max (whose birth in 1910 had been mercifully without incident) – moved in. The young First Deputy was now properly established as a great figure in the panoply of – admittedly parochial – Cologne.

But there were other grounds for self-congratulation in the timing of Adenauer's assumption of office. Nineteen hundred and nine saw the start of a clear recovery in the German economy, fuelled not least by the Kaiser's armament programme. The incorporation of the industrial suburbs on the right bank of the river had, for Cologne, come at the right time. The demand for steel, for machine tools, for combustion engines and for chemicals – precisely the products for which the companies in Deutz and Mülheim were well equipped – had taken off. The resulting economic activity in the Cologne suburbs generated financial activity in the city itself. Both the industrial firms and the banks were in a good mood as a result. So, indeed, was the city's administration. The extra tax revenue generated in the recovery allowed the city, after a deficit of 1.5 million marks in 1907, to present a balanced budget for 1910. Thereafter, it was a matter of building a surplus, and of planning for an expansion of the regional economy – a second bridge over the Rhine to the new communities on the right bank, a publicly-owned lending bank, the acquisition of shares in local transport companies and utilities. All in all, the period 1909 to 1914 was a prosperous period for Cologne and for its First Deputy.

Prosperous it may have been, but Cologne did not live in a vacuum. It was, after all, the major fortified city defending the Rhine against any attack from France or the Low Countries. Parochial as its concerns were, it could not afford to ignore the outside world in the way other, less strategically placed, cities could; and the outside world, as it happened, was even then hurtling towards catastrophe. Kaiser Wilhelm II* had adopted what is generally known as a 'forward policy' in foreign affairs. 'Your grandson,' the Prussian Crown Princess had written to her mother Queen Victoria in London one month after Wilhelm's birth in 1859, 'is exceedingly lively and, when awake, will not be satisfied unless kept dancing about continually.'[11] As such, it is a fair description even of the Kaiser in the years leading up to the First World War. The result had been a succession of dangerous international scrapes. True, as Queen Victoria's grandson, he enjoyed the patronage, and friendship, of the British Royal Family, not least of his first cousin, the future King George V. Furthermore, within Germany, or at least Prussia, he commanded respect, loyalty, and even enthusiasm. In particular, his visits to Cologne – since he was not one to neglect his Rhine Province – evoked the most enthusiastic demonstrations of patriotism.

But the 'forward policy' had dangers as well as advantages. Certainly, the Kaiser's programme for German armament, and in particular the building of more battleships to counter what was perceived as Britain's unhealthy domination of the high seas, brought prosperity to Cologne and the surrounding

---

* Wilhelm II, Friedrich Wilhelm Viktor Albert (1859–1941): Emperor of Germany. Born in Potsdam. Educated in Kassel and then Bonn University. 1880: Entered Prussian army. 1885: Colonel of Prussian Guard Hussars. 1888: Became Kaiser after the death of his father, who had ruled for only ninety-nine days. 1914: Bellicose statements contributed to international tension. 1917: Approved policy of unlimited submarine warfare, which had the effect of bringing the USA into the First World War. 1918: Abdicated, and fled to Holland. Strong on the divine right of rulership; even in 1918, there were some who still believed in him.

Rhineland. There was, however, some disquiet over the way the Kaiser seemed from time to time to take foreign policy entirely into his own hands. 'Foreign policy,' he said to his new Chancellor, Theobald von Bethmann Hollweg, in 1909, 'you can leave to me!'[12] That might have been what the Kaiser wanted, but, as it turned out, it was hardly a recipe for peace.

That particular controversy had only limited echoes in Cologne, or with Adenauer himself. The Kaiser was, after all, both the King of Prussia and the German Emperor. For a senior civil servant, such as Adenauer now was, loyalty to the Kaiser was what he had sworn; and that oath had to be kept. As it happened, it was also Adenauer's inclination. As First Deputy to the Mayor of Cologne, and as a nephew-in-law of the mayor, he was certainly not going to rock any boats. In later years he was to say that 'the 1914–1918 war was a war which was brought about by the stupidity of everyone',[13] but that was certainly not his – or anybody else's – mood in the years leading up to 1914. Adenauer was for Prussia and for the German Empire; and, if that meant war, so be it. Like other Germans of his time, he was deeply worried about the prospect of 'encirclement', of military co-operation between France and Russia against Germany. Moreover, the available evidence indicates that he was very much in favour of the German Empire acquiring colonies 'at all costs'.[14] All in all, in the years leading up to 1914 he was almost certainly a supporter of military action to protect the German Empire against what he and others perceived as a deliberate threat to its existence. He was certainly no pacifist nor even an advocate of a negotiated peace.

It is difficult to say at what precise point Adenauer realised that war was inevitable and that preparations had to be made for the maintenance of good order – and safety – in Cologne during what would inevitably be a difficult period. At the age of thirty-eight he was too old to be drafted for military service, and in any event he was needed for the administration of the city. The fortifications had to be kept in good shape, and although this was primarily the responsibility of the military, the civil administration had a most definite interest. Furthermore, Cologne would be a major transit point for military units going to and from whatever front there might be in the west, either in Belgium or in northern France. It is impossible to believe that the First Deputy to the Mayor was unaware of the complications which would ensue, and that he was not making preparations – perhaps even covert – for the event.

But if Europe was hurtling towards war, the Adenauer household was hurtling towards its own personal tragedy. Emma had given birth in 1912 to a daughter – Maria, or, more familiarly, 'Ria'. The birth had been even more difficult than that of Konrad six years earlier, or of Max, her second son, two years earlier. This time there was no recovery. From then on Emma looked, and was, seriously ill. She spent her days moving with difficulty from bed to sofa and back to bed again. There were all the signs of an advancing cancer. Adenauer tried to avoid talking to her about her illness, let alone its gravity. But Emma was no fool. She knew that she was unlikely to recover, and insisted on speaking with her husband about the future of the children after her death. Adenauer forced himself to an 'outward display of composure, even cheerfulness'.[15] But even he occasionally broke down. After a particularly difficult interview with her doctor, he was heard by his son to mutter, in tones of deepest depression: 'So she has to die after all.'[16] War, for Adenauer, was to bring not only the bitterness of defeat for his country but also the bitterness of the death of his wife.

5

A TIME OF TRAGEDY

'... wahre Hölle'*

'WAR IS LIKE Christmas,' wrote a newly commissioned German officer to his family in August 1914.[1] Three weeks later he was dead, killed by an accidental gunshot on his way to the Belgian front. But his letter home sums up more graphically than any other the enthusiasm which seized not just many in authority but a large section of popular opinion in all the belligerent countries at the start of what, in the end, was to become one of the most gruesome wars in history. True, there had been much opposition in all countries during the previous July. For instance, 'thousands of workers' had 'overfilled meetings and on the street demonstrated against war and for peace' in Berlin on the 29th.[2] Yet once war had been declared, patriotism demanded that criticism be muted – although it was never wholly suppressed – and enthusiasm manifested.

Even with the benefit of hindsight, the enthusiasm is difficult to explain, let alone justify. Perhaps in part it was simple ignorance of what modern war

---

* '... true hell': Adenauer, describing life after Emma's death in 1916; quoted in P. Weymar, *Adenauer*, p. 58.

was; in part, too, it may have been an explosion of excitement at the start of a great venture; there may also have been a feeling of relief that the problems which had accumulated during the years of peace would be quickly and easily resolved in a matter of months; and finally it was, without a doubt, an unpleasant reflection of the self-confidence, and self-righteousness, which was the legacy of the fat years of the previous decade. To this already heady mixture was added the belief, firmly held by all the belligerents, that theirs was the just cause. They were fighting not for self-interest or aggrandisement – even the thought was unworthy – but for what was right. They were also, they were told, fighting for God. At least on that point each national church was singing the same tune, even if in a different key; they all believed that God was on the side of their country, and were not reticent in saying so. That the countries, and therefore the churches, were on opposite sides did not, at the time, seem to be a problem for Christendom in its broader perspective, although the Vatican was wise enough not to take sides, but simply to pray for peace.

There is no reason to suppose that Adenauer was immune from the tide of general enthusiasm. After all, Cologne was very much at the centre of things. The regiments which had been stationed there left for the Western Front amid scenes of great jubilation. They marched through the streets singing at the top of their voices their songs of war: '*Morgenrot*', '*Kein schön'rer Tod ist in der Welt als wer vorm Feind erschlagen*', and so on.[3] (It was a feature of German war songs, compared with those of other countries, that they seemed to dwell very much on the concept of 'noble' death. Perhaps Wagner had reached more deeply into the German psyche than was realised at the time.) Women and old men lined the streets to cheer them on. Emma Adenauer herself even managed to leave her sofa and stand with her friends handing to the soldiers as they passed by glasses of – strangely enough – raspberry juice. Trains packed with figures in field grey crossed the Hohenzollern Bridge at the rate of one every ten minutes. The *Kölnische Volkszeitung*, the newspaper most closely connected to the Centre Party, published articles with titles such as '*Englands Schuld*',[4] '*England, der Feind der Neutralen*',[5] or '*Belgien und die deutschfeindliche Verschwörung*'.[6] In short, the sense of excitement that all this activity engendered was almost impossible to resist.

But there was practical work to be done as well, and the First Deputy to the Mayor was keen, and more than keen, to do it. Cologne had resumed its old role of fortress-city. It was also the main railway junction linking the north German plain, and the military camps that were being set up there, with the fronts which were opening up in Belgium and northern France. Further, as the casualties came wandering back from the front, they had to be looked after; civilians, too, had to be fed; Cologne's industry had to convert to war production; even the cathedral's five-ton bell had to be melted down to make shells.

The most urgent matter was the provision of food. Adenauer took this as his own personal responsibility. In August 1914 a decree was promulgated to stop any form of food from being taken out of the fortified area of the city. Simultaneously, there was a vast programme of purchase, financed by borrowings, of almost everything that was immediately available. Flour, rice, lentils and peas all piled up in the warehouses along the Rhine at Rheinau dock. Dairy cows were bought from Holland, cabbage was bought from Neuss. Calves were herded into the Gürzenich and allowed to graze in the city's parks. At the same time, under Adenauer's instruction, forestry firms, which had closed down or reduced their activity in the pre-war period, were to work again at full output. Other firms raised money from their employees 'for the war expenses of the city of Cologne'.[7] By October it was reported that the Cologne Automobile Club was to form an ambulance corps: all its members were urged to provide their cars to go to France and Belgium to bring back the wounded. By November, a group of Italian journalists on a visit to Cologne, dignified by a greeting from the mayor himself, were shown a factory with the message at the gate, in large letters: '*Die unermüdlich durcheinander wirbelnde Menschenmenge*'. The lesson was that the economy was in fine fettle and that all the people of Cologne, men and women, were working unanimously and tirelessly for the victory of the Kaiser and the Reich.[8]

Nevertheless, although it all started well enough, before long people started to wonder how long the whole thing was going to last. Complaints started when savings had to be made and belts had to be tightened. To be fair, the Adenauer house showed no reluctance in tightening belts. Although he was First Deputy to the Mayor, Adenauer's family's standard of life was no better, as his son remarked, 'than that of a small official'. Adenauer himself never drank or smoked; his clothes were always simple; his shoes were worn until their tips started to turn up; and once a fortnight an employee of the city who had formerly been a hairdresser turned up to give father and two sons a close crop – 'It is hygienic and cheap,' he pointed out if anybody complained about the result.[9]

The one activity on which Adenauer was prepared to spend money was on his inventions. It is a curious, and indeed unlikely, feature of the man, but for almost all his life Adenauer was convinced that he had a talent for invention. The fact that nobody else believed in this talent or that none of his inventions made the fortune which he confidently expected did not deter him. In 1904, for instance, he had invented a new type of streamlining for cars. Then he invented a new type of hairpin, which, he claimed, was impossible to lose (and which Emma was required to wear). Of course, in anybody else this activity could just be regarded as a mild form of eccentricity; but it is all the more surprising to find such eccentricity in what was in other respects a well-ordered and disciplined character.

Given what he regarded as his inventive talents, at the beginning of the war Adenauer turned them to the important problem of the supply of food. As the war ground on, and turned into static trench warfare on the Western Front, food shortages became widespread. At that point Adenauer invented the 'Cologne Sausage', a tasteless affair consisting mostly of soya flour, and 'Cologne Bread', an equally unprepossessing concoction of maize, barley and ground rice, of which he seems to have been particularly proud and for which, in fact, he registered a patent.[10] Until 1916, Cologne Bread was available without limit, but after Romania entered the war the supply of maize dried up and the bread was put on ration. In order to discourage consumption – not that the qualities of Cologne Bread had ever been much appreciated – Adenauer further ordered bakeries to sell only bread that had been kept in store for two days, and was therefore stale. He also set up vast kitchens in working-class areas of Cologne to churn out a particularly unpleasant, but nutritious, form of paste. They were not a great success, but Adenauer did not seem to be discouraged. Indeed, during 1915 he wrote a series of articles for the *Kölnische Zeitung* (not by any means a Centre Party supporter), subsequently published by the Berlin publishing house Concordia under the hopeful title of 'New Regulations for Our Food Supply Economy'. In these he argued in detail, and at considerable length, for greater local control of the purchase of foodstuffs, and less interference from Berlin.

But in truth, in spite of his creative efforts, there was little that the First Deputy could do about the underlying problem. Even as early as 1915, food shortages were commonplace and a black market was operating. In October of that year the Association of Rhine Province Municipalities met to discuss rising prices and the poverty of the popular diet. It was, of course, to get much worse in 1916. Horse meat became a regular part of the Cologne diet, along with a vegetable substitute instead of potatoes and coffee made of barley and chicory. The First Deputy, who had achieved a respectful popularity for the way he had organised the distribution of food in 1914, inevitably came under severe criticism when supplies of the food which Cologne had been used to for centuries simply ran out.

In all this, Mayor Wallraf had managed to take for himself the credit for Adenauer's successes and to make sure that Adenauer took the blame for perceived failures. In fact, the mayor took a lower and lower profile as the war dragged on. It was up to the First Deputy to organise the city, and he should be in no doubt about the nature of his job. Recognising this, Adenauer set about organising his first cross-party alliance. This was to be something of a new venture. The partners whom he had to cultivate were not just the Liberals, hitherto the powerful force of the industrial and commercial *bourgeoisie*, or the Centre Party, the political wing of the Catholic movement whose membership spread across the classes, but the disenfranchised representatives of the industrial working class whose political weight had greatly increased since the incorporation into Cologne of the industrial communities on the right bank of the Rhine. Those representatives formed the heart of the Social Democratic Party in Cologne, a party which hitherto, as a good Catholic, Adenauer had regarded as representatives of something close to the Devil. As it happened, in this new venture Adenauer was once again fortunate. Instead of a group of aggressive Marxists he found, obviously to his surprise, reasonable people who in general supported the Kaiser and the German war effort; and the leader of the loyalist faction within the Social Democrats was Wilhelm Sollmann, 'one of the most splendid men I have ever met', reported a senior civil servant, 'manly, courageous and direct'.[11]

Sollmann was, in age, Adenauer's contemporary. He had been born in 1881, in Thuringia, and had become an apprentice in Cologne, leaving the Gymnasium early on the grounds that he was better off learning something sensible. He was teetotal and Christian (of an obscure evangelical sect known as the Good Templars). As local editor of the *Rheinische Zeitung*, he had put forward the Marxist view of political history, and its relevance to the events of the day, with a good deal of venom. Furthermore, in 1913 and 1914 he had been a leading figure in the harrying and subsequent conviction of a group of corrupt officers of the Cologne police force. To be sure, at first sight he was not a promising partner for the Catholic and conservative Adenauer, in spite of the general view that he was 'a decent man'.[12] But Sollmann was sensible enough to realise that there was a deal to be struck, and Adenauer was sensible enough to know that unless there was a deal, the practical, as opposed to the political, administration of Cologne under wartime conditions would become impossible.

The deal was done. In return for Social Democrat co-operation in the running of the city, Adenauer agreed that the Social Democrats would be entitled to three seats in the City Council at the elections to be held in 1918. Moreover, the whole Prussian system of election by three classes was agreed to be badly out of date, and would be replaced by a more equitable system of voting. Finally, Adenauer recognised that the poorest in the city had borne the greatest burden of domestic life in the wartime period, and gave assurances that they were not in the future to be neglected. On the basis of these three undertakings, Sollmann and the Social Democrats pledged their co-operation with the authorities for the duration of the war.

Nevertheless, although co-operation with the Social Democrats, and, by extension, the trade unions, was of vital practical importance in the administration of the city, the old antagonists, the Liberals and the Centre Party, still controlled the City Council, and were still, whatever the urgencies of the war, fighting their old battles. The Centre Party in particular were riding high. Their two most important figures were Hugo Mönnig, a lawyer in the mould of Hermann Kausen a decade earlier – tough and devious, and Johannes Rings, a former printer's supervisor who came from the largely craft-based membership of the party. Together they controlled a reasonably disciplined and cohesive organisation. In truth, neither of them much liked Adenauer, who was too ascetic and unsociable for their taste, but they recognised the First Deputy's diligence and conscientiousness. Besides, nobody could get rid of him; so, like him or not, they had to work with him.

The Liberals were much more diffuse in their organisation and in their leadership. Their members were predominantly from the *haute bourgeoisie*, many of them making good profits out of the war. Nevertheless, they exercised great influence in the affairs of Cologne, and the one who exercised the greatest influence was without a doubt the brightest star in their constellation, the banker Louis Hagen.

Hagen, of Jewish origin (he changed his name from Levy when he married the daughter of a Catholic industrialist and himself converted to

Christianity), was the most successful among the new 'money aristocracy' of Cologne. A banker by trade, his speciality was organising mergers between industrial companies. By the time war broke out, Hagen was a very rich man, a director of no fewer than thirty-nine companies and president of the Cologne Chamber of Commerce. He was also top of the Cologne social tree; an invitation to the Hagen home was one to be treasured, and to speak freely about to friends and neighbours. As a benefactor, he was generous (his gifts ranged from the university to the zoo). In this he was as successful as he was in his business dealings, and there were few men in the city who were not in one way or another indebted to him. One such, for instance, was a lawyer named Bernhard Falk, the chairman of the Liberals and the most respected member of the Jewish community. It also happened that Falk had another advantage: his wife was one of the main figures in the women's organisations of Cologne.

These were the men, Mönnig, Rings, Hagen and Falk (with Sollmann in the background), with whom Adenauer had to work in the wartime administration of the city. Indeed, more and more, it was Adenauer himself who took the leading role, as First Deputy rather than as representative of the Mayor, since Wallraf spent an increasing amount of time on national business in Berlin.

It was also these men who, in February 1916, started to reflect on the mayoral elections due in 1919. Of course, they thought, it was always possible that Wallraf might wish to serve another term, but Mönnig and Rings were unwilling to endorse his candidature on the grounds that he was not a member of the Centre Party, which had a clear and legitimate majority on the City Council; and they pointed out that the confused conditions under which Wallraf had emerged as a compromise candidate in 1906 no longer applied. Their choice, as they made clear to their colleagues in the Centre Party on the City Council, whatever their own personal likes or dislikes, was the obvious one: Adenauer.

It was at this point that there was an unexpected diversion. The Mayor of Aachen, Philipp Veltmann, suddenly died of a heart attack. The Centre Party, the dominant party in what was, after all, the city of the great Charlemagne, sent a message to Adenauer inviting him to put his name forward as a candidate. If he did so, they went on, he would be assured of their support. The offer was certainly attractive. Aachen was a pleasant enough city of some 160,000 inhabitants; Adenauer would be his own master rather than a second-in-command; he could serve three years in Aachen and then put his name forward for Cologne when Wallraf's term of office came to an end in 1919; and, in the meantime, he would be enjoying a salary of 40,000 marks per annum, over twice what he was earning in his present job. All in all, it was not an offer to be turned down easily.

Yet turn it down he did. There were, to be sure, long conversations with Mönnig, Falk and others about the prospects in Cologne itself. He also spoke with Wallraf, who advised him against taking the job on the grounds that Aachen would not suit him (in other words, he did not want to lose his indefatigable First Deputy). Wallraf even held out the further bait that he might not stand again in 1919. Indeed, there may have even been hints that, as a former senior Prussian civil servant and as Mayor of Cologne a member of the Upper House of the Prussian *Landtag* (parliament), some promotion to Berlin might be in the offing. Furthermore, Wallraf went on, if Adenauer left Cologne that in itself might leave the way clear for Wilhelm Farwick, Adenauer's predecessor as First Deputy, and an obvious Centre Party candidate for mayor should Adenauer be unavailable. But Wallraf would not give the final assurance which his nephew-in-law wanted: that he would stand down early, in 1917 or 1918, in Adenauer's favour.

The whole matter was thrown into confusion in early May by Wallraf's decision to go to a sanatorium in Freiburg for a rest cure. It was further complicated by Wallraf's subsequent decision to finish his cure by going shooting, which resulted in a minor accident, but one which did nothing to improve his temper. The butt of his rifle escaped from his shoulder and struck him in the face, giving him a badly bruised, and hence very black, eye. After that, the mayor was in no mood to give any assurances to anyone about his future ambitions. By the time he had recovered his temper, and had written to Adenauer along the lines of their previous conversations – 'the particular Aachen milieu would not suit either him or Emma'[13] – it was already July and the Centre Party in Aachen were getting tired of waiting for an answer to their offer. In the end, Adenauer, while thanking them profusely, called the whole thing off. In November 1916 Wilhelm Farwick was elected Mayor of Aachen.

The whole negotiation, and its result, was of the greatest importance to the forty-year-old Adenauer's position and future in Cologne. While Mayor Wallraf was recuperating from his shooting accident, the First Deputy was, to all intents and purposes, Mayor. Nevertheless, the whole episode, and, indeed, the whole of Adenauer's burgeoning career in these years, has to be set against the general context of the time. City politics, for this is what they were, may be fun, but even the most absorbed of city politicians has to take at least some notice of the major events of the day; and in the years of 1914 to 1918 there was only one event that merited attention: the war.

Sadly – the adverb comes with the benefit of hindsight – that event seems to have been wholly ignored at the time. In any reading of the first-hand accounts, whether they be the letters from one Cologne politician to another, or the Cologne newspaper reports of events, or even the memoirs of the participants in the disputes about the mayoralty in Aachen or Cologne, it is difficult to find any reference to, let alone any concern about, the dreadful carnage that was, even at that moment, taking place not more than 200 miles from Cologne itself.

In mid-February 1916, for instance, just at the time when Adenauer was being solicited by the Centre Party in Aachen, the German Army launched its major offensive on the weakest point of the French front, where it hinged southwards at the salient of Verdun. There followed a ten-month battle, recorded in the history of warfare as the bloodiest battle of all time. The whole area to the north-east of the city of Verdun is, even today, scarred for mile upon mile. The slaughter was seemingly endless, but time after time both sides mounted hopeless and suicidal attacks to gain no more than a few yards of ground. The fort at Douaumont, for instance, was captured by the Germans in March 1916 and recaptured by the French in October 1916. Throughout those eight months the fighting around the fort had been relentless, and by October the casualties were such that trenches could not be dug because corpses lay in layers on the spot.

The German wounded, or at least those who survived the miserable conditions of mud and neglect in field hospitals, were brought back from Verdun to hospitals behind the front line. One of the clearing stations for serious casualties was Cologne. The hospitals were full of desperately wounded, often blinded, burned and smashed bodies. The scenes in the hospitals must have been quite heart-rending. Yet, throughout this carnage of their countrymen, there is no record of the seniors of Cologne, Wallraf, Adenauer, Mönnig, Rings, Hagen, Falk or Sollmann, ever having visited any of the hospitals to give any comfort at all to the wounded and the dying, to encourage the doctors and nurses or even to see whether they were being properly looked after. They may have done so, and their solicitude may have gone unrecorded, but if such attention was never offered it is a shameful chapter in the lives of Cologne's leading figures of the time – of whom Adenauer was one.

Be all that as it may, Adenauer at least arguably had an excuse in his problems at home. Emma was by early 1916 a permanent invalid. Adenauer himself had to give parental attention to his three children, and at the same time to keep Emma company in the evenings. By then, too, Emma, in the last year of her life, had refused to be nursed; and Adenauer, in his lunch hour, had to change the poultices on the sores which she had developed and 'do all the little jobs that the care of a sick person requires'.[14] He repeated the task in the evenings, and stayed with her, holding her hand, until she went to sleep. On Sundays, weather permitting, he took his children for long walks in the Siebengebirge and told them stories about his childhood and the trees and flowers that they saw. Not, of course, that there was any extravagance. Their food was always carried in a knapsack and, if they did stop, 'no landlord was likely to make a fortune from us'. Nevertheless, Adenauer felt able to shake off his troubles and worries, and even laugh out loud as he told his children stories; 'He talked to me,' his elder son said, 'as he would to a grown-up friend.'[15]

It could not last. All the known treatments of the day, including prolonged visits to spa towns to take the waters, were to no avail. During September 1916 Emma's condition deteriorated at an accelerated pace. She could no longer get out of bed, and was in constant pain. At lunchtime and in the evenings, Adenauer sat by her bedside for as long as he could, holding her hand, often far into the night. By the middle of October, the situation was desperate. But it was just at that moment that Adenauer was summoned to Berlin for a meeting. While he was away, on 16 October, the family ate a meal consisting of little more than mushrooms. The mushrooms turned out to be toxic and, although the rest of the family recovered quickly, the shock was too much for Emma's system. Her kidneys gave up the struggle and, at the age of thirty-six, she died.

Adenauer took Emma's death with a sense almost of despair. On his return he sat for long hours by the bed where she lay, the bed covered with roses. At the requiem and funeral, he led the procession of mourners, and then immediately ordered his family into mourning for the prescribed full year and after that a further six weeks. Ria, only four years old, was put into a black frock. There were no more Sunday walks in the Siebengebirge;

Adenauer spent his Sundays, after Mass, sitting gloomily with his brother Hans speaking about his loss and seeking whatever spiritual comfort he could find. All domestic arrangements were left to his mother. She probably did her best to look after the children and run the house, but she was old, had continual rows with the servants and could not stop them from their petty pilfering. Adenauer later described the whole period as 'true hell'.

The winter of 1916–17 was grim in almost every respect. True, the ten-month carnage at Verdun had come to its inconclusive end; but the new carnage on the Somme had sent more broken bodies back to Cologne, and it seemed that there would be no end to the melancholy procession. Adenauer continued in his job, still in the deep depression which had followed Emma's death. In the winter, he did make some sort of effort with his children, taking his elder son Konrad for sleigh rides when the snow came to the Siebengebirge, but his heart was not in it. In a photograph taken at the time his eyes show the deep marks of depression, and fierce anger. He had lost weight, and his hair had started to thin at the temples. All in all, it is the face of a man who has been deeply hurt, working through the sad process of anger and bereavement.

But worse was to come. In mid-March 1917, Adenauer unaccountably failed to return home to Max-Bruch-Strasse at lunchtime. The family waited for him for nearly two hours before a telephone call came from the Trinity Hospital: the First Deputy had been admitted after a car accident and was at that moment on the operating table. The precise details of the accident they did not know, but they would keep his mother informed of his progress.

There was, as might be imagined, consternation in the Adenauer household. Throughout the whole afternoon Adenauer's mother was on the telephone to anybody she could think of – the police, doctors, anyone who the police thought might have been a witness to the accident. Gradually the story was pieced together. Adenauer, it appeared, had been coming back home for lunch when his driver had fallen asleep at the wheel of his official car. The car had careered straight into the path of an oncoming tram, and had been completely wrecked. Somehow, the driver had emerged unscathed from the disaster, but Adenauer had been thrown through the glass partition which separated him from the driver in front. Both his cheekbones and his nose had been broken, his lower jaw had been impacted, he had lost several teeth and his eyes had been damaged.

Later that day Adenauer's mother and his son Konrad went to the scene of the accident. The fire brigade had cleared away most of the wreckage, but there was still a pool of blood and some splinters of glass in the middle of the road. The owner of a nearby gardening shop told them the details of the event in a state of near hysterical excitement. 'There was a terrible crash,' he said, 'as though a shell had landed in the middle of the street. The car was no more than a pile of twisted metal. I would never have thought that even a mouse could have lived through that. But then a man slowly crawled out of the wreckage, stood up straight and, streaming with blood, walked away, stiff like a puppet. It was First Deputy Adenauer. The driver, who was only slightly injured, allowed himself to be carried away on a stretcher.'[16]

The two went quickly to the hospital, where the shopkeeper's account was confirmed. Adenauer had indeed arrived at the hospital on foot. Furthermore, because of the loss of blood from deep cuts in his head and face, a surgeon had had to stitch up the wounds while he was still conscious – and without anaesthetic. It was only when the operation was over that Adenauer fainted from the pain.

Three days later, his mother and son were allowed to visit him in hospital. When they saw him, 'We wanted,' his son reported, 'to turn around straightaway [to go home]. The man who looked at us from the pillows was a total stranger.'[17] Indeed, the accident and the subsequent surgery had given him an entirely different face. His already high cheekbones had been lifted further, his eyes were narrower, his nose was slightly bent in the middle, and the lower part of his face ended in thin lips and a more pointed jawline. Of course, the swelling in his face and the welter of stitches and bandages which were only normal after such extensive reconstruction made the effect all the more shocking, and must have made him look to his son 'a total stranger'. Nevertheless, the change in his features, however good a job the surgeons had done, was to be permanent.

During the first week of his recovery, Adenauer, as he later wrote himself, 'hovered between life and death'.[18] In his conscious moments he was in great pain, and his eyesight was badly affected. Yet, 'the first days after my accident were full of spiritual quiet and spiritual peace such as I had not known since the summer of 1913, since my wife became seriously ill'.[19] The streak of fatalism in Adenauer's character is never more evident. The simplest way out of the depression which had taken hold of him since Emma's death

71

was to die. In that way he could not only be with her in the next world but could rid himself of the burdens of this.

Oddly enough, Adenauer recorded those words soon after he had achieved his (and his dead father's) ambition, of becoming Mayor of Cologne. After weeks spent in hospital, recovering slowly from his dreadful accident, he had decided to convalesce in a sanatorium at St Blasien in the Black Forest. But it was just at that moment – early August 1917 – that Max Wallraf was summoned to Berlin and offered the job of Under-Secretary of State in the Ministry of the Interior. The matter was, of course, of the utmost urgency. Wallraf accepted immediately. His appointment was announced on 8 August, and his farewell party was held in the Gürzenich Hall on the following day. But as far as Cologne was concerned the upshot was clear: the city had to find itself a new mayor.

At this point, the same set of characters as before moved on stage: Mönnig and Rings for the Centre Party, Falk for the Liberals, with Hagen (and, to a minor extent, Sollmann) hovering in the wings. The Centre Party was clearly in favour of Adenauer, provided – it was an obvious and powerful reservation – that his accident had not affected his ability to do the job. Since the main physical damage had been to his head, and since it was known that his eyes had been affected, there was the unspoken fear that he might have suffered some form of brain damage. The only way to resolve the problem was to go and see Adenauer to find out.

So it was that Mönnig and Rings quickly made the journey to the Black Forest to the sanatorium where Adenauer lay. They first saw his doctor, who gave them a favourable report on the patient, and then went in to see Adenauer himself. Their visit came as no surprise to him. Hagen had already written to him to outline the new situation in Cologne, so he was well prepared. He also guessed the purpose of the visit, and was not at all taken aback when his visitors engaged him in conversation about the weather, the progress of the war, the finances of the city of Cologne, and almost any other matter which they could think of. After two hours of this, Adenauer had had enough. 'Gentlemen,' he announced drily, 'it is only outwardly that I am not quite normal.'[20] The others got the point, laughed – perhaps nervously and in some embarrassment – and immediately offered him the Centre Party nomination for the mayoralty.

Mönnig and Rings reported back favourably to the Centre Party group on the Cologne City Council, which immediately endorsed the nomination. It

was then time to square the Liberals, since, although the Centre Party could
have elected Adenauer by its simple majority on the council, it was obviously
better for the mayor to enjoy support from all sides. The broker in this exercise was to be Hagen. Falk recognised Adenauer as a 'tolerant, candid and
progressive man'[21] and did not need to be persuaded, but there were others
who were concerned that he was too close to the Centre Party. Hagen then set
about the age-old political process of trading on the goodwill which his
dealings and munificence had won for him. One by one those in the 'money
aristocracy' were politely convinced by Hagen that Adenauer would be better
for business than any alternative Centre Party candidate, and in that process
no doubt certain hints were dropped about past favours, and possible future
rewards.

The Liberal group on the council was won over. The last remaining
problem was the matter of the mayor's salary. Adenauer's negotiating position was robust: he wanted very much more than Wallraf's 25,000 marks,
and justified his position by referring to the inflation that had occurred
during the course of the war. But he was dismayed to find out, when he made
a list of the salaries of the mayors of the major cities in Prussia, that only
the Mayor of Berlin earned the 40,000 marks which the city was prepared
to offer Adenauer. The letters went from Cologne to St Blasien and back as
the haggling continued. Finally agreement was reached on a pensionable
salary of 42,000 marks, to be topped up by a director's fee of 10,000
marks from Rheinische Braunkohlen AG. It was a most generous settlement.
There was no doubt: Adenauer was now to be a rich man.

On 18 September 1917 Konrad Adenauer was elected Mayor of Cologne
by fifty-two out of a possible fifty-four votes, with two abstentions. On 18
October he was sworn in by the District President in the Hansa-Saal of the
City Hall. There were lengthy speeches: Mönnig reminded the audience of
dignitaries that 100,000 of Cologne's citizens were in Germany's armed
forces fighting for their country (not that he had ever cared much about the
wounded in hospital); Falk (presumably speaking for the Jewish community,
with unconscious irony given the later history) proclaimed that what was
important was not life but being a German; and the District President
announced the dawn of a new age which would follow the horrors of war.

When Adenauer spoke, he was not slow to pick up the operatic tone of
the whole event. He assured his audience that Cologne, as the metropolis of
the Rhineland, indissolubly linked with the German Empire, would always

feel itself to be part of the great German fatherland. He went on, at some length, to recapitulate the views of Carl Hilty (without mentioning the source) on the organisation of life and the importance of work. But it was his peroration which brought the assembled company to its collective feet. He showered praise on the heroic courage of the German people in war. 'We on the Rhine,' he declared, 'consider this with particular gratitude, since the enemy's onslaught and thirst for conquest is directed above all against the Rhine and its metropolis. There can be no better way to honour this decisive hour for Cologne than to make a passionate declaration of loyalty to Kaiser and Reich.'[22] The civil servant had by now, quite obviously, become a politician.

6

THE MANAGEMENT OF DEFEAT

'Excellenz, ich habe bei Ihnen nichts mehr zu suchen'[*]

AT THE END of 1917, Adenauer had every reason to be pleased with himself. He was, after all, at the age of forty-one not just the Mayor of Cologne but the youngest mayor in the whole of Prussia. He had become *ex officio* a member of the Provincial Assembly of the Rhine Province and was soon to become a member of the Prussian Upper House. Furthermore, as Mayor of Cologne he had the opportunity to move on to a wider stage, both in German domestic politics and even internationally. This in turn allowed him to broaden his range of acquaintance, to meet and get to know the powerful owners of German industry and commerce, and to speak with them as equals. Physically, he had regained his strength after his accident, although his face was not quite repaired (he had again grown a moustache to hide the scars around his lips), his eyes were still giving trouble and he had bad headaches from time to time. But he made an impressive figure, tall, slim as he was – and still clad in the solemn black of mourning. He gave every

---

[*] 'Excellency, I have no more business with you': Adenauer to the Commander of the Cologne garrison, 6 November 1918; quoted in P. Weymar, *Adenauer*, p. 63

appearance of somebody who was used to giving orders and seeing them obeyed.

Nevertheless, although he may have been pleased with his achievements, Adenauer certainly was not, in any sense of the word, happy. Indeed, he was deeply unhappy. In the fragment of a diary which he wrote at the end of 1917, he groans almost audibly in what can only be described as a trough of despair. 'Nineteen seventeen,' he wrote, 'was difficult, very difficult for me, full of physical torture and anguish. The whole year was filled with pain and suffering and longing for my dear wife . . . work was a drug to alleviate my suffering . . . Ever since I was appointed to a high position while still young I have been much envied, but I am wretched, terribly wretched.'[1]

The words could hardly be stronger; nor is there any reason to distrust their substance. The underlying theme is beyond dispute: Adenauer, more than a year after the event, was still not reconciled to his wife Emma's death. Just as his accident had left clear physical scars, so Emma's death had left equally clear emotional scars. Nothing could demonstrate more convincingly the depth and intensity of their relationship. Furthermore, it is perhaps not too much to say that the emotional, as opposed to the political, Adenauer never, for the rest of his long life, truly recovered from the loss of his first wife.

Nevertheless, leaving aside his private grief, Adenauer would have been quite content with the position of Cologne as 1917 moved painfully into 1918. The harvest of 1917 had been good, although the potato crop had been varied, and that in itself had gone some way to alleviate the food shortage in the city – at least until official supplies ran out and the black market cornered the remainder. By the autumn the shortage had re-asserted itself. 'What are we living on?' asked the *Kölnische Volkszeitung* in November, pointing out that the titbits which had helped people get through the first three winters had by then vanished.[2]

But it was not until the hard frosts set in during December and January that the situation again became desperate. Adenauer's response to the crisis – to give local communities the responsibility for distributing the available food rations – had gone some way to reassure the city that the matter was directly in their hands, and that the citizens themselves were responsible, not some idle bureaucrat (the fact that this arrangement served to protect the better-off, and was in clear contradiction to Adenauer's assurances to Sollmann and the trade unions, was conveniently forgotten). But, whatever the virtue of the new arrangement in terms of public relations, it did not serve to fill many stomachs.

On the other hand, the military threat to Cologne had, at least to some extent, been lifted by the German successes on the Western Front during 1917. The French offensive under General Nivelle had ended in fiasco followed by mutiny; the British attack in southern Belgium had floundered in the mud of Passchendaele; and the Italian Army had been broken at Caporetto. Elsewhere, the Marquess of Lansdowne – a former British Foreign Secretary – had publicly urged the British government, in the light of the military stalemate, to explore possibilities for a negotiated peace; and, although this was far from Cologne and the Rhine, the Bolsheviks had seized power in Russia, immediately signalling that, as far as they were concerned, the war was at an end.

At the turn of the year, Adenauer's assessment of Germany's war prospects seemed to shift according to his mood. At one point, in early January 1918, he is reported as saying to his predecessor Wallraf that 'the war was going to be lost, and with it the monarchy would be finished';[3] at another, at about the same time, he is reported as thinking that the beginning of 1918 marked 'the most favourable situation for us since the beginning of the war, with the prospect of a good, honourable peace'.[4] The latter view relied very much on confidence in future military success, since by then it seemed to be common knowledge that the German Army would launch an offensive to end the war on the Western Front in the spring of 1918. Under the overall command of Field Marshal Paul von Beneckendorff und Hindenburg* and directed by the abrasive but ruthless General Erich

---

* Hindenburg, Paul von (1847–1934): Soldier. Born in Posen, East Prussia. 1858: Entered Prussian cadet corps at age eleven. 1878: After rising steadily through the officer corps, appointed to the general staff of the Prussian army. 1903: Promoted to the rank of Lieutenant General. 1911: Retired. 1914: Recalled as Field Marshal. 1919: Retired again. 1925: Elected President of the Weimar Republic. 1932: Caved in to Hitler. In history, will go down as the last symbol of Prussian supremacy in Germany, and as the one person who might have successfully opposed Hitler.

Ludendorff,* who together had demolished the Russian armies, and with the reinforcement from the troops released from the Russian front, Adenauer assumed that the German Army would have little difficulty in sweeping the enemy aside. On the other hand, it perhaps also occurred to him that the offensive would almost certainly be the Germans' last throw of the dice. Nineteen eighteen would see the build-up of American land forces in Europe – fresh troops in vast numbers, who would without any doubt and in the course of time tip the balance decisively against Germany and her allies.

In the meantime, there was not much to be done in Cologne, other than make sure that essential services were maintained and that whatever food was available was distributed as quickly as possible. Nevertheless, the sense of the time was that, whatever the result, the end of the war was in sight. The armies which had been fighting since the summer of 1914 were exhausted; and the political will to go on fighting had disappeared in virtually every country in Europe. It therefore only made sense to prepare for the peace, and this Adenauer set himself to do.

'After the war,' he told the Cologne City Council on 6 March 1918, 'things will never be as they were before. The war will transform the relations between states, as well as political, economic and social conditions within states in a total and lasting way.'[5] He was not just thinking of his discussions with Sollmann: the October Revolution in Russia had introduced a system of government the like of which had not been seen since the French constitution of 1792 – and then, of course, under very different circumstances. It was all very well to say that it could not happen in Germany, that people were so disciplined that, as one Russian remarked,

---

* Ludendorff, Erich (1865–1937): Soldier. Born in Posen, East Prussia. 1882: Entered Prussian army. Studied under Schlieffen. 1908–12: Chief of division within the Reich general staff responsible for mobilisation programme. 1914: Chief of staff to Hindenburg, and regarded as architect of German victory at Tannenberg and subsequent negotiations leading to the Brest–Litovsk settlement of 1917. 1923: Supported Hitler in abortive putsch. 1925: Potential Nazi candidate for President of the Reich, but fell out of favour with Hitler. One of the last Prussian dinosaurs.

'when German revolutionaries plan to storm a railway station, they start by buying platform tickets.'[6] Adenauer knew very well that the conditions which had served to breed violent revolution in Russia were on his doorstep in Cologne: starvation, resentment at the war, class hatred, and the emancipation of women who had played their full part in the wartime factories.

But revolution of such a radical nature had somehow to be avoided, not least – a crucial consideration for Adenauer – because it would mean the suppression of the Catholic Church. Yet for all the clarity of his analysis, he had no particular solution to offer. His only identifiable conviction was that the inevitable changes would take a long time to achieve. His one firm suggestion was the creation of an Institute for Social Research (not, as it happened, an original proposal). It seemed that his approach to the unknown social problems of the future was to be through careful intellectual analysis, followed by detailed policies which had been properly thought through. He was in this still the civil servant; the politician would have quickly understood that neither the pace nor the direction of events can be so easily controlled.

Fortunately, and perhaps wisely, the Social Democratic leadership in Germany was far from devising a German version of the Bolshevik *coup d'état* in Russia. Apart from all else, they lacked the steel of a Lenin or a Trotsky. They had also taken a firmly supportive line on the war. But it was by no means clear that they were wholly in control of their rank and file; and Adenauer, for one, knew perfectly well that it was in practice a beaten army rather than social conditions, however grim they were, which had sparked the turbulence in Russia, and it had been a mutinous Russian Navy which had secured the revolution. The great uncertainty in his mind was how the German Army would react if the coming spring offensive failed and the Reich went down to defeat.

It was matters such as these which Adenauer was able to discuss not just with Sollmann, who noted cogently, in the same March debate in the City Council, that it was 'a sign of the times when the mayor of a great Prussian city feels himself so much affected by the powerful upheavals of the war years',[7] but with his acquaintances in the business world. One of his closest confidants was Louis Hagen, who, though still nominally a Liberal, was moving in spirit closer to the Centre Party; but there were now others: August Thyssen, Hugo Stinnes, Albert Vögler, all of them figures of power and substance in the heavy industry of the Rhineland. But the two men Adenauer trusted most in such discussions were not in Cologne at all. One lived in Berlin, and the other in Brussels.

Johann Hamspohn was thirty-six years Adenauer's senior. Although he had been born in Cologne, he had spent most of his working life in Berlin. By the time the two men met, in 1907, Adenauer was First Deputy of Cologne and Hamspohn was head of the electrical engineering company Union Elektrizitätsgesellschaft AG (UEG) and on the managing board of its parent, Allgemeine Elektrizitätsgesellschaft AG (AEG). In other words, he was a very successful businessman, with contacts throughout Western Europe. The relationship of the two men was close: when Adenauer went to Berlin he would usually see Hamspohn and even stay at his house on the Wannsee. With his knowledge of international affairs – a knowledge which Adenauer conspicuously lacked – Hamspohn was an obvious person to consult about the post-war future for Cologne, and it comes as no surprise to find that the two were corresponding on the matter regularly from 1917 onwards.

Hamspohn provided Adenauer's entry into the Cologne Jewish community; in turn he introduced Adenauer to an even more useful friend, Dannie Heineman. Heineman had been born in 1872 in Charlotte, North Carolina, of a Jewish father whose family had migrated to the United States from Germany two generations earlier – but which had preserved its Judaism unswervingly – and an equally Jewish mother who had been imported, as it were, from Bremen to the United States to preserve the purity of the strain. For the first seven years of his life Heineman had spent an idyllic childhood in North Carolina. But his father had then died, whereupon his mother decided to return with her two sons to her home in Bremen.

Heineman had ploughed his way through the Prussian education system and ended by studying electrical engineering first at Brunswick and then at the Hanover Technical College. From there he joined UEG, where he was spotted by Hamspohn as a young man of great inventive flair who was also an intensely hard worker. Hamspohn sent Heineman off to electrify the horse-drawn tramway systems in Liège, Naples and Koblenz – all of which he completed successfully. In 1905, however, he left UEG and changed the direction of his career, joining the small Brussels investment company Société Internationale et Financière (SOFINA). The change brought spectacular success: when he joined in 1905 the company had three employees;

when he retired in 1955 it had forty thousand. Heineman had set himself the task of building a small investment company into a large industrial concern. He achieved the task brilliantly.

By the time Adenauer and Heineman first met, at Hamspohn's introduction, Heineman already had a wide range of acquaintances. He was not, it is true, the easiest of companions, aggressive in his business dealings, short, stocky and bald in appearance, with an abiding dislike for bankers and politicians. But he was a man 'of great versatility, a social conscience and a passion for art';[8] in short, he was the sort of man who had hitherto been outside Adenauer's limited acquaintance. Heineman, for his part, obviously found in Adenauer a rare animal: a politician to his liking. Adenauer, in turn, found a sharp and analytical mind which had been honed by experience in a world he knew nothing about; and was duly fascinated. Furthermore, even beyond mutual fascination, there developed between the two a trust which survived the years, and on which Adenauer was to rely in his later, darkest days.

During the war Heineman kept his distance from the German military occupiers of Brussels. But he was free with advice to Adenauer on how the post-war political landscape might develop. Not all of it, however, was wholly realistic. For instance, he and Adenauer seemed to agree that the historic relationship between Cologne and the Low Countries – not to mention the religion shared with Belgium and a large section of the Netherlands – made Cologne, in Adenauer's words, the obvious 'centre of attempts to revive cultural and economic ties with neighbouring countries after the war'.[9] But, as with his previous views on the future, it made sense to the civil service eye, but neither Adenauer nor, perhaps more surprisingly, Heineman had begun to appreciate the animosity towards Germany felt in Belgium – and, more important, in France. Both these countries were much more interested in what they regarded as Germany's 'war guilt' and the reparations which would have to be paid to expunge it. Any talk of future cultural and economic ties with Germany – even with a Catholic Rhineland – was no more than a sour joke. The only relationship the French envisaged with the Rhineland at this stage of the war was outright annexation.

The unrealistic nature of Adenauer's ideas for a post-war settlement highlighting the role of Cologne as its centre was borne in on him during the first few months of 1918. The truth was that the city was starting to break down as a coherent and governable unit. The crime rate was by now frighteningly high, both in street violence and in pilfering of any food that was not closely guarded. Factories, too, found their equipment mysteriously disappearing. Furthermore, in the spring of 1918, there were anything up to 20,000 deserters in the Cologne district, many of them armed. So serious had the situation become that it was even suggested that there would soon have to be a citizens' militia to cope with it.

Everything now depended on the much-heralded spring offensive. On 21 March the offensive began, with a mighty artillery barrage directed at the British positions in northern France between the towns of St Quentin and Arras. The barrage was followed, as was customary in the warfare of the time, by an infantry assault on the British positions. In its early stages, the offensive was successful. The British 3rd Army was pushed aside and the 5th Army reduced to disorderly retreat. The line of the upper Somme, the hinge between the British and French armies, was taken, and the way looked to be open to Paris. But the hinge itself did not snap, and Ludendorff's reserves were not up to the task of breaking through the battle-hardened armies – now including the Americans, who were starting to adapt themselves to the realities of battle in the mud and desolation of what was once the staid and civilised landscape of the northern French plain.

By mid-April, Ludendorff concluded that the way through to Paris was barred to him. Like other commanders before him, he then made the mistake of deviating suddenly from his initial plan and shifting the thrust of his attack. He decided to move to attack the British positions in Belgium. But the British held their ground at Ypres, and Ludendorff switched again. This time he went for the French armies, in a series of attacks between Soissons and Reims. In May, he managed to push his advance units far enough forward so that they were able to cross the river Marne in the first week in June. At that point, ironically enough, they were within sight of the positions which their armies had reached in the first, heady months of the war in September 1914. All those bloody years had yielded nothing.

In Cologne these events were followed with a mixture of hope and fear, depending on the gossip that came from the front. When the news filtered through, mainly from the wounded who were suddenly overloading the Cologne hospitals, that the German offensive had been halted once more at the Marne, morale in the city seems to have broken. There was no longer any belief that the war could be won. Worse than that, there was a view gaining credence that the war itself had, in some way, been Germany's fault.

It was also noted, since by then it had become perfectly obvious, that the major slaughter in the west had taken place not on German soil but on French and Belgian soil. It had not been German towns and villages that had been reduced to rubble and desolation, with innocent civilians gassed or shelled, but French and Belgian villages. Furthermore, there was the beginning of a view that all this had happened not because the French and Belgians, or the British for that matter, had invaded Germany, but because the Germans had invaded Belgium and France. The idea that the western powers had had territorial ambitions in Germany itself, and had launched the war to satisfy them, seemed suddenly to be no longer wholly credible.

By the summer of 1918, it was clear that the spring offensive had failed. On 8 August, British and French armies struck at the German lines east of Amiens, supported by a mass of the new weapon, the tank. By the beginning of September, all German armies were on the retreat, in front of the British on the Somme, in front of the French in Champagne Ardenne, and in front of the Americans in Meuse Argonne; and more American reinforcements continued to arrive almost every day on troopships into the western French ports. At the end of September, even Ludendorff gave up. He signalled Hindenburg that the campaign was stalled and would not succeed; an armistice was the only realistic outcome. Hindenburg in turn advised the Reich government that the war was lost and that the Kaiser should sue for peace.

The news that the Reich government was seeking an armistice soon leaked out. The realisation that the war, after all the blowing of trumpets and the oratorical bombast, was irretrievably lost destroyed whatever remained of morale within Germany. It also had the effect of removing all restraints on anti-government sentiment. To be sure, Ludendorff had advised that the terms of any armistice would be easier for Germany if a government was formed with the participation of the majority parties in the *Reichstag* (the national parliament), who hitherto had been reduced to the role of bystanders during the war; and this was done. Quite unexpectedly, the Social Democrats, the Progressives and the Centre Party discovered that they were being requested to implement reforms which they had been advocating unsuccessfully for years. During October, under the Chancellorship of Prince Max von Baden, they rushed through a series of laws, abolishing the Prussian three-class electoral system (thus redeeming the promise that Adenauer had given to Sollmann in Cologne), providing for ministerial accountability to the Reichstag, and virtually removing the Kaiser's power of command over the armed forces without reference to the civil power.

This sudden spring-tide of legislation was not enough, however, to douse the fire of radical reform which was beginning to rage. Had the Kaiser realised at that point that the game was up, and that his own position was untenable, the situation might not have run out of control. As it was, he clung on, nurturing his obscure fantasy that he would himself march with the German Army and restore the loyalty of his inherently faithful subjects. But, as Adenauer had earlier suspected, it was precisely in the defeated armed forces that the trouble really started.

At the beginning of November 1918, the German High Sea Fleet, a large part of which had been sitting in Kiel harbour for well over a year, was ordered by Admiral Reinhard Speer, Chief of the Admiralty Staff, to get up steam, sally forth and engage the British fleet in battle in the open sea. As a plan, it was suicidal. The Kiel sailors were understandably reluctant to commit suicide, and they mutinied. The authorities made the usual mistake of clapping the ring-leaders of the mutiny in prison, whereupon the remaining mutineers formed a sailors' council, demanding not just the release of their leaders but, well beyond the original source of the mutiny, the immediate conclusion of an armistice and – treachery indeed – the immediate abdication of the Kaiser.

What started as a mutiny had now become a rebellion, and the government was immediately drawn into the dispute. Prince von Baden pleaded with the Socialist majority leader in the Reichstag, Gustav Noske, to go to Kiel and attempt to restore at least a semblance of order and discipline. This Noske did by the simple procedure of getting himself elected chairman of the sailors' council, legitimising it, and then inviting the authorities to negotiate with it. But the mutiny at Kiel had set the pattern for others: a sailors' council took effective control of Germany's largest naval base at Wilhelmshaven; sailors and workers marched on the City Hall in Hamburg and demanded that a council be put in charge of food distribution; there was mutiny in Hanover – the commanding officer was arrested and put in prison;

there were riots in Munich. But for Cologne the most sinister development by far was the sally by a group of sailors from Kiel to seize the police head-quarters in Brunswick. With the bit now firmly between their teeth, the mutineers were no longer prepared to restrict their activities to their own localities. They were out to create a national revolution, and Cologne was an obvious target.

Cologne, in fact, already had its own convulsions. There had been a 'flu epidemic in the second half of October – more than 300 people had died in a week – which had already strained the resources of the hospitals and of the city administration itself. There were some 45,000 troops forming the garrison, jittery and on the edge of mutiny, under the uncertain com-mand of Lieutenant General von Kruge. If, as had happened elsewhere in Prussia, the soldiers made common cause with the industrial workers, the city administration would be easily overrun. For Adenauer, therefore, the problem was to try to block such a move, and the key to any solution of the problem lay in the hands of the Social Democrat leader, Wilhelm Sollmann.

Certainly Sollmann was a strong enough leader to keep his local party under control. Outside intervention, however, was a different matter. Sure enough, on 6 November, word quickly spread that a trainload of sailors from Kiel were already on their way to Cologne. Adenauer went at once to see Von Kruge to ask him to deploy troops to halt the train before it neared Cologne. Von Kruge in turn telephoned the President of the State Railways with the request. But nothing could be done – or, at least, nobody was prepared to take the responsibility for doing anything. The train would have to arrive at Cologne's main station, in the centre of the city, on its appointed schedule. 'And what,' asked Adenauer, 'are you thinking of doing in such a situation, Excellency?' 'I will strengthen the guard at the station,' came the reply, 'and give orders that nobody wearing a red rosette shall pass the barriers.' 'And that is all?' 'Certainly all I can do for the moment.' Von Kruge looked, and sounded, like a defeated man. 'Excellency,' Adenauer con-cluded, 'I have no more business with you,' and, white with anger, turned on his heel and left.[10] By the afternoon, the Kiel sailors were in control of the centre of Cologne; they had simply taken off their red rosettes when leav-ing the station. They were immediately joined by soldiers from the garrison. Twenty-four hours later, the Republic was proclaimed by a crowd in front of the cathedral.

In Cologne, the onlookers to these events could only stand about waiting for further developments in the city. On the wider scene, however, there were onlookers who were aghast at what appeared to be the disintegration of the social order, not just in Cologne, but in most of the other major cities in Germany. Those onlookers were, of course, the disparate group of countries which had been fighting to exhaustion the war against the Reich and its allies. It suddenly became clear that diplomacy had to take up the running from military campaigning; and for this the Western Allies were woefully ill-prepared.

The diplomacy was further complicated by the decision of the German government not to seek an armistice through the channel of some neutral embassy – Switzerland would have been an obvious choice – but to signal on 4 October a positive response to the 14 Points which the US President Wilson* had set out in January 1918 as constituting the United States' war aims. As it happened, French decoders were able to intercept and unravel the signal between Berlin and Washington (the Americans were not immediately disposed to release the text to their allies), and were therefore able to pass the contents on to the British so that the two governments were able to consider their response once the contents of the signal were officially communicated to them by Washington.

The upshot was that, because of the urgency of the situation and the clear possibility of the emergence of 'Bolshevism' in a defeated Germany, the French Prime Minister, Georges Clemenceau,† with powerful support from

---

* Wilson, Woodrow (1856–1924): Academic and politician. Born in Virginia, USA of Scottish–Irish parents. Educated at Princeton, University of Virginia and Johns Hopkins University. 1885–88: Professor of history and political economy, Bryn Mawr College. 1888–90: Professor at Wesleyan College. 1890–1910: Professor of jurisprudence and politics, Princeton. 1911–13: Governor of New Jersey. 1913: Elected President of the USA; served until 1920. His record in history can best be described as doubtful.

† Clemenceau, Georges (1841–1929): Journalist and politician. Born in the Vendée and educated in Nantes. 1865–69: Lived in the USA. 1876–93 and from 1902: Member of National Assembly; founded a number of newspapers, notably *L'Aurore* in 1903. 1916–19: Prime Minister of France. Known as 'The Tiger', or, more potently, '*Le Père de la Victoire*'. Rightly, one of France's great heroes.

the Allied Commander-in-Chief, Marshal Ferdinand Foch,* was able to persuade the British Prime Minister David Lloyd George to support a (temporary) occupation of the Rhineland, which, hitherto, the British government had consistently opposed. In fact, such was the worry that a British conscript army would want to go back home as soon as an armistice was signed that the Commander of the British Expeditionary Force, Sir Douglas Haig, made the strongest representations to Lloyd George on the grounds that the German defensive position – since he was still thinking about the paper strength of the German armed forces – would be much more powerful if confined to the eastern bank of the Rhine than if they were left 'astride the river holding the . . . frontier of 1870'. Furthermore, Haig suspected, perceptively, that 'on the whole' Foch's arguments were 'political', as indeed they were.[11]

The fact was that the French – particularly Foch, but with Clemenceau's tacit support, were aiming for an independent French-orientated Rhineland; the main British concern, on the other hand, was the neutering – and preferably the destruction – of the German High Sea Fleet; and the Americans wanted a return to stable frontiers in the west and to pre-1914 frontiers in the east (not that anybody was entirely clear what these were) and a general move towards democracy. It was only at a long series of meetings between the three, which ended on 4 November, that the final terms of the armistice to be put to the German government were agreed; and these included, apart from the immediate transfer of Alsace-Lorraine into French hands, Allied occupation of all the territory on the left bank of the Rhine, a neutral zone

---

* Foch, Ferdinand (1851–1929): Soldier. Born in Tarbes in the south of France. Educated at Jesuit school in Metz, but left temporarily to enlist in the army during the Franco-Prussian War of 1870; then at the Polytechnique. 1873: Joined artillery. 1885: Went to Ecole de Guerre. 1895: Returned to Ecole de Guerre as teacher. 1908: As brigadier general, appointed head of Ecole de Guerre. 1911: Divisional commander. 1913: Commander of 20th French Army Corps. 1915–16: Commanded Northern Army Group. 1917: Appointed chief of the war minister's general staff. May 1918: Commander-in-chief of all Allied armies on Western and Italian fronts. August 1918: Commanded final offensive; made Marshal of France. Showered with honours; numerous statues (including one in London).

on the right bank but with Allied bridgeheads at the major cities of Mannheim, Mainz and Cologne. As it turned out, the French had achieved almost all of their aims.

Nonetheless, Foch made one tactical mistake. His original plan, when it came to carving up the Rhineland between the different armies, was to occupy the three major bridgeheads with a joint Allied force. At this point Haig, who had taken little part in the discussions, put his foot down. Experience had shown, he said, that the command and control of joint forces had never worked and he, for one, was not going to have it. Foch conceded the point, and the bridgeheads were split between the different armies. In what was to prove a decision of the greatest significance to the future of the Rhineland, and of the life of the young mayor, Cologne was awarded to the British.

On 7 November 1918, the armistice terms were presented to the German government. But that particular government had only two more days to run. On the same day, the radical journalist Kurt Eisner led a revolutionary *coup d'état* in Munich, which in practice took Bavaria out of the German Empire. On 9 November, Prince Max von Baden threw in the towel; not only that, but in his resignation statement he announced that the head of the Social Democratic Party, Friedrich Ebert,* was to become Chancellor and, at the same time, was to summon a Constituent Assembly to work out a new constitution. Later that evening, the Kaiser, Wilhelm II, accepted what had by then become inevitable, packed his bags and fled across the Dutch border. The Kaiser's Germany had come to an end, even before the final surrender at Réthondes in the early morning of 11 November.

Although there was much rejoicing at the end of the long and miserable war, it would be wrong to assume that the outcome was altogether to everybody's liking. The French were probably best pleased, apart from the

---

* Ebert, Friedrich (1871–1925): Politician. Born in Heidelberg. Joined Social Democrats in 1889. Elected to the Reichstag in 1912. 1913: Chairman of SPD. 1916: Leader of SPD parliamentary group. 1918: Chancellor of the Reich. 1919: Elected by the Weimar Assembly as President of the Reich; held the post until his death. Down-to-earth, determined to maintain the integrity of the Reich and democracy, but much resented by the Prussian upper class.

concession of Cologne to the British. The Americans were already looking for ways to 'get our boys home' and were irritated by suggestions of future commitments in Europe. But the British were probably the least content. At a War Cabinet meeting on 10 November, the day before the signature of the armistice, Lloyd George warned that 'marching men into Germany was marching them into a cholera area. The Germans did that in Russia and caught the virus – of Bolshevism.'[12] Winston Churchill went so far as to say that 'we might have to build up the German Army, as it is important to get Germany on her legs again for fear of the spread of Bolshevism'.[13] All in all, it was a very doubtful British Cabinet which committed troops to the occupation of Cologne. Furthermore, when Haig heard the guidelines laid down by Foch's staff for the civilian population he noted, in a rare outburst of humour, that 'the only possible way for a German to avoid contravening one or other of the many bylaws will be to stay in bed' and, even then, 'he will only escape provided he does not snore'.[14]

No one in the British Cabinet, of course, had the remotest idea of the conditions which their exhausted troops would find when they finally arrived at their new posting in Cologne. Had they known the truth, they might have been even more reluctant than in fact they were. The truth was that once the Republic had been declared in the afternoon of 7 November, nobody had any clear idea about the immediate future, let alone the longer term. Mass demonstrations were planned for the following Saturday, 9 November, but nobody knew for what purpose. Fortunately – since otherwise the prevailing anarchy would have quickly given way to street violence – Sollmann persuaded a group of Social Democrats in Mülheim, one of their strongholds, to formulate precise political demands: immediate release of all 'political' prisoners (the old revolutionary cry), immediate abdication of the Hohenzollerns, a National Assembly elected by universal suffrage and, whatever it meant, 'the creation of a Greater German Socialist Republic'.[15]

Sollmann had, in fact, played his hand very cleverly. This was not the time to resist the madder political ideas of frustrated party activists. The essential point was to try to regain some sort of control of a highly combustible political situation. It was therefore no accident that the Mülheim resolution included a clause to ensure that 'in the Cologne area the unstoppable revolutionary movement proceeded without bloodshed and in an orderly fashion'.[16] Moreover, a proposal to storm the prisons was turned down.

Adenauer, on the other hand, was at this point still in favour of using military force to impose what he regarded as the legitimate government of the city. While random groups of soldiers, workers, sailors, and anybody else who had come to see the fun, milled around the city in the afternoon of 7 November and well into the night, waving red flags, demanding the arrest of officers and shouting revolutionary slogans, Adenauer had telephoned the military commandant to point out that there was a battery of field artillery in the courtyard of the Apostelgymnasium awaiting orders. Why, asked the mayor, were they not ordered to fire on the mob?

Fortunately for Adenauer (and for the future of Cologne), the governor failed to follow up the mayor's clear request. He replied that he thanked the mayor for his message, but that there was nothing he could do. The governor was not being cowardly. He knew, as Adenauer, without any military experience, could not possibly know, what carnage would have resulted if the artillery had opened up on an undefended and infuriated mob. The retribution would have been terrible. The governor's view was obviously that the mayor, for his part, might wish to be torn limb from limb, but that he himself was certainly not prepared for such certain and brutal martyrdom. Sensibly, the troops were ordered to retire to their barracks.

Adenauer finally accepted that this was time not for heroics but for sensible negotiation. The city was by then in chaos. Soldiers wearing red rosettes manned the major crossroads and public squares, tearing the epaulettes off the shoulders of any officer they could find; military prisoners, still in prison uniform, roamed free in the streets. The Neumarkt and Hohe Strasse were jammed with crowds who, in the end and after a great deal of debate, called on Sollmann and four of his colleagues to form a workers' and soldiers' council alongside five soldiers who had been acclaimed as leaders by the troops assembled at a meeting in the Gürzenich Hall.

It may have been, and indeed was, chaotic, but at least there was a body with some sort of mandate to negotiate with the mayor about the future conduct of the city's affairs. Adenauer's oath to the Kaiser was conveniently forgotten – he had decided to negotiate with the new council the day before the Republic had been declared in Berlin – but in reality he had no choice. Either he negotiated or he would be swept aside in the revolutionary spasm. There was no other possible outcome.

This, then, was the Cologne which the British had agreed to take in hand when they put their signature to the armistice of 11 November 1918. It was teetering on the edge of revolution, perhaps just kept from the brink by the joint efforts of Sollmann and Adenauer. But for Adenauer himself it represented almost the first, albeit faint, smell of failure in his life. He had become mayor, but was now only mayor on sufferance. His city was in chaos. He had lost his wife. His country had been defeated in war. His home town was to be occupied by foreign troops. The Kaiser's Germany, which had nurtured him for more than forty years and in which he had risen to prominence and wealth, lay in ruins. The future could only have looked bleak, but nobody at the time could possibly have realised how bleak, in the event, it was to turn out to be, for him and for Germany.

PART TWO

Weimar Germany

I

THE AFTERMATH OF WAR

'Ich werde Ihren Befehl ausführen soweit es mein Gewissen zulässt'*

DEFEAT IS NEVER, under any circumstance, an easy pill to swallow. But it was the more difficult for Germany in 1918, as it was for Russia in 1917, in that defeat had led to the collapse of the old order and the old certainties. It is therefore hardly surprising that the only identifiable theme, if it can be called that, running through what remained of the German Empire from the immediate pre-armistice period up to the signature of the Peace Treaty in June 1919, was one of chaos and confusion.

The confusion was compounded, of course, by arguments between the Allies about the basis of the armistice itself, and, in the subsequent discussions over the proposed peace treaty, by each belligerent's pursuit of different war aims. But it was further compounded by the breakdown within Germany itself. After the Kaiser's ignominious departure and Eisner's coup against the Wittelsbach king in Bavaria, and after other, less eminent, princes had been

---

* 'I will carry out your order as far as my conscience permits': Adenauer to General Lawson, 3 November 1918; quoted in P. Weymar, *Adenauer*, p. 69.

bustled off their shaky thrones, the Bismarckian Empire had quite clearly fallen apart.

There was little that the new Chancellor, Friedrich Ebert, could have done about that – even if he had wanted to – since, apart from anything else, such was the corresponding breakdown in communication that nobody in Berlin had any idea what was going on from day to day in Munich or Brunswick or, for that matter, in Cologne, let alone the less important parts of the former Empire. Not that it was of much consequence either way, since the main threat to the whole fragile construction was to its foundations, in Berlin itself.

For Ebert, this was the matter immediately to hand; it was in Berlin that the seemingly orderly transfer of power from Prince Max von Baden to Ebert (in reality of doubtful constitutional propriety) was openly challenged by the forces of the left, the most formidable of which was the avowedly revolutionary Spartacist movement. For many weeks there were riots, strikes and violence in the streets. Indeed, it was not until the following January that the main Spartacist threat was finally put to rest, by the murder of their two charismatic leaders, Karl Liebknecht and Rosa Luxemburg. In the meantime, the Ebert administration had its hands full to maintain some sort of order in the capital itself.

Under those circumstances, Cologne – give or take the long series of confused and sometimes contradictory signals from the government and the Army High Command in Berlin – was during those months left to its own devices; in other words, to its mayor. But Adenauer, much as he might have liked to, could not run the city single-handed. There was also the City Council – its role now uncertain. There were, too, the workers' and soldiers' councils, potential hotbeds of violent revolution which were in the outlying areas of the right bank of the river, strongly Spartacist in mood. Added to all these were the regular crowds of thousands who assembled around the City Hall, and even invaded the offices themselves, clamouring for bread. 'Adenauer's office,' reported the obviously shocked Captain Otto Schwink, sent in after the armistice by the Allies to help with the repatriation of German troops and the transition to occupation, 'looked like an operational headquarters on the day of battle.'[1]

In all this, the responsibility of managing the city was the mayor's: and the first, and overriding, priority was to create an administration that functioned. This Adenauer managed to do by forming a 'Welfare Committee for the City of Cologne'. On to this committee he invited representation from the various interests of importance: the City Council, the state authorities, local industry, bankers, trade unions and, of course, the workers' and soldiers' councils. As mayor, Adenauer presided over this unwieldy and motley group (deliberately wearing the armband of the workers' and soldiers' councils), and somehow managed to make it work. One of its first acts, for instance, which must have been particularly difficult for the 'workers and soldiers' to accept, was to set up a citizens' militia to stop looting, control riots and ensure the safety of the streets. In practice, since the militia was made up mostly of old men and discharged soldiers, it was — unsurprisingly — not particularly effective. But it was a start.

The major impact of the new committee was to mollify the revolutionary mood which had threatened the city in the second week in November. To be sure, the Spartacist element still remained strong in the industrial suburbs of the right bank, but the involvement of the workers' and soldiers' councils in the practical administration of the city served to moderate their revolutionary enthusiasm. Decisions had to be made, and in due course were made, by the Welfare Committee about the repatriation of foreign workers, public health (including a programme of delousing and the future of brothels), the organisation of the port and shipping on the river, and, above all, on the supply of food. The difficulties in making decisions of such a nature tend in the end to calm even the most strident revolutionary spirits.

In setting all this up, Adenauer had an unexpected bonus. When the terms of the armistice finally became known in early November 1918 there was in Cologne a definite and pronounced reaction of angry complaint. The complaints were on three grounds. First, the terms were thought to be unfair (people in Cologne, as elsewhere in Germany, had simply not understood the extent of the resentment against them). Second, they now realised that they were going to be occupied for the foreseeable future. The only consolation, if consolation it was, seemed to be that they had avoided outright annexation by France, which had to be content with taking back the lost provinces of Alsace and Lorraine, themselves annexed to Germany by Bismarck in 1871. And third, they thought that they were being victimised for their unwitting involvement in a war which had not been of their own making, but of their imperial masters in Berlin.

Out of these angry complaints grew a resurgence of patriotism. In this, circumstances played in favour of Adenauer and the Welfare Committee, since, in reality, by far the most important part of the committee's activity was to plan for the retreat of the German Army; and the last thing that Adenauer wanted at that moment was a hostile civilian population. More than half a million men and almost as many horses – the remnants of the 6th and 7th armies – were due to pass across the Rhine on their way east into what was to be unoccupied Germany. Four German Army corps were to come through Cologne itself.

It was a formidable challenge. The troops had to be fed; they had to receive the back pay which was owed to them; and they had to be out of the territory forming the bridgehead opposite Cologne on the right bank of the river before the British arrived – otherwise they would be interned. As an extra measure to forestall disorder among the demoralised troops, Adenauer insisted that they all be disarmed before they left Cologne. Also in preparation for the event, Adenauer (wisely) ordered all stocks of alcohol, three quarters of a million litres of spirits, let alone large quantities of cognac, to be tipped into the Rhine under cover of darkness.

The first German troops arrived back in Cologne on 21 November 1918. Although they were tired, demoralised and ragged, they were given a heroes' welcome. Flags – even imperial flags – were flown, church bells were rung, crowds cheered. It was as though they had won the war rather than lost it. Cologne almost immediately became an extended military camp. As more and more came shambling in, field kitchens were everywhere, working day and night, to provide basic food for the soldiers and for the starving civilians who huddled around them. To get the raw materials for the kitchens Adenauer and the Welfare Committee sold off any available army property, lorries, cars, horses, anything that could be sold except arms. Admittedly it was illegal, and most of it went straight to the black market, but it was the only way to keep going.

Adenauer himself made the most of the occasion, taking on, perhaps for the first time, the public mantle of a politician. He gave an outspoken welcome to the 'courageous warriors', his speech to the City Council on the day the warriors arrived going some distance beyond the truth. 'Our brothers in field grey,' he announced, 'are coming home . . . they are coming home after four years of defending house and home with their bodies . . . they are coming home to us, not defeated and not beaten.'[2]

It was, of course, the greatest nonsense, as Adenauer knew perfectly well, since the war had been fought nowhere near 'house and home' and the German Army had been decisively defeated. But in politics nonsense from time to time has its place. Unfortunately, it was also dangerous nonsense, since it encouraged the feeling that the armistice and the coming peace might not be the end of the story, and that another chapter might unfold (as, indeed, it did), and it further irritated the French, whose territory the German Army had invaded and whose land had been ravaged. But the justification of the nonsense was simply that the speech played well with the crowd, and with the returning troops.

In truth, this was the point of Adenauer's whole exercise – to raise the battered morale of the city and the defeated army. In the further pursuit of this objective, he arranged a particular welcome for the remnants of the 65th Division, which had been stationed in Cologne before the war. Again, the mayor appeared, to make a speech that appeared to be full of emotion, beating the patriotic drum and thanking the troops on behalf of the whole city. 'We will never forget them, what they have done for Germany, what they have done for the Rhineland.'[3]

But, apart from raising morale, Adenauer also had a subsidiary purpose. The officers of the returning units, commissioned, as they had been, under the Empire, were understandably determined to confront 'Bolshevism' head on, by armed attack if necessary. Had they been allowed to do so, all plans for the orderly withdrawal of their units across the Rhine would have been scrapped. Cologne would then almost inevitably have lapsed into what Adenauer most feared: civil conflict followed by revolutionary government. In the event he seems to have achieved what must at the time have seemed impossible, succeeding, even at the price of bending the truth, both in raising morale and in calming the spirits at what was without a doubt a particularly highly-charged moment.

Captain Schwink was bowled over with admiration. 'Konrad Adenauer is one of the bravest men I ever knew,' he said many years later. '[He] explained to me his view that hundreds of thousands of armed men, without work and without adequate food, roaming around in the big cities, constituted an acute social danger.'[4] It certainly was not the time to bemoan the war – let alone raise the matter of possible war guilt.

In fact, even if it had been the time, it is doubtful whether Adenauer had, at best, more than a very slender feeling of 'war guilt'. If he took a view at all, it was that the stupidity of all parties lay at the origins of the war, that the German armed forces had fought bravely, but had been badly let down by the 'inexplicable, shameful, disastrous flight of its supreme leader, Kaiser

Wilhelm'.[5] The idea that the French or the Belgians resented the German invasion of their countries in 1914 did not seem yet to have occurred to him. Indeed, he claimed, only eighteen months later, that France hated Germany herself, while all that Germany wanted was a stable system by which she would be free to work. He had, of course, yet to travel outside German territory apart from his holidays with Schlüter and his honeymoon with Emma, and had yet to see the devastation of Verdun. The narrowness of his upbringing and experience were perhaps, to put it no more strongly, blinding him to the cataclysmic realities of what had happened in the previous four years.

The now disarmed units of the German Army, which had paused in Cologne on their eastward migration, gradually moved out. On 3 December the last regiment left. It was an emotional occasion. They formed up in the Domplatz ready to move. 'A charming children's choir sang,' wrote Schwink later, 'no louder than the December rain that splashed down; a cry of "hurrah for our Germany" was again heard around the cathedral; and the last German troops paraded at a brisk pace before the history of Cologne. "Auf Wiedersehen!" cried the children. The adults, who could scarcely believe what was happening, watched with aching hearts.'[6] The small crowd went home. The Empire was finally dead.

As it happened, on the previous day the first units of the British 2nd Army under General Sir Herbert Plumer had crossed the German frontier at Malmédy, on their way to the Cologne. There was concern about possible German snipers in the forests which they crossed, but they marched with fixed bayonets, colours flying and bands playing. The British generals, in truth, were more worried about how their own men would behave once they reached their destination. 'Our men,' wrote General Sir Richard Haking, the British representative on the Armistice Commission, to Field Marshal Haig, 'have been killing Germans for four years and they think no more of killing a German than squashing a fly.'[7] The omens were not favourable.

The occupation certainly got off to a bad start. Adenauer, still fearful that the vacuum resulting from the German withdrawal would lead to a swift revolutionary take-over, 'sent a request to the British troops asking them to hasten their arrival in Cologne'.[8] The result was that on 6 December, at about 11am, one armoured car carrying two young officers drove through the empty streets of the city, arrived at the City Hall and, in halting German, its occupants demanded to see the mayor. Then not only did they march into the mayor's offices, but they immediately sat down on a sofa, lit cigarettes and flicked the ash on to the mayor's carpet. Adenauer, not unreasonably, was deeply offended by this show of bad manners. In his iciest voice he said to one of his staff, 'The gentlemen want an ashtray,' and then kept his silence.[9] The young men were suitably abashed.

Things could only improve, and they did. About an hour later the rest of the British advance party, consisting of six armoured cars of the 2nd Cavalry Brigade under the command of Brigadier-General Algernon Lawson, arrived in front of the City Hall. The atmosphere was now quite different. Not only did the mayor feel that his dignity was being respected by the fact that he was now speaking with a general, but Lawson was a man of natural, and rather old world, courtesy – educated at Harrow and commissioned into the Scots Greys – who recognised the sensitivity of Adenauer's situation.

The two men got on very well. There were, of course, difficult issues. Lawson insisted that the militia should be disbanded, and that the workers' and soldiers' councils should have no part in discussions with the occupying force. Adenauer in turn requested an immediate parade of the advance party through the city, simply to show that they were there; but Lawson thought that that was exceeding his brief – and was concerned that there might be ugly scenes between the British soldiers and the gangs of young German men still in the city. Better, he thought, to await the arrival of the main body of the British force. Adenauer then wanted to know, for the purposes of arranging billeting, how many British troops would be stationed in Cologne. Lawson at this point was evasive. He merely replied that his own squadron should be regarded as the 'hors d'oeuvre to an unknown number of dishes'.[10]

During the next few days, three British divisions marched into the city, watched by the crowds in sullen silence. On 11 December the Military Governor, General Sir Charles Fergusson, and his staff set up their headquarters in the Hotel Monopol, turning out anybody who happened to be staying there as well as removing the furniture and putting in desks in their stead. By 14 December British troops had reached the outer edge of the bridgehead on the right bank of the river, and had started to set up control points, dig trenches and lay barbed-wire defences. By the third week of December martial law had been established throughout the zone. When Adenauer protested that the people of Cologne were 'somewhat different to other German tribes'[11] and should be treated more leniently, he was gruffly told by Fergusson that the British were only doing precisely what the

Germans had done during the war in Belgium. In other words, as *The Times* in London pointed out, the normal pattern of occupation was being followed, in that 'British rule settles on a district as softly as snow, but freezes as hard as ice'.[12]

Nevertheless, given Adenauer's mood of co-operation and the restoration of reasonable order on the streets of the city, the full rigours of occupation were to some extent relaxed. The curfew, for instance, from 7pm to 5am, was not insisted on. The rule requiring adults to raise their hats to a British officer, a particular feature of the equivalent wartime German regulations in Belgium, was abandoned. But the main burden of the regulations remained. The Cologne police were put under the supervision of the British Provost Marshal; Cologne courts only exercised jurisdiction in cases of offences against the existing penal code, offences against the occupying power being reserved to courts martial; and, for the first time in their history, citizens of Cologne were required to carry identity papers which could be inspected on demand.

But in spite of all this, and of the rigours of a cold late autumn and a continuing shortage of food, the stability of occupation was at least in some respects not unwelcome to Adenauer and the City Council. The revolutionary threat had been warded off. The workers' and soldiers' councils had been reduced to no more than a cipher. But, above all, the British had followed, in Cologne as elsewhere, their policy of dealing only with the legally constituted local authority. This had been made clear by General Fergusson in his first meeting with Adenauer on 12 December. Cautious as he was, Adenauer took pains to ensure that the official interpreter kept proper records of the meeting. 'The governor decided at the end,' runs the minute, 'that they wanted to deal with me alone, as I alone bear the responsibility for the obeying of all regulations.'[13] Adenauer even so sought confirmation. The minute was confirmed. 'The governor would prefer to deal directly with the mayor.'[14] It was perhaps the most important statement of policy that the British authorities had hitherto made, since it re-affirmed the principle, not just that they were not prepared to accept illegal plans for the governance of Cologne, whether put forward by the Spartacists on the right bank or the workers' and soldiers' councils on the left, but that they were not prepared to countenance the moves of local separatists in the Rhineland to take the territory out of Prussia altogether.

The importance of Fergusson's message lay in the last point. The future status of the Rhineland was without a doubt one of the most difficult political problems with which the Allies and the new German government had to deal in the immediate aftermath of the war. To be sure, the whole problem had its origins in the mists of history, but what brought it to a position high on the political agenda of late 1918 were the aspirations of two quite different groups, who may or may not have been in close contact at the outset, but probably were as the plot unfolded. The first group was the French High Command and, in particular, Marshal Foch. The second group was a heterogeneous collection of journalists and politicians in the Rhineland itself.

Foch's view was quite simple, and was expressed in a memorandum to Clemenceau on 28 November 1918. In it he argued that a series of client states should be created along the left bank of the Rhine which should be in irrevocable military alliance with Belgium, Luxembourg and, of course, France. These would serve as a permanent buffer against any future Prussian-led German attack. Clemenceau broadly supported the proposals, although he drew the line at introducing conscription in the 'Rhenish Republics' which were to be formed. But he rightly realised that neither the British nor the Americans would be at all enthusiastic. Indeed, when the first high-level negotiations on the peace treaty started, in London in early December, both Lloyd George and Andrew Bonar Law, the leader of the Conservative Party, were unimpressed. When Foch claimed that he would avoid creating a new 'Alsace-Lorraine' by precautions to conciliate the feelings and interests of the Rhinelanders, Bonar Law remarked gloomily 'that Germany had said exactly the same thing. We ourselves had tried for years to conciliate the Irish.'[15]

Coincidentally (or, according to some versions, in tandem) the *Kölnische Volkszeitung* led a campaign for a Rhenish Republic, the high point of which was a rally in the centre of Cologne on 4 December – between the withdrawal of the German troops and the arrival of the British – at which Karl Trimborn, a long-standing member of the Centre Party, spoke about the dismemberment of the old Empire and claimed that the future must be decided by the inhabitants of the localities affected. This was seen as giving support at least to the notion of a Rhenish Republic. The plan, if indeed at this stage there was a coherent plan, did not command the support of the Social Democrats, who staged a counter-demonstration of their own on 6 December, but that only served to encourage support for it in Cologne's business community, who seemed to see it as a device to preserve the influence of the Liberals and Centre Party against all comers – particularly those coming from the left.

As might be expected, well before these events, and even before the signature of the armistice, Adenauer had been approached by his supporters in the Centre Party, Mönnig and Rings, and by the editor of the *Kölnische Volkszeitung*. The argument was straightforward: the only way to prevent annexation by France was to create a separate Rhineland state divorced from Prussia. Adenauer thought the whole project far-fetched, but he was careful enough to report the conversations to the Social Democrat Sollmann and the Liberal Falk. The upshot of their discussions was that the idea should only be seriously considered if the basic assumption was correct, that this was the only way to prevent the Rhineland being incorporated into France.

As it happened, the terms of the armistice had, at least temporarily, invalidated that assumption. The immediate threat of French annexation passed, and Adenauer was able, for the moment at least, to resist any further moves within Cologne, and the Rhineland generally, towards a Rhenish Republic. But the French were certainly not going to let the issue die. It was far too important for that. The scene therefore shifted to the inter-Allied discussions on the proposed peace treaty, mostly held in private during the months of December, January and February. Clemenceau raised Foch's proposals repeatedly, but without making any headway.

Faced with this brick wall, the French then moved to a more subtle approach. At a conference in Paris on 25 February 1919 they tabled a memorandum which suggested that in the treaty the western frontier of Germany should be fixed at the Rhine, that the bridgeheads should be occupied by Allied troops, but that no permanent annexation or other political arrangement should be 'forced' on the Rhineland. Quite how this was meant to work was not altogether clear, but the British certainly took it to imply that it would be open for the Rhineland, at some future stage, to vote to rejoin Germany.

The British government was still wholly opposed to military commitments in Germany of anything resembling a long-term nature. Lord Curzon considered the idea of a permanent military presence in the Rhineland 'intolerable'; Austen Chamberlain was firmly of the view that no British government could keep troops on the Rhine 'beyond the period required to extract reparations and indemnity'; and Winston Churchill thought that the French might be satisfied with the construction of a channel tunnel through which a British Expeditionary Force could move quickly in the event of a future German attack on France.[16] None of this, of course, was at all satisfactory to the French government, which returned to the charge at the next Allied Conference on 11 March. André Tardieu, the French delegate, insisted that 'the drawing of the German frontier on the Rhine, the constitution of an independent Rhenish state and the Allied command of the bridges were three legs of one plan and stood or fell together'.[17] But the British still objected in principle – and the Americans, if the truth be told, were getting tired of the whole thing.

The wrangling continued for another month, until Clemenceau finally gave way. In spite of fierce opposition from Foch, he accepted a compromise: an Anglo-American military guarantee of French security, together with a fifteen-year occupation of the southern Rhineland, a ten-year occupation of the central Rhineland and a five-year occupation of the northern Rhineland (which included Cologne). Foch was furious.

The negotiations had been followed with the greatest interest by the Mayor of Cologne. Indeed, Adenauer had done his best to influence events, his particular aim being simple: to avoid French annexation. His attitude towards a separate Rhineland state fluctuated in inverse proportion to his perception of the French threat. In late December 1918 he was in a pessimistic mood, not least because he felt that the Ebert government in Berlin was doing nothing to help. He had again reverted to the view that the French would win the argument on annexation, and he therefore kept in close contact with the *Kölnische Volkszeitung*, particularly the deputy editor, Josef Froberger, who was the main advocate of separatism in the newspaper. But he also saw the state prosecutor of Wiesbaden, Dr Hans Adam Dorten.

That move was, as it turned out, a dreadful mistake. Furthermore, it was a mistake which was to cost Adenauer dearly in the future. Dorten was a dubious character, with a reputation for double-dealing. He claimed, in seeking a meeting, that his aunt had met Adenauer during a summer holiday in 1900. This in itself might have been enough to put Adenauer on his guard; but, as Falk was to remark, 'though [Adenauer] regarded people he did not know with a healthy degree of mistrust, his judgement was formed too quickly. Quite a few people were able to impress him and use this to achieve important positions. But a rapid rise was very often followed by an abrupt fall. He went through a lot of people in a short period . . .'[18] In fact, there is little doubt that Dorten was in league with the French occupying force in the southern zone of the Rhineland, the zone which included Wiesbaden and Mainz; nor is there much doubt that the officers of that force were taking orders directly from Foch – behind Clemenceau's back.

By the end of January 1919 the political temperature in the southern zone was nearing boiling point. Sensing this, Adenauer – in his capacity as Mayor of Cologne, and therefore the senior political figure in the Rhineland – at the end of the month summoned a number of influential dignitaries to meet in Cologne: the delegates from the Rhineland who had in mid-January been elected to the new National Assembly at Weimar, which was to decide the constitution of post-imperial Germany; the chairman of the Rhine Province executive committee; and the mayors of Aachen, Bonn, Trier, Mönchengladbach, Neuss, Rheydt, Saarbrücken and Koblenz – in other words, the established authorities on the left bank of the Rhine. The Mayor of Cologne invited them to meet at the City Hall on 1 February 1919 to discuss the whole matter of the Rhineland and its future. It was an invitation which was impossible to refuse.

The meeting was long, and there were many speeches. The separatists were encouraged by that morning's *Kölnische Volkszeitung*, which was believed to represent Adenauer's views and those of the Centre Party, and which had come out in favour of a Rhenish Republic. But Adenauer's own speech, which lasted for no less – and possibly more – than three hours, adopted a rather more subtle line. He analysed in turn what he took to be the attitudes of the French, the British and the Americans. France obviously wanted the Rhine to be the strategic frontier between herself and Germany. This was perfectly understandable, since not so very long ago Germany was thinking of controlling, or even annexing, Belgium to provide a strategic frontier between herself and France. Britain, on the other hand, was divided between her traditional policy of siding with the weaker continental power to preserve the balance, which in this case meant Germany, and her recognition that France needed protection against the clear desire for revenge which a resurgent Germany would harbour. The Americans, finally, were anxious to wash their hands of the whole problem.

After this lengthy analysis, Adenauer's solution to the problem was to create a federal Germany, of which a 'West German Republic', incorporating territory on both banks of the Rhine, would be a part. This solution, understandably, took the assembled company by surprise. But that was precisely Adenauer's intention – to make maximum impact on the delegates who were about to set off for Weimar to debate the new German constitution. Unfortunately, there were three major objections to the plan which soon became evident: first, that the eastern part of Germany would not be economically viable without the relatively affluent west; second, that any such suggestion would send a clear signal to France that the Rhineland was prepared to see some sort of separation from Prussia; and third, although this was only whispered at the time, that the whole scheme was no more than a vehicle for Adenauer's own self-advancement, since he would be the obvious candidate to lead the proposed 'West German Republic'. Certainly, Adenauer's 'intense personal ambition was well known' to the British.[19]

The result of the meeting was that a committee was formed 'with the task of preparing plans for the establishment of a West German Republic within the constitutional framework of the German Reich and grounded in the Constitution of the Reich to be drafted by the German National Assembly'.[20] The committee's chairman – unsurprisingly – was to be none other than Konrad Adenauer. In other words, the whole issue was active, but was to lie on the shelf until the Weimar Assembly had decided what the shape of the future Germany was to be. All options, at that point, were held open.

Only two weeks later the armistice was renewed. The renewal, however, was not without difficulty. The British had wished to see substantial moves towards German disarmament as a pre-condition for renewal – Lloyd George said directly that 'all he wanted was to get the guns away from the Germans so that it might not be necessary to maintain huge armies'.[21] The French government, on the other hand, was adamant that the occupation and the appropriate war footing should be maintained. The compromise was brokered by the Americans, who suggested what became the Inter-Allied Military Control Commission (IAMCC), a temporary arrangement which, as it turned out, was to remain permanent in Germany until 1927.

The renewal of the armistice came as something of a relief to Adenauer. He was at that moment trying his best to convince the British occupiers that the conditions under which the people of Cologne were obliged to live were on the edge of intolerable. It was not just the restriction of liberties involved in military occupation. That was bearable, if unpleasant. What was aggravating an already difficult problem was the isolation of the occupied Rhineland from the unoccupied Ruhr. The two areas had always formed one economic unit, and it made little economic sense to split it in half. By the end of January 1919, the time of Adenauer's conference on the whole future of the Rhineland, the Cologne economy was in crisis. Unemployment was rising fast; the continuing Allied blockade was preventing essential supplies of food and fuel from reaching the city; and the industrial suburbs – the seedbeds of revolutionary activity – were seeing starvation on the streets. Unless the British took some action, Adenauer told Fergusson, hunger and unemployment would deliver Cologne into the hands of the 'Bolsheviks'. Louis Hagen, then president of the Cologne Chamber of Commerce, endorsed the bleak message.

Adenauer's view of the threat of 'Bolshevism' was not idle. Indeed, it was confirmed by British military intelligence reports. Furthermore, even when the British troops had entered Cologne the previous December they had noted that the bakeries were producing 'abominable flourless, sugarless concoctions' (presumably a reference to Cologne Bread) and had seen 'the little child skeletons' waiting patiently around 'the Officers' Messes for crusts and refuse'.[22] By the end of February Fergusson's Chief of Staff, General Sidney Clive, noticed that 'the schoolchildren whom we passed in walking to our office had entirely stopped running about and playing on their way to school'.[23] There was by now no doubt that the situation was critical. Fergusson's response was to send Frank Tiarks, a London merchant banker who had been seconded in January to his staff to advise on financial and commercial matters, to see Lloyd George and persuade him to sanction the immediate delivery of food supplies to Cologne.

But it was not as easy as that. For a start, the French government was unsympathetic, on the grounds that this was only what the German aggressors deserved, and that furthermore any available funds in the Rhineland should be used to pay reparations rather than to buy food. Then there was the matter of how any food might equitably be distributed. Even by the time of Tiarks' mission to London, the British troops in the Cologne Zone were starting to lose heart. In January 1919, if the weekly postal censorship reports are any guide, they were reasonably contented, but in February there was a clear increase in drunkenness and minor mutinies. The reason was obvious: they wanted to go home. But the British, as the occupying force, provided the only available mechanism for the overall protection and supervision of food distribution.

The response of the British Cabinet was to adopt a plan which they thought would ensure that the British force in Cologne was fully capable of supervising a food distribution programme. Astonishingly enough, their solution was to adopt a plan under which Cologne would be garrisoned in the future by what was in practice a new army, consisting mainly of conscripts who had joined too late to fight in the war, the 'old soldiers' being repatriated and demobilised. The difficulty, of course, which nobody seemed to have spotted, was in the transition from what was virtually one type of army to another.

The change was never going to be easy. But it happened to coincide almost precisely with the decision, reached on 14 March in spite of strenuous French objections, that Germany was to be treated as one unit for the purpose of the supply of food, and that some 200,000 tons of potatoes and surplus army rations were to be released immediately for delivery to the British and American zones of occupied Germany. The result was, as might be imagined, administrative chaos. Indeed, such was the chaos that even this limited gesture made little impact. The potatoes did not arrive until April, and were not unloaded until 'they were rotting the sides out of their barges'.[24]

The military and administrative weakness of the British presence in Cologne was well understood by Adenauer. But he was equally aware of German political weakness. To him it came as no surprise when the government in Berlin, presented with the terms of the peace treaty by the Allies on 8 May, first of all objected, then prepared for armed resistance, and then caved in. The terms were, of course, humiliating: the army was to be reduced to 100,000 men, without aircraft or armour; the navy was to have no ships above 10,000 tons and no submarines; there were to be extensive financial reparations; and the Emperor and other war leaders were to be surrendered to face charges of violating the laws of war.

In response, the outraged German generals were even in favour of rejecting the treaty out of hand, and prepared for renewal of war. The Allies did the same, moving troops into the bridgeheads on the right bank of the Rhine, ready to invade unoccupied Germany. Further, they refused all modifications to the draft treaty, and finally issued an ultimatum that it should be signed by 23 June. At the last moment, the German government realised that they had no alternative. The Treaty of Versailles was duly signed – triumphantly by the Allies, but grudgingly by the Germans.

As it happened, the Rhineland, and the French, had had one more surprise in store before the signature. On 30 May the committee which

Adenauer had set up in February met for the first (and last) time. It was to discuss the results of a meeting that Adenauer had had with French military officials to review his plan for a West German Republic, and the subsequent debate in the Assembly at Weimar. Neither event had produced any positive move. The idea was in practice dead. But on the following day, Dorten, supported by the Commander-in-Chief in the French Zone, General Charles Mangin, quite unexpectedly took the extraordinary step, by simultaneous proclamations in Wiesbaden and Mainz, of announcing nothing less than the immediate establishment of a Rhenish Republic.

Both Adenauer and the British were taken aback by Dorten's move. Clive had specifically warned Mangin's Chief of Staff a few days before that 'we are here to keep order and that is what we shall do'.[25] To be sure, he was sufficiently concerned about the political implications to make a special trip to Paris to seek instructions from Lloyd George. Lloyd George's reply was unambiguous: Britain would not support any move towards a separate Rhineland. But Clive was also instructed to be very careful in handling the French; in particular, he was certainly not to be hurried into precipitate military action. Clive took the sensible course: he ordered the Cologne newspapers merely to report the event without comment, and then let it be known that no constitutional change in British-occupied territory would take place without the prior consent of the occupation authorities. There was now no doubt. Without Cologne there could no separate Rhineland; and without explicit British authority there would be no Cologne. Dorten's gambit, bold as it was, had been met and countered — for the time being.

In all this Clive had tactfully taken the trouble to keep Adenauer informed, and to listen to his advice. The separatists in Wiesbaden, of course, were well aware of Adenauer's role, and thought it no more and no less than a betrayal. At a farcical 'Revolutionary Tribunal' in Koblenz Adenauer was tried, found guilty of treason to the Rhenish Republic, and condemned to death. 'This verdict,' Adenauer was to say later, 'was worth more to me than a decoration.'[26] Politically, that view may have been right. But, even at the time, Adenauer's mind was, at least to some extent, engaged in a project which was much more personal than political. He was thinking of getting married again.

2

LIFE HAS TO GO ON

'Aber Deutschland wird sich erholen . . .'*

THERE IS LITTLE doubt that Emma's death in 1916 had affected Adenauer much more deeply than he was prepared to admit, perhaps even to himself. Photographs even as late as the early 1920s – taken in private – show a face still hurt and depressed. The formerly cheerful moustache only appears again in minimal form, obviously to hide the scars on his upper lip; the eyes are dark and fierce, the left eye still slightly angled towards the bridge of his nose, with the lower eyelid lifted and puffed from the surgical reconstruction of his left cheek; his mouth is turned down at both corners; and, as though to add almost deliberately to the ferocity of his expression, his close-cut hair recedes at the temples and is flecked with grey above his ears. It is not, on any view, the face of a man at peace with himself.

As might be expected, in public Adenauer's face took on a different expression. No sign of personal emotion was allowed to show. On those

---

* 'But Germany will recover . . .': Adenauer, in a speech to a meeting of Rhineland representatives, 1 February 1919; Konrad Adenauer, *Reden, 1917–1967: Eine Answahl*, ed. Hans-Peter Schwarz (Stuttgart, Deutsche Verlags-Anstalt, 1975), p. 27.

occasions, it was as though he was wearing a mask. He assumed, consciously or semi-consciously, an air of remoteness and authority which he thought to be appropriate to his position; and his figure, tall, slim and spare (and the formal top hat, worn like a large chimney extended above his head), helped to give him the degree of dignity suitable for the first citizen of Cologne. The world, he clearly considered, demanded no less; appearances had to be maintained. But at the end of the official day there was the return home; and it was here that the official mask could be dropped and sadness be allowed to set in.

To be sure, quite apart from the current circumstances, Adenauer's home in Max-Bruch-Strasse could hardly ever have been described as a haven of good cheer. The house, after all, had been built for Emma and the growing family, and Emma herself had been almost as ascetic in taste and habit as her husband. Creature comforts had been kept to no more than a bare minimum. As what seems like a precaution, Adenauer had made certain that the house, itself of ample proportions, had a wing which was to serve as his own working quarters. But the larger and taller structure was designed for family life. Indeed, it was in many respects a fine construction. It was more than simply commodious; it was expansive and gave every appearance of luxury. At its back, the house had a large garden, where children could play in safety. There was room, too, for Adenauer's increasingly frail mother. All in all, had Emma lived, it would have been an ideal home for a devoted couple and a Catholic family life; but on the inside it was austere to the point of gloom.

The house, of course, had its own memories. It was the house in which Emma had suffered, and in which she had died; and during the years after her death an atmosphere of ghostly depression pervaded the whole place. The children, deprived of their mother, were looked after by a succession of governesses and, to a limited extent, by their grandmother, while their father busied himself with his work. Life obviously had to go on, but there were no concessions to comfort, let alone luxury. The only recourse for the children was to find neighbours in the same street with whom they could play.

As luck would have it, there were indeed neighbours, not just in the same street but next door, who fitted the bill. Their house had been built at the same time as Adenauer's and more or less to the same dimensions. But if the house was similar in dimensions, the father of the family which lived in it, Ferdinand Zinsser, was in character almost the opposite to his neighbour.

First of all, he and his family were Lutheran; then he had, it seems, 'a cheerful temperament, open and hospitable'.[1] He was also fond of music, and – again quite unlike his neighbour – of a good evening's chat about nothing in particular. He regularly invited to his house friends, students, and almost any musician or artist who happened to be around, for the general entertainment of himself and whatever company might be with him. Children, too, were invited, and Zinsser took great pleasure in entertaining them with stories and clever conjuring tricks. Further, even when Zinsser himself was fighting in the war, his house remained what must have been a welcome refuge for the Adenauer children from the austerity of their own home.

The relationship between the two families had blossomed in the early years of the war. The Zinsser children, Auguste, Lotte and Ernst, all had been taught to play musical instruments – Auguste, known familiarly as Gussi, the violin, Lotte the piano and brother Ernst the cello; and there had been musical evenings in the Zinsser house, which in turn, and in the course of time, spilled over into the Adenauer house next door. The quality of the music was no doubt uncertain, but at least it served to occupy the dark wartime evenings – and, during Emma's prolonged illness, to amuse the otherwise sombre Adenauer. Indeed, he took to asking the two girls, Gussi and Lotte, to sing for him. It was nothing too complicated: just a few simple tunes, and particularly Rhineland folk songs. But it was pleasant and, above all, ensured that Koko, Max and Ria, the Adenauer children, had close and happy, if rather older, friends, who would look after them in the difficult moments of their mother's illness. In return, Adenauer made sure that Frau Zinsser was adequately supplied with coal while her husband was away fighting the war.

Suddenly, with Emma's death, the whole thing had collapsed. Adenauer had cut off all contact, and had retreated into mournful isolation. For the children, this meant endless hours of lonely play in the large and haunted house where their mother had died. Children, however, have their own way of breaking out, and it was not too long before the three of them sneaked across into the Zinsser house to renew acquaintance with their old friends, the two Zinsser sisters. Indeed, it was the sisters that looked after the Adenauer children after their father's dreadful accident of March 1917, when the children thought that they were to be orphaned. Gradually, through the medium of the younger generation, neighbourly relations between the Adenauers and the Zinssers had been re-established. There was, of course, a difference in ages: Gussi, for instance, the eldest Zinsser child, had been born in 1895 while Koko, the eldest Adenauer child, had been born in 1907. But for the purposes of neighbourly and (suitably conspiratorial) childish companionship, the age difference was of no apparent importance.

The difference, however, became important when Adenauer took what seems to have been a conscious decision: that as Mayor of Cologne it looked odd, in the context of the time, for him to remain unmarried. But, although it was a simple matter to arrive at the decision, it was not at all easy to see how the end could be achieved. Fifteen years earlier, the younger man had been able to join in the jovial and flirtatious gatherings at the tennis club. The present Mayor of Cologne was now not just older, and furthermore a widower, but he was so busy with his official work that, even had he felt inclined, there was nothing remotely resembling a tennis club that he could with any dignity or decency join for the specific purpose which he had in mind.

In the event, it was his garden which provided the solution. During his time as a widower, Adenauer had relieved the frustrations of his work and his life by creating an attractive garden. To some extent (although almost certainly exaggerated in official histories) he had already been interested in what seemed to be the mysterious workings of nature, as a town boy often is; and he had, over the years, gone to the trouble of reading books on botany. He had also started to take a particular interest in roses. But after Emma's death his garden had changed its role in his life. Previously, it had been a source of intellectual interest; now it had become a source of emotional solace and relaxation. The war might be what it was; Cologne's troubles might be what they were; his family might impose whatever burdens they did; what was immutable, predictable and reassuring was that flowers would grow in the spring and die back in the autumn, that trees would obey their own particular seasonal cycle, and that the grass would flourish from year to year.

Gussi Zinsser had some of the same sense of the rhythms of nature, but in her case the perspective was that of young adulthood rather than that of the threshold of middle age. In truth, by 1918 Gussi had grown into something near – but perhaps only near – to a mature woman. She was, after all, nearly twenty-three; but the sheltered nature of her late adolescence, and the restricted social opportunities of the war years, had left her shy and ill at ease in masculine company. Nevertheless, she was by any standards an attractive young lady: quick to laugh and to cry, and quick to give sympathy where sympathy was needed. Physically, she was pretty rather than beautiful, of average height, slim but with a small, rounded face and large, dark eyes always seemingly on the point of laughter. She dressed conventionally, in the ankle-length dresses which were the fashion of the time; but her hair was parted in the centre and waved into curls that fell, with suitable decorum but nonetheless with studied and fetching delicacy, around her ears and forehead. All in all, she was an obvious target for her distinguished but dissatisfied neighbour.

Conversations between the two started over the fence separating their respective gardens. Adenauer, on his way out to work, paused to offer Gussi advice, first of all, on how to hoe potatoes, which she happened to be doing at the time. It was a matter, he said, of how to handle the hoe. Gussi duly reported the conversation to her parents: 'I had a long conversation with Dr Adenauer today.'[2] A few days later there was a further conversation, again about gardening. As the days and weeks went by, the gardening conversations seemed to get longer and longer. Gussi's mother started to take note, but all she could get out of her daughter was that the conversations were entirely concerned with gardening. 'Beans and potatoes,' she said.[3]

Frau Zinsser, of course, suspected that there was much more to it than beans and potatoes, and her suspicions were amply confirmed when Gussi, in an almost throwaway remark, announced to her parents that she wished to convert to Roman Catholicism. The news was not well received; indeed, it came as something of a bombshell. Gussi's mother was firm on the matter. It was perfectly obvious, she asserted, that Gussi had fallen under the spell of the next-door neighbour; and that, not to put too fine a point on it, she had fallen in love with him. In fact, Gussi's mother was quite right. Gussi had indeed fallen in love with the grand, aloof and austere character next door. It was also true that marriage had indeed been discussed; but Adenauer, in making what seems to have been a proposal, had pointed out that he could not possibly marry a Protestant. It was certainly an unconventional way to declare love – if that was what Adenauer was trying to do – but by then Gussi was too far gone to worry about that. 'He is the best, the cleverest, the most chivalrous man I know,' she had told her sister, and then, after a pause, '. . . he and Father.' '"Father" came in a bit late there,' Lotte replied.[4] She meant it as a joke, but it did not go down very well with her sister.

The matter had obviously become serious, and, as the situation warranted,

Professor and Frau Zinsser embarked on what was no doubt an intense debate about their daughter's future. Gussi, her mother said emphatically, should be sent away to bring her to her senses. Dr Adenauer was all very well; he had indeed been a good friend during the war, held a position of the utmost distinction and, although this was perhaps only mentioned in a whisper, may have had something to do with Zinsser's appointment as professor of dermatology in the newly established Cologne University (for the foundation of which, indeed, Adenauer had been responsible, earning thereby, incidentally, the first of his many honorary doctorates).

But, against that, he was almost twice the age of their daughter, already had three children, and, what was more, had had a previous marriage which everybody acknowledged had been one of the deepest love and affection. Gussi could not possibly compete with that. Besides, she went on, Adenauer's children would not accept Gussi as a mother, if it came to marriage, since they had played together as equals, in spite of the age differences. There was also, she pointed out, the matter of religion. Adenauer was a Catholic by inheritance and conviction. Emma had been a devout Catholic as well. It was impossible to believe that Gussi, brought up as a Lutheran, could fit into such a religious straightjacket.

Needless to say, Frau Zinsser's opinions won the day. Gussi, it was decided, was to be packed off for six months to cool down (and possibly meet a more suitable prospective bridegroom). She was given the choice of Vienna or Wiesbaden; the Zinssers had relatives in both places where she could stay. When offered the choice, Gussi chose Wiesbaden; and there she went. But the arrangement did not go to plan at all. Within a few weeks she turned up again at home, and told her parents, with much spirit (and courage), that 'I will never give up Adenauer'.[5] At this point, her parents realised that the battle was clearly lost, and that surrender was the only possible course. From then on, her engagement was no more than a formality. Soon afterwards she was received into the Roman Catholic Church, after suitable instruction from Adenauer's brother Hans.

Once received and re-baptised, Gussi threw herself with enthusiasm into her new faith, joining, and becoming an active member of, the Society of Catholic German Women. From then, it was only a matter of weeks before, on 25 September 1919, she and Konrad Adenauer were married. There were still, however, surprises in store. The wedding took place not, as might have been expected, in one of the grand churches of Cologne but in the chapel of the Trinity Hospital. Furthermore, the service was kept as simple as possible; it was conducted by Hans; and the bride wore grey rather than white. There was no official reception, and only the closest relatives were invited to the subsequent muted celebration. Those who were there noted that Adenauer was forty-three. Gussi was not yet twenty-four.

After the event the couple departed. But it was to be nothing like the extended honeymoon of Adenauer's marriage with Emma. In fact, it was only to be two days in a hotel a few miles down the road in Bad Godesberg. Adenauer felt that he could not be away from Cologne for long, and even during the two-day break officials arrived to brief the mayor on the current events in the city. For the new bride it was something of an awakening. 'Often,' she sighed later, 'I wished that Konrad had become a gardener.'[6] Furthermore, on their return to Cologne, she found that her new husband hardly had time for her. There was a long working day; messengers came and went; trips to Berlin were frequent and often lasted several days. And, as if all this was not enough, she found herself managing a large house in which the servants, by then used to running the place in their own way, refused to accept the authority of 'this twenty-year-old'.[7]

To cap it all, the difficulties with Emma's children turned out to be just as bad as Gussi's parents had predicted. For them to move from calling the Zinsser sisters 'Gussi' and 'Lotte' to calling them 'Mother' and 'Aunt' was altogether too much. Max, the second son, told Frau Zinsser that if she ever had another child he could not possibly call it 'uncle' or 'aunt', while Koko, who had, as a ten-year-old, vivid recollections of his mother's illness and death, said flatly that he could never call Gussi 'Mother' since 'I have seen her going to school with her satchel'.[8] Besides, they did not think their new stepmother 'very intelligent' and much preferred to regard their aunt Mia, Emma's sister, as their 'surrogate mother'.[9]

It was hardly a deliriously joyful start to a marriage. But Adenauer had a great deal to occupy his mind. Of course, he ought to have warned Gussi in advance, and not allowed her to plunge into marriage with him, against the advice of her parents, without due time for preparation and understanding of the life she was thereafter to lead. But that was not his style; and, as it happened, it was Gussi's own character, full of patience, warmth and kindliness, that enabled her to surmount the problems which she encountered.

'She was the most unselfish person,' said an old family friend, 'that I ever knew. Her guide was God. Only sometimes,' he went on, 'was there perhaps a doubt that the place of God in her heart had been taken over by her husband.'[10] The comment is not unfair. Gussi was deeply, almost heroically, in love with her husband. In the mornings and afternoons, when he went off to work in his official car, she would watch at the window until the car was out of sight. Half an hour before he came back, either at midday or in the evening, she would leave her work and prepare for his return – do her hair, make up her face, and put on a fresh dress or blouse. Her life was devoted to one cause – pleasing Adenauer.

This was, to be sure, far from an easy task. For a start, Adenauer's day was organised with meticulous, even neurotic, care. It started with breakfast (with Gussi), after which he took his sheepdog for a fifteen-minute walk in the park. (Adenauer liked dogs but hated cats. Furthermore, when told that sheepdogs were 'decadent' he instantly replaced his with a Rottweiler.) At 8.45am his car drove him to the City Hall. The return journey was at 1.45pm, at which point he lunched with Gussi and Emma's three children. After lunch he retired to the terrace or his bed, depending on the weather, and slept for half an hour or so, his eyes covered with a bandage to keep out the light and his ears stuffed with earplugs to keep out the noise. At 2.45pm his car was waiting for him to take him back to the City Hall, where he worked until 8pm – later if necessary. He returned for supper, but on many evenings would have to go out again to official functions. He liked, however, to be in bed no later than 11pm.

It was not a simple matter for a new wife to adjust to the timetable. Such a regimented life would no doubt be very irritating in a modern family. But in those days it was probably something of a relief to be able to predict precisely the movements of the head of the house. What was more difficult were Adenauer's frequent shifts of temper. He was at times benevolent and sympathetic, at other times irritable, and, from time to time, prone to outbursts of intense rage. Some of this was directed at his family, since he followed his own father in insisting on strict discipline at home; but most of it was due to the pressure of his work and, indeed, to the multitude of problems with which he was confronted and with which, given his particular character, he felt he had to deal single-handed.

Strange as it may seem, given Adenauer's explosively energetic mood of the time, the easiest problem he had to deal with was the British occupation. True, there were irritations. The Military Governor and his staff had requisitioned the most elegant villas and the larger hotels, and the use of nearly a hundred schools in the whole area as barracks for British soldiers had given rise to understandable resentment. There were also regrettably high spirits among the younger officers – one night in January 1919, for instance, an obviously drunken group had placed, with accompanying gales of laughter, chamber-pots on the heads of the statues of Kaiser Wilhelm and Kaiserin Auguste. More serious, of course, were the sporadic episodes of looting by British troops, careless driving by British lorries leading to traffic accidents, or the occasional shooting at innocent citizens because for one reason or another they had failed to obey an order to stop and be searched.

Such incidents, and countless others, were probably inevitable given the fact of occupation, and they were dealt with sensibly by the Occupation Department at the City Hall, set up by Adenauer for the purpose of sorting out such difficulties. Despite all this aggravation, however, by the summer of 1919 visitors from Britain to Cologne were surprised at the relatively friendly relations between the occupiers and the occupied, particularly once fraternisation had been permitted in July, and soldiers returning home to Britain reported that for the most part they had been treated with friendliness, and indeed warmth, by the Rhinelanders.

Official relations during 1919 and 1920 were 'on the whole . . . satisfactory and harmonious'.[11] Unofficial relations were, of course, another matter. The occupied had no more love for the occupiers than the occupiers had for the occupied. There were severe tensions, particularly on how the labour unrest and the food problem could be surmounted.

To some extent, the establishment of a civilian High Commission in Koblenz to oversee the military government of the occupied zones, and the gradual implementation of an agreement on the Rhineland – signed at the same time as the signature of the Treaty of Versailles itself on 26 June 1919 – seemed to make occupation at least marginally more palatable to the occupied. The Rhineland agreement, for instance, although it fell far short of a guarantee of civil rights, did go some way to set up the mechanisms for consultation between the occupying powers and the local Rhineland authorities – while reserving the occupiers' right 'to enter into relations with any local authority whatsoever'.[12] Nevertheless, there was nothing which could make the occupation more popular.

There were, as well, continuing arguments between the British and the French, which intensified after the United States Senate refused to ratify the Versailles Treaty, leaving a vacuum in the administration of the Rhineland which the French government was quite happy to fill. Fortunately for Adenauer, the British held their political ground (while reducing their military force) and thus prevented the French from infiltrating military detachments into what they claimed were empty barracks in the city. That was welcome. In fact, Adenauer's attitude at the time is probably best summed up in an interview he gave to the correspondent of the Paris magazine *Eclair*, duly reported to the British government in the daily press summary of 24 March 1920: 'He [Adenauer] said that France, unlike that politic [sic] country England, did not want to reach an understanding with Germany . . . France hated Germany herself.'[13]

The comparative stability of Adenauer's relations with the British occupiers allowed him to devote a large part of his by now formidable energy to what can only be described as his master plan for the development of Cologne itself. In 1918 and 1919 Adenauer had worked it out with the greatest care. Leaving aside the foundation of a university to compete with Bonn, the plan was designed to take advantage of the clear, and fortuitous, opportunities provided by the settlement at the end of the war. For instance, the outer city fortifications were, by order of the Allies, to be demolished. Then subsidies for railway freight to the north German ports of Hamburg and Bremen were, again by Allied order, declared illegal. Even by themselves, these two quite unrelated events left Adenauer with an opportunity which no Mayor of Cologne had enjoyed since Mayor Becker at the turn of the century.

First, the destruction of the outer fortifications, which had enclosed the city and its satellites on both banks of the Rhine, allowed not only the forced acquisition of the land which they occupied but also enabled the city to use the land already acquired when the inner wall had been demolished by Mayor Becker well before the war. By buying up all the land thus freed, the city was able to use it for whatever purpose seemed appropriate; and Adenauer certainly had a purpose in mind – a 'green belt' to surround the city. Second, it was quite obvious that the Rhineland was going to enjoy an economic resurgence and equally obvious that Cologne, if transport to the north German ports was no longer to be economically viable, would be the main port of exit to the North Sea, and the Atlantic beyond, for the goods so produced. That meant a new, enlarged port. Both of these were major projects in their own right but, as though that were not enough, it became obvious that the major industrial development of post-war Cologne would have to be to the east rather than to the west – in other words, on the far side of the river from the city itself. To do this, the community of Worringen on the right bank would have to be incorporated into Cologne, and houses built for the workforce which was going to man the new factories.

The whole plan was massive, even for a city as rich as Cologne. But, whatever the concept, Adenauer badly needed an experienced urban planner who could understand what it was all about, and reduce grand and sweeping designs to the level of practical drawings. He was shrewd in picking his man. His choice lighted on Fritz Schumacher.

Schumacher was from Hamburg, by then a port largely deprived of its ocean trade. The alternative was the river trade which Cologne, in its privileged position, was about to attract. The temptation was too much, and Schumacher agreed to pack his bags and set up his office in Cologne – but, cautiously, for no more than three years. Before he did, he was warned of the problems he would face: the British were the final arbiters of everything he would wish to do; unemployment was severe and probably endemic; separation from unoccupied Germany meant that Cologne could not rely on the mineral riches of the Ruhr; and the mark was starting to slide in the currency markets. 'If I came,' he later reported, 'I would see the things I was supposed to work on burst like bubbles.'[14]

There were, as always in such matters, many high hurdles which had to be jumped. At first, the British – and the French – in Koblenz just wanted the fortifications to be blown up and left as rubble. In Cologne, although legally permissible, the compulsory purchase of large tracts of land gave rise to vocal opposition from those who were to lose out. In Berlin, 'the confusion in the authorities is terrible'.[15] The only positive sign for Adenauer and Schumacher was the depreciation of the mark, which, at least in its early stages in 1920 and the first half of 1921, was gentle enough to make the purchase of German assets, and inward investment, attractive to foreign companies.

On 8 June 1920 Adenauer wrote an article for the *Kölner Stadtanzeiger* setting out his vision for Cologne. The city, he wrote, was at a turning point. It could become a 'giant desert of stones' or it could become 'a city whose inhabitants can lead an existence fit for human beings'.[16] The answer, of course, was obvious to him, but it was significant that he felt it necessary to engage in such an effort of persuasion. Not all were convinced. The City Council in particular were terrified at the huge expenditure to which

Adenauer and Schumacher were committing their city, and during the long debates on the matter tempers became more and more frayed. The language, too, deteriorated: Adenauer was at first called simply 'Utopian'; but that soon became 'a reckless gambler and speculator', and finally 'Germany's most expensive mayor'. Nor were the public all that enthusiastic. Indeed, when plans were announced for a vast athletics stadium at Müngersdorf, on the western edge of the city, there were those who asked whether the money would not be better spent on ensuring proper food and housing for the city itself. But Adenauer was not to be deterred. As Schumacher later wrote, 'If he had lived in earlier centuries he would have been a great church dignitary, one of those men with two great qualities: the craft to pursue their objectives as resolute politicians in the cut and thrust of German politics and the strength to translate their boundless will into deeds.'[17]

Adenauer's energy in the pursuit of his grand ideas for Cologne is all the more remarkable in that while all the critical debates were going on there was a family crisis in the Max-Bruch-Strasse. In the spring of 1920, by now expecting her first child, Gussi became suddenly and seriously ill. The doctor was summoned, and promptly diagnosed malfunction of the kidneys. It was all horrifyingly reminiscent of Emma. Fortunately, after this scare, Gussi's illness was contained, but the birth of the baby, on 4 June 1920, brought with it another problem. The baby, a boy, was clearly very weak; his chances of survival were slim. He was immediately baptised – the highest priority – and given the name of Ferdinand. Since both mother and son were in need of constant attention, Lotte, herself a trained nurse, moved in to help. Adenauer spent what time he could with his wife, but was frequently called back to the City Hall.

But when he came back late in the evening on 7 June, he found that the doctor had given up hope for his son's life. He went straight to the room where the baby was, only to find the night nurse asleep in an armchair next to the cradle. Adenauer woke the obviously exhausted woman, sent her off to bed and himself sat by the cradle keeping watch. Around midnight the baby's breathing grew heavy. Adenauer ran out to telephone the doctor, who replied that he would willingly come round, but that his visit would be fruitless. Adenauer went back to the baby's room, picked him up out of his cradle and held him in his arms until death finally came early the following morning. An hour or so later, Adenauer went to his wife, who was sleeping fitfully in the next-door room. He wanted to break the news to her himself.

She woke as soon as he entered. He did not have to say anything. Gussi simply whispered: 'He's dead.'[18] Adenauer nodded, then sat down on the edge of her bed and held her hand for a long time in silence.

Several times during that morning his office sent urgent messages for him to return immediately, and in the end, return he did. In fact, the urgent calls were justified. While the tragedy of Ferdinand's death was being played out in Max-Bruch-Strasse, the whole political complexion of Germany had changed. On 6 June elections had taken place for the new Reichstag – the first since the ballot for the Weimar Assembly eighteen months earlier, and only a few months after the ratification of the Peace Treaty. The period between those two elections had, to say the least, been unhappy. The main problem had been that the armed forces, and particularly the army, had been unable to reconcile themselves to what they regarded as a treaty which was no less than humiliating. The Ebert government's attempts to comply with the terms of the treaty had met with outbreaks of mutiny. It had not just been the disenchantment of those who had fought in the war. Others had joined in various unregulated militias, known as 'free corps'. The overall result had been continual – and sporadically violent – tension throughout 1919 and into 1920.

Matters came to a head in March 1920, when two of these 'free corps', the Baltikum Brigade and the 2nd Marine Brigade, were ordered by the Ebert government to be disbanded, to comply with the requirements of the treaty. This had been too much for the commander of the 2nd Marine Brigade, Captain Hermann Ehrhardt von Döberitz, who instantly appealed to the choleric General von Lüttwitz. He, in turn, consulted a somewhat louche East Prussian politician, Wolfgang Kapp. The result was that Kapp and Lüttwitz decided, in the name of German nationalism, to launch an attack on Berlin. Captain Ehrhardt was only too happy to join in the fun, and led his troops on the forward march to the capital.

In the event, the capital fell to them without a shot being fired. General Hans von Seeckt, the Chief of the Troop Bureau of the Reichswehr and, in practice, the army's Chief of Staff, pronounced that under no circumstances could German soldiers fire on their wartime comrades. At that point, Ebert took the only sensible decision. The government abandoned Berlin, moving first to Dresden and then to Stuttgart. From there, they ordered all civil servants to down tools, and appealed to the 'working class' to support the Republic. Not all civil servants respected the order, but enough did to make government, in any reasonable sense, impossible.

The 'working class' were only too happy to respond to a call from the Social Democratic Party for a general strike. In fact, they responded in strength. Since neither Kapp or Lüttwitz had any idea what they would do if they found themselves in power, in the face of the general strike the whole effort collapsed in confusion. The 'Government of National Unity', set up on 13 March, lasted no more than four days. But, such had been the success of the general strike in bringing down the Kapp administration in Berlin, the 'working class' mobilised the strikers into what was tantamount to an army, and by 20 March not only had occupied the main industrial centres of the Ruhr but openly dominated the areas immediately to the east of Düsseldorf. General von Seeckt, however, reluctant as he was to use his army against their wartime comrades, was quite happy to let them loose on the 'Red Army' on the right bank of the Rhine. This he did, and successfully. But the lesson was not lost on those who were trying to construct a new republic. The army was quite clearly no longer a servant of the civil power but an independent unit, prepared to intervene whenever it, and it alone, felt that its own perception of what constituted civil responsibility was at stake.

Under normal political circumstances, it would have been reasonable to expect the voters to support a government which had been so rudely dislodged and reinstated. But the political circumstances were far from normal. In the confusion that surrounded what became known as the 'Kapp Putsch' in Berlin the national electorate decided that governments, at whatever level, had not been performing adequately. The major sufferer in the elections of June 1920 was Ebert's own party, the Social Democrats, whose vote dropped from 11.5 million in 1919 to 6.1 million in mid-1920. Ebert himself then quite properly decided that he could no longer continue to lead a government dependent on a Reichstag in which the majority was now held by the parties to which he was opposed.

The result of the June elections was, of course, one matter; but the major split in the Reichstag, in truth, was not between left and right but between those who supported the Republic and those who did not. What until the elections of June 1920 had been the coalition formed to support the Republic now only controlled 205 of the Reichstag's 452 seats. The shift to the right, whatever in those circumstances 'the right' might in practice mean, was evident. Ebert did not feel that there was still sufficient support for the Republic itself to put together a viable coalition. He therefore resigned as

Chancellor; but, such was the goodwill towards him personally that a new shaky coalition government, under the veteran and venerable Centre Party politician Konstantin Fehrenbach, swore him in as President without delay.

The results of the Reichstag elections of June 1920 were, as might be imagined, of intense interest to the Mayor of Cologne. What obviously became clear to him — even during the days of Ferdinand's short life — was that the future government in Berlin would be formed from the parties of the centre and right. One of those parties was, of course, the Centre Party, of which he was, as mayor of one of Germany's major cities, a senior and prominent member. The time and circumstance were therefore ripe for him to make a major move; in other words, to concentrate his energy not merely on Cologne but on Germany itself. This the by now restless and energetic mayor set out to do.

3

THE REPARATIONS CRISIS

'Sie gehen zu schnell, Herr Meier; Sie werden Ihr Ziel nie erreichen'*

'MY LORD, I have the honour to transmit herewith for your Lordship's information an account of an interesting conversation which took place between the Commissioner at Cologne and Dr Adenauer, the Oberbürgermeister of Cologne.'[1] So begins a report in May 1921 from Arnold Robertson, the British member of the Inter-Allied High Commission in Koblenz, to the Foreign Secretary, Lord Curzon. The language, of course, is appropriate to its time, and to its author. Robertson was a professional diplomat, originally deputy to the first British High Commissioner, Sir Harold Stuart, but something of an expert, as had been Stuart himself, in blocking French efforts to dominate the High Commission's proceedings. 'It is hardly a secret,' Robertson had acidly observed in his first speech to the Commission in October 1920, 'that this is almost the only Inter-Allied Commission which has progressed without any serious disagreement.'[2] For obvious reasons, therefore, he and his staff were considered by Adenauer to be on his side.

---

* 'You are going too fast, Herr Meier; you will never reach your goal': Adenauer to an official, quoted by his brother-in-law Dr Suth; quoted in P. Weymar, *Adenauer*, p. 93.

The conversation referred to was between Adenauer and Julian Piggott, Robertson's deputy in Cologne. It was certainly interesting; so interesting, indeed, that Piggott called it, also in suitably diplomatic language, 'somewhat remarkable'. Apart from all else, it showed that Adenauer's political skills were by now quite up to the task of dealing with the British occupiers, and of playing them off against his, and their, French opponents. But it was more than that. 'The most striking part of the interview,' Piggott records, 'was Dr Adenauer's frank admission that for the past two years Germany had not done her best to fulfil the obligations imposed by the Peace Treaty.' The cause, Adenauer had gone on to say, was to be found in the 'extreme weakness' of successive German governments. The conversation did not end there. Adenauer went on: 'The only salvation for Germany now lay in the creation of a government which would have almost dictatorial powers.' So interesting was the account of the conversation that Curzon (annotating Piggott's report of Adenauer's view as 'a remarkable admission') felt it right to pass it on not just to the British Cabinet but to King George V.[3]

The background to Adenauer's conversation with Piggott is extremely complex. The obligations to which Adenauer was referring in the conversation were the reparations demanded by the Allies to compensate them for the damage which, in their view, the Germans had been guilty of inflicting on them in the war. But while the general principle of reparations seemed to be freely accepted – other, of course, than by the Germans, who only accepted under duress – the amount and method of payment were the subjects of protracted dispute both among the Allies themselves and between them and successive German governments. Even during the discussions leading to the Peace Treaty there had been no unanimity of Allied opinion. As an exasperated American observer remarked, 'Some of the delegates wanted to destroy Germany, some wanted to collect reparations, and others wanted to do both. Some wanted to collect more than Germany had agreed to pay or could pay; and others wanted to take all her capital, destroy her, and then collect a large reparations bill.'[4] Furthermore, the whole matter of reparations, if one of his biographers is to be believed, filled Lord Curzon with 'bewildered distress'.[5]

The upshot of these arguments had been that a Reparations Commission was set up in August 1919, to report by I May 1921 with a recommended sum and a recommended method of payment. In the meantime, Germany was to pay 20 billion gold marks (the 'gold mark' being fixed at the pre-war exchange rate of 4.1 marks to the dollar) between August 1919 and the date on which the Commission was to report. In return, the Allies were prepared to accept a proportion of that sum in kind rather than in cash, particularly in deliveries of coal, chemicals and wood. All had seemed to be going well until the Kapp Putsch and the subsequent general strike had intervened. The strike had led inevitably to shortfalls in deliveries of coal and wood. By the middle of 1920, Germany had fallen badly behind.

The whole thing had by then developed into a serious and bad-tempered mess. The only way out of the mess, so it seemed, was to convene yet another conference to see what could be done. This was duly held in July 1920 at the Belgian town of Spa. As it turned out, the conference was a fiasco. The incongruous British duo of Lloyd George and Curzon turned up (described, perhaps unfairly to Lloyd George, as 'Impudence and Dignity'[6]) willing to make some sort of compromise with the German government. The French, on the other hand, were unsure of their general position, since they were now led, if that is the right word, by Alexandre Millerand, who regarded himself as something of a peacemaker ('not a Clemenceau or a Poincaré'[7]). Nevertheless, given all the circumstances, there might perhaps have been the making of a compromise between the Allies and the defaulting Germans.

What immediately destroyed all efforts to find it was the appearance of the German delegation. It was led by Chancellor Fehrenbach and his Foreign Minister, Walter Simons, soberly dressed for such an important diplomatic occasion; but they were accompanied by General von Seeckt and several of his staff ostentatiously wearing full military uniform with accompanying medals for distinguished service in the war. As if that was not enough to infuriate the British and French delegations, Hugo Stinnes, the owner of much of the Ruhr coal-mining industry, who for some reason had been invited to the Spa conference as an 'expert', delivered a long lecture to the British and French delegations in a loud and peremptory voice on what he perceived to be the arrogance of victory. That was more than enough. It provoked an immediate ultimatum from the British and the French to the effect that unless the default in coal deliveries was made up within seventy-two hours, they would occupy the Ruhr – whatever Herr Stinnes might say. The ultimatum was withdrawn after a fierce row, but the damage had been done. There was no longer any deal acceptable to all sides.

After the Spa débâcle, there were further conferences, at which both sides continued to present sharply different views of what reparations should be paid, and how. But the real difficulty came with the report of the Reparations Commission at the end of April 1921. Their recommendations were complex; indeed, there were few who could truly be said to understand them. They involved A Bonds, B Bonds and C Bonds, with different maturity dates and different (but all enormous) amounts. The bonds themselves were denominated in 'gold marks', which by 1921 were of no more than historical interest. It soon became clear that to pay what the Reparations Commission recommended would have required no less than $12.5 billion, or 750 billion paper marks, given mid-1921 exchange rates. In short, the burden which was to be imposed was, by any reasonable standard, impossible for Germany to bear.

But this was far from the end of the story. In presenting the bill to the German government on 5 May 1921, the Allies demanded not just the acceptance, without any amendment, of the total package, but the transfer to their account within twenty-five days of $250 million. The Fehrenbach government appealed to the United States for mediation, but by then Washington was no longer interested. Support for his government in the Reichstag was slipping away. The only way out was to accept the Allied conditions and then resign. This Fehrenbach did. But, in order to meet the immediate Allied demand, the government sold paper marks on the foreign exchange markets and borrowed from domestic banks to make up the deficit in its accounts. The effect on the value of the paper mark, both internal and external, was catastrophic. The great German inflation had begun.

It was at this point that Adenauer was invited to become Chancellor of the Reich. On 9 May the Centre Party group in the Reichstag held a meeting to discuss the succession. Fehrenbach had, after all, been a member of their party; it was only right that they should determine who should be his successor. But the arithmetic was difficult. After the elections of June 1920, the Centre Party, together with the Bavarian People's Party, could command only 85 seats in the Reichstag out of a total of 452. It was obvious that another coalition would have to be assembled, but the question was whether the Centre Party could achieve one without the participation of the Social Democrats, who still had 102 seats. In other words, either they plumped for a coalition of the parties of the centre right, in which they would still numerically be the largest party (although the conservative German National People's Party came close with 71 seats and the new German People's Party, the successor to the old National Liberal Party, was not far behind with 65 seats), or they tried to do a deal with the Social Democrats.

It was an important choice. Its importance lay in the Centre Party's own position. Soundly based, as it claimed to be, on the two Catholic principles of good order and social conscience, it could conveniently go either way – to the right or to the left. In fact, it is no exaggeration to say that the Centre Party was the political hinge around which the various coalition governments of the Weimar Republic swung. May 1921 was, in that respect, no different from the various coalition crises which persisted right through the Weimar period.

Adenauer was, of course, a committed member of the Centre Party. He was also the elected mayor of one of Prussia's, and Germany's, largest cities. It therefore came as no surprise that, at their meeting on the evening of 9 May, Heinrich Brauns, Minister of Labour in the Fehrenbach government and himself from Cologne, suggested that the party decide for the Social Democrat option – and proposed Adenauer as the candidate who would be most acceptable. As it happened, Adenauer was in Berlin at the time, and, over dinner, discussed with Brauns and his colleagues the general idea and its ramifications. With due caution, he would, he said, like to think the matter over.

Events then moved at some speed. The following morning President Ebert heard that his own party, the Social Democrats, were refusing to join any coalition with the Centre Party such as Brauns had suggested. He tried to knock heads together. He announced that he was not to be made a fool of; that Germany had to have a government – and quickly – and that he 'would resign his office if it proved necessary'.[8] In short, his party should come to its senses and accept an Adenauer-led coalition.

But heads were not so easily knocked together. Indeed, Adenauer, having slept on the problem, took a clear and contrary position. Of course, he said, he would be prepared to accept the honour of the Chancellorship; there could be no greater honour. But (and Adenauer had by then become good at 'buts') there was a caveat. His caveat, as it emerged, was contained in a series of conditions which in practice made it impossible for his candidature to be acceptable to any of the main parties, and succeeded in offending almost everybody. He offended his own Centre Party by saying that the

Chancellor must be free to choose ministers 'from whatever party he thought fit' (and sack them accordingly, if he thought fit). He offended the Social Democrats by saying that there should be 'no more further talk of socialisation for the present'; and he offended all parties by saying that the statutory working day 'for officials and workmen' should be scrapped in favour of a nine-hour day 'if this measure should be found necessary to balance the budget'.[9]

That was the end of the Adenauer candidature of May 1921. After further negotiation, the result was that the Social Democrats joined a coalition government led by the Centre Party's Joseph Wirth. Nevertheless, Adenauer seems to have come out of the whole incident without serious damage, and perhaps with some credit. He was able to argue – not, perhaps, wholly persuasively, but at least with a show of conviction – that he had only been being honest about the problems facing Germany at the time, and had only tested the will of party politicians to face up to them. More important, however, he had been politically adroit. He had shown his hand for the future, indicating that he would under certain circumstances be prepared to give up his position in Cologne for an uncertain future in Berlin, provided it was on his terms. In truth, he was happy to be well out of it. Adenauer was never a great expert in economics, but even he could tell that this was not the moment to be in charge of the Reich's affairs.

He had, nevertheless, achieved his main objective in going to Berlin. He had put himself firmly in the ranks of Germany's leading politicians. It had not just been a question of bidding, or not bidding, for the Chancellorship; he had succeeded in the original purpose of his visit to Berlin, to secure election as President of the Prussian *Staatsrat*, the upper house of parliament of what was, after all, by far the largest German state. In terms of the politics of the Weimar Republic, it was a shrewd move. The Staatsrat had replaced the old Prussian Herrenhaus of the Wilhelmine Empire and met in the same building as its predecessor. Unlike its predecessor, however, it was elected annually, not by direct suffrage but by the assembly of each Prussian province, on the basis of one delegate for every 500,000 inhabitants, with a minimum of three. Each province was therefore represented, but, because of the complicated electoral system and the rounding of population figures, the number of members varied at any one time around the figure of 75–80.

In practice, the Staatsrat never had very much to do. It was described by one commentator as a 'bloodless legal construction'.[10] Debates were mostly confined to windy resolutions only of concern to Prussia at the time; and it had no say in the decisions of the Reich except in so far as they affected the Prussian state. Nevertheless, it met every month for anything between two and five days in its chamber in the Leipziger Strasse, just around the corner from the Potsdamer Platz and the Wilhelmstrasse, two of the main centres of government. As a result, its members, particularly the senior ones, had ample opportunity to mix with those who wielded power and influence in the Reich itself.

At its first meeting, on 6 May 1921, the Staatsrat decided to elect a President, and the process took place the following day. As is frequently the case on such occasions, there was a wrangle about which members had been properly sworn in and were therefore entitled to vote. In the end, seventy-two members were allowed voting papers. Although the Social Democrats were the largest party there was no overall majority, and, as one of the members from the Rhine Province, Mayor of Cologne and a senior figure in the Centre Party, Adenauer was an obvious candidate around whom the other right-wing parties could coalesce. So it turned out. He won a clear majority on the first ballot of members. (Once established, he was not to be dislodged, and was re-elected each year for the following twelve years.) Having achieved his election and avoided the Chancellorship, and no doubt satisfied with both results, he took the train back across the Rhine to Cologne – and to Gussi.

The 'somewhat remarkable' conversation with Julian Piggott took place immediately after Adenauer's return from Berlin on 11 May 1921. From Adenauer's point of view its purpose was clear. The Allied demand of 5 May had raised again the spectre of an occupation of the Ruhr if the required tranche of reparations was not paid. But the Ruhr was an essential provider to Cologne both of brown coal for the generation of electricity in the city itself and semi-manufactures for the heavy industry on the right bank of the Rhine. If the area were occupied, particularly by the French, and its products diverted to France and Belgium, Cologne would for all practical purposes be bankrupt. The only possible recourse was to the British, in the hope that either they would be able to prevent their Allies from taking such a drastic step or, if they could not, at least they would come to the economic rescue of Cologne. Adenauer was at pains, therefore, to assure the British that the blame for the situation rested with Germany, with the result that the Allies 'and the rest of the world had, with some justice, refused to believe in Germany's good faith'.[11] The underlying but unstated themes, of course, were that Cologne looked to the British rather than to weak German governments, and that he, Adenauer, would have done very much better in power than the Reich governments of 1919 to 1921.

Although the name of Adenauer was, as he had intended, now firmly on the map of political Berlin, Cologne was still his main interest and concern. As it happened, he returned from Berlin in May 1921 to a number of pressing problems. The first, perhaps irritatingly in the light of his conversation with Piggott, was with the British occupiers. Officially, of course, relations between the occupiers and the occupied were considered to be 'on the whole . . . satisfactory and harmonious'. 'Oberbürgermeister Dr Adenauer' was reported by the British, somewhat patronisingly, to be 'a competent official . . . and only on rare occasions has it been found necessary to complain'. 'The German officials and the Cologne citizens,' the report continues, 'repose a considerable amount of confidence in the British authorities, to which the excellent discipline of the British soldier and the correct deportment of the British official have largely contributed.'[12]

This rather smug assessment was true only up to a point. Certainly, in general relations were friendly, but it was a distant friendship, and by 1921 the British soldier had become thoroughly bored. Before the Peace Treaty was ratified, there had been little contact between the British Army and the people of Cologne, and what there was had been friendly enough. The soldiers had led, on the whole, a comfortable and self-contained life. They had their own cricket and football matches, and other more or less innocent pastimes characteristic of units of the British Army on foreign postings.

But after ratification, when their families came, they brought their own interests and tastes with them from Britain. Relations with the Germans were still amicable, but there was a particularly British life in the middle of it all. There was, for instance, a Mothers' Union, a Boy Scout troop and a Girl Guide section, a drama group, a sizeable school in the Frankstrasse and a military store in the Hohe Strasse. There was even an off-licence and a bakery specialising in scones, crumpets and white bread. By early 1921 there was in all a British population in Cologne of some 15,000, and it was inevitable that at times there was friction. A source of particular irritation was the system of billeting families in suites of rooms in private houses. The Occupation Bureau was inundated with complaints from angry German housewives about the way in which British families treated their furniture and, above all, their kitchens. The behaviour of the soldiers deteriorated. Prostitution was rife, and the 'soldiers seemed very young and nearly all seemed to have had too much to drink'.[13] Finally, there were cases of clearly criminal behaviour: a clerk who stabbed his German mistress to death; an officer who fired some warning shots at a passing group of boys, one of whom was fatally wounded; and, in May 1921, a civilian who was trying to stop a street fight finding himself arrested for assaulting the son of a British sergeant.

The only solution to such problems was to segregate, as far as was possible, the occupiers from the local population. Adenauer, with the approval of the British authorities, decided on a programme to build houses specifically for British military families. There was little more he could do, but even so the decision was unpopular, given that at the time there were some 12,000 Germans in Cologne who were living on the streets. To aggravate the problem, by May 1921 there were up to 2,500 ex-British Army personnel who had decided that they liked Cologne so much they wanted to stay there on demobilisation rather than return to their home country. Lastly, there was a strange population of repatriated German prisoners of war who had become anglicised, to the point where many of them referred to England as 'home' and talked English not only to the British soldiers but among themselves as well. It was all very confusing and, at times, very irritating.

These were perhaps only pin-pricks in the 'spirit of goodwill and understanding'[14] which official reports emphasise, but pins can on occasion hurt. More serious were the domestic political problems. The news of the conditions Adenauer had placed when the Chancellorship was being discussed soon leaked out to the press. When the Social Democrats in Cologne heard about his proposal to extend the statutory eight-hour working day to nine hours, there was uproar. The tramwaymen called it 'a declaration of war on the whole German proletariat';[15] and Social Democrats on the City Council demanded that he be called to account. Adenauer was unrepentant. He was particularly angry at the tramwaymen. He was, after all, their ultimate employer; they ought, he said, to have come to see him and talk the matter over. Besides, he went on, the extension of the eight-hour day to nine hours was only intended as a temporary measure to make it easier to pay the reparations which the Allies demanded. Finally, he said, 'the German working class has more interest in a continuing Germany . . . than allowing a temporary change in the eight-hour day to impede it'.[16]

But perhaps the most difficult problem with which Adenauer had to contend was the developing financial crisis. The work that he and Schumacher had planned was moving rapidly ahead. The years from 1919 to 1923 saw the construction of the new university, the school of music, the inner ring road, the exhibition grounds at Deutz, and a new harbour at Köln-Niehl. In addition, the 'green belt' – the project of which Adenauer was most proud – was laid out. Finally, all this activity had served to attract major industrial investment to the Cologne area.

In terms of financing, the last was perhaps the easiest, since it made little demand on public funds. To secure the investment, Adenauer went out of his way to cultivate the industrial barons of the Rhineland – Klöckner, Thyssen and, of course, Louis Hagen. But he also went out of his way to develop a relationship with Hugo Stinnes. In this there were clear political risks. Stinnes had advocated during the war, with his customary bluntness, the policy of annexing wide tracts of Belgium. Nevertheless, although his views had irritated the Allies and although he had made something of a fool of himself at Spa, there was a certain logic in his ideas. It did, after all, make sense to integrate the coal and steel industries of the Ruhr, the Saar, Luxembourg, Belgium and eastern France; and the obvious axis around which such an integration could take place was the basin of the Mosel and the Rhine. Adenauer was not slow to appreciate the importance to Cologne of such a grand scheme, and was particularly attentive to Stinnes, much to the fury of the Cologne Social Democrats, in whose demonology Stinnes occupied a particularly privileged position.

The importance of these relationships was demonstrated in the pace of Cologne's development in the early 1920s. Although domestic housing in the private sector was subject to strict rent control, no such restrictions applied to industrial or commercial building. The return to investors in ambitious building schemes was handsome, and the Chamber of Commerce, the Stock Exchange, as well as the larger business concerns, were by 1921 busy putting up large and impressive blocks of factories or offices. But if private money was available for industrial and commercial projects, public money for housing, let alone Adenauer's more ambitious schemes, became more difficult as inflation took hold. The greatest problem, in terms of Cologne's social needs, lay in public housing. Adenauer was perfectly aware of this, and although the difficulty of finding accommodation was met 'on the whole in a practical manner', as the British reported, '[the] question still remains a problem'.[17] But there remained also the matter of raising funds for Adenauer's great plans for the city.

The whole financial problem had been made more acute for Cologne by the reconstruction of the Reich tax system at the end of the war. Previously it had been largely a matter for individual states and communes. The new system was designed to shift the burden from indirect taxation to direct taxation; not only that, but both the setting of the rate and the collection of the tax itself was centralised in Berlin. The proceeds, amounting to some 60 per cent of the total Reich tax revenue, were then re-distributed. There were, of course, drawbacks to the scheme: there were the inevitable disputes between central and local government over each commune's share, and since the process of allocation was annual nobody could be sure about their budget from one year to the next.

For the Rhineland, this uncertainty was to some extent balanced by the increase in purchases by foreigners (generating tax revenue for the city) as the mark depreciated and German goods became cheaper in terms of foreign currencies. But this source of funds carried its own risks. The attractions were obvious. In July 1921 the month's average quotation was 76.7 marks to the dollar; by January 1922 it had become 191.8. Even during 1921 there were wild fluctuations. By November, when the mark touched its lowest point of the year, there had been such an influx into Cologne of Dutch, Belgian and Danish shoppers eager to buy almost anything in sight that the Rhineland authorities, with the approval of the Inter-Allied High Commission, imposed restrictions on foreigners buying essential food and clothing to avoid prices rising to such an extent as to put them beyond the reach of the majority of their own people. The tax revenue to Cologne from foreigners dried up as a result.

There was a further problem specific to the occupied territories: customs receipts were lost to them for the simple reason that the Reich, the normal collecting authority, had no sovereignty in their area. The provincial budget was consequently in permanent deficit, which was made up by loans from the Reichsbank. The overall result was that Adenauer found himself in the uncomfortable position of trying to run Cologne on the basis of an uncertain subsidy to its annual current expenditure. Not only that, but he had planned major capital expenditure under one financial system and now had to complete it under another – worse still, one over which the city had almost no control.

It was Cologne's financial problems which, in April 1922, led Adenauer to make his first clearly anti-Prussian speech. In the course of setting out the parlous state of Cologne's finances to the City Council, he claimed that 'Prussia is planning a further attack on the finances of the communes . . . The financial situation of Prussia is so good that I wish the town of Cologne was in the same position . . . Prussia began by giving up its railways – a property capable of large profits – to the Reich, but at the same time she handed over all her debts . . . She then proceeded to take from the Reich income tax a far greater share than [the amount] she previously drew from state income tax.' He went on to complain that Cologne was hampered in dealing with its housing problem because of lack of support from Prussia and indeed that 'the system governing the existing financial relations . . . was unsatisfactory and untenable . . .'. As a final sideswipe, he accused Prussia of inefficiency in collecting adequate revenues from its forests and mines. 'I wish I rented a Prussian estate,' he said. 'I cannot imagine anything better at the present moment.'[18] It was certainly heady stuff, the more so since it came from the President of the Prussian Staatsrat himself.

Adenauer's speech caused something of a sensation. It gave hope and comfort to those who argued that a large part of the financial burden of the Rhineland was due to its umbilical connection with Prussia, and that if this could be severed, the Rhineland would be free of occupation and given generous economic assistance by the Allies. Whatever its merits, this was certainly the view of a number of industrialists in the Rhineland. This view was reinforced by the arrival of Raymond Poincaré* at the head of the French government in January 1922. Poincaré had provided a clear signal, and continued to provide signals, of a much tougher policy towards Germany. The Treaty of Versailles, and the conclusions of the Reparations Commission, he made it clear, must be enforced to the letter. The failure of yet another conference at Genoa in April and the collapse of the Wirth government in Berlin in November confirmed the Rhineland industrialists in their view. By

---

*Poincaré, Raymond (1860–1934): Lawyer and politician. Born in Bar-le-Duc. Barrister at the Court of Paris. Various ministries from 1893 onwards, including (1894 and 1906) Minister of Finance. 1911–13: Prime Minister. 1913–20: President of the Republic. 1922–24: Prime Minister and Minister of Foreign Affairs. 1926–29: Prime Minister. A hawk on everything German.

the late autumn of 1922 a 'director of a very important Westphalian industrial concern' gave it as his 'well-considered opinion that the French would have achieved their object in the creation of a buffer state in the Rhineland within a year'.[19]

The political ice was by now very thin. There was much talk of a French occupation of the Ruhr. The new Reich government, led by the chairman of the Hamburg-American Shipping Line, Wilhelm Cuno, was considered to be politically inept. It was widely believed that France's ultimate objective was to knock out Germany once for all. In short, there was danger in skating on the ice at all.

Nevertheless, there were many who were still prepared to take the chance. One of those was Adenauer. He, as others were in the Rhineland, was convinced not just that France would occupy the Ruhr but that 'the one aim of France is the dismemberment of the German Reich'.[20] In the face of that threat, three quite different solutions were advanced to Piggott in Cologne on 11 December 1922. The first in line was Dr Karl Müller, the chairman of the Arbeitgeber Verband for the Rhineland, the main organisation for Rhineland employers. He argued that, in view of 'the impending French occupation of the Ruhr, and the consequent resentment in Germany, the Reich should turn its attention to the reconstruction of Russia in preparation for what would inevitably be a "freedom-war"';[21] and that, therefore, negotiations should be opened with the Soviets to that effect. As a serious proposition, however, Müller's ideas were little short of fantasy.

The second in line was Dr Paul Silverberg, a close friend of Stinnes. He followed Stinnes' view, arguing that the French occupation of the Ruhr would bring about 'the inevitable *Verständigung* ["understanding"] between French and German industry . . . to the exclusion of, and directed against, Great Britain . . . [There is] no other choice.'[22] He, Stinnes and Klöckner were prepared to go to Paris on any convenient occasion 'to enter upon direct negotiations regarding reparations'. Silverberg went on to inform Piggott that he should feel at liberty, should he wish, to impart 'this piece of information . . . to His Majesty's Government'.[23] This, again, was a remarkable piece of skating – to suggest that two or three industrialists would take over the whole business of negotiating the tangled problem of reparations.

The third in line, Adenauer, took a completely different view. He reverted to the idea, formulated in 1919, that the only real defence of the Rhineland against any serious French incursion was the creation of a state of

Rhineland–Westphalia within the German Reich. At was what turning out to be close to the eleventh hour, he was prepared to advance that solution again. Furthermore, he advised Piggott, he would use all his influence with President Ebert and the Cuno administration to make some – admittedly far-reaching – offer of such a nature to dissuade the French from the step that Poincaré was obviously determined to take.

Whatever the merits of the different solutions, the striking point that emerged was, in Piggott's words, 'the immense importance attached by each of my three visitors to the maintenance of the British occupation in Cologne. Shortly put, it is the last bulwark of Western Germany against the Napoleonic plans of the French government.'[24] The message could hardly have been more clear. That was all very well; but the British were anxious to protect their relationship with the French (not least because of delicate negotiations about the Middle East which were even at that moment taking place in Lausanne), and were certainly not in the mood to put any sort of substantial block on Poincaré, however much they disapproved of his aggressive anti-German policies. In fact, even the Belgians, aggrieved as they were after the German assault on their neutrality at the beginning of the war, were doubtful.

The outcome of the crisis was perhaps what Poincaré had wanted all along and what everybody else had tried to avoid. On 2 January 1923 the Cuno government offered a staged payment of 20 billion gold marks ($5 billion), to be raised by an international loan. Conditional to this offer was the immediate Allied evacuation of Düsseldorf, Duisburg and Ruhrort, and assurances about the future evacuation of the Rhineland. But it was all to no purpose. The Reparations Commission had already declared Germany in default on 26 December 1922, and Poincaré did not even bother to look at the new German offer. The Commission's decision was confirmed by the French, Belgian and Italian governments on 9 January. On 11 January, French and Belgian troops moved in force into the Ruhr.

4

1923

'Wenn die Reichsregierung schon den traurigen Mut aufbringt, Teile
Deutschlands preiszugeben, dann soll sie allein vor dem ganzen Volk
*dafür einstehen'**

THE REACTION IN Germany to the Franco-Belgian occupation of the Ruhr was, in the words of one historian, 'a scream of indignation'.[1] The nation was united as it had not been since August 1914. Indeed, only one discordant note was struck, by an otherwise obscure Austrian-born ex-soldier by the name of Adolf Hitler, who mounted a table in a Munich beer hall on the day after the event to proclaim that the call should not be 'Down with France' but 'Down with the traitors in Berlin'. That aside, the protests were all in one direction.

On the face of it, they were amply justified. Quite apart from the fact itself, the pretext for the occupation was not far short of ludicrous. It was, after all, allegedly undertaken only in support of a motley group of French, Belgian and (rather reluctant) Italian engineers who, according to the reports, were to supervise 'the action of the coal syndicate for the purpose of

---

* 'If the government of the Reich musters the melancholy courage to sacrifice parts of Germany, it should itself justify this before the whole German people': Adenauer to the Reich Finance Minister, 13 November 1923; quoted in P. Weymar, *Adenauer*, p. 124.

securing coal reparation deliveries' and to make up for the undoubted fact that only 65,000 telegraph poles had been delivered out of 200,000 ordered.[2] The reality, of course, was that the French believed the Germans were determined to evade paying adequate reparations at all; but it is hardly surprising that the Germans reacted with fury. The effect of the occupation was equally dramatic. From January to November 1923, and into early 1924, accelerating inflation formed the backdrop to a period of domestic and international turmoil.

There was an immediate rash of spontaneous local strikes in the Ruhr. When these appeared to have popular backing, not least from the press of unoccupied Germany and the Rhineland, the Reich Cabinet, with President Ebert presiding, announced a policy of 'passive resistance', in other words an instruction that workers in the Ruhr should not work for the intruding for-eigners. The announcement was greeted in Germany with demonstrations of popular support. That was all very well in the heat of the moment, but the consequence of 'passive resistance', perhaps at that point unforeseen, was that the 'passive resisters' would have to be financially supported by the Reich when their jobs vanished – to be taken over by French and Belgian person-nel – or, as indeed happened, when they were harassed and bullied by French troops and officials.

The effects of the Ruhr occupation on Cologne were precisely those which Adenauer had expected and feared. Coal was immediately diverted to France. Food became harder to come by. Employment started to fall as the industrial links between the Cologne Zone and the Ruhr were cut. Last, and most damaging of all, the support to the 'passive resisters' in the Ruhr – who lost their jobs almost overnight – led to a massive increase in the Reich's public expenditure which could only be met by the expedient of printing banknotes. As a result already serious inflation turned, in a few weeks, into hyperinflation.

As it happened, it was at this perhaps inconvenient moment that an event occurred in the Adenauer household which would normally be assumed to be one of unalloyed joy. On 18 January 1923, seven days after the occupa-tion of the Ruhr, Gussi Adenauer gave birth to her second son. Unlike the drama of the birth (and almost immediate death) of Ferdinand two and a half years earlier, all went smoothly. Gussi had been in good health through-out her pregnancy and the baby boy, later to be christened Paul, was free from illness and suitably chubby – perhaps even on the verge of overweight.

Gussi herself had in fact filled out from the slender girl of 1919. Marriage obviously suited her. The flighty young lady had turned into the dignified young wife. Indeed, she had filled out more than she would perhaps have liked; there was the suspicion of a double chin and an altogether more ample proportion in her waist and upper arms. Although her smile and her eyes still flashed with humour, she seemed, even in her mid-twenties, well on the way to developing the physical characteristics of the placid German housewife.

None of this should be a matter of surprise. To be sure, her husband had been preoccupied during the period of her pregnancy with other matters; but in those days affairs of the family were, unless disaster intervened, normally left to the women, and the women, with little interest outside the home and with no involvement in their husbands' professional lives other than on ceremonial occasions, formed distinct and decidedly feminine social groups. Their meeting-places were in the cafés of Cologne, which at the time were the height of elegance. In their meetings, however, there was a tendency, not to put too fine a point on it, to eat a large number of cakes.

By contrast, Adenauer was growing ever more spare in his physique. The worry of the events of 1922, taken together with the burdens – in some ways self-imposed – of the administration of the city of Cologne, were taking their physical toll. He looked even thinner than before; the moustache had almost disappeared; the top hat seemed to fit more awkwardly on his head; and his lips were pursed more tightly than ever. In short, he looked depressed and angry. Certainly, the house in Max-Bruch-Strasse was not a place where he could find much comfort from the problems of his political day. Gussi's pregnancy and Paul's birth seem to have been viewed by him from a distance. If all was well, there was no need for him to intervene. But, again, this should come as no surprise; it was the customary attitude of the German father of those days, particularly of a father whose early character had been formed in the certitudes of the Kaiser's Germany.

But what the father had to do was to ensure, as far as he was able, that his family was secure financially; and this Adenauer did, to the point where they were immune from the financial chaos which surrounded them as the year progressed. Certainly, Adenauer had always been careful – some would say mean – with his money. But he also seems to have been, on negotiating terms for his assumption of public office, particularly astute. When he was elected mayor in 1917, he had exchanged the mayor's right to free accommodation in the city in a modest apartment in the centre of Cologne for the right to live and occupy his house in Max-Bruch-Strasse, to be treated, in terms of his financial privileges, as though the two types of property were equivalent – which, it need hardly be said, was far from the case. He had also persuaded the City Council to change the general rule that his remuneration as representative of the city on any board of directors should be the property of the city, to allow him to keep it as his own. All remuneration and expenses were, of course, indexed.

Since those two early concessions, Adenauer had quite openly pursued the advantages thereby gained. Expenditure on his house, and the expenses of using it (including, on one instance, the repair of his garden chairs) were paid for by the city. His official car was upgraded to a grand six-litre Mercedes-Benz. His house had to be extended for official purposes, at a cost (to the city) of 103,000 marks. Furthermore, the city had bought three plots of land in 1921, Schreckenberger, Bosch and Schütte, for nominal sums – the clear reason being that they were neighbouring plots to the mayor's home in Max-Bruch-Strasse. Moreover, the city agreed to pay the interest on the credit which Adenauer had taken out to build a further private extension.

It did not end there. As a further financial burden, the city was required to support Adenauer's costs in representing the city of Cologne as mayor, costs which, as it happened, turned out to be far from trivial. Moreover, in submitting the claims, he always asked for the receipts back. Since the receipts have disappeared, it is no longer possible to say precisely what they were for. But, at the very least, it is clear that he was playing the system for all it was worth.

These manoeuvres kept the finances of the house in Max-Bruch-Strasse in exceptionally good order; and Gussi, when she had recovered from Paul's birth in January, kept the family – her stepchildren Koko, Ria and Max, as well as her new baby – in good heart. By 1923 the relations between the stepchildren and their stepmother (apart from Koko's continuing resentment) had been smoothed over. They now regarded Gussi as their friend rather than as an interloper. Apart from her natural charm, it had all been helped by Gussi's efficient management of the household. With only one cook and two maids, she was almost obliged to do the daily shopping herself. Apart from that, she made sure that proper vegetables were grown in the garden and that there was adequate milk from the domestic goat (later to be replaced by a sheep). Whatever else was to go on in Cologne later in the year, there was never any shortage of food in Max-Bruch-Strasse.

Of course, domestic matters, unless there was a crisis, did not loom large in Adenauer's mind. His major concern at the time, which quite clearly overrode events at home, was political: to find some sort of strategy which would protect the interests of Cologne, and, perhaps, if all went well, at least contribute to the solution of the Ruhr problem. Initially, he hoped that the British might be resolute in riding to the rescue, to mediate with the French and perhaps to ease the economic consequences for Cologne of the Ruhr occupation. As far as mediation was concerned, however, he was to be disappointed. The British simply did not want to get involved. On 11 January there was an instruction from the Foreign Office in London to the British High Commissioner in Koblenz. 'It is the intention of His Majesty's Government,' he was told, 'to minimise, so far as it may lie within their power to do so, the adverse effect upon Anglo-French relations of French independent action.'[3] So that, as far as it went, was that.

But Adenauer was not prepared to give up so easily. He knew perfectly well that it was only the British presence in Cologne which had prevented French occupation of the city, and which was allowing an admittedly minimal supply of food and fuel by river. He also felt that Cologne, being as it was under British occupation, might be a major factor in arriving at some sort of settlement of the Ruhr problem, and that he, as mayor, might well seek in some way to play a decisive role. But he also knew that relations between the two major occupying powers were far removed from the cordiality of the immediate post-war period. They were still on speaking terms, but on occasions only through gritted teeth – as, for instance, during the tortuous negotiations over the passage by train of French troops and supplies through Cologne on their way to the Ruhr. Under those circumstances, it was a difficult minefield through which to tread.

Adenauer's first step was to spell out to the British authorities his pessimism about the likely future course of events. When asked by Piggott in early March 1923 for his views, Adenauer replied: 'For Germany it could hardly be worse.'[4] He was reported as foreseeing 'the destruction of Germany by France and Europe's return to Napoleonic conditions; England, France and Russia would remain as the main states . . .'[5] Of course, such expressions of gloom were perhaps no more than a deliberate tactic to impress the British and to spur them to some form of action. If so, or even if they were genuine, they seem to have made little impact. The gloom, however, was accompanied by a constructive suggestion: a possible solution to what was turning into a diplomatic deadlock – and, moreover, a solution which required no more than avuncular diplomatic activity from the British, something which he assumed that they thought they were particularly good at.

Adenauer's constructive suggestion was that there should be an 'armistice'. France would withdraw her troops from the Ruhr but leave civilian officials there, while on her side Germany would cease 'passive resistance'. This, he argued, would allow both a cooling of tempers and a space in which substantive negotiations covering the Ruhr and the related problem of reparations could take place. In a rational world the idea might have been welcomed. But the world at that point was far from rational. The Americans had withdrawn their troops from the occupation of the upper Rhineland in protest at the Franco-Belgian action (and in response to domestic political pressures) – only to see the French take their place. The Cuno government in Berlin had clearly lost control, and seemed to be more concerned about possible Polish incursions from the east than with events in the Ruhr.

But by far the greatest difficulty was that Poincaré was in no mood to negotiate rationally. 'Germany,' he declared to manic applause in a speech at the dedication of a war memorial in Dunkirk, 'will wait in vain for us to vacillate even for a moment . . . France will walk this road to the end.'[6] Furthermore, the strongly nationalist press in both occupied and unoccupied Germany was unanimously against the solution which Adenauer had in mind. Their message on reparations was quite simple: 'We will not pay.'

Lord Curzon, for his part, made a speech to the House of Lords in April – tip-toeing carefully so as to preserve neutrality – in which he tried to point the way to a settlement, urging the German government to accept arbitration on the matter of reparations by a neutral authority. The Reich government welcomed this, with much acclaim, as an indication of British support. But Cuno, while accepting the principle, made yet another proposal. The Reich, he insisted, would only accept a neutral authority if its role was confined to lowering rather than raising any figure which Germany might put forward. The response was unanimous. It simply was not good enough. The only receptive audience was Poincaré, since it allowed him to insist that he would consider no German proposals until and unless 'passive resistance' was called off. Curzon considered Poincaré to be 'not capable of a generous gesture or a genial thought'.[7] The deadlock was then complete. By the end of May it was clear to Adenauer that, at least for the moment, there was no further role for him on that particular part of the international stage.

Meanwhile, Cologne still had to be run, and Adenauer knew only too well that it was his job to run it. To secure food supplies he turned to his old ally Louis Hagen, who negotiated vegetable and fruit supplies from the Netherlands and from the Bavarian Palatinate. He relied on the British to guarantee safe passage on the Rhine. He turned to Hugo Stinnes to negotiate coal supplies from wherever he could find them; and again relied on the British to ensure that they reached the city without interception. In all this, Adenauer acted in public almost as a dictator. Although he did not speak often in the City Council – even in the eleven debates which took place in 1923, in the early stages about the 'deficit' and in later stages about what was curiously called the 'greater deficit' – he was able to move discussion from the council itself to a series of committees, over which he could exercise greater control.

In public, too, he was fierce in defying all opposition. To the City Council he was scathing, pointing out in mid-June, for instance, that they might be concerned about increased charges for baths and hospitals, but they should not forget that if the financial system broke down then the whole bath and hospital system would collapse too. In private, it was a matter of relying on what friends and allies he had in order to secure for Cologne the basic necessities of life. This was done, and, on the whole, done successfully.

Oddly enough, ordinary life in Cologne – unlike life, for instance, in the Ruhr – went on in a relatively normal manner, at least for those who were able to adjust to the hyperinflation. Wages and salaries were indexed and paid daily, and from April onwards, when the spiral accelerated, twice a day; and there was an interval after payment during which those who were paid were allowed by employers to go out and spend their money immediately. Cologne, like other cities, had its own printing presses, authorised by the Reichsbank to print notes – signed, it should be noted, by Mayor Adenauer – to the extent needed to keep the roundabout going. Furthermore, Adenauer's programme of public works went on apace, maintaining not just public sector employment but employment in supporting industries.

Moreover, as though whistling to keep its spirits up, the city was a place of almost hysterical gaiety. Anybody who had any money to spend had to spend it quickly, and the quickest way to spend it, if it had not been spent at lunchtime, was to unload it in the garden restaurants and nightclubs, or in the cafés which proliferated along the banks of the Rhine, before it lost its value yet further in the following afternoon or morning's quotation. There was much dancing: the Charleston was in vogue, as was any new musical import from America. The songs of the moment were wholly frivolous: 'Yes, We Have No Bananas Today', 'My Parrot Eats No Hard-Boiled Eggs', and, a particular German favourite, the nonsense ditty '*Was tut der Meyer im Himalaya?*'. It was, needless to say, not an attitude which found much sympathy with Cologne's mayor.

There was, however, another side to it. The lights may have burned through the night, but the savings of the middle classes were, to put it bluntly, wiped out. The sick suffered dreadfully, since the cost of medical treatment escalated beyond the means of anybody but the most privileged; but nobody else seemed to care very much. As a result the suicide rate went up, and deaths from starvation and hunger-related ailments were common; but there was no particular concern beyond the charitable activities of the churches and, to give him his full due, the mayor. For those who were unable to protect themselves, it would be idle to pretend that life in the Cologne of 1923 was anything other than a continuing story of misery – and Adenauer himself, at the end of October, personally authorised the distribution of 30,000 meals a day to those who were starving.

But, generally, for those who were able to enjoy some form of protection from the ravages of hyperinflation, Cologne – at least until the autumn – was not such a bad place in which to live. For those who were clever enough to know how to play the system, profits were there for the taking; and one of those who knew was one of Adenauer's most faithful supporters, Hugo Stinnes.

To be sure, even before 1923 Stinnes had been a man of considerable substance. But the 1923 hyperinflation allowed him to borrow on the security of his extensive property, to use the funds to buy more property or industrial assets and then to borrow on the security of those to repay the original loans in depreciated currency. It was almost childishly simple – so simple, in fact, that by the time he died in 1924 Stinnes controlled, apart from his coal interests, some 150 newspapers and periodicals, 69 construction companies, 66 chemical, paper and sugar factories, 57 bank and insurance companies, 83 railway and shipping companies, and more than 100 other businesses. He was a man of immense power; so much so that when he died the satirical magazine *Simplicissimus* carried a cartoon showing St Peter summoning all the angels of heaven with the words: 'Stinnes is coming! Wake up, children, or in a fortnight he will own the whole works!'[8]

But if it was simple for Stinnes to finance his ever-increasing commercial and industrial empire, it was correspondingly difficult for cities such as Cologne to manage their daily, let alone monthly, accounts. The complicated structure of the Reich institutions dealing with finance, from the Reichsbank to state banks and the national loan bureaux, led to an extensive and cumbersome bureaucracy, which in turn seemed to many to have as its main purpose the delay of payments which were due, particularly to the municipalities. The result was a chaotic system of credits flying in all directions. In one case in early 1923, for instance, the Prussian State Bank gave Prussian municipalities over 4 billion marks in prepayments on municipal bonds which had not yet been issued. At the same time the bank agreed to accept (in other words, guarantee) Special Municipal Credit Certificates issued by Prussian municipal authorities, which it then used as security to borrow from the loan bureaux, which in turn were financed by the Reichsbank. The resulting credit mountain simply grew larger and larger.

It was not only the credit mountain. The volume of notes in circulation also grew exponentially. By the late spring of 1923 the printing presses were churning out banknotes twenty-four hours a day, including weekends. In Cologne alone the daily requirement for the Zone, including the British occupiers, was at one point between 8 and 10 billion paper marks, which could only be met by the Cologne presses and trainloads of notes from Berlin. Employees, whether in private firms or in municipal offices, collected their money in buckets, washing bowls or any other container large enough for the purpose. A relatively small payment to the Reparations Commission for expenses for a train journey and a car, for instance, needed seven bank officials to deliver the money in waste-paper baskets. British soldiers found that they could buy a bottle of champagne for the equivalent of less than two pence.

By mid-July the mark was trading at around 4 billion to the dollar – and falling hourly. As if that was not bad enough, the French suspected that banknotes were being smuggled out of Cologne to pay those who were the unwilling victims of 'passive resistance' in the Ruhr. They were determined to stop the traffic, even to the extent of refusing authority for trains loaded with notes to cross the frontier from unoccupied Germany into the city. It was only the intervention of the British in the High Commission that saved the situation; they would, they said, inform London that 'the entire responsibility for any disturbance which might occur in Cologne must rest on the shoulders of the French and Belgian authorities'.[9] (It was only in September that it was revealed, much to British embarrassment, that the Reich government had been paying the British-owned Instone Airlines to fly bundles of banknotes to Cologne from Berlin via Amsterdam and that the funds had been laundered though banks in Trier, Koblenz and Aachen to pay the 'passive resisters'.)

During the summer, the economic situation in Cologne deteriorated noticeably. Even after indexation, the real cost of food, particularly potatoes, was rising. There were strikes and riots throughout the occupied territories, even to the point where in Solingen a company of British soldiers had to reinforce the German police. The last of all the straws was a printers' strike in Berlin in early August. The Reich government presses ground to a standstill. No more notes were printed. The Cologne presses were not able to make up the shortfall. On finding that there was no money to pay them, municipal workers, railwaymen, construction workers and hospital nurses decided that they, too, would go on strike. By late summer Cologne was near to breaking-point. There were rumours in the city – firmly discouraged by Adenauer, but widespread nonetheless – that Cologne would follow Danzig in becoming a 'free city'. In the rest of the Rhineland, the separatist movement was again gaining ground. The British were told by the police in the Zone that they 'could only see a fortnight ahead; if there was another slump in the mark, there would inevitably be increased rioting'.[10] The outlook from Adenauer's office was, to say the least, extremely bleak.

It was no better in Berlin. On 11 August the Social Democrats in the Reichstag withdrew their support from the Cuno government, which collapsed forthwith. Cuno's replacement as Chancellor was Gustav Stresemann.*

---

* Stresemann, Gustav (1878–1929): Businessman and politician. Born in Berlin. 1907: Elected to Reichstag after successful early career in business. 1918: Founded the German People's Party, conservative but not denominational. 1923: Chancellor of the Reich. 1923–29: Foreign Minister, and joint winner in 1926 of the Nobel Peace Prize. One of the successes of the Weimar Republic. It is said that the world might have been different had he not died prematurely.

On the face of it, it was an unlikely choice for President Ebert to make. Stresemann, although an orator of undoubted distinction, with a command of every rhetorical register from sarcasm to pathos, was the leader of one of the smallest parties in the Reichstag, the German People's Party. Furthermore, he was a Berliner to his fingertips – his father had owned and run a beer shop in the Köpenicker Strasse, a working-class district of the city – and he had a Berliner's knack of irritating and sarcastic humour. Physically, he was short and bald. He looked, some said, like an ageing Italian waiter.

Moreover, his political career had been, to put it at its mildest, chequered. As a National Liberal before the war, he had supported Germany's imperialist ambitions, and during the war had not only advocated the German annexation of Belgium but had been so uncritically supportive of the German Army that he became known as 'Ludendorff's young man'. As it turned out, however, he was, right up until his death in 1929, the most successful politician of the Weimar Republic. He never ceased to be a German nationalist, but he was clear-sighted in his view that Germany could only achieve what she wanted by convincing her neighbours that they need not again fear German aggression. He was, above all, courageous.

It was Stresemann's decision to end the policy of 'passive resistance', a decision announced on 26 September. The now rabidly aggressive German press responded to the news this was even on the agenda with predictable fury, but Stresemann could reasonably reply that the currency had ceased, for all practical purposes, to function, that the policy had ruined the middle classes and brought the major cities of Germany to their economic knees, and that the cost of supporting the policy could no longer be borne by the Reich. Furthermore, he introduced, through his Finance Minister, Hans Luther, a reform of the currency which was, in the course of a few months, to bring an end to the hyperinflation.

But there was one further hint from Luther. Under existing financial constraints, he let it be known, Reich financial support for the Rhineland could no longer be taken for granted. This hint, when leaked, came as something of a shock. Certainly, Adenauer had, during this whole critical period, been thinking seriously about reviving the idea which he had had in 1919 of a Rhineland–Westphalia state within the Reich. There had also been a meeting – admittedly somewhat tentative in nature, but arranged by the British and sanctioned by Stresemann – between Adenauer and Paul Tirard, the French chairman of the High Commission, to discuss the possible issue of Rhenish banknotes. But Luther's hint changed the nature of the debate. Rhineland separatism was again firmly back on the political agenda.

As if this were not enough, it was at this crucial moment for the future of Cologne and the Rhineland – and the Reich itself – that Adenauer was taken into hospital with appendicitis. Fortunately for him, his comparatively healthy diet, and the fact that he drank very little and did not smoke, helped him sustain the physical shock of the operation. In those days, of course, depending on the severity of the condition, the operation itself was dangerous. In fact, it was frequently fatal; but it had to be done, since the alternative, if the burst appendix was left untreated, was peritonitis – and certain death. To be sure, as mayor, Adenauer was able to command the best available medical attention, but it is also a measure of his physical resilience that he was able not only to support without difficulty a complicated operation to remove his appendix but to recover from it abnormally quickly. After only two weeks in hospital he was discharged; he then had only eight days of convalescence, from 15 to 23 October, with Gussi at the Mariahilf monastery in Bad Neuenahr before events called him back to Cologne. He could not possibly have been fully fit; but, as he would perhaps have put it to himself, duty took precedence over health (his wife's views probably not being asked).

During Adenauer's illness and absence much indeed had happened. The Stresemann government had fallen – only to be revived again within three days. The fresh government, with Luther again as Finance Minister, had picked up a previous idea of the Nationalist politician Karl Helfferich: a Rentenbank, which would receive an interest-bearing mortgage on all German agricultural and industrial land and would issue Mortgage Banknotes (*Rentenmark*) on the back of it. But Helfferich had suggested that the value of the Rentenmark should be based on the price of rye – the chief product of German agriculture. This was plainly absurd. But Luther, together with Hjalmar Schacht – still in mid-October a minor banker in Darmstadt but subsequently President of the Reichsbank – re-worked Helfferich's scheme, basing the Rentenmark on gold. As early as 15 October the Rentenbank had been set up, and a date fixed for the introduction of the Rentenmark in mid-November. It was to be the basis for the currency reform which was a pre-condition for a successful cure to the inflation.

All this Adenauer might have ignored in his convalescence, and, indeed, approved of. But the real fireworks had been on the political scene. On 21 October the 'Free Rhineland Movement' under Leo Deckers had seized the City Hall of Aachen and declared a 'Rhineland Republic'. The next day two other buccaneers, Josef Friedrich Matthes and Adam Dorten, not to be outdone, ordered their followers to seize the main public buildings in Wiesbaden and Trier, and then in Bonn and Mainz. There was further trouble in Koblenz and, although the British general officer commanding told London that in Cologne 'the majority of people here are all for a quiet life',[11] the pot there was certainly simmering. Furthermore, and most worryingly, large posters were put up with the message that Tirard and the French were encouraging the movement (which was certainly true) and that Tirard had specifically approved the constitution of the Provisional Government of the Rhineland (which was certainly untrue).

On 22 October representatives of all properly constituted political parties in the occupied territories met in Cologne to assess the situation in the light of the separatist explosion and the widely leaked 'hint' that the Reich was to cease its financial support. In Adenauer's absence, the meeting was chaired by his Centre Party colleague Mönnig. The result of the meeting was to request an immediate meeting with Stresemann in the Rhineland itself. Such was the urgency that Stresemann agreed immediately. The date set was 25 October.

The problem, however, was to know what the meeting should be about. No fewer than fifty-three Rhinelanders appeared at a preparatory meeting on 24 October in Barmen, under the chairmanship of Karl Jarres, the Mayor of Duisburg. Jarres argued for a total break from the French, and a Rhineland independent of both the Reich and France. But by that time Adenauer had turned up, and proceeded to argue the opposite: negotiation with the French. The solution he proposed was certainly radical. It was the creation of an independent Rhineland state, if possible within the Reich; in return, the High Commission was to be wound up, military occupation brought to an end, and the new state demilitarised. He demanded finally that the Rhinelanders should be given full powers to negotiate the package.

Needless to say, there was an immediate row, not least because Adenauer had clearly said that 'in the worst case separation from the Reich must also be considered'.[12] The Social Democrats and Democrats accused him of being an outright separatist. Others supported him. In the event, the meeting broke up without any conclusion about what to say to Stresemann the following day. In fact, things were no better in Berlin, where the Reich Cabinet was meeting at the same time. It was generally recognised that the occupied territories would have to be relinquished, but nobody could say how or in what form. All Stresemann could say was: 'We cannot continue this struggle any longer; the objective must be to part in love rather than in hatred.'[13]

The meeting took place on 25 October at Hagen, a joyless industrial town a few miles to the south of the occupied Ruhr. The choice of site for the meeting was intended as a gesture of defiance to the French. But as a gesture it was no more than feeble, and all the participants were too depressed to make much of it. There was, indeed, much to be depressed about. Stresemann knew that his government was being challenged openly, not just in the Rhineland but also in Bavaria, Saxony and Thuringia. Luther had remained in Berlin, but had pressed Stresemann to ensure that the meeting agreed an early deadline by which payments to the occupied territories would cease. Adenauer, for his part, gloomily envisaged the break-up of the Reich.

The meeting itself went about as badly as possible. Jarres, in the chair, opened by recounting – at some length – the menace of the separatist movement and its growing strength. Stresemann, when he came to reply, accepted the obvious fact that the Reich and the Rhineland were in crisis, but said quite bluntly that all suggestions for a separate Rhineland state were unrealistic, and that he was not prepared to allow it. He told Jarres that to break with France would be tantamount to repudiating the Peace Treaty, and would incur the wrath of Britain. He told Adenauer that the idea of a neutral Rhineland state was nonsensical, since France would always wish to keep a military force on the Rhine. Finally he said that payments from the Reich to the occupied territories would be maintained – even increased, in view of the level of unemployment in the Ruhr.

It was, of course, a complete volte-face; so much so, indeed, that nobody believed him. But he was right. In fact, he had received, a short time before he spoke, a letter from Luther, who had revised the arithmetic and found the result better than previously thought. Adenauer insisted that the Reich could not keep payments going for long, and that the separatists would grow in strength in the intervening period of uncertainty. The Rhinelanders, he said, must have authority to negotiate directly with the French. There followed an acrimonious wrangle between Stresemann and Adenauer, each accusing the other of what amounted to hypocrisy. The meeting then ended in some confusion, Stresemann finally agreeing that a 'Committee of Fifteen' Rhineland leaders should be set up with a remit to negotiate with the French. The difficulty was that there was no indication what they were meant to be negotiating about. It is little wonder that Stresemann collapsed with severe angina after the meeting, and that Adenauer sighed, 'As a convalescent, I have been too much caught in a maelstrom which exhausts body and soul.'[14]

The fifty-two Rhinelanders wasted no time. They formed the 'Committee of Fifteen' and elected Adenauer as chairman. On 26 October, Adenauer, Arthur Meyer, the chairman of the trade union association in the occupied territories, Louis Hagen and five other members of the Cologne City Council requested an immediate meeting, on behalf of the committee, with Tirard. To their astonishment – and, indeed, offended shock – Tirard refused to see them. The reason for the refusal, although the Rhinelanders could not possibly have known it, was in fact quite simple. Poincaré had only the day before given instructions to Tirard to give unqualified support to the separatists. The drawbridge to the representatives of Rhineland official-dom was immediately raised.

It was not until 3 November that Poincaré, by then sensitive to the intense British irritation at the turn of events, allowed Tirard more latitude. Adenauer, on hearing of the change of climate, sent Louis Hagen to Koblenz to negotiate with Tirard. Hagen referred openly to 'the future state',[15] but said clearly that if this was to come about the separatist movement would have to end and the sovereignty of the Reich over the new state be recog-nised. Furthermore, he added, almost as an aside, that the head of the new state should be none other than the Mayor of Cologne. Tirard merely lis-tened politely.

On 8 November the assembly of the Rhine Province approved another measure: the establishment of a Rhineland Bank to issue currency based on gold. French banks would have a 30 per cent holding in the new bank – the total foreign stake being set at 45 per cent – which would give them a dom-inant influence. The proposal was warmly welcomed by Tirard and Poincaré, the more so since the British showed no interest in participating. Piggott was almost at the end of his tether: 'astonishment is felt that more interest is not being displayed by British official quarters'.[16] Silverberg wrote to Adenauer, after a discussion with British officials in Cologne, that he was convinced that 'the British had completely surrendered to the French'.[17] The lack of interest was all the more painful in that Tirard had successfully blocked the introduction of the Rentenmark in the occupied territories on the grounds that its legal basis needed careful scrutiny by the High Commission.

By now, inflation was patently out of control. Larger and larger sums of *Notgeld* ('emergency money') were issued – the city of Cologne alone issued some 7 trillion marks in the month of November alone. It was only Adenauer's success in convincing the Reichsbank that Notgeld should be legal tender until January 1924 which prevented the city from going into outright bankruptcy. Indeed, by mid-November the economic situation in all the occupied territories was one of desperation. Unemployment was over two million, public servants were unpaid, separatism was rapidly gaining ground, and law and order was breaking down.

Adenauer decided on one last throw. He went, with members of his committee, to Berlin to face Stresemann and the Reich Cabinet for what might be the last time. Even President Ebert was in despair. 'Poor Germany,' was all he could say.[18] But the encounter, on 13 November, was as barren as the Hagen meeting. Stresemann collapsed again and had to be helped outside by his aides. Luther announced that there would be no more payments to the occupied territories as from that day; Adenauer replied that Luther's ulterior motive was to abandon the Rhineland to be rid of reparations and save his currency. Braun, the Prussian Minister-President, when asked how he could take responsibility for the surrender of two Prussian provinces, simply shrugged his shoulders. Adenauer and his colleagues were left to form their own conclusions. They were now convinced that the Reich was preparing to abandon them, and they were therefore unanimous in seeking an appointment to see Tirard the following day.

As it happened, Tirard was, again, not particularly pleased to see them. He had his own ideas for a Rhineland constitution; he was also aware that the British on the High Commission, particularly Lord Kilmarnock, who had replaced Robertson in 1921, were increasingly hostile, and that this hostility was having its effect in London and in Paris; he also knew that contacts were being made in Paris over his head by Adenauer's allies Louis Hagen, Stinnes and Albert Vögler, apparently with Adenauer's encouragement. Besides, he was firmly of the view that Adenauer was Britain's man. It is hardly surprising that the negotiation started in suspicion and ended in doubt.

On 23 November events took another turn. The Social Democrats in Berlin removed their support from Stresemann, who promptly resigned. Almost in panic, a new Reich government was formed under Wilhelm Marx, a Centre Party politician of no great distinction and little charisma. He was, however, from Cologne and, from Adenauer's point of view, he had the advantage of not being Stresemann. The change of government encouraged Adenauer to persist with Tirard, but it gradually became obvious that the process was going to be fruitless. The objectives of the two sides were too far apart. Adenauer continued to argue his old solution of a Rhineland state within the Reich. Tirard, on the other hand, wanted an autonomous confederation of several states in the Rhineland, each with a sovereign parliament, currency and administration.

Not only were the two sides far apart, but time and events started to move against Adenauer. The separatist movement was losing ground. Wilhelm Marx had come out firmly in favour of the unity of the Reich, and, almost worst of all, Adenauer's Committee of Fifteen had been dissolved by the new government and replaced by an amorphous Committee of Sixty, chosen by members of the Reichstag. By the first week in December 1923, the negotiations between Adenauer and Tirard had no platform on which to rest. In short, Adenauer's 'Rhineland state within the Reich' was at best moribund, if not totally dead. 'Theoretically very good,' Marx pointed out with unaccustomed crispness; 'not workable in practice.'[19]

5

COLOGNE IS FREE!

*'Für mich wäre die Übernahme des Kanzlerpostens ein sehr
schwerer Entschluss'**

NINETEEN TWENTY-FOUR began badly for Adenauer. His negotiations with
Tirard were sinking into the dust of fruitless discussion and postponed
interviews. To try to rescue his scheme of a 'Rhineland state within the
Reich', and by now aware that the Marx government was hostile to the
whole idea, Adenauer decided on a different tactic. He recruited a number
of industrialists and bankers from the circle of those he considered close
allies, Stinnes, Vögler, Silverberg, Hagen and Heineman, as unofficial ambassadors. They would be able, he thought, to use their powerful contacts in
Paris to advance the cause on his behalf. The tactic was, to say the least,
unusual, but it was also painfully naïve. Understandably, Adenauer in 1924
had little experience of international diplomacy; but, worse still, he had no
experience in business, and quite clearly did not understand that if he used
businessmen, they would use him. Furthermore, the French government was
deeply perplexed to receive approaches at different times and in different

---

* 'For me to take the post of Chancellor would have been a very difficult decision':
Adenauer, quoted in P. Weymar, *Adenauer*, p. 132.

places from intermediaries who appeared to have no official status at all. Tirard, of course, when he heard about it all, was furious.

It was Stresemann who put an end to the resulting confusion. As Foreign Minister in the Reich government, he rightly considered himself to be in charge of negotiations with the French, and was not prepared to allow Rhineland industrialists to blunder about in a shop full of such delicate china. He also understood with clarity that their main motive was their own personal financial advantage. Accordingly, he vetoed a plan for Stinnes and Vögler to go to Paris to pursue negotiations. 'We would be asked,' he wrote to Marx on 16 January, 'on the basis of what mandate . . . we had given the Stinnes concern the right to conduct negotiations with France.'[1] Tirard was equally blunt. On 19 January he told Adenauer that the French government would only agree to negotiations on reparations with Stinnes and Vögler if they were formally introduced as representatives of the Reich government, a status which Stresemann had specifically refused to give them. At that point Adenauer realised he could go no further. On 24 January, he wrote despairingly to Marx that he and his Rhineland colleagues would in future refrain from all diplomatic activity.

Things were going no better with the proposed Rhineland bank of issue. On 2 January Schacht, by then President of the Reichsbank, visited London. He convinced Montagu Norman, the Governor of the Bank of England, that the creation of a Gold Discount Bank in Berlin, which would allow the Rentenmark to be pegged to the gold standard, would make a Rhineland issuing bank superfluous. Norman agreed. He consequently refused an invitation from the Banque de Paris et des Pays Bas to participate in the proposed Rhineland Bank, undertook to raise '5 million for Schacht's new bank, persuaded other central bankers to participate as well, and then informed Schacht that he had now "killed the Rhenish Bank".'[2] Hagen and Schröder accepted defeat in their turn, and told their French counterparts that the project was to be laid to rest.

In truth, the French themselves were no longer in a position to negotiate. 'Separatism', which they had supported, had collapsed. The franc was under pressure. Curzon had left office along with the Conservative government, and the new Labour government under Ramsay MacDonald seemed determined to improve Franco-British relations. 'I am bound to say,' wrote Charles de Beaupoil de Saint-Aulaire, the French Ambassador in London, 'that I have never . . . found such goodwill in the English government.'[3] Poincaré could not simply ignore this new approach from his powerful ally, and was obliged to tone down his hitherto aggressive rhetoric. Besides, he was by then clearly facing defeat in the French elections due to take place in May.

Finally, and conclusively, an international 'committee of experts', with a brief to find ways of bringing the German budget back to equilibrium – in other words, to re-examine the whole reparations issue – had started their meetings on 14 January. Since the chairman was an American, the Chicago banker General Charles Dawes, and since the French themselves had agreed to the brief and had two representatives out of a committee of ten, all negotiations to do with reparations and the Rhineland had to be suspended until the Dawes Commission, as it became known, completed their deliberations and reported.

Adenauer's first foray into international diplomacy thus ended in failure. But, that aside, his part in the whole episode had revealed in him two major weaknesses. First, his inability to speak any foreign language (apart from a smattering of French) had led to an equal inability to comprehend the thought processes of those he was dealing with. He simply could not understand how the French or the British or the Americans looked at the world, and this in turn caused him to promote ideas or opinions which were unrealistic – and, at times, downright silly. The second was his exaggerated respect for the small and closely knit group of the most powerful families of Cologne, mostly bankers and industrialists, who tended to assume that, whoever might be mayor, in practice they controlled the city. He seemed, perhaps because of his origins, to have harboured a belief that they belonged to a higher caste of human being; and there is little doubt that in the 1920s it was his ambition to be regarded as a member of that caste.

Be all that as it may, it was now no longer a question of playing a grand international role but of concentrating on the city itself. But even here, grandeur was not far from Adenauer's mind. On 11 May the Cologne Trade Fair opened in the new exhibition halls on the right bank of the Rhine. The opening ceremony was as fine as it could be in the circumstances of the time. President Ebert was invited, as were Wilhelm Marx and other ministers of the Reich and Prussia. In the large main hall, crammed to the doors, Ebert made a powerful speech. He congratulated, as was to be expected, the organisers of the Fair. But he went on to lament 'the conditions of the Peace Treaty [which] had laid cruel burdens on German industry; and nowhere were these burdens heavier than in the Rhineland and the Ruhr, the twin hearts of the nation's economic life'.[4] The speech was received ecstatically and with loud applause by all his listeners – except the French and the British, who considered that 'it went beyond the bounds of what is proper in the occupied territories'.[5] Adenauer replied to Ebert in kind, saying that the entire occupied area was solid in its support of the policy pursued by the Reich. That, too, was enthusiastically applauded, particularly when he went on to say that if there was any doubt there should be fresh elections to consult the German people on the matter.

After the event the two men, President and mayor, walked through the crowd, which had grown larger by the minute. They made an odd couple. Ebert, with his fine head of hair and an almost bucolically round face, snub nose and eyebrows full of humour, seemed to shamble along. He wore a shabby overcoat; his trousers had clearly not been pressed for some little time; and he clasped in his hand a rather battered bowler hat. His smiles to the crowd, however, were full of warmth and friendliness. Adenauer, on the other hand, his thin, tall figure easily topping Ebert's, was as stiff as a matchstick. He was impeccably dressed – a grey overcoat, a walking stick hanging on his left arm, gloves and top hat carried in his left hand to leave his right free for shaking others, his trousers pressed to a knife edge. His smile, unlike Ebert's, was thin and humourless, almost disapproving. The contrast could hardly have been more marked. (As a matter of fact, Adenauer was disapproving. After the event he compiled a list of all the things that had gone wrong during the ceremony and berated his staff for them.)

The whole thing had been highly irregular, and quite contrary to the assurances given to the occupying powers that Ebert's speech would be 'ceremonial and that he would say nothing political'.[6] Piggott complained to Adenauer about Ebert's speech, but was told firmly that the President had to think of wider circles in Germany over which it was of the utmost importance that he should retain his influence. 'A milk-and-water speech,' Adenauer went on, 'would have exposed him to violent attack.'[7] The French raised the matter, in terms of sullen resentment, at the following meeting of the High Commission, but to no great effect.

What neither the British nor the French had yet understood was the new mood of confidence in both occupied and unoccupied Germany. The currency had been stabilised; in fact, the mark was even appreciating against sterling and the franc. Even in the Rhineland, in spite of Tirard's efforts to block the introduction of the Rentenmark, Schacht had succeeded in holding the paper mark at a stable one billion to the newly revived gold mark. Confidence in money returned; the price of food was falling steeply; and the number of people fed in Cologne's soup kitchens was declining daily. In April the Dawes Commission reported with what seemed to be a sensible way forward to deal with the complex problems surrounding reparations; and in the French elections of May Poincaré was duly defeated and replaced by the more conciliatory Edouard Herriot. In short, events seemed to be moving Germany's way. The press and public scented the shift in the wind and reacted accordingly.

This new-found confidence was reflected in a number of ways. The British occupiers in Cologne noted that 'cases of insolent behaviour were not infrequent'. There were 'contemptuous remarks about the weakness of sterling and the depreciation of the French and Belgian franc'.[8] An incident at the village of Möderath, hitherto a sleepy and peaceful enough place, is typical of the changing times. A four-year-old child took it upon himself to throw a stone at the car of a British officer. The officer leapt out of his car and tried to grab the child, who immediately scuttled into his home. The officer pursued him and tried to drag him out, whereupon the villagers rushed to the child's defence. Other soldiers appeared on the scene; there was a brawl; and the overall result was the arrest of two hundred villagers and a ten-day curfew on the village.

Oddly enough, the situation was aggravated, rather than improved, by the general agreement to the 'Dawes Plan' at a conference in London in August 1924. Among its provisions the plan, together with a side agreement between Stresemann and Herriot on the evacuation of the Ruhr within a year, set January 1925 as the date for the end of the British occupation of Cologne. By now it was clear that French post-war policy towards Germany had failed in its ultimate objective, the solution to the eternal problem of the security of France from future attack from the east. The only remaining possible solution, it seemed, was a Germany which was militarily powerless.

This, in turn, depended on how far the Germans had fulfilled, or were prepared to fulfil, their Peace Treaty obligations on disarmament. As it happened, the Military Control Commission made a general inspection of German factories and military installations shortly after the Dawes Plan had been approved by the Reichstag. In November 1924, in a preliminary report, they noted such extensive evasions and violations that the Herriot government had no option but to demand a postponement of the British evacuation of the Cologne Zone; and the British government, now Conservative again with Austen Chamberlain as Foreign Secretary, had no option but to accede to the French demand.

The decision to postpone the evacuation of Cologne was greeted with a storm of anger in the German press throughout January and February 1925. Even in London it was felt by many that 'an injustice has been perpetrated on Germany for a bagatelle'.[9] In Cologne the main political parties held simultaneous protest meetings. Since these took place at the beginning of the pre-Lent carnival season, Adenauer was concerned that there would be a good deal of drunken rioting, and promptly closed all the municipal halls and cancelled many of the carnival balls. In fact, the meetings went off without incident, and such was the indifference of the Cologne public to the high politics of the occasion that it was the interruption of the carnival which was the major grievance of the day.

In all this, the steadying hand of President Ebert was missing. He had died suddenly in February 1925. A campaign for election to the presidency immediately followed. The consequence, of course, was that tempers were further inflamed. Adenauer's tone in his speeches became much more abrasive. In welcoming the new Reich Chancellor Luther (Marx having declared his candidature for the presidency), Adenauer asserted roundly that the continuation of the occupation was 'intolerable' and that the population of Cologne were labouring under the strain of lack of freedom – 'a remarkable statement,' the British report runs, 'in view of the carnival festivities now in progress'[10] – and resented the treatment meted out to them. It was only one example, as the British wearily noted, of the terms which were becoming familiar whenever the mayor spoke in public.

As it happened, and almost as a sideshow, a row broke out during the presidential election campaign which was to have repercussions for Adenauer in the future. One of the candidates, Jarres, claimed that Adenauer had proposed during the critical period of 'passive resistance' in 1923 that negotiations with the French should take place with a view to creating an autonomous Rhineland state outside the Reich. Adenauer replied with some ferocity in a speech on 24 March, challenging Jarres to produce his evidence and threatening to mention 'well-known names' in his defence against Jarres' attack.

Further, he asked Luther to make public details of the negotiations which had taken place at the time. Only then, he claimed, could the German nation pass a verdict on who had preached the policy of 'surrender' and who had not. The whole unedifying row centred around what had occurred at Barmen on 23 October 1923. As such, it was no more than a passing event with no particular significance; but Adenauer's reaction demonstrated his sensitivity to any imputation that he had promoted or encouraged Rhineland separatism. He was right to be sensitive. There had indeed been a moment when he had veered in that direction, but he had swiftly retracted. But the retraction had not satisfied everybody, and the ferocity of his repudiation of Jarres only served to increase the scepticism of his opponents.

As it turned out, neither the row nor anything else was of help to Jarres in his campaign. The result of the election, to general surprise, was that Field Marshal Hindenburg, who had been wheeled out by his friends at the age of seventy-seven to put his name forward in the interests of national stability, found himself the winner by a narrow margin over Marx. From Adenauer's point of view, it was a result which he could hardly welcome. He had lost an admittedly Social Democrat President but one whom he respected and trusted, and had gained a President whose military background and age certainly did not augur well.

But life in Cologne, whoever might or might not be President of the Reich, had to go on; and throughout the rest of 1925 Adenauer pursued his programme for the grandeur of the city. In the summer, he mounted a 'Thousand-Year Exhibition of the Rhineland' to celebrate the millennium of the Rhineland's union with Germany. Whatever the historical accuracy of the grounds for celebration, it was again to be a platform for Cologne's self-assertion. Indeed, President Hindenburg himself was invited to attend the event. But at this point the Allies drew the line. Hindenburg, after all, was still technically on the Allied list of war criminals. Chamberlain went so far as to try to stop the celebrations altogether, but, once the invitation to Hindenburg had been discreetly cancelled, it was pointed out to him that 'one could not easily prevent the population after a long period of repression from organising harmless festivities'.[11] The event went ahead, opening on 16 May in the presence of the Reich Chancellor, with many speeches, including a number from Adenauer, along familiar lines.

By the spring of 1925 it had already become clear that the British occupation of Cologne was in a period of twilight. Indeed, in March the garrison and its support facilities were already being wound down. Four canteens and an English school were closed, and both Barclays and Lloyds banks had written to their customers to ask them to 'liquidate their accounts'.[12] It was now only a matter of time before the occupation would finally end. But time, in fact almost another year, was needed before the event could take place.

During the summer of 1925 the time was spent in digesting the final report of the Military Control Commission on German disarmament, which had appeared, after some haggling between the British and French representatives on the Commission, the previous February. From the Allies' point of view it was far from satisfactory, but the British were now so anxious to leave Cologne that they adopted a proposal from Stresemann for a multilateral non-aggression pact between France, Britain, Belgium, Italy and Germany. By early May a draft security agreement had been drawn up in London, and in August the French government was finally persuaded to agree to its basic principle, that the British would only come to France's aid if, in their view and that of the other guarantor powers, there was evidence either of German re-militarisation of the Rhineland or the launch of an unprovoked German attack against France itself. The Reich government was accordingly invited to negotiate the small print of the agreement at a conference to be held in Locarno on 5 October.

In public, the British insisted that the question of disarmament and the evacuation of Cologne 'have, in fact, no relation to the negotiations for a security Pact . . .'[13] In private, it was recognised that the three matters were inextricably linked. The Locarno conference itself went without a hitch, since all the essential principles of the agreement had been settled beforehand. It was only in side meetings after the main event that Stresemann argued strenuously for a softer approach by the Allies to alleged German disarmament defaults and for a definite commitment to evacuate the northern zone, including Cologne. The ensuing negotiations were at times difficult and protracted, revolving around the provision in the Peace Treaty that before leaving occupied territory the Allies must be certain that it was fully de-militarised, but the conclusion was inevitable. On 16 November the Allies informed the Reich government that evacuation of the Cologne Zone would begin on 1 December.

It was not until the end of January 1926 that the final detachment of British troops left the city. There had been delays, primarily in fixing up accommodation for the troops in Wiesbaden, where they were to take over from the French in the occupation of the southern zone (only leaving finally in 1930). But there had also been two further problems: the Allies were worried about the Cologne police force, which had grown in size over the years and which, as the French General Nollet had warned a year earlier, 'was numerous and well-armed [and] would constitute a very severe danger for our security';[14] and they were equally worried that the Nazi Party had, since the ban on its organisation had been lifted in Prussia in January 1925, started to assemble a powerful paramilitary presence in the city.

The difficulties were finally glossed over, and on 30 January 1926 at 3pm, a cold and slate-grey afternoon, the Union Flag was hauled down in a brief ceremony at British Army headquarters. On the lowering of the flag a great cheer arose from the Germans present at the ceremony. But 'it was in no sense a jeer', as the British were at pains to emphasise.[15] The remaining detachment then marched, with bayonets fixed and led by an officer with sword drawn, through the Domplatz to the railway station. A large crowd had come out to witness the event, well wrapped against the winter chill; the windows of neighbouring buildings were bursting with curious onlookers; a large force of Cologne police kept the approaches to the station clear. As the troops marched past, cheering broke out again, and there was much waving of handkerchiefs. By 3.10pm the soldiers were all on the station platform and boarding their military train. As the train moved out of the station, there were renewed cheers and shouts of farewell. By 3.30pm the flag of Cologne had been hoisted where the Union Flag had flown for seven years. The British occupation of Cologne had ended.

The ceremony itself was described by the Germans who were there as 'very dignified'. It was also very friendly. The British General Staff Intelligence report told of a tour of the local cafés by British soldiers on the eve of their departure: 'They received an effusive welcome ... Almost every party of Germans asked [the soldiers] to do them the honour of coming to their table for refreshment ... In at least one café the Germans locked the door so that [the soldiers], whom they seemed to delight in entertaining, should not depart too early.'[16] It was a very typical example of Rhineland hospitality – particularly when the occupiers were leaving.

Six hours later, as the cathedral clock struck twelve, the midnight festival of liberation began in the Domplatz. The square itself was crammed, and the crowd spilled over into the streets which led into the square and even beyond. This was a moment to be savoured, and Adenauer savoured it with exquisite theatricality. As the last stroke of twelve died away, he mounted the steps leading to the cathedral's west front, stopped at the step from which the

Kaiser had spoken in 1880, turned and spoke to his city. 'Hear me!' he proclaimed. 'Cologne is free! The hour, so warmly, so fervently longed for, has come; the day of freedom has dawned! Our hearts rise to God the Almighty . . . We have had for seven long years to bear a heavy burden under the hard fist of the victor . . . We have borne suffering in common . . . Let us swear unity, loyalty to the nation, love to our Fatherland! . . . Cry with me: "Germany, dearest Fatherland! Hurra! Hurra! Hurra!"'[17] The crowd duly joined in. At the end of the hour of celebration 'there rang out over Cologne the muffled tones of the new, five-hundredweight bell of St Peter, the most powerful bell in Germany'.[18]

Of course, the rhetoric might seem today to be somewhat overblown. For its time, however, Adenauer's speech was perfectly pitched, both in length and in language. Indeed, the speech of Otto Braun, the Minister-President of Prussia, which followed Adenauer's, was long-winded and flat by comparison. Furthermore, Adenauer, sensing the mood of the city, had slipped in a compliment to the British occupiers: 'Yes, we will be just; in spite of much that has befallen us, we will recognise that in political matters the departed opponent has acted justly.' Braun failed to give them even a passing nod. But, all in all, it had been a moving moment. Adenauer himself considered it to be, according to one of his biographers, 'the high point of his life'.[19]

The ceremonies marking the end of the occupation of Cologne were far from over. On 21 March President Hindenburg paid a formal visit to the city. It was another splendid occasion. Hindenburg by then had allayed all fears that he would turn out to be a monarchist and an ultra-reactionary; he was loyally adhering to the Weimar constitution. As a Field Marshal and the victor of the battle of Tannenberg he was accorded almost reverential respect. Besides, unlike Ebert, he could always be relied on to bear himself as the military man that he was — upright, smart and appropriately dressed for each occasion, his grey moustache trimmed in the form of a sabre, as was the custom among the officers in the Kaiser's army. As he drove with Adenauer through the streets of Cologne in an open-top car he looked the very picture of an old-fashioned and honourable military gentleman. Nothing at that moment could have had greater appeal to the man, or woman, in the Cologne street, and he was duly rewarded with rapturous applause.

Not only was Hindenburg quite different from Ebert, but the Adenauer who greeted him was quite different from the Adenauer who had greeted Ebert a year earlier. The end of occupation, and the consequent increase in his own standing in the city, had brought with it an air of confidence which showed itself in his face. This was no longer the 'terribly sad' and 'rather tired' man that a British visitor had noted in 1923,[20] nor the thin and stiff figure that had walked with Ebert in 1924; his face had filled out to something near to sleekness and his body had put on valuable weight. The smile was still not exactly warm, but it was recognisably a smile, particularly when the crowd demonstrated their admiration of their mayor – even if it was admiration rather than affection.

There was a rally in the morning in the main building of the exhibition hall, but it was the dinner in the evening, at the Gürzenich Hall, which was the highlight of the day. It was lavish on an unprecedented scale. The guest list stood at around six hundred. Adenauer had required all invitations to be engraved on hand-made cards; next to each place setting there was a bottle of eau-de-Cologne; the menu was sumptuous; and, at the end, the male guests were invited to smoke specially made cigars whose band carried a picture of Adenauer's head. Apart from the touch of vulgarity, it was a worthy successor to the state dinners that had been given in the same hall by Adenauer's predecessors for the Hohenzollerns and the Habsburgs. Ever conscious of his status, Adenauer could not help feeling pleased. As he wrote to the dying Johann Hamspohn, 'it was truly overwhelming'.[21]

It may be that the whole event went to Adenauer's head. At the morning rally, in contrast to Hindenburg's uncontroversial and neutral speech, Adenauer was outspoken in tone and content. He went back to the beginning of the occupation, and described in lyrical vein the departure of the last German regiment from Cologne and the depression felt at the arrival of British troops. He referred to the 'pride of the victors' as being 'unbearable'. Equally unbearable, he went on, were 'the triumphant blare of their regimental music', 'the hard fist of the victor', 'the burdens and mental martyrdom of countless families', and 'many hundred years' imprisonment awarded by British courts'. He then paid tribute to 'the no small number of men and women who lost their lives under the British occupation'. Finally, Adenauer explained the reasons for recounting in full his grievances. It was done, he said, 'not to incite or revile, but because we owe it to history at this historical moment to speak openly and with truth, so that the whole world should recognise that an occupation by a foreign power is never an instrument of peace and of understanding . . . Away with this source of unrest, away with the whole Rhenish occupation.'[22]

The British, of course, were listening, and listening with care. In that one speech Adenauer managed wholly to destroy his previous reputation with the British for fairness and objectivity. Kilmarnock, one of the listeners, and a man of mild manners who had done his best over the years to favour the cause of the Rhineland and Germany against the French, sometimes against the instinct of his masters in London, was almost apoplectic with anger. His outrage echoes down the years even in the formal language of his report of 23 March to the Foreign Secretary, Austen Chamberlain. It is blistering in its condemnation of Adenauer. It castigates the 'cynicism of his attitude' which was increased 'by the well-known fact that he himself telegraphed to General Plumer asking him to hasten his arrival in Cologne'. As for the reasons which Adenauer gave for saying what he did, Kilmarnock's outrage was even greater. 'The hypocrisy of this pretext,' his report goes on, 'recalls the well-known device of those writers who seek to justify the publication of offensive literature on the ground that they hope thereby to bring about the remedy of the abuses which they describe with gusto.'[23] Kilmarnock's report was duly noted by the British government – and filed for future reference. There it lay for many years; but there is little doubt that, as part of the 'Adenauer' file in the British Foreign Office, Kilmarnock's report of Adenauer's speech on 21 March 1926 played a part in events which took place twenty years later.

Nevertheless, if Adenauer was now thoroughly disliked and distrusted by the British, he was all the more popular both in Cologne and in the wider Germany. It so happened that in May 1926 there occurred one of those supremely ludicrous moments which illustrate the fragility of the Weimar Republic. It concerned the national flag. Under the Weimar constitution the German merchant navy – but only the merchant navy – was allowed to fly a flag of the old imperial colours of black, white and red, with the new national colours of black, red and gold in a rectangle at the upper corner of the flag nearest to the flagpole. But on 5 May there appeared a Presidential Order, counter-signed by Chancellor Luther, to the effect that German legations and consulates outside Europe and in European seaports should display the flag of the merchant navy rather than the national flag of the Republic.

The decree caused uproar. Hindenburg was known for his attachment to the imperial colours, but as long as he kept it to himself nobody was particularly worried. But the fact that the decree was countersigned by the

Reich government was an altogether different matter. Things got worse when Hindenburg wrote to Luther on 9 May, in a letter intended for publication, explaining that he had no intention of changing the national colours but that the whole argument over the decree had shown 'how threatening and dangerous to our people the unresolved question of the colours has become'.[24]

There was a furious debate in the Reichstag on 11 May. Luther, in his reply to a series of impassioned speeches, all of them critical of his government, failed to find the right tone to soothe his opponents. He appeared almost indifferent to what by then had come to be seen as a challenge to the Republic. The Democrats in the Reichstag immediately moved a motion approving Hindenburg's intention to settle the issue peacefully but condemning the Chancellor 'who through his behaviour on the matter of the flag . . . made any final solution . . . more difficult and who, in these troubled times, gratuitously kindled a new conflict'. The hitherto fragmented opposition parties coalesced, and the motion was carried. Luther had no choice but to resign. He later remarked to one of his colleagues: 'I do not understand how they could put a government out of office on account of such a bagatelle,' to which the colleague replied: 'That's exactly why.'[25]

At a quarter to eleven on the morning of Thursday 13 May Adenauer received a telegram from two of his Centre Party colleagues in Berlin, Theodor von Guérard and Adam Stegerwald, requesting his presence in the capital. He knew perfectly well what they wanted: to persuade him to accept the Centre Party nomination for the post of Reich Chancellor. His immediate response was to play for time. In a telephone call to Stegerwald, he explained that he had received the telegram too late for him to travel to Berlin on the same day, but he would take the following day's train. With that done, he went home to discuss this momentous invitation with his wife.

The reason for bringing Gussi into the discussion was quite simple. If he were to accept the offer which was now being extended, it would mean resigning as Mayor of Cologne. This, in turn, would mean giving up the house in Max-Bruch-Strasse, as well as the income and expenses which made their family life so secure. In return, of course, he would occupy the highest political office in the Reich, with all the dignity and prestige which that entailed. But the decision to leave Cologne would be final. He could not hope to return as mayor and, given the vagaries of Reich politics, his tenure of office might only be for a few months, after which he would have to look to his allies in Cologne for a job in one or other of their banks or in one or other of their portfolio of industries. Either way, his political career would be effectively finished.

Gussi was all for taking the risk, but Adenauer was much more cautious. In the event, he decided that they should both go to Berlin to explore the ground. By that time, he had almost certainly made up his mind that he would only accept the job if he could be assured of a stable cross-party coalition running across political boundaries, from the Social Democrats through the Centre Party and as far as the German People's Party. To be certain of this, he would have to have discussions with the leaders of the other parties in the Reichstag, not least the Social Democrats. But he knew enough about political life to realise that there could not be a vacuum. Everything would have to move at speed.

Once arrived in Berlin, Adenauer reviewed the situation with Guérard and Stegerwald in his usual resting place in the capital, the Hotel Kaiserhof. The meeting did not go easily. Preliminary soundings with the Social Democrats and the German People's Party had shown that they were hostile to an Adenauer Chancellorship. On the other side, the German National People's Party were hostile both to the German People's Party and to the Centre Party. Furthermore, Stresemann, after all that had happened, was not prepared to serve under Adenauer as Chancellor.

Adenauer then spent the next four days in Berlin in an attempt to resolve the difficulties, but the efforts of himself and his colleagues came to nothing. In the end, the project foundered on the rock of Stresemann's resistance. As he came out of the decisive meeting of the German People's Party caucus, Stresemann was heard to say, with satisfaction: 'Today we stopped Adenauer becoming Chancellor.'[26]

Adenauer tried to salvage what he could from the wreckage in a memorandum on the whole affair. In it he claimed that the sticking point had been his views on the Locarno security pact, to which he was unsympathetic, as apparently was 'well known'.[27] It was an odd point to make, not least because he had spoken in favour of Locarno during Hindenburg's visit to Cologne two months earlier, and nobody could quite understand why his position had shifted since then. But he went on to complain not just about the substance of German policy but about the way it had been conducted. This, of course, was a frontal attack on Stresemann.

Not content with that, Adenauer also claimed that the reparations programme set by the Dawes Plan could not conceivably be met. The claim is hardly convincing, since he had little detailed knowledge of the Reich finances of the time nor indeed, as Mayor of Cologne and President of the Prussian Staatsrat, did he have access to the figures which might substantiate his claim. Indeed, the memorandum seems to be little more than an exercise in self-justification. As such, its content should be taken with more than a pinch of salt. In reality, the truth was that no credible Reich government could be formed without including Stresemann as Foreign Minister, and Stresemann and Adenauer shared a mutual dislike, which neither was prepared to put aside. As Adenauer put it in his memorandum, 'Stresemann had to stay in the Cabinet [but] I could see difficulties arising if I was unable to reach agreement with him.'[28] Such a situation was all too likely to arise.

Adenauer abandoned the project after the wearisome days of wheeling and dealing among the parties in Berlin had produced no conclusion which he felt he could reasonably accept. He therefore told his Centre Party colleagues, and President Hindenburg, that he was out of the race. Accordingly, on 17 May 1926 Wilhelm Marx was yet again named Chancellor, with Stresemann yet again as Foreign Minister. It was to be the thirteenth government of the Weimar Republic; and there were to be six more before the whole edifice collapsed under the weight of its own contradictions. Adenauer decided that it was time for him and Gussi to go home to Cologne, and home they duly went.

6

THE PRIVATE AND PUBLIC MAYOR

'Wenn Sie Schatten für mein Bild brauchen . . . dann gehen Sie zu
Herrn Görlinger. Der wird Ihnen genügend dunkle Farben für mein
Porträt liefern'

AT SOME POINT in the sixth century BC, the lugubrious Athenian statesman
Solon is said to have given advice to King Croesus of Lydia on the subject
of happiness. 'Until a man completes his life,' his advice went, 'forbear to call
him happy, but only call him fortunate.'[1] Solon's aphorism is, of course, of
general application, but it has particular resonance in the life of Konrad
Adenauer. To be sure, he was fortunate. On his fiftieth birthday on 5 January
1926 he could reasonably have said to himself that he had been granted
many gifts, and that he had used those gifts, through his own endeavours, to
the greatest possible effect. On what is usually regarded as the threshold of
middle age, Adenauer, like others before and since, probably made for himself a personal balance sheet reflecting his life to date; and in 1926 the
Adenauer balance sheet would have looked to be one of reasonable equilibrium, the positives satisfactorily outweighing the negatives. Whether he was
happy or not was, as Solon had pointed out all those centuries ago, another

---

* 'If you need shadows for my picture . . . go and see Herr Görlinger. He will supply you
with enough dark colours for my portrait': Adenauer, quoted in P. Weymar, *Adenauer*, p. 107.

matter. All that can be said is that, according to his son, 'He was happier in the years 1926 to 1929 than at any time in his life other than during his period as Chancellor.'[2]

On the positive side, Adenauer had established himself as an authoritative and effective mayor of one of Germany's major cities. He had seen Cologne through the various traumas of the post-war period; he had played the occupying powers with some skill; he had embarked on a programme of expansion and redevelopment of the city which had excited those who had seen it unfold; and he had been invited twice to accept the highest political office in the Reich. Furthermore, he had used his legal training to good effect: he was always a master of his briefs, however complicated they were. This showed notably in speeches to the City Council, dry and uncompromising though they might be. Indeed, it was only on rare occasions, such as the celebration on the night of 30 January 1925, that he allowed his emotions to break through the carapace of habitual reserve. But, among those who heard him that night, there were few who could doubt that those emotions ran very deep, however hard he might try to contain them.

Equally positive, from his point of view, was his life at home in Max-Bruch-Strasse. Gussi, his wife, had fulfilled all his expectations of her. She was dutiful, cheerful, and was seen as an eminently suitable spouse for the mayor at the official functions she was obliged to attend. True, their relationship was one of affection and mutual respect rather than undying and passionate love. But Gussi was sensible enough to realise that her husband's one and only love had been for his first wife Emma, and that her role was to occupy the place of privileged and devoted companion to a man she respected and admired.

There were, however, negatives. Towards his subordinates in the administration of Cologne he was something of a bully. His temper, when aroused, was fearsome. Furthermore, as he developed in authority after the end of the British occupation, he tended to treat the elected members of the City Council as little more than a necessary but regrettable nuisance. If they complained in public about the debts which the city was incurring to finance his ambitions for Cologne, or indeed the manifestly lavish remuneration of the mayor, they were treated to sarcastic speeches and brutal put-downs. At all costs, the discipline of authority had to be maintained.

This discipline was carried through to Adenauer's life at home. His

routine, indeed, even with the arrival of children and his second marriage, had hardly changed over the years. During the working week, he
would leave the house at nine o'clock sharp, walk through the neighbouring park for ten minutes or so to his official car, and be driven to the City
Hall. His children, in the meanwhile, would go off to their respective
schools: the eldest, Konrad, and the younger Max to the (boys only)
Apostelgymnasium, Ria to the girls' school Lyceum 3; and Paul would go
to his primary school. Lotte, the youngest child, born in 1925, was still a
baby and stayed at home. Adenauer returned at about two o'clock, by
which time the children had come back from school. The family then
assembled for lunch, and, after Grace, sat down to what usually turned out
to be an interrogation about the children's educational progress. It was not
a moment which they particularly enjoyed. If they recorded a mark of 'satisfactory' they were told that it was not good enough; they must, he said,
do better. When one of them had the temerity to remind Adenauer that
his own marks at school had been no more than 'satisfactory', he brushed
the comment aside, as many fathers do, with a crisp remark that standards
were much higher in his day.

Grace was said again after lunch. Adenauer would then retire to his customary rest, while the children got on with their homework. He would leave
again for his office at about four, usually returning home at around eight
o'clock unless there was an official dinner which he had to attend. He would
have a quick supper with Gussi, and then settle down to read his papers for
the following day. The older children were in the evenings generally left to
their own devices, although from time to time they were required to show
what they had learned in their weekly piano lesson – which in practice was
not much, since they only had a quarter of an hour's lesson each week from
a particularly uninspiring teacher, and they only bothered to practise for a
few minutes prior to going to their lesson. That apart, they amused themselves as best they could. With that, the day ended, and the household
retired to bed.

The older children, Koko, Ria and Max, were in this period inclined to
seek out their neighbours for companionship. That was only normal at
their age. But they were the more so inclined when their home was empty,
apart from Lotte and her nanny, on the occasions when their father and
Gussi were at official dinners or receptions. From time to time, on summer
evenings, they could go to play tennis at the courts nearby, but such was the

crowd that it was unlikely that they would each get more than a quarter of an hour on court. Adenauer himself had little interest in sport of any kind, and played none himself. Besides, he no longer had any need, or inclination, to join any of the Cologne tennis clubs since he had no further interest in meeting eligible young ladies – which had been the point of the whole exercise in his youth. If his children wished to do so, that was something not to be discouraged; what was discouraged was for them to bring any friends they might have met there back to their home.

As a result of all this, there was in Max-Bruch-Strasse little that might be called social life. In the City Hall, of course, there were official dinners from time to time; but they were what they were – long and tedious. Adenauer 'had no small talk', 'was shy' and 'over-sensitive about his health',[3] to the point where at dinners where there were speeches and toasts, and where wine was served for the purpose, he would at best have only one glass, and even at times have his glass filled with water, hoping that nobody would notice. Anyway, he much preferred small meals at relatively frequent intervals, since he thought such a regime to be better for his health. Large dinners were just a necessary but boring (and in his view unhealthy) part of his mayoral duty. But even in his own home, Adenauer had little time for social activity. Perhaps four or five times a year he and Gussi would be invited to dine at the house of one of his banking or industrialist allies, but that was about the sum of it.

Adenauer's asceticism was at times certainly daunting, particularly to his children. Their allowance of sweets, for instance, was carefully monitored. On the day of Santa Barbara it was the custom for children to leave their shoes outside the door of their room – to find them full of sweets in the morning. The custom was duly observed in Max-Bruch-Strasse (provided the shoes were clean), but two days later, on 6 December, the feast of St Nikolaus, the apportionment of sweets was kept to a minimum, on the grounds that they had had their fill on the earlier saint's day. If they felt aggrieved about that, they were reminded that they had been out only three weeks before Holy Barbara's day, on the feast of St Martin, to sing in the street with their neighbour's children – also for sweets. Enough was enough; and even on occasions part of their stock of sweets was removed by parental command.

The greatest event in the winter calendar was, of course, Christmas. Again, a careful ritual was observed. On Christmas Eve the tree was decorated during the morning, Gussi supervising the efforts of the children. On occasions, by way perhaps of escape, Gussi would visit her family next door, and would play her violin with her brother and sister, as she used to before her marriage. The all-important ceremony, however, took place precisely at 5pm. The whole Adenauer family assembled around the tree. The older children were then asked each to recite a suitable poem (baby Lotte, naturally, being excluded) and play pieces on the piano, which by 1926 had grown from a simple upright to a proper grand. Carols were then sung, mostly by the children but with the parents occasionally joining in, much to the amusement of the children, since Gussi had never had a good singing voice and Adenauer had obviously lost the voice which had won him good marks forty years earlier at school. Presents were then opened, and a meal followed. It was then time to prepare for the serious spiritual business of the next morning.

On the following day, the whole family went to High Mass at the Apostelkirche at half-past ten. The Mass was long, and, of course, conducted in the elaborate language of ecclesiastical Latin. Nevertheless, even after that, the family attended two further Low Masses which followed in succession immediately after the High Mass. Their religious duty thus completed to Adenauer's satisfaction, they made their way, presumably in a state of grace but also of physical exhaustion, back to their home. Their exhaustion must have been the greater in that Adenauer refused to use his official car to transport them, on the grounds that his driver 'deserved his Christmas as well', and they all had to walk.[4]

Christmas done, the next event was the New Year. The celebration was quite simple, since New Year's Eve was not a religious feast of great consequence: the whole family stayed up until midnight and, on the stroke of twelve, exchanged good wishes for the coming year. After that, Cologne was launched into the carnival season. Although the carnival had taken some time to re-establish itself after the war, since there was neither the money nor the will to mount the customary events, by 1926 it was almost back to pre-war normality. From January onwards the carnival companies, based originally on old parish boundaries but by then with a somewhat random membership, organised their parties, as now, in one or other of the large halls or restaurants of the city. The climax of the carnival came, again as now, with the parade (and accompanying celebration) on *Rosenmontag*, the Monday preceding Ash Wednesday. Nowadays, the Mayor of Cologne is almost obliged to attend every ball and actively encourage the parade. Adenauer, on the other hand, was barely to be dragged to one, or at most two, parties in the year, and watched the parade stoically from the balcony of the City Hall. His children, in contrast, enjoyed every minute of it.

It was only on his holidays that Adenauer felt able to relax. These were normally taken in August or early September. In the years immediately after the war, the family would go to the Eifel (to be near Cologne in case the mayor's presence was required in the city). In 1921 and 1922, Adenauer had felt able to go as far as the Black Forest. But holidays then could never be taken outside Germany because of the daily depreciation of the mark. By July 1924, however, it was possible to embark on foreign holidays, and Switzerland – perhaps with its memories of Emma – was Adenauer's choice. In particular, he chose the little hamlet of Chandolin, high in the mountains of the Valais, at that time only accessible on foot or on pack animal. Here he would not be disturbed. 'I have fulfilled my obligations towards people,' he was apt to say. 'On holiday I would like for once to be alone.'[5]

From 1924 onwards, for the next few years, summer holidays were always at Chandolin. Each year, it was a strange, almost biblical, caravan which made its way up the mountain from the lower slopes. Adenauer and Gussi led the older children; they were followed by a nanny, carrying Lotte until she was old enough to walk by herself, and a large number of porters supervising the twelve mules which were needed to carry the chests and suitcases. Once arrived at the ambitiously named Grand Hotel, however, the family could relax. To be sure, there were still rituals. Year after year, they stayed in the same rooms; they slept in the same beds; they ate at the same table at all meals; and Grace was said as at home – only seated and silently, with hands kept carefully under the table so as not to annoy their hosts or any other guests. There were daily walks, Adenauer leading the way with his mountain walking stick, singing from time to time in his unreliable baritone and joking all the way, and occasionally picking up dried cowpats on the end of his stick and throwing them at his sons. All in all, his daughter Ria summed it up well when she wrote to her uncle from Chandolin in 1928: 'Father is much more cheerful than in Cologne.'[6]

It is no more and no less than the truth. Once returned to Cologne, Adenauer immediately took on again the burdens of his office and the disciplines, both at work and at home, that went with them. He was again driven by his work. But, by the middle of 1926, the popularity which he had achieved at the time of the British evacuation had started to wane. The City

Council, in particular, had become fractious. Furthermore, the council had found a more aggressive leader of opposition in Robert Görlinger.

Görlinger was, in every sense of the expression, a Social Democrat. He came, and was proud to come, from the Cologne working class. He had worked his passage through the trade unions which had been reconstituted, and had achieved rapid increase in membership, in the years immediately following the war. Although small in height, and physically far from attractive, he was as sharp-witted as Adenauer, and an equal master of the sarcastic retort. As earlier with Stresemann, Adenauer disliked him personally – and the dislike was amply returned.

For a time, Adenauer could afford to ignore Görlinger, and indeed he did. He continued to go his own way. Always fond of ceremonies, particularly those which served to enhance Cologne (and his own prestige), he took pains in 1926 to take centre stage in the inauguration of the new Cologne airport, even to the point of taking to the air in a special flight to circle the airport and to make an uncertain landing on the half-finished runway. There was also the task of laying out ambitious plans for the new building for Cologne University, and there were the ceremonies of welcome for the foreign investors who were increasingly interested in establishing manufacturing ventures on the outskirts of the city.

But Adenauer could not ignore Görlinger and the City Council for ever. The projects for the enlargement, aggrandisement and beautification of the city seemed to have no end, and a number of councillors wondered aloud where the money was coming from. During the period of inflation the answer had been easy enough. Money was either printed or borrowed to be repaid in devalued marks. But with the stabilisation of the currency in 1924 both those avenues were closed. The only remaining possibility, since the Reich, on Schacht's urgent advice, refused to finance Adenauer's ambitious projects, was to borrow and borrow again. The figures speak for themselves. From a debt of 180 million gold marks in 1924, the city's net liabilities had grown to 262 million by 1926, and escalated to 280 million in 1927.

The first real battle between Adenauer and the City Council came over the affair of the Mülheim Bridge. This time, it was not particularly a matter of money; nor was it a matter of whether or not there should be another bridge over the Rhine to the industrial suburb of Mülheim on the right bank. That had been conceded when Mülheim had been absorbed within the city boundaries. What was at issue was the design of the bridge. To arrive at a balanced view, the council set up in late 1926 a committee of experts, consisting of five architects and four representatives of the city, of whom Adenauer was one. The committee quite properly decided to put the design of the bridge to open competition. The winner of the competition, by a vote of seven to two, was a design by the Krupp company for an arched bridge standing on columns resting on the river bed. One of those voting against the Krupp design was the mayor himself, who had tried, and failed, to persuade the committee of the aesthetic merits of a beautiful but more costly suspension bridge. The City Council then made what was assumed to be the final decision, and by a large majority approved the committee's choice.

Adenauer, however, was not going to let the matter rest there. He wanted the suspension bridge, and was prepared to use all the tricks that he knew to get it. First, he invited city councillors one by one to his office, or even to Max-Bruch-Strasse, for a glass of wine and a 'chat'. The 'chat', needless to say, was a long exposition from Adenauer on the beauty of the suspension bridge. But that was not the main objective. Adenauer had by now learned the essential politician's ability of personal charm when it was required, and councillors who had hitherto been rather frightened of their overpowering mayor came out of his office or home convinced that he was human after all. The weaker ones started to waver, and declared that they were prepared to reconsider the design of the bridge, bearing in mind what the mayor had said.

His next target was the trade unions, and in particular the works' council of the Cologne firm of Felten & Guillaume, which would be a major beneficiary were the suspension design to be adopted. He pointed out that Krupp was not a Cologne firm, and that one of his objectives was 'to guarantee work for the industry of Cologne'.[7] In response, the works' council lobbied the Communist block of city councillors to vote for the suspension bridge. They also persuaded the Christian trade union movement to support them, and to ensure 'that the work is kept in Cologne as far as possible, so that Cologne workers gain employment'.[8]

His last manoeuvre was to request the city architect, who had already expressed some doubts about the Krupp design, to review in detail the Krupp calculations. Although it was a Sunday in the middle of the carnival season, Adenauer instructed him to stay in his office until he had produced his results. The architect's report was clear in its conclusion: the bed of the river would not support the weight of the Krupp bridge. His report and accompanying calculations were then read out to an astonished council by one of Adenauer's supporters at a meeting in April 1927. The council voted to re-open the matter, and approved the suspension design by a decisive majority. That done, work on the Mülheim Bridge started immediately.

The affair of the Mülheim Bridge is the best illustration of Adenauer's ability to master the Cologne City Council, but it was far from the only one. On a number of occasions he had to use the same tactics: a mixture of chastisement in public, of charm and flattery in private conversations, of subtlety in identifying the right levers of influence, and of the timing of events. But in the case of the Mülheim Bridge, at least in the way he had gone about getting what he wanted, he had offended many councillors. His justification was, to say the least, Jesuitical. 'If the decision of the council is to be final,' he said, 'then the council must take full responsibility for it; equally I, for my part, have the duty to ensure that the council arrives at decisions which I believe to be right.'[9]

It was a clever try, but the damage had by then been done. On 14 December 1927 Görlinger encapsulated the feelings of the offended councillors in a brutal letter. He complained about 'aimless activity' and 'the excessive haste with which a number of projects were pushed through'. Public transport in the suburbs, he went on, had been neglected, resulting in a 'transport catastrophe'.[10] Furthermore, the situation had been made worse by Adenauer's restrictions on the activities of his deputies; they were now little more than highly paid servants of the mayor. In short, Adenauer was behaving in a dictatorial and offensive manner.

Görlinger, and others who supported him, certainly had a point. Adenauer was indeed behaving in a dictatorial manner, which to many was offensive. He had no great respect for the city councillors, be they or be they not elected by the citizens of Cologne. He was the mayor, and, as such, was entitled to run the city in the way that he wanted. But the objections were not confined to Görlinger and the Social Democrats; even Adenauer's hitherto faithful colleagues in the Centre Party were also restive, particularly about the city's finances. In early 1928, for instance, his closest ally in the Centre Party, Johannes Rings, was protesting almost hysterically about the whole of Adenauer's programme of development. 'What will happen,' he wrote agitatedly, 'if a stop is not put to this development?'[11]

As always when attacked from many sides at once, Adenauer went on the offensive. He ignored Görlinger's reproaches, but directed his assault to where it would most hurt – his own party. In a letter to Rings, he pointed out not only that his own party had failed to discuss their concerns in an amicable manner with their mayor but that he had suffered the indignity of receiving a letter from them 'which contains a series of wholly false figures and goes on to base its comments on this false picture'. He was, he went on, 'very offended'.[12]

By way of further counter-attack, Adenauer pointed out that the only way to bring the city's finances back into what his colleagues considered to be order was to cut back on social expenditure in the city. He had already, in March 1927, criticised the Reich government for its 'craving for concentration', claiming that Berlin imposed welfare burdens on the city without allowing the means to support them.[13] The only solution, he now claimed, was to reduce or even stop social security payments to anybody who was not in proven need, and to raise gas and electricity prices all round. This solution, as Adenauer well knew, would infuriate the Social Democrats and even upset the more liberal-minded in the Centre Party. In the event, he was prepared to concede on the social security issue if the council met him on the issue of fuel prices. The matter was settled accordingly; and, as a consequence of this manoeuvre, Adenauer succeeded in undermining popular support for the council itself, and, in doing so, reinforcing his own.

By the beginning of 1928 Adenauer's relations with the City Council were on a swift ebb tide. But things were no better for him in Berlin. Schacht complained about Cologne's borrowings – due to rise by a further 40 million marks during the year – and Stresemann was asking openly whether the extravagance of Cologne's mayor was not impeding the Reich's efforts to reduce the level of reparations payable under the Dawes Plan. Both Schacht and Stresemann were particularly critical of the exhibition hall at Deutz, and were shocked to hear that there was to be a new building for Cologne University and, apparently, a 'Rhenish Museum' in the old cuirassier barracks on the river bank. Worse still, much of the financing for these projects was in US dollars – which might be all right, as Schacht pointed out, while the economy was growing and the mark remained strong, but would be disastrous in a recession or if the mark were to lose its value against the dollar.

Once begun, of course, projects such as these are difficult to stop; and Adenauer, for one, had no intention of stopping them. In fact, he went further. During 1928, in addition to the major projects already under way, there was the launching of the naval cruiser *Köln* at Wilhelmshaven on 23 May; the

'German Gymnastics Festival', from 21 to 28 July, to which many thousands of gymnasts from all over Germany came to competitions held in the Müngersdorf stadium; and, by way of a climax, there was the 'International Press Exhibition' in the exhibition hall at Deutz.

Of all these, the Press Exhibition understandably attracted the most attention. The exhibition was opened on 12 May and went throughout the summer and into the autumn, only closing on 14 October. It was a mammoth affair, designed to present all aspects of the press, both national and international, and it was mounted seemingly almost without regard to cost. For instance, the charge on the city for the entertainment of visitors alone came to nearly 800,000 marks. Visitors, indeed, came from far and wide. Even the Soviets sent a delegation – much to the dismay of the right-wing German press and to the outspoken disgust of the Nazi Party. Edouard Herriot, by then the Minister for Education, arrived with a suitably large posse of French officials. Others, from almost all the countries of Europe, followed in their wake.

It was at the formal dinner for Herriot, during his visit to the Press Exhibition, that Adenauer made an appeal for a general reconciliation of nations. To be sure, he had made speeches in the early 1920s which seemed to advocate Franco-German co-operation, but those were in the context of his efforts to promote the standing of his unofficial ambassadors in the cause of the Rhineland. In private, however, and indeed to the British, he had been very critical of successive French governments and of French policy generally while the occupation lasted. In 1928, however, he seems to have been genuine in his advocacy of 'peace and reconciliation'. 'Many people in Germany,' he said, '[and] I was one of them myself, initially regarded these ideas with great doubt and caution, but we have been convinced.'[14] It was a long way from the views he had expressed two years earlier on the Locarno pact, but consistency of view has never been, nor will it ever be, a necessary condition for success in politics, and Adenauer certainly was by now enough of a politician to be able to put forward contrasting views – after a suitable passage of time – without blushing.

As a politician, however, he was fully aware that his term in office as Mayor of Cologne might be coming to its end. The election for the office of mayor was due to be held in November 1929. Even in mid-1928, therefore, he was starting to address the matter seriously. Certainly, he continued to adopt a high profile as the city's mayor. He started to make visits abroad, some as a private – but well-publicised – citizen, for instance to London in the spring of 1929, ostensibly to see his son Koko who was then studying there; others as an official visitor from the city of Cologne – equally well publicised – for instance to Amsterdam in the autumn. That was all very well; but the real work for his re-election had to be done at home.

The arithmetic was always going to look doubtful. Adenauer had upset so many councillors that there seemed to be too many fences which needed to be mended. Nevertheless, he set about the task with his usual thoroughness. He knew that there were to be elections for the City Council in November 1929, and that the then elected council would proceed, as first business, to elect their mayor. His approach was therefore simple – and familiar to anybody who has stood for elective office. His office worked through the list of councillors, identifying those who were likely to be re-elected; the trawl was widened to include those who were not councillors in present office but who might be likely to be elected. The fact that public money was used for the purpose was, as was usual in those days, conveniently ignored.

Even Görlinger, who was to stand against him in the mayoral election of 1929, admired Adenauer's meticulous campaign. 'He did not forget a birthday or a bereavement,' Görlinger said later. 'He congratulated them on the good news and sympathised with them on the bad; he answered all letters quickly and in detail.'[15] There were also little presents on suitable occasions and, where possible, jobs for those of his supporters who were eligible for municipal posts. He also went out of his way to engage his list of possible future council members in intimate conversation – a technique at which he could show himself at his best. Opposition Social Democrats were not excluded. Indeed, Görlinger himself was subjected to the Adenauer treatment. 'It was then,' he reported subsequently, 'that I understood the secret of Adenauer's personal success.'[16]

Hitherto, Görlinger, like others, had regarded the mayor as cold, infinitely reserved and without any feeling which could easily be identified as human. In those interviews, however, Adenauer revealed 'an extraordinary gift of generating warmth and friendliness'. In his account, however, Görlinger was swift to emphasise that this gift was only used 'towards people who might be useful to him; and as soon as they have fulfilled their function the sympathy speedily died away'.[17]

Nevertheless, and whatever the techniques, there remained the simple matter of electoral arithmetic. Adenauer still had to ensure that he would command a majority. But by the autumn of that year it was clear that there was an international economic crisis, and that Cologne could not be immune from its effects. As Schacht had warned, the financing of Adenauer's grand projects was turning into an albatross around the city's neck, as tax revenues declined and social security payments to the growing number of unemployed increased. Although the full impact of what came to be known as the Depression of the 1930s had yet to be fully felt in the Rhineland, there was already a marked shift in the hitherto favourable economic breeze. Scenting the shift, the Cologne press had started to blame the mayor. The *Rheinische Tageszeitung* inveighed against the 'vast lack of scruple of the Renaissance Man'.[18] The *Kölnische Zeitung* was also starting to publish critical articles – not quite mentioning Adenauer by name but making it clear by oblique reference precisely who it was they were talking about.

Adenauer managed to shore up his position with his Centre Party colleagues in a long and defensively aggressive speech in October 1929. Their support was, of course, vital. In the event, at the council elections of 17 November, the result revealed a delicate balance. The Centre Party won 25 seats, up 4 on 1924; the Social Democrats marginally improved on their 1924 position with 21 seats; the Communists fell to 13; the German People's Party and the Democrats together won 10, and their Liberal allies 3; independents of one sort or another won 8 – and the Nazis won 4.

It was obviously going to be a tight squeeze in the mayoral election which followed, particularly since Görlinger was standing against Adenauer and would be certain of both Social Democrat and Communist votes. In other words, Adenauer, leaving aside the minor parties and independents (and Nazis), was facing a minority of 25–34. The Nazis could go either way; so what Adenauer needed was the votes of the German People's Party, the Democrats and the Liberals to tilt the balance – in the hopes that the independents would vote against Görlinger and hold firmly on to what they had.

To secure that support, Adenauer had to make concessions. He agreed to surrender to the city his remuneration as a director of Rheinische-Westfälische Elektrizitätswerke (9,200 marks per annum) and of the Deutsche Bank (10,700 marks per annum). Financially, Adenauer could at the time support this loss of income, particularly since his elder children were near the point where they could earn their own living. But he was not one to give up easily any personal financial advantage, and for him the sacrifice must have been particularly painful.

These concessions made, Adenauer did, in the event, just scrape through. He was supported by the Centre Party vote, along with the German People's Party, the Democrats and their allies, and all the independents. The Social Democrats, Communists and Nazis voted against him. The deputy mayor, Matzerath, exercising his statutory vote as representative of the 'municipality', went for Adenauer. The result was: Adenauer 49, Görlinger 47.

It was far from a glorious victory, but at least Adenauer had achieved a further term as Cologne's mayor. In Solon's terms, he had been fortunate. But, as the events of his second term unfolded, he was to demonstrate the truth of Solon's aphorism. The next few years, in fact, were to be the least happy of his whole life.

7

DUBIOUS MANOEUVRES

'Das Verhängnis ist nicht mehr aufzuhalten'*

'FOR ME, IF I can put it in a single word, Adenauer has always been a gambler.'[1] Thus Robert Görlinger's considered view – in later life – of his political opponent of the 1920s. On the face of it, it is a surprising view, given Adenauer's widely acknowledged reputation for caution. But Görlinger had a point. He could reasonably claim that Adenauer, during his many years as Mayor of Cologne, had been prepared to take risks: risks in his plans for the development of the city, risks in his own standing in the city at large, and risks, in particular, in his relations with the City Council. These risks were part of Adenauer's political character.

To be sure, taking such risks is part of any successful political career. But what neither Görlinger nor anybody else suspected was that in the late 1920s Adenauer was prepared to gamble in a different sense, not just in his political career but with his own and his family's personal finances. Unlike his political adventures, which at that time could reasonably be regarded as

---

*'The dreadful destiny can no longer be prevented': Adenauer, quoted in P. Weymar, *Adenauer*, p. 147.

successful, his financial adventure ended in almost total disaster. Indeed, but for the timely intervention of his trusted allies, by the middle of 1930 Adenauer would have had to declare himself bankrupt, and would have had to accept, as an inevitable consequence, that his political career had come to an abrupt and untimely full stop.

The facts of the matter are beyond dispute. By the end of 1927 Adenauer had accumulated, by one means or another (including, presumably, Gussi's dowry), a substantial portfolio of securities valued at some 1.3 million marks. Against that portfolio, he had a bank loan of just under 300,000 marks. In itself, the debt might seem large, but it could reasonably have been justified by the cover provided by his portfolio. There were those, of course, who thought that the mayor should not be borrowing at all, let alone from the Deutsche Bank of which he himself was a director and which managed his investments. But such comments could be shrugged off. The comfortable reality was that his financial position (even leaving aside his house in Max-Bruch-Strasse) had been at that time very healthy – net liquid or near-liquid financial assets of just over 1 million marks.

Certainly, the whole thing had been carefully done. Adenauer's instructions to the Deutsche Bank on the management of his portfolio had been simple. The bank was only to buy bonds whose standing was impeccable or shares in companies in which he felt he could have confidence – in other words, to put it in perhaps rather crude terms, in which either he or the bank had access to inside information. As he wrote in 1924 to his portfolio manager at the bank, Albert Ahn, he wanted to invest in 'machine and crane building, Elberfeld dyes, Cologne gas and Düsseldorf machines',[2] all safe, unspectacular and, above all, local companies on which he and the bank could keep a careful eye.

By the end of 1929, however, the healthy position of two years earlier had turned into a catastrophe. The market value of his portfolio had fallen to 1.1 million marks, and his liability to the bank had risen to 1.9 million marks. Instead of holding net financial assets of more than a million marks he was in net debt – to the very large extent of 800,000 marks. Apparently, during the years of 1928 and 1929 the cautious Adenauer had engaged in unsuccessful financial speculation on a truly heroic scale – and had seemingly watched on the sidelines as his whole carefully accumulated fortune had been wiped out.

The arithmetic certainly tells its own depressing story; but the apparent picture of hectic gambling, and consequent nemesis, is in fact some way short of the truth. The truth is that Adenauer had attempted to apply in the international arena the same principles of investment which had served him so well in German securities; but in straying beyond the boundaries of his own knowledge he had, like many others before and since, failed dismally.

The track is not hard to follow. As early as the spring of 1928 Adenauer had decided to change his investment strategy. He had seen the sharp rise on the world stock markets in the previous few years, and considered that he could afford to expand his portfolio, both geographically, to the United States, and industrially, to the newer companies manufacturing synthetic fibres. It so happened that at the time one of his colleagues on the local board of the Deutsche Bank was Dr Fritz Blüthgen, the General Manager of the large Cologne synthetic fibre company of Vereinigten Glanzstoffwerke. Blüthgen had been particularly helpful in advice on how to raise private money for the new building for Cologne University, and in Adenauer's eyes was the ideal of the public spirited industrialist. The natural course was to ask him for recommendations for investment. This Adenauer had done.

Blüthgen suggested that Adenauer might profitably invest in two US subsidiaries of Glanzstoff which he was sure would do well. Cautious as he was, Adenauer had then taken further advice from the local executive director of the Deutsche Bank, Dr Anton Brüning. Brüning in turn had told him that if Blüthgen thought that the proposed investment was good there was no reason to doubt his judgement. Furthermore, Brüning went on, the bank would lend him extra cash for such an investment if the need arose. Adenauer then instructed the bank to sell almost his entire German portfolio and put the proceeds into the two Glanzstoff US subsidiaries. This was done, albeit with some difficulty, since the shares of the two companies were very narrowly traded – for the most part in Amsterdam – and were not quoted on any of the German stock exchanges.

At first all had gone well. But in October 1928 things had started to go wrong. One of the subsidiaries in which Adenauer had invested, American Glanzstoff, made an issue of new shares. Adenauer had immediately decided to exchange his holding in the other Glanzstoff subsidiary into the new issue. He even cabled Blüthgen in New York: 'The exchange is proving difficult; please do all possible to arrange for me a tranche of the new issue.'[3] In addition, more cash was required on top of the shares which Adenauer was prepared to surrender in the exchange. He had therefore drawn yet again on his credit line with the Deutsche Bank.

The new issue completed, the price of American Glanzstoff shares started to fall. Adenauer drew further on the Deutsche Bank to buy more shares as they fell – a common enough technique known as 'averaging down'. By the spring of 1929, he had started to worry about his holding, but Blüthgen had reassured him – even to the length of transferring a sizeable part of his own general portfolio (held, as it happened, in an illegal account in Holland) to secure a further loan for Adenauer to buy even more shares. Whatever Adenauer was to say later, Blüthgen was genuinely optimistic about the future of Glanzstoff in the United States; indeed, he had kept a large holding himself in the same American subsidiary in which Adenauer had invested so heavily.

But things went from bad to worse. The New York Stock Exchange collapsed in late October 1929, taking with it what remained of the value in American Glanzstoff (which by then had been merged with another Glanzstoff subsidiary). In fact, when Adenauer was standing for re-election as mayor, although few were aware of it, he was teetering on the precipice of bankruptcy. By December 1929 the financial situation of the newly re-elected mayor was beyond any visible means of recovery.

It was Louis Hagen, together with another Cologne banking ally, Robert Pferdmenges, who put together a rescue plan. Adenauer complained bitterly about Blüthgen to Dannie Heineman, but both Hagen and Heineman told him that they had good reports of Blüthgen, and that he had only been trying to help. Adenauer also threatened to sue the Deutsche Bank for allowing him to borrow so extensively, but Hagen's wiser advice prevailed – he pointed out that such an action would inevitably mean the end of Adenauer's political career. On the other hand, the Deutsche Bank knew perfectly well that it would do its reputation no conceivable good to force the Mayor of Cologne (and President of the Prussian Staatsrat, not to mention his directorship of the bank) into what would be a much publicised bankruptcy. There was therefore the makings of a deal.

Hagen's rescue plan certainly had financial elegance, even if it required some lack of scruple – from all parties. He and Pferdmenges persuaded Oscar Schlitter, one of the Deutsche Bank's managing directors in Berlin and himself also from Cologne, to transfer Adenauer's worthless American shares and the greater part of his debt, together with Adenauer's remaining German shares and Blüthgen's illegal portfolio, to a suspense account in the bank's head office branch in Berlin. The whole package could remain there indefinitely without detection, and without disturbing the bank's auditors. It was hardly orthodox banking, but the deed was done. Adenauer's bankruptcy was headed off – without anybody other than those involved having any inkling of how the trick had been managed. But there was a cost. Adenauer himself was now left without capital, apart from his house and furniture. He had only his mayoral salary to support Gussi and his family – augmented in May 1928 by the birth of another daughter, Libet. The consequence was clear: his prime objective had to be to protect his own job.

But if Adenauer's personal finances were in a mess it was as nothing compared with the state of the finances of the city of Cologne. The same forces that had destroyed the prospects for American Glanzstoff were destroying Cologne's cash flow. The rapid fall in domestic demand and the stock market crash of October 1929 led to precisely the situation which Schacht had warned against. Dollar credits which had been so easily obtainable in earlier years were withdrawn, and the funds repatriated to the United States. Added to the difficulty of finding replacements for short-term dollar loans was the extra difficulty of a sharply rising bill for welfare payments.

The result was that throughout the first half of 1930, Adenauer engaged in a frantic round of visits and discussions with lending banks, the Prussian Finance Ministry, the Rheinische Provinzialbank, the Prussian Landesbank, and anybody else who might be prepared to lend Cologne money. In desperation, he even asked Dannie Heineman to invest in the city's electricity company – but was horrified to find that Heineman would only do so if he could take majority control. He negotiated a loan from the Deutsche Bank secured on a note issued by the Prussian Central Co-operative Fund (as it turned out, a transaction of doubtful legality). As a last resort, however, Adenauer was forced in mid-1930 to turn in the direction he least wanted – to the Reich government.

The timing and the circumstances could hardly have been worse. The Reich itself was in a period of the greatest difficulty. The fourth Marx government had fallen in the spring of 1928, to be superseded by another uncertain coalition led by the Social Democrat Hermann Müller. It was never a government to inspire much confidence, and its own disintegration in turn seemed only a matter of time. Throughout the rest of 1928 and into 1929 unemployment had been rising; both the Nazis and the Communists, from different ends of the political spectrum, were making gains in local elections; and there were regular street fights in every major city between armed supporters of both extremist parties. By the end of 1929 Wilhelm

Groener, Müller's Defence Minister, had come to the conclusion that the country was on the brink of civil war, to the point where he issued a general order to the armed forces warning them not to become infected by party political battles. They should remember, he proclaimed, that the Wehrmacht was 'the necessary and most characteristic expression' of national will and unity.[4]

As a matter of fact, throughout the winter months of 1929–30 Groener and the head of the political bureau of the Defence Ministry, General Kurt von Schleicher, had been quietly plotting against their own government. Of the two, Schleicher was very much the cleverer; but they both considered that the proper solution to the Reich's problems was certainly not the government which they were presently serving but a government which was free from the constraints of party allegiance and would govern in the national rather than any sectional interest. In addition, they added, such a government would have to support without equivocation the necessary appropriations of public money for the armed forces.

This formula, of course, has been the favoured political solution of generals down the ages. But in this case the military had three factors working in its favour. First, and perhaps foremost, was the prestige of Hindenburg, who was, after all, one of their kind (although he had regrettably become apt to bouts of weeping, particularly on public occasions). The second was that the Müller government was clearly unable to suppress the street violence. Moreover, the rising misery and unemployment were driving more and more voters to take sides in the ballot box for one extreme or the other. The third was that there was to hand a potential Chancellor who could be relied on to lead a government to their taste: his name was Heinrich Brüning.*

---

* Brüning, Heinrich (1885–1970): Politician. Born in Münster. Volunteered for military service in 1915. 1919: Active in Christian trade unions. 1924: Elected to Reichstag for Centre Party. 1929: Became leader of the Centre Party parliamentary group. 1930–32: Chancellor of the Reich. Fled to Holland in 1934, then to the US to take up a professorial chair at Harvard. 1951–54: Returned to Germany as professor of political science in Cologne. Made an attempt to re-engage in German politics, but was frozen out by Adenauer, who thought him primarily responsible for Centre Party's acquiescence to Hitler's Enabling Act of 1933. 1955: Left Germany to live permanently in the US.

Brüning had all the qualities which Groener and Schleicher liked and admired. He was young – not yet forty-five years old – and energetic. Even at that age he had become leader of the Centre Party in the Reichstag. Furthermore, his credentials were undoubted: he had led a machine-gun company in the war, winning an Iron Cross (1st Class) in the process, was an ardent Roman Catholic, and was wholly hostile to Social Democracy. Moreover, he had the intellectual equipment, which previous Chancellors since Stresemann had lacked, to allow him not just to understand the technical problems which confronted him but to master them. Groener told his friends that he had never known 'a statesman, chancellor, minister or general who combined in his head as much positive knowledge and political clarity and adaptability as Brüning'.[5] The American Ambassador informed Washington that Brüning was 'the discovery of Europe, a really great man'.[6]

The Müller government had nearly collapsed after Stresemann's death in October 1929, but it managed to stagger on until March of the following year. By that time Schleicher had persuaded Hindenburg that Brüning was Müller's obvious successor. When the call came on 27 March 1930 Brüning was fully prepared. He could only accept the post of Chancellor, he announced to Hindenburg, if the office were given the emergency powers available only to the President under the Weimar constitution. The old man just managed to swallow Brüning's demand – 'but naturally only in so far as it is consistent with the constitution, which I have sworn before God to maintain'.[7] At that point, Brüning was invested with virtually dictatorial powers.

Brüning's appointment should by all rights have been welcomed whole-heartedly by Adenauer in Cologne; and so, at first, it was. Here at last was a Chancellor of his own Centre Party, obviously able and obviously prepared to adopt strong measures. The difficulty, as it turned out, was that the two men did not much take to one another. Adenauer had in 1929 tried to interest Brüning, in his capacity as leader of the Centre Party in the Reichstag, in Cologne's affairs, but without success – Brüning warily refusing an invitation to visit the city. Adenauer was offended, but Brüning was unsympathetic to what he regarded as Rhineland bleating. Besides, he was determined to pursue a policy of severe austerity, and had no time for hand-outs to rich cities such as Cologne. Hand-outs, on the other hand, were precisely what Adenauer was after.

By the time Brüning became Chancellor the relationship between the two men had further cooled. The cause had not been a matter of great moment, and certainly one which could have passed by amicably if there had been a degree of mutual trust. After all, it only concerned a clerical appointment. But the underlying issue was deeper than that. It was, in Brüning's view, a challenge to his ultimate control of the Centre Party.

Between November 1929 and April 1930 Adenauer had gone to great lengths to promote the appointment of the Chairman of the Centre Party, Ludwig Kaas, to the deanery of the cathedral of Cologne. It was an odd move, since Kaas was hardly an obvious candidate for the job. He was, admittedly, an ordained priest, but he had chosen a political as well as a clerical career (apart from his constant and prolonged absences in pursuit of his hobby of collecting antiques). Physically, he was small and squat; and, with his bowler hat, thin face and heavy spectacles, gave the appearance of a down-at-heel pawnbroker. Nevertheless, he was no fool, and indeed in terms of party politics he had made something of a success. He had identified himself with the right wing of the Centre Party and, in doing so, had risen to be elected as its chairman – while still retaining a post as the leading authority in canon law in the diocese of Trier.

As far as Adenauer was concerned, Kaas had two important qualities: first, he was a Rhinelander and, second, he was in favour with the Vatican (he was, for instance, loud in his endorsement of the 1929 Concordat between Pius XI and Mussolini). As such, and possibly because of his outspoken right-wing views, Adenauer considered him to be an ally. Brüning, however, from the perspective of his constituency of Breslau in East Prussia, saw the proposed appointment of Kaas as part of a deep plot towards the self-assertion of the Rhineland, of Cologne – and of its mayor. Above all, he saw it as a move by Adenauer to extend his own influence at the heart of the Centre Party, which was, of course, Brüning's own power base. The appointment had to be resisted; and so it was.

It was against this unpromising personal background that Adenauer, on 9 July 1930, wrote a long letter to Brüning detailing the miseries of Cologne. The number of its citizens on welfare benefit, he claimed, was so great, and the financial situation of the city so precarious, that within a few months there would be no more funds with which to pay benefits. Unless the Reich and Prussian governments helped out, he went on, there would be 'the most serious unrest'.[8] It had been – and still was – Adenauer's persistent fear, ever since the near breakdown of social order in 1918.

Brüning, on the other hand, had no such fears. Cologne's plea was rejected. 'He will maintain the value of the currency,' was Adenauer's bitter comment, 'and let go the reins of politics.'[9] Brüning maintained firmly that if Cologne was in trouble it was Cologne's own fault. For his part, his policy was very clear: to bring the Reich's finances to order by a programme of severe retrenchment. Taxes were to be raised and public expenditure cut. In fact, he had presented these measures to the Reichstag only a month earlier. In a fit of collective disgust, they had in their turn voted down most of them. Brüning had then gone over their heads and promulgated his budget under his emergency powers. The Reichstag had then voted in favour of a resolution to abrogate the emergency decree. There was only one further procedure open to Brüning: to call elections to the Reichstag. This he did, and the date was set for the last constitutionally available day: 14 September 1930.

It was to be the crossroads for the Weimar Republic. As Brüning wrote later, 'The election contest became a plebiscite on the emergency decrees, but at the same time a fight between a senseless form of parliamentarianism and a sound and judicious democracy.'[10] In the event, the fight was comprehensively lost. Quite unexpectedly, the main beneficiaries were the Nazi Party (or, to give it its full name, the Nationalsozialistische Deutsche Arbeiterpartei). On a turn-out of 82 per cent out of 35 million votes cast, the Nazi Party polled 6.4 million. As a result, instead of 28 seats in the old Reichstag, they were entitled to 107 seats – which they took in a staged event when the new Reichstag assembled in October, all of them wearing the brown shirts which were the uniform of their movement. Furthermore, during the whole afternoon and evening Nazi demonstrators ran riot in Berlin, smashing the windows of Jewish-owned shops and, in a mass rally in the Potsdamer Platz, shouting, '*Deutschland erwache*', '*Jude verrecke*', '*Heil! Heil!*' in scenes which recalled 'the days shortly before the revolution, the same crowds, the same Catilinarian types lounging about and demonstrating'.[11]

It was the first time that Adenauer had had to face up to the powerful appeal of National Socialism. To be sure, the Nazis had done slightly less well in Cologne than in the rest of Germany, and the Centre Party had held its position. Nevertheless, a jump from 4.6 per cent in the local election of

November 1929 to 17.6 per cent in the national election of September 1930 could hardly be regarded as insignificant. Yet Adenauer felt able to write to Heineman only three days after the result was declared: 'In many respects I do not think that the result of our election is quite as bad as it appears on the outside . . .' He went on to write that if the economic situation improved it would be possible to regain control 'over the dangers inherent in the entire situation'.[12]

To say that this attitude was naïve, although certainly true, is to miss the point. Adenauer undoubtedly still thought that the Communists, who had polled 17 per cent in Cologne in the September Reichstag election, were the major threat, and that by reaching some sort of accommodation with the Nazis he could induce them to assist him in defeating the threat. What he had not realised was that the Nazis were not prepared to play that sort of game. In their view, that was the game of the old politics which they were out to destroy.

Furthermore, they were masters of black propaganda, and in Cologne that propaganda was directed against Adenauer himself. He was attacked almost daily by the local Nazi newspaper *Westdeutscher Beobachter*. Almost any pretext would do: extravagance, holidays in Switzerland, excessive salary and expenses, self-advertisement and, of course, support for Rhineland separatism. But the one assault which commanded the Nazis' main attention was Adenauer's association with the Jewish community in Cologne.

The accusations were many, and to a large extent based on known facts. It was certainly true that Adenauer had allies who were Jewish by origin and often by religion. It was true that Cologne's economic, cultural and academic life had been enriched by many Jews who were long-standing and respected residents of Cologne, and, as such, encouraged by the mayor. It is also true that Adenauer had become, at the invitation of Ludwig Kaas, a member of the 'Pro Palästina' society, which supported the altogether reasonable view that Jews who wished to emigrate from Germany to Palestine should have the ability to do so and should be guaranteed safe residence when they got there. But in the hands of the Nazi propaganda machine, which rarely missed a trick, these innocent and often laudable activities were turned into heinous sins. As the climax to the campaign, Adenauer was labelled as the worst of all beings: a 'blood Jew'.[13]

Confronted with this barrage, Adenauer treated it in the same way as he had treated similar – although less venomous – Communist barrages. He simply ignored it. Indeed, the Centre Party as a whole seemed determined to treat the Nazi movement as a minor affair which would disappear once the economy came to rights. In the meantime they would tolerate it as a petulant but unimportant and temporary nuisance. While doing so, moreover, they seemed quite content to continue their old wrangles. Brüning was determined to pursue his long-term economic strategy of reducing public expenditure. Others, notably Luther and Adenauer, opposed the policy, recommending by contrast a major programme of public expenditure to create employment. The row, such as it was, rumbled on.

It came to a head in December 1930. Brüning promulgated a decree, to come into effect on the 20th of the month, setting overall spending limits for the Reich. Concurrently, the Prussian government, to meet the terms of the decree, issued a series of mandatory budgets for municipalities within its jurisdiction – which, of course, included Cologne. Expenditure was to be cut. But Adenauer needed money for Cologne's welfare payments, and therefore decided to raise Cologne's taxes before the decree could come into effect. Brüning was outraged. 'Despite his position as the President of the [Prussian] Staatsrat,' he wrote later, '[Adenauer] raised taxes for his municipality against the spirit of the decree . . . That was open defiance of state authority.'[14] Adenauer replied that if he had not done so Cologne would have been insolvent within months. Brüning did not even bother to answer Adenauer's letter. A further angry exchange took place in September 1931, when Adenauer, in a rare confession, admitted that 'the city of Cologne has over-extended itself in one case or another' and asked for the help of the Reichsbank.[15] The request was again curtly refused.

By then the situation was desperate. At the end of 1931 in Cologne the employment figures were frightening: close to 100,000 registered unemployed; nearly 25 per cent of the population living on benefits. Financially, the city was threatened with a deadline of August 1932, when 40 million marks of short-term loans were due for redemption. Hardly a week went by without random attacks and even murders committed by thugs wearing swastika armbands. True, Hitler, in a speech to the Industry Club of Düsseldorf in January 1932 (the industrialists were already hedging their bets), pledged that the leadership of his party would abide by the law; but no attempt was made to restrain the violence of his local organisations or the lorry-loads of *Sturmabteilung* (SA) and *Schutzstaffel* (SS) which roamed the streets in the evenings.

Adenauer seems, on all available evidence, to have closed his mind to what was going on around him. He still imagined that his strategy of dealing with the Nazis would work – ignoring them and concentrating on the Communist threat. He seems even to have been unruffled when, in March 1932, the election to the presidency of the Reich failed to produce an immediate majority for Hindenburg, who was only re-elected in the April run-off by 19.4 million votes to Adolf Hitler's 13.4 million, or when, in the elections to the Prussian Landtag in the same month, the Nazis came out only just short of an overall majority of seats. At this point, it is clear that Adenauer's main priority was the city of Cologne – and his own job.

It is not difficult to see why. In 1932, Adenauer was fifty-six years old. He had a large and comfortable house and, on the whole, a large and comfortable family (augmented yet again in 1931 by the birth of his son Georg). He realised that he was out of favour with his own party in Berlin, and that at any moment there might occur the same kind of social disruption as he had had to fend off in 1918; only this time it might well be successful. If that occurred, his tenure of the office of Mayor of Cologne would be terminated in an instant. Since he no longer had any capital to fall back on, thanks to his unwise financial adventure four years earlier, the clear priority was to ensure his only source of income.

It was never going to be an easy task. The Nazi successes in the April Landtag elections had further changed the political landscape. Although Adenauer's preoccupation was with the Communists, as President of the Prussian Staatsrat he could hardly afford to ignore the electoral verdict. Nevertheless, he was surprisingly slow in his reactions, and by the time he had woken up the landscape had shifted yet again. The Landtag election results had also caused ructions in Berlin. In the face of the now obvious Nazi threat, Brüning took what he thought would be decisive action. He published a decree banning Hitler's SA and SS. As it turned out, it was his fatal mistake, since Hindenburg refused to sign it. On 29 May 1932 he told Brüning that no more emergency decrees would be signed. That was Brüning's death knell; he had no alternative but to resign.

In truth, it was Schleicher who was behind the whole manoeuvre (as with most political manoeuvres in Berlin at the time), and it was Schleicher who persuaded Hindenburg to appoint Franz von Papen* as Brüning's successor. The choice, as Schleicher well knew, suited almost everybody. Papen's credentials were admirable: he was a Catholic nobleman and a former officer in the Imperial Guard; he was on the right wing of the Centre Party; and his wife was the daughter of a Saarland industrialist. He was also much liked by Hindenburg – possibly because of his monarchist sympathies. If the truth be told, it also suited Schleicher that Papen was not very clever. Indeed, as Adenauer wrote later, he was a man of 'abnormally limited intelligence. Unfortunately many people allowed themselves to be deceived by his obliging manner and his pious talk.'[16] None of this perhaps mattered very much, since it was Schleicher himself, now Minister of Defence in the Papen government, who held the true reins of power. Indeed it was Schleicher who had secured Hitler's tolerance of the new Papen government. The price, however, had been high: new Reichstag elections and the revocation of the decree against the SA and SS.

Schleicher then persuaded Papen to intervene in the affairs of Prussia, on the doubtful grounds that the SPD-led coalition was unable to maintain public order. His evidence was the recent bloody clash between Nazis and Communists in the town of Altona – in fact provoked by the Nazis. Papen promptly issued a decree deposing the Prussian government and appointing himself as Reich Commissioner with full powers over the state. As it happened, this spectacularly unconstitutional move was surprisingly successful. There was little resistance. The SPD realised that there was nothing to be gained by armed resistance and had recourse to the courts, but the ensuing

---

* Papen, Franz von (1879–1969): Politician. Born in Werl in Westphalia of aristocratic parentage. Education no different from others of his kind – emphasis on Prussian military values. 1913–15: German military attaché in Mexico and Washington. 1915–18: Staff officer in First World War. 1921–32: Member of Prussian Landtag. 1932–33: Chancellor of the Reich. 1934–44: Diplomatic posts as minister, then ambassador, in Vienna and Ankara. 1946: Sentenced at Nuremberg to eight years' hard labour. 1949: Released. Spent his last years in obscurity. Weak and rather sad character, who rowed with the tide, which was too strong for him.

legal action was bound to take time; and the trade unions who had resisted the Kapp Putsch in 1918 had been weakened by mass unemployment. Adenauer, as President of the Staatsrat, was silent. There was a meeting of Centre Party leaders in Frankfurt, but nothing came of it beyond vapid speeches of conciliation. There was also some talk of 'standing up to Hitler', but again the plans were vague (and included a scheme to transfer the seat of the Prussian government to Cologne, which Adenauer had 'apparently agreed to'[17]). But there was little conviction, and very little sense, in any of it.

But Adenauer was, after all, President of the Prussian Staatsrat and a senior member of the Centre Party. He could not avoid becoming embroiled in the constitutional crisis in Prussia which Papen had provoked. The problem became more acute after the Nazi Party had more than doubled its representation in the Reichstag in the elections of 31 July 1932. Adenauer as a result came to the conclusion that the Nazis had to be included in the government of Prussia if Papen's 'Reich Commission' was to be lifted and normality restored. On 2 August he therefore held a meeting with his Centre Party colleagues to review their position.

The meeting was held in the house of the banker Kurt von Schröder. Schröder, as a partner in the respected Stein banking house and as such a member of the Cologne financial community which Adenauer much admired, was somebody to be listened to. But there was a problem. Apart from Schröder's known right-wing views, which might be accommodated, his wife had become a committed Nazi. The whole discussion was therefore pushed in one, perhaps uncomfortable, direction. The result was recorded by Adenauer himself in a note written on Schröder's personal writing paper. The conclusion was clear – and went well beyond the immediate problem of Prussia. If a Reich government were to be formed by a coalition of Nazis and Nationalists, the Centre Party, Adenauer's note reads, 'would be prepared to tolerate it and to judge it wholly without bias by its deeds alone'.[18]

That particular outcome was headed off at a meeting on 13 August between Papen, Schleicher and Hitler. Hitler was offered no more than the Vice-Chancellorship in a continuing Papen government. Hitler and his colleagues, of course, were not going to stand for that, and on 12 September broke off their truce with Papen – thus provoking yet another round of Reichstag elections, which were then set for 6 November 1932.

There is no doubt that it was a moment of the greatest political tension both in Prussia and in the Reich itself. But nothing, it seemed, could stop holidays; and in mid-August Adenauer and his family went on their annual holiday to their customary retreat at Chandolin. In the circumstances it was, to say the least, a surprising decision. Not only were the affairs of Prussia and the Reich in suspense, but Cologne itself had failed to meet its financial deadline and was therefore legally insolvent. A budget for the city had been passed in June, but it had been hopelessly optimistic in its forecast of revenue and expenditure, providing only for a deficit of 25 million marks. By August, the estimate of the deficit had risen to 30 million, and the lending banks were already in the process of calling creditors' meetings to start the difficult negotiations on a settlement which might allow them to recover their money without crippling the city in the process. While this was all happening, the mayor, who many thought had been responsible for the whole thing, was out of all reasonable touch.

The family return to Cologne in September 1932 was hardly the happy event that it had been in previous years. The propaganda barrage, from all sides, had intensified; even Adenauer's allies were distancing themselves; the people of Cologne had patently lost confidence; the City Council were asking unpleasant questions about his association with the Deutsche Bank and his private finances; and the problem of the governance of Prussia was still unsolved. Under the circumstances, difficult and depressing as they were, all Adenauer could do was to hold on and hope that things would get better.

It was by now plain that the decisive event would be November's Reichstag elections. If Hitler won anything close to an outright majority, the game would be up. The Reich would have its first Nazi government, with all its as yet unknown consequences. If the Nazis could be badly defeated, then there was the alternative of forming a government without Nazi participation. If, on the middle view, the Nazis could be contained, there might be a continuing Papen government with a controllable Nazi participation.

When the event came, the Nazis lost nearly 2 million votes but managed to hold on to all but 34 of their Reichstag seats. The scene was thus set for the middle view. Everything might then have progressed smoothly. But at that point, almost immediately after the November elections, Papen produced his bombshell: what can only be described as a most bizarre scheme. It was, apparently, the only scheme he could think of which would ditch Hitler. His proposal was for a wholly new Reich constitution, implemented by presidential decree. It would do away with all forms of democracy and entrust the government of Germany to an élite whose membership would be confined to owners of large tracts of property. In other words, he was proposing a return to the old Junker formula of property-based feudalism.

Schleicher had not been consulted on Papen's scheme; and when he heard about it thought it must be some sort of joke. 'What do you think?' he said to one of his friends. 'Little Franz has discovered himself.'[19] But it was not a joke. Besides, Hindenburg was rather attracted by the idea. Schleicher took the only decision possible: in crude terms, to dump Papen as his protégé. His tactic in doing so was admirably subtle. He commissioned a study from his own Defence Department, the result of which was to demonstrate that Germany would be in danger of civil war, and certainly unable to contain the industrial action which the Papen plan would provoke without extensive deployment of the armed forces. The result would be, the study went on, that Germany's eastern frontier would be left undefended, allowing the Poles to march on Berlin if they so chose.

However fantastic the hypothesis, it was enough to convince Hindenburg. The old Field Marshal was certainly not going to go down in history as the President who had left Germany unguarded. When the study was presented to him on 2 December, he burst into tears. Papen was immediately sacked. 'But I am too old,' he went on, 'to assume responsibility for a civil war at the end of my life. So we must, in God's name, let Herr von Schleicher try his luck.'[20]

In those tense moments of December 1932, Schleicher had one, and only one, plan: to split the Nazi Party. Since August he had been in discussion with one of Hitler's aides, Gregor Strasser. Strasser held a central position inside the organisation of the party, and was able to tell Schleicher that there was both dissension and impatience at the slow movement of events. Strasser even went on to say that he might well defect and that, if he did, he would not be alone. Schleicher's plan was therefore to lead a coalition of interests, supported by the Catholic and the independent trade unions, and part of the Nazi movement. In that way he would isolate Hitler.

Ignorant of Schleicher's master plan, the Centre Party executive met on 8 December to consider the situation in the light of his appointment as Chancellor. Adenauer referred to this meeting when he wrote to Ludwig Kaas on 12 December. The discussion had taken place around two issues concerning Prussia, but it went further than that. The first issue had been the matter of immediacy, that there should be a properly constituted government of Prussia to allow the withdrawal of Papen's decree appointing a Reich Commissioner (now, of course, Schleicher). The second issue was much wider: whether that matter of immediacy should be disregarded and the formation of a Prussian government put off 'until the question of the entry of the National Socialists into the Reich government is resolved in a positive sense'.

As if this was not enough, Adenauer's letter to Kaas went on to assert that all those responsible had the duty 'to ensure that, as soon as the political situation permits, a government including the National Socialists is formed in Prussia . . . Subsequent negotiations with the National Socialists regarding their participation in the Reich government would not be damaged, in my view, and might even be promoted, by the procedure in Prussia. I also think it correct for the National Socialists in Prussia, as the less dangerous place, to show whether they are really in a position to cope with such high offices.'[21] At the time of writing, of course, Adenauer knew perfectly well that if his view prevailed, the new Minister-President of Prussia would be one of Hitler's principal adjutants, Hermann Göring.

The conclusion, whatever the subsequent apologia, is inescapable. As President of the Prussian Staatsrat, Adenauer was prepared to encourage the formation of a Nazi-led Prussian government, headed by Göring, as a testing ground for a Nazi-led Reich government, headed by Hitler. As one of his biographers has written, 'this was an enormous error'.[22] But the 'enormous error' needs at least some explanation. The charitable explanation is that Adenauer was fixed in his anti-Communist mindset. Any combination was better than a 'Bolshevik' take-over. There is, however, a less charitable explanation: that Adenauer's undoubted Catholic and humane instincts were at that point subordinated to the problem of his own financial position. Sad, but true; he needed to keep his job; and he was prepared, as a gambler, to play with whatever devil appeared in front of him. As a gambler, of course, he always thought that he would win.

8

CONFRONTATION

'Es ist wirklich schwer, die Menschen zu kennen und sie
nicht zu verachten'*

SURPRISING AS IT may nowadays seem, Adolf Hitler is said to have admired Adenauer. Albert Speer, who came to know Hitler's mind perhaps as well as anyone, wrote as much during the years he spent in Spandau prison after the Second World War. According to Speer, Hitler thought that Adenauer was 'an able man'; he was full of praise for what Speer called Adenauer's 'obstinacy'; he was also much taken with the 'grand design' for the city of Cologne, and much regretted that Adenauer's 'political folly' prevented a constructive relationship between them.[1] There is no reason to believe that Speer was misrepresenting Hitler's views. At that point, indeed, there was no reason for him to do so. But Speer's account, if accurate, perhaps goes to show that Hitler, whatever his other faults, was quick to recognise ability when he saw it, and that Adenauer had not been left off the list of potential recruits to the 'new politics' – provided that he had felt able to cross the final bridge which led to them.

---

* 'It is really very hard to know the human race and not to despise it': Adenauer to Heinrich Billstein, quoted in P. Weymar, *Adenauer*, p. 151.

It is also odd, perhaps, that Hitler and Adenauer never met. Although Hitler made two well-publicised visits to Cologne in early 1933, and Adenauer, as President of the Prussian Staatsrat, went regularly to Berlin, their paths never crossed. To be sure, if they had met, it is unlikely that they would have found much in common. The austere, Catholic, disciplined mayor would have had little time for the little Austrian whom Hindenburg persisted in referring to as 'the corporal'; nor would Adenauer have appreciated Hitler's particular form of political genius: his instinct for shifts in public mood and his patience and subtlety in calculating the right moment to unleash his venomous strike.

Certainly, an occasion for a meeting between the two presented itself in Cologne on 4 January 1933. It was the day on which Hitler was in the city for a conference with Franz von Papen. There is no doubt that Adenauer was fully aware of Hitler's visit. It was not in any way secret; indeed, it had been heavily advertised by what were known as 'the usual signals'. When it came, crowds of enthusiastic supporters turned out in the streets. The city, according to eye-witnesses, 'looked like a sea of flags'.[2] The police had their hands full simply in maintaining order. Moreover, it was a matter of general knowledge that Hitler's meeting with Papen was to take place in the house of Adenauer's banking ally, Kurt von Schröder.

Nor was the reason for Hitler's visit a particular secret. Schleicher's efforts to assemble a coalition of interests to support a Reich government which would exclude the Nazis had foundered during December 1932 on two rocks: first, after some initial interest, both the Social Democrat unions and the Catholic unions were reminded that Schleicher had prompted Papen to abolish the democratically elected Prussian government, and was therefore not to be trusted; and, second, Strasser had failed to deliver on his promises. In fact, not only had he neglected to mobilise enough support within the dissidents in the Nazi Party for Schleicher's venture, but when he was most needed he had gone off on holiday to Italy. Hitler had then been able, in a display of terrifying rhetoric and an accompanying display of cool administrative acumen, to bring his party into line under a new lieutenant, Rudolf Hess. By the end of 1932, Schleicher's cause was clearly lost.

It was at that point that Papen, probably with Hindenburg's knowledge, prepared to negotiate with Hitler. Papen was Hindenburg's favoured candidate to succeed Schleicher; and Hindenburg was almost certainly in secret conversations with Papen throughout January 1933 – as Schleicher alleged when submitting his angry resignation at the end of the month. But Papen at least knew enough to realise that the only Reich government which had a realistic chance of survival was one led by Hitler.

The Cologne meeting of 4 January between Hitler and Papen thus had an obvious agenda: to negotiate terms on which Hitler could reasonably be invited to become Chancellor of the Reich. For his part, Hitler knew perfectly well that an invitation from Hindenburg was essential if he was to avoid blocking opposition from the German armed forces, which were still loyal to the President. An attempt at a putsch simply would not be successful. He also knew that Papen had Hindenburg's ear. Papen, for his part, was still convinced that he could embrace Hitler into a Reich coalition government and, in the process, neutralise him and the Nazi Party. The meeting therefore duly took place, and a deal done to the satisfaction of the two participants. Hitler was confident that he had secured an invitation to the Chancellorship when Schleicher finally gave up the struggle, and Papen was equally confident that any such invitation would be hedged around with so many conditions that Hitler would be tamed.

The fact that Adenauer was not at the meeting in Schröder's house raises a question. From Hitler's point of view, there might have been advantages. Adenauer was, after all, President of the Prussian Staatsrat; and he was also an important figure in the hierarchy of the Centre Party, on whose support Hitler might initially have to rely. From Adenauer's point of view, the advantages were perhaps more evident. Only three weeks before, even after the personal attacks levelled at him, he had expressed his view to Kaas that the Nazis should be accepted into the government of Prussia and then into the government of the Reich. It was no more than good sense to meet the man who would run the whole show. But apart from all else, it would have been normal courtesy to meet, in his own city, one of the major political figures of the Reich. A simple telephone call from Adenauer to Schröder would have been all that was needed to test out the ground, and, if appropriate, to secure an invitation. But the call was apparently never made or, if it was, met with no response.

Of course, for Hitler, Papen was the softer target; Adenauer might have been a harder negotiator. Papen also had the key to Hindenburg's door; Adenauer hardly knew him. Furthermore, Papen could be persuaded to join a Hitler government as Vice-Chancellor (and Reich Commissioner for Prussia); it is impossible to believe that Adenauer would have accepted a similar offer. For all these reasons it is reasonable to suppose that Hitler was inclined to play one fish at a time. Adenauer was not the largest fish in this particular river and, for the moment, could be left to swim.

Events went according to Hitler's plan. Schleicher got wind of the negotiations, thought that Hindenburg was involved in them behind his back, and resigned on 28 January 1933. Hindenburg still wanted Papen as Chancellor, but Papen persuaded him that that was no longer an option. By 30 January Hindenburg had reluctantly conceded the point, and had given his assent to Papen's proposal for a new coalition Cabinet. Hitler was to be Chancellor, Papen was to be Vice-Chancellor and Reich Commissioner for Prussia; Alfred Hugenberg, the press and film baron, now head of the German National People's Party, was to be Minister of Economics; and the other places were to be filled by relative makeweights. Apart from Hitler, there were to be only two Nazis in the new Cabinet: Wilhelm Frick as Reich Minister of the Interior and Hermann Göring as Minister Without Portfolio but – significantly – as Minister of the Interior in Prussia. 'We have him framed in,' exulted one of Papen's friends.[3]

The remark was foolish and, with the hindsight of history, foolish almost beyond belief. Papen and his friends had quite clearly no understanding at all either of Hitler's lack of scruple or of his political agility. Even before taking the oath of office, Hitler hectored his new colleagues into demanding an immediate dissolution of the Reichstag. Hugenberg was the only one who put up serious resistance; he knew that the main loser in the subsequent Reichstag elections would be his own party. But even he crumbled in the end, as did Hindenburg, who was obliged, under the Weimar constitution, to accede to the new Chancellor's request. The presidential decree for dissolution of the Reichstag was accordingly signed; and the date for elections to a new Reichstag was fixed for 5 March 1933.

The stage was then set for what would be one of the most unpleasant, violent and fraudulent election campaigns in modern European history. Hitler was the Chancellor of the Reich, properly appointed by President Hindenburg, with all the authority which his position, and the legality of his appointment, commanded. He had also, thanks to Papen's position as Reich Commissioner for Prussia, total control over electoral procedures in the largest state in the Reich – with Göring effectively in charge. Furthermore, he had no hesitation at all in using the constitutional advantages which he had inherited from previous Chancellors.

On 1 February, Hitler made a long speech condemning the politics of the Weimar Republic; the new politics, he said, had been correctly defined by Frick as 'the will and strength to act'.[4] On 3 February he went on to make another long speech to senior commanders of the armed forces, to the effect that their own interests were best served by the 'strictest kind of authoritarian leadership', on the grounds that that was the only way to be rid of Communism, pacifism – and the Versailles Treaty.[5] Göring followed up by sacking fourteen senior police officers in Prussia and appointing a 'Commissioner on special assignment' whose job was to purge the police of 'undesirable elements'. On 17 February, a further decree ordered all Prussian police officers to co-operate with the SA and the SS, to combat the Communists 'if necessary, by the resort to the unconditional use of weapons'.[6] In explaining the decree, Göring went on to say that 'every bullet that now leaves the mouth of a police pistol is my bullet. If you call that murder, then I am the murderer, for I gave the order, and I stand by it.'[7] In practice, this meant that SA units now had official licence in Prussia to break up any meeting, and muzzle any speech, of which the Nazis disapproved.

In those days of early February 1933 Adenauer appears finally to have recognised that all talk of compromise with the Nazis was fruitless. The City Council of Cologne had been dissolved over his head by a decree from Papen on 5 February, and new elections announced for 12 March – a week after the results of the Reichstag elections were due to be declared. Furthermore, the Prussian Landtag had also been dissolved. Adenauer's position as President of the Staatsrat was thus under a suspended guillotine, the blade of which would only be released if and when his position as the elected Mayor of Cologne was legally overturned.

Given the change in Adenauer's view of the Nazis, the dissolution of the Prussian Landtag on 6 February, although perhaps of minor importance in the political context of the day, had not been an easy event. Under the constitution of Prussia, the decision to dissolve the Prussian Landtag had to be taken by a committee consisting of the President of the Upper House (Staatsrat), the President of the Lower House (Landtag) and the Minister-President. The first of the three, of course, was Adenauer. The second was by now a Nazi, Hans Kerrl. The third position had become vacant after the decree of July 1932, removing all functions of the Prussian government and transferring them to the Reich. Papen, as Reich Commissioner, asserted the right to exercise in the committee the vote attributable to the Minister-President – a view supported by the Prussian Supreme Court. That was all very well, in Adenauer's opinion, if Papen could be relied on to support the Weimar constitution. But the situation changed after Hitler's appointment as Chancellor of the Reich. But Papen had by then switched sides.

The proposed dissolution of the Prussian Landtag seems to have been Adenauer's final sticking point. At the meeting of the three-man committee on 6 February, Papen and Kerrl did their best to convince him 'for an hour and a half'[8] that dissolution in Prussia was the obvious and only possible consequence of the dissolution of the Reichstag and of the municipal councils in the state. Adenauer stubbornly argued against dissolution, on the grounds that Papen's assumption of the Minister-President's vote was unconstitutional. The wrangle went on until Papen and Kerrl forced a vote. At that point, Adenauer claimed that any decision would be constitutionally unlawful, got up and walked out of the room. Papen and Kerrl immediately resolved that the Prussian Landtag should be dissolved and new elections held.

Thereafter, apart from a visit to Berlin on 25 February to protest to Papen and Göring about Göring's decree authorising the use of guns in Prussia, Adenauer spent the election campaign, such as it was, in Cologne. He spoke at a large Centre Party rally on 7 February, not, admittedly, to great effect. Nevertheless, he came out in clear party political colours. This was no more than honest, but inevitably made it more difficult for him to resume the role of a city mayor above party politics should protocol require it.

It so happened that on 17 February protocol did require it. Hitler was due to arrive in Cologne on that day for a Nazi election rally. It was the second occasion on which Adenauer might, with all propriety, have met Hitler to discuss matters which might have been of mutual interest. Adenauer had to make a difficult decision: either he would go to the airport, as mayor, to welcome the Reich Chancellor, which would have been customary protocol, or he would not go, on the grounds that Hitler was just another party leader on the election trail. In the event, signalling his final belief that no possible deal could be done with the Nazis, he took the decision not to go. He sent instead one of his deputy mayors, Heinrich Billstein, who was responsible for security at the airport. Hitler, needless to say, immediately claimed that he was deeply offended. He refused to stay in Cologne, and went on to spend the night in Bad Godesberg.

That was just the prelude to the main row. Having taken the decision not to meet Hitler on his arrival at the airport, Adenauer then had to accept the consequences. As mayor, he had to forbid the display of party flags on buildings which were the property of the city. Furthermore, the Rhine was not to be floodlit, whatever the distinction of the visitor to Cologne. All this led to a most embarrassing incident. Overnight, on 17 February, two flags appeared on pillars of the bridge which crossed the Rhine from the old city of Cologne to the new suburb of Deutz, and its large exhibition hall, where the Nazi rally was to be held. The flags carried the swastika. Adenauer ordered the offending flags to be removed. This was done, although a unit of the SA was in attendance at the event, noting carefully the individuals who had been ordered by the mayor to carry out the act.

But it did not stop there. As a compromise, it was accepted on all sides that the swastika could legitimately and reasonably be displayed in front of the exhibition hall in Deutz where Hitler was to speak. That was all very well. But it appeared that there were no available flagpoles considered large enough to carry the flags in suitable flamboyance. The only solution was to call in the fire brigade. In the end, after some delay, the fire brigade produced and erected poles of adequate length to carry the swastika flags in a manner which was to the Nazis' satisfaction. In other times, of course, the whole incident would have been a simple matter of humorous comment. Farce, after all, is a common feature of election campaigns. In this case and in this campaign, however, farce was not welcome. The whole episode was summed up by the *Westdeutscher Beobachter*: 'Herr Adenauer might like to know that such challenges will be avenged in future.'[9]

The campaign came to its climax with the torching of the Reichstag building on the night of 27 February. Whoever was the culprit, the occasion gave the Nazis an opportunity which they were only too eager to exploit. Göring immediately claimed that the Communists were responsible, and ordered the arrest of 4,000 of them before dawn. By noon on the following day, Hitler had persuaded Hindenburg that he should sign a decree giving the Reich government almost unlimited power. Under the terms of the decree, the Reich could unilaterally take over the functions of a state government if it felt that the state was no longer able to maintain order. Even that might have been acceptable if it had stopped there. But the decree went on to specify particular crimes which would be subject to long terms of imprisonment or the death penalty: assault on members of the

Reich government, arson on public buildings, incitement to riot, and so on. Not the least of the crimes specified was resistance to the decree itself.

The decree once signed, the police in, for instance, Cologne were able (in co-operation with the SA) to arrest any person and keep him or her in detention for an indefinite period. Relatives need not be informed where somebody might be or whether he or she had been arrested at all. He or she could be treated with whatever brutality the police and SA chose – or be shot if that was thought appropriate. Furthermore, as a result, hostile press articles were silenced; Social Democrat and Centre Party meetings could be broken up on the order of a minor police official; the official Communist Party was declared illegal; violence in the streets was stepped up; meetings were regularly broken up; and marches of Nazi supporters were held almost daily, escorted by the police. As election day approached, it was becoming obvious that units of the SA and SS 'would be stationed around the polling stations on the day'[10] – as Adenauer complained to Papen on 1 March, in a letter which, as it happened, was the last letter which he wrote in his capacity as President of the Prussian Staatsrat.

When they came, the results of the Reichstag elections of 5 March 1933 were rather less impressive for Hitler than he might have hoped and expected. In spite of all Nazi attempts to terrorise the opposition, both the SPD and the Centre Party won close to the number of seats which they had held in the previous Reichstag. Certainly, the Nazis and their allies won a simple majority (celebrated by looting of Jewish shops and further beatings of any opponent who dared to appear on the streets). But it was not enough to force changes in the Weimar constitution through the Reichstag.

Nevertheless, it was enough to allow wholesale disruption of subsequent elections for the Cologne City Council. Sollmann and other Social Democrats were taken into 'protective custody'. The *Westdeutscher Beobachter* screamed 'Away with Adenauer . . . Down with huge salaries . . . National Socialists into City Hall.'[11] Collection boxes were passed round to gather money for 'a bullet for Adenauer'.[12] A troop of SA was posted outside Adenauer's house in Max-Bruch-Strasse, supposedly for his protection. A Centre Party meeting billed for 10 March, at which Adenauer was to make a long defence of his record as mayor, was cancelled at short notice on the grounds that it would be a threat to public order. Furthermore, the Nazi campaign was having its effect. Old acquaintances 'turned away when they met Frau Adenauer in the street'.[13] Adenauer himself was ostracised by all but his closest allies, and abused if he showed himself in public.

On 10 March, after the cancellation of the Centre Party rally, Adenauer realised that he and his family were in serious physical danger. Indeed, he was warned that the SA wished to take him to a Nazi rally in Cologne's Neumarkt and put him publicly on display as 'an enemy of the people'. He quickly left for Bonn with Gussi – but not before he had taken their children to shelter in the Caritas Hospital in Hohenlind.

On Sunday 12 March, the day of the municipal elections, Adenauer was back in Cologne. He was told that he was still in danger, and was advised to disappear quietly. In spite of this advice, he went to a memorial ceremony in the Gürzenich Hall for those who had died in the war. At the ceremony he was ignored by everybody but one of his deputies, who warned him that the Nazis were planning to 'liquidate him by an assault squad in the City Hall . . . as soon as he arrived at his office'. Apparently, 'they were going to throw him out of the window into the street'.[14] In addition, he was refused the police protection which he had asked for. The warning signals were clearly evident.

In the event, the elections to the Cologne City Council went largely as expected. The Nazis came out as the largest single party, but failed to win a majority. Nevertheless, by declaring the outlawed Communist seats 'dormant' they created a majority for themselves. For Adenauer, the conclusion was clear beyond doubt: he was about to lose his job as Mayor of Cologne. But he was still President of the Prussian Staatsrat; and on the morning after the results of the Cologne council elections were announced he decided to go to Berlin to protest to Göring about the whole conduct of the elections in Prussia. In truth, it is far from clear what he hoped to achieve; but, whatever his motive, he had to evade the SA troop which was still encamped on his doorstep. This he managed to do, and was taken by a car provided by Pferdmenges to Dortmund railway station to catch the train to Berlin.

When he arrived there, he went to the elaborate and dreary formal apartments reserved for the President of the Prussian Staatsrat rather than his usual rooms in the Hotel Kaiserhof. He thought it wise to be in Wilhelmstrasse – and only two doors away from Göring. But there was to be no immediate meeting with Göring. In fact, he was kept waiting for three days. As it happened, while he was kicking his heels he heard on the radio that the Nazi Gauleiter in Cologne, Josef Grohé, had occupied the City Hall and had announced from the balcony that the mayor, Dr Adenauer, had been dismissed. His replacement, Günther Riesen, was apparently prepared to take on the job without salary.

When Adenauer finally saw Göring, he was told that there was to be an investigation into his 'financial malpractice'. Adenauer, of course, denied any malpractice, and complained in turn about the illegality of his apparent dismissal as Mayor of Cologne. Göring made it clear that he had had no prior knowledge of the event – and that it certainly was not his doing. However, he went on to say, 'My further decisions will depend on the results of the investigation'.[15] With that, the interview came to an end.

Adenauer thought it best to stay in Berlin. At least he would be safe, since the police in the Wilhelmstrasse were there to protect official visitors – whatever the SA might say or wish. But while he was there, living – by that time with Gussi – in the somewhat absurd formal apartments in Wilhelmstrasse, surrounded by the artistic relics of the old Prussian Empire, he learned that his own party, the Centre Party, voted on 23 March in favour of Hitler's Enabling Act, designed to give him nothing short of total and all-embracing dictatorial powers. Brüning and the Centre Party in the Reichstag had apparently been persuaded to do so by Adenauer's supposed ally, Ludwig Kaas. Kaas had argued that if Hitler did not get what he wanted legally he would take it by force, and it was therefore better to vote with him – in the hope of favours in return. This the Centre Party did – signing, in the process, the warrant for its own extinction.

On 23 March 1933, with the passing of the Enabling Act, the Weimar Republic finally came to its stuttering end. Anything that was done by the Hitler government was now legally sanctioned. Consequently, on 4 April, the District President for the Rhineland sent Adenauer a formal letter announcing legal action to remove him from the office of Mayor of Cologne. Pending the result of the action, he was suspended for an indefinite period. The city of Cologne stopped all payments to him, and the Deutsche Bank froze his account. He was told that he would have to leave the official apartments of the President of the Prussian Staatsrat in Berlin no later than 25 April. He had no money, no home and no job. As he wrote to Heineman, 'my position, inwardly and outwardly, is frankly desperate'.[16] It is not surprising that when his son Max visited him at the time, he found his father, at the age of fifty-seven, in the deepest of deep depression.

PART THREE

Hitler's Germany

I

DESCENT INTO DARKNESS

'Ich habe keine besonderen Bedürfnisse, nur den einen Wunsch nach Stille'

IN 1906 KONRAD Adenauer had embarked on a political career which had taken him steadily up the rungs of what had turned out to be a far from easy ladder. He had risen to be a formidable Mayor of Cologne; he had become a major and respected figure in the Centre Party, the party which was pivotal in the politics of the Weimar Republic; he had twice been offered the Chancellorship of the Reich itself; he had had the satisfaction of seeing Cologne, his native city, become one of the greatest and most innovative cities in Europe; and, as a bonus, he had built for himself a substantial fortune. All this, moreover, had kept him fully occupied, even to the point of depriving his growing family of the companionship which he might – and they certainly would – have wished.

By April 1933 it had all gone. Adenauer himself was out of work, virtually bankrupt, and separated from his family. He was faced with a serious charge relating to his financial management of Cologne during his mayoralty

---

* 'I have no particular needs; only a wish for peace and quiet': Adenauer to Herwegen, requesting sanctuary at Maria Laach, 17 April 1933; AiDR, p. 111.

(with a charge of 'separatism' thrown in as an extra); he had been deserted by almost all those whom he had thought to be his friends; he was living in uncomfortable apartments in Berlin, a city he disliked, with only occasional visits from his wife; his party, with whom he 'had worked shoulder to shoulder for nearly twenty-seven years' he now thought guilty of 'cowardly betrayal';[1] he was afraid to return to his home because of the threats against him; and he had no prospect whatever of finding a job.

It is hard to imagine a picture of greater gloom. There were no more than a few isolated shafts of light. One or two of his former friends and colleagues in Cologne stood by him, and wrote long letters of sympathy to him in Berlin: the Cardinal Archbishop of Cologne, Karl Joseph Schulte; the banker Robert Pferdmenges (and particularly his wife Dora); Benedikt and Ella Schmittmann; and, of course, his sister Lilli (and her husband Willi Suth) and his brothers Hans and August. These letters were undoubtedly welcome, and were replied to at length and with gratitude. But the plain fact was that Adenauer's letters in return were copious in number and long in text mainly because there was not much else to do.

A major concern, of course, was to mobilise his defence against the charge levelled against him. His determination had been increased by a ferocious letter he received in late March from Günter Riesen, the 'Acting Mayor of Cologne', a three-page diatribe which ended with the words: 'You are a criminal, guilty of crimes against your family and your wife, for whom, in her blissful ignorance, I can only feel sorry. You are guilty of crimes against our Lord God and against all those who have come into contact with you. You are the accused; I am your accuser; the people are your judge. That is the position between us.'[2]

Adenauer spent a great deal of time and care writing a detailed defence to the charge. He had, reasonably enough, been much angered by Riesen's letter. In a letter to the Reich Ministry of the Interior of eighteen closely written pages, dated 17 April, he answered one by one the ten points which had been produced to justify the charge laid against him. He was even more upset when Gussi reported that Riesen had contacted her in Hohenlind to offer his protection. Adenauer, who had been so powerful, was now powerless even to defend his wife. It is little wonder that his letters of the time show clearly the depressing combination of suppressed fury and sheer boredom.

From the practical point of view, the most timely – and crucial – support came from Dannie Heineman. Heineman responded to Adenauer's desperate plea for help by turning up in Berlin on 12 April. 'He said,' Adenauer wrote many years later, 'without my having spoken of my financial worries, that he imagined that I was in a difficult financial situation.'[3] In writing this, of course, Adenauer had conveniently forgotten his two letters written immediately before Heineman's visit; the first asking openly for Heineman's financial help, and the second moaning that he was living in Wilhelmstrasse 64 'as a refugee'.[4] Heineman duly arrived with a 'loan' of 10,000 marks – in cash, to avoid Adenauer the embarrassment, and possible danger, of a visit to a bank. Adenauer, whatever his previous appeal to Heineman, was obviously taken aback by this sudden act of almost overwhelming generosity. He could only stutter that he had no idea whether and when he could repay it. Heineman replied that he was sure the money was well invested, put the banknotes down on the table, shook Adenauer's hand, and left.

It was indeed a remarkable gesture. Although Adenauer later described Heineman as 'my good friend',[5] at the time the relationship was more professional than personal. Unlike his letters to friends such as the Schmittmanns, or to sympathetic acquaintances such as Peter Klöckner, or to his family, Adenauer's correspondence with Heineman was formal both in language and in tone. What is remarkable is not that Heineman had a genuine admiration for Adenauer, but that he was prepared for that admiration to be translated into extreme financial largesse. Over the next three years his generosity was to be called on a number of times – and never failed; and as an American citizen, although a Jew, he was free to travel into and out of, and within, Germany without fear of attack from the authorities. It is no exaggeration to say that without Heineman's support during the years 1933 to 1936 Adenauer and his family would have been destitute.

Nevertheless, although his financial problem was for the time being solved, Adenauer had to find somewhere to live. Cologne was obviously impossible: it was too dangerous. Riesen's letter had shown that all too clearly. But he had soon to leave the apartments in Wilhelmstrasse. The upshot was that when Gussi made a visit to Berlin on 14 April the two of them settled down to a serious marital discussion. That there was a discussion at all is perhaps a measure of the changed balance in their relationship that events had provoked. The Adenauer who was Mayor of Cologne would almost certainly have merely told his wife what he was going to do and what in turn she was to do. The dispossessed Adenauer of Berlin had lost that confidence. His wife had assumed the role of counsellor and friend to her weakened husband. As a result, their relationship was probably closer and more affectionate than at any time since they had married fourteen years earlier.

This being so, their first – joint – decision was to give priority to the safety of the children. The three eldest, Emma's children Konrad, Max and Ria, were by then more or less able to look after themselves, aged as they were twenty-six, twenty-three and twenty-one respectively, and all of them studying. Konrad was finishing his legal training in Berlin, having followed in his father's wake in Freiburg and Munich. Max was following a similar path of legal study, but in Cologne; and Ria was reading modern languages at the University of Heidelberg. Both Max and Ria, when they were not away in their studies, were able to live in safety in the family house in Max-Bruch-Strasse. Gussi's four children, on the other hand, needed looking after and protecting, since the elder two were at school in Cologne and might easily, in their parents' view, be used in some way in the Nazi attack on their father. The conclusion was therefore clear: Gussi would have to spend as much time as possible with them in Cologne, either in Hohenlind or, when it was prudent to return, in Max-Bruch-Strasse.

But, that settled, there was then the matter of where Adenauer himself should live. It was Gussi who finally persuaded her husband that he should seek a safe haven, even if this meant that the family would have to split up. The decision was, by its very nature, difficult; but, once persuaded, Adenauer set about finding the safe haven for himself which his wife had wished. It so happened that a former school companion of his at the Apostelgymnasium, Ildefons Herwegen, had become abbot of the Benedictine monastery of Maria Laach. After trawling through the alternatives, it was to Herwegen that Adenauer appealed. In a letter dated 17 April, he told Herwegen that he had been advised not to go back to Cologne, and that he needed bodily and spiritual recuperation, which he would not be able to find in a hotel. 'Besides,' he added (perhaps not wholly tactfully), 'it would not be too far from Cologne.' It seems that geographical convenience was for Adenauer at the time on a par with spiritual refreshment. Be that as it may, he asked Herwegen if he could stay for 'one to two months' at Maria Laach.[6] Herwegen agreed. The agreement achieved, on 19 April Adenauer and Gussi took the overnight train from Berlin across the Rhine at Düsseldorf to Neuss. From there they were driven in a car provided by Pferdmenges –

carefully skirting Cologne – down towards Koblenz and to the abbey which was to be his new home.

Maria Laach lies some twenty kilometres to the west of the Rhine, where the volcanic massif of the Eifel descends gently towards the plain leading to the point at which the long and beautiful Mosel joins its majestic parent river at Koblenz. The abbey itself rests on the edge of what was originally a crater but over the centuries became a lake. It is a quiet enough place, with gardens watered by streams which run off the surrounding hills into the rich volcanic soil, and a pond suitably stocked, in the monastic tradition, with old and venerable carp. But, unlike its Benedictine counterparts in France, Maria Laach cannot boast great Gothic beauty. The buildings themselves have their own character: solid and impressive rather than elegant. The large basilica was built in the twelfth century in the severe Romanesque style of the Rhineland, of dark ochre stone roofed with grey slate. Its interior is long, cavernous, penumbral and virtually without ornamentation. Nothing, it seems, had been allowed within it which might attract attention away from the solemnity of the monastic office.

The outbuildings are rather less severe, particularly those constructed for the lay servants who helped the monks in their cultivation of the gardens and the surrounding fields. The monks' cells are, as might be imagined, free of distracting ornament – but not wholly uncomfortable. There is, however, a general air of asceticism about the place, even in the summer when the gardens flower with roses and the sun is bright on the surrounding hills. In short, as is proper, the shadow of the founder of the Order, St Benedict, seems never to be far away.

Abbot Herwegen was the elected head of a community of some forty monks. He was large and bluff in appearance, conservative – and even monarchist – in his political views. In fact, he too had been infected by the sudden wave of enthusiasm which greeted Hitler's new administration in the spring of 1933. If the *Westdeutscher Beobachter* is to be believed, he preached that people and state were united in 'the great Führer, Adolf Hitler' who was 'the father of the nation'.[7] Admittedly, his enthusiasm did not last more than a few months, but it is indicative of the strength of the so-called 'national awakening' of early 1933 that so many otherwise sensible people could speak in such lyrical tones. Nevertheless, and in spite of his current political views, Herwegen was prepared to offer shelter to his old school colleague in his moment of distress. St Benedict would have demanded no less.

Konrad and Gussi Adenauer arrived at Maria Laach on 20 April 1933. They said their farewells at the gate of the monastery. She returned to Cologne and to her children; he moved in to the solitary room which Herwegen had allocated to him. It was a sad moment for both of them. But at least Adenauer could feel that he was now safely within the precinct of a religious house. To be sure, he had known more luxurious accommodation; but, set as it was slightly apart from the main living quarters of the monks, his room was one of reasonable comfort. It was larger than a monastic cell, with a carpet and panelled walls. The furniture, however, was little short of the basic minimum: apart from the bed, the desk and its accompanying chair, there was only a *prie-dieu* by the wall and a small bookcase. It was all very different from his former office in the Cologne City Hall and his home in Max-Bruch-Strasse; but it was what it was, and he had to make do with it.

Equally different was the pace of life, which in a Benedictine monastery moves in a slow and gently undulating rhythm. It revolves around the twin principles of the Order – work and prayer. Much time is spent in silent meditation, to achieve the particular spiritual peace of the contemplative vocation. The Greater Silence is observed between Compline in the evening and breakfast in the morning, and the Lesser Silence during the afternoon. Meals are also eaten in silence, while an appointed monk reads passages from an improving book or from the Rule of St Benedict. The high points are the daily morning Mass and, to a lesser extent, the evening Vespers. In short, it is a life which seems on occasions to be closer to the next world than to this. But it was this rhythm to which the former almost hyperactive Mayor of Cologne had to adjust.

It was far from easy. At first, Adenauer found the long periods of lonely silence difficult to endure. He was still interested in the politics of the day, and the regular and repetitive monastic offices were of little relevance to the excitement of the world which he had known. True, he attended most of the daily offices – the early Matins at 5am was altogether too demanding – but then only sitting in the organ loft where he would not be seen. He was free to walk in the gardens as he wished, but was advised that he should not wander outside the precinct of the abbey. In this constricted and otherworldly atmosphere Adenauer found it difficult to settle down. He wrote letters – many of them. In particular, he wrote, and sent flowers, to Gussi, who replied in the most affectionate terms. She wrote about events and gossip in Cologne. He heard from her how upset she was that Benedikt

Schmittmann had been taken into custody, that his wife Ella was hardly allowed to speak freely, and that the Schmittmann house was under constant guard. He was worried about money, and wrote again to Dannie Heineman telling him so – and pestered Gussi to hear whether Heineman had been in contact at all. But a few days later, on 16 May, he was writing to Dora Pferdmenges about German foreign policy and how disturbing it all was.

Apart from writing letters, walking around the gardens and attending the offices and the daily Mass, there was little for Adenauer to do other than read. Here there was another adjustment to be made. In his previous active life, his reading, in so far as it was not confined to official papers, was of what his son has called 'thrillers',[8] in other words detective novels for which little intellectual effort was required. He never had been – nor would he ever be – in any sense what the world would call an 'intellectual'. Philosophy passed him by. Metaphysics, political theory, abstract theology – all these were of little interest.

The difficulty was that it was precisely books of that sort which were in the library of the abbey. Detective novels were not part of monastic study. Adenauer was therefore reduced, if that is the right word, to reading literature of a serious nature, for the most part works of history or theology. As it happened, there were books which he could read with something near to enthusiasm. The life of Cavour, for instance, was one; and of particular interest, given the collection of paintings which he had acquired during his time at his home in Max-Bruch-Strasse, were books about the history of painting. He made it a task, for instance, to study the life of Rembrandt.

But by far his most important reading, in the context of his future political life, were the two Papal Encyclicals *Rerum Novarum* and *Quadragesimo Anno*. These were the two great Encyclicals which defined the attitude of the Roman Catholic Church to the social and political problems of the day. Certainly, neither of them make easy reading, but Adenauer had plenty of time at his disposal, and could afford to spend it studying the two documents in detail. This he did; and it is no exaggeration to say that he found in them both an echo of what, as a Catholic, he instinctively felt and also a theoretical and authoritative underpinning to the practical policies which he was to espouse in the future.

Rerum Novarum, On the Condition of the Working Classes was published by Pope Leo XIII in 1891.[9] As its title implies, it addresses the problems of the industrialised world of its time, and offers a Christian solution to them. The

Introduction is entitled 'The Worsening Condition of the Workers', and sets the tone for the whole Encyclical: one of sympathy with the 'plight' of those at the bottom of the social scale, who are 'tossed about helplessly and disastrously in conditions of pitiable and undeserved misery'.[10]

Somewhat surprisingly, however, Part I of the Encyclical, instead of out-lining the facts and reviewing possible remedies, launches immediately into a fierce attack on 'Socialism', which argues 'that the remedy for this evil is the abolition of private property'. This notion is condemned outright. There is then a parallel defence of private property as 'a right which a man receives from nature'; and, finally, an assertion that 'there is no case for introducing the providence of the state . . . Before the state came into existence, man had already received from nature the right to make provision for his life and liveli-hood.'[11]

But the prominence given to the themes of Part I leaves the Encyclical in an ambiguous position. 'Socialism' is to be shunned; the role of the state is to be minimal (later to be defined as only helping those who are destitute); private property is the natural order. Yet it is precisely the rise of 'a tiny group of extravagantly rich men able to lay upon a great multitude of unpropertied workers a yoke little better than slavery itself' which Leo defines as the evil which he is trying to remedy.[12]

Part II of the Encyclical is therefore devoted to an attempt to resolve this dilemma. Leo's answer is contained in four principles. The first is that the Church has an active role to play in the resolution of class conflict. By call-ing constantly on all classes to remember 'the duties they owe to each other', the Church can help to calm the conflict.[13] Moreover, the Church is not only concerned with the care of souls. 'She wants expressly to see the unpropertied workers emerge from their great poverty and better their con-dition.'[14] The second is that the state should devote itself to providing good general administration, minimising the need for intervention to cases of help for the poor. 'Rich people can use their wealth to protect them-selves . . . but the mass of the poor have nothing with which to defend themselves and have to depend above all on the protection of the state.'[15] The third is the obligation of the workers themselves. They should aim at ending their proletarian condition through solidarity and responsible action. 'Christian workers can form their own [associations] and, with united strength, free themselves courageously from . . . injustice and intol-erable oppression.'[16] Fourth, and last, 'wealthy owners of the means of production and employers must be mindful of their duties'. But in the end, the Encyclical concludes, 'religion alone is able totally to eradicate the evil . . . all men must be persuaded that the first thing they must do is to renew Christian morals'.

If the conclusion seems lame, it is not difficult to see why. The dilemma of reconciling the defence of private property and initiative with sympathy for the plight of its victims seems to have proved insoluble. Furthermore, Leo's Encyclical, although much studied in theological colleges, turned out to have little practical effect. Indeed, the 'condition of the workers' could even be said to have deteriorated over the following decades. This being so, a further effort was therefore made by Pope Pius XI in his Encyclical *Quadragesimo Anno, On Reconstruction of the Social Order*, published in May 1931.

Quadragesimo Anno has a tone altogether different from *Rerum Novarum*. The title itself (translated, vulgarly perhaps, as 'Forty Years On') indicates the content of the Encyclical. Certainly, it starts with a fulsome acknowledgement of Leo XIII's effort, occupying several pages ('The Apostolic voice did not thunder forth in vain'). But it then slips into a different mode: '. . . and so it happened that the teaching of Leo XIII, so noble and lofty and so utterly new to worldly ears, was held suspect by some, even among Catholics, and to certain ones it even gave offence'.[17]

The Encyclical then goes on politely to demolish many of Leo's conclusions. True, it recognises the impetus that had been given to the foundation of Catholic trade unions, but its general conclusion is that 'certain doubts have arisen concerning the correct meaning of some parts of Leo's Encyclical or conclusions to be deduced therefrom, which doubts in turn have even among Catholics given rise to controversies that are not always peaceful'.[18] In other words, Leo had got much of it wrong.

Pius XI was concerned to correct Leo's errors. He first of all asserts the Church's authority over social and economic matters: 'The deposit of truth that God committed to Us and the grave duty of disseminating and interpreting the whole moral law, and of urging it in season and out of season, bring under and subject to Our supreme jurisdiction not only social order but economic activities themselves.'[19] He then goes on to amend Leo's defence of private property by asserting that the right of property is 'social and public'.[20] Furthermore, 'public authority, under the guiding light always of the natural and divine law, can determine more accurately upon consideration of the true requirements of the common good, what is permitted and what is not permitted to owners in the use of their property'.[21] As if that was not enough, Pius XI went on to award the state a much greater role than Leo was prepared to give it. Although the state should delegate as much as possible 'concerns of lesser importance', the purpose would be to allow the state 'more freely, powerfully and effectively [to] do all those things that belong to it alone because it alone can do them: directing, watching, urging, restraining, as occasion requires and necessity demands'.[22] After that, the Encyclical embarks on a detailed analysis of what would nowadays be known as competition policy – complaining that monopoly domination has succeeded free competition.

But it is in the analysis of 'Socialism' – left, in contrast to *Rerum Novarum*, to the end of the Encyclical – that Pius XI agrees wholeheartedly with his predecessor. There is a section entitled 'Changes to Socialism'. In it, the definition is drawn between Communism ('the more violent section') and Socialism ('the more moderate section'). Obviously, Communism is condemned out of hand. Socialism, in its rejection of violence, equally obviously needed more careful treatment. It was a difficult matter, not least because many good Catholics had joined Socialist parties – such as the Social Democrats in Germany. The response, however, was firm. The Encyclical describes this development as 'most lamentable'.[23] 'We have also summoned Communism and Socialism again to judgement and have found all their forms, even the most modified, to wander far from the precepts of the Gospel.' As if that were not enough, Pius states unequivocally that 'Religious socialism, Christian socialism, are contradictory terms; no one can be at the same time a good Catholic and a true socialist'.[24] In other words, Communists and Social Democrats were consigned to the same theological dustbin. The best they could do would be to return 'to the maternal bosom of the Church'.

If the Encyclicals provided the theological basis for Adenauer's politics, there was another quite unrelated and arguably more relaxing product of Adenauer's stay at Maria Laach: his study of its flowers. In his walks in the gardens of the abbey, he applied the same intensive examination of detail to the flowers as he had previously to the documents of the city of Cologne. True, he had always shown an interest in gardening (witness his wooing of Gussi in 1918), but he had never had the time or occasion to look in detail at the way nature could be harnessed in a confined environment. In fact, the whole thing came to him as something of a revelation. 'I have never,' he wrote to Dora Pferdmenges in mid-May, 'been able to watch the entirety of nature as I have here, where I live in the midst of nature.'[25] He went on to write that he was 'moved and shaken by the enormous power which nature has shown in these last six weeks, nearly every day a completely different picture'. The town gardener had suddenly understood the power of nature in the countryside. In particular, of course, he had found in the abbey gardens the old roses, and their cultivated derivatives, of which he became so fond in later life.

Adenauer felt able to write to Dora Pferdmenges in a way which is quite different from his letters to Gussi. Dora's letters to him have not survived, but were, on any reasonable supposition, in similar style. She was entrusted with Adenauer's most serious reflections, not just about past theatrical productions in Cologne or general gossip about shared acquaintance, but about the state of the world, ranging from his sudden perception of the beauties of nature to his views on the current state of Germany. Indeed, it was to Dora that he wrote his first letter from Maria Laach, and it was Dora who was his first visitor there in mid-May.

The background to Adenauer's friendship with Dora Pferdmenges still remains to be unravelled. All that is known about her origins – enquiries are met with deep silence from her descendants – is that Dora was born in Gladbach (now Mönchengladbach); that her maiden name was Brenkes (or Bresges, as recorded on her son's birth certificate); that her family was of Dutch origin; that she met her future husband Robert at a tennis club in Gladbach and, when he was posted to London by his bank in 1905, promptly followed him there. They were married in Gladbach in 1909, and returned to London, where their first child was born in Forest Hill, on the outskirts of London, in October 1910. Robert Pferdmenges was a strict, and, in truth, a rather ponderous Lutheran. Dora, too, was Lutheran, but perhaps less strict (and certainly less ponderous) – given that she had pursued her future husband to London. Needless to say, such behaviour was, in the context of the time, distinctly unusual.

It was perhaps this independence of mind and spirit which appealed to Adenauer. There is no suggestion of impropriety in their relationship and, indeed, Dora was also Gussi's friend. But, whatever the background, Adenauer's letters to Dora from Maria Laach reveal a particularly trusting friendship. For instance, after Gussi had brought him the formal notice of his dismissal on 24 July, in spite of an intervention from her father on his behalf and another visit to Berlin to refute the charge against him, he wrote a long and emotional letter not to Gussi but to Dora. Furthermore, he had written to her, not to Gussi, only a few weeks before about his worry that the Hitler administration would in the end have serious problems with first the Lutheran and then the Catholic churches. Most remarkably, he confided to Dora, in writing, that 'in my view our only salvation is a monarch, a Hohenzollern or as far as I am concerned even Hitler, first as president for life; then comes the next stage. In that way the whole movement would reach calmer waters.'[26]

Quite apart from the trust in Dora not to reveal any of this to the Nazis, the ideas themselves come as something of a shock. That Adenauer in 1933 seemed prepared to consider, and indeed favour, a return to the Wilhelmine Empire is startling enough. What is even more surprising is his belief that Hitler would make an acceptable 'president for life'. To be sure, both ideas have to be seen in the context of the time. Adenauer, like many others, had become disillusioned with the Weimar Republic; therefore a return to pre-Weimar days was a solution preferable to the post-Weimar chaos. Furthermore, Adenauer, again like many others, clearly thought that Hitler was a moderating influence in the Nazi movement rather than its main driving force. Finally, long and lonely hours in a monastery can lead even the most practical mind to bizarre theoretical constructions. In spite of reading the daily newspapers, Adenauer was far removed from the realities of the 'new awakening'. Nevertheless, even with these caveats, the fact that he was prepared not just to think these thoughts but to put them in writing rather than keeping them to himself is a strange revelation of his mental and psychological state at the time.

Visitors to Maria Laach were few and far between. Apart from Dora's visit in May, Gussi (and Dora) came with Paul and Lotte in early June with a picnic – 'it is so expensive [to eat] in the hotel'.[27] Gussi came again in late July, bringing with her his formal notice of dismissal from the mayoralty of Cologne under paragraph 4 of the Law of 7 April on the 'reconstruction of the Civil Service' (celebrated by the *Westdeutscher Beobachter* by the headline 'Adenauer sacked – an unholy era finally at an end'[28]). His lawyer, Friedrich Grimm, spent a week there in the autumn discussing his defence. Gussi came to see him again in October. But beyond that, there was little other than continued correspondence with Gussi, Dora and numerous officials in Berlin about the charge lying against him. What was to begin with 'one or two months' dragged on to a stay through the summer and autumn, and further on into the winter.

Adenauer's presence at Maria Laach had not gone unnoticed. It had indeed been noted in the *Westdeutscher Beobachter* in its edition of 20 August ('the monastery seems like a place of escape'[29]). The paper also noted later, with disapproval, that the city of Cologne had agreed to pay him a monthly pension of just over 1,000 marks, starting on 1 November. But the real difficulty came at Christmas 1933. Adenauer had spent most of the month of December in Berlin, trying, without success, to resolve the joint problems of the charges against him and his consequent financial difficulties. He had tried to see Schacht, by then President of the Reichsbank, and had been refused. He had met Heineman, to discuss the possibilities of a job, but without any response other than sympathetic noises. He had had to stay in another religious house, the Maria Viktoria hospital. All in all, the month had been a depressing waste of time and energy.

Even before his return to Maria Laach he and Gussi had decided to celebrate the festival of Christmas in a grand manner, come what may thereafter. As he recalled later, 'I had been hunted and banned from my home city.'[30] The least they could do was to re-unite the whole family in the way they had in older and happier days. Gussi and the children put up a Christmas tree in a room in a neighbouring hotel. There were few presents, but at least the family was together for the first time after almost nine months apart. But the main event was to be in the basilica of Maria Laach. Invitations had been issued for the High Mass of Christmas Eve. To those who accepted, special entry cards were allocated, since it was meant to be kept private. As it happened, the response was almost overwhelming: the basilica was 'full to overflowing',[31] with visitors from Cologne, Koblenz and other industrial towns in the area. There is no doubt that the response was a clear demonstration of support, not just for the abbey, but for Adenauer himself.

The Mass lasted from 10pm to 2am. The liturgy was sung in full, with 'our beautiful German Christmas hymns'. At the end, everybody went out into the clear night. Snow was lying on the ground, the stars were shining, and 'a great and wonderful stillness lay over the hills and the lake'.[32] All in all, it was a moving event – not least to Adenauer and his family.

But that too did not go unnoticed. Almost immediately, Herwegen was told by the Nazi authorities in Koblenz that Adenauer's presence at Maria

Laach was undesirable, and indeed could be damaging to the monastery itself. For Herwegen a nod was certainly more effective than a mere wink, and he told Adenauer that, for everybody's good, he should now move on. Adenauer accepted Herwegen's decision, but quite where he was to move on to was a difficult problem. He was convinced, probably rightly, that if he returned to Cologne he would be taken without delay into 'protective custody'. Even Bonn and Bad Godesberg had their dangers. In the end, he decided that the safest place for him was Berlin. He therefore left Maria Laach on 8 January 1934 to take up temporary residence in another hospital run by a religious Order, the Franziskus Krankenhaus.

The year 1933 had drawn to its unhappy close. In a letter to Heineman in mid-October Adenauer had summed up his stay in the monastery: 'I have lived this whole time separated from my family, in uncertainty about my family and my future and in an inactivity which is almost no longer bearable . . . I cannot sleep without sleeping pills and then only for a few hours. I am nearly at the end of my powers of resistance. My poor wife is the same; she remains brave, but she is nearly finished . . .'[33] It was certainly in this mood of depression that Adenauer left Maria Laach for Berlin. Nineteen thirty-three had certainly been bad, but the question in his mind was whether 1934 would be any better.

2

THEY START TO CLOSE IN

'Hitler wird keinen seiner früheren Gegner aus den Augen verlieren'

WHEN ADENAUER LEFT Maria Laach for Berlin in early January 1934 he still believed that Hitler's 'revolution', like other revolutions in history, would soon devour itself. As a consequence, he believed that his own return to an active political life would not be long delayed. True, he had been somewhat shaken in this belief by the view of his former Cologne Centre Party colleague Rudolf Amelunxen. In the course of a long walk in the woods on the banks of the Laachersee, Amelunxen had said that Hitler might last at least two years. In response, Adenauer had exclaimed: 'Two years! In two years' time I will be too old to return to politics.'[1] Amelunxen's view was obviously a novel thought, and one which, for understandable reasons, Adenauer was reluctant to accept. In simple terms, the conclusion was clear. If Amelunxen was right, and Hitler stayed in power beyond 1936, Adenauer himself, by then aged sixty, would have no clearly identifiable political future.

It was a difficult conclusion for the still ambitious politician. But one

---

* 'Hitler will let none of his former opponents out of his sight': Adenauer in early July 1934; quoted in P. Weymar, *Adenauer*, p. 175.

thing was clear. Pending the disappearance of the Hitler regime, however long it took, his energies had to be directed elsewhere: to his defence against the Nazi legal attack, to the safety of his wife and children, to his financial position, to the restoration of his own personal reputation, which had been damaged by his dismissal from Cologne, and to his own personal security.

In terms of his own security, Berlin was the obvious place for him to go. In the large city, far from his Rhineland home, he could perhaps remain unnoticed and therefore reasonably safe. Besides, he was still hopeful of finding some sort of job, and was encouraged in this by an offer to his son Konrad of a trainee position in a large Berlin-based firm. Moreover, he was nearer to the seat of power, and perhaps better able to pursue his defence against the charges against him.

Even so, he did not intend to stay there for more than a few weeks. The Franziskus Hospital, although it was another safe haven, could hardly have been said to be a home from home. But, as it turned out, he stayed there throughout the months of January and February. The reason was that during those two months there was something of a break in the clouds. There were indications from Cologne that there was 'no further political interest in pursuing the criminal proceeding'.[2] In Berlin, he tried to find out more, particularly the precise state of his case, but again without success. The Nazi authorities were not going to give him more information than was strictly necessary. His enquiries, both direct and indirect, were met with an uncompromising stone wall.

Early March therefore saw Adenauer back at Maria Laach. Arriving there, he found an unexpected conversion. Abbot Herwegen, previously so enthusiastic about the new regime, had come to realise the dangers of National Socialism, and had declared himself firmly opposed to the Hitler government. But Herwegen's conversion (described oddly by Adenauer as a Wagnerian 'Twilight of the Gods'[3]) had made Adenauer's retreats to the monastery more rather than less dangerous. Maria Laach was now under constant surveillance. Indeed, at one point there was anxiety that it might be closed down altogether. That, and the fact that it was Lent, cold to the marrow, with deep snow and grey skies, made for a depressing stay, and after a few days Adenauer decided to go back to Berlin. As he wrote to Dora Pferdmenges, with something close to bitter irony, 'I will celebrate the anniversary of my "departure from Cologne", 13 March, in Berlin.'[4]

Nevertheless, by the end of March he was back at Maria Laach, this time in a more cheerful frame of mind. He had found a house which might serve as a more comfortable refuge not just for him but for his wife and family as well. It was in the prosperous Berlin suburb of Neubabelsberg, on the south-western side of the Griebnitzsee where the flat terrain merges almost imperceptibly into the old imperial town of Potsdam. There were, as it happened, a number of properties left vacant by Jewish bankers and traders who had wisely decided to emigrate. The owners of the house which Adenauer had finally chosen, Augustastrasse 40, were about to do the same, and, in negotiations, declared themselves happy to see their house rented by a known opponent of the Hitler government. The contract was duly signed for a year's rental at a very reasonable price, and it was agreed that Adenauer and his family would move into the house in May. His hope, of course, was that, once the family was re-united, life could resume a more or less normal course.

The move to Neubabelsberg took place in two stages. Adenauer himself was the advance party, and travelled from Maria Laach to Berlin on 3 May. Gussi, still in the Caritas Hospital at Hohenlind, followed him with her four children two days later. When the family finally arrived, they found a house which was large and well-furnished. There was a substantial garden – sadly neglected over the years – a swimming pool, and enough room for the family to relax in comfort. True, Gussi's children had difficulty in adjusting to their new schools, and Adenauer was still worried about his future. But at least they were all together.

In addition to the reassuring company of a family living under the same roof, there was for Adenauer an immediate further bonus. On 9 June he received a letter from Cardinal Schulte telling him that three days earlier the criminal charges against him had been thrown out by the Cologne court for lack of evidence. It was not wholly unexpected, but it nonetheless came as a great relief; and there was occasion for celebration, which was duly, if modestly, observed. At least one anxiety could be laid to rest.

It was, however, only one anxiety. There was still no sign of a settlement of his financial claims on the city itself, or any recognition that his dismissal from Cologne had been anything other than a political manoeuvre. Furthermore, unless and until a financial settlement could be reached, the family's position would continue to hover on the edge of disaster. Indeed, Adenauer sold some of his pictures and part of the garden in Max-Bruch-Strasse just to keep going. Gussi's jewellery had been stolen – but fortunately it had been insured, and her claim was paid. Heineman sent another 'loan' from Brussels. It was all bits and pieces, but one way or another they managed to scrape along.

To be sure, it was better than Adenauer's previous lonely and precarious life; so much so that he started again to show signs of his old self. Jobs in the household, for instance, were carefully allocated: Adenauer himself looked after the shopping and – above all – getting the garden into some sort of shape; Paul cleaned shoes for the whole family; Lotte did the washing-up; Libet did the dusting; only Georg, now three years old, was relieved from all duties. Pocket money was also carefully calculated – 'one never gets anything for nothing in life', he would say to his children.[5] He helped them with their homework, taught them all to swim (including Georg), and took them for long walks, pointing out, as he went, the wild flowers which they saw on their way. In fact, June 1934 was the first month since Adenauer had left Cologne that he was able to spend time with his family in relative tranquillity.

It was also to be the last for some time. On the final day of the month Hitler struck at one of his closest associates: the leader of the SA, Ernst Röhm. Hitler's strike was harsh, brutal and decisive. That said, and seen in retrospect, it was not without its own political logic. The dispute between Hitler and Röhm had been boiling up over the previous year or so. Hitler had been trying to keep the support of the senior officers of the German armed forces. He wanted to succeed Hindenburg as President of the Reich, and knew perfectly well that he could not afford to offend Hindenburg's generals. Röhm, on the other hand, was a revolutionary. He wanted the SA to take over as the dominant military force in the Reich. Furthermore, he had expected that, on coming to power, Hitler would allocate all high offices to his supporters, of whom Röhm considered himself to be the most faithful. Admittedly, he himself had been rewarded with ministerial office, but his cronies in the SA had been ignored.

Röhm had been deeply offended. Worse still, he had been public in his offence. He accused Hitler of 'associating with the reactionaries', of 'cuddling up to the East Prussian generals', and complained that Hitler was throwing away the 'opportunity . . . to make something new and big that will help us lift the world off its hinges'.[6] Not content with offending Hitler ('Adolf is a swine'[7]), Röhm had also succeeded in offending precisely those senior officers whom Hitler was trying to keep on his side. Finally, Röhm had succeeded in offending Göring with his pretensions and, fatally, offending another close associate of Hitler, Heinrich Himmler, by his boasts that the SA were more powerful than Himmler's SS.

On the night of Saturday 30 June Röhm and other SA leaders were dragged from their beds in Munich and unceremoniously shot that same night in the Stadelheim prison by SS troopers. As was subsequently revealed, the army had provided transport and weapons to the SS for the purpose. The generals had also placed regular army units on alert to intervene if the SA resistance proved too difficult to overcome. What they had perhaps not yet realised was that they were, by that simple action, surrendering the traditional position of the military – that it should stay aloof from politics. Moreover, in their relative innocence they had not realised that the Nazis were using the occasion to get rid of many supposed troublemakers who had no connection at all with the SA. From that time on, the German armed forces were hopelessly compromised – the more so when the Defence Minister General von Blomberg issued an order of the day on the following morning praising Hitler's 'soldierly decision and exemplary courage' in wiping out 'mutineers and traitors'.[8]

In Neubabelsberg it became clear, as early as the morning of 30 June, that something unusual was happening in Berlin. Motorised SS units were seen roaming around at high speed; columns of troopers were marching in the streets. Later on in the evening, in fact, Kurt von Schleicher and his wife, near neighbours of the Adenauers (and innocent of all connection with the SA), were gunned down in their home; Erich Klausener, the leader of Catholic Action and a confidant of Papen, was shot in his office in the Prussian Ministry of the Interior; and every hour there came rumours of further arrests and shootings in Berlin.

It was at about seven o'clock in the evening that a small car arrived in front of Adenauer's house at Augustastrasse 40. A man in civilian clothes got out and rang the bell at the gate. Before anybody could open it he climbed over it and walked straight up to Adenauer, who was in the garden watering his flowers, as was his habit every summer evening. 'Gestapo' was the first word uttered – as the stranger produced his tin badge of identification. After that: 'You're under arrest. Pack your suitcase and follow me at once.' There was nothing much that Adenauer could do. He put down his watering can and the two men walked towards the house, where Gussi was anxiously waiting on the terrace. 'What do you want of my husband?' she asked the Gestapo agent. 'Provisional arrest,' was the reply. When she pressed him further, asking, 'Do you think that my husband will come back soon?', she received an equally evasive reply: 'I fear it will be longer.'[9]

Adenauer did as he was asked. He packed a suitcase, said his quick farewells to a distraught Gussi and the bewildered children, and then left. He still seemed quite calm, telling Gussi that 'there was no need to be worried'.[10] Just before he got into the Gestapo car he gave them another wave from the garden gate. The car drove off into the woods in the direction of Potsdam. After a few minutes, the Gestapo agent asked Adenauer whether he was carrying any weapons. 'At that moment,' Adenauer told his family later, 'I felt that my life was over.'[11] He well knew that he could be taken into the woods at gunpoint and shot 'while attempting to escape'. But the moment passed, and the car drove on. Soon afterwards, however, the family heard shots fired close by. Already in a state of shock, they could only fear the worst. As it turned out, it was the murder of Schleicher and his wife that they heard.

Adenauer spent Saturday night and Sunday locked up with thirty or so other prisoners in a house requisitioned for the purpose by the Gestapo, the prison at Potsdam being already full. On Monday morning he was taken to the Police Headquarters in Potsdam, kept incommunicado for several hours in a small cell, and then interrogated by another Gestapo agent. Gussi in the meanwhile was beside herself with worry. While Adenauer was being held in Potsdam, she decided to go there to find out where he was and what had happened to him. She was met with a brusque response. Nobody would tell her anything, either where he was or what the charge against him was. She returned to Neubabelsberg and told her children that she had no news of their father. Prayer, she thought, was the only possible solution.

But, to everybody's surprise, on Monday evening another car drew up at the gate of the house. It was bringing Adenauer back. He had been freed following a general order from Hitler to release all those arrested during the attack on Röhm and the SA and to cease further harassment of all suspects. He was unhurt and, apart from looking worn out from lack of sleep, seemed in good spirits, and able to tell his relieved family at length what had happened. They in turn hoped that their father would now be left in peace. Adenauer himself was less sanguine. He had now seen the Nazi machine at close quarters. 'Hitler,' he replied, 'will let none of his former opponents out of his sight.'[12]

There is little doubt that Adenauer's experience during what became known as the 'Night of the Long Knives' finally killed off any lingering sympathy he might have had for Hitler and the National Socialist Party. Up until that point, he had clearly found it difficult to take Hitler entirely seriously. Hitler was, after all, a wholly unusual phenomenon, outside the range of Adenauer's previous political experience. Furthermore, the whole of Adenauer's upbringing and education had led him to believe that, whatever the political circumstances of the time, the rule of law would in the end always prevail. This belief had been reinforced by the decision in his favour of the Cologne court; and, even when arrested on 30 June, he had reassured Gussi with the words 'I have done nothing wrong'.[13]

But the events of 30 June to 2 July 1934 had demonstrated conclusively and with ruthless brutality the true nature of Hitler's regime. In particular, the rule of law had been totally disregarded. Röhm, whatever his faults, had not received anything resembling a trial, let alone a fair one. Nor had Klausener, who had been one of Adenauer's Centre Party colleagues. Moreover, the truth about the new order was confirmed when Hindenburg finally died, at the age of eighty-eight, on 1 August. Within the hour Hitler had been proclaimed by the Reichstag as both President and Chancellor with the new title of Führer und Reichskanzler. The armed forces took an oath of loyalty to Hitler in person on the following day.

In the light of all this, not only were Adenauer's eyes finally opened about Hitler and his government but he realised that he himself had to move not just with caution but with the greatest care. His arrest had come as a sudden but intense shock, however coolly he behaved in the event. It was obvious that he was on some kind of Nazi blacklist – not perhaps at the highest level but certainly with those in lower reaches, particularly those who had either been briefed on his reputation or who bore grudges against him. It needed a change of tack; it was no longer any good relying on the rule of law; more political skills were required.

Those political skills were immediately applied. He set himself the task, to which he devoted his attention during the whole month of July and into early August, of establishing his *bona fides* at the highest level in the new Reich. If, he clearly thought, he could do that, and in so doing could salvage his damaged reputation as a German patriot, he might achieve at least freedom from future attack. The result of long hours in his study, and long cogitation while he watered his flowers in his garden, was a detailed letter to Wilhelm Frick, composed in the knowledge that Frick was not only at that time Prussian Minister of the Interior but also a close associate of Hitler himself.

Adenauer's letter to Frick of 10 August 1934 has excited much controversy. In later life, Adenauer was prepared to admit, without going into details, that he had written to Frick on the matter of his pension due from the city of Cologne. As far as it goes, that is all very well. But, whatever the state of Adenauer's memory at the time, the text of the letter does not support his retrospective interpretation. The truth is that, given his new perception of Hitler and the Nazis, he simply wanted to do some sort of deal which would keep him and his family out of any present or future trouble.

His letter to Frick sets out on this path. It starts with a long account of his attitude towards the Nazi Party in Cologne. He quotes the relevant parts of Article 4 of the Law for the Restoration of the Civil Service under which he was dismissed. He then goes on to claim that he was never in breach of the law, on the grounds that a public official's entire political activity has to be considered. There follows an extensive recital of how he had 'always treated the Nazi Party correctly':[14] he had repeatedly opposed ministerial orders and orders from the Centre Party group on Cologne City Council to act against them; he had put sports facilities at their disposal against the orders of the then Prussian Ministry of the Interior, and allowed them to display their swastika banners on city flag-poles for their events (as the city archives would prove); he had for years released city announcements, against ministerial orders, to the *Westdeutscher Beobachter*; and, although he had ordered swastika flags to be removed from the Deutz bridge during the Reichstag elections of 1932, he had allowed similar flags to be put up by city employees in front of the exhibition hall.

The letter goes on, at some length, to rehearse the history of 'separatism'. Adenauer claims that he advised against the signature of the Versailles Treaty; and that in October 1923 there was a French and separatist plot to cut Cologne off from the rest of the Rhineland, to assassinate him or at least to put him up for trial before a Rhenish revolutionary tribunal and have him shot. And so it goes on. The conclusion which Adenauer then asserts is that his characterisation as 'nationally unreliable' under Article 4 is undeserved; he therefore asks that his case be reviewed.

Adenauer's letter to Frick, whatever the interpretations to be put on it by his opponents in the future, was an attempt by a skilled but threatened politician to curry favour with the authorities who quite clearly governed, in the most arbitrary fashion, the lives of himself and his family. Of course, the question which Adenauer's opponents have repeatedly put remains unanswered. If Frick had responded with an offer to restore all his rights, to admit that his dismissal from the mayoralty of Cologne had been a judicial error, to give him the pension rights which he was due, to assure security for his wife and children, but in return had insisted that he joined the Nazi Party, his opponents have suggested that he would have done so.

In the event, Adenauer was not offered the choice. Frick did not bother to answer his letter until early November, and then only with a curt refusal to re-open his case. Indeed, it was possibly while he was waiting for a reply in August that Adenauer received a warning from Herwegen (which in turn was probably a leak from a Catholic source in the Nazi administration in Koblenz) that he was still in danger. According to his son Paul, Adenauer decided that, in the face of this unknown danger, his only sensible course of action was simply to disappear. He accordingly left Berlin 'a hunted fugitive',[15] and went from place to place, not stopping anywhere for more than twenty-four hours. Nobody knew where he was until he finally surfaced on 4 September at a guest-house in Kappel in the Black Forest. By then the danger Herwegen had warned about had apparently passed, since he was joined there by Gussi, and planned to return to Berlin 'by 14 September at the latest'.[16]

But the danger had not passed. In fact, it did not come from Berlin but from Cologne. On his return to Berlin Adenauer received a summons from the Cologne court. He was to attend as a witness in the trial of Anton Brüning, the former director of the Deutsche Bank in Cologne, who had been arraigned on charges of embezzlement. On the face of it, the summons seemed innocent enough. Adenauer had no love for Brüning; he had indeed blamed Brüning for negligent encouragement of his own disastrous speculation of 1929. He was therefore quite prepared to go to Cologne as a witness in Brüning's trial.

Nevertheless, he smelled something of a rat. When he found out that Brüning was claiming that Adenauer had personally received 55,000 marks in return for favours to the Deutsche Bank granted by the city of Cologne, the rat became more apparent. Adenauer immediately got in touch with his two brothers, August, the lawyer, and Hans, the canon of Cologne cathedral, asking them first to find out what was going on and second to ensure that his presence in Cologne would remain undetected by the press.

Hans immediately assured his brother that he was welcome to stay with him as long as he wanted. August went to the chairman of the court to negotiate about the procedure to be adopted. The upshot was that the examination of Adenauer as a witness would take place in Hans's house in the Domplatz. When Adenauer arrived on 23 November, with his usual punctuality, he found in front of him not just the judge of the Cologne court but the State Prosecutor, Brüning himself with his own lawyer, and two officers of the court. There followed what can only be described as an unusual legal process. Instead of an examination of the 'witness', it turned into the examination by the 'witness' of the defendant. In this Adenauer was in his old and experienced legal element. Besides, he had prepared himself in detail, in the knowledge that he had to break Brüning's case.

Adenauer's interrogation of Brüning lasted some six hours. He questioned Brüning repeatedly about the accounting procedures at the Deutsche Bank and the accounts which the bank had held in his name. Subjected to this long and persistent onslaught, Brüning finally buckled. After six hours of hectoring attack, he had had enough. He withdrew his allegation against Adenauer. The whole process then ended in a shambles, with the State Prosecutor shouting at Brüning that his retraction would be the worse for him.

It was hardly a dignified affair. In fact, in legal terms the process was not far short of ludicrous. Of course, the grounds for Brüning's allegation against Adenauer have never been objectively examined, for the simple reason that most of the records have disappeared. All that can be said is it would have been wholly out of character for Adenauer to have accepted any money to which he was not entitled. Certainly, he took all that he was entitled to – down to the last pfennig – but that is a different matter. Nevertheless, Adenauer had to use all his considerable powers of legal and rhetorical experience – and stamina – to get himself off what was a very nasty hook. If Brüning's allegation of financial impropriety had held up, Adenauer knew, as did everybody else present at the event, that he was in for a long period in prison.

But even though Brüning's allegations had been withdrawn, Adenauer was not going to just let the matter go. There were unwelcome press reports. It turned out that the story had been leaked to the press in Cologne and Berlin, who had reported it with a distinct anti-Adenauer slant. (The *Berliner Tageblatt*, for example, published its version under the headline 'Adenauer's financial affairs'.[17]) Immediately he saw the reports, Adenauer wrote to the court from Maria Laach with complaints on four counts against the press, and asking the court to ensure that they were corrected. He followed his letter up on his return to Neubabelsberg with a further letter to the editor of the *Kölnische Zeitung* when the paper repeated its errors a week later; and he went further, pointing out that he had instructed his brother August 'to be in touch with you'.[18]

Adenauer was understandably angry about the whole Brüning affair. Indeed, he only seems to have cooled down by the end of the year. But, the Brüning affair apart, he was still pursuing with vigour his defence against his supposed 'separatism'. He had earlier in the year called in aid Julian Piggott, who had duly produced a 'statement' in April certifying that Adenauer had 'never shown the slightest interest . . . in the separatist movement'[19] – although Piggott was careful enough to point out that he had left Cologne in February 1925 (and had not therefore heard Adenauer's 1926 rhetorical onslaught on the British occupiers).

Furthermore, in January 1935, Adenauer was in touch with General (by then Sir Sidney) Clive, and, indeed, met him briefly in Berlin. Clive too produced a memorandum of support, stating that during his period as military Governor of Cologne in late 1918 and 1919 Adenauer had steered a perfectly proper course. Clive followed this up with a letter to the German ambassador in London, who in turn reported the matter, at Clive's request, to the Foreign Ministry in Berlin. Other British officials, who had heard Adenauer in 1926, were apparently – and unsurprisingly – not asked for support; nor, for obvious reasons, was there any request for support from any of the French participants in the events of the 1920s.

Whatever their different degrees of enthusiasm, none of these messages of support had any evident effect. By early 1935, it is clear that Adenauer was fighting what amounted to a lone battle. If the truth be told, nobody was any longer particularly interested in what happened to him. Time and events had moved on. But the next question was whether his presence in Berlin served any useful purpose and, in particular, whether the year's lease on the house in Neubabelsberg should be renewed.

At the beginning of March, Gussi's father had picked up a rumour that she was moving back to the Rhineland and asked whether they 'had already found a new home'.[20] The decision had, in fact, already been made. Adenauer had asked Josef Giesen, who had been in charge of the Cologne gardens when Adenauer was mayor, to keep his eye open for a suitable Rhineland property. He responded with one or two ideas, whereupon Adenauer and Gussi went what would now be known as 'house-hunting'. They stayed at obscure villages — Stadtwaldgürtel and Plittersdorf — before arriving at the Abbey of the Holy Cross at Herstelle for a few days' rest.

By then the new home had already been chosen. It had been Max, Emma's second son, who had discovered a house in the village of Rhöndorf, on the eastern side of the Rhine where the hills of the Siebengebirge fall towards the river. The house — Löwenburger Strasse 76 — was 'very small and modest',[21] but it had enough space to accommodate the family, and, above all, it was cheap. It had a good view across the Rhine towards the distant Eifel, which was its main attraction, but it was, in truth, shabby and run-down; it was also almost permanently in shade, and damp from the stream that ran down from the hill behind.

The Adenauers moved from Berlin to Rhöndorf, with a few pauses on the way, in April 1935. They were recognised and well received by their new neighbours in the village. Indeed, they might well have thought that, what-ever the disadvantages of the house, they were now safe from further intrusion from Nazi authorities. As Adenauer wrote to Dora Pferdmenges on 5 May 1935, 'The wonderful spring compensates us all for the past weeks. We are fairly well installed; there is much in the house we must get used to; but we are rooted in nature and that is frankly enchanting.'[22]

It almost hardly needs to be said, but Adenauer's move to Rhöndorf had been carefully tracked. Whatever he and Gussi might have thought, their troubles were far from over. Within three months they were to find out how and why.

3

HE NO LONGER MATTERS

'Ich will versuchen, in Maria Laach zuerst mein Inneres, mein religiöses Gleichgewicht wiederzufinden . . .'*

ON 21 MAY 1935 a senior official of the Cologne Gestapo wrote to a subordinate official in Siegburg. Cologne, he said, had been informed by the Potsdam Gestapo that the Adenauer family had been signed off to move from Neubabelsberg to Rhöndorf (am Rhein), which lay within the Siegburg administrative area. Cologne wanted to know whether Adenauer had arrived there. On the assumption that this was so, the letter went on, it was no longer necessary to watch his mail, since his mail hitherto had revealed no trace of 'separatist' activity. Nevertheless, 'he should be kept under confidential surveillance, to establish clearly whether he is engaged in any occupation and [if so] who his associates are'.[1]

None of this, of course, was known to Adenauer. He probably did not know that his mail had previously been watched in Neubabelsberg, but he may have suspected that it might be watched in his new home in Rhöndorf. All that can be said is that there were no more letters to Dora Pferdmenges

---

* 'I want to try in Maria Laach first of all to find again my inner self, my religious equilibrium . . .': Adenauer to his wife, 29 August 1935, AiDR, p. 264.

and others commenting on events or the government policy of the day. For instance, when Gussi visited her parents in Tübingen in mid-June, he wrote to her what for him was a chatty letter; about the family, how he had seen the Schmittmanns (and what a nice car they had), describing in glowing terms the flowering of the vines on the nearby slopes, and wishing her a few fine days before her return to Rhöndorf. In short, he was being as cautious as he could be.

His letter to Gussi – starting, as usual, with 'Dear wife' and ending 'Your husband' – was at least some indication that, at least as far as the Adenauer family was concerned, all was quiet and peaceful. But the peace and quiet were not to last for long. It so happened that each year, then as now, Rhineland villages had annual celebrations, sometimes related to a particular Catholic saint whom the village in question venerated, and sometimes related to nothing in particular. In these *Kirmessen* (perhaps best, but inadequately, translated as 'fairs') there were parades; flags were waved; bands played; songs were sung; and the villagers came out to enjoy themselves – and drink. To be sure, the music at such an event was not perhaps of the highest quality, and probably too much was drunk, but the whole thing was jolly and, on the whole, good-tempered. All in all, the annual village fair was a bit of harmless Rhineland fun, and, after an appropriate interval for recuperation, everybody felt better for it.

In Rhöndorf the date of the annual fair in 1935 was 8 July. As part of the fair there was a ceremony, again particular to the Rhineland, which involved waving a flag and saluting it to the accompaniment of loud music from a band. In the Rhöndorf fair of that year the main performers were an enthusiastic group known as the Association of Young Marksmen; and they were aided in their efforts by the – admittedly uncertain – music of the band of the Bad Honnef Fire Brigade. As part of the whole event, the Young Marksmen had asked Adenauer if they could perform the flag ceremony and serenade him and Gussi in their garden.

At first, Adenauer was reluctant to agree, since for obvious reasons he had no desire to draw attention to himself. But in the end he conceded, largely for the sake of the children. After all, there was not much else by way of amusement for them in Rhöndorf. In the late Sunday afternoon of 8 July, therefore, the Young Marksmen duly turned up with the Fire Brigade band (complete with helmets, a bass drum and an unwieldy tuba), gathered in a semi-circle in front of the Adenauers, and proceeded with their flag ceremony. By way of encore, as it were, the band played Hitler's favourite, the Badenweiler March.

The scene was observed by a member of a group of Nazi activists from Honnef – perhaps even hiding behind a hedge for the purpose. The rest of the group were immediately alerted, and they equally promptly reported the matter to the head of the Nazi Party in Siegburg. He, in his turn, protested to the Kreisleiter in charge of the Siegburg administrative area. By that time, what had been a short and cheerful ceremony performed by not more than twenty young men had been blown up into a flagrant anti-Nazi parade. The Association of Young Marksmen and the Honnef Fire Brigade were considered to be hotbeds of anti-Hitler resistance. Furthermore, the Fire Brigade band had played the Badenweiler March – which was forbidden. As final proof of the unpatriotic nature of the event, it was reported that Adenauer had 'donated 80 marks and 100 bottles of wine' for the occasion.[2] The party in Siegburg demanded an immediate investigation of what they considered to be a determined and provocative unpatriotic demonstration. Understandably, the Siegburg Kreisleiter complied with the demand, and required a full report from the Mayor of Bad Honnef.

The Nazis in Honnef and Siegburg clearly thought that they had smoked Adenauer out as an active resister to the new patriotism. But the police report from Honnef, when it came on 29 July, proved to be something of a disappointment. The sergeant in charge, who had been specifically detailed by the mayor for the purpose, wrote that he had made exhaustive enquiries. The fair, he pointed out, had taken place annually for a hundred years. The Young Marksmen and the Fire Brigade band had had an active and exhausting afternoon prior to the event in question. They had performed their flag ceremony on several occasions during the day – for instance, in front of the Hotels Wolkenburg, Bellevue and Löwenburg – before arriving at Adenauer's house. Moreover, the Fire Brigade band had not known that playing the Badenweiler March was forbidden. 'I myself,' he modestly adds, 'had no knowledge of this prohibition.'[3] Besides, it appeared that the Badenweiler March had been played in the village many times during the day, and at the Adenauers' house at Frau Adenauer's request.

As the police sergeant pointed out with some delicacy, there was really nothing in it. The episode was no more than a small part of an annual event without any political significance. The allegation that Adenauer had contributed 80 marks and 100 bottles of wine was, given Adenauer's parsimonious nature, little more than idiotic. In fact, Adenauer gave no more than 10 marks and, in typical fashion, no more than one – carefully measured, no doubt – glass of wine to each participant, as was the custom. He himself drank a toast to the flag 'but did not make a speech'.[4]

Nevertheless, however absurd the allegations, and however honest the report of the Honnef police sergeant, the Kreisleiter in Siegburg refused to accept defeat. The police had not reported in the way he wanted; he therefore simply ignored their report. A further inquiry was launched. This time there were two days of interrogations. But the second enquiry produced the same result as the first. Needless to say, the Kreisleiter ignored that as well. On no evidence whatsoever, he asked the Provincial Governor in Cologne to expel Adenauer from the administrative area within his jurisdiction. The Governor acceded to his request, and in an order, dated 10 August, required Adenauer to leave the Cologne administrative area within ten days. Failure to comply would incur a fine and, 'if need be', a period of 'protective custody'.[5] No grounds for the order were given.

A policeman from Honnef delivered the order to Adenauer on the morning of 14 August. In doing so, he said that the Honnef police had received a second order from the Provincial Governor instructing them to make sure that the order expelling Adenauer from the Cologne area was properly complied with. 'The order,' Adenauer wrote, 'hits me extraordinarily hard.'[6] He had taken the house in Rhöndorf for a year but had only been in it for three months; he would lose money if forced to move; his children were at schools in Honnef, and any change would damage their educational progress; he was going regularly to a dentist in Bonn who was the only one who could understand the irregular structure of his mouth which had been the result of his motor accident of 1917; in short, his whole life was going to be yet again disrupted, and for no apparent reason.

From the evidence available, at this point Adenauer may have been starting to break. The continued and random attacks on him were taking their toll. Nevertheless, in compliance with the expulsion order, he packed his bags yet again and on 19 August left Rhöndorf and his family to seek solace at Maria Laach. Even so, the now familiar silence of the monastery failed to restore his spirits. His letters to Gussi in Rhöndorf tell the story. Rather than chatty, they show clear signs of deep depression. He even tries to justify himself to his own wife, who had been unfailingly loyal and affectionate. He wrote that he was deeply hurt that he should have been thought to be unpatriotic, since he had wished, since his dismissal from Cologne, to be 'far removed from politics';[7] he could not sleep, and if he did he was plagued with nightmares; he was consumed with worry about the future; he was even struggling every day to maintain 'his faith in God';[8] he thought he should go to a sanatorium, but felt that, before paying attention to his body, he should get himself into some sort of reasonable mental shape.

Things only got worse when his brother August reported on a meeting he had had with the Provincial Governor, Rudolf Diels. As a *Justizrat* still practising in Cologne (and therefore, however unwillingly, a member of the Nazi Party), August had sought and obtained an audience with Diels. It had not been a success. Diels had told August that there was nothing further that he could do. When August had insisted that Adenauer should have his rights, Diels, according to August's report of 29 August, just 'laughed'.[9]

By that time, and on receipt of his brother's report, Adenauer was showing all the signs of teetering on the edge of a breakdown – his 'nerves are suffering under these constant attacks'.[10] He was indecisive; his letters rambled, almost to the point of incoherence. Perhaps, he thought, his expulsion order would be lifted in a few weeks; perhaps it would not. He did not know where to go; perhaps two more weeks at Maria Laach and then to a sanatorium; but 'what I will do then', he wrote to his mother- and father-in-law in Tübingen, 'I do not know.'[11]

In the event, Gussi was worried enough to take her husband to the Kurhaus St Elisabeth in the Black Forest resort town of Freudenstadt, where they both registered on 19 September. As it happened, his wife was up to the task of averting what looked to be a serious nervous crisis. The air was healthy; there were long, peaceful walks, and gentle conversations; and in their three weeks together there Gussi seems to have managed to calm her husband down, and even to have restored something of his faith in himself.

Nevertheless, Freudenstadt was a summer resort. As winter approached, they both knew that Adenauer had to find somewhere else to rest his head. Even if his appeals for the expulsion order to be lifted had succeeded, he knew that Cologne was out of the question. Apart from the danger, the house in Max-Bruch-Strasse had been put under official administration by the Cologne court for failure to pay taxes due. The only option was Rhöndorf, which, of course, he would have been only too happy to accept. But his appeal had failed. Gussi could go back to Rhöndorf, as indeed she did, to look after the children. For him, the problem remained. Maria Laach was no longer a possibility, as Herwegen himself was under suspicion and Adenauer's presence there would be an embarrassment – 'which I well understand'.[12] They had to start looking again. Finally, they found a rest house for Catholic priests in the little village of Unkel, on the right bank of the Rhine and some twelve kilometres south of Rhöndorf.

For the casual summer visitor, Unkel am Rhein is an attractive enough place. It is typical of many Rhineland villages, with its half-timbered houses, old archways bearing the coats of arms of a forgotten nobility, and narrow streets wandering here and there without any particularly apparent purpose. In the high summer months it is full of flowers, and altogether pleasant and colourful. But its misfortune is that it lies in the shadow of the Siebengebirge, and, as the sun drops in the late summer and autumn, it becomes dark and gloomy. When Adenauer arrived there, the sun was already dipping early in the afternoon behind the surrounding hills. He could only look forward to shorter days, withering flowers, and autumn mists. It was a bleak prospect. Nevertheless, for him Unkel had two clear advantages: it was not far from Rhöndorf, and it was outside the Cologne administrative area. Indeed, Unkel was to be his home for ten long months.

The Pax Home, as it was called, was in use mainly during spring and summer for priests who were either convalescing from illness or had nowhere else to go for a holiday. As such, it was familiar territory to Adenauer, who had spent so much time at Maria Laach. The Home itself was a large house directly overlooking the river. It was owned by the Pax Society but managed by nuns of the Sisters of the Heart of Jesus, who provided the simple food common to such establishments – no doubt nourishing but far from exciting. There were some twenty-five rooms, a chapel (with three altars for the residing priests to say their daily Mass), a spacious dining room, several sitting rooms, and a small library with a stock of religious books. But in autumn and winter it was little used, not least because the climate in the Rhine valley is unhealthy, with constant rain and with the river frequently shrouded in a cold grey mist. As a result, the Home when Adenauer moved in on 24 October was gaunt and empty.

Adenauer was allocated one of the best rooms, a corner room on the first floor of the house. Its main feature was a large window. The view across the Rhine, and of the little island of Nonnenwerth, was certainly impressive. But the room could hardly be said to have been luxuriously furnished: a bed, a bedside table, a wardrobe, a cupboard, and a small table with two upright chairs. Furthermore, apart from staring at the view or reading religious books, there was absolutely nothing to do.

Adenauer's stay in Unkel during the late autumn of 1935, as he himself later said, was one of the lowest points in his life. True, his most serious nervous crisis had been averted in his three weeks with Gussi in Freudenstadt. Nevertheless, in Unkel he was living in almost total isolation, without anybody to talk to, throughout the grey Rhineland autumn and with the prospect of winter ahead. Certainly, there were daily visits from Rhöndorf, either by Gussi or his son Paul, but these entailed long bicycle journeys in the rain and on muddy roads, the autumn of 1935 being exceptionally wet. Moreover, the visits could not last long since the return journey had to be completed before dark.

Beyond that, there was no more than the daily walk along the bank of the Rhine. A car would have served no purpose. There was nowhere particular to go and, besides, he had never learned to drive. Many years later, Adenauer told Josef Giesen how in November 1935 the feeling of frustration nearly broke his spirit. 'He was sixty years old,' Giesen recalled him saying, 'without office, without an objective, and his future seemed hopelessly dark.'[13] It is little wonder that his son Max, on one of his visits, found his father 'in tears'.[14]

To be sure, there were a few diversions. When Lotte developed a bad throat infection, he applied for leave to go to her. His application was refused; but he was, as some sort of compensation, allowed to spend three days (but no more than three days) with his family in Rhöndorf at Christmas. Next, on 5 January 1936, Adenauer, Gussi and Ria were taken for a drive by a relatively new acquaintance: a young man by the name of Paul Franken, at that time, and significantly, the leader of the Confederation of Catholic Student Associations of Germany. Franken drove them along the valley of the Mosel to Cochem, where they had lunch to celebrate Adenauer's sixtieth birthday. They all went on to spend the afternoon with Herwegen at Maria Laach.

But these were only temporary diversions from the tedium of life at Unkel. The first real break only came at the beginning of February. Adenauer realised that he had to get away. He therefore decided to go to Berlin. It was, however, not just a casual trip; he was going with a purpose. It was, in truth, the first real purpose he had had for many months.

In his early life, Adenauer had considered himself to be something of a dab hand as an inventor. He had, after all, studied physics at school, and had seen no reason why he should not put what he had learned to practical effect. Up until 1908 he had toyed with one or two ideas ('The Elimination of Dust Generated by Automobiles', 'Reactive Steam Engines', 'Improved Cylinders for Vehicles Powered by Steam', and so on), but had given them up when his job in Cologne occupied all his time and energy. In 1935, having nothing else to do, he took them up again. Nowadays, his efforts would no doubt be described as occupational therapy, and perhaps they were. But it would be wrong to think that Adenauer was frivolous in his researches. He genuinely thought (despite continuing scientific evidence to the contrary) that he had a gift for invention and that at some point he would make a great deal of money out of it.

The 'Reactive Steam Engine' was revived. Failing any serious attention to that project, he embarked on the 'Procedure and Installation for the Prevention of the Pollution of the Air by Emissions, Soot etc. from Fireplaces'. This involved closing overhead chimneys and 'connecting them to the sewage system below'.[15] Not content with that, he developed an idea to destroy aphids and slugs by the use of an electrically powered brush. The current in the brush, he thought, 'would kill the animal organism without inflicting appreciable damage to that of the plant'.[16] Indeed, he was so enthusiastic about the brush that he requested a patent for it, prepared practical trials, and rejected outright all objections to his scheme.

The electric brush was, indeed, the reason for Adenauer's trip to Berlin – and, again, to the Franziskus Hospital – in early February 1936. He wanted to persuade an old acquaintance, Fritz Spennrath, who held a senior management position in AEG, that the invention should be taken up commercially. Spennrath duly submitted the project to experts, who were unanimous in their view that it was, to put it bluntly, not much more than fantasy. They were probably right, but Adenauer was not discouraged, and thought that only practical tests would be the proper way to determine the value of his invention. He therefore persevered with it. As always, he was reluctant to admit failure.

Adenauer's visit to Berlin, whatever the merits of the electric brush, had not been a great success. True, he had had the company of his son Konrad. He had also seen another doctor, who pronounced that whatever symptoms he had were due to 'a nervous condition',[17] whatever that meant. But AEG had finally turned his invention down. He therefore wrote to Gussi on

I March that he was going back to Unkel. However, he wrote pointedly, the return journey was not to be direct. He wanted to see Paul Franken again, this time in Bad Ems. The train timetables being what they were, he asked Gussi to pick him up at Niederlahnstein, and from there he would go back to Unkel.

Adenauer arrived back to his room at the Pax Home to hear, a few days later, that Hitler had declared that the conditions of the Locarno Treaty had now been satisfied and that the German Army was moving in to the previously demilitarised west bank of the Rhine. On hearing that there was to be no French challenge, as he said later, he claims to have come to the conclusion that another war was by then 'inevitable'.[18] Such claims, of course, have to be considered with the benefit of hindsight. What is clear, however, is that the re-militarisation of the Rhineland, and the absence of any challenge, gave Hitler's standing in Germany, hitherto still uncertain, an undoubted lift. In Adenauer's later words, '1936 was a decisive year for Hitler's megalomania, for his conviction that, with force, everything can be done'.[19]

In fact, the re-militarisation of the Rhineland had, for Adenauer, an unexpected effect. Only a week or so later, in the general euphoria that ensued, his expulsion order was suddenly rescinded. He was free – to go home to Rhöndorf, and to his wife and family. The weight had at last been lifted. On Easter Saturday, 11 April, he was able in all sincerity to send his best wishes to Herwegen and the Community at Maria Laach for a 'truly happy' Easter.[20] True, he knew that it was not all to be peace and quiet. His house would be, and was, under continued and constant surveillance by the SS. Even when he and Gussi went with their son Paul to Freudenstadt in mid-May for a few weeks they were carefully trailed. In Rhöndorf they were checked whenever they went out.

Nevertheless, whatever the relief, and whatever the suspicions about further 'surveillance', by then Adenauer's political mind was working again. The meeting with Franken at Bad Ems, on the way back from Berlin, had been no accident. Franken, in fact, was trying to organise a network of contacts from the remnants of the old Centre Party to oppose the Hitler government. It was, to say the least, a delicate task, but an obvious contact for him to make was the former Mayor of Cologne. The meeting of the two men at Bad Ems was part of this process. In the summer of 1936, Franken had seemed to be making progress, to the point where, at Bad Ems, he managed to persuade Adenauer to discuss matters with Jakob Kaiser,* a former leader of the Catholic trade unions in the western part of Germany. He had, he said, been in contact with two senior generals, Kurt von Hammerstein-Equord and Werner von Fritsch, both of whom were apparently alarmed by Hitler's adventurism, not least his proposed intervention in the Spanish Civil War.

At some time before the Adenauers' southern German holiday in September 1936, Franken and Kaiser, together with another former Centre Party colleague, Heinrich Körner, arrived on foot at Adenauer's house in Rhöndorf. In order not to attract the attention of the SS, they came at different times and by different routes. When they were all assembled, Adenauer took Kaiser aside, leaving Gussi to entertain Franken and Körner. Adenauer and Kaiser then had a conversation which lasted the best part of three hours. Kaiser explained the substance of the network which had been built up and mentioned the support of the generals. He was, he said, convinced that Hitler could only be overthrown with the help of the leadership of the German armed forces. The objective was to ensure that enough of them would support the idea so as to ensure its success.

The conversation was, from Jakob Kaiser's point of view, a deep disappointment. Adenauer was far too cautious to engage in doubtful conspiracies. Furthermore, he had known Kaiser in the 1920s and had no great faith in his abilities. If this was not enough, after his arrest in June 1934 he had been confined for a day or so with a number of generals, and his general impression had been that they were both cowardly and stupid. 'Have you ever,' he asked Kaiser, 'seen a general with an intelligent face?'[21] The question, thus put, marked a clear end to the long conversation.

It was also the end of Adenauer's flirtation with Kaiser's improbable efforts to overthrow Hitler. He was far too clever, and also far too vulnerable, to allow his name to be associated with a group which had limited

---

* Kaiser, Jakob (1888–1961): Politician. Born in Hammelburg in the Rhineland. 1906–12: Bookbinder in Nuremberg. 1912: Member of Christian unions. 1924–33: Executive within Christian unions. 1933–45: Stayed in Germany leading underground resistance. 1945: Founder and chairman of CDU in Berlin. 1949: Elected to Bundestag. 1949–57: Minister for German Affairs, and deputy chairman of national CDU. Main competitor to Adenauer from the Christian Socialist wing of the CDU.

credibility and no apparent substance. Kaiser and his two colleagues left Rhöndorf with the view, as Kaiser expressed it, that 'he cannot be counted on'.[22] Adenauer, in turn, went back to his family and to his inventions.

By then, Adenauer had quite clearly come to the conclusion that the resistance movements within Germany, such as they were, would be unable to dislodge Hitler. From this one conclusion there followed two further conclusions, each equally clear: first, and most important, that he should do nothing further which might in any way compromise his own safety and that of his family; and, second, that the only solution of the Hitler problem lay in external intervention. If that meant a war, then war it would be.

There is no doubt that, after the conversation with Jakob Kaiser, Adenauer decided to keep himself to himself, and to devote his time to the solution of his dispute with the city of Cologne and finding a more permanent home in Rhöndorf. There were to be no more flirtations with possible resistance movements. Moreover, he could not abandon his home and live abroad, as others had done and were doing. It was against all his instincts; it would have uprooted Gussi and her children from their homeland; and it would have put Emma's children under political suspicion. The only course of action was to keep quiet – and, above all, out of trouble.

The negotiations with Cologne dragged on into 1937. As long as Riesen was mayor there was little possibility of a settlement. Fortunately for Adenauer, Riesen left the city in early spring, to be replaced by the much more accommodating Karl Georg Schmidt. Adenauer was encouraged enough by this to ask his brother August to raise the whole issue again. Schmidt admitted privately that Adenauer had been badly treated, 'but, of course, officially I could never admit this'.[23] The way was now open for a deal.

It still took time. Negotiations were suspended when Adenauer's brother Hans died in March at the age of sixty-three, and were only resumed after the appropriate period of mourning. Yet Adenauer felt confident enough to attend his brother's funeral in Cologne Cathedral – as the Swiss consul Franz-Rudolph von Weiss pointed out, it was his first public appearance for 'four years'.[24] Negotiations resumed in May, first through the intermediation of lawyers, and then directly between Adenauer and Schmidt on the neutral ground of the town hall in Bonn. Finally, on 28 August, a settlement was reached. Adenauer and Schmidt celebrated with one glass each of Deutscher Sekt.

Schmidt accepted that part of Adenauer's salary had been unlawfully withheld and that he had been denied his full pension rights. Adenauer accepted that he had not paid mortgage interest or taxes when they were due. The upshot was that Adenauer was to receive a capital sum of 153,886 marks and an annual pension of 10,000 marks. The city would take over his house in Max-Bruch-Strasse in return for the cancellation of the mortgage and waiver of the taxes due. All in all, it seems a fair arrangement for both sides, although Adenauer continued to grumble about it.

The deal left Adenauer in a position, at long last, of financial security. But even before the final negotiations Adenauer had felt sure enough of a successful outcome to buy a sizeable plot of land in Rhöndorf, at number 8a Zennigsweg. It was cheap enough, at 50 pfennigs a square metre. As soon as his deal was done, he set about planning and building a new house. It was to be his retirement home. In fact, he was to live there for the next thirty years. His financial future was secure. As a footnote, however, there is no evidence that Heineman's 'loans', which had kept him and his family going for the best part of four years, were ever repaid.

1. The young schoolboy.

2. The first communion.

3. The Abitur class of 1894 (Adenauer seated, third from right).

4. The law student.

. With Emma in 1902.

6. President Ebert visits Cologne in 1924.

7. Hindenburg and Adenauer on presidential visit to Cologne in 1926.

8. Opening the Mülheim Bridge.

). Gussi and family.

10. Adenauer's children (and dog) visit Maria Laach.

11. Exile in Berlin.

12. Brigadier Barraclough.

13. Adenauer's first post-war political speech, 12 May 1946.

14. With Kurt Schumacher and Carlo Schmid.

15. ... with French Foreign Minister Schuman.

16. ... with President Eisenhower.

17. ... with Secretary of State Dulles.

18. Adenauer in Moscow, September 1955.

19. Khrushchev, Bulganin and Adenauer. Bulganin makes a point.

20. Praying …

21. Tending his roses …

22. With his dog, Cäsar …

23. Signature of the Treaty of Rome, 1957.

24. First meeting with de Gaulle, Colombey, September 1958.

25. With David Ben-Gurion in New York, 1960.

26. Rheims Cathedral, 8 July 1962.

27. Adenauer with Kennedy …

28. … and Secretary of State Dean Rusk.

29. De Gaulle and Adenauer embrace after
signing the Franco-German Treaty, 1963.

30. The Chancellor goes on holiday.

31. Adenauer with his successor, Ludwig Erhard.

32. Puzzling over his memoirs.

4

KEEPING OUT OF TROUBLE

*'Ich rate euch, früher zu fahren und zwar ins Ausland. Am besten kommt
ihr gar nicht zurück'*

THERE IS A photograph, taken probably in Rhöndorf in the summer of
1936, of Adenauer, Gussi and four of his children: Konrad, Ria, Paul and
Libet. Like many family groups of the time, it is taken against a conventional
background: a small meadow with trees in the near distance. As such, it is
both dull and flat. Nevertheless, in its own way, it reveals something of the
characters as they were at that particular moment.

Adenauer himself stands at one end of the group, slightly in front of the
others. His look is one of suspicion, with only a feeble attempt at a smile.
His arms are folded across his chest, his eyes narrowed; his face and close-
cropped hair look grey with age and worry; his suit and tie are their
customary dark charcoal, as though he were permanently in mourning.
Furthermore, his stance is one which might be described as aggressive
defence, mingled with just a suggestion of contempt: half sideways to the

---

* 'I would advise you to travel abroad sooner rather than later. It would be best if you didn't
come back at all': Adenauer to the Schmittmanns, summer 1939; quoted in P. Weymar,
Adenauer, p. 192.

camera, his right shoulder, hip and foot pushed slightly forward, as though challenging the photographer. It is a picture of a bitter and unhappy man.

Alongside his father, but just behind and partly obscured by him, is Paul, in a double-breasted jacket and the almost knee-length shorts and long socks which were the fashion of the time for teenage boys, even those who were not in the Hitler Youth (which Paul had managed to avoid). His face is earnest; his smile is perhaps a little forced; and he is looking towards his mother. Gussi stands next to him, her hair by now greying at the edges and with the crinkly permanent wave which was the fashion of the day, dressed in an obviously cheap and rather dowdy long frock, but laughing cheerfully at something Ria is saying. Ria herself comes next in line, and beyond her stands Konrad, as tall as his father and dressed in the same manner, his dark hair now obviously thinning, his right hand tucked uncomfortably into the fold of his double-breasted jacket, the left in his trouser pocket, clearly doing his best to look nonchalant but, on the photographic evidence, not wholly succeeding. At the far end of the line is Libet, gawky in figure and dress, ignoring everybody else and sticking out her tongue at the camera.

The star of the show is undoubtedly Ria. Although she was tall, she had inherited her mother Emma's good looks; and in the photograph her gesture – she is obviously telling a story or a joke – shows a relaxed and stylish charm which neither Gussi nor her children could match. The others are all looking at her, clearly enjoying her performance – apart, that is, from Adenauer himself (eyeing the camera suspiciously) and Libet (playing a schoolgirl prank).

Ria, in fact, had every right to be the main performer on that particular stage. She had the confidence that comes from the knowledge that she was attractive; and her time at Heidelberg had given her a social sophistication which others in her family – particularly her father and stepmother – had found difficult to achieve. But there was a further reason. There was, to use rather old-fashioned language, a man in her life. She was at the time considering marriage to a successful engineer from Mönchengladbach, Walter Reiners. Reiners was by any standards very well off. He was the owner and manager of the company founded by his father, Schlafhorst KG, a manufacturer of textile machinery. He could afford the good things in life, and had apparently no wish to deprive himself of them. Certainly, Ria, throughout her life, was well cared for financially.

Fortunately for her, Adenauer approved of Reiners. He had always admired successful businessmen. Furthermore, he found the prospective addition to his family particularly agreeable since he thought that, with his expertise in engineering, Reiners would be able to help his new father-in-law with his inventions. The parental consent to the daughter's betrothal was duly given. After a suitable period of engagement, Ria's wedding took place in the late summer of the following year: the civil ceremony on 27 August 1937 and the religious ceremony in Maria Laach a few days later. On the whole, Adenauer seemed content enough to see her married – 'she has made a good choice'[1] – although he wrote at the same time that 'it is difficult to give away a daughter'.[2] Ria's wedding, however, had a special significance. However distant the relationship between the two while Ria had been in Heidelberg and Adenauer in Unkel, Ria was the living reminder of Emma. Her leaving her father for her own husband and home was not, in this case, just a daughter exchanging one home for another. It was the severing of the last link with her mother.

Ria's wedding was also significant in another way. At the civil ceremony the official in charge solemnly handed to Ria a copy of Hitler's book *Mein Kampf*. This was the point at which the marriage (and patriotic) oath was to be taken. That done, Ria handed the book to her father. Twenty years later Adenauer could still remember the moment when he braced himself to hold in his hand Hitler's testament. He did so, apparently, without flinching. In fact, there was nothing else he could do. *Mein Kampf* in those days was given to every couple at their wedding.

In fact, this was only one sign of Adenauer's changing tactic towards the Nazis. Certainly, he had decided to lie low. But he had realised that that in itself might not be enough. In other words, he had to make some gesture or gestures which might be approved by the Nazi authorities. In 1936, his name appears on the members' list of the local branch of the NSV (Nationalsozialitische Volkswohlfahrt). The NSV was an organisation founded by the Nazis in 1933 to group together various voluntary organisations (including Caritas and the Red Cross) which had worked in the field of charitable help to the poor. Of course, as the years went by, it had become something of an instrument of social policy – its charity, for instance, did not extend to Jews. But Adenauer, as a mere member of a local branch, could have had no influence there. Then, in 1937, he started to sign his letters, at least all formal letters, with the expression '*mit deutschem Gruss*' ('with German salute'), which was the officially recommended style. All this was no more than an extension of his policy to keep out of trouble. It was as far as he could go, other than to join the Nazi Party itself; and that was a step which he was certainly not prepared to take.

Ria's wedding took place while Adenauer was in the middle of building his new house in Rhöndorf. Although the timing had been fixed well in advance, and could not be changed, the wedding came at an awkward moment, since the construction of the house was at a critical stage. Even the earlier stages had not been without difficulty. Adenauer had asked his brother-in-law, Ernst Zinsser, who was a partner in an architect's firm in Hanover, to draw up plans for the new house in early 1937. These were duly sent to Adenauer on 12 February, were revised in discussion on 13 February, and were submitted to the Honnef town architect on 17 March. They were given official approval, marked '*Baupolizeilich geprüft*' ('approved by the building police'), only on 10 April.[3]

Even before the official approval, however, Adenauer had been negotiating with a number of contractors. It need hardly be said that the negotiations were long and difficult. In the end, Adenauer settled on a Rhineland building firm, Rheinische Baugesellschaft GmbH für Hoch- und Tiefbau, with whom he signed a contract on 1 April. The contract specified payment in instalments of 23,800 marks, on submission of regular accounts and only to start after official approval of the project. The house was to be completed by 1 October 1937; the architect in charge was to be Dr Fritz Wolfgarten from Bad Honnef; and the construction engineer was to be Professor Josef Pirlet.

The project ran into trouble from the start. Adenauer, having nothing else to do, took a proprietorial and detailed interest in the minutiae. For instance, since the house was to be built on a steep hill, and therefore on several levels, Pirlet insisted on a strong retaining wall to protect against subsidence. Adenauer disagreed, on the grounds of extra expense. There were long arguments, but Pirlet won the day — fortunately, since during the construction of the house itself there were two episodes of subsidence which, unless there had been a retaining wall, would have taken the whole construction down the hill and into the valley below.

Furthermore, Adenauer continually changed the specifications. He wanted the terrace in re-enforced concrete, which involved a variation to the original permit, granted on 11 October. He wanted a garage (although he had no car) and received an additional permit for this on 20 October. Finally, he decided at a very late stage to convert an outlying basement into a cellar, ostensibly for storing fruit but designed with thick concrete walls, so that it could be turned in the future into an air-raid shelter, as the building regulations had required in the first place. As these changes of mind were conveyed to the architect, the engineer and further down to the workforce, costs escalated accordingly.

As if all this was not irritating enough for his architect and engineer, Adenauer insisted on going through the accounting returns in the greatest of detail. Lists with quantities of materials purchased, the prices at which they had been purchased, and their dates of delivery were minutely scrutinised. At one point Adenauer went so far as to protest to the builders about the number of nails that had been ordered and delivered – and to make extensive enquiry as to the purpose to which they had been put. Adenauer also disputed at length with his neighbour about the access to the site. He also refused to pay his bills on time if he was dissatisfied. Indeed, one of the painters on the site was so short of cash that he had to discount with a bank his unpaid invoices simply to keep going. The greatest sufferer, however, was the architect Wolfgarten. Even twenty years later he was complaining that Adenauer had not paid him what he was due.

In the end, thanks to Adenauer's changes in the specification and his general meddling in the construction, the building cost a total of 95,000 marks, and was not completed until the end of 1937. However, such was their impatience, the Adenauer family moved in, so the police recorded, on 6 December. To be sure, the place was still something of a shambles – 'the usual depressing appearance' of an incomplete house, Adenauer wrote;[4] workmen were there from early morning until late in the evening, no doubt in a hurry to finish the job in order to avoid the irritating attention of the owner. Fortunately for them, Adenauer was by then intent on laying out his new garden.

The building of the new house, and the laying out of the new garden, had given Adenauer an identifiable and clear task – something which he had not had for many years. It acted as a tonic. He obviously enjoyed arguing with Wolfgarten over his fee, with Pirlet over the construction of the retaining wall, with the contractors over the price and quantity of the materials, and with the workmen generally about the quality of their work. The whole thing had cheered him up. Although by Christmas they had not yet achieved 'the enjoyment of having one's own house',[5] they were settling in well. Gussi had allocated rooms to her four children; others were reserved for Emma's children when they wished to pay a visit; Adenauer's pictures had arrived (in particular a Dutch 'Madonna and Child' and a portrait of King Charles I of England, as well as what Adenauer considered to be his 'Rembrandt', all inherited from Emma); the extra furniture needed was on order and the curtains already made up.

Zennigsweg 8a was the first house that Adenauer could truly claim to be 'his own'. Up until then, he had either been living in rented houses or in Max-Bruch-Strasse in Cologne. There was nothing wrong with renting accommodation; but Adenauer had seen enough uncertainty over the years to wish to be sure of a roof over his and his family's heads, come what may. Max-Bruch-Strasse had been a pleasant enough home, but it was to a large extent a perquisite of the mayoralty of Cologne. Without the job Adenauer could not have afforded to live there. The tenure, to put it simply, was conditional and, as it turned out, not more than short-term.

Adenauer's new house in Rhöndorf gives further hints about the owner's character. It is, to say the least, somewhat spartan in its appearance. More or less rectangular in shape, it has four storeys, the uppermost being reserved initially for servants but subsequently for grandchildren. The second floor is given over to a series of bedrooms, each of them with the main characteristic of the place, the view across the Rhine to the Eifel. The rooms themselves are surprisingly small – there is only one room of size even on the ground floor, the formal drawing room. Other rooms, for instance Adenauer's study, along with the kitchens and dining room at the back of the house facing the hill behind, could quite easily be part of a much smaller building. The entrance hall is narrow, and the front door far from welcoming. Besides, in order to get to it, the visitor has to walk up a long and steep flight of steps from the Zennigsweg. In the lower ground floor there were cellars at the back – without natural light since they were almost part of the steep hill behind – and rooms for the children in front, again with their view over the Rhine.

The decoration of the interior is equally restrained. The furniture is sparse and uncomfortable, with few concessions even to what might have been modernity in the 1930s. The contrast with other Rhineland houses of the time, built indeed in the same period of growing opulence, is very marked. The only concessions to elegance are the drapes which cover many of the walls – particularly upstairs; a handsome three-piece suite which Adenauer had made for what was called the 'music room', and which still survives; and a succession of small wooden pieces of minor religious sculpture which still occupy most of the sharp corners of the interior. St Sturmius, for instance, an eighth-century missionary to southern Germany, stands in the entrance hall, looking – rather disapprovingly – at the front door.

But if the house gives an impression of coldness, perhaps of an occupant who was not particularly interested in his domestic surroundings, the garden and the site itself give quite the opposite impression. The garden is carefully terraced to match the contours of the slope on which the building rests. It surrounds the house, and is planted carefully (particularly with roses) where the sun is most direct and with shade-tolerating shrubs in the areas under the shadow of the hill. Rivulets run off the hill and are diverted here and there to small fountains, giving something of a Mediterranean character to the whole construction. It is perhaps true to say that even in 1937 it was clear that Adenauer was more at ease in his garden than in his house. The garden, after all, was of his own design (although with the advice of Josef Giesen) and, over the years, almost entirely of his own creation; and, although it is somewhat formal, it reveals a certain warmth and delicacy of touch which is wholly missing in the house itself.

Nevertheless, it is the site and the views which command the most attention. Behind is the volcanic outcrop of the Siebengebirge, dominated by the craggy summit of the Drachenfels, easily visible from the terrace of the house. In front, the hill drops sharply towards the village of Rhöndorf. Nowadays, the space of a kilometre or so between Adenauer's house and the Rhine is built up, and the trees carefully manicured. In 1937 the space was empty, and Adenauer had a full view of the mighty Rhine and the Eifel beyond – with the attractive (but architecturally undistinguished) Rhöndorf parish church just visible at the foot of the hill.

When Adenauer and Gussi moved into the house in late 1937, it was with her children only. Emma's children had by then left home. Konrad was well into his career with AEG, travelling from time to time – for instance, to Paris in late November to supervise the audit of AEG's French subsidiary; Max had been invited to visit the United States, where he had spent several months ('on a student's visa'[6]), and was by then looking for a permanent job; and Ria was safely married.

Once they had moved in and settled down, life took on a steady and uneventful rhythm; and there was enough outside help to keep it so. Apart from one maid who lived in, Gussi preferred to recruit her help either from her daughters – each had a 'duty year' – or from Rhöndorf village. It was, after all, cheaper and more convenient, and there was no lack of well-disposed ladies there prepared to earn a few marks, even if it meant a laborious trudge from the village up to the house. The day, of course, was organised around Adenauer's own activities. A bad sleeper, he got up early and wandered around his garden, observing in detail the passing of the seasons and how his plants were faring. Mealtimes were observed punctually, with breakfast and supper on the small terrace adjoining Adenauer's study. Lunch was in the more formal dining room. In the evening, before supper, he worked on his inventions. Indeed, an unannounced visitor in late 1937 was astonished to be told, when he called at the new house, that he could not be admitted because 'between five and six Herr Oberbürgermeister works on his inventions'.[7]

Adenauer's move to his new house seems to have dispersed in large measure the cloud of political suspicion which had hung over him since 1933. On 13 January 1938 he learned that his portrait was to be hung again in the Cologne City Hall. 'What a [great] sign! We are speechless,' wrote his friend Busley on hearing the news.[8] True, few of his old acquaintances from Cologne came to visit him. The exceptions to the rule were the Pferdmenges and the Schmittmanns. But there was a new, although carefully restricted, circle of acquaintance from Bonn and the surrounding villages. Busley, the art historian, and his wife were part of it, as were Adenauer's dentist from Bonn, Johann Vollmar – indeed, the Adenauers and the Vollmars holidayed together in the summer of 1938. The circle was Catholic and, above all, discreet.

The most overt sign of the lifting of the political mist was that Adenauer was able to travel outside Germany. The matter was clearly no longer of importance to the authorities. In January 1938 he and Gussi were invited by the Heinemans to visit Brussels, which they did. Similarly, in July they were on holiday again, with the Vollmars, in Chandolin, their trip arranged by the Swiss Consul Weiss. It was, in fact, an extended holiday, which took them on a six-week tour through Switzerland, staying at Basel, Montreux and finally Lausanne, where again they met the Heinemans. (Of course, meetings with Heineman were not altogether by chance: given the restrictions on foreign exchange transactions which were then in place, it is reasonably certain that

Heineman provided Adenauer with the foreign currency for his long periods abroad.)

All in all, 1938 passed agreeably enough for Adenauer and his family. It was the life of a retired couple. 'In Switzerland it was marvellous,' he wrote to Herwegen on his return.[9] In Rhöndorf the garden was coming on well ('The garden in full bloom!' was Busley's enthusiastic comment[10]); Ria was expecting her first child, and Gussi was looking forward to becoming a step-grandmother. For the moment, it seemed that life was treating Adenauer well.

But the world, and in particular Hitler's Germany, was moving on. Busley records Adenauer in March as being 'very pleased'[11] with what amounted to the annexation of Austria (although the event was presented to the public in rather different terms). In September came the meeting between Hitler and the British Prime Minister Neville Chamberlain in Bad Godesberg, at which Chamberlain agreed to the separation of the Sudetenland from Czechoslovakia and its return to Germany. Many years later Adenauer said that he had been 'shattered by Chamberlain's ignorance of the nature of Hitler and the Nazi Party'.[12] At the time, however, his view was, to say the least, not nearly so clear-cut. For instance, at tea with Busley in Rhöndorf on 9 November 1938, in the wake of the agreement between Hitler, Chamberlain and the French Prime Minister Edouard Daladier at Munich, his view of the international situation was that it was a 'tremendous success for Hitler in the history of Germany . . . smashing of the Versailles Treaty . . . utter failure for Paris and London', and so on.[13]

It is, of course, by no means uncommon for politicians in later years to attribute to themselves in retrospect views which they did not hold at the time. It needs hardly to be said that in such cases it is best to rely on contemporary evidence. The evidence, such as it is, points to two conclusions. It is clear that Adenauer of 1938 disliked both the principles of the Nazis (witness his comments on the Berlin Olympics and the Nuremberg rally of 1936) and their methods. Indeed, that particular dislike had been born of his own personal experience. On the other hand, the evidence also tends to the conclusion that he rather admired Hitler's successes in foreign policy. There is no contemporary record, for instance, of Adenauer's disapproval of the dismemberment of Czechoslovakia (it is only twenty-five years later that he recalled saying to General Hans Günther von Kluge in

January 1939 that it was 'clear madness to . . . imagine that Germany can conquer the whole world'[14]); and he certainly approved of the Austrian *Anschluss*.

It is even harder to know what the Adenauer of 1938 felt about the treatment of German Jews. He must have been aware of what was happening; after all, there was no particular secret about it at the time. The Reichsbürgergesetz of 15 September 1935, which confined the privilege of full citizenship to those of Aryan blood, had been properly published. So, for that matter, had the 'Law for the Protection of German Blood and German Honour', published on the same day, which forbade marriage between Aryan German citizens and German Jews and which made it, and extra-marital relations between Aryans and Jews, punishable by imprisonment. There had been also the principle, laid down by Hitler in a memorandum of August 1936 and subsequently put into a decree, that the Jewish community as a whole should be responsible for any damage done by individual Jews to the German economy, a principle which led to the wholesale expropriation of Jewish foreign exchange holdings.

To be fair, given Adenauer's own troubles of 1935 and 1936, it is reasonable to suppose that these relatively minor pieces of legislation might perhaps have passed him by. But the situation changed suddenly and decisively in 1938. The Aryanisation of Jewish businesses started in earnest in June of that year. Notice was given to Jewish doctors a month later that they would not be allowed to practise beyond October. A similar notice was given to Jewish lawyers in September. Göring then announced in October that Jews must be 'completely removed from the economy'.[15] There followed the dreadful pogrom of Kristallnacht on 9 November, and the subsequent fine imposed on the Jewish community of 1 billion marks for the disturbance caused by the damage to, and looting of, their own property. Finally, promulgated two days later, was the decree on 'Eliminating Jews from Economic Life'.

Taken together, these measures meant that by the end of 1938, German Jews had not only been abused and seen much of their property looted or expropriated, but had been deprived of their basic legal rights and of the means of making a living. At least by then Adenauer must have known about all this – the decrees were published and events such as Kristallnacht were widely reported in both the German and foreign press. Indeed, on that night the synagogues of Cologne were torched. What Adenauer thought about it all is still a mystery. He certainly was not anti-Semitic in personal relationships – in the sense that he had always had Jewish acquaintances, some quite close, in the Cologne business community. But there is no recorded reaction from him on any of the measures taken against the Jews, not even when the Jewish banking house of Sal. Oppenheim changed its name to Pferdmenges in order to carry on business, although Robert Pferdmenges was an old friend of Adenauer's (and one of the few regular visitors to Rhöndorf), or even when a Jewish butcher in Rhöndorf was forced to close.

To be sure, after the Second World War Adenauer fully and explicitly recognised the horrors inflicted on Jews, but by then the whole story had changed with the discovery of the 'Final Solution'. What he felt in 1938 can only be guessed at. As one commentator has put it, 'presumably . . . with the conclusion of the Munich Agreement Adenauer took the view that . . . the system of terror would last until the bitter end, and finally [Germany] would have to carry out a cleansing process by her own efforts, as well as punishing the guilty'.[16] If that is the case, then silence was the only possible reaction. Given the Catholic hierarchy's acceptance of the Hitler regime after the Concordat of 1933, and the fact that the official Vatican view was that Jews were guilty of Deicide, it is perhaps not surprising that Adenauer, whatever disgust he felt at Nazi behaviour, kept his views to himself.

By early 1939, there was much talk of war. In March, Germany demanded from Poland the return of the port of Danzig to the Reich. At the end of the month, Chamberlain offered a Franco-British guarantee to Poland against any aggressive attack. On 3 April Hitler ordered the German Army to make contingency plans for the destruction of the Polish armed forces. On 28 April he made a powerful speech attacking a United States suggestion that Germany might contribute to world peace by guaranteeing the integrity of the states surrounding her.

There was then a pause in what seemed to be an irreversible drift towards war. As Hitler said on 11 August to his High Commissioner in Danzig, Carl Burckhardt, with revealing candour, 'everything I undertake is directed against Russia. If the West is too stupid and too blind to comprehend that, I will be forced to come to an understanding with the Russians, to smash the West, and then, after its defeat, to turn against the Soviet Union with my assembled forces.'[17] Indeed, it turned out as predicted. On 21 August German radio announced that the Soviet Foreign Minister Vyacheslav Molotov* and the German Foreign Minister Joachim von Ribbentrop had signed a non-aggression pact. The following day Hitler said to his senior military commanders: 'Now Poland is in the position in which I wanted her . . . I am only afraid that at the last moment some swine or other will submit to me a plan for mediation.'[18] On I September, German forces invaded Poland.

While all this was going on Adenauer, Gussi, Konrad, Ria and Walter Reiners were on their annual holiday, which started in early July. Adenauer wrote to Heineman from Chandolin on 15 August that they would stay there until the 21st, then go on to Glion, from there 'probably' to Geneva, and from there back home. The length of their stay in Switzerland, he went on, 'is a question of francs' – hinting that Heineman ('dear friend') might send him some more Swiss francs for a 'short extension' of his stay.[19] Heineman duly obliged.

However, it appears that all did not go according to plan. On I September Adenauer and Gussi were stuck in Schinznach bei Olten, just outside Basel. They were then forced to spend a week there, since all trains had been commandeered by the Swiss government for the mobilisation of its armed forces. It was not until 8 September that they were able to cross back into Germany at Bregenz and stay the night at Lindau on Lake Constance – from where they sent a cheerful postcard to the Busleys, noting with particular admiration the onion domes of churches in Lindau, but saying that they were hoping to return to Rhöndorf the following day. It all seemed wholly innocent.

There is, however, another version of Adenauer's movements. In this version, Adenauer invited the Schmittmanns during the summer of 1939 to his house

---

* Molotov, Vyacheslav (1890–1986): Born as Scriabin (he was a distant relation of the composer of that name). Son of a shop assistant. Changed name to Molotov ('The Hammer') at the time of the October Revolution in 1917. Involved in the liquidation of the Mensheviks in Petrograd and subsequently the elimination of the Zinoviev faction in what was by then Leningrad. In 1931 appointed Chairman of the Council of People's Commissars. Responsible for Soviet foreign affairs, with various titles, from 1939 to 1956. Ambassador to Mongolia 1957–61. Never cured a bad stammer, and persisted in wearing ugly *pince-nez*. Trotsky described him as 'mediocrity incarnate'. Others were less complimentary.

in Rhöndorf, and after dinner told them that he was certain that war would break out very soon. 'The moment war breaks out,' he continued, 'Hitler will arrest all political suspects and send them to concentration camps.' Schmittmann was on their list, as was he himself. 'The point is that one mustn't be available at the crucial moment. After a period of waiting for things to settle down, one would probably be able to return without much risk.'[20]

Schmittmann apparently did not take Adenauer's advice. After a holiday in Austria he and his wife returned to Cologne, where he was indeed arrested on the day on which Poland was invaded – 1 September. He was taken to the concentration camp in Sachsenhausen, where he was reported as 'dying of a heart attack' on 13 September. Adenauer, on the other hand, was out of the country at the apparently crucial time, and learned later that his name had been on the list of those to be arrested but had been crossed off by an unknown hand.

The two versions are, of course, incompatible. On the evidence, Adenauer had every intention of returning to Rhöndorf by 1 September, and was only prevented from doing so by Swiss mobilisation and the consequent disruption of the railway timetable. Furthermore, if he had been on the list of suspects to be arrested, seven days would have been neither here nor there. The fact remains that he was not arrested; nor was there any attempt to do so, in spite of his resumption of his normal and regular life in his house in Rhöndorf.

The truth is that Adenauer suspected in the summer of 1939 that war could well be imminent. He had probably worked for some time on the assumption that there would be a war, but Hitler's manouevrings over Poland had led him to conclude that the time was not far off. Furthermore, he was probably aware that Schmittmann was more involved in resistance movements than he was, which was why he referred to Schmittmann as a 'political suspect' and why Schmittmann admitted that he was 'on the Gestapo proscription list'.[21] Under the circumstances it made sense to advise Schmittmann to go abroad – and not return at all.

What made no sense was for Adenauer himself to go abroad and then return to Germany at the crucial moment when war broke out if he had been, as he later claimed, on the 'Gestapo proscription list'. The sensible course of action would have been to stay in Switzerland. Schmittmann ignored his advice – and paid the price. Adenauer, too, ignored his own advice – and was left alone. The conclusion must be that Adenauer by then was not on any proscription list. His tactic of lying low had worked. As far as the Nazis were concerned, Adenauer was no longer any sort of threat.

5

A Quiet War

'Ich finde dass, je älter man wird, desto rätselhafter Welt und
Menschen werden'*

IN THE LITTLE village of Rhöndorf the first few months of the Second
World War passed by in relative calm. True, from time to time there were
food shortages, particularly in the hard winter of 1939–40. Travelling, too,
was difficult. As for the Adenauer family, there were some discomforts, but
no more than might be expected. Konrad had scarlet fever in Berlin – coincidentally only a few weeks after his half-brother Paul in Rhöndorf; Max had
been posted from the east, with the rank of 2nd Lieutenant in the
Panzergrenadiers, and was doing guard duty, without much apparent purpose, on a Rhine bridge near the Dutch frontier, and waiting for further
orders; Ria was still in Mönchengladbach, but was ready 'from day to day' to
move to Rhöndorf with her child if things became too 'uncomfortable'
where she was;[1] and Gussi's children were all at home, going peaceably to
school in Honnef. Adenauer himself, for his part, was working on his inventions, and his garden.

---

* 'I find that the older one becomes the more baffling are the world and its people':
Adenauer to Dora Pferdmenges, 11 January 1941, AiDR, p. 365.

Regrettably, the inventions continued to be a disappointment. 'Now I have invented something wonderful,' he would exclaim from time to time.[2] For instance, he was particularly happy to have 'discovered' a device by which a mirror was perched by a typewriter, so that a secretary could see the text as well as the keys on the machine. All that sounded admirable – until it was explained to him that any competent secretary could type using her eight fingers and two thumbs, without needing to look either at the keyboard or the text in front of her. Other 'inventions', conceived with the same enthusiasm, met the same unhappy fate.

Work in the garden, however, seemed to be less frustrating. Indeed, Adenauer spent a great deal of his time there, even in winter, and continued to do so right through the war. As with his 'inventions', however, there is in his gardening an air of mild and old-fashioned eccentricity. Advancing age, and limited opportunities to allow him to keep active and alert, may have been starting to take their toll. For instance (like others in their time), he insisted on wearing the same pair of gardening trousers long past the moment when they could reasonably have been thrown away. They had to be mended with increasing frequency as they wore out – and as he reiterated his refusal to wear a new, or even a different, pair. In the summer, an old straw hat was brought out, which he wore in the garden to protect his balding head.

All in all, in contrast to his uncompromising, and sometimes fierce and autocratic, demeanour during his period as Mayor of Cologne, it was a gentle and benign Adenauer who saw through the early years of the Second World War. He seemed to have detached himself from the world outside his home, family and a small circle of friends. Even when that world changed suddenly on 10 May 1940, with the German assault on France, Belgium and Holland, Adenauer was on the same day engaged in drafting a letter to the Reich patent office requesting a patent for his new invention, a spray nozzle. Furthermore, on the date that the letter was sent, 31 May, the British Expeditionary Force was in the middle of the desperate evacuation at Dunkirk. (Although Adenauer was not to know it, it was at Dunkirk that his son Max was severely wounded in the neck – so seriously, indeed, that the doctors in the field nearly despaired of his life.) At the time, the garden in Rhöndorf was rejoicing in its own explosion – in the glorious spring sunshine; and Adenauer had to spend almost all his waking moments keeping it in some sort of order. For him, the war was very far away.

Nevertheless, the tone of his letters started to change with the tempo of events. 'Our nights are only disturbed at a distance,' Adenauer wrote to Ria on 6 June. 'The poor people of Bonn, however, have already had two unquiet nights this week. The port of Neuss has been hit with great accuracy ... We have still heard nothing from Max.' He still spends most of the letter telling her about domestic matters – Gussi's hay-fever, the weather (hot and dry), the lack of cherries, the strawberries just starting, the roses flowering, the summer arriving 'with giant strides', but at the end he does revert to the war. 'By September England must be occupied or it will not be possible at all before the spring.'[3]

Adenauer's letter to Ria accurately reflects his mood at the time: he was still taken up with his inventions, the garden and the affairs of the house, but he could not help being fascinated by the march of outside events; and the fact that he was no longer involved certainly irked him. 'I find it extraordinarily difficult,' he had written the previous March, 'to remain mentally fresh and productive while everything that I do is so far removed from my previous life, from "action".'[4] Tending his garden and inventing spray nozzles or slug exterminators was all very well, but there was clearly part of him which felt that there was more to life than doubtful inventions, however much he tried to convince himself that they were of the greatest scientific importance.

To be sure, there were some necessary duties: in late June he went to visit Max, by then recuperating in a hospital in Schwäbisch Gmünd, near Stuttgart; and in October he went to Duisburg for the funeral of Peter Klöckner, his old Cologne ally, who had died at the dignified age of seventy-seven. Then Christmas saw the family coming together again as usual. Konrad came from Berlin; Max, now recovered and engaged to be married to Gisela Klein – 'a very sweet girl' from Cologne[5] – was on leave from his depot at Königsberg; Paul, after passing his Abitur with good marks, was still at home, but was waiting to go into a seminary; and the younger children were on holiday from school. Only Ria and her husband were missing; she had to stay in Mönchengladbach with her child.

It was certainly a pleasant enough reunion; and, with it, 1940 drifted into 1941. On 5 January Adenauer celebrated his sixty-fifth birthday. It was a quiet occasion, as befitted the time, and only his nearest family were there. Indeed, at the age of sixty-five, his thoughts seem to have been turning towards death. 'It is a great comfort to see the miracle of transformation when taking leave of the dead. I have experienced it twice; one never forgets it . . . One longs for the spring and for work in the garden, but this is probably foolish. The spring will probably bring such unrest as to make one yearn for the calm of winter. Yet behind this unrest lies peace; let us trust in it.'[6] Lurking behind those words is without a doubt the perception of mortality.

But it was not all gloom. Life in Zennigsweg 8a, grey and uneventful as it must have been, was at least to some extent enlivened by the presence of two or three French prisoners of war. Adenauer had, in the middle of 1940, applied for the services of POWs, on the grounds that he was a householder (one of the conditions of the application), that he was of pensionable age and that he had to maintain members of his extended family without proper assistance. The request had been granted by the Siegburg authorities, and the French prisoners moved in.

Their tasks were mainly in the garden, and their accommodation was in one of Adenauer's cellars. Surprisingly, supervision was minimal: it seemed to be accepted that the prisoners would not try to escape (they knew that they would be shot on sight if caught) and that Adenauer's cellar was preferable to the insanitary conditions of a prisoner-of-war camp – to which they would return after their allotted period of relative freedom. Adenauer himself was careful to show kindness to the prisoners, as a number of them testified at the end of the war. He was equally careful to make sure that he was reimbursed by the authorities for the expenditure which he had incurred in their upkeep.

The French brought with them, perhaps, a little bit of fun; but, that apart, there was little else to keep everybody amused. Paul entered his seminary, but his journey to the priesthood was to be interrupted by a period of compulsory public work, in lieu of military service, on the island of Sylt, off the North Sea coast. Konrad was moved by AEG to a job in Aachen. Max was duly married in late August 1941, after being sent back from the east before the German attack on Russia in late June and, much to his and his father's relief, put in charge of military administration in Brussels. Lotte, Libet and Georg (known to everybody by his nickname of 'Schorsch') went on holiday to Switzerland – arranged and supervised by the Swiss Consul Weiss, by then known as 'Uncle Toni', but somewhat spoiled by Schorsch's homesickness. In general, however, Adenauer accurately summed it up in a letter in early December: 'About us, I know of hardly any news to report to you.'[7]

Nineteen forty-two was much more eventful. As the German advances in

Russia faltered and the United States became an active belligerent, the effects of the war were more apparent, even in isolated Rhöndorf. The industrial installations of the Rhineland began to suffer heavy bombardment. On 31 May a thousand British bombers raided Cologne. 'The disaster which has hit Cologne,' Adenauer wrote, 'is truly terrifying.' Adenauer's sister Lilli and her husband Willi Suth lost everything, although they themselves were fortunately away at the time. A large area in the financial and industrial districts was demolished – 'dead', as Adenauer put it.[8]

It was following that raid, and subsequent and continuing attacks, that there was a proposal to bring Adenauer into the movement of active resistance to Hitler. In the autumn of 1942 a meeting took place in Cologne under the auspices of a group of Catholic dissidents in the old – but still surviving – Kettelerhaus. Apart from the Provincial of North German Dominicans, Laurentius Siemers, there were present Canon Otto Müller and two laymen, Nikolaus Gross and Karl Arnold,* both Catholics of high standing in the old Centre Party. Once they were assembled, in conditions of the greatest secrecy, they invited their guests to come in. These were Jacob Kaiser, who was already known to them, and a stranger, Dr Karl Friedrich Goerdeler.

In spite of all that has been written about him, Goerdeler is not an easy figure to assess. In some ways, he seemed to have, in full measure, both the good and the bad qualities of his native East Prussia. He was certainly courageous and robust in his views and actions. Born in 1884, he had fought bravely on the eastern front in 1915, and from there he had followed the career of a successful local politician. Politically, he was very right-wing; indeed he was a member of the German National People's Party in the Weimar Republic. This was obviously to the taste of Leipzig, where he was elected mayor in 1930. The record was certainly good; but there was some-

---

* Arnold, Karl (1901–58): Trade unionist and politician. Born in Herrlishöfen in Württemberg. 1920–33: Various posts in Christian union movement. 1933–44: Kept head down, working in business. 1945: One of the founders of the CDU. 1946: Mayor of Düsseldorf. 1947–56: First Minister-President of North Rhine–Westphalia. Christian Socialist, hence on the left wing of the CDU. Intelligent and witty; his early death left a gap.

thing about the man – a leaning towards prevarication and indiscreet boasting – which made him difficult to deal with. His square, hard face, his wide-set eyes and the close-cropped head seemed to inspire fear rather than trust.

Although Goerdeler remained Mayor of Leipzig until 1937 (and was forced to resign only after his protest at the destruction in Leipzig of the statue of the composer Mendelssohn), he was never at ease with the Nazis. Indeed, he was so reactionary that he persistently argued the case for Germany's return to its pre-1914 frontiers and, by extension, a return to the Hohenzollern monarchy. After his resignation as Mayor of Leipzig, he had fallen in with a group of similarly-minded German generals, whose recognised head was the army chief of staff until 1938, Ludwig Beck. Thus was the 'Stauffenberg Plot' born. It was to come to its unhappy climax on 20 July 1944.

At the meeting with the clerics in Cologne, there was a discussion about who might be in charge of the Rhineland once Hitler had departed – in one way or another – an outcome which Goerdeler assured the others would not be long delayed. Lists were drawn up. Needless to say, the name that came top of the list was that of the former Mayor of Cologne, Konrad Adenauer. The meeting discussed the matter at length. In conclusion, Goerdeler was invited to contact Adenauer in Rhöndorf that very day.

This he did; but, downcast, he reported back to the meeting later in the evening that 'Dr Adenauer had refused to receive him'.[9] Adenauer, in truth, wanted none of it. For a start, he had known Goerdeler when they were colleagues on the Prussian Staatsrat before the Nazis came to power, and had not been impressed. Secondly, he knew that Goerdeler was unable to keep his mouth shut – indeed, Goerdeler had let it be known, even in the late 1930s, that he was in touch with certain British and French industrialists with a view to mounting a diplomatic campaign against Hitler. Finally, he had no confidence that generals could do anything other than obey orders; taking the initiative was, in his view, beyond them.

Adenauer told Paul Franken as much in a conversation they had at the home of Adenauer's dentist in Bonn, Josef Vollmar. 'He repeatedly urged me to move with caution,' Franken wrote later, 'since he trusted neither the military nor the civilian leaders of the group, especially Karl Goerdeler . . .'[10] Adenauer reiterated this view to two visitors to Rhöndorf in the autumn of 1943. Of course, his attitude could be interpreted as a convenient way of avoiding all risks, however attractive the invitation and however well-led the conspiracy. Certainly, some have taken this view. As it turned out, however, Adenauer's assessment of Goerdeler, Beck and Jakob Kaiser was right. On the other hand, however much he tried to distance himself from the conspiracy, he was, as it happened, unable to avoid some of the consequences of its failure.

Nineteen forty-three was moving steadily and sadly on. Konrad was married early in the year to Carola Hunold (nicknamed 'Lola'). They had met in Aachen the previous year, but Lola had followed Konrad to Berlin and by then was working as a secretary in the Central Chamber of Auditors. Lola's parents in Aachen, for their part, were opposed to the marriage, on the grounds that Konrad was sixteen years older than Lola, but also on the unspoken grounds that they were worried about the political implications of an association with the Adenauer family – particularly since Konrad carried his father's first name. For his part, when Adenauer heard that his proposed daughter-in-law was called 'Lola' he thought that she must be a circus dancer – or worse.

Nonetheless, a written invitation was issued to 'Lola' to visit her prospective parents-in-law at Rhöndorf. Like all such occasions, it must have been particularly daunting for the twenty-year-old girl from Aachen. Indeed, the visit got off to a bad start. It was normal for the bride-to-be to bring a bunch of flowers for her future mother-in-law. This Lola had omitted to do. However, Adenauer was so obviously and immediately impressed by the young lady that he rescued the situation by surreptitiously stealing a bunch from one of the vases in the house and slipping it to Lola – who promptly, and with great presence of mind, presented them to Gussi. After that, Adenauer's approval of the marriage was only a formality.

Konrad and Lola's honeymoon did not last long. Konrad was soon called up as a Panzergrenadier, but after his initial training was posted to Riga for onward movement to the eastern front. In fact, he was lucky enough to be sent to Norway as an interpreter – since he had learned some Norwegian, and good English, when he had been sent to Oslo by AEG. By May, Adenauer had three sons in the armed forces: Konrad in Riga, Max in France and Paul as a medical orderly with an anti-aircraft battery in Bonn. Furthermore, Lotte had been called to do her period of compulsory public work.

The second major British bombing raid on Cologne took place on the night of 29 June 1943. It was, as Adenauer told his friend Weiss, 'much worse than [the raid of] 30–31 May 1942'. The main hall of the Gürzenich had been destroyed; the Rathaus was in ruins; the whole of Hohe Strasse had been burned down; the cathedral had suffered a direct hit which had destroyed the organ; around the cathedral the railway station, the Domhotel and the Hotel Excelsior were still in flames; the Apostelkirche had been wrecked, along with other churches 'with a history of a thousand years'.[11]

There is no doubt that Adenauer felt deeply about the destruction of Cologne itself. How far, even subconsciously, he blamed the British for destroying his city – British incendiary bombs were in the following October to reduce the house in Max-Bruch-Strasse to ashes – remains an open question. Certainly there were those, even in Britain, who were doubtful about the tactic of carpet-bombing German cities, regardless of the civilian casualties thereby inflicted. On the other hand, even those Germans who protested at the onslaught of the British and American bombers would have been aware of the anger in Britain at the similar onslaught on British cities two years earlier.

Adenauer, of course, was particularly sensitive about his personal achievements in Cologne. As he said in July 1943, just after a visit to the city, 'Just think: I did not recognise it, and I had trouble finding my way about – and Cologne was my life's work. Now that has been destroyed.'[12] Furthermore, the city was in chaos. In the aftermath of the June raid, there were some 100–150,000 people without homes, families whom Adenauer had tried to look after in the years following the First World War. Bad Godesberg, for instance, at that time a small town of some 25,000 inhabitants, suddenly found 2,000 refugees on its doorstep. Rhöndorf expected a similar number at any time. Cologne was no longer a safe place in which to live, and its inhabitants were desperate to escape to the safer countryside. Even the Swiss Consul Weiss took refuge in Rhöndorf, now not just one of Adenauer's acqaintances but one of his neighbours.

At that point there started a process in Zennigsweg 8a which was to continue until the end of the war. Adenauer's female dependents – his wife, daughters, daughters-in-law and their children – were gradually assembled in his house. When the bombing of Berlin increased in intensity, pregnant women were ordered out of the city, and Lola, by then expecting her first child, arrived in Rhöndorf; then came Gisela, Max's wife; Ria was to come later. The house was near to bursting, since Lotte was learning nursing in

Bonn, while living at home; and Libet and Georg were still at school. 'Everyone just moved a little closer together,' Lola recalled, 'and soon every room in the house was filled to capacity' – except, she added, Adenauer's study.[13]

In the event, the family migration to Rhöndorf was not unwelcome. Adenauer felt himself to be in the role of the father of this extended family, and, as such, the protector of the females in his charge. In this role he showed the most affectionate side of his character. There was, of course, no question about who was in charge, but his exercise of authority was benevolent and mild. There were, apparently, hardly any flashes of temper. Everybody was kept busy. Self-sufficiency was the order of the day. Vegetables came from the garden or from trustworthy friends such as Josef Giesen. A ewe was acquired, given, like all her subsequent successors, the name of 'Nelke'. Nelke provided milk, and was shorn in the late summer for her wool; from her wool a yarn was then spun which was used for knitting socks and pullovers. Later in the year she was put to the ram, and the male lambs were duly slaughtered in the following spring, providing much needed fresh meat; and the ewe lambs were kept for their milk and for future breeding.

All this, of course, involved a great deal of work, and Adenauer made sure that it was done to a regular timetable. Even when a visitor came to see one of the family, Adenauer would entertain the guest 'with great patience'[14] in the music room until the work was done and the others were free to join him. But this apparent intrusion was performed with the greatest courtesy. Adenauer, by his upbringing, was always particularly courteous to women, especially the women of his own family. Nor was it just a matter of courtesy. When in late 1943 Lola had her baby in Honnef hospital, Adenauer visited her every day, walking down the hill to the tram since there were no longer any taxis, bringing her milk or preserved fruit – in one instance a jar of marmalade which he had stolen from the family cupboard without anybody's knowledge – and walking back again up the hill to his home. In short, as Lola recalled, 'he was charming and most delightful'.[15] Courtesy, at least in Lola's case, had become kindness – and even love.

By the beginning of 1944 it was clear to Adenauer that Germany was going to lose the war. Since the family had only one resident maid, and since the house was set apart from Rhöndorf village, Adenauer was able to listen without danger to foreign broadcasts – not least the BBC German Service.

Admittedly, the procedure was still dangerous. He had to keep his ear close to the radio, and sat with a blanket over his head. But at least he knew, whatever the German radio might put out, that the eastern front was collapsing, that Italy was to all intents and purposes lost, and that an Allied invasion of France was only a matter of time. Moreover, he had started to think what role he might play when the war was finally over. As a clear sign of this change of mood, by early 1944 he had ceased work on his inventions.

6

'THE WAR IS OVER!'

*'. . . das deutsche Volk von Grund auf zum Frieden zu erziehen'**

THE BEGINNING OF the end of the Third Reich finally came with the hammer blows of the Soviet tanks in the east and the Allied invasion of Normandy in the west in early June 1944. Within Germany itself, more and more people were questioning the purpose of the war, and were fearful of the consequences of defeat. Indeed, it was at that moment that the plot to assassinate Hitler was coming to something near to fruition. But it had been a long time in the planning, and the combination of the length of the gestation period, Goerdeler's loquacity and the large number of people by then privy to the secret had ensured that rumours of an impending military putsch were widespread. Security was accordingly tightened; old lists of suspected enemies of the Reich were dusted down in Gestapo offices all over the country; and one name that was on an old list in the headquarters of the Gestapo in Cologne was that of Konrad Adenauer.

---

* '. . . to educate the German people from the ground up to the idea of peace': Adenauer to Lt-Col. Tuhus and Capt. Emerson, when asked to explain his ambition: Dr Werner Bornheim; diary entry, 16 March 1945; AiDR, p. 434.

After the brave fiasco of the assassination attempt of 20 July, the Gestapo launched an immediate series of investigations – many of them followed by random arrests. On 21 July Adenauer learned by telephone that Josef Giesen had been arrested for 'demoralisation of the troops'. It appeared that a letter he had written to his son, which contained an unwise reference to the successful bombing of the Wesseling refinery near his home in Urfeld ('this time the English have tailored the job to measure'[1]), had been intercepted by the censors. Before being led away by the Gestapo Giesen had managed to whisper to his wife, 'Warn the Adenauers.'[2] This she had done.

In Rhöndorf there was near panic. 'We were all terrified by this news,' Lola recalled.[3] The vegetables and fruit which Giesen had been supplying from his own farm had immediately to be hidden away. That done, the next job was to make sure that any document that might be in the least compromising was burned. It was not an easy task. Over the years Adenauer had, like a squirrel, assembled thousands of papers in cardboard box-files – old receipts, bills and other useless papers which would 'normally be put in the rubbish bin'.[4] Books which might appear subversive were also put on the same bonfire. The radio was rapidly re-tuned to the Reich Radio Service.

In the event, the Gestapo acted with a surprising lack of urgency. It was not until after one o'clock on Sunday 24 July that they finally turned up at Zennigsweg 8a. By that time, all potentially incriminating documents had been disposed of. When they arrived – seven of them, led by a senior official from Bonn (made more sinister in appearance by the fact that he only had one arm) – they did not bother to ring the front door-bell, but walked round to the terrace where the family were sitting, in the middle of their lunch. 'We have orders,' the one-armed official announced, 'to search your house.' He produced a stamped piece of paper, which he claimed to be his authority. 'Furthermore,' he went on, 'we require some information from you.'[5] Adenauer immediately got up from his lunch and went with two Gestapo officials into the house, leaving his family in bewildered silence.

The other Gestapo agents started their search. It went on until 4.30pm that afternoon. They went through every room, from the attic to the cellar. Every cupboard was opened, every wardrobe, chest or box was investigated. In the meantime, Adenauer was being interrogated in his study. But he was asked nothing about the Stauffenberg plot; he was only questioned about his relationship with Giesen and his acquaintance of earlier times. Even the old accusation of 'separatism' was raised.

In truth, the interrogation was little more than bluster. At the end of their day, the Gestapo officials sealed Adenauer's study door, took with them a number of books, and said that they would come back the following morning. At 10am on the Monday, they duly re-appeared. Once more, they went through the whole house, breaking only once at midday and finishing at about 5.30pm. They found nothing of any particular interest, and left with a few more books and some innocent papers. By now, as Adenauer later wrote, they were 'very polite and correct', and told him that 'before anything was done against me on the basis of my correspondence . . . they would seek information which might possibly resolve the matter'.[6]

Nothing more, for the moment, was heard. The whole exercise had been fruitless. The Bonn Gestapo had obviously received instructions to go and investigate Adenauer but without any instruction about what it was they were meant to investigate. As a result, they had dredged up an old agenda from their files and, when that proved to be to no purpose, had gone off with a few books and papers simply to show to their superiors that they had done their job. As they left, Adenauer told them, with only a hint of acid in his voice, that 'I would not keep anything in future, which would save me from these investigations and them from extra work'. The sally went over their heads. They replied that 'they thought [the proposal] quite reasonable'.[7]

Adenauer might have escaped for the moment, but there was much more to come, and this time from a different and more serious angle. After the failure of 20 July Goerdeler had sought refuge in his homeland in East Prussia; but he succeeded in evading capture only until 12 August. His interrogation by the Gestapo before his execution was, as might be imagined, dreadful in its brutality. Under severe torture, Goerdeler mentioned many names of accomplices; he was prepared to admit to anything his torturers wanted. The old names of the Centre Party, many Social Democrats and churchmen – all were now on the list of Gestapo targets; and among those was, of course, the former Mayor of Cologne.

On 23 August 1944 the Gestapo launched Operation Thunderstorm. Anybody and everybody who might have been, or might in the future be, a threat to the Reich was to be arrested. On that morning – early, before the rest of the family was awake – Adenauer answered an urgent ring on his doorbell. Facing him were two policemen, one the local policeman from Rhöndorf and the other, whom Adenauer did not recognise, in plain clothes. The Rhöndorf policeman was apologetic. 'I'm very sorry, Herr

Oberbürgermeister,' he said, 'but I am afraid we shall have to take you with us . . . A general measure, it seems . . . There's six we have to collect in Rhöndorf and Honnef alone.'[8]

Lola helped her father-in-law pack a small suitcase, under the watchful eyes of the plain clothes – obviously Gestapo – agent. That done, he was taken to the Gestapo headquarters in Bonn. It was already crowded, mostly with old men who had been dragged out of their beds and arrested, for no reason that they could understand. At around midday, they were assembled in the courtyard and told to line up in alphabetical order. A roll call was taken. They were then shepherded to the railway station and put on a train to Cologne. From Cologne station they were marched across the bridge to the Trade Fair grounds in Deutz, which had been turned into a detention camp. Inside there was a whole army of former politicians, churchmen – and Russian and Polish prisoners of war. The contingent from Bonn was herded in with them. The former mayor now found himself a prisoner inside the very Trade Fair grounds which had been his own brainchild.

In Rhöndorf, Gussi was bewildered almost to the point of hysteria. In the afternoon, she and Lola went on the tram to Bonn to try to find out where Adenauer was. But he had by then been shipped off to Cologne. They then wandered aimlessly through the streets of Bonn, asking questions of any-body they met. Finally, the owner of a bookshop told them that he had seen a column of men marching towards the railway station, and thought that Adenauer was among them. The Bonn station-master confirmed the story: there had been a number of elderly men, under guard, boarding a special train for Cologne. They were going, he thought, for detention in Deutz. Gussi and Lola made an immediate decision: they took the next train to Cologne. Once there, they walked across the Deutz Bridge and stood help-lessly outside the wired enclosure of the Trade Fair grounds until late in the evening. It was only when darkness fell that they gave up in despair and went home to Rhöndorf.

Adenauer himself was by then deeply depressed. He assumed that he would never see his family again. Things got worse as the days went by. He could not sleep; the camp was infested with lice; he had nothing to do; he could only pace up and down along the wire fence. Fortunately, however, there were detainees of long standing who were entrusted with supervising the new arrivals, and, as luck would have it, Adenauer had been assigned to the Communist Eugen Zander, who had formerly been a municipal worker in Cologne (and had worked in the garden in Max-Bruch-Strasse). Zander realised that Adenauer was in bad shape, and managed to get him billeted in his own room in the clothing depot. It was a generous gesture, but, although it made him more comfortable, the change did little to relieve Adenauer's depression. After the six o'clock morning roll call 'he would return to our room and just sit there quietly for hours'.[9]

Gussi and Lola made the journey to Cologne regularly to wait outside the wire fence hoping to catch sight of him. After a few days they did see him, pacing up and down. They waved and shouted, but as he moved to speak to them a guard came up and chased them away at rifle point. There was nothing to do, and they went away in tears. Adenauer returned to his room in the clothing depot and told Zander about the event, explaining in a gloomy voice that he had been unable to exchange a single word with them. 'I looked at Adenauer as he sat there in front of me on the bed,' Zander recalled later. 'He was as thin as a skeleton; his clothes were flapping loosely about him; and, with his collarless shirt and his soup spoon stuck in his breast pocket, he must have been a heart-breaking sight for his wife.'[10]

But at least food parcels started to arrive from Rhöndorf, and, even during the weary days of August, Adenauer's mood seemed to improve. In order to pass the time, he organised discussion groups in the clothing depot. The subjects covered were almost endless: religion, history, art and science. One matter which was certainly not discussed, for fear of the informers in the camp, was the current state of the war and what might happen afterwards. Nor was the matter of the daily disappearances, or the times when special squads would at night drag somebody from his bed and take him away – his dossier later to be marked 'shot while attempting to escape'. Life in the camp also took on a momentum of its own, with even a dance on one evening and a concert on another (one of the Polish prisoners being particularly proficient on the violin). Furthermore, visits were allowed: Libet and Lotte were driven by 'Uncle Toni' Weiss to Cologne on 25 August and spent half an hour with their father; Gussi was also driven by him to Cologne station on 28 August, walked across the bridge and spent an hour with her husband.

But it was at the beginning of September that Zander, with his privileged access to the camp office, discovered that against Adenauer's name there was marked the expression 'return not wanted'. In other words Adenauer was due for deportation. Once on a train bound for the east, he would disappear for ever. The only possible solution was for him to report sick without delay. This he did, with good reason, in fact, since by then his health had seriously deteriorated. A doctor in the camp – another detainee – went with Zander to the room in the clothing depot. The doctor immediately diagnosed 'pernicious anaemia'[11] and pronounced him 'unfit for imprisonment'.[12] The official camp doctor agreed; an ambulance was called, and the patient was taken to the hospital in Hohenlind.

The problem then was what to do next. The diagnosis of the two doctors was at best vague. It had, to be sure, secured for him the medical opinion that he was 'unfit for imprisonment', but Adenauer knew that, particularly in the circumstances of the time, diagnoses could change. It might only be a matter of days before the doctors in Hohenlind reversed the opinion of the camp doctors and decided that he could safely be returned to detention. This being so, he needed to get himself out of Hohenlind – and to freedom – as soon as possible. He knew that American forces were close – they had already occupied Liège, Maastricht and Luxembourg; it was only a matter of time before they were into German territory. He therefore decided, after a long discussion with Gussi in Hohenlind, to escape from the hospital and to go into hiding until the Americans arrived.

The escape plan and its follow-up were theatrical – almost to the point of farce. On a fine afternoon in early September a car drew up, with much screaming of tyres, in front of the main entrance to Hohenlind hospital. A Luftwaffe major emerged, wearing thick dark glasses. He summoned the director of the hospital, and told her that he wished the prisoner Adenauer to be handed over to him immediately, producing as authority an order from the German Army High Command stating that Adenauer was required in Berlin for interrogation. (The order was, of course, forged.) Adenauer was duly brought down, also wearing dark glasses, prescribed for an invented 'inflammation of the eyes'. He got into the car, with an appropriate show of reluctance. Once there he found, in the back seat, a heavily disguised Gussi.

The major in question was Hans Schliebusch. He had known the Adenauer family before the war, and, when Gussi had asked him, had been quite happy to co-operate in the escape plan. 'If it's a question of cocking a snook at the Nazis,' he had said, 'you can count me in.'[13] The plan had been hatched and duly carried out. With Adenauer – dark glasses and all – safely in the car, Schliebusch drove off, with his unlikely cargo, at breakneck speed and with more impressive squealing of tyres.

But it was all very well to be out of the hospital and of captivity. The new problem was that they had not decided where they should then drive him to. After some debate, they decided to go to Adenauer's dentist in Bonn. The dentist, Josef Vollmar, was understandably horrified when he saw them appear at his door. 'Haven't you thought,' he asked angrily, 'of the danger which you are exposing me to?'[14] The truth was that that had been the last thing on their minds. Vollmar gave them only one night; and then they must leave. There was much discussion. Finally, it was Gussi who came up with the idea that Adenauer should hide at the Nister Mühle, a small hotel near Hachenburg in the Westerwald. The proprietor, Josef Rödig, had known Adenauer in the old days and would not give him away. It was agreed. They drove off and, as Gussi had thought, Rödig allowed Adenauer to sign in as 'Dr Weber' and took care that he remained as far out of sight as possible.

In the event, the whole thing turned out to be a dreadful mistake. At first, all went well. Adenauer settled down at the Nister Mühle, went for long walks in the autumnal woods and even, on 16 September, wrote to Ria under the pseudonym K. Zennig. But it could not last. By escaping from Hohenlind Adenauer was implicitly admitting guilt. The Gestapo response was predictable. It was normal procedure. Failing the gander, they arrested the goose. On the morning of 24 September two of them arrived at the house in Rhöndorf. They did not bother to say who they were, or to produce any authority. They simply asked Lola, who answered the door, where Gussi was and, when she appeared, asked her where Adenauer was. Gussi pleaded ignorance, but almost before she could get the words out she was told to pack a bag and come with them.

They took her to Honnef for her first interrogation, and then, in the late afternoon, on to the Gestapo headquarters in Cologne. There she was put in the cellar along with criminal cases – mostly prostitutes. It was foul-smelling and noisy. Some of the girls were singing and dancing to the sound of a radio in the guardroom above; others sat huddled against the walls. In a corner there were two white enamel bins; there was no other furniture. The cellar was lit by one naked electric bulb.

It is hardly possible to exaggerate the shock Gussi must have felt. She had never in her life met people like that, let alone been shut up with them in a dark cellar smelling of urine and excrement. She was frightened and disgusted in equal measure. It was almost a relief when she was summoned for a further investigation by the Gestapo Commissar Bethke. But the relief was short-lived. Sitting behind a desk, in darkness but with a bright light shining directly into Gussi's face, he demanded to know where Adenauer was. She refused to answer, and after a long and threatening silence, broken only by the steady tapping of his pencil on the desk, the Commissar told her to think it over. She was taken back to the cellar.

By that time the other women had stretched out on the floor. Some of them were already asleep. There was no room for Gussi, who had to remain standing. Two hours later she was sent for again. This time the Commissar was more direct. He asked Gussi how old her daughters were. 'Nineteen and sixteen,' she replied.[15] The Commissar then told her that either she revealed where Adenauer was hiding or the house at Rhöndorf would be confiscated; furthermore, and this was the breaking point, Lotte and Libet would be arrested and kept in the cellar indefinitely. At that, Gussi cracked immediately, and told him where her husband was. She was then taken to the prison at Brauweiler, a converted convent just to the west of Cologne.

Orders were quickly given, and on 25 September Adenauer was re-arrested by the Gestapo at the Nister Mühle. Three of them came for him just before first light, driving at speed along the track leading to the small hotel, then switching on a powerful spotlight directed at the window of his room. On hearing the all too obvious sounds and seeing the fierce light, Adenauer panicked. He snatched up his clothes and in bare feet scampered up the wooden stairs leading to the attic, hoping that they would believe he had escaped into the woods behind. But they were not so easily fooled. They searched the place from bottom to top, finally shining a torch on a shadowy figure hiding behind the attic chimney stack. 'But really, Herr Oberbürgermeister'[16] was the heavily ironic comment from the Gestapo officer. The former Lord Mayor of Cologne had been caught without any reasonable shred to clothing to cover his dignity.

They took him to the prison at Brauweiler, explaining on the way, in carefully oblique terms, that his wife was also being held there and that it was she who had told them where he was — neglecting, of course, to add that she had only done so when arrested herself and threatened with the further arrest of her two daughters. As the day dawned, dull and grey as only Rhineland weather can be, the prisoner and escort arrived at the Gestapo prison. On arrival, Adenauer was taken to the clothing depot, where he handed in his braces, shoelaces, tie and pocket knife. He was then led to a narrow nun's cell with one barred window high up on the wall, a small cupboard and a plain bed. Although the cell had no heating, in terms of Brauweiler prison it was relative luxury. But on the way to the cell the Gestapo commissar was blunt. 'Please do not kill yourself,' he said, 'you would only cause me a great deal of trouble.' Adenauer asked what made him think that he might take his own life. 'He replied', Adenauer recorded later, 'that as I was now nearly seventy years old and had nothing more to expect from life, it seemed reasonable to suppose that I would put an end to it.'[17]

Adenauer and his wife thus spent a week in the same prison – without seeing one another. Mortified by what she regarded as her treachery, and depressed by the solitary confinement in which she was held, Gussi tried to kill herself. Her first attempt was by swallowing a whole bottle of a relatively mild painkiller, Pyramidon. All this achieved was to make her dizzy. Undeterred, she had another shot. When she was taken down to her daily task of repairing clothes, she took a pair of scissors in her right hand and crudely slashed at her left wrist. One of the two arteries in the wrist was severed, and she lost a great deal of blood. But it was not enough to kill her. She was saved just in time.

Suffering painfully, ill and depressed, Gussi, her arm bandaged and in a splint, was finally allowed to see her husband at the end of the week. After a few tearful moments with Adenauer, during which he tried to assure her that she had done nothing wrong in revealing his hiding place, she was taken away again to her cell. Only a few hours later, she was told that an order for her release had been received. By then Libet had managed to get to Brauweiler, just as her mother was about to be released. She was able to take Gussi back to Rhöndorf. 'She looked pale and worn,' Libet recalled, 'her eyes were red and swollen from crying. Her hair, always so carefully done, hung loose and unkempt, and was tied at the nape with a shoelace.'[18] For many days after her return home she was only able to speak in frightened sentences – or even just in monosyllables. Her former good cheer had completely deserted her.

Adenauer set himself to live through the long days and – worse – the even longer nights, punctuated as they were by the screams of those who were being tortured on the floor below him, waiting always for the banging on the door which would tell him that he was to be transported eastwards to almost certain – and probably violent – death. But, although he did not know it at the time, the Gestapo administration was already breaking down in the face of the Allied advance. As it turned out, the timing was fortunate, since, as he later learned, his name had been on the list for 'elimination' and he had only avoided death because of the Gestapo's hurried withdrawal from Cologne.

The question for the family at that point was how to get Adenauer out of Brauweiler. Again, it was Libet who had provided the answer. Soon after Gussi's arrest she had sent a telegram to her half-brother Max. Although in coded language, it made clear that both parents had been arrested. Max received the telegram on 4 October, and immediately applied for compassionate leave. This was at first refused, but, after his wife Gisela had intervened with Max's commanding officer to explain the facts of the case, it was granted on 24 October. Max was in Brauweiler two days later.

Surprisingly, he was allowed to see his father almost immediately. In fact, after the first series of investigations, Adenauer had been treated relatively leniently. His insistence on his distance from the Stauffenberg plot was apparently accepted by his interrogators. Furthermore, the prison doctor had requested his transfer to a heated room, a special diet (for invalids) and daily walks. He was given books to read and paper and pen. Finally, when Max came to see him, they were left alone without supervision, and spent three hours together.

They agreed that Max should go immediately to Berlin to intervene on his father's behalf. This he did. Private contacts proving ineffective, he went on 2 November directly to the Gestapo headquarters on Prinz-Albrecht-Strasse. From there he was referred to another branch, where he went the following day. By then it was clear that the charge against Adenauer of complicity in the Stauffenberg plot could not be sustained; the only charge against him which might stand up concerned his implicit admission of guilt in his escape from Hohenlind. But Max was able to use, and use convincingly, the argument which he and his father had agreed on. There were himself and two brothers, he told them, serving in the armed forces. 'How do you think,' he asked them, 'a soldier in the field, fighting the enemy, feels when he hears that one of his family at home has been arrested for no reason at all and thrown into prison?'[19] Max won the day. An order for the prisoner's release was immediately issued.

Adenauer finally left Brauweiler prison on 26 November. Still without braces, shoelaces or tie, he made his way in a borrowed van back to his home at Rhöndorf. He avoided Cologne, which was dangerous territory, and crossed the Rhine upstream at Bonn. When he arrived at Königswinter he sent a telephone message to his family to tell them that he was on his way, but such was the flooding on the road along the east bank of the river to Rhöndorf that he was forced to turn back on his tracks. He then had to undertake a long diversion, driving round the whole of the Siebengebirge range of hills and approaching his home from the south through Honnef. His family had almost given him up for lost, afraid that he had been spotted at a Gestapo checkpoint. It was late in the evening when he finally arrived at Rhöndorf. 'It was,' he recalled, 'a wonderful end; it was like a dream to be home again; and it often seems like a dream still.'[20]

It was time again to lie low. But it was not to be for long; nor was it to be quiet. The day after Adenauer's return from Brauweiler, Ria and her two children arrived to take shelter in Rhöndorf. In January 1945 Lola's second child was born. Adenauer and Gussi had to walk with her to the hospital at Honnef, stopping every five minutes because of her pains – and hearing the rumble of gunfire from the distant front. Transport was by now impossible to find; the railway had ceased to function and there was no petrol for cars. Lola stayed in hospital for no more than a few days before being walked back to Rhöndorf with her baby son.

The guns came closer with the launch of the American spring offensive in March. Adenauer calculated that the two main lines of attack would be by the British through the Belgian lowlands, leading on to the Ruhr, and by the Americans across the Rhine at Mainz, leading on to Frankfurt. The middle Rhine (including Rhöndorf) would on this reasoning escape serious military action. What he had not guessed was that the Germans would leave a bridge on the middle Rhine intact – the railway bridge at Remagen. On 7 March an American tank squadron arrived at Remagen expecting to see the bridge destroyed. They found it intact, but defended on the right bank by a company of German infantry. It took almost a day of close quarters infantry fighting before the Americans were able to secure the bridge and start moving their tanks across. Once the bridge was safe, however, the Americans moved rapidly to widen the bridgehead on the right bank. By 9 March, Adenauer's sister telephoned him from Unkel: 'We are already free; the Americans are here . . .'[21]

Adenauer's military calculations had to be sharply revised. It became obvious that the Americans would expand the bridgehead from Remagen (which by then had extended as far as Unkel) and would direct their thrust towards the Cologne–Frankfurt motorway, which ran north to south directly behind the Siebengebirge. In other words, Rhöndorf, on the Rhine side of the Siebengebirge and still in German hands, could expect to be at the centre of an American assault. Adenauer knew perfectly well that American field commanders insisted – reasonably enough – on heavy bombing raids and a prolonged artillery barrage before moving troops or armour forward. The conclusion was clear. At any moment, Rhöndorf could be bombed or shelled into oblivion.

Adenauer immediately ordered the fruit cellar in the basement of the house to be converted to its other purpose, an air-raid shelter. Chairs, mattresses, blankets and provisions were installed in readiness. The entire family, apart from Adenauer himself, Gussi and young Georg, were instructed to take refuge there. On the evening of 9 March, the shell bursts were getting closer. By nightfall, the artillery barrage was increasing in intensity – and creeping towards Rhöndorf. At four in the morning the house was starting to shake from the continued shelling. Adenauer, Gussi and Georg retreated to the cellar to join the terrified family. A direct hit was expected at any moment.

When daylight came, Adenauer emerged to see what was going on. He noted that the German troops had withdrawn to positions in the hills behind the house but that a German tank was in place next to the Rhöndorf parish church. That particular day – 10 March – was quiet, apart from the arrival of five escaped French prisoners of war, one of whom, Louis, had worked in the garden at Adenauer's house. They pleaded for shelter. Unable to think of another solution, and also unwilling to turn them away, Adenauer shovelled the five into a garden shed just above the house, and told them only to come down to the house if they were in desperate need of food.

In the evening the American bombardment resumed, and the whole family re-assembled in the cellar. Shells were by now landing not far from the house itself. On the following morning, Adenauer and Gussi went up to get breakfast for the family and to boil some potatoes for lunch. No sooner had they returned to the cellar than the house suffered a direct hit, the shell destroying a bedroom and a whole corner of the first floor. In the afternoon, the house was hit again, and several trees were destroyed in the garden. At dusk, the five Frenchmen appeared, saying that the garden shed was terrifyingly unsafe and asking to be taken into the cellar. Adenauer agreed. They could not, in all Christian conscience, be refused. The population in the fruit cellar at that point rose to nineteen.

The 'battle for Rhöndorf' lasted for nearly a week. Adenauer observed its progress by means of a daily sortie from the cellar. He would go up to the top of the garden, survey the scene and report back to the group in the cellar. None of the others, of course, was allowed to go out. After a day or two of this the American artillery observers on the other side of the Rhine saw this strange figure standing in an advantageous position of observation. Guns were immediately targeted. Three shells landed within a few yards of Adenauer – he later claimed that he saw one of them coming towards him – who immediately retired to the cellar 'pale and mud-spattered'.[22]

It was the Swiss Consul Weiss who mediated between the two warring sides. Waving his Swiss flag by way of passport, he pointed out to the American commanders that there were large numbers of wounded in military hospitals in the area, and that continued bombardment could only be regarded as inhumane. He also managed to convince the German commanders to withdraw from their strong and entrenched positions on the Drachenfels once their wounded had been evacuated. The hospitals were to be in a 'neutral zone'. The result was that Rhöndorf, both the village and Adenauer's house, was damaged but not flattened, and the party in the cellar was able to emerge, which they did on the morning of 15 March to the noise of American tanks rumbling through the streets and little Georg shouting, 'The war is over!'[23]

But there were to be further surprises. At three o'clock in the afternoon of 16 March – as it happened, in beautiful early spring weather – a US Army jeep drew up at the entrance to Zennigsweg 8a. Two officers and the Mayor of Honnef got out and walked up the steps to the house. Adenauer was talking to a visitor, the art historian Werner Bornheim, when they arrived at the front door. They introduced themselves as Lieutenant-Colonel Tuhus and Captain Emerson. They were there, they explained, as emissaries of the new US Military Governor of Cologne, Lieutenant-Colonel John K. Patterson. Their particular mission on his behalf was to invite Adenauer to resume office as Mayor of Cologne.

Once over his surprise, Adenauer asked them into the house, and, apart from the Mayor of Honnef, they all went in to the drawing room. There Adenauer replied that, however grateful he was, he could not accept the American offer. The officers' reaction to this reply was one of offended astonishment. They tried to convince him to change his mind. At that point, Adenauer asked Gussi to come in. She listened to the arguments – and stubbornly supported her husband. They had three sons in the armed forces, and reprisals against them were almost certain if Adenauer took on the job of mayor. That was the end of the matter. But, before they left, the officers asked Adenauer what his ambitions now were. Perhaps somewhat pompously, he replied that it was to educate the German people from the ground up to the idea of peace. Pompous or not, it was clear that he was already looking beyond the narrow confines of Cologne. (His future assertion to his secretary that it was his dream to become Mayor of Cologne again seems to be little more than a retrospective comment from the vantage-point of old age.)

He was finally persuaded to take a serious interest – as an adviser – in the reconstruction of Cologne by one of Patterson's adjutants, Captain Albert Schweizer. An architect by profession, he managed to rekindle in Adenauer an enthusiasm for the rebuilding of Cologne along the lines which Adenauer himself had conceived in the 1920s. Adenauer in the meanwhile had received a visit from the Archbishop of Cologne, Josef Frings, who argued in the same direction. His brother-in-law, Willi Suth, added to the pressure. Schweizer finally persuaded him to make a three-day visit to Cologne with Gussi. They were to be put up at the expense of the US Army in the Caritas Hospital in Hohenlind.

The journey into Cologne of 27 March 1945 was quite clearly an emotional moment for both of them. In the former Gestapo headquarters in Appellhofplatz, they looked at the office of their former tormentor, the Commissar Bethke. There was a photograph of Reinhard Heydrich still on the wall. Adenauer took it down and smashed it against the edge of the table. Their house in Max-Bruch-Strasse was a burned-out wreck. The inner city was almost wholly destroyed. The only redeeming feature was the cemetery at Melaten, where the graves of his parents – and Emma's too – were undisturbed.

Adenauer was by now convinced. He would do what he could. Willi Suth would hold the position of mayor; Adenauer would stand behind him as his adviser. But the arrangement was only to be temporary. When hostilities ceased Adenauer would formally resume his post as mayor. On 3 May 1945 Adenauer accepted the post and was formally appointed. He had – in a sense – finally come home. But the homecoming was not all that he might have expected. He had no particular illusions about those who had won the war; they were from a new generation. He had no illusions about the venom of the Allies towards Germany. Furthermore, he had no illusions about the virtues of the victors in the war; the behaviour of some American GIs in Rhöndorf had removed any that might have remained. Indeed, he had no particular enthusiasm for the job of Mayor of Cologne. The city was shattered beyond his belief. Reconstructing it, he knew, would certainly be the task of a younger man.

Before Adenauer resumed his office as Mayor of Cologne, he had made clear his views on the future of Germany to a junior American officer on 28 March. There were, he told Lieutenant Just Lunning, two Germanies: 'the Germany which is fundamentally based on the Roman cultural inheritance, and the Germany of Prussia, which imposed its own will'. The ideal solution, Adenauer had gone on, would be 'a combination of Austria, parts of Prussia, Westphalia and the Rheinland, and Southern Germany'. This, he claimed, would 'neutralise' the 'un-German' influence of Prussia.[24]

In that one conversation, Adenauer had set out his stall. As he approached his seventieth birthday, it was clear that he had only one further ambition. Cologne was now just a port of passage. With Hitler's suicide in a bunker in Berlin, Hitler's Germany had passed. Adenauer's Germany was about to begin. But there was a small footnote. When the Americans arrived at Rhöndorf, the French ex-prisoners wanted to leave immediately. Adenauer stopped them. They should sign, he said, 'a paper, in which they certified that they had lived [at Rhöndorf] and were concealed during the last days of the war'.[25] Nothing, clearly, was to be left to chance.

PART FOUR

Adenauer's Germany

I

SACKED BY THE BRITISH

'Ich wollte, dass einmal ein englischer Staatsmann von uns als Westeuropäern gesprochen hätte'*

ON 10 JULY 1945 the eighty-year-old General Sir Charles Fergusson sent a memorandum to the British Foreign Office. From an account in the Scottish *Daily Express* of Monday 2 July of a correspondent's interview with 'one Herr Adenauer', he had learned that Adenauer had been re-appointed Mayor of Cologne. He himself, his memorandum explained, had been Military Governor of occupied German territory from early December 1918 until he had handed over to his successor, Lieutenant-General Clive, at the end of July 1919.

Fergusson reported that during that period he had come to know Adenauer well. He did not deny, his memorandum went on, Adenauer's ability; but he recalled Adenauer saying, more than once, 'We will never forget. If it takes us five or ten or twenty years, we will never rest until we get our revenge.' Fergusson finally gave his considered opinion: 'I am quite certain that unless he has changed very much in the last twenty-five years his

---

* 'I wished that an English statesman might once have spoken of us as Western Europeans': Adenauer's account of Associated Press interview of 5 October 1945; quoted in P. Weymar, *Adenauer*, p. 281.

293

hatred of Britain is far deeper than any other feeling. He is clever, cunning, a born intriguer and dangerous. I suggest that too much reliance should not be placed on him, and that in their dealings with him our authorities should be on their guard.'[1]

Of course, Fergusson's memorandum has the flavour of disappointed old age. He even misspelt his name in signing it – it came as 'Ferguson' rather than 'Fergusson'. Coming from such a distinguished source, however, it could not be ignored. It made its way through the British Foreign Office, and finally was passed to the British Military Government in Germany, where it arrived in late September 1945. But in London it provoked further research. This revealed that Adenauer had had a reasonable relationship with Fergusson's successors (and a particularly good one with Julian Piggott); but, on the other hand, he had made an inflammatory speech when the British left Cologne in 1926. All this was noted, and duly passed on to the British in Germany.

Adenauer's views about Britain were certainly not as extreme as Fergusson described. True, he had blamed Britain (and France) for not intervening in the Rhineland in 1936, and felt some resentment against the British bombers which had destroyed Cologne; but he had, on the other hand, trusted the BBC German Service during the war. True, he did, in a private conversation in May 1945, describe Winston Churchill as a 'German-hater' while at the same time pronouncing Stalin to be 'Germany's friend';[2] but these throwaway remarks – both of which were patently untrue – could not justify any description that he was unremittingly 'anti-British', any more than he could be described as 'pro-Russian'.

The fact is that Adenauer's knowledge of countries outside Germany, already limited, had, if anything, been further eroded during the isolation of the Nazi years. Twelve years of retreat into his Rhineland shell, from 1933 to 1945, had served to set his previous ignorance into a cast of something close to insularity. But, if insularity it was, there was one constructive product. It had concentrated his thoughts on the future of his own particular patch – the Rhineland. Towards the end of the war he had come to brood at length about the future of Germany; and, after due reflection, had come to the conclusion that his old, post-First World War ideas of some sort of Franco-German concordat still made sense. That, he considered, was the only way to counter Prussian supremacy in Germany.

Indeed, for post-war Germany, the one important political result of

Adenauer's twelve years in his particular wilderness was the unconcealed dislike of Prussia and the values which Prussia represented. He had come to believe that Prussian militarism had given rise to Hitler, and that the Prussian bureaucracy, both civil and military, had been craven and stupid in the face of the Nazi threat. His attachment to the Rhineland and its interests became as a result more marked – as did, by way of emphasis of that attachment, his Rhineland accent.

The future of Germany, however, was one thing. The present – 1945 – was another. Adenauer, as the re-appointed Mayor of Cologne, now had to deal with Americans; and about Americans he was wholly ignorant. When the two US officers first arrived on his doorstep, they seemed pleasant enough, and initially he was glad to find Americans in charge of Cologne. Furthermore, in spite of the fact that he spoke no English, he formed friendly relationships with Lt-Col. Patterson and Captain Schweizer. He was also pleased that American intelligence had placed him first on their 'white list' for Cologne, and also first on the consolidated 'white list' for Germany – although it may not have occurred to him that the reason for his apparently exalted position might have been that his name began with the first letter of the alphabet.

But, as the spring of 1945 turned into early summer, it became irritatingly clear that the Americans had no understanding of what Adenauer regarded as 'the German mentality', and quite clearly no experience or aptitude in running a large German city. He quickly revised his previously favourable opinions. As he told Weiss, the Swiss 'Uncle Toni' of Rhöndorf, 'The Americans are the purest children in administration'.[3] He found almost all their decisions – on the clearance of the streets, on the supply of food, or the restoration of some sort of transport system – quite nonsensical. The Americans then became not just children but 'big, bad children'.[4] He was pleased to see the back of them when the control of Cologne passed into British hands on 21 June.

Again he was to be disappointed. He had hoped for a renewal of the previous relationship with the British as an occupying power. But he had not appreciated that circumstances were now quite different. In 1918, Cologne had been intact, with a viable administration in place; and the occupying power had been able to ride on a loose rein. As mayor, Adenauer had controlled the administration of the city without too much interference from the occupying power. In 1945, on the other hand, Cologne was largely a pile of rubble; the population had fallen from a pre-war 790,000 to somewhere close to 30,000; even that small number was living largely in caves dug out of the rubble; there was no administration worthy of the name; furthermore, as the horrors inflicted by the Nazis fully came to light, there was a wave of revulsion against all Germans, guilty or innocent. There was to be no frater-nisation between the occupying troops and German citizens, and there was to be a thorough programme of 'de-Nazification' and 're-education'. The prevailing attitude of the British military was tersely summed up in a mem-orandum from Brigadier John Barraclough of early November: 'No German is persona grata with Mil. Gov.'[5]

Furthermore, the physical circumstances made the task of reconstruction all the more difficult. There was no telephone, no writing paper and above all, no staff. Almost all those who had remained had been Nazis, and hence barred from holding any official post. The mayor's office was installed in a building belonging to an insurance company. Adenauer and Gussi them-selves, when in Cologne, stayed in two rooms in Hohenlind Hospital. It was depressing, and, for a man nearing seventy, exhausting. Moreover, Adenauer was not master in his own house; everything he did, or tried to do, was sub-ject to the closest control of the occupying power. It is hardly surprising that he started to lose interest and heart in the reconstruction of his native city.

In truth, he was considering the wider perspective for the future. For instance, he was aware that the Yalta Conference of February 1945 had allo-cated to the French a small zone of occupation carved out of the British and American zones. He was also aware that the French – particularly General Charles de Gaulle – considered that it should be larger. When the French general Pierre Billotte told Weiss during the summer of 1945 that he thought that Cologne and Aachen would be added to the French Zone, 'Uncle Toni' faithfully reported this to his friend the Mayor of Cologne.

Adenauer thought that the chance was there for the taking. Surprising as it may seem, given that he was an appointed Mayor of Cologne now under British auspices, between August and early October 1945 Adenauer met French staff officers on no fewer than six occasions, usually accompanied by Weiss. The first occasion was at a private dinner organised by Weiss in Bad Godesberg, at which Gussi was present. After that, there was a series of dis-cussions in different places – all in the French Zone – at which future economic co-operation between France and the Rhineland was the main agenda. On 1 September, according to the French Capitaine Goussault,

Adenauer claimed that the British in 1945 were far inferior in education and knowledge to their predecessors in 1918. It followed that, if a series of small states could be created in Germany, one of which would consist of the Rhineland, the Ruhr and a sizeable piece of Westphalia, he personally would welcome a deal with the French. It was quite clear whom he had in mind as head of such a state.

Weiss elaborated on these ideas in a memorandum of 22 September which he sent to his government in Berne, a memorandum which in fact was probably drafted by Adenauer himself. 'On the construction of a Rhineland State,' it ran, 'two further states could probably be set up from the remaining parts [of Germany] . . . All three states would have to pursue a foreign policy independent of the others, and each in particular would have its own foreign representation.'[6]

Not unnaturally, the Political Department of the Swiss Foreign Ministry was horrified at this intrusion by a consular official of a neutral country into the affairs of the great Allied powers. Weiss was treated to a thunderous broadside from his superiors in Berne. 'We do not approve of your initiative in this matter,' he was informed in the curtest possible language, 'and urgently request you to cease your active attempts to influence both parties but also all mediation in the issue [of separatism].'[7]

Weiss was suitably abashed. But Adenauer, too, was playing a dangerous, even foolhardy, game. If the British had discovered his intrigues, he would certainly have been immediately – and rightly – dismissed, on the grounds that he was engaged in discussions with another occupying power without permission. As it happened, in fact, Adenauer's relations with the British authorities were worsening steadily throughout September 1945. As mayor, he refused to assent to a British request to allow trees in the Cologne green belt to be felled for use as fuel, although there is some evidence that the intention was to use them not as fuel but as 'timber for pit props'.[8] The British were further irritated by the programme of street clearance, which was falling behind; and the provision of shelter for the thousands of former inhabitants who were returning to their homes after the cessation of hostilities was almost non-existent.

Furthermore, although the British were unaware of Adenauer's flirtation with the French, they were certainly aware of what they described as his 'political intrigues'[9] within the area of their Military Government. As Mayor of Cologne, he was in a perfect position to receive visitors, not least from those whose main purpose was to sound him out about the political future of the Rhineland. He also made frequent visits to Bonn and Bad Godesberg, where there was embryonic, but intense, political activity. Furthermore, there was a group in Königswinter, led by a school teacher, Leo Schwering, which was already discussing the formation, when it was permitted, of a Christian Democratic Party. All this the British knew about. For the time being they were prepared to turn a blind eye, but the charge of political intriguing – when it was prohibited – was to figure prominently in subsequent events.

It was on 28 September 1945 that General Fergusson's memorandum of 10 July arrived at the headquarters of the British Military Government of the North Rhine Province in Düsseldorf. Its arrival posed something of a problem. Certainly, if the circumstances of Adenauer's intrigues with the French had been known, Fergusson's verdict would have been emphatically endorsed without further ado. Failing that knowledge – since the French had been suitably discreet – the reaction in Düsseldorf was more measured.

At the time, the North Rhine Province of the British Military Government was commanded by Brigadier Barraclough. In the ensuing years, of course, Barraclough has been portrayed as one of the main villains in Adenauer demonology. The picture, like many of its kind, has been over-done. He was certainly a professional soldier – 'a stocky regular officer apparently of conventional pattern'[10] was one description of him – short, square-jawed, with a pugnacious face and an aggressive military moustache; but he was far from the inhuman monster that some have portrayed.

Barraclough's military record was most distinguished. He had risen from the ranks during the First World War, winning a Military Cross in 1918, had been severely wounded in Iraq in 1920 but had recovered to serve further in Palestine, Egypt and India. At the beginning of the Second World War he was a battalion commander in the Middle East, and was one of the heroes of the siege of Tobruk in 1941, Mentioned in Despatches five times and winning the Distinguished Service Order – and wounded again. By the end of the war he was commanding a brigade in the offensive across the Rhine. But, whatever his military valour – which was considerable – he could hardly be described as a politician. Furthermore, like many British soldiers who had fought through the war, he was not enamoured of Germans – whoever they might be.

Nevertheless, as a soldier through and through, Barraclough had a proper sense of responsibility for those under his command. Military discipline, of course, had to be maintained; but he had been trained to ensure that his subordinates, of whatever nationality, were properly looked after. His reaction to Fergusson's memorandum, which arrived on his desk on 28 September 1945, was therefore guarded. 'I know Dr Adenauer well,' he wrote back to his ultimate authority, the Main HQ, Control Commission for Germany. 'As General Ferguson [sic] says,' he went on, 'Adenauer is a man of undeniable ability. I very much doubt that he exercises any very great influence at the moment. He impresses me as being tired and dispirited, and no doubt he has lost a good deal of the fire which he had when General Ferguson knew him twenty-five years ago.'[11]

So far, so mild. There was, however, a sting in the tail of Barraclough's letter to Main HQ. 'I have written to Hamilton, the Mil. Gov. Commander in Köln, for his views. My inclination at the moment is to get rid of Adenauer on grounds of inefficiency rather than political undesirability.'[12] Indeed, Barraclough wrote to Colonel Hamilton that very day. 'As you know,' his letter runs, 'I have always had doubts about Adenauer. I think we would be well advised to get rid of him, and I propose to do so unless you hold very strong views to the contrary. Please let me know your views. I will take no further action until I hear from you.'[13] With his letter, Barraclough enclosed a copy of Fergusson's memorandum. Both letters were dated 1 October 1945.

Hamilton made no objection to Barraclough's proposal. Accordingly, Barraclough summoned Adenauer to Hamilton's office in Cologne on the morning of Saturday 6 October. But, as it happened, the summons came too late. Adenauer was already on his way to Bonn to attend a Requiem Mass for his former rescuer Major Schliebusch. He had crossed the Rhine and was heading in the direction of Bonn and Koblenz when he was stopped at a British checkpoint and escorted at speed by outriders from the British Military Police back to Cologne. Barraclough, it need hardly be said, was sitting in Hamilton's office, fuming at the delay.

At that point, Adenauer was under the impression that there was to be a discussion about his opposition to the felling of trees in the Cologne green belt, possibly to discuss the results of the first meeting of the new City Council which had taken place the previous week, or perhaps even to debate Adenauer's plans for the long-term architecture of the city of Cologne which he had previously shown to Barraclough. As he soon found out, however, the reality of Barraclough's summons was quite different. He also found out that Barraclough's temper had snapped.

When Adenauer arrived, Barraclough did not get up. He sat behind a desk with two other British officers, Colonel Charrington and Major Lawson, beside him. An interpreter stood behind. Adenauer moved to take a chair and sit down himself. Barraclough stopped him. '"Don't sit down" he said curtly.'[14] He then proceeded to read out to Adenauer a letter of dismissal. It started by saying that he, Barraclough, was not satisfied with the progress made on the repair of buildings, the clearance of streets and the general task of preparing for the coming winter, and that he had warned Adenauer two months previously of his responsibilities. It went on to say that 'in my opinion you have failed in your duty to the people of Cologne', and that he was therefore dismissed as mayor.[15]

It was a brusque and bruising affair. In itself, of course, it was simply following the procedure of a British military tribunal, which Barraclough had conducted hundreds of times. For Adenauer, on the other hand, it was grossly insulting. Having read out the letter, Barraclough asked him whether he had anything to say – again, standard military procedure. Adenauer simply replied 'No', signed the original of the letter, turned and walked out of the room. He cleared his desk, and, in reasonable calm, went to lunch with Weiss in Rhöndorf, together with Gussi and Lieutenant-Colonel Gouraud. He and Gussi were late, 'which he explained as being by act of God'.[16] The lunch lasted four hours, during which the whole story presumably came out.

Apart from the humiliating circumstances of the event, and the fact that the grounds for his dismissal was incompetence, there were three provisions in Barraclough's letter of dismissal which Adenauer felt to be particularly offensive.

The first was that he was that he was to 'leave Cologne as soon as possible, and in any case not later than 14 October'.[17] The expression was ambiguous, since it was unclear whether it was a matter of giving Cologne up as a residence or whether he was barred from entering Cologne at all. If the latter, as he pointed out in a letter to the Military Government, he would be prohibited from accompanying his wife Gussi for treatment at Hohenlind, and would further be prevented from seeing his lawyer in Cologne to pursue the claims which he still had against the city for 'damages . . . on account of my political opinions'.[18] But when his request to accompany her for her treatment was transmitted by Hamilton to Barraclough, with a recommendation that it be granted and, incidentally, with the return of Fergusson's memorandum, Barraclough was adamant. 'I think it is most undesirable,' he replied, 'that Dr Adenauer should be allowed to come into Köln with his wife for medical treatment. There is no objection to his wife coming in alone, or coming in accompanied by someone other than her husband. If we give permission to Adenauer to come in with his wife, we shall find that the lady requires medical attention five days out of six.'[19]

The second prohibition was equally clear but more limited in scope: 'After you have handed over to Herr Suth [the newly appointed mayor] you will take no further part in the administration or public life of Cologne or any part of the North Rhine Province.'[20] That might have hurt Adenauer personally, but in political terms it could be shrugged off.

It was the third prohibition which was the widest and the most damaging of all. It was emphatic: 'You will not indulge either directly or indirectly in any political activity whatever.'[21] In practice, this meant that he would be unable to take part in the activities of the fledgling Christian Democratic Party, although in mid-September it had been authorised by the British in their zone and although he was an obvious candidate as its leader. It seemed that, at least in that respect, the ghost of Fergusson's past had won. Adenauer's earlier 'political intriguing' in Cologne during the summer had been stored up and now was used against him.

So there it was; but it was not to be quite as simple as that. Adenauer himself was convinced that the reason for his dismissal, and the accompanying prohibitions, was entirely political. He suspected the newly elected Labour government in Britain of wishing to favour the SPD, and therefore wanting their main opponents out of the way. Some twenty years later, in his memoirs, he claimed that his old opponent Görlinger had written a report for the British Secret Service on the situation in Cologne specifically condemning Adenauer's policies, not least his re-introduction in July 1945 of confessional schools at the primary level. He also unearthed his own account of an interview he had given on 5 October 1945 – the day before his dismissal – to journalists from the News Chronicle and Associated Press, in which he reports himself as saying that 'the Allies had no intention of giving the German population coal for cooking . . . that de Gaulle had just made a speech at Saarbrücken . . . he had said that Frenchmen and Germans must remember that they are Western Europeans . . . I wished that an English statesman might once have spoken of us as Western Europeans.'[22]

Nevertheless, Adenauer's view of his dismissal, however politically convenient in terms of his subsequent career, cannot be sustained. It is inconceivable that Görlinger was ever asked to do any work for the British Secret Service, let alone write a report on the situation in Cologne. Cologne was, after all, under British Military Government. If any information about the city was required, the military authorities were the ones to give it. It may well be that Görlinger wrote a memorandum to the British, but there is no record of it, direct or indirect, other than in Adenauer's own memoirs and his personal files in Rhöndorf. As for Adenauer's summary of his interview with the two journalists, the *News Chronicle* did not publish any account of it, although the paper had a special correspondent writing a series on conditions in the British Zone at the time, nor did Associated Press put out a report. Again, the only evidence of the interview is from Adenauer's own memoirs – and his 'authorised biography'.

In truth, whatever Adenauer and his apologists might contend, there is no doubt that he was dismissed – rightly or wrongly – on the grounds of incompetence. As Barraclough wrote in 1959, 'Dr Adenauer's attitude was rather that of a man who says, "I am doing my best – if you don't like it, it is just too bad".'[23] The British plainly had not liked it. When General Gerald Templer, the Director of Military Government, visited the Rhineland in early September he had found that in Düsseldorf, Essen, Dortmund and other cities progress was being made, but he was shocked to see how far Cologne was lagging behind. In his own words, 'The city was in a terrible mess; no water, no drainage, no light, no food. It stank of corpses.'[24]

There is, of course, the matter of who took the final decision. On his way back to his headquarters in Lübbecke after his inspection of the Rhineland, Templer had stopped off at Barraclough's office in Düsseldorf. It is still unclear, and will for ever remain unclear, whether he said to Barraclough 'If the old man's no good, you must get rid of him' or 'The old man's no good; you must get rid of him.' Barraclough thought the former, and maintained that the decision was his. Templer was always convinced that it was he who had given Barraclough a firm instruction. There, failing further evidence, is where the matter rests.

The responsibility – between Templer and Barraclough – for the decision to dismiss Adenauer as Mayor of Cologne stays unresolved. But where Adenauer certainly had a point was in the blanket prohibition on any political activity wherever it might take place. Although he was deeply angry at the charge of incompetence, it was at least comprehensible. The total pro-hibition on political activity, direct or indirect, apparently in whatever jurisdiction, was devoid of all sense – and of doubtful legality, since British Military Government jurisdiction only extended to the frontiers of the British Zone.

Certainly, Adenauer's previous 'political intriguing' had been resented by the British and was the prime reason for the prohibition contained in his letter of dismissal. But it is also reasonably certain that the *News Chronicle* correspondent and the journalist from Associated Press realised that the whole content of their 5 October interview with Adenauer was seditious; it was, after all, ille-gal for any German to criticise an occupying power. It followed not only that reports of the interview could not possibly be published, but that it was wise to consult the appropriate authority of the occupying power. The 'appropri-ate authority' in question was Brigadier Barraclough in Düsseldorf.

Whatever the truth about the circumstances of the dismissal, the British almost immediately started to retreat. Barraclough's decision to sack Adenauer, and the way it had been done, had not gone down well with the British officers in Cologne itself, nor with the Political Division of the Control Commission in Berlin. 'Good God!' was Lt-Col. Noel Annan's reac-tion in Berlin when he heard the news.[25] There were many telephone calls between Cologne, Düsseldorf, Lübbecke and Berlin. The result was that on 11 October Barraclough wrote to Adenauer, at the 'suggestion' of the Control Commission, modifying the original order and allowing him to take part 'in legitimate political activity outside the Regierungsbezirk of Köln'.[26] That dealt with part of the problem, but did not address the prob-lem of Gussi's illness. By then her condition had deteriorated, and she had been admitted as an in-patient to Hohenlind Hospital. There was then a fur-ther concession. On 15 October, Hamilton wrote to Barraclough saying that he had given orders allowing Adenauer to visit her 'on three days next week between stated hours'.[27] At that point, Barraclough's whole position was starting to disintegrate.

After a few weeks to allow at least some of the dust to settle, Annan vis-ited Rhöndorf. On his way, he had been to a conference in Düsseldorf. There he had been briefed by Captain Michael Thomas, a German refugee, born as Ulrich Holländer, who had left Germany after the anti-Semitic Nuremberg decrees, joined the British Army and who by then was on Templer's staff. Thomas had been the first to see Adenauer after the

Barraclough interview. Initially, he had gone to Adenauer's office on a routine call, but had found the mayor's desk cleared. On enquiry at the British headquarters, Thomas was told that Adenauer had been sacked three days earlier. Realising that fences needed to be mended, he then went to Rhöndorf to visit Adenauer, whom he found 'still in a state of shock over his brusque dismissal'.[28] As the conversation continued it became clearer and clearer to Thomas that Barraclough had made a major political blunder. That was his message to Annan. Annan concurred. Adenauer was, in his view, undoubtedly one of the potential leaders of a rehabilitated Germany, but the military administration had not been far-sighted enough to appreciate it. In fact, they were working on the premise of a long period of occupation; indeed, with this in mind, Barraclough had taken the view that 'new blood is required in the German administration in Köln'.[29]

The blunder had to be put right, and Annan called on Barraclough to tell him so. Barraclough replied that he could not climb down as far as to reinstate Adenauer as Mayor of Cologne. This Annan accepted; once the judgement had been made about Adenauer's competence, it could not be reversed. But the restrictions on his movements and his political activity had to be lifted.

In early December Lt-Col. Annan — at the age of twenty-eight — called on Adenauer — at the age of sixty-nine — at his home in Rhöndorf. He was received by Adenauer 'gravely, without any recrimination or coldness but with what is usually referred to in diplomatic circles as reserve'.[30] But he was, as Annan later remarked, 'a shaken man'.[31] Adenauer observed that if politics were to be discussed they should go immediately to Unkel, which was outside the Cologne administrative area, and where he was entitled to talk freely. Annan thought that this was some sort of joke. Adenauer then insisted that he was under threat of court-martial if he offended.

Having surmounted that hurdle — not without some of Adenauer's sharp irony — Annan was listened to 'with dignity'.[32] Annan pointed out that military government was by its nature difficult. They were faced with enormous problems, for which they were not particularly equipped. Nevertheless, Annan went on, the prohibition on his political activity would be lifted immediately. When he remarked that his dismissal by the British as Mayor of Cologne would help him in his efforts to gain political support, Adenauer 'permitted himself to smile faintly'.[33] After that, the conversation became more general. Annan referred to the concern that after the First World War

Adenauer was perceived to be anti-British. This was denied, but Adenauer admitted that 'he found difficulty in seeing Britain as a European state'.[34]

The interview lasted no more than an hour. But the consequence was immediate. On 14 December, Barraclough again sent for Adenauer. This time the meeting was more cordial. The ban on his political activity had been raised, and 'Dr Adenauer may take part in any legitimate political activity within or without Köln Regierungsbezirk'. Furthermore, 'Dr Adenauer may now live in or visit Köln whenever he wishes to do so'.[35] Barraclough's initial position had not just disintegrated but by then had been completely demolished.

As it happened, the lifting of Adenauer's political ban was fortunately timed. The Christian Democrat party groups which had been formed throughout Germany were to hold a meeting in Bad Godesberg on 14 December. As a result of the lifting of the ban, Adenauer was able to attend. Nevertheless, the tone of the meeting was not at all to his liking. The most important speech was that of Andreas Hermes* from Berlin; but it had to be read out because Hermes had not been given permission by the Soviet authorities to leave Berlin. Moreover, the theme of most of the speeches was, on any judgement, decidedly Christian Socialist. Even Jakob Kaiser, who had managed to escape the consequences of the Stauffenberg plot, was in the vanguard of the movement to the left. Adenauer, on the other hand, opposed it. His, and others', opposition was in the end effective. The only definite result of the Bad Godesberg meeting was the decision to adopt the name of 'Christian Democratic Union' for the whole movement. The ideological battle was left for another day.

Relations between Adenauer and the British were still far from harmonious.

---

* Hermes, Andreas (1878–1964): Politician. Born in Cologne. 1905: Doctorate in agricultural studies. 1911: Director of agricultural institute in Rome. 1920: Appointed Reich Minister for Agriculture. 1922: Also Reich Minister of Finance. 1924: Member of Prussian Landtag (Centre Party). 1928: Elected to Reichstag. 1936–39: Lived in Colombia. 1939–44: Returned to join resistance against Hitler. 1944: Arrested and sent to concentration camp. 1945: Released by Allied forces; founded CDU in Berlin. 1948–54: President of German agricultural trade union. Honourable, but on the left wing of the CDU, and no match for Adenauer.

In early 1946, therefore, the British made another effort. This time it was the Foreign Office in London which took the initiative. They instructed the head of the Control Commission Political Division, Christopher Steel, to make contact with Adenauer to try to patch things up. Steel turned to Annan, who in his turn asked Lt-Col. Ronald Grierson, then based in Cologne with Military Intelligence, to invite Adenauer to lunch.

This Grierson did, and the four men sat down in the Officers' Mess in Cologne. The lunch started at 1pm and ended at 7pm. During that period Adenauer gave the three British officers a long discourse on history – with a substantial section on the Holy Roman Empire. When Adenauer left, the exhausted officers sat down together, each with a much needed whisky and soda. It was Steel who had the last word. 'We can't do business with him,' he said. 'He keeps on insisting that the future must lie with "occidental Christianity". That's no good to us.'[36] What Adenauer thought of the meeting is a mystery; the real truth was that he no longer felt the need for British support. He was too busy founding his own political party.

2

ANOTHER POLITICAL BIRTH –
ANOTHER PERSONAL DEATH

'Der Grundsatz, dass die Würde der menschlichen Person über allem, auch
über der staatlichen Macht, stehen muss, ist aus dem Wesen des
abendländis chen Christentums entwickelt'*

'NO, CERTAINLY NOT' was Adenauer's response in 1962 when asked whether
he would have become Chancellor if he had not been dismissed in October
1945.[1] The response may or may not have been genuine – Adenauer by then
was a master of half-truths. But what is certainly true is that between his dismissal and the lifting of the ban on his political activity in December he was
far from idle. Indeed, now that the political bit was firmly between his teeth,
he seemed to recover much of the energy of earlier years. True, he spent a
good deal of time in his garden, but he was no longer tempted to return to
his inventions. Instead, he devoted time and thought to setting out a political philosophy for the new CDU; indeed, he wrote it all out in his own,
elaborately sloping, hand.

Admittedly, the document so laboriously produced was not particularly
original. It seemed closely to resemble *Quadragesimo Anno*, the Encyclical of
Pius XI which he had read all those years before at Maria Laach. There is the

---

* 'The principle that the dignity of the individual must be the paramount consideration,
even above the power of the state, is one that derives naturally from occidental Christianity':
Adenauer, *Erinnerungen*, Vol. I, p. 52.

same emphasis on the relationship between the individual and the state, limiting the power of the state 'by the dignity and inalienable rights of the individual'. There is, too, the same emphasis on 'the principles of Christian ethics and culture . . . which must pervade the life of the state'.[2] Similarly, Socialism and Communism are both condemned, much in the way Pius XI would have wished.

Nevertheless, there were points of difference with the Encyclical. Adenauer, and, indeed, all the founders of the CDU, were determined to embrace as wide a variety of political and religious views as possible. They wished, in particular, to distance the Union from the old Centre Party, which, although still in existence, had been tainted by its support for Hitler's Enabling Act of 1933, and was, in a British view, 'in a rickety condition'.[3] There was therefore no question of the Union becoming a confessional political grouping. Protestants, trade unions, the middle classes and business were all to be part of the act; and the act was one which built on the spontaneous political scenes which had been playing, admittedly on small stages, ever since the débâcle of 1945. As it happened, it was precisely the development of democracy at the grass roots which was the movement most favoured by the occupying authorities.

Adenauer himself was, however, careful to keep the support – in extensive conversations – of Archbishop Frings, who turned out, in fact, to have no great love for the Centre Party. The Rhineland was a particularly sensitive area, as the population was predominantly Catholic. There was, therefore, in Adenauer's remarks, a nod towards Pius XI – and, indeed, towards Leo XIII's *Rerum Novarum* – on the liberation and development of the working people, but there was nothing about the Christian duties of private ownership, on which Pius XI had been particularly clear. Yet the important principle, which Adenauer spelled out at length, was that personal freedom should not be endangered by the activity of the state.

Adenauer's programme rowed somewhat heroically against the political tide of the time. In line with the general post-war belief in Europe that the capitalism of the 1930s had failed, the prevailing and recommended solution – of all but the American occupiers – to the problems of the Germany of 1945 was to emphasise social cohesion rather than individual enterprise. In practice, of course, such an approach took many forms and shapes. But it is fair to say that the approach in the west of Germany came from two predominant directions: one religious, the other political. The essential point, however, was the same: in contrast to Adenauer's view, and that of Pius XI and Leo XIII, their common assertion was that the interests of the community should come before the interests of the individual.

It was, at the time, a matter of heated discussion. The 'Christian Socialist' view gained theological justification from the Dominican Provincial at Walberberg monastery, Laurentius Siemer. Siemer had been involved in the early stages of the Stauffenberg plot with Goerdeler in 1942, but somehow, perhaps because of his monastic vocation, had escaped the penalties which others had suffered, and had gone into hiding until British troops came to his rescue. But in 1945 – although for an admittedly short period – he was a powerful figure, so much so that his enemies dubbed him 'the white cardinal'. Siemers was in no doubt of his theological authority. It was no less a figure than St Thomas Aquinas. Whether the medieval theology of St Thomas was of any real support was, of course, open to argument.

The theological basis might be debatable. But Siemer was far from a lone voice in the political wilderness. In Germany, the Walberberg view was supported by many of the new Christian Democrats in all zones, let alone the SPD. Moreover, it had the further advantage of promising some sort of reconciliation with the Soviets to the east. This made it particularly attractive to the Berlin CDU, whose leader was one of the ablest politicians of the day, Andreas Hermes, and whose deputy leader was Siemer's old accomplice of 1942, Jakob Kaiser. In fact, it was Hermes' speech, read out at the December 1945 meeting in Bad Godesberg, which set out most clearly the Christian Socialist position.

Running parallel to this doctrinal dispute was the organisational question: whether the new CDU should be run centrally from Berlin or whether each zone should have its own independent structure, albeit linked federally with those of other zones. Hermes and Kaiser were in favour of the former, Adenauer of the latter. Of course, the question went well beyond the simple matter of organisation. It was a matter of power.

Adenauer was perceptive enough to see the crucial importance of the British Zone. After all, it contained the whole of the industrial area of the Ruhr and Cologne, and all the North Sea ports except for the American enclave of Bremen. Given that Bavaria was determined to maintain its own party structure, it followed – at least in his view – that whoever controlled the British Zone CDU would almost certainly end up by controlling the whole organisation in the west of Germany. Ambitious as he had now again quite clearly become, Adenauer set out to prevent control of the British Zone CDU from going to Berlin – and at the same time to secure control of it for himself.

Both tasks required skills in political in-fighting. In his career as Mayor of Cologne, Adenauer had never had to confront his opponents in public. He had been, after all, the master of events, and, within reason, could hire or fire as he wished. That was no longer the case. Everything he did was now in the public arena, and also under the scrutiny of the occupying powers. Nevertheless, and remarkably – given his age – he seemed to take almost naturally to the skills required.

The first step, of course, was to identify his rivals. Both Hermes and Jakob Kaiser were by origin Rhinelanders and therefore potential candidates to lead the British Zone CDU; but both were members of the Berlin CDU and would have to change to one of the British Zone parties to be serious contenders. In any event, they were both in favour of overall Berlin control of the national CDU when it emerged. Hermes, however, had been forced out as chairman of the Berlin CDU – and expelled from Berlin – by the Soviets for opposing their programme of land reform, and his position was in consequence weakened. That left Jakob Kaiser as the most powerful voice of the Berlin CDU. He would be a formidable rival to Adenauer in any national CDU, but not in the British Zone CDU. Leo Schwering had been one of the founder members of the Cologne Christian Democrats, and was obviously throwing his hat in the ring. Friedrich Holzapfel, the stubby and bad-tempered Mayor of Herford, was another, and the tall and aristocratic Hans von Schlange-Schöningen – 'almost a perfect English gentleman'[4] – would be a potential candidate from Schleswig-Holstein. For the moment, that seemed to complete the list.

Adenauer's supporters, on the other hand, were more difficult to identify. He was, after all, an old man, and had lived in seclusion during the years when a new generation was growing up. But there was one old friend, however, on whom he could rely: Robert Pferdmenges. Pferdmenges set about rustling up support in Cologne. The result was that by Adenauer's seventieth birthday, 5 January 1946, a number of members of what was by then the executive of the Rhineland CDU signalled a wish that Adenauer should assume the chairmanship of the CDU for the whole of the British Zone.

Adenauer had been astute enough to invite them to his home in Rhöndorf for the occasion, thus putting himself in the chair for the meeting and hence in a natural position of authority. Of their number, the most important were, without a doubt, the former trade unionists, Karl Arnold and Johannes Albers, both of them on the Christian Socialist wing of the party. Nevertheless, in the ensuing discussion, Arnold and Albers, backed up by their colleagues, agreed that they would suspend discussion of policy until a later date. This was precisely what Adenauer had hoped to achieve – the support of the left wing of the party for the chairmanship of the zonal CDU but without any concessions on policy.

The next step was to choose representatives of the Rhineland CDU as candidates to serve on a new body which the British Military Government had set up to advise on the general conduct of affairs in their zone. The Zonal Advisory Council, as it was called, was in practice an embryonic zonal government. Its importance for the future could not be over-emphasised. At a meeting on 8 January, the Rhineland CDU executive committee met to make the decision. By that time Adenauer, Arnold, Albers and Pferdmenges had fixed it. There was, of course, a row. But the list of candidates, when it emerged, included Adenauer, Pferdmenges, Arnold and three others who had been at the birthday meeting in Rhöndorf. Schwering, on the other hand, was only nominated as a deputy. His stock was falling fast. At the same meeting the Rhineland CDU executive nominated their delegates to a meeting of the CDU from the whole British Zone in the town of Herford in Westphalia, to take place on 19 and 20 January 1946. By then it almost went without saying that Adenauer would be nominated, as indeed he was.

As it happened, the Herford meeting offered Adenauer an unexpected opportunity – which he was quick to grasp. When the meeting finally assembled in Herford town hall, the scene was little short of chaotic. Few of the delegates knew each other; they had come from all over the zone – Schleswig-Holstein, Lower Saxony, Westphalia and the Rhineland. Moreover, they were not at all sure what the agenda of the meeting was apart from the main purpose, which was to constitute an executive for the British Zone CDU. Finally, when they all arrived, they found that there was no chairman to guide them in their deliberations.

When the dark-suited – and without exception male – delegates gathered on the first morning, they found that the large chair at the centre of the long top table was empty. Somehow it seemed to be assumed that the Mayor of Herford, Holzapfel, would occupy it. But in the general and nervous hubbub that is usual at the beginning of such meetings Adenauer marched up to the top table and sat down in the central chair. He then stood up, called the meeting to silence, and announced: 'I was born on 5 January 1876, so I am probably the oldest person here. If nobody objects, I will regard myself as president by seniority.'[5]

It was done with such grace and charm, as though it was an elegant joke, that all the delegates burst into relieved – but rather nervous – laughter. They were obviously relieved that their difficulty had been resolved in an elegant manner, and that order, as they understood it, had been restored. On the other hand, they were perhaps a little nervous that Adenauer had asserted his authority so decisively and so soon. What none of them fully appreciated was that, once they had accepted his initial bold move, it would be almost impossible to dislodge him, and that he had in practice appointed himself chairman of the British Zone CDU.

Adenauer was now in a position of strength. He was able to rule that one of his main rivals, Andreas Hermes, was a visitor from the Berlin CDU and therefore not entitled to take part in meetings of the committee of the British Zone CDU. Hermes thereupon left in a huff. The Schleswig-Holstein delegation declared that the electoral procedure inside their Land party had not yet been resolved, and that they were therefore only there as observers. That ruled out Schlange-Schöningen, who left on the second day of the meeting. Holzapfel agreed to be deputy to Adenauer. The result of the elections to the British Zone CDU executive committee was thus a foregone conclusion. Adenauer was elected unanimously as its 'temporary' chairman, with Holzapfel as his deputy.

Adenauer had by then quite clearly occupied the high ground. The opinion of Josef Kannengiesser, the secretary of the Westphalia CDU, that the election of Adenauer only as 'temporary' chairman had 'averted the danger of a false start to the right by the new party'[6] was no more than whistling in the wind. What Kannengiesser had not understood was Adenauer's determination both to hold on to office and to ensure that his 'Rhöndorf programme' was adopted. Such innocence was easily out-manoeuvred by an old hand such as Adenauer.

In the meantime, the matter of the leadership of the Rhineland party was being handled by his ally Karl Arnold, who adroitly postponed any firm decision until after the zone party meeting at Herford. In the week following Herford, Adenauer arranged with the Rhineland Protestant Otto Schmidt for the Protestant vote to come his way in return for a position for Schmidt as one of his two deputies. Schmidt was flattered by the offer, and persuaded his colleagues that Adenauer wanted a genuine co-operation with the Protestant community. The deal was done, and on 5 February at a meeting in a suburb of Krefeld, Adenauer was elected chairman of the Rhineland CDU, with Schmidt and Holzapfel as his deputies. Leo Schwering promptly resigned all his offices in the party. 'Yesterday,' he wrote to Albers on the following morning, 'was a black day for Christian working people and a victory for reaction all down the line.'[7]

One by one, all Adenauer's rivals were being carefully disposed of. Hermes, Holzapfel, Schlange-Schöningen, Schwering — in one way or another they were quietly shunted into political sidings. By early March 1946 only Jakob Kaiser remained as a serious contender. He, of course, was inextricably linked with the move to control the CDU centrally from Berlin and to a left-wing programme for the party. To achieve the control he needed Adenauer had to defeat both.

His first move was to summon a meeting of the British Zone CDU executive committee. This took place on 1 March 1946 in a convent in the small Westphalian town of Neheim-Hüsten. The convent was chosen not because of its undoubted religious aura but because the nuns would be able to provide the delegates with proper sustenance — important in the context of the almost starvation rations of the day. But, for all that, Adenauer was to write of the meeting at Neheim-Hüsten that it was 'one of the most decisive meetings of the CDU. We overcame the groups that advocated a strong dose of socialisation and so prevented a break-up of the party.'[8]

Nevertheless, in spite of Adenauer's apparent optimism, his battle was far from won. The meeting accepted the bulk of Adenauer's programme, particularly the 'return to the foundations of Western Christian culture', but was badly divided on the one issue of public ownership. After a long wrangle, it was Albers who succeeded in finding common ground between the two sides. It was finally agreed that there was nothing practical that could be done on the 'urgent question of a socialisation of parts of the economy, because the economy was not free'.[9] In other words, the whole issue was kicked conveniently into touch. But where Adenauer had won, as he himself later put it, was in achieving Point 10 of the Neheim-Hüsten economic programme: 'Property-holding is one of the essential safeguards of the democratic state. The acquisition of a moderate amount of property by all who toil honestly should be facilitated.'[10]

Adenauer felt confident enough after the meeting in Neheim-Hüsten to make a major speech. A few days after the meeting he delivered a long address, lasting just over two hours, to an audience of some four thousand listeners in the still damaged main hall of the University of Cologne. Physically, it was a remarkable effort – at times analytical, at times passionate, but above all exhausting. He had taken a great deal of trouble with it, and, even now, half a century later, it reads as it must have sounded – a fine platform speech.

First, he asked his audience some awkward questions. 'How was it possible,' he demanded, 'that the German Republic which we established in 1918 only lasted fifteen years?'[11] How, he went on, was the Third Reich possible? Why had Germany embarked again on a war 'which, despite dazzling early successes, was inevitably lost?'[12] From there Adenauer turned to the 'Prussian view of the state', militaristic, urban and materialistic. 'Nationalism found the strongest intellectual resistance among those Catholic and Protestant parts of Germany which had fallen least under the spell of the teachings of Karl Marx – of Socialism! That is absolutely certain!'[13] Of course, it was far from certain; in fact, it was wholly untrue. Bavaria, after all, was one of the most Catholic parts of Germany and at the origins of National Socialism. But by then Adenauer's audience was too carried away – and exhausted – to attend to nice points of detail such as that.

It followed, he went on, that the return to the values and sense of justice of Western Christendom was the way forward. Each human being was unique and irreplaceable. It therefore followed in turn that the only party which could rebuild Germany from the ashes of the Third Reich was the Christian Democratic Union. The underlying theme, of course, was that there was only one person qualified to lead it.

Towards the end of his speech, Adenauer turned his fire on the Social Democratic Party. He knew, as did his audience, that they would be the CDU's main opponents in future elections. They must therefore be attacked without mercy. But there was one further reason for Adenauer's determined

314

onslaught: they were led by one of the most charismatic politicians in the Germany of the day – Kurt Schumacher.*

Schumacher was in a number of ways the direct opposite to Adenauer. To start with, he was a Prussian, born in 1895 in the West Prussian town of Kulm on the river Vistula. Unlike Adenauer, he had served in the Kaiser's army in the First World War. Badly wounded, he had lost an arm and had been invalided out. He had gone on to study law and economics in Berlin and later in Württemberg, where he had joined the SPD. He was elected to the Reichstag in 1930 and was chairman of the SPD in Württemberg at the time the party was banned in 1933. He was then arrested by the Nazis, and – again unlike Adenauer – spent ten out of the twelve Nazi years in concentration camps, eight of them in Dachau. By sheer determination, he survived the starvation, frequent illnesses – and torture – of the camps, until the Nazis released him from Dachau in March 1943, believing him to be on the point of death.

He survived. But his body was dreadfully broken after all those years of torture. He was without his right arm; there was no more than a stump in its place; his face was haggard, etched with suffering. 'His high forehead, with penetrating, glowing eyes, flickering a little, tense, nervous, poised to spring, watchful as to who might enter, prepared to attack or defend his convictions . . . I understood the obsession of this man . . . With all due respect and regard to Adenauer's sober approach, and regardless of the fact that I was politically closer to Adenauer's way of thinking, I felt, already at the first meeting with Schumacher, a personal warmth that I was never able to feel towards Adenauer.'[14] Thus Michael Thomas, on first meeting Schumacher in November 1945.

---

* Schumacher, Kurt (1895–1952): Lawyer, economist and politician. 1914–18: Fought in First World War; lost an arm. 1918: Member of Berlin worker and soldier council. 1920–24: Journalist in Stuttgart. 1924–31: Member of Baden-Württemberg Landtag. 1930–33: SPD member of Reichstag; voted against Hitler's Enabling Act. 1933–44: Imprisoned in concentration camp. 1945: Re-organised SPD in Berlin and elsewhere. 1946: Became chairman of national SPD. 1949: Stood against Heuss for Federal Presidency and lost. 1949–52: Member of Bundestag. Possibly the most charismatic figure of the early post-war Germany.

Politically, too, Schumacher was Adenauer's opposite. To be sure, he was a socialist in the Marxist tradition. But he was an unremitting nationalist, deeply opposed to Communism, and wholly committed to a united, strong and centralist Germany. His opinions were expressed in an almost hysterical tone, which many British officers privately compared to Hitler's speeches. On the other hand, he was a realist. He fully understood that the heartland of the SPD was now buried in the Soviet Zone, and that any attempt to split Germany would deprive the SPD of a large measure of its electoral support. Adenauer, needless to say, had reached the same conclusion. In consequence, the two were fundamentally at odds on Adenauer's notions of a Rhineland–Westphalian state anchored firmly to the West. Where Adenauer regarded Jakob Kaiser's Christian Socialism as 'a vanity: the man, he said, had been breathing too much oriental air',[15] Schumacher felt that he could make common cause with Kaiser.

Moreover, the two men disliked one another personally. Lt-Col. Annan recalled how the two were invited to Berlin in July 1946. 'Beside me,' he wrote, 'was Adenauer, impassive, in formal dress, overcoat and homburg hat, as always dignified and calm . . . On the other side stood Schumacher, his thin hair blowing in the wind, hugging, as he often did, the stump of his right arm with his left hand . . . each gesture revealing his demonic energy and sardonic, impatient disposition . . . his sallow colour, his bad breath . . . Throughout the journey, in the aircraft and then by car, neither Adenauer nor Schumacher spoke a word to the other.'[16]

The occasion for their meeting, at Lübbecke airport, was an invitation by the British to the two leaders to explain, as a matter of courtesy, that they were forming a new Land: North Rhine-Westphalia. Schumacher objected violently, but this, of course, was just what Adenauer had argued for all along. Prussia had been abolished by an Allied Control Council Law in February 1946; the Soviets were busy integrating their zone into a Communist system by forcing a merger between the SPD and the Communist Party; it was becoming clear that Four-Power rule was simply not working; it was also becoming evident that Germany would be split for the foreseeable future. The creation of a major power centre in the western part of a split Germany was therefore essential.

The British decision was on those grounds very much to Adenauer's taste. But there were further reasons for his approval. If there was to be an economic powerhouse in the west of Germany, he certainly welcomed it – provided, of course, that he was in charge. In anticipation of the event, he had, during the spring of 1946 after Herford and Neheim-Hüsten, embarked on a hectic timetable of visits to CDU groups throughout the British Zone. That had gone well. But the truly decisive meeting had been on 3 April in Stuttgart, where he had met Christian Social Union leaders from Bavaria and CDU leaders from Baden and Württemberg. At that meeting it was agreed that the site of the CDU party leadership should not be in Berlin, but 'in some place near the [river] Main'.[17] Furthermore, the Bavarians would have nothing to do with Jakob Kaiser's programme for 'Christian Socialism'. Finally, if the two parties were to work together, as they should, they should remain as CDU in the British Zone and CSU in the American Zone. Adenauer was deputed to convey all this in person to Jakob Kaiser – which he did with what was obviously considerable personal satisfaction.

By the time of Adenauer's visit to Berlin in July 1946, he was therefore almost – but not quite – in total control of the CDU in the British Zone. As Albers wrote to Jakob Kaiser in August, about the mood in the CDU membership: 'They virtually worship Adenauer.'[18] But Adenauer's campaign, since that was what it had been, was not without cost. Since March, he had travelled up and down the country – in his old Horch car, and to the exhaustion of his driver – to public appearances, party meetings, rallies, negotiations with other groups, meetings with the British, and to meetings of the Zone Advisory Council and the Rhine Province Provincial Committee. As a programme it was, to say the least, more than punishing, particularly for a man of seventy. But in spite of the acknowledged success of his tour in political terms a personal tragedy was lurking in the background. The truth is that the one person who seemed to be entirely left out of his equation was his wife Gussi.

Gussi had, in fact, never really recovered from the traumas of 1944. Even when the wound from her second attempt at suicide had healed, she was left with post-traumatic symptoms: depression and insomnia. But it was worse than that. The Pyramidon on which she had overdosed while in prison at Brauweiler – and which she almost certainly continued to take – turned out to be heavily toxic. As a result, she unknowingly inflicted on herself a serious illness, known medically as agranulocytosis. In lay terms, the condition reduces the ability of the bone marrow to produce the white blood corpuscles which serve to counteract infections. By the summer of 1945 the agranulocytosis had been diagnosed, and was treated with medication and blood transfusions. The treatment was successful in controlling the condition, and, although infections occurred from time to time, they were dealt with. Nevertheless, a permanent cure even then seemed no more than a remote possibility. Throughout the summer and autumn, Gussi suffered.

Yet Adenauer, whatever his sympathies for his wife in her travails, was preoccupied with the municipal elections – the first elections in the British Zone since the war – which were to take place in November 1945. In the event, the CDU did well in the British Zone, but badly in Berlin. The result was another episode in the political war between Adenauer and Jakob Kaiser, between the British Zone CDU and the Berlin CDU. Kaiser argued angrily that the CDU should move to increase its electoral support in Berlin and in the Soviet Zone by siting its headquarters in Berlin and adopting a programme of 'socialising' the heavy industry of the Ruhr. Adenauer responded in an interview in *Die Welt*, in which he claimed that his most important difference with Kaiser concerned Germany's 'centre of gravity'. Berlin was no good, he said, because of its 'Prussian spirit'.

'It is my belief,' he went on, 'that Germany's capital should be situated in the south-west rather than in Berlin . . . somewhere in the region of the river Main . . .'[19] The response to Kaiser was Adenauer at his most subtle. He was not advocating the Rhineland, which would have caused the greatest irritation, and he was living up to his agreement with the Bavarians seven months earlier. The fact that he had little intention of implementing the agreement, and had only agreed to it as a matter of political tactics, was for the moment neither here nor there.

The new Land of North Rhine-Westphalia, of course, required a new administration, and the British Military Government appointed Rudolf Amelunxen as its head. Amelunxen was an old schoolfriend of Adenauer's, and they had kept in touch during the Nazi years. But his politics were not to Adenauer's liking: he had, after all, been private secretary to Otto Braun, the Social Democrat Minister-President of Prussia during the Weimar Republic, and had shared Braun's political views. As a result, the CDU – and Adenauer – stayed out of the new administration.

The difficulty was that the British decided to allocate seats in the new Landtag of North Rhine-Westphalia in proportion to the votes cast in the September municipal elections. There could no longer be any argument: the CDU had to be part of the administration. But Adenauer continued to refuse office. The result was that Karl Arnold, already Mayor of Düsseldorf, became Deputy Minister-President of the new Land, appointed by the British. Arnold was by now becoming, in Adenauer's terms, a rival. Furthermore, he was an open supporter of co-operation with the SPD, as well as the rump of the Centre Party — and he was a friend of Jakob Kaiser.

None of these manoeuvres, of course, took place in an international vacuum. There were Four-Power conferences in Paris in April 1946, and in Paris again in June into July. Nothing of moment came out of them, except the British and American realisation that the Soviets were not playing the game whose rules had been set out at Potsdam a year earlier. This being so, the Americans proposed, and the British accepted, a merger between the economies of their two zones — henceforward to be known, inelegantly, as the Bizone. Lt-General Sir Brian Robertson,* the deputy Military Governor of the British Zone, announced this to Adenauer and others at a meeting in Hamburg of the British Zone Advisory Council in August.

At the same time, it was revealed that France was to take full control of the Saarland subject to final resolution at the signature of a Peace Treaty. Finally, and most encouragingly for Adenauer, the US Secretary of State, James F. Byrnes, made a speech in Stuttgart in early September in a tone quite different from anything that the Germans had heard before from the occupying powers. 'The American people,' he said, 'want to help the German people to win their way back to an honourable peace among the free and peace-loving nations of the world.'[20] The tone, and the content, were echoed in a statement by the British Foreign Secretary, Ernest Bevin,† to the House of Commons in the following month.

---

* Robertson, Brian (1896–1974): Soldier. Distinguished record in First World War. 1933: Retired from British Army to become managing director of Dunlop South Africa Ltd. 1935: Returned to army in administration. 1941–43: Served as such in Middle East. 1945: Restored to active list in British Army. 1947–49: UK High Commissioner in Germany. 1949–50: Commander-in-Chief Middle East Land Forces. 1953: Retired; various subsequent positions. 1961: Became Lord Robertson of Oakbridge. Respected as fair, firm and charming.

† Bevin, Ernest (1881–1951): Trade unionist and politician. 1910–20: National organiser of Dockers' Union. 1921–40: General Secretary of Transport and General Workers' Union. 1940: Elected to House of Commons. 1940–45: Minister of Labour and National Service. 1945–51: Foreign Minister. One of the British Labour Party's great historic heroes.

The net result of all these moves, seen from Adenauer's perspective, was to make it all the more important for the future Germany, which was obviously not far from independent reality, to be created in his image. In other words, he had to win his battles, not just with Schumacher and the SPD but with Jakob Kaiser and his deputy Ernst Lemmer from Berlin, and with others in his party who wanted to move the entire edifice to the left.

But that whole matter, for the moment, would have to wait. Adenauer realised that some sort of compromise between him and Jakob Kaiser – between Rhöndorf and Walberberg – had to reached before the North Rhine-Westphalia Landtag elections of April 1947. In the event, the compromise was worked out by Albers from the trade union 'left' and Pferdmenges from the industrial and banking 'right' – both closely watched by Adenauer. It was presented to the British Zonal Committee in early February 1947, in the small mining town of Ahlen in Westphalia, and was agreed.

The Ahlen Programme, as it became known, was certainly a radical proposal for economic and social change. The three most important parts of the programme were the transfer of the coal industry to public ownership, anti-cartel legislation, and the right of workers to 'co-determination' on the major issues concerning the companies which employed them. There is no doubt that, in assenting to the Ahlen Programme, Adenauer had done much to calm the spirits in the left wing of his party. There is, however, equally little doubt that, once the elections were over, he would do all in his power to undermine the whole programme.

So it turned out. In the April Landtag elections, the CDU won 92 seats out of 216, the SPD won 64, the Communists (KPD) won 28, the Centre Party won 20 and the Liberals (FDP) 12. The result was, in practice, a defeat for Adenauer. Although he remained chairman of the CDU group in the Landtag, he could not prevent an alliance between his party, the SPD and a group in the Centre Party. Arnold was in consequence elected as Minister-President of North Rhine-Westphalia – an outcome much to the satisfaction of the British. Adenauer remained on the sidelines. As a result, not only did his personal relationship with Arnold collapse, but he deliberately set out on a programme of obstruction to the new Minister-President. Sniping from the flanks was the new order of the day.

The main target for the sniper was the Ahlen Programme. When the Landtag assembled, Adenauer, as leader of the largest party, introduced no fewer than three Bills which purported to implement the Programme, but which contained modifications to bring the whole thing back to what Adenauer regarded as good sense. The SPD immediately proposed a far more radical Bill, going beyond the Programme and advocating more extensive nationalisation. They had fallen into the trap. Adenauer, of course, was able to persuade the CDU to oppose the SPD Bill. The debates were long and profoundly tedious, but Adenauer ended by achieving his purpose. The Ahlen Programme remained as an important part of the CDU objectives, but on Adenauer's terms.

By the end of June 1947, although the debates on the Ahlen Programme and the associated legislation were only just starting, it was time for a holiday. Adenauer had applied for permission from the British just after the Landtag elections, and, in view of Gussi's poor health, it had been granted. In fact, Gussi was in better health than for some time, and the couple were able to set off in cheerful spirits – once again for the Swiss village of Chandolin, for a stay of three weeks. It was their first journey outside Germany since July 1939, but they found Chandolin 'almost completely unchanged . . . astonishingly beautiful in the wonderful weather . . . Everything is available, although expensive . . .'[21] Gussi, too, was equally enthusiastic. 'It is like a dream!' she added. 'Here in Chandolin the world has stood still.'[22]

The euphoria was not to last long. On her return, Gussi was taken ill again. Her white blood count was still dangerously low. Menacing skin infections had started to return, and in early October she started to run a high temperature. In mid-October her doctor called a consultant, who recommended immediate admission to the Johannes Hospital in Bonn. There was an operation to remove infected tissue, and for some weeks she was treated with blood transfusions, not least with blood given by Lotte and Libet. But the infection had gone deeper, and its manifestations steadily became more serious.

Over the winter, there were good days and bad days. Other consultants were called in – one a professor from Switzerland. They did their best, and by the end of 1947 it seemed that the patient might be on the mend. In early February 1948, however, things took a turn for the worse. There was a further operation, and massive blood transfusions, but it was to no avail. During the month her condition continued to deteriorate, and on 1 March all the doctors agreed that further treatment was useless. On the same day she lapsed into a coma and, on 3 March 1948, she died.

It was to be her last return to her home in Rhöndorf. Her body was brought back, the family was assembled, and the appropriate rites were observed. She was buried in the forest cemetery, beside Adenauer's first wife Emma, with due ceremony and with the solemn liturgy of the Catholic Church.

Gussi, by any standards, had been a good wife to Adenauer. She had lived, in the view of her daughter-in-law, 'selflessly for others, mainly for her husband and her children. She was natural, simple and uncomplicated, full of goodness and peace . . .'[23] Nevertheless, it would be wrong to compare Gussi's death in 1948 with Emma's death in 1916. Emma had been the passionate love of Adenauer's youthful life. Gussi had been the steady wife of his middle age.

As a matter of fact, while Gussi was going through her final agonies, Adenauer's mind was elsewhere. The London Foreign Ministers' Conference had been adjourned *sine die* on 15 December 1947, and he was busy considering the prospects of a further conference on the 'German Question' to be held – again in London – between the United States, Britain, France, Belgium, Holland and Luxembourg. It was left to the children, Paul – who postponed his novitiate at Maria Laach – Lotte, Libet and Lola to carry the burden of Gussi's final illness. Adenauer came when he could.

Adenauer certainly cared deeply for Gussi, but somehow it was difficult to find the time to sit with her in the hospital in Bonn. On the other hand, it is hard to believe that anything would have stopped him sitting all day and night with Emma in her dying moments in 1916. Therein, perhaps, lies the difference between the two Adenauer marriages.

3

THE BEGINNINGS OF THE NEW GERMANY

'Ich hielt [den] Rat für richtig, mit der Arbeit zu beginnen'*

GUSSI ADENAUER'S DEATH in March 1948, however long expected, came, as do all such events, as a shock. The immediate effect of the shock was to drive Adenauer further into his protective shell. Even at her funeral at Rhöndorf he snapped at one of the attending mourners. Moreover, during the days following her funeral, apart from his family he was only prepared to see those who came on urgent matters of business which could not be delayed.

But that retreat could only last for the immediate aftermath of her death. When he resumed his busy political life he still had to make the long-term personal adjustment. He had, after all, married twice, and he had seen both wives buried. In one sense, Emma's death, however emotionally painful, had been easier to deal with. At least there had always been the possibility of a future. Gussi's death, on the other hand, was more difficult. It took little imagination for him to see that he would be unlikely ever to marry again. He therefore had to come to terms, not just with bereavement, but with loneliness.

This Adenauer did, certainly slowly, and over the whole period of months

---

* 'I thought the [Robertson's] advice to get down to work was good': Adenauer, *Erinnerungen*, Vol. I, p. 145.

and years which made up the rest of his life. But he did so by convincing himself that Gussi's fatal illness had been entirely due, and was the direct consequence of, her experience in Brauweiler in 1944. Objectively, of course, this view is not supported by medical evidence. Chronic agranulocytosis is not caused by a single overdose of toxic material but by continuing absorption over months and even years. But it is no more than a truism to say that everyone who lives a long life has to deal at some point with grief, and the guilt that may be associated with it, in his or her own way. This was Adenauer's way.

Whatever his state of mind, at the time of Gussi's death and thereafter, he was able to persuade himself that it was the Gestapo who had been responsible for the illness which led to her death. It was a convenient road to self-absolution, if that was what was required; and he took it. Indeed, his continuing self-absolution was such that even when – many years later – he came to write his memoirs he persisted, again contrary to the evidence, in maintaining that she had become 'ill without hope of recovery'[1] as a result of her imprisonment by the Gestapo in the last stages of the war.

In the period of mourning after their mother's death Adenauer did his best to look after his children. He made time for lunch with them at Rhöndorf, to keep the family show, as it were, on the road. But, although the effort was made, the road turned out to be bumpy. In the period of his wartime inactivity he had appeared to them as a kindly, grandfatherly old man. Now his temper was frequently frayed and, as Lola remarked about him later on, 'you could be happy if you were not the target of his attack'.[2] In place of the battered gardening clothes, the trousers which could never be thrown away and the much loved old hat, there appeared the traditional dark suit, three-quarter-length overcoat and the formal homburg. Lunches with his family at Rhöndorf seemed to be less the relaxed affairs which they had known during the war; they were more like formal meetings of a Cabinet.

Indeed, it was as though the change in dress was marking a change in character, or at least the re-emergence of the character of the former Mayor of Cologne. For instance, he resumed his aggressiveness in political warfare. In fact, the tempo of his aggression was raised a notch or two. To be sure, his weapons were, on the face of it, the same as they had always been. But what previously was legitimate irony became sarcasm – at times fierce to the point of vulgarity; the personal attacks on his opponents became more wounding; and – to put it bluntly – he was prepared to play the game of political dirty tricks. To mention only one instance, his assertion that his party colleague

Jakob Kaiser had been talking to officials of the Soviet Military Government and to former generals in the Wehrmacht was no more than an invention (but it was enough to destroy Kaiser's credibility in the CDU). Adenauer had not just learned how to play the political game but seemed now prepared to play it in the most unscrupulous manner.

This transformation required a difficult adjustment on the part of his family. The gentle old grandfather of 1943 had, within five years, turned into a hard and unforgiving old politician. With hindsight, of course, it is not hard to detect in this the effect of the loss of his second wife. She had undoubtedly been a mollifying influence on her husband, calming him down in periods of stress. She had also been the central figure around whom the whole extended family, which gave Adenauer such emotional security, could unite in friendliness – and even love. Without her, the family could only unite on the basis of obedience to Adenauer himself. Lola again: 'My father-in-law behaved . . . wholly differently to the way he behaved when I first got to know him.'[3] Indeed, the one child to whom his father was closest, his (and Gussi's) son Paul, was the gentlest one of the family. He was on the verge of the priesthood, committed to celibacy, poverty – and patience. As such, in Adenauer's newly aggressive character he was almost destined to be his father's favourite son.

If it is true that Adenauer felt the need to justify to himself his behaviour at the time of Gussi's final illness until the crisis arrived, the reason was not far to seek. The whole period was one of intense political activity, all of which he wished, his character being what it was, to absorb in the greatest detail. Internationally, 1947 had been a year of almost bewildering movement, the long-term implications of which were difficult to foresee. The Byrnes speech at Stuttgart had been followed by the 'Truman Doctrine', announced by President Harry Truman* in March 1947 and summed up by

---

* Truman, Harry S. (1884–1972): Lawyer, farmer and politician. Born in Missouri, USA. 1906–17: Managed family farm. 1918: Served in France in First World War. 1922–34: Judge in Jackson County, Missouri. 1934: Elected to US Senate from Missouri; various committees in the Senate. 1944: Elected Vice-President of the USA. 1945: Acceded to the presidency on Roosevelt's death. 1948: Elected for a second term as President. Baptist, Freemason, homespun, but surprisingly robust.

the single word: 'containment'.[4] In parallel, an ambitious plan for US economic aid to Europe had been set in train by Secretary of State George Marshall in June 1947.*

Domestically, events had moved equally fast. Certainly, in terms of the narrow politics of the CDU, Adenauer had achieved a victory. He had managed to win the battle with Kaiser over the Berlin claim to run the CDU from the centre. In December 1947, Kaiser and Lemmer had finally been removed by the Soviets, on an invented pretext, from their positions as Chairman and Deputy Chairman of the CDU in the Soviet Zone, and prohibited from any further political activity there. There had been no longer any question of a CDU controlled centrally from Berlin. As though to show that Adenauer had been right, the Soviets went on the offensive. Between 1948 and 1950 some six hundred members of the Soviet Zone CDU were arrested by the agents of an organisation known as K-5, set up by the Soviets in August 1947 for the declared purpose of de-Nazification, but in practice for the convenient disposal of opponents to the new regime. Indeed, the majority of those arrested 'probably . . . found their way into Soviet . . . labour camps'.[5] It was more than enough to prove Adenauer's case.

Aside from internal CDU politics, there had been a further domestic event which turned out to be of long-term significance: the first meeting of the Bizonal Economic Council in Frankfurt in June 1947. The black, red and gold colours of the German Republic had been raised for the first time for fourteen years – until the Americans noticed the flag and ordered it to be taken down. But, apart from this almost revolutionary gesture, there had been a further development which was to have profound implications for the future of the new Germany. When the Council came to choose its

---

* Marshall, George (1880–1959): Soldier. Born in Uniontown, Pennsylvania. 1897: Virginia Military Institute. 1902: Commissioned into infantry. 1917: Chief of operations in US 1st Division on Western front. 1918: Chief of operations in US 1st Army. 1919–24: Aide to General Pershing. 1927–33: Assistant commandant at infantry school, Fort Benning, Georgia. 1939–45: Chief of Staff of US Army. 1947–49: Secretary of State; main architect of the 'Marshall Plan'. 1950–51: Secretary of Defense. 1953: Awarded Nobel Peace Prize. Regarded as aloof in manner, but with fierce temper when he let it go.

directorate, the SPD had refused to join in coalition with the CDU/CSU and had assumed the role of opposition. Finally, the Council had passed, and the Military Governments had accepted, what was called the Transitional Law, the first post-war piece of legislation which legalised a federal authority over the Länder. It seemed, even at the time, to be a decisive move towards a sovereign federal state.

There had been, however, one dispute still causing ill-feeling on all sides: the programme of the dismantling of all plant which had been built for, or converted to, military purposes, a programme which had been announced by the Americans and the British in October 1947. It was particularly severe in the British Zone, and Adenauer had protested vigorously. On top of the continuing and severe food shortages, and the fact that industrial production was little more than one third of its pre-war level, the dismantling programme had come as a bitter blow. Even Lord Pakenham, the British minister responsible for German Affairs in London, had had his doubts. 'My own conflict of mind,' he subsequently wrote, 'was very intense.'[6] But, as Adenauer pointed out with impeccable logic, the dilemma was there: the dismantling programme was in direct contradiction to Marshall's European Recovery Plan.

All this had been enough to occupy Adenauer's full attention in the months and weeks before Gussi's death. But in early 1948 the political landscape shifted yet again. In February, just a few weeks before her death, the Communists seized power in Czechoslovakia; 'Friendship, co-operation and mutual assistance' treaties were then signed between the Soviet Union and East European states. In March, Marshal Vassili Sokolovski – known, rather irreverently, by his Western colleagues as 'Soko' – walked out of a meeting of the Control Council in Berlin. In April a Soviet Yak fighter collided with a British passenger aircraft as it was coming in to land at Gatow airport in Berlin; both sides blamed the other in an acrimonious exchange of notes. The downhill slope of relations between the Western occupying powers and the Soviets was becoming dangerously steep.

It became even steeper when a conference of Western allies was convened in London to discuss the future of Germany. The Soviets, after their refusal to accept aid under the Marshall Plan, were pointedly not invited. General Robertson, by then Military Governor of the British Zone, explained the situation on 7 April to the North Rhine-Westphalia Landtag. 'Come forward,' he said to them, 'determined to make the best of that larger part of your country which is on the right side of the Iron

Curtain. The rest will come in time. We offer you our good will and co-operation.'[7] It was a reflection of the new Allied view of the Soviets and, as Adenauer later wrote, 'the speech contributed greatly to reviving our courage'.[8]

At the same time, a new figure was about to occupy the attention of the domestic political audience – at least those who were interested in economics: Ludwig Erhard.* He, in truth, came from no recognisable starting point. The first director of the Bizonal Economic Council, the erratic Johannes Semler, had at least come from the Bavarian CSU; but he had made the mistake of criticising the economic policies of the two Military Governments. He had been particularly angry at the American offer of maize, which in pre-war Germany had been considered only good to be fed to chickens. Moreover, he discovered that the Germans were expected to pay for the chicken feed. It had all been too much for him. 'It is about time,' he proclaimed, 'that German politicians refrained from offering public thanks for this kind of food subsidy.'[9] He was promptly sacked by General Lucius Clay, the US Military Governor.†

Adenauer wanted one of his CDU allies, the admittedly colourless

---

* Erhard, Ludwig (1897–1977): Economist and politician. Born in Fürth in Bavaria. 1928–42: First assistant and later director of Nuremberg Institute for Economic Studies. 1942: Dismissed by Nazis, then headed a market research firm. 1945–47: Minister for Economic Affairs in Bavaria. 1947: Economics minister in Bizone. 1949–63: Minister for Economic Affairs in Federal Republic. 1957–63: Federal Deputy Chancellor. 1963–66: Federal Chancellor. 1966–67: Chairman of CDU/CSU parliamentary group. Outgoing, cigar-smoking, in character the opposite to Adenauer.

† Clay, Lucius (1897–1978): US General. Born in Marietta, Georgia. 1918: Graduated from US Military Academy at West Point. Various engineering assignments in US Army. 1940: Head of US national civil airport program. 1942: General in charge of army procurement. 1945: Deputy military governor in Germany. 1947: Appointed military governor of US Zone. Retired in 1949. 1961–62: Kennedy's personal representative in Berlin, with rank of ambassador. Much respected in Germany, not least because of his role in the Berlin airlift in 1948, although at times the fuse was short. Sometimes known as an 'independent warlord'.

Hermann Pünder, to get Semler's job. Pferdmenges tried to rally support for Pünder, but without success. Erhard was much cleverer, and even prepared to take greater risks. Furthermore, he was a Franconian – and therefore came from the American Zone – and he was, like Semler, something of a bruiser. He had lain low during the war, discreetly spending most of the time as the chairman of an obscure institute studying the long-term economic problems of the city of Nuremberg. The result of his studies turned out to be a tedious paper on the problems of war debt and of economic policy in a defeated country. Thereafter, he spent a short and unremarkable period in the provisional government of Bavaria between April 1945 and January 1947 before staring an academic career in Munich. The omens for a successful political career were far from favourable.

Nevertheless, the Americans liked his ideas, and he was suddenly projected in October 1947 from his honorary professorship at the University of Munich to be the head of the Special Bureau for Money and Credit in the Bizone Economic Council. It was all very surprising. But as it turned out, the result of Erhard's appointment as Director of Economics of the Economic Council was little less than spectacular. By June 1948 the Allies had planned the reform of the currency and the introduction of the Deutschmark, and Erhard had successfully implemented the plan by arranging for 500 tons of the new banknotes to be printed in the United States and airlifted to Frankfurt.

The Deutschmark duly became the legal currency in the three western zones on 20 June 1948. At the same time, Erhard was responsible for abolishing virtually all rationing and lifting price controls. It was an astonishingly bold manoeuvre, the more so that a great deal of it had been done without the prior agreement of the Military Governors. In fact, when Clay told Erhard 'my advisers tell me that what you have done is a terrible mistake' and asked him, 'What do you say to that?', Erhard replied without hesitation: 'Herr General, pay no attention to them. My own advisers tell me the same thing.'[10]

Adenauer himself played little part in the currency reform. He was, however, astute enough to realise that in the portly, cigar-smoking Erhard there was the potential of a capable and energetic economics minister. This realisation was tucked away in his mind for future reference – only, in fact, to be acknowledged later. Conveniently enough, Erhard's ability would

allow Adenauer to concentrate on the wider politics of international relations. To him they were much more interesting than the dry calculations of
economics.

Adenauer's first serious venture into international politics, apart from
parochial discussions with Christian Democrats from other European countries (or chattering with the French over the Rhineland), was in his leadership
of the CDU delegation to the congress of the United Europe movement in
The Hague in early May 1948. The event was certainly a grand affair.
There were no fewer than eight hundred delegates, one hundred and forty
from Britain alone, led by Winston Churchill and including Anthony Eden,*
Harold Macmillan† and, for some obscure reason, the conductor Sir Adrian
Boult and the Poet Laureate, John Masefield. Paul-Henri Spaak** was there
from Belgium, Léon Blum and Edouard Herriot from France, and Alcide de

---

* Eden, Anthony (1897–1977): Politician. Educated at Eton and Oxford. 1915–18: fought
in First World War. 1923–57: Member of House of Commons. 1925–33: Numerous
appointments in British Foreign Office. 1935: Appointed Foreign Secretary – resigned in
1938. 1940: Re-appointed as Foreign Secretary, and served until 1945. 1951: Again
Foreign Secretary. 1955–57: Prime Minister. 1961: Became Earl of Avon. Good-looking,
Rolls-Royce negotiator, but had serious health problems.

† Macmillan, Harold (1894–1986): Publisher and politician. Educated Eton and Oxford.
1914–18: Served in British Army in First World War (wounded three times). 1924: First
elected to House of Commons. Thereafter combined politics with publishing career in
family business. 1940: Various ministerial posts, including, notably (1942–45) Minister
Resident at Allied HQ in Algiers. 1951–57: Minister in Conservative government; Foreign
Secretary (1955) and Chancellor of the Exchequer (1955–57). 1957–63: Prime Minister.
1984: Became Earl of Stockton. Shrewd operator; presented himself as an aristocratic Tory
grandee and at the same time as descendent of Scottish crofters. Great political actor.

** Spaak, Paul-Henri (1899–1972): Lawyer and politician. Born in Schaerbeck, Brussels.
1921–31: Practised law in Brussels. 1932: First elected as socialist deputy for Brussels.
1935–38: Various ministries in Belgian government. 1938–39: Prime Minister of Belgium.
1939–46: Foreign Minister (from May 1940 in Belgian government in exile in London).
1947–49: Prime Minister of Belgium. 1952–54: President of the Common Assembly of
the ECSC. 1954–57: Belgian Foreign Minister. 1957–61: Secretary-General of NATO.
1961–66: Deputy Prime Minister and Foreign Minister of Belgium. Rightly believed to be
one of the genuine 'Fathers of Europe'.

Gasperi,* the Italian Prime Minister. All in all, it was an impressive gathering.

Churchill's opening speech lived up to the occasion. It was long, idealistic about the unity of Europe, and suitably orotund. He was particularly warm in welcoming the delegations from Germany. For the European Movement, he said, 'The German problem is to restore the economic life of Germany and revive the ancient fame of the German race without thereby exposing their neighbours and ourselves to any rebuilding or reassertion of their military power of which we still bear the scars.'[11] Churchill also received Adenauer personally. Adenauer was duly impressed.

Although his private opinion of Churchill remained cautious – he remembered Churchill's remark that 'the German is either at your throat or at your feet' – he asked Lord Pakenham, who was also present, to convey to Churchill his and his colleagues' deep gratitude. 'We were Hitler's prisoners,' he said, 'and but for Mr Churchill we would not be alive today.' When Pakenham asked why he did not say that directly to Churchill, Adenauer replied, with some dignity: 'I did not feel that I would be serving my country's interests if I had appeared fawning or fulsome in the moment of national humiliation.'[12] Furthermore, on his return to Germany, he wrote to Silverberg: 'Of Churchill I gained a good impression. But he is already very old.'[13] (As a matter of fact, Churchill was seventy-three at the time; Adenauer was a mere seventy-two).

In general, Adenauer found the conclusions of the Hague congress much to his liking, as he reported soon afterwards to the British Zone CDU executive. In particular, he agreed with the conclusion that Germany's future lay

---

* De Gasperi, Alcide (1881–1954): Politician. Born in Trento, Italy (but then part of Austria-Hungary). Educated at Trento and then University of Vienna. 1911: Elected Deputy for Trento to Austro-Hungarian parliament in Vienna. 1919: Elected Deputy for Trento to Italian Parliament; Secretary of Partito Populare Italiano. 1926: Arrested on dissolution of Italian political parties and imprisoned. 1945–53: Prime Minister of Italy. 1954: President of the Common Assembly of the ECSC. Together with Adenauer and Schuman, ranks as a founder of the ECSC, and hence a 'Father of Europe'. One of the great post-war Europeans, whose place in history has been underestimated.

in a European federation. 'European nations,' the congress declared, 'must transfer and merge some of their sovereign rights so as to secure common political and economic action.'[14] Adenauer echoed the sentiment: 'In truth, in [the unification movement] lies the salvation of Europe and the salvation of Germany.'[15]

At the time, too, Adenauer seemed to be getting on better with the British, at least at the personal level. His relationship with Robertson was cordial – and was later to develop into something close to friendship. He also liked Lord Pakenham, not least because of their shared Catholicism, and invited him to a farewell tea in Rhöndorf when Pakenham changed jobs at the end of May 1948. Nevertheless, it was only a relative change; there remained a residue of deep suspicion – on both sides.

But even these personal relationships, not to mention the relationship with British officialdom, were put under strain in the weeks following the Hague congress. It was not a matter of 'dismantling', however irritating that was. The London Conference of the Western Allies, reconvened on 20 April, produced what became known as the London Agreements at a press conference on 7 June. These made three recommendations: first, that a constituent assembly should be convened; second, that the Military Governors would set out an Occupation Statute to define their residual powers once the proposed new constitution had been agreed; and, third, that an international Ruhr authority, in which Germany would participate, should be set up to allocate the coal and steel production of the Ruhr between the various countries of Western Europe. It was the proposed Ruhr authority that stuck in Adenauer's craw. It was in his view no less than the rape of the major industrial area of the valley of the Rhine.

As it happened, the London Agreements were announced only a fortnight before the currency reform was implemented. Both the Agreements and the currency reform irritated the Soviets, who in retaliation promptly tightened their stranglehold on Berlin. There is little doubt, nor was there much doubt at the time, that the world seemed at this point to be trembling on the brink of a Third World War. But Adenauer was single-minded. He had little involvement in the Berlin blockade (and airlift) of 1948. He was much more concerned about the proposed Ruhr authority. 'The Versailles Treaty,' he wrote, 'is a bed of roses by comparison.'[16] The tribal leaders were summoned: the CDU Länder organisations in both zones of the Bizone met three days after the publication of the London Agreements under Adenauer's chairmanship at Bad Königstein. They immediately issued a statement which 'sharply rejected' the provisions for a Ruhr authority.[17] Adenauer went on to try to associate the SPD with the protest, but Schumacher was ill, and nobody was prepared to take a decision without him.

Given the crisis over Berlin, Adenauer's efforts over the Ruhr authority appear little more than complaints about the functioning of the parish pump. The protest was in any case futile. After so many months of negotiation between themselves it was, to say the least, simple-minded to believe that the occupying powers would change their minds, however strong the protests from the country they still regarded as the defeated enemy. The London Agreements were patently only negotiable at the edges, whatever Adenauer might say or think.

Among the many detailed points in the Agreements was a provision to wind up the Zonal Advisory Council. Its last meeting took place on 29 June 1948. Robertson turned up for the occasion, and told them firmly to stop behaving like children. The Military Government was also sending the message out to the Minister-Presidents of the Länder to cease 'restrictive and discursive criticism'.[18] Robertson pointed out to the meeting that he knew perfectly well that they would not like the arrangements for the Ruhr, but it was the price which had to be paid to secure France's agreement to the package as a whole. The message went home. After reflection, he 'thought that [Robertson's] advice to start our work was right';[19] and this they promptly did.

There was, of course, much to-ing and fro-ing about the specific terms of the London Agreements. The formal documents were handed to the Minister-Presidents of all the Länder in the three western occupied zones. They in turn called a meeting at Koblenz on 8 July which lasted three days. That was followed by a meeting between the Minister-Presidents and the Military Governors in Frankfurt on 20 July which lasted six days. There was a further meeting of constitutional experts on 10 August on the Herreninsel, the island in the Chiemsee near Munich, which lasted thirteen days. As a result of all these meetings, a draft constitution was produced, and the Western governments in turn made one concession: they agreed to abandon their original idea of a national referendum on the new constitution if and when it was produced.

Adenauer himself took no part in these meetings. Nor could he have taken part; he had no governmental position. Not only that, but Karl Arnold, the Minister-President of North Rhine-Westphalia, was not prepared to be dictated to – even by the chairman of his own political party. Furthermore, Adenauer found the Bavarian Minister-President, Hans Ehard, boorish and stupid, although they in turn saw eye to eye in joint dislike of Josef Müller, the chairman of the CSU. Since Adenauer had no possible authority over the SPD Minister-Presidents – nor, for that matter did Schumacher – he was almost without influence on the course of events.

It was a frustrating time. He could make pronouncements, summon meetings of the Zonal CDU, negotiate with other parties and with Christian Democrat parties in other countries, but he had no official position which would allow him to argue with authority against the Military Governors in Germany or with their parent governments. For instance, he knew nothing about the administration of the American Zone and had not yet met General Clay. (Nor had Clay ever signalled that he wished to meet Adenauer.) It is hardly surprising that his family found him fractious and bad-tempered.

The frustration turned to activity when the Minister-Presidents decided on 26 July that they would comply with the Allied government wishes and summon a constituent assembly, to be known as the Parliamentary Council, to meet in Bonn on 1 September 1948. This was to be a council of party representatives rather than government officials, elected by the Landtage; there were to be twenty-seven CDU/CSU delegates, twenty-seven SPD delegates, five Liberals and two each from the Centre Party and the Communists – reflecting with as much accuracy as possible the proportions of seats held by each party in the totality of the Landtage of the zones. The choice of Bonn was only made in mid-August after intense lobbying by the North Rhine-Westphalian administration. Indeed, Adenauer himself would have preferred Koblenz, since it was in the French Zone, and meetings there would help to bind the French to its conclusions; but he was not yet in a position to intervene.

Needless to say, the jockeying for position within the Parliamentary Council started almost immediately. Behind Adenauer's back, and much to his irritation, the CDU and SPD had swapped a seat in Württemberg for a seat in Hamburg to allow in to the Council an SPD expert in constitutional

law, the genial and portly professor from Tübingen, Dr Carlo Schmid.*
The SPD then announced that they would support Adenauer for the presidency provided that Schmid was accepted by the CDU as chairman of the main working committee. 'We've made Adenauer President,' one SPD delegate remarked, 'to put this old nagger and squabbler in a place of honour where he is safely out of the way. The real work will be done in the steering committee, and there our own Carlo Schmid presides.'[20] Besides, the SPD thought that Adenauer was too old to have much of a political career left. Thus was Adenauer elected to what, at the time, was the prime position in German politics.

But it was not so easy to muzzle the old man. Admittedly, Schmid and his committee did the essential work on what was to become known as the Basic Law, but Adenauer was the titular head of the Council, and used his position to get himself better known outside the British Zone to the public and the press. He was also able to discuss matters directly and officially with the Military Governors who, naturally enough, took a close interest in the ebb and flow of debate within the Council. Lastly, as Theodor Heuss† later pointed out, 'although as yet without a precise

---

* Schmid, Carlo (1896–1979): Lawyer and politician. 1923: Doctorate in law. 1927–40: At Kaiser Wilhelm Institute for international law. 1940–44: In military administration in Lille; made contacts with resistance movement in Germany. 1946–53: Professor of international law at Tübingen. 1949: Elected SPD member of Bundestag. 1949–66 and 1969–72: Vice-president of Bundestag. 1966–69: Minister for Internal Affairs. One of the main architects of the post-war SPD. Portly, jovial and charming, but perhaps lacked political steel.

† Heuss, Theodor (1884–1963): Journalist and politician. Born in Brackenheim in what is now Baden-Württemberg. 1905: Doctorate in political science. 1905–21: Journalist, supporting middle-of-the road politics. 1921: One of the founders of the Berlin Hochschule for political education. 1924–28: Member of Reichstag. 1930–33: Again member of Reichstag. 1933–45: Returned to writing, biographies and non-political articles under a pseudonym. 1945: Minister for Culture in Baden-Württemberg. 1946: One of the founders of the FDP. 1948–49: Member of Constitutional Council; at the same time, professor of modern history and political science in Stuttgart. 1949–59: First President of the Federal Republic. Respected by all who knew him; gave stability to the early years of the new country.

"appointment" . . . [Adenauer] had become the obvious and acknowledged spokesman with the Western powers for the Federal Republic which was being born'.[21]

Adenauer was helped in all this by a new figure on the stage: Herbert Blankenhorn.* At the age of forty-four, coming as he did from a comfortable bourgeois family of wine merchants and growers in Baden – his grandfather had developed successfully, by means of grafts from California, a regeneration of the Müller-Thurgau vine after the native variety had been destroyed by phylloxera – Blankenhorn had seen life from the outside. His uncle had been German ambassador in Washington between 1937 and 1939, and he himself had been accepted into the diplomatic service at the early age of twenty-five. There, if the truth be told, he kept his head down. Prior to, and during the war there were postings in Athens, Washington, Helsinki and Berne. He was intelligent, charming – and anglophile. He certainly had a future of distinction in the foreign service of the new Germany. In view of this, none of his many British friends could understand why he chose to leave the Foreign Service and throw in his lot with an old reprobate and reactionary like Adenauer.

Whatever his motives, Blankenhorn was an instant success. Appointed by Adenauer as general secretary of the British Zone CDU, he then became private secretary to the President of the Parliamentary Council – namely Adenauer himself. He became responsible for maintaining close links with the Military Governors' liaison staffs, and for steering Adenauer through the murky waters of the Allied rivalries of the time.

It was almost certainly through Blankenhorn that Adenauer was introduced to a number of foreign journalists. The first encounters were not, it must be admitted, a great success. One American journalist, with experience in Egypt, reported that Adenauer looked like a wrinkled mummy with a disconcerting capacity for breaking into speech. Another, with experience in

---

* Blankenhorn, Herbert (1904–91): Diplomat. Born in Baden. 1929–48: Reich Foreign Office. One of the founders of the CDU: General Secretary, 1948–52. Adenauer's closest foreign policy adviser until they fell out over Britain's exclusion from the EEC. 1953: Federal Republic's permanent representative at NATO (1953–58 as ambassador). 1958–70: Ambassador in Paris, Rome and London. Suave, cultivated, anglophile.

China, thought that he was 'oriental': 'very grey, clean, immaculate, ageing, starched detachable collar'.[22] In his interviews, Adenauer never made even the vestige of a joke, but gave his audience a solemn lecture on the issues facing Germany. The journalists obviously thought him something of a temporary and expendable nuisance, and waited for the younger generation which would surely take over.

Moreover, during the period of deliberation in the Parliamentary Council over the winter of 1948–49, Adenauer, divorced as he was from the committee work of the Council and only required to preside over the intermittent plenary sessions, went, on Blankenhorn's advice, on a number of foreign expeditions. In fact, nobody knew where he was from time to time. He would re-emerge in unlikely places – in Switzerland or in Luxembourg. During these disappearances – which irritated his CDU colleagues doing the hard work in the Parliamentary Council – he would talk to many of those who, in truth, held the future of Europe in their hands. Some of them he had met earlier at the congress in The Hague, Alcide de Gasperi for instance. But, for the future, the most important contact he made during the autumn and winter was with the French Foreign Minister Robert Schuman.* As it turned out, Adenauer, Schuman and de Gasperi were in the future to make a formidable triumvirate.

Adenauer's meeting with Schuman took place in the utmost secrecy. The venue was Bassenheim on the river Mosel, in a castle constructed – in perhaps doubtful taste – by the Oppenheim family but at the time occupied by the French Governor of the Rhineland Palatinate, Hettier de Boislambert. So secret was the meeting that Adenauer travelled in a large car wrapped in a travelling blanket, his homburg hat crammed down over his head. Schuman

---

* Schuman, Robert (1886–1963): Lawyer and politician. Born in Luxembourg. Educated in German universities of Bonn, Munich and Berlin. 1919: Elected to French National Assembly. 1940: Arrested by Gestapo. 1942: Escaped and joined the Resistance. 1945: Founded Mouvement Républicain Populaire. 1946 (July to November): Minister of Finance. November 1947–July 1948: Prime Minister. 1948–52: Foreign Minister. 1958: President of fledgling European Parliament. Thanks to his bilingual ability in French and German, and his Alsatian background, was able to build bridges between post-war Germany and France.

flew in from Paris to the nearby military airport of Niedermending. The two men then settled down to a discussion which lasted the best part of two days.

Adenauer and Schuman found that they talked the same language, literally as well as metaphorically. Schuman had been born in Luxembourg in 1886. His mother language was German. Not only that, but his education had been in German, in Metz, Munich and, finally, at the University of Bonn. He had been a reserve officer in the German Army in the First World War – indeed, his enemies accused him of having been a military judge. When Alsace and Lorraine reverted to France at the time of the armistice, Schuman had worked as a lawyer in Metz, practising mostly in industrial disputes, and was elected as a deputy to the National Assembly for the Moselle district in 1919.

As a character, Schuman evades easy classification. He was nervous where Adenauer was cool and dignified, anxious about details where Adenauer seemed able to stand above them. 'This strange, melancholy, quixotic figure, half politician, half priest' was the opinion of a British commentator.[23] Nevertheless, he had served France well during the war. He had been arrested by the Gestapo in September 1940, had escaped from prison camp in 1942, and had thereafter been an active member of the French Resistance. He was certainly not lacking in courage; but by the time he met Adenauer, even though he was France's Foreign Minister, he was full of doubts.

The first subject of their conversation was Adenauer's long-standing belief that the traditional enmity between France and Germany must cease; that French fears over the security of their eastern frontier were understandable, but could be overcome by economic integration; and that such policies were more acceptable to the population of the Catholic and Roman west of Germany, those to the east being more affected by Marxism and nationalism. Schuman was impressed, but cautious. He would still like to see a Germany divided into three parts, and grumbled about Adenauer's attitude to the Ruhr authority. Nevertheless, he was more flexible on the Saarland. It might in due course, he said, return to Germany provided French economic interests were safeguarded.

The meeting ended, inevitably, without any conclusion. But the two men had struck up a cordial, as well as a thoughtful, relationship. Adenauer, with this in mind, wrote to Schuman after the event, 'I spoke to you about economic integration as the most secure basis for good neighbourly co-operation,'[24] and reported his conversation, and its context, to the US ambassador Robert Murphy the first time he met him on 24 November. In December, he met General Clay for the first time – and explained his views yet again.

While its President was embarking on these high diplomatic manoeuvres, the work of the Parliamentary Council was grinding on. Although Schmid's committee took longer than the Military Governments would have liked, there was a reasonable degree of consensus on what were to become the essential provisions of the Basic Law. That this was so was to some extent due to the absence of Schumacher, who was ill almost throughout the winter. He would certainly have put the SPD case with greater force – and would certainly have been more entertaining. Even as it was, however, there were inevitably acute points of political difference between the two main parties which often took weeks of bitter argument to resolve.

The first and most ferocious dispute turned on the relations between the Länder and the central government. This was brought to its final focus in the almost endless debates on the composition of the Bundesrat, the Upper Housen. Adenauer argued to the CDU delegation that the United States Senate, which provided for two delegates from each state regardless of its size, was the wrong model. If Berlin was included, he said, it would make for a natural SPD majority. If then, he went on, the SPD won a majority in the Bundestag, the Lower House, they would have unfettered power to shape Germany in their own image. The debate was long and bad-tempered, but, in the end, the CDU delegation accepted an SPD compromise – behind Adenauer's back. Delegates to the Bundesrat would be chosen by Land governments, but the number of delegates from each Land would be weighted by size of population. Adenauer was furious, but was obliged, with the greatest reluctance, to accept the agreed formula.

The second dispute related to the influence of the Military Governors on the course of debates within the Council. Adenauer saw, quite rightly, that if the Basic Law was to be approved by them they would have to be kept in close touch with what was going on. The SPD, on the other hand, thought that the Western governments had some very clear ideas on what sort of constitution they would like to see, and were using Adenauer as a vehicle for promoting their ideas. The matter came to head after a visit by Adenauer to Frankfurt on 16 December for a discussion with the Military Governors.

The result was that the Military Governors felt that, on several counts, the Parliamentary Council was not following their advice. When Adenauer reported his meeting, the SPD objected, on the grounds that Adenauer was canvassing support for his own opinions on the nature of the Bundesrat. They issued a statement expressing no confidence in Adenauer as spokesman. Adenauer was forced to defend himself – which, in fact, he did successfully. The row then simmered down over the Christmas break.

The third dispute again involved the role of the Military Governors. When a draft document was presented in March 1949, the Governors pointed out that the proposed boundary of fiscal jurisdiction between the Länder and the new federal government was not consistent with the guidelines from the Western governments issued at the time of the publication of the London Agreements. The SPD, understandably, made the same objections as before – that the Allies had their own agenda. There was another row. In fact, this particular crisis nearly broke up the whole process of the Parliamentary Council. Realising the danger, the Military Governors beat a hasty retreat.

The last controversy concerned the site for the new federation's capital. It was, of course, to be designated as a 'provisional capital', pending reunification of the whole country. The two candidates were Frankfurt and Bonn. The SPD favoured Frankfurt on the grounds that it was the site of a number of Bizonal offices which could be easily converted. The CDU (apart from the Hessen CDU) wanted Bonn. Adenauer then read out to the joint delegation a leaked report – which may or may not have been true – that Schumacher had claimed that the choice of Frankfurt would be a serious defeat for the CDU/CSU and a triumph for the SPD.

That nearly swung it for Bonn, but what finally tipped the scales was the British statement that they would release the Bonn area from the British Zone. It would become autonomous, wholly under German sovereignty. The Americans were unable to give the same undertaking for Frankfurt. Even so, voting in the Council was closely balanced, was 'long and tedious and took until nearly midnight'.[25] In the end, Bonn won by a narrow margin. Adenauer indignantly – indeed, perhaps rather too indignantly – denied the suggestion that he had thrown his weight behind Bonn for the simple reason that it was near his home. But immediately after the decision he wrote to Archbishop (by then Cardinal) Frings that all had gone well – 'because I know the interest you also take in this matter'.[26]

The Basic Law was signed with a good deal of pomp and circumstance on 23 May 1949 in the presence of the three Military Governors. Adenauer then promulgated the Law, and in so doing ushered in the Federal Republic of Germany. In his final speech, he claimed that 'our work constitutes a major contribution to the reunification of the German people'.[27] In fact, of course, precisely the opposite was true. The Basic Law laid down the principle of one Germany, but in practice, since it was to become the constitutional basis of the Federal Republic, made reunification more difficult. This suited Adenauer well. 'In every speech,' Annan wrote later about Adenauer, '[he] proclaimed his dedication to the ideal of a united Germany. By every action he did his best to make it politically impossible. Why should he want the traditionally socialist Germany east of the Elbe to thwart his scheme of a Catholic-dominated West Germany?'[28]

The two other parts of the London Agreements were gradually falling into place. The Occupation Statute, redefining the role of the three Western occupying powers, substituting an Allied High Commission for Military Government and only reserving rights which were essential for security, was published on 8 April 1949. The merger of the French Zone with the Anglo-American Bizone had been agreed in principle at the same meeting in Washington which had given the Occupation Statute its final blessing. The way was open for the first free national elections to a national parliament for sixteen years. They were set for 14 August 1949.

They were not to be easy. The fact was that nobody had any real experience of running elections. Furthermore, local interests within the new German Federal Republic loomed as large as national issues. It was understandable, given that different political alliances had been formed in different areas as occasion demanded, and it was difficult to know, in any particular locality, who was fighting whom, and to what purpose. There was also the question of what sort of coalition might emerge: whether it should be a CDU/SPD coalition, which was the successful formula for North Rhine-Westphalia under Karl Arnold as Minister-President, or an SPD/FDP (Free Democratic Party) coalition as in Hamburg and Bremen, or a CDU/FDP coalition as in Baden. It was all a matter of intense but confused discussion.

The main event within the CDU prior to the campaign itself was the final defeat of the Christian Socialist wing. As chairman of the British Zone CDU, Adenauer had asked Erhard to a meeting at Königswinter in February. Erhard had been so impressive in his attack on socialism that only Albers raised serious objections – claiming that the Ahlen Programme was being thrown into the wastepaper basket – which, of course, was true. Adenauer responded that he stood 'entirely'[29] by the Ahlen Programme – which was wholly untrue. Others, bemused by the debate, fell into line; and a committee was set up to draft what became the Düsseldorf Principles, announced at a press conference on 15 July. In these, the CDU in all three zones committed itself to Erhard's programme of economic liberalism. The Bavarian CSU, itself riven by internal disagreements, signed up to the Düsseldorf Principles soon after.

The election campaign was by then well and truly launched. Adenauer set out the themes of his own campaign in a speech to celebrate the concordat between the CDU and the CSU, delivered at Heidelberg on 21 July. 'The main enemy,' he said, 'will be Social Democracy . . . we will ensure that 14 August does not under any circumstances signal the birth of a socialist economy.'[30] A powerful underlying theme, however, was an attack on the British, with particular focus on 'dismantling'. His claim, put most clearly in a letter to Heineman a month earlier, was that the British were actively supporting the SPD, that 'the Labour Party is providing large sums of money . . . [and] the British government has placed the media in the British Zone almost entirely in the hands of Social Democrats'.[31] None of this, of course, had any basis in fact, as Adenauer knew full well, but it made for good electioneering.

But if Adenauer went to the limits of honesty, and perhaps sometimes beyond those limits, so too did Schumacher. Not only did he use the most extravagant language in his assault on the market economy and on Adenauer personally, but he made the mistake of launching a violent attack on the Catholic Church, dubbing it 'the fifth occupying power'[32] and railing against denominational education. As one participant remarked, 'The Liberals [FDP] got a shock when they were told that they owed the market economy to religious schools.'[33] All in all, neither campaign was a source of much pleasure or edification. Foreign commentators were certainly far from impressed.

In the event, the result of the Bundestag election, so eagerly awaited, caused the greatest dismay. Of the 31.2 million eligible voters, 24.5 million valid votes were cast – a turnout of 78.5 per cent. The CDU/CSU won 31 per cent, the SPD 29.2 per cent, the FDP 11.9 per cent, and twelve other parties and independents won collectively 27.3 per cent. It seemed like

Weimar all over again. In order to prevent chaos, four Minister-Presidents from the CDU, including Arnold in North Rhine-Westphalia, came out for a coalition with the SPD. Adenauer, needless to say, was wholly opposed.

Once the calculation of Bundestag seats had been made, in accordance with the complex formula in the Basic Law designed to preserve a degree of proportionality, Adenauer realised, perhaps before anybody else, that it would be possible to construct a viable non-socialist coalition. He therefore telephoned Hans Ehard, the CSU leader and Minister-President of Bavaria, proposing that there should be a coalition between the non-socialist elements in the Bundestag. If Ehard agreed to support the idea, Adenauer said that he would propose to the CDU that they should nominate, and support, Ehard as chairman of the Upper House, the Bundesrat. Ehard agreed, apparently without discussion.

But even if such a coalition could be formed, and could command a majority in the Bundestag, there remained the question of who would be the proper candidate for Chancellor – to be elected in the Bundestag in its first plenary session. A further initiative was needed, which Adenauer duly took. He invited the main actors in the drama to coffee on the afternoon of Sunday 21 August 1949 – in his own house, and on his own home ground, in Rhöndorf. The purpose was made clear: it was to decide who would be in charge of the new Germany.

4

THE FEDERAL CHANCELLOR

'Der einzige Weg zur Freiheit ist der: im Einvernehmen mit der Hohen
Alliierten Kommission unsere Freiheiten und Zuständigkeiten
Stück für Stück zu erweitern versuchen' *

THE PARTICIPANTS AT the afternoon coffee party on 21 August 1949 in Rhöndorf had been carefully chosen. Adenauer was, of course, acting in his capacity as chairman of the British Zone CDU, there being no national organisation at the time. But even so his position was one of authority, partly because of age and experience and partly because the British Zone CDU was the largest of the CDU zonal groups. It was also a reasonable consequence of his position that the meeting should be held at his own home. Nevertheless, he, and everybody else, knew perfectly well that the whole procedure gave him a decisive advantage over his potential rivals.

In all, twenty-six had been invited. In his selection, Adenauer had been careful to ensure a proper geographical spread, while making equally sure that the majority of the twenty-six favoured a centre-right coalition rather than a 'grand coalition' with the SPD. The most notable absentee was Karl Arnold, the Minister-President of North Rhine-Westphalia, one of the most

---

* 'There is only one way to freedom: in close co-operation with the Allied High Commission to try to regain our freedoms and responsibilities piece by piece': Adenauer, 20 September 1949; *Reden, 1917–1967*, p. 167.

vociferous advocates of the grand coalition, and therefore out of Adenauer's favour. Needless to say, Pferdmenges had been invited, and Blankenhorn was instructed to hover discreetly in the background. When they had all arrived, they were seated around a large table in the sitting room, Adenauer, of course, taking the chair. Nothing was to be left to chance.

To some extent, the decisions which were due to be taken at the Rhöndorf conference had been pre-empted by a private meeting in Frankfurt between Adenauer and the CSU leader Ehard in Frankfurt on the previous day. At that meeting Adenauer had succeeded in persuading Ehard that it would be impossible for the CSU to put forward a candidate for Chancellor since they had voted against the Basic Law. Realising that he himself, as leader of the CSU, was therefore out of the running, Ehard then agreed to support Adenauer as Chancellor and a coalition of the CDU/CSU with the FDP, and, perhaps, the small Deutsche Partei ('German Party'). Adenauer undertook in return to propose Ehard as President of the Upper House, the Bundesrat. To lure the FDP into the net, they both agreed to offer the FDP leader Theodor Heuss the federal presidency. Finally, in order to weaken the leadership of the CDU in Hesse, who were pressing for the federal capital to be their own Land capital of Frankfurt, it was agreed that Erich Köhler from the Hessen CDU was to be offered the presidency of the Bundestag. In short, Adenauer had stitched the thing up, at least with the leader of the CSU, before the twenty-six even arrived at Rhöndorf.

Even so, there was work to be done to bring his CDU colleagues into line. Adenauer therefore made a long opening statement at the meeting in favour of a centre-right coalition, setting out all the arguments – yet again – in the greatest detail. He announced, furthermore, that Ehard supported his solution and that even Schumacher himself was opposed to a grand coalition. At the end of his speech, however, as he later reported in his memoirs, 'the applause was none too strong'.[1] He was followed by Peter Altmeier, the Minister-President of the Rhineland Palatinate, who took the opposite view and spoke in favour of a grand coalition. This speech was apparently 'received with strong applause'.[2] There was then an argument which lasted some four hours, Adenauer employing his customary technique with opponents, repeating the same arguments over and over again until he wore them down, as much as anything by sheer boredom.

What became clear towards the end of the discussion and in the subsequent break for dinner, during which Adenauer carefully lobbied his most determined opponents, was that the advocates of a grand coalition were losing heart. Their resolution weakened further when Adenauer told them that not only was Schumacher committed to opposition but that if there were to be a grand coalition the SPD would demand for themselves the direction of economic affairs. That seems to have clinched the argument. Certainly, Adenauer felt able to resume the discussion after dinner on the basis that he had won the day. In one of those bold moves of which he was a master, he proceeded immediately to a discussion of the principal offices of state – and who should hold them – on the assumption that a centre-right coalition had already been agreed.

In his memoirs, Adenauer claimed that he was 'surprised' when 'someone . . . proposed me as Federal Chancellor'.[3] To put it mildly, his version is barely credible. He already knew that he had the backing of the CSU, and was reasonably confident that he could count on support from the carefully chosen representatives of the British Zone CDU. Much more plausible is the version of Gebhard Müller, the Minister-President of one of the French Zone Länder, who took notes at the meeting. According to his report Adenauer referred to a suggestion that he should be Federal President, and said that he did not want the job. 'Our party,' he apparently went on, 'is not yet so well established that we could fulfil the great long-term tasks that were set before us if I left [party politics].' On that basis he considered that he should be Chancellor, not least because 'I have sharper elbows than I thought'.[4] Furthermore, he had consulted his doctor and had been advised that he could do the job for two years or so.

Nobody seemed to want to take issue with this. Adenauer had bemused them into agreeing to his Chancellorship almost by default. He then quickly went on to put forward Heuss's name for the presidency. There was little discussion of this either, except to question whether Heuss was aware of the suggestion. He was not, came the answer. (In fact, he would learn of it later, and then only from the press.) Finally, there was the matter of drafting the press release. This was a delicate business, since the gathering at Rhöndorf had no official status. It therefore had to be described as 'the conference of CDU/CSU politicians at the house of Dr Adenauer at Rhöndorf'. Nevertheless, the message was unequivocal: '. . . an unambiguous endorsement of the social market economy as opposed to a socialist planned economy'.[5] Karl Arnold was left to read about it in the newspapers.

As he said a courteous goodbye to his visitors and sat down to analyse the situation with Blankenhorn, Adenauer allowed himself a smile of satisfaction.

'I was very satisfied with the result of this hot summer day.'[6] But Arnold and other supporters of a grand coalition were offended, and started immediately to mount a counter-attack. The main target was the Heuss candidature for the presidency. If they could torpedo that, the FDP, they considered, could be weaned away from a coalition with the CDU/CSU and the whole project would collapse. As a target it had a great deal of merit, since Adenauer was quite clearly using the presidency, which was meant to be above politics, as a party political bargaining counter. Even the Allies thought that Adenauer was behaving improperly. In the event, however, the counter-attack hardly got out of the trenches, since Adenauer continued his offensive in a speech to the CDU group within the Landtag of North Rhine-Westphalia, and secured their approval of the Rhöndorf decision; and Arnold made a dreadful political blunder by admitting that he proposed to have a meeting with Schumacher – going over the heads of, and thus offending, the whole CDU hierarchy.

Nevertheless, there was still some fighting to do when the CDU/CSU joint party group in the new Bundestag met in Bonn for the first time on 1 September. By that time Adenauer knew that the FDP and the German Party were prepared to join in coalition with the CDU/CSU. But he was 'having anything but an easy passage'. There were objections to his use of the presidency, and to his arbitrary behaviour. But, in the end, 'somewhat grudging agreement was apparently reached on Heuss'.[7]

There was then, however, a setback. When the Länder representatives and the members of the Bundestag met in Unkel on 6 and 7 September to elect the Bundesrat President, instead of a calm acceptance of Adenauer's candidate Ehard, there was an unexpected contest. At the last moment Karl Arnold put himself forward as a candidate, on the grounds that North Rhine-Westphalia, as the largest of all the eleven Länder, should have the post. The SPD backed him, and he was consequently elected by a large majority. Ehard, of course, felt badly let down. Although Köhler was safely elected as President of the Bundestag on the afternoon of the same day, Adenauer realised that Ehard needed placating, and it took another meeting between the two to smooth ruffled feathers. The price of the smoothing was to offer the Ministry of Finance to the CSU when the new government came to be formed.

By then, Arnold 'was believed to be somewhat appalled at the result of his own action, and to be considering resigning from his office as President of the Bundesrat in an effort to undo some of the damage'.[8] On 9 September, Adenauer, certainly not in the sunniest of moods, had a three-hour meeting with the abashed Arnold. Although angry, Adenauer thought that he ought at least to try to mend fences with an important member of his own party. As a result, he reluctantly accepted Arnold's suggestion that he should have a meeting with Schumacher. Through Arnold's good offices, this was arranged for the following day.

The meeting, as might be expected, was not a success. Adenauer was accompanied by Fritz Schäffer of the CSU, and Schumacher had with him Carlo Schmid. In the event, there was a good deal of polite skirmishing, but no fundamental questions were discussed, and the whole thing amounted to no more than a reasonably polite encounter between two antagonists who had refused to speak to one another for more than two years. There was, however, one indirect consequence of the meeting: neither side was prepared to nominate a candidate for the presidency who was acceptable to the other. By Sunday 11 September it was certain that Heuss would be the candidate supported by the parties of the centre-right; on the morning of the 12th, the SPD decided to nominate Schumacher himself.

The ballot in the Bundestag took place in the afternoon of the 12th, and Heuss was duly elected. But the next, and much more important event, was the election of the Federal Chancellor. Heuss followed meticulously the provisions of the Basic Law. On the morning of 14 September he consulted the leaders of all the party groups. His conclusion was that Adenauer was the only candidate who seemed able to command a majority in the Bundestag. Late that evening he formally put in his nomination. It was to be decided the following day.

15 September 1949 was a day was of high drama. It was, after all, a long time since a freely elected German parliament had been called upon in its turn freely to elect a head of government of a new German Republic. There was a meeting of the CDU/CSU party group at 9.30am. Possible Cabinet appointments were discussed. The Protestants of the CDU, with Holzapfel to the fore, complained that they were being overlooked. Blankenhorn noted that three members of the group were absent. For the first time Adenauer showed agitation, and called for greater effort to win over the votes of the maverick Bavarian Party. It was a distinctly nervous meeting which broke up only one minute before the session of the Bundestag which was to decide the issue of the Chancellorship – at 11am.

When the vote came, it was as tight as could be. Adenauer's family, Konrad, Ria, Max, Paul, Lotte, Libet and Georg, with their respective children, were all assembled anxiously in the gallery. There was the usual hubbub as the votes were counted. Finally, the result was announced. Out of 402 members of the Bundestag, Adenauer received 202, a majority of one vote. He had just squeezed in. Blankenhorn noted that thirteen members were absent for one reason or another. Adenauer – reasonably enough – had voted for himself.

It had been tight, but there was some compensation. When the news went out through the wire services, the Soviet News Agency TASS issued a statement: 'American puppet Adenauer is Chancellor of the West German separate "government"'[9]; and *Pravda's* political commentator, Viktor Mayevski, characterised Adenauer as 'a partisan of Mussolini and Hitler' and the Bundestag as a 'bastard Bonn Parliament'.[10] Adenauer's credibility was thus established. All in all, it had turned out, after some alarums, as Adenauer had hoped.

There was little time for celebration. Adenauer had a quick lunch with his family before hurrying back to a meeting of the CDU/CSU party group at 3pm. They were assembled to discuss future Cabinet positions. But time was short. Immediately after his election Adenauer had agreed with Heuss that his formal appointment as Chancellor would be on the following morning, and that the next meeting of the Bundestag would be on the Tuesday of the following week, 20 September. At that meeting, Adenauer promised, he would announce his Cabinet.

In some respects, it was a tall order. There had, of course, been numerous discussions between the parties involved, and within the parties themselves. But by Sunday 18 September it looked as though he had managed to negotiate his way around most of his problems. Needless to say, in doing so he had upset almost everybody in his own party. At the meeting of the CDU/CSU party group in Bonn on that day, the 'general atmosphere' was one of 'unanimous but wearily resigned opposition to Adenauer's arbitrary behaviour'.[11] Pünder was 'visibly enraged', saying that he might speak his mind freely since he had not been offered a Cabinet post. Lehr said that 'talking was a waste of time, since Adenauer had already decided what he proposed to do'.[12] That was enough to irritate the meeting, which then voted unanimously that Lehr, Adenauer's choice, should not become Minister of the Interior, but that the job should go to Gustav Heinemann. Anton Storch was voted in as Minister of Labour, in the knowledge that he was not Adenauer's appointee.

On the whole, however, by the end of that Sunday, whomever he had upset,

Adenauer had got more or less the Cabinet that he wanted. The new government was therefore presented to the Bundestag on 20 September 1949, along with a statement from the Chancellor on his government's general policy stance. It was a carefully thought-out performance, although Adenauer was amending drafts right up until the last moment. He was surprisingly moderate in tone on the matter of dismantling. He was firmer on the question of Germany's eastern frontier, running along the line of the rivers Oder and Neisse, saying that it was unacceptable – but saying it in such a way that he realised that there was not much anybody could about it. The British noted rather sourly that 'as usual Adenauer considers that his bread is spread entirely with American butter',[13] although he referred with pleasure to the meeting he had had with the British Foreign Minister, Ernest Bevin, when Bevin had paid a flying visit to Berlin. Generally, however, having sat on the edge of their collective chair, the Allies breathed something of a sigh of relief.

The new government was duly presented to the occupying powers on the following day in their plush offices in the Hotel Petersberg. With the entry into force on the same day of the Occupation Statute, the Military Governments were wound up, and replaced by a High Commission responsible for the general oversight of the new Federal Republic, and for reporting to their respective governments on German foreign policy, for which under the Statute the Allies had continuing responsibility.

There was also a changing of the guard. Of the three Military Governors only Robertson stayed on as High Commissioner – now reporting to the British Foreign Office. Generals Clay and Koenig were replaced by two civilians, the American John McCloy and the Frenchman André François-Poncet.* In fact, it had been Robertson's job, since Bonn was in the British Zone, to find office accommodation for the new High Commission.

---

* François-Poncet, André (1887–1978): Diplomat. Born in Provins. Fought in First World War. 1924–31: Deputy to National Assembly. 1931–38: French Ambassador to Germany. 1938–40: Ambassador to Italy. 1941: Member of French National Council. 1943: Arrested by the Gestapo and imprisoned. 1945: Liberated by Allied armies. 1949–55: French High Commissioner in Allied High Commission and subsequently, until September 1955, French Ambassador to Bonn. Tough, caustic and verging on cynical – but very able.

He had chosen for them the extravagant hotel at the top of the Petersberg, one of the Siebengebirge and conveniently just outside Bonn. It was so luxurious that Robertson's choice had provoked something of a diplomatic incident. The commander-in-chief of the Belgian occupying force, who had requisitioned the place for himself and his staff, had happily settled in there – but was now summarily turfed out. Bevin himself had to explain the whole thing to the Belgian government.

Of the three High Commissioners, Robertson was the one whom Adenauer knew best. After a difficult period in the early stages of the occupation, when Robertson appeared stiff and palpably anti-German, Adenauer had come to appreciate his good manners and his integrity. McCloy was something of an unknown to Adenauer. In fact, although he was a banker by profession, he had been assistant secretary to Franklin Roosevelt's War Secretary, Henry Stimson. As such, his career had not been without problems. In May 1944 he had personally turned down a request for American bombers to bomb the railway lines which by then were known to be transporting Jews to the extermination camps. 'The War Department is of the opinion,' he had written, 'that the suggested air operation is impracticable . . . diversion of considerable air support . . . doubtful efficacity.'[14] That said, however, McCloy was genial enough, and Adenauer, after an initial period of reserve, warmed to him.

With François-Poncet relations were certainly less easy. He had been French Ambassador in Berlin from 1933 to 1939, spoke fluent German and had a ready wit. Small and always immaculately turned out, he was inclined to somewhat feline spite. In fact, Adenauer was used to such treatment from French officials. It had happened before. But the saving of what could have been a difficult relationship came with François-Poncet's attacks on Schumacher, whom he called a 'Faustian schizophrenic', while Schumacher maintained that François-Poncet had appeased the Nazis in the 1930s. Anybody who attacked Schumacher was a friend of Adenauer, even if only by default.

So it was that on the morning of Wednesday 21 September 1949 Adenauer and five of his colleagues arrived at the Hotel Petersberg to present themselves as the new government of the Federal Republic of Germany, and to receive formally the Occupation Statute. In presenting the members of his Cabinet Adenauer pointed out that this was indeed the first contact between the Federal Government and the High Commissioners. He wished it to be known that his government would do its part to create conditions to apply the Occupation Statute in a liberal and generous manner. He went on to express Germany's gratitude for the 'immense assistance' rendered by the Allies in keeping Germany from starvation, and that he had been particularly conscious of the social and economic problems caused by the large number of refugees.[15] He again advocated an effective European Federation by transforming the Ruhr Statute into an organism embracing the basic industries of other European countries as well. He did, however, emphasise that Germany would not be prepared to join the Ruhr authority in its present form. All in all, it was a dignified performance.

In his reply, François-Poncet, the chairman of the High Commission for that month, announced the entry into force of the Occupation Statute and the consequent simultaneous establishment of the Allied High Commission. He went on to say that the revision of the Occupation Statute which the new German government wished, and which would be designed to hand over a greater measure of sovereignty, would be 'earlier and more generous in proportion as its terms were meanwhile scrupulously observed'.[16] The champagne bottles were then opened, toasts were drunk, and the proceedings ended with as much jollity as is possible on such occasions.

There had, however, been a curious incident at the beginning of the ceremony. A carpet had been laid, on which the High Commissioners were to stand. According to Adenauer, he was only to step on to the carpet once François-Poncet had made his speech presenting the Occupation Statute and accepting the – partially sovereign – Federal German government. Until that time, it was reserved to the High Commissioners. The first part went according to the agreed choreography. Adenauer and his colleagues were ushered into the room, and indeed the three High Commissioners were there, standing on the carpet. After that it all went wrong. François-Poncet stepped forward to shake Adenauer's hand, whereupon 'I saw my opportunity, went towards him, and thus stood on the carpet as well'.[17] Adenauer made much of what was, after all, a childish gesture – intended symbolically to proclaim Germany's equality with the Allies. Although Adenauer thought it something of a triumph, the others present did not notice, or, if they did, failed to see the gesture's significance. Robertson, for one, did not mention it in his report.

The debate in the Bundestag on the government's policy statement opened on 22 September. It was a rowdy affair, made rowdier when the first speaker, Schumacher, lost his temper and called the CDU 'the real Nazis'. It took several minutes for the President, Köhler, to restore order. Fortunately, the chairs and desktops had been screwed to the floor, and therefore could not be hurled at opponents. The only remaining possibility was verbal assault, of which there was plenty. Throughout the whole row Adenauer sat in silence, his face inscrutable. When, in the end, he rose to reply to the debate, he let his annoyance at the continued heckling show only once, referring to an exchange in the old Kaiser's Reichstag, when a deputy had claimed that it was his job, as a representative of the people, to express the feelings of the German people, but it was the Chancellor's job to repair the damage which resulted.

The conduct of the debate set the pattern for the Bundestag over the following few years: raucous and ill-disciplined. But there was one issue in 1949 on which all members felt equally strongly: dismantling. Adenauer used this unanimity as support in his arguments with the High Commissioners. He was so persistent, in spite of 'mud-slinging'[18] from François-Poncet, that the Allies agreed to re-open the issue at the meeting of the Western Powers due to take place on 9 and 10 November in Paris, to review the basic course of future Allied policy towards the new Germany. Robertson and his political adviser, Christopher Steel, wrote a cogent memorandum for the meeting arguing that if the Allies did not end dismantling on their own initiative soon, German resistance would grow to the point where it would become impossible to implement the policy at all.

Schuman was convinced by the argument (although other French ministers took a harder line); so was Bevin. The Americans had never thought much of the policy anyway. The result was that the dismantling list was substantially reduced, and, as a bonus, the Federal Republic was allowed to build ocean-going ships again. Furthermore, there was an invitation to become an associate member of the Council of Europe, a body which had had its genesis in the Hague conference of May 1948; and permission to establish consular representation abroad.

The conclusions of the Paris meeting were the nucleus of what became known as the 'Petersberg Agreement'. In formal terms, the Agreement was the response to letters from Adenauer to all three governments insisting on an end to dismantling, and the final text was only agreed after difficult negotiation with the High Commissioners. 'It is a very hard task,'

François-Poncet sighed at one point, 'giving presents to the Germans. It is also a thankless task.'[19] Although it did not go as far as he wished, Adenauer was astute enough to realise that it was only possible to proceed towards full German sovereignty in a series of small steps. The step which the Agreement allowed the Federal Republic to take was its re-appearance as an acceptable member of the international community. It was to become a member of the Organisation for European Economic Co-operation, the World Health Organisation, the International Labour Organisation, the World Bank and the International Monetary Fund.

The debate in the Bundestag on the Petersberg Agreement followed the usual pattern. Schumacher accused Adenauer of abandoning the 18 million East Germans, of meekly accepting the Ruhr Statute, and of surrendering to international capitalism. Furthermore, one of Schumacher's colleagues, Adolf Arndt, claimed that Adenauer had behaved unconstitutionally in signing such an agreement without first consulting the Bundestag. The row became so fierce that in the heat of the moment Schumacher called Adenauer 'the Federal Chancellor of the Allies'.[20] Invited to withdraw the remark on the next day, Schumacher refused, and was suspended for twenty sitting days. In truth, it was an own goal. Without Schumacher, the SPD attack fizzled out.

But the SPD had a point. There was one provision in the Petersberg Agreement to which Adenauer had put his name but which, on the subsequent evidence, he had no intention of honouring. 'The Federal Government,' it went, 'declares its earnest determination to maintain the demilitarisation of the Federal Territory and to endeavour by all means in its power to prevent the creation of armed forces of any kind.'[21] So far, so clear. But, as a matter of fact, Dean Acheson,* the US Secretary of State who had

---

* Acheson, Dean (1893–1971): Lawyer and diplomat. Born in Connecticut, USA. Studied at Yale and Harvard Law School. 1919: Private Secretary to Supreme Court Judge Brandeis. 1921: Practised law in Washington, DC. 1933: Under-Secretary of the US Treasury. 1941: Assistant Secretary in US State Department. 1945: Under-Secretary. 1949–52: US Secretary of State. 1952: Returned to practise law, but continued to act as foreign policy adviser to successive presidents. Generally, and rightly, respected; fiercely anti-Soviet.

succeeded Marshall, told Adenauer in a visit he made to Bonn just before the Paris meeting – and told Bevin and Schuman at the Paris meeting itself – that as far as the US was concerned West Germany was now an ally against the Soviet Union. That meant, in one form or another, German rearmament.

The fact was that the Berlin blockade had given the Allies a new determination. They had earlier watched with apprehension while in the Soviet Zone the SPD was merged with the Communist Party to form the Sozialistische Einheitspartei Deutschlands (SED) in March 1946, and their intelligence sources had told them that pressure had been building in eastern Germany for a more aggressive stance towards the West. This had certainly been true; indeed, at the time it had been the view of at least some high-ranking Soviet officers. For instance, although the evidence is not wholly secure, it appears that some time in 1946 there had been a meeting of the Soviet political and military leadership, at which Marshal Semyon Budennyi regretted the 'error' made at the end of the Great Patriotic War. In other words, he is said to have argued, the offensive to the west should have been continued – against the Allies. 'I wish,' Budennyi is reported as saying, 'that we had slashed [them] with the sabre from the neck to the arsehole.' The language was crude but the message simple: that 'error', he said, should now be 'corrected'. It had taken Stalin himself, ever the pragmatist, to refute his argument with the decisive question: 'And who will feed Europe [then]?'[22]

But although the Soviet hotheads had been restrained in 1946, there was still pressure from the Germans in the Soviet Zone over Berlin. In response, the Soviet Foreign Ministry developed an elaborate plan, set out in a memorandum dated 12 March 1948, designed to secure the restoration of the four-power regime in Germany (on Soviet terms, of course) or to lay on the Western Allies the blame for its collapse. But, for Stalin, it was all too complicated. When a delegation of the SED, led by Wilhelm Pieck,* arrived in

---

* Pieck, Wilhelm (1876–1960): Politician. Joined SPD in 1895. 1906–10: Member of Bremen assembly. 1910: Moved to Berlin. 1914: Organised anti-war demonstrations; expelled from SPD; deserted from German Army to found the German Communist Party. 1921–28: Member of Prussian Landtag. 1928–33: Member of Reichstag. 1933: Fled to Paris and from there to Moscow. 1945: Brought back to Soviet Zone as chairman of KPD. Jovial front man for Ulbricht's hardline Communism in the GDR.

Moscow on 26 March, to tell Stalin that 'they would be glad if the Allies left Berlin', Stalin replied (although precise versions differ), 'Let's try together; perhaps we will drive them out.'[23] It was that simple answer which had led to the Berlin blockade.

As it turned out, it was a miscalculation. Not only did the Berlin blockade fail to drive the Allies out of Berlin; it had unnecessarily reinforced Allied suspicions of Soviet intentions towards Germany. Suspicion grew into hostility when the Soviets set up their own 'German Democratic Republic' (GDR) in October 1949. Adenauer was not slow to grasp the feeling of the moment. 'In November 1949,' run his memoirs, 'the foreign press suddenly began to discuss the rearmament of Germany.'[24] Indeed it did, not least because Adenauer wanted it to do so. Since under the Occupation Statute foreign policy was reserved to the occupying powers, Adenauer used the press to convey his views to the world. In an interview with a correspondent of the *Cleveland Plain Dealer* he announced that although he could not agree to a free-standing army of the Federal Republic, he was prepared to consider a German contribution to an army of a European federation. He repeated this view at a press conference in early December, and to a correspondent of the *Frankfurter Allgemeine Zeitung* two days later. But – again covering his tracks – he went on to tell a CDU meeting in Düsseldorf on 8 December that a contribution by the Federal Republic to the defence of Western Europe under no circumstances diminished the government's opposition to war.

There is no doubt that Adenauer, whatever the Petersberg Agreement might have said, thought that some sort of West German military capability was a pre-condition of full political sovereignty. He was fortified in this view by a series of memoranda, compiled by Generals Hans Speidel and Adolf Heusinger – both involved in the 20 July plot against Hitler – arguing that the new Germany must think about its security from attack from the east. Even in December 1948, Speidel had pointed to the overwhelming superiority of conventional Soviet forces in eastern Germany over the forces of the Allies.

Oddly enough, this view was reinforced by the East Germans. Instead of advertising its military weakness, which was the truth, East German intelligence chose to exaggerate the GDR's strength. They spread it about that their Volkspolizei ('People's Police') was very much stronger than it was. Furthermore, they reported to Moscow that in November 1949 the strength of West German 'police and other formations of military type' was 'not less than 470,000 men'.[25] The number was, of course, grossly inflated; but reports of this nature, however inaccurate, served to create a climate of tension, which in turn, of course, helped to support Adenauer's position.

In short, the East Germans seemed determined to heighten rather than lower the tension; so, for that matter, was Adenauer. 'Which is the greater danger,' he asked, 'the Russian threat to the Western World or the existence of German military contingents joined with units of armed forces of other countries?'[26] But, whatever the basis for his claim that there was a 'Russian threat to the Western World', by the end of 1949 Adenauer's rhetoric was being heard with dismay by the French and the British, particularly Bevin, who jumped to the conclusion that Adenauer was a German after all, and that the Germans were again up to their old tricks.

It was not altogether true. Adenauer was relying on a series of reports which had been written for him in 1948 by General Hans Speidel, assisted by General Adolf Heusinger, on the strength of Soviet forces and East German paramilitary formations in the then Soviet Zone. Admittedly, Speidel's reports were alarmist, but they provided ammunition for Adenauer in his campaign to promote what he regarded as full West German sovereignty. The case was stronger in that the North Atlantic Treaty Organisation (NATO), which came into being in April 1949, had accepted the Speidel conclusions and had based its strategic planning on the defence of Western Europe against a massive Soviet assault.

Nevertheless, in the face of British and French hostility in the first half of 1950 to any form of German rearmament, Adenauer decided to let the issue lie. As it happened, the French Foreign Minister, Schuman, visited Bonn for the first time in mid-January of that year. Unlike their meeting at Bassenheim in October 1948, the meeting between Adenauer and Schuman in January 1950 was far from cordial. The stumbling block was the matter of the independent territory of the Saarland. Far from hinting that its future was negotiable, as he had at the earlier meeting, Schuman told Adenauer about the 'Saar Conventions' which the French government was putting in place. These were designed to ensure that the territory, although nominally autonomous, would be in practice be run virtually as part of France. At the same time, Schuman suggested that the Saarland should become a member of the Council of Europe at the same time as the Federal Republic. Needless to say, Adenauer was furious at what he regarded as

Schuman's betrayal. The whole visit turned what had been friendship into bad-tempered dispute.

In the early months of 1950, Adenauer looked an isolated figure. Politically, he was under constant attack. Both the CDU and the CSU were losing local elections. Schumacher was accusing him of betrayal over the Ruhr and the Saar. His relationship with Schuman had broken down. The High Commissioners were distant: Robertson was about to be replaced by Sir Ivone Kirkpatrick,* McCloy was frequently travelling, and François-Poncet seemed always to be looking for ways to be offensive. Until Schuman's visit Adenauer's office had been in the Museum Koenig in Bonn, a museum of natural history which he had had to share with a group of stuffed bears and giraffes. Even when his new office was ready at the Palais Schaumburg, it was still uncomfortable – and there was a row about the silver which had been brought from Cologne on Adenauer's own instruction but which the architect considered unsuitably vulgar. When he arrived home in the evening it was to a house with all its memories of Gussi, and even Libet deserted him in March 1950, when she was married to a nephew of Cardinal Frings.

It was in this mood of frustration and disappointment that Adenauer put forward a most extraordinary proposal. Four days after the signature in Paris of the Saar Conventions, in an interview on 7 March with the head of the European bureau of the International News Service, Kingsbury Smith, Adenauer suggested no less than a complete union between France and West Germany. The two economies would be managed as one, their parliaments would be merged and citizenship would be in common. There was only one condition: the Saarland must first be returned to West Germany.

The proposal was met with stunned silence in France, apart from General de Gaulle, who was dreaming in Colombey-les-Deux-Eglises of a revival of

---

* Kirkpatrick, Ivone (1897–1964): Diplomat. Irish Catholic. 1914–18: Fought in First World War. 1919: Entered British Foreign Office; thereafter, various posts, notably 1932–33 as First Secretary in British Embassy in Berlin. 1948: Permanent Under-Secretary Foreign Office (German Section). 1949: UK High Commissioner in Allied High Commission in Germany. 1950–53: Permanent Under-Secretary of State, British Foreign Office. Known as a smooth operator and mender of damaged fences.

the Carolingian empire – with France playing the leading role. Apart from de Gaulle, nobody took Adenauer seriously, and assumed that he was playing an elaborate game designed to impress the United States. Adenauer therefore had another shot with Kingsbury Smith on 21 March. This time his proposal was more modest. He referred to the German *Zollverein* (customs union) of 1834, which he claimed as the precursor of German unification, and suggested that as a model for an arrangement between France and West Germany. But the French were not going to give up the Saar Conventions lightly. Furthermore, the war was still far too fresh in people's minds to make Adenauer's proposals palatable in any form. No French government would have survived the storm if it had taken Adenauer's proposals seriously.

It is not easy to see why Adenauer felt it necessary to go out on such a weak limb in the first place. Certainly, there was pressure on him and his government to take the decision to join the Council of Europe; and, equally certainly, Adenauer had his doubts about the move, not only because of the dispute with France over the Saarland but principally because he realised that joining the Council of Europe, in whatever capacity, would send a clear signal to the Soviets – if further signal was needed – that the Federal Republic was part of the constellation of the Western Allies. The sub-text, of course, was that the defence of West German territory against any incursion from the east would rise rapidly to the top of the agenda. That, in turn, meant West German rearmament. Since the Allies, particularly the French, regarded that with horror, any diversionary tactic would do to avoid West German membership of the Council of Europe until an accompanying programme of rearmament was accepted.

By this time, the British and French were starting to get irritated. François-Poncet was quick to point out that the Allies were doing Adenauer a favour 'only to get their ears boxed'.[27] Kirkpatrick told Blankenhorn in April that, as far as the British were concerned, their security was protected by a nuclear strike force in North Africa which could and would destroy Soviet industrial plants in Rostov and put out of action the oilfields of Baku – and that the Soviets knew it. There was no need for German rearmament, and, furthermore, the Federal Republic ought to get on with its application to join the Council of Europe without delay. Delay was no longer possible, and on 8 May 1950 Adenauer signed a memorandum, for submission to his Cabinet, advocating West Germany's application for associate membership of the Council.

It was a diplomatic defeat, in that it made no demands either on the question of the Saarland or on West German rearmament. The attacks on the Federal Government became more strident. But Adenauer's own position, unpopular as it then was both domestically and with the European Allies, was rescued by a new French move. That same afternoon two letters were delivered to Blankenhorn for the attention of the Chancellor. They came from Schuman. The first was personal, signed 'with my most cordial regards';[28] the second was more formal. It proposed that the entire French and West German production of coal and steel should be placed under a joint high authority. Other European countries would be invited to take part in the scheme if they so wished. Schuman went on to say that his proposal had yet to be submitted to the French Council of Ministers, but he was confident that they would approve it if Adenauer's reaction was favourable.

The whole thing came as a complete surprise. But once he had talked through its implications with Blankenhorn, Adenauer saw that Schuman's initiative, if successful, would solve four distinct but interrelated problems: first, it would put into practice what Adenauer had for long been advocating – an anchor for Germany to the west; second, it would remove once and for all French fears of resurgence of the German war machine based on coal and steel; thirdly, but equally helpfully, it would provide at least an interim solution to the Saar problem; and finally it would help his own case in defending West German membership of the Council of Europe.

Adenauer replied to Schuman on the evening of 8 May also with two letters. 'The Federal Government,' he wrote, 'will give thorough consideration to the French plan as soon as its details are known.'[29] His caution is perhaps surprising, given that what Schuman was proposing was, after all, what Adenauer had consistently advocated for some thirty years: a Franco-German *rapprochement*. He had, however, learned that the chief figure behind the whole scheme was Jean Monnet.*

---

* Monnet, Jean (1888–1979): Born in Cognac. Worked in family brandy business until First World War. 1917–18: French representative on Allied Maritime Transport Council. 1919–21: Deputy Secretary-General of League of Nations. 1925: Became European partner of the investment bank, Blair & Co. 1929: Vice-president of Bancamerica–Blair Corporation. 1939: Appointed chairman of Franco-British Economic Co-ordination Committee. 1940: Sent by Churchill to Washington to organise US supplies to Britain.

At the time, Monnet was head of the French Central Planning Agency; and there was at least a suspicion in Adenauer's mind that Monnet's aim might be to hold back the development of Germany's key industries and to build up French interests in their place. When Monnet arrived in Bonn on 23 May for his first meeting with Adenauer, he found that 'the man before me was not self-assured . . . Clearly he could not believe that we were really proposing full equality; and his attitude was still marked by long years of hard negotiation and wounded pride.' But as the conversation progressed, 'I saw the old man gradually relax and reveal the emotion that he had been holding back.'[30] When they had finished, Adenauer rose to his feet. 'Monsieur Monnet,' he said, 'I regard the implementation of the French proposal as my most important task. If I succeed, I believe my life will not have been wasted.'[31]

1943: Sent to Algiers to work with Fighting France. 1947: Set up national planning authority for France. 1950: Proposed outline of ECSC to Robert Schuman. 1952–55: President of High Authority of ECSC. 1956: Set up Action Committee for the United States of Europe. Frequently referred to as the 'Father of Europe'.

5

BUILDING EUROPE – AND FACING
THE BEAR

'Nur wenn sich Europa unter Einschluß eines freien Deutschlands bildete,
konnte es ein Damm gegen die rote Flut sein'*

ADENAUER HAD ALWAYS been careful about his health, at times even to the point of hypochondria. In his later years his care was as evident as it had been in his youth. His diet was controlled; he avoided rich food as far as possible and drank wine – which he was now enjoying – no more than sparingly. Moreover, since he had not had a holiday for nearly two years, he took longer rests during the working day, and, perhaps more important, tried to exclude the world of politics from Rhöndorf at weekends. As for exercise, the steps leading up to his house and his walks around his garden had always given him all that he needed to keep at least his outward appearance in healthy shape; but he made sure that his walks were brisk.

The result of all these careful measures was that physically his figure had hardly changed over the years. For a man of seventy-four he still stood tall and spare. If his face was lined they were only the natural furrows of old age. Mentally, too, he seemed still to have the ability to concentrate with patience on the matter to hand, and to put it out of his mind when necessary. In

---

* 'Only if Europe were formed with the inclusion of a free Germany could it be a dam against the red flood': Adenauer, *Erinnerungen*, Vol. I, p. 382.

other words, as Annan wrote, reversing Lord Randolph Churchill's verdict on William Gladstone, he was 'an old man not in a hurry'.[1]

Certainly, Adenauer had needed all his patience and stamina in the first few months of 1950. His government was by then trailing badly in local and Land elections; so much so that he had felt the need to desert Bonn and the Rhineland, and to travel to other parts of Germany. His travels took him far and wide. But, most notably, in April he visited Berlin. There, in an openly nationalistic speech, he encouraged an enthusiastic crowd to sing the third verse of the traditional German national anthem, the 'Deutschlandlied'. Of course, he knew, as did everybody else, that the crowd would launch immediately into the first verse: 'Deutschland, Deutschland über alles'. This, indeed, they did.

There was then a row, since performance of any kind of the 'Deutschlandlied' was officially banned. Adenauer, however, when summoned by the High Commissioners, explained that the third verse of the anthem had been explicitly banned by Hitler; and, therefore, in calling for the crowd to sing the third verse only, he was doing nothing wrong. Nobody, of course, was convinced, least of all the foreign press. 'Incorrigible old nationalist' was one of the politer expressions used about him after the incident.[2]

Then there were the implications of the Schuman Plan. Although he was attracted to it in theory, Adenauer realised that it would be something of a risk. When Monnet told him in May that the British were most unlikely to participate, the risk for him became greater. It seemed to him more than likely that the French would attempt to run, and perhaps succeed in running, the proposed High Authority for their own benefit. When Lord Pakenham paid him a courtesy visit in Rhöndorf, Adenauer 'pleaded with me to use my influence to get Britain into the Schuman Plan'. But when Pakenham returned to London he found a memorandum from the British Treasury saying flatly that 'it is not in our interests to tie ourselves to a corpse'.[3]

It was a game which the British were obviously not going to play. That given, for Adenauer it was then a question of defending German interests as resolutely as possible; and, to do this, the right negotiating team had to be found for what would inevitably be long and detailed discussions. Both Schuman and Monnet advised Adenauer to retain overall control of the negotiation but with a capable deputy who could spend time in Paris. This certainly suited Adenauer (and indeed was what he had been determined to do in the first place).

The problem then was to find the deputy. Blankenhorn said that he did not want the job. If Blankenhorn did not want it, Adenauer was inclined to choose his friend, the banker Hermann Abs. But Abs's war record as manager of the Deutsche Bank in Berlin had been far from spotless, and the French, when consulted, said that they would not have him. In the end, Adenauer turned to Walter Hallstein,* a professor of law at Frankfurt and a visiting professor at Georgetown University. Hallstein agreed – just in time. The first plenary session of the negotiating committee took place in Paris on 20 June 1950, under Monnet's chairmanship.

The Schuman Plan apart, Adenauer's preoccupation in those months was the defence of Western Germany. Up until the middle of 1950, the Allied High Commissioners were not prepared to entertain any proposal for West German defence which involved German soldiers appearing on a battlefield wearing German uniform. Adenauer's solution to this problem was to appoint a security adviser; perhaps, if he chose, a committee of security advisers. The remit would be to keep the West German government informed of any threat to German security, and allow Adenauer to request appropriate assistance from the Allies. The solution was agreed.

But the Allies could not agree on who should be the chief adviser. The Americans suggested General Reinhard Gehlen, who had run an intelligence operation on the German eastern front during the war and had built an extensive information network in the countries of eastern Europe. At the end of the war, American intelligence had latched on to him, and had financed a private operation run out of Munich – in return for information about Soviet troop movements and any other relevant intelligence. Adenauer, however, was suspicious of the freelancing Gehlen, and was more attracted by the British proposal: General Gerhard von Schwerin, formerly Field Marshal Erwin Rommel's Chief of Staff and known to have held anti-Nazi views.

---

* Hallstein, Walter (1901–82): Academic, lawyer and politician. Born in Mainz. 1930–41: Professor of law in Rostock. 1941–48: Similar position in Frankfurt. 1948–49: Visiting professor at Georgetown University, USA. 1950: State Secretary in office of Federal Chancellor. 1951–57: State Secretary in Federal Foreign Office. 1957–67: President of European Commission. 1968–72: Member of Bundestag. Very able, if on occasions dry and even prickly; convinced Euro-federalist.

Besides, he spoke good English. So Schwerin it was – although only for a few months.

The rearmament issue, apart from continued sniping from the SPD and the Evangelical Martin Niemöller ('[the Federal Republic is a child] conceived in the Vatican and born in America'[4]) remained quiescent until the outbreak of the Korean War on 25 June 1950. Suddenly the atmosphere changed. Adenauer's arguments in favour of West German rearmament suddenly took on new force. If the North Koreans could take the South Koreans and all the Western Allies totally by surprise, there seemed to be no reason why the Soviets should not do the same in Germany. The mere thought was enough to cause something very close to panic. The US State Department, hitherto seemingly committed to the Potsdam formula of German demilitarisation, issued in mid-August a paper recommending a European army which included West German contingents. Without such a force, the US Department of Defense, it was said, considered that a Soviet tank assault could not be stopped before it reached the Pyrenees.

At that point, in early July 1950, Adenauer's persistent bronchial troubles led to a bout of what was diagnosed – rightly or wrongly – as pneumonia. At the time, it did not seem to be of much consequence, and certainly nothing that penicillin could not put right, but he felt himself so weak that in the middle of the month he took a holiday. He went, accompanied by his daughter Libet, to the Bürgenstock, in the hills overlooking Lake Lucerne in Switzerland. The holiday, at the Palace Hotel on the high point of the Bürgenstock, lasted for almost a month, before events called him back in mid-August.

During his convalescence and on his return to Rhöndorf Adenauer took time to reflect on his future tactics. It was clear that the Korean War offered a new range of options. From Adenauer's point of view, it forced the Americans to reconsider their previous position on West German rearmament, since Western Europe could not be defended without West German troops if the Soviets decided to launch an attack on that front while the US was at the same time fighting a war in Korea. One theatre of war was surely enough. Besides, he knew that the US State Department thought that the Korean assault was only a single part of a co-ordinated Communist plot to conquer the world. There were reds to be found, apparently, under every bed.

However bizarre the theory, Adenauer was quick to grasp an opportunity for the new West Germany. To put it bluntly, there was a case for blackmail, however gently expressed. He knew that there was to be a meeting of the three principal Western foreign ministers in New York on 9 September. He therefore sent to McCloy, for tabling at the meeting, two memoranda, one dealing with the issue of European security against Soviet attack, and the other dealing with the general state of relations between the Federal Republic and the occupying powers. The two memoranda were drafted hastily and in secret by Blankenhorn and Charles Thayer, the US liaison officer to the Federal Government, with 'occasionally the Old Man himself [coming in] to lend a hand'.[5]

In his first memorandum Adenauer repeated his request for permission to form a federal police force. He also offered to raise twelve German divisions as a contribution to a joint Western European army. But his second went much further. He demanded a revision of the Occupation Statute, for full sovereignty for the Federal Republic in all matters except for defence, for a formal end to the state of war and for the existing occupying forces to remain in Germany for its protection. The blackmail was indeed delicate: the implication was that there would be no German troops while Germany was an occupied country. America had to decide.

Although they were secret, the general tone of Adenauer's memoranda soon leaked out – and caused immediate uproar, not least because he had consulted neither the Cabinet nor the Bundestag. Rearmament was in any event an unpopular domestic issue. There were still large numbers of German prisoners in Soviet camps, and the war was still fresh in people's minds. An opinion poll showed some 70 per cent of adults opposed to any German rearmament. Certainly, Adenauer had powerful support from Cardinal Frings, who preached an emphatic sermon restating the Catholic belief in the 'just war', and claiming that neither states nor individuals should plead the horrors of modern warfare as an excuse for tolerating injustice. Furthermore, President Heuss also assured his Chancellor of full support. But none of that seemed to blunt popular opposition.

Whatever the popular view, Adenauer had three specific concerns. The first, which he shared with the Allies, was of a massive invasion of West Germany by the Red Army; the second, about which the Allies were sceptical, was that the GDR's Volkspolizei would make incursions across the border; and the third, about which the Allies were much more than dubious, was that there would be domestic Communist uprisings, possibly provoked by such incursions or followed by them. (Adenauer had enduring memories of the Kiel mutiny in 1918 which had almost engulfed Cologne.)

In fact, all three of Adenauer's fears were unfounded. Once the 'Budennyi plan' for a drive to the west in early 1946 had been rejected, Soviet units in the Soviet Zone (and then in the GDR) were instructed to deploy defensively to repel any attack from the west. The 'Operational Plan for the Actions of the Group of the Soviet Occupation Troops in Germany' of 5 November 1946 makes this quite clear.[6] Furthermore, the railway system in East Germany was downgraded to a single track, which made any substantial troop movements by rail almost impossible. It was done, of course, because the Soviets wanted the track; but it certainly ruled out a military offensive to the west by the Red Army.

This being so, it seems clear, as modern Russian historians have pointed out, that 'there was no military threat to the United States and to the West as a whole from the Soviet Union at the end of the 1940s and the beginning of the 1950s, at the very start of the Cold War'.[7] In other words, the figures for Soviet troops which Speidel, Heusinger and their researchers reported to Adenauer and which Gehlen reported to Washington may have been accurate in themselves, but the authors had wholly misread Soviet intentions. Adenauer's fear was groundless.

So too, for that matter, was his fear of incursions by the Volkspolizei. In fact, at that time the Soviets were far from hostile to Adenauer and his government. For instance, at a conference of foreign ministers of eight Soviet bloc countries held in Prague on 20–21 November 1950, there was a debate about West German rearmament. When the draft communiqué was finally discussed, the Polish delegation proposed inserting words to the effect that the West Germans were recruiting 'war criminals'. Molotov, who was leading the Soviet delegation, intervened decisively. 'I would like it understood,' he said, 'that our draft does not include a single critical or offensive word against the Adenauer government. Our whole document should be directed to criticising the three occupying powers – the USA, Great Britain and France . . . Furthermore, in our specific conclusions, point four, we are more or less inviting this government to take part in establishing the All-German Constituent Council. It is not expedient to go in for criticism of the "West German Government" or the "Bonn

Government".[8] The other delegates, needless to say, accepted Molotov's words as concluding the discussion.

Also at the Prague conference was Georg Dertinger, then Foreign Minister of the GDR. Although Molotov was ready to add that 'it does not stop the GDR delegation from combatting Adenauer'[9] there was no suggestion that the GDR were going to encourage cross-border raids by the Volkspolizei. Besides, they were most unlikely to do so without Soviet approval, and Molotov's words had been sharp enough for Dertinger to take the hint: the Soviet Union did not want the Adenauer government to be destabilised. Finally, although the Adenauer government was unpopular domestically, there is no suggestion that either the Soviets or the GDR were trying to incite local Communist parties to insurgence.

Nevertheless, if Western fears were unfounded, it does not mean that they were not real. In fact, so real were they that even before the September conference of foreign ministers in New York President Truman approved preparations for incorporating new West German armed forces into a NATO framework. Furthermore, he announced that US forces in Europe would be strengthened. When the conference itself assembled, it approved many of the proposals which Adenauer's memoranda had put to them through McCloy. The Federal Republic was recognised as the only legitimate German government. As such, it could set up its own foreign ministry and ambassadorial presence abroad. Steel production quotas were removed. Such was the panic in the first months of the Korean War that Adenauer had been able to achieve at least half a loaf, and perhaps rather more.

Much to his disappointment, however, the Allied foreign ministers baulked at authorising a major West German defence effort. Instead, they gave rather grudging permission for the creation of a federal police force of not more than 30,000 men. It was all the French would stomach. Quite what the force was meant to do was left in the air; but even its mere creation was too much for Gustav Heinemann, Adenauer's Minister of the Interior, who had been opposed from the start to any form of West German rearmament. After an acrimonious exchange, with Heinemann expressing his total opposition to rearmament, resignation was at first offered and refused — and then demanded.

At that point, embarrassed by criticism of its position in New York, the French government produced its own plan. On 24 October 1950, René

Pleven,* the French Prime Minister, made a speech to the National Assembly proposing the creation of a European Army under the authority of a High Authority similar to that envisaged in the Schuman Plan. He went on to say that 'the contingents supplied by the participating states would be incorporated in the European Army at the level of the smallest possible unit'.[10] In fact, the main author of what came to be known as the 'Pleven Plan' was none other than the seemingly ubiquitous Jean Monnet. The idea, apparently, was to satisfy the Soviets that any German troops would be incorporated into a friendly institution, and to satisfy French public opinion that German rearmament, if it happened, would be carefully controlled.

It was not one of Monnet's happier ideas; and, as it turned out, the Soviets were not particularly concerned with what would obviously be 'the Babelic confusion in a multi-lingual fighting force'.[11] True, the mere thought of German soldiers facing east, whatever cosmetic arrangements there might be, was enough to send Soviet military planners into overdrive, but the political reaction was much more muted. On the evidence, the Soviet Foreign Ministry was less concerned about the fact of German rearmament than about how it could be used as propaganda material. Nor was French public opinion more sympathetic; the whole project was simply too complicated to understand. For their part, the British chiefs of staff thought it was hardly worth bothering about.

But the Soviets also had their card to play. Hearing of the Pleven Plan, they proposed a four-power meeting of foreign ministers to discuss the total withdrawal of occupying forces from German territory. As a follow-up, they induced the Volkskammer, the GDR parliament totally controlled by the SED, to pass a resolution proposing free elections in all four zones of

---

* Pleven, René (1901–93): Businessman and politician. Born in Dinan, Brittany. Business career until 1940. 1940: On commercial mission to London at the time of the French Armistice; decided to stay and join the Free French. 1941–44: Various portfolios in de Gaulle's shadow administration. 1944: Minister of Finance. 1946: Minister of Defence. 1949 and then for a few months 1951–52: Prime Minister. 1958 (for a few months): Foreign Minister. Anglophile, but also favoured Franco-German reconciliation; rightly or wrongly, de Gaulle thought him weak and ineffective.

Germany. This was precisely what Adenauer opposed. He believed that such a Germany would quickly fall under Soviet influence and possibly control. His rejection of both proposals was therefore emphatic. Jakob Kaiser, on the other hand, supported by Schumacher, thought the proposal of the Volkskammer worth exploring. In truth, there is no evidence that the Soviets expected either proposal to be accepted. They were simply good propaganda, which had its effect in splitting the West Germans and impressing public opinion. But the British and French showed enough interest to agree to a conference, or at least to a preparatory meeting, and fixed a date for it to be held in Paris at the Marbre Rose palace in the following spring.

During the winter of 1950–51, therefore, there were three different and complicated sets of negotiations in which Adenauer was directly involved, and a fourth in which he was intensely interested: negotiations over the Schuman Plan, in which the West German negotiating team was led by Hallstein; negotiations to try to make sense of the Pleven Plan, in which the West German team was led by Theodor Blank,* a former trade unionist and now a CDU member of the Bundestag; negotiations with Schumacher, Pastor Niemöller and other opponents of rearmament, which Adenauer felt, in view of its importance, that he had to carry on himself; and, finally, the looming prospect of a possible four-power meeting which might destroy everything that he had been working for. Furthermore, the domestic economy was suffering under mounting trade deficits and trade union militancy. It is little wonder that the worry lines on Adenauer's face were deepening, and that he started to develop eczema.

In the event, the first half of 1951 saw some lifting of the gloom. The Korean War had allowed German heavy industry to increase its exports. The resulting economic upturn softened trade union attitudes, which were further mollified by an agreement in January on the extension of co-determination

---

* Blank, Theodor (1905–72): Trade unionist. Born in Elz (Hessen). One of the founders of the Westphalia CDU. 1949: Elected to Bundestag. 1950: Adviser to Federal Government on matters concerning Allied troops. 1951: Led German delegation to negotiate EDC. 1955: First Defence Minister. 1957–65: Minister for Employment and Social Affairs. 1965–69: Deputy Chairman of CDU/CSU parliamentary group. Plodding but honourable.

in the coal and steel industries. Moreover, by the beginning of April the treaty establishing the European Coal and Steel Community (ECSC) was ready for signature. As a bonus Adenauer discovered at the same time that the Marbre Rose meeting with the Soviets was already in stalemate.

Adenauer's visit to Paris for the formalities surrounding the signature of the ECSC treaty was without a doubt one of the highlights of his political life. By then, following the authorisation given by the Allies the previous September, Adenauer had been formally appointed by Heuss as Foreign Minister of the German Federal Republic. It was therefore not just as Chancellor but as Foreign Minister with plenipotentiary powers that he arrived in Paris on 11 April 1951.

The precedents for German visits to Paris were not altogether happy. Bismarck had been there after the Franco-Prussian War to proclaim the German Empire. Brüning had been there in 1930 to ask for a loan. Hitler had been there on the day after the French surrender in June 1940. Altogether, the three acts, in their different ways, were difficult to follow. The French were not altogether happy either. When Adenauer's plane landed at Le Bourget airport, he found only Jean Monnet waiting to greet him. Monnet had, in fact, found a room for him at the Hotel Crillon, one of the Germans' favourite haunts during the occupation. There was then, on the following day, a quick tour of Paris, during which François-Poncet was always at Adenauer's elbow. The French President, Vincent Auriol, could only manage to invite Adenauer to breakfast – not the greatest of French feasts. Adenauer then went on a sightseeing tour, rather different in atmosphere, as was noted, from Hitler's tour of 1940.

All in all, the visit was not a great success. François-Poncet and Blankenhorn tried to interest Adenauer in the tourist trip around Notre Dame, the Sainte-Chapelle and the Louvre, but without arousing much obvious enthusiasm. They took him for lunch to Lucas-Carton in the Place de la Madeleine, and persuaded him to forgo for the occasion his strict dietary regime; but Adenauer was not really interested in the food or the wine. The highlight was a visit to the splendid dignity of the Elysée palace and the Quai d'Orsay. As Mayor of Cologne, he had realised only too well the importance of elegant surroundings for the conduct of diplomacy.

There was, however, a subsidiary but important event. Adenauer had for some time been pondering on the reparations which Germany should pay to Israel for the dreadful crimes committed by Germans during the war. He had himself, after all, benefited from Dannie Heineman's generosity, and had been supported in Cologne by the Jewish banking community. It was therefore 'on his own initiative'[12] that in Paris he met David Horowitz, director-general of the Israeli Ministry of Finance, in the strictest secrecy, to tell him that he wanted an early conclusion of an agreement on reparations. The amount, of course, remained to be negotiated, since the figure of $1.5 billion, put forward by the Israeli government to the governments of the occupying powers during March, was more than half the amount West Germany had received in Marshall Aid.

All that was to be followed up later. In the meantime, it was something of a humble departure from Paris. Rome, which Adenauer visited in June, was, in terms of deferential ceremony, much better. To start with, Italy was not an occupying power; Adenauer was therefore received by de Gasperi with all the pomp and circumstance which by then he perhaps thought he deserved. Moreover, de Gasperi spoke fluent German, having been born and educated near Trento, when it was part of Austria-Hungary. To cap it all, de Gasperi was, like Adenauer, a Catholic in the tradition of *Rerum Novarum* and *Quadragesimo Anno*. In Rome, therefore, Adenauer was received with full ceremony – and a cordiality which until then he had never encountered. It almost, if such a possibility were conceivable, went to his head.

Dealing with the Israelis and making ceremonial visits to Italy were all very well, but the defence of West Germany was still the main priority. During the summer of 1951 Blank and Hallstein were in almost constant negotiation with Monnet and the Allied governments to see what, if anything, could be salvaged from the Pleven Plan. The negotiations, although difficult, went surprisingly fast. By the end of July an interim report had been agreed between all the parties. A 'European Defence Community' was to be set up, which would incorporate a German contingent. For Adenauer, things were definitely moving in the right direction.

But it was not enough. During his holiday in August, again on the Bürgenstock, Adenauer thought again about his tactics. Various officials were required to attend what amounted to a seminar on the future of Germany. Blankenhorn, Hallstein and Blank were there; also, for the first time at such debates, Wilhelm Grewe, a professor of international law at Freiburg. There was consultation and debate; and then Adenauer handed out instructions. He reverted to the ideas which he had put to McCloy and the Allied foreign ministers a year earlier. There should be, he said, a general treaty which would recognise West German sovereignty, accept German contingents into the EDC on equal footing, allow West German entry into NATO, end the Occupation Statute and conclude a peace treaty.

It was, to say the least, an ambitious agenda. Nevertheless, the assembled company of officials sat down to draft the text of a treaty which would reflect Adenauer's views. But when it was handed to the High Commissioners on 30 August, the reception was icy. As it stood, the whole thing was quite impossible. All that they could do was to promise negotiations; but when negotiations came to the point, as they did on 24 September at François-Poncet's residence at Castle Ernich, the response was clear. On the basis that Adenauer had set out, there was no deal. Adenauer would have to moderate his demands if he wanted an agreement.

But Adenauer was now playing from strength. The Americans were still aiming for a West German armed force, after their costly experience in the Korean War. Adenauer was out to see what political price they would pay. He instructed Hallstein, for onward passage to Blank in Paris, that there would be no German agreement on the EDC unless there were agreement on a treaty incorporating the provisions which Adenauer had given out on the Bürgenstock in August. The two treaties were, he said, interlinked. The gambit was effective. The Allies agreed to parallel discussions on both treaties. Again, the discussions went surprisingly quickly; by the end of November 1951 the General Treaty was ready in draft and detailed agreement had been reached to set up the EDC. So far, again, so good.

By then it was evident that Adenauer had achieved almost all he wanted. The General Treaty, or, to give it its full name, the 'Convention on Relations with the Federal Republic of Germany', terminated the occupation regime, acknowledged West German sovereignty in international affairs and recognised the Federal Republic as an ally within the EDC. Furthermore, the Allies agreed to work with the Germans towards a common aim, a reunited Germany with free and democratic institutions within the Western community. Admittedly, the treaty was not signed until May 1952, as there were some loose ends in the protocols to be tied up, but the principle of the simultaneous signature of the General Treaty and the EDC Treaty, and the interlinking of the two, had been firmly established. Ratification, of course, as events were to show, was another matter.

As it happened, Adenauer, at least for the moment, had to leave further negotiations on the loose ends to Hallstein and Blank, since he had been invited on his first official visit abroad – to Great Britain. It was a moment to savour. On 3 December he arrived in London, to be greeted by Churchill, now reinstalled as Prime Minister, and Anthony Eden, the Foreign Secretary. His welcome, he felt, was 'a truly cordial one'.[13] He gave an address at Chatham House, and even had an audience with the ailing King George VI.

There were, to be sure, one or two unpleasant incidents. The British press was hostile. In Oxford, where he visited Balliol College – his nephew Hans had been an undergraduate there – New College and Oriel, a group of undergraduates at the gates of Oriel became abusive. But the upshot was amusing. The police thought that it might turn into a riot, and asked for the official cars to be moved through Canterbury Gate into Christ Church. Adenauer was then shown around the college, but as it was not on his original itinerary, the Dean was not there and it was left to an undergraduate to be his guide. Fortunately, the undergraduate spoke good German, and was able to point out Gladstone's rooms and the statue of Dean Liddell. He went on to explain to Adenauer that the deanery garden was at the origin of a well-loved part of English heritage, imagining that Adenauer would never have heard of Alice Liddell. 'Dr Adenauer stopped,' the undergraduate later wrote, 'turned and, putting his hand upon my shoulder and with a twinkle of triumph and delight in his eye, started quoting to me from *Alice's Adventures in Wonderland* in German.'[14] The undergraduate was as astonished as the Germans in the party – although there were sceptics in the party who suspected that the Chancellor had been carefully and efficiently briefed on all Oxford matters by the anglophile Blankenhorn.

On his return to Claridge's in London, Adenauer had another clandestine meeting with a representative of the Jewish world. In this case it was with Dr Nahum Goldmann, a German by birth but resident in New York. Goldmann was head of the World Jewish Congress and president of the newly established Conference on Jewish Material Claims against Germany. In fact, Adenauer and he had nearly met once before, at the hotel on the Bürgenstock where both happened to be staying in the summer; but, in spite of Blankenhorn's efforts at mediation, Goldmann refused to meet Adenauer unless and until the principle of reparations had been publicly agreed by Germany.

By the time of the London meeting, Goldmann's condition had been satisfied. The Bundestag in September had passed unanimously a resolution accepting the obligation. Nevertheless, the meeting was still secret.

Goldmann was only accompanied by the Israeli ambassador – under an assumed name, for fear of resentment in the London Jewish community if news of the meeting seeped out.

From the Jewish point of view, the meeting was a complete success. Without consulting his Cabinet, let alone the Bundestag, Adenauer decided on his own authority, and confirmed in writing to Goldmann, that the Federal Government considered that a claim of $1.5 billion was an acceptable basis for discussion, and that final negotiations should take place in the following spring. One billion dollars would be paid to the Israeli government and $0.5 billion to Jewish organisations outside Israel.

When the news of Adenauer's commitment reached Bonn, the Cabinet were incredulous. The Finance Minister, Fritz Schäffer, was beside himself with anger. Abs, whom Adenauer had appointed to lead the West German delegation in negotiations to settle the problem of Germany's residual wartime debts, tried to reduce the amount. But Adenauer would not budge. He had committed the government in writing, and that was that. There were mutterings about the Chancellor's financial irresponsibility, and, at least in the corridors, there was talk of Cologne in the 1920s. Schäffer thought that Adenauer was taking the Federal Republic down the same path – towards insolvency. Certainly, it is not clear that Adenauer had fully understood the financial implications of what he was doing, any more than he had when he was Mayor of Cologne. What he was trying to do was to re-establish Germany's reputation with the rest of the world. Money, he seemed to assume, would simply have to be found for such a vital project.

Of course, the rest of the world with which he wished to establish his country's reputation did not include the Soviet Union; and it was during his discussions in London with Churchill and Eden that Adenauer talked at length about relations between the Soviet Union and the West, and the general Communist threat. Admittedly, he found Churchill a difficult interlocutor. 'His way of speaking is jerky,' Blankenhorn observed, 'sometimes stuttering, hesitating, indecisive, until suddenly four, five sentences emerge which are reminiscent of the big stones of an enormous building.'[15] Nevertheless, however difficult the conversation, both Churchill and Eden understood clearly the message which Adenauer wanted them to hear. In his view, he said with the greatest emphasis, full integration into Western Europe was a precondition of the reunification of Germany. Without European integration there could be no reunification. It was clear enough, but it also raised the question of how the Soviets would react if such an event were to occur. The answer was that nobody really knew.

On present evidence, the answer would be that the reaction would have been fierce. After they had tested an atom bomb in 1949 and satisfied themselves that it could be effectively delivered, the Soviets shifted their view from the European theatre as the major strategic problem to the global threat – from the only other significant nuclear power, the United States. Furthermore, the previous emphasis on purely military defence in Europe shifted quickly to emphasis on what might be called economic defence. In other words, a German army was no longer feared; what was worrying was an economically powerful Germany locked into the philosophy of the West.

It is this that explains why the Soviets seemed unruffled by the EDC, but much more concerned about the Schuman Plan. Stalin was certainly unlikely 'to accept the integration of the reunited Germany into the European community as it began to take shape with the ECSC in 1950–1951'.[16] Moreover, it may explain why Soviet intelligence on the offensive capability of the Allies in West Germany became more and more slipshod. The archives show wild variations in Soviet assessments of western military capability. For instance, the number of bridges in western Germany prepared for destruction in the event of war – the favourite item in the public exposure of Western militarism – varied from 'over 60' to 'over 630'.[17]

The change in emphasis prompted the Soviets into what was by far their most telling post-war diplomatic initiative. It came, significantly, while the details of the General Treaty were still being finalised – and before signature. On 10 March 1952 the Soviet government sent a note to the other occupying powers offering to discuss urgently 'the question of a peace treaty with Germany'. It included a draft of such a treaty: Germany – west of the Oder–Neisse line – would be reunited; the reunited Germany would be neutral; all foreign forces would be withdrawn, to permit 'free activity of democratic parties and organisations'; 'all former Nazis' would be granted amnesty; and, most surprisingly, Germany would be permitted 'to have its own national armed forces (land, air and sea) which are necessary for the defence of the country'.[18]

'Stalin's Note', as it became known, caught everybody in the West by surprise. Nobody seemed to have any idea what was behind it. As far as Adenauer was concerned, as he explained to a Cabinet meeting the following day, it was primarily aimed at France 'in order to bring it back to its old traditional policy towards Russia'.[19] It should not change Federal Government policy at all. This attitude failed to satisfy Jakob Kaiser, who thought that the government must at all costs take the note seriously, and even said so on the radio on 12 March. But by that time Adenauer had seen the High Commissioners to explain that the Cabinet was unanimous in rejecting the contents of the note; that its main aim, the neutralisation of Germany, was unacceptable; that the Federal Government did not want its own national army; and that it pandered to ex-Nazis and militarists. In short, the Western governments should have nothing to do with it, and should say so quickly. Having done that, Adenauer held another Cabinet meeting on 14 March to slap down Kaiser, and state categorically that he, and only he, was authorised to speak for the government on this matter.

It soon became clear, however, that in his flat rejection of the note Adenauer was out of step with German public opinion. It was not just Kaiser who was against him, nor even Schumacher who, while rejecting future neutrality, thought all possibilities should be explored. A large section of the press which normally supported his government was also up in arms. Expressions such as 'lost opportunity' were freely bandied about. Lastly, he found the Allies much more flexible on the matter than he was. Certainly, none of them knew what it was about, but at least the British and the French were prepared to try to find out.

By now, it was clear that Adenauer had made a bad mistake. Recognising this, his approach started, however subtly, to change. Instead of preaching total rejection he started asking questions. How would an all-German government be formed? Would there be free elections? Would there be a commission from the United Nations to supervise? What was really meant by 'neutrality'? Would the ECSC be ruled out?

In all this, Adenauer was trying hard to come round to the position held by the British, and which they proposed when the Western foreign ministers met in Paris on 20–21 March to prepare their response. Adenauer was invited – much to his pleasure. He still attempted to argue to Eden and Schuman that acceptance of German neutrality would inevitably lead to the withdrawal of the United States from Europe, but they saw this as yet another version of his basic position, that no reunification of Germany was possible on acceptable terms for the foreseeable future. It added nothing to the debate. As a result, the Western governments accepted the British suggestion that their reply should concentrate on what was meant by 'free elections' and should further make reference, as Kirkpatrick had argued against Adenauer's objections – Adenauer wanted the issue taken up later with a 'free Poland' – to the Oder–Neisse line and the fact that it had not in any sense been accepted as permanent.

The Soviets responded with a second note on 9 April. It was courteous in tone, and clearly stated that the Soviets wished to open negotiations without delay. Schumacher wrote a pleading letter to Adenauer in favour of the four-power talks. But even if Adenauer was inclined to accept his view, which he was not, all opportunity for initiative had passed out of his hands. The United States was starting to make the running. At the same time as the arrival of the second Soviet note, Dean Acheson pointed out that the US Congress was due to go into recess on 3 July. Time for ratification of the two treaties was running out. But the US itself was by now facing both ways. They wanted the treaties, but Acheson, having started as a sceptic, was now also proposing to take up the Soviet proposal that representatives of the High Commissioners should meet in Berlin to discuss the modalities of 'free elections'.

There followed a confused few weeks of intense diplomatic activity between the Western governments, which Adenauer could only sit and watch. All he could do was to complain from time to time to McCloy about the US attitude. In the end, however, it was the British and the French who called it a day. They would rather have the two treaties signed and sealed than a prolonged period of uncertainty in central Europe, with a possible US withdrawal at the end of it. The Western reply to the Soviets was finally sent on 13 May 1952. There was to be no meeting of High Commissioners in Berlin. The matter could now be finally put to rest.

From the Soviet point of view, Stalin's note offensive had been a resounding diplomatic success. It had held up – and nearly torpedoed – the two treaties which were to cement the Western Alliance; it had created division between Britain and France on the one hand and the United States on the other; it had exposed the differences of opinion within the Federal Republic and made Adenauer look doctrinaire, old and out of touch; and it had drawn attention to the continued possibility of a return to four-power rule should events lead that way. All in all, Stalin and the Soviet Foreign Ministry were pleased with their efforts.

But, more subtly, the offensive may also have been directed at the GDR leadership. In truth, the Soviets were finding the GDR something of a nuisance, 'since its ruling élite (or, at least a part of it) quickly learned to make use of the West German developments for polite but firm requests of concessions from the Soviet side, and the situation of the open frontier largely precluded the traditional procedures of "disciplining" by mass bloody purges'.[20] They needed reminding that at any stage the Soviets could sell them out to the West, or at least into 'democratic' neutrality, unless they were careful.

Stalin, of course, realised perfectly well that the note would not be accepted by the West. In a meeting with GDR leaders on 7 April 1952, two days before the second note was sent, he was clear on the matter. 'Irrespective of any proposal that we can make on the German question,' he asserted, 'the Western powers will not agree with them, and will not withdraw from Germany in any case. It would be a mistake to think that a compromise might emerge or that the Americans will agree with the draft of the peace treaty. The Americans need their army in West Germany to hold Western Europe in their hands . . . [they] will draw West Germany into the Atlantic Pact. They will create West German troops. Adenauer is in the pocket of the Americans . . . The line of demarcation between East and West Germany must be seen as a frontier . . . a dangerous one. One must strengthen the protection of this frontier.'[21] Stalin further stressed the point in a conversation with Chou En-lai on 19 September 1952. 'The Americans,' he said, 'are not likely to agree to the unification of Germany. They robbed Germany; if the Western and Eastern Germans unite, Germany could not be robbed any more. Therefore, the Americans do not want the unification of Germany.'[22]

Of course, the motives and calculations behind the Soviet note offensive have been matters of controversy, and differing interpretations have been put forward. But one thing is certain. It remained a short-lived episode. Indeed, the episode concluded, the Allies turned their attention again to the treaties. On 26 May 1952 the General Treaty was signed. On the following day, the EDC Treaty was also signed. The wind was set fair for an end to occupation, for the resumption of sovereignty and for the security of West Germany under the umbrella of the European Defence Community and, through that, of the United States. The first stage of Adenauer's Chancellorship was triumphantly over. The next stage would be to build on the ECSC and the EDC to achieve the political union of Europe.

6

AT HOME AND AT WORK

'Reden Sie mit dem Herrn Globke'*

'HE IS ALWAYS the rational man,' wrote Sir Ivone Kirkpatrick of Adenauer. 'The argument is conducted on the plane of reason with courtesy, humour and understanding. The tall figure sits stiff as a ramrod at the table. In carefully articulated German the sentences fall from his lips – impassive, authoritative sentences with a flavour of Chinese detachment.'[1] The British were thus awarding Adenauer his spurs. Indeed, during the events leading up to the signature of the two treaties in May 1952 he had established himself as a formidable politician in his own right. True, he was not yet a European leader, but he had escaped from his previously perceived role as a mere servant of the occupying powers. He was also, albeit somewhat warily, recognised as a subtle and determined negotiator. Furthermore, he was thought, at least by the Western Allies, to be sound on the essentials of policy. 'Your father,' remarked an American journalist to Adenauer's son Georg, 'is a great democrat.'

---

* 'Speak to Herr Globke': Adenauer's stock response to political requests; H.-P. Schwarz, *Adenauer*, Vol. I, p. 660.

Georg's reply was tart. 'Yes,' he said, 'but when the door of the house is closed the democrat stays outside.'[2] This was certainly true; but it would be wrong to expect anything else. There was nothing in Adenauer's upbringing which would suggest that a family might be a democratic body in which there could be open debate and, if necessary, disagreement. If that had been permitted, he had been taught, the position of the head of the family would no longer be respected, and domestic anarchy would ensue. It had been thus when he was a child in the patriarchal Wilhelmine Empire, and he saw no reason to change. Furthermore, the older he became, the more deeply were entrenched the received ideas of his childhood. However much the politician was able to envisage new and sometimes radical solutions to the international problems of the day, the old family dog was unable, and unwilling, to learn new tricks.

Adenauer's domestic life in old age thus took on the almost monastic rhythm of his childhood. Everything had to happen at the right time and in the right sequence. He woke in the morning at 5am, after no more than six hours' sleep – helped by a generous dose of sleeping pills. He rose, ran cold water into his bath, and sat on its edge to allow his feet and lower legs to dangle in the water. This, he maintained, encouraged the circulation of the blood. Once dressed, and weather permitting, he walked around the garden and inspected the flowers, paying particular attention to the roses which flourished in the well-drained soil and the hot summer sun. These morning walks allowed him to examine and assess the work of his gardener, who was subsequently taken severely to task if, for instance, any of the roses had mildew or looked undernourished.

That done, Adenauer sat down at his desk and began his working day. Between 6 and 7am messengers would arrive from Bonn, bringing a press digest and messages requiring urgent action on this or that matter. These were assembled carefully and brought in to him at 7am. He would read through them, perhaps telephone Blankenhorn in Honnef to discuss a point, and then dictate memoranda and letters to his long-serving personal secretary, Frau Hohmann-Köster. This process lasted an hour or so. Leaving her to get on with the typing, he would then have a cup of coffee, with one or other of his children if any were there, and then prepare to leave for his office in Bonn.

At 8.30am he walked down the steps of his house to his official Mercedes and, preceded by a security car, made his way at speed to the Dollendorf ferry, which was on permanent instruction to leave for the trip across the river as soon as the two cars were safely on board. He was so uncaring of his own personal safety, and so enthusiastic about the speed of his journey, that it was not until 1951 that a third car with armed police was attached to the procession, after an intelligence report that a Czech hit squad was planning to ambush him during his journey and the security services pointed out that they could not guarantee his safety without this extra protection.

Once in his office, the strict regime was continued. Lunch he took alone, in a small room next to his office. Official lunches were unwelcome, and avoided unless absolutely necessary. After lunch, he went into a second small room behind his office, which was specially equipped as a bedroom, and changed into pyjamas. After an hour's sleep, he emerged, dressed again, drank a cup of tea and went for a walk of three-quarters of an hour in the surrounding park. He then went back to his office to resume the official day.

The return to Rhöndorf in the evening was conducted with equal precision. Unless he had an official engagement, Adenauer would arrive back at about 8pm. Once there he ate a light dinner, cooked by his housekeeper, after which he spent half an hour with his children questioning them about their studies or the village news. 'He always wanted to know about other things,' Lotte recalled, 'whether the weeding had been done, or whether the chickens had laid any eggs, or whether the carrots were growing properly.'[3] That done, he sometimes listened to records, Haydn, Mozart, Schubert or Beethoven, but never, it seems, Brahms – let alone Wagner, whose music he regarded as tainted by its association with Hitler. Alternatively, he might just sit and look at one of his paintings. It was then to his rather spartan bedroom, to read a poem or two, by Schiller or Heine, and to go quietly to bed.

There was no social life to speak of. Adenauer did not want to be disturbed while he was at home. Nor did he have many friends. Most of those he had known were dead, and in his mid-seventies he was not going to make new ones. He still corresponded with Dannie Heineman, but Heineman was by then back in the United States. His one close friend was the one he had known for decades, Robert Pferdmenges. The two old men spent birthdays together and their families often joined forces to go on holidays; or they simply sat and talked over a cup of coffee.

In fact, those moments of quiet, mulling over things with Pferdmenges, listening to music or looking at his paintings, were the only true relaxation that Adenauer seemed able to allow himself during the week. Furthermore, the weekly rhythm was as controlled as the daily rhythm. Saturday was for catching up on reading official documents or drafting speeches. Sundays were for church and for his family, both for those who still resident – Libet until her marriage in 1950, Lotte until hers in 1954, Georg until his in 1957 – and for those already married and living their own lives, Konrad, Max and Ria, who took it in turns to visit him.

When July came round, it was holiday time. Holidays were for a strict minimum of four weeks. Chandolin was by then too strenuous – and too redolent of Gussi. Besides, the Bürgenstock overlooking Lake Lucerne or the Bühlerhöhe in the Black Forest were easier to reach. Each summer therefore a party set out from Rhöndorf, in the early 1950s to the Bürgenstock and in the mid 1950s to the Bühlerhöhe. Since Ria was far from anxious to spend a month away from her own family, Lotte and Libet took it in turns to be Adenauer's main companion, and hostess if visitors were present. After Lotte's marriage in 1954, Libet was his preferred companion. She in turn seemed to be ready to leave her own family whenever Adenauer asked her. What her husband thought about these prolonged absences at the behest of her father is, to say the least, far from clear.

There were some holidays, of course, which were turned into prolonged seminars, with ministers and officials travelling to and fro loaded inconveniently with bundles of papers. Others, when the political temperature was relatively low, were periods of genuine relaxation. Even then, however, Adenauer would not let go the reins of his authority as Chancellor. Anything 'significant'[4] was to be referred to him – and, of course, he was the sole arbiter of what was significant. Ministers who remained in Bonn were left to chafe at their particular bit.

The winter holidays, Christmas and New Year, were celebrated in Rhöndorf. Of the two, Christmas was, for a Catholic family, much the more important, and the ritual was elaborate and solemn. The whole family was expected to be on parade, children and their husbands or wives, and all the grandchildren. A large crib was constructed in an alcove in the main living room, and appropriate devotions were said around it which complemented attendance at High Mass in Rhöndorf parish church. Admittedly, the proceedings were interrupted by Adenauer's Christmas message, which he worked on right up to the moment of its broadcast on Christmas afternoon, and Adenauer himself was usually nervous – sometimes bad-temperedly so – because of it. But the Christmas celebration, however lugubrious at times, was part of what was expected of a family, and the thing had to be done.

More elaborate, since it was a public event, was Adenauer's birthday on 5 January. It was a ceremony of almost royal style – rather to the annoyance of Heuss, since it tended to overshadow his own New Year reception. In fact, it lasted the whole day, starting with a horn call at 9.30am and ending with a reception in the Palais Schaumburg. There were presents from all over the Federal Republic, from the diplomatic corps, the Bundestag and the Bundesrat, and from anybody else – and there were many – who thought that it would do them some good. The celebration of his seventy-fifth birthday in 1951 was particularly lavish. It lasted no less than ten hours, during which Heuss had congratulated Adenauer 'in the name of the German people', Adenauer had gone so far as to refer in his speech to his Cabinet as 'my friends', and Schumacher and the SPD had, equally remarkably, sent him seventy-five tea-roses.[5] By the end, everybody was exhausted.

Adenauer, of course, realised the political importance of the celebrations, particularly in 1951 when he and his government were deeply unpopular. Failing bread, there should be circuses, and if the circus could be attached to a celebration of himself, so much the more effective. Nevertheless, there were the lesser birthdays, as it were, those of his family, and Adenauer was always meticulous in sending his congratulations as they occurred. Name-days, too, were important, and his family in turn were expected to remember Konrad's day on 26 November.

The lasting impression of Adenauer's domestic life in the early 1950s is of a dutiful and affectionate father and grandfather; it is not one of outward and visible love. In his life he had known such emotion – but it had been many long years ago. The spring had dried up with the loss of his two wives. There was no intimate companion with whom he could share the process of growing old. As a result, there was perhaps not enough laughter in his home; there was too much obedience and respect from his children; and his grandchildren were frightened of him. Indeed, frivolous as it may sound, it is perhaps not too much to say that the affective side of his character found at least part of its outlet in his love of roses. At least they were free from tragedy.

Once across the river and into Bonn, Adenauer entered his political world. His car moved, again at breakneck speed, through the streets and into the large park on the southern edge of the town. Almost in the middle of the park was the Palais Schaumburg, which he had chosen in 1949 to house the Chancellor's own office and those of his staff. The building itself is solid, large and undistinguished. Indeed it was built in the style of its time, the late nineteenth century, by a rich German textile trader, Wilhelm Loeschigk, whose only serious claim to historical fame was the fact that his partner's wife, Mathilde Wesendonk, was Wagner's mistress.

The subsequent history of the house had been chequered. In 1890 it was bought by the young Prinz Adolf zu Schaumburg-Lippe, a scion of one of the most noble families of northern Germany who had ruled a tiny prince-dom on the bank of the river Weser since the twelfth century. The occasion was his marriage to one of Queen Victoria's many granddaughters, and sister to Kaiser Wilhelm II, Wilhelmine Victoria. 'On 12 March 1891,' so it was reported, 'the pair made their proud entry into the Palais Schaumburg.'[6] That was the high point in the place's history. After the Prince's death in 1916, the house was inherited by Wilhelmine, who, now in her fifties, fell in love with and married a Russian adventurer by the name of Alexander Zoubkov. He managed to spend her large fortune in a few glori-ously extravagant years before returning to Russia, leaving Wilhelmine to die in poverty in 1929. After that the house was let to various tenants before it was bought by the German government in 1939.

It was in this unprepossessing mansion, painted all in white, looking like a giant wedding cake, that Adenauer decided to settle. Its one advantage, which appealed greatly to him, was the park leading down to the banks of the Rhine. From his office on the first floor of the building he could look out over a rolling expanse of green lawn and a profusion of noble trees. Indeed, it was about the only advantage of his office, which was small and uncomfortable, and almost unadorned. His chair was upright, of nine-teenth-century design, easy to sit in but far from luxurious; in front of it was a bow-legged table, on which papers were kept to a minimum, but with a blotter, an inkstand, and a table lamp, all of which looked very much as though they were survivors from the 1920s.

Nonetheless, this office, simple as it was, became the centre of the com-plex which was the Federal Government. Adenauer's own staff was small – in the early 1950s not more than twenty – but he made sure that in all his appointments he had supporters in the right places. For instance, in the departments in which he had been obliged to appoint ministers who were not to his taste, the senior official, or state secretary, was carefully selected by

Adenauer. Heinemann, Storch, Thomas Dehler and even Erhard were shad-
owed by state secretaries selected for their loyalty. Large numbers of senior
civil servants who were members of the SPD were posted elsewhere and their
places filled by CDU sympathisers. All appointments of officials even of
middle ranks were approved by the Cabinet – allowing the Chancellor to
have his say.

At the centre of this web, of course, lay Adenauer himself, supported by
his own trusted officials. Of these, the most senior was Blankenhorn, who
had been with Adenauer during the formation of the CDU and had
guided him in the early forays into international affairs. But Blankenhorn
was distrusted by the West German press; he had been a member of the
Nazi Party, and a former diplomat in Hitler's Foreign Ministry. Because of
that, although in May 1950 an Office for Foreign Affairs was formed,
Adenauer did not give Blankenhorn the job of heading it. The job therefore fell to another trusty: Hallstein – precise, academic, kind, and a
convinced supporter of European integration. He was known as 'The
Professor'.[7]

In February 1952 Adenauer strengthened his staff by the appointment of
Felix von Eckardt as Press Secretary. In fact, press relations has been badly
handled during the first years of the Federal Republic. Indeed, Adenauer was
reported as saying: 'One should be careful with small boys and journalists.
They will always take a shy at you with a stone afterwards.'[8] Von Eckardt had
all the social ease and instinctively easy charm that Adenauer lacked. He was
never at a loss for a witty sally or a deft turn of phrase, but what Adenauer
liked about him above all was that he seemed never to be at a loss, either for
the right words or the right gesture for every occasion.

The one appointment which Adenauer came to regret was that of Otto
Lenz to the most important job of all, State Secretary to the Chancellery, in
the autumn of 1950. On the surface, Lenz had all the right qualities for the
job. He had an outstanding legal mind and a detailed knowledge of, and
interest in, the news media. During the war he had served in the Reich
Ministry of Justice until 1938, after which, from his new base in a private
law firm in Berlin, he had become associated with the resistance group led by
Goerdeler and Jakob Kaiser. Arrested after the 20 July assassination attempt,
he had been sentenced to several years in prison, but was released by the
advancing Red Army. He then settled in Munich, working with the law firm
of Joseph Müller. But although both Kaiser and Müller had formerly been

opponents of Adenauer, Lenz himself was prepared to fight hard for Adenauer's policies, and fight as hard and as brutally as was necessary. On one occasion, for instance, he bullied a member of the Bundestag into agreement simply by keeping him up drinking all through the night.

Yet Lenz was not a success. He was too gregarious for Adenauer's liking, was often indiscreet, and – sin of all sins in Adenauer's eyes – unpunctual. Nevertheless, he had been recognisably the best candidate in what had been a long and wide-ranging search. Not that Adenauer had wanted a search at all. The reason for the search was quite simple: the obvious man for the job, the one whom Adenauer wanted, was ruled out because of his Nazi past. It was Hans Globke.*

As a character, Globke was quiet and unpretentious; he would have passed unnoticed in a crowd. He had been born and brought up at the turn of the century in Aachen, where his father was a well-to-do cloth merchant. His education completed, Globke had followed a career in the civil service. He had entered the Prussian civil service in 1921 and had been transferred to the Prussian Ministry of the Interior in 1929, which was merged with the Reich Ministry of the Interior in 1934. He was then put in charge of the section dealing with matters of personal and legal status and from 1936 to 1939 he co-authored all papers on 'general racial issues'. In the words of one commentator '[Globke] was actively involved in organising the implementation of Nazi racial policy – and the persecution of the Jews which it entailed'.[9]

Globke was also a devout Catholic. He had joined the Centre Party in 1922, and remained a member until 1933. During the Third Reich he had remained in his employment – in his account at the request of the Catholic Church – to act as their source of confidential material obtained in the course of his employment. He certainly did not need the salary from his job,

---

* Globke, Hans (1898–1973): Lawyer and civil servant. Born in Aachen. 1932–45: Official in Ministry of the Interior in Third Reich. Later, de-Nazification certificate issued. 1949: Appointed to organise Federal Chancellor's office. 1953–63: State Secretary in Federal Chancellor's office. Always protected by Adenauer, to whom he owed his position (and perhaps freedom from prosecution). True extent of his commitment to the Nazis continues to be in doubt.

thanks to a felicitous marriage to an heiress in 1934. In other words, he claimed to be the Catholic 'mole' in the Reich Ministry of the Interior. The fact that he tried to join the Nazi Party in 1940, only to have his application rejected by Martin Bormann, was, in his view, neither here nor there.

After the war, in the process of de-Nazification, Globke was able to produce affidavits to show that he had never joined the Nazi Party and that he had provided the Church with a constant stream of important and crucial information. Moreover, as Cardinal von Preysing witnessed, 'He disclosed to me and my fellow workers plans and decisions made by the ministry and certain proposed Bills of a highly confidential nature . . . he rendered valuable assistance in our relief work for the persecuted Jews and half-Jews by giving timely warnings.'[10]

All that may have been true. There were, however, two difficulties. The first was the extent of Globke's knowledge of the Nazi intentions towards the Jews and what, if anything, he did about it. If he was able to give warnings to the Church about the Jews presumably he must have known what was happening to them. But there is no evidence that he did anything about it except pass the information on. The second was perhaps more serious because it was more public: he had been largely responsible for the official commentary on the infamous Nuremberg Decrees, the race laws, of 1935, and, indeed, had helped in their drafting. He had even been commended in the official *Ministerial Gazette of the Reich* of 11 March 1936 for his work in drafting the decrees.

In his defence, Globke claimed that he had not been able simply to opt out. He could perhaps, he said, have refused to work on the decrees, but that would have put him under suspicion. Besides, he 'imagined that the Nazi regime would become more liberal as time went on'. But his main defence was that of many others: the ruthless pressure exerted on an 'un-Nazi' official by the Nazi policy of 'administrative indoctrination'.[11]

Globke had been investigated a number of times after 1945, but nobody had been able to disprove his story. Certainly, the results of the investigations satisfied Adenauer that Globke was innocent of malign intent. Nevertheless, his reputation was tarnished. Globke himself realised this, and when questioned by Adenauer, advised him to appoint Lenz to the position which would otherwise have been his. Globke himself moved from his post-war job as city treasurer of Aachen to become, in title at least, a subordinate official in the Ministry of the Interior. In practice, Lenz let him do much of the work and, in doing so, allowed Globke to establish a close relationship with the Chancellor himself.

Globke soon took the opportunity to make himself indispensable. He knew instinctively where the levers of power were and somehow made himself the recipient of all the gossip. He made it his business to know those who carried weight in each individual Land chancellery, and assembled the information about which they were sensitive. As such, he was Adenauer's eyes and ears – and quickly became his preferred companion on the afternoon walk.

But in setting up an intimate network to control the actions of his government, Adenauer also knew that he had to control the unruly Bundestag. As far as he himself was concerned, he had little difficulty in dominating the assembly when he was speaking. If attacked when not speaking, he adopted his customary unblinking passivity. If, on the other hand, he was heckled while speaking, his riposte came in the form of withering sarcasm. His Cologne accent became more pronounced. Only Carlo Schmid for the SPD could match him in parliamentary performance.

Nevertheless, the CDU/CSU group in the Bundestag could not be allowed to run riot. They needed guidance and, not to put too fine a point on it, to be controlled. Here too Adenauer had his own man: Heinrich Krone. Krone was a former deputy general secretary of the Centre Party who had, like Adenauer, spent most of the period of the Third Reich keeping his head down. He had been one of the founder members of the CDU in Berlin in 1945, and had been elected to the Bundestag in 1949. Unlike the chairman of the CDU/CSU group in the Bundestag, Heinrich von Brentano,* Krone had little appetite for government office. Adenauer therefore felt safe with him, and by the early 1950s Krone had become the main conduit of information between the Chancellery and the party in the Bundestag – in other words the equivalent of a chief whip.

---

* Brentano, Heinrich von (1904–64): Politician and lawyer. Born in Offenbach. Kept low during the Second World War. One of the founders of CDU Hessen. 1946: Elected to Hessen Landtag. 1949: Elected to Bundestag. 1949–55 and 1961–64: Chairman of CDU/CSU parliamentary group. 1955–61: Foreign Minister. Honourable but generally thought (particularly by Adenauer) to be weak.

Then there was the Cabinet. Most of them were Adenauer's men. Even Jakob Kaiser had come round, although from time to time he threatened resignation – only to withdraw when it seemed that it might be accepted. As a result, they were reasonably docile. Adenauer was a firm chairman, but not overbearing. At the weekly meeting on Wednesday mornings ministers were expected to speak to their briefs, shortly and to the point, but not to intervene in the business of other departments. Only the hot-tempered Schäffer broke this rule, but as he was Minister of Finance Adenauer was prepared to accept his interventions. At the end of each discussion Adenauer wound up with his own view – which then became the Cabinet decision.

Cabinet meetings usually lasted the whole morning. Even on the coldest days Adenauer insisted on keeping a window open, and smoking was discouraged – Adenauer disliked the habit and was anyway prone to bronchitis. Occasionally, someone would slip out of the meeting for a cigarette and smoke in the corridor, but generally ministers respected Adenauer's feelings and overcame their addiction just for the morning.

Nor did Adenauer neglect his party base. Adenauer insisted on remaining chairman of the British Zone CDU and when the national CDU was formed in Goslar in the autumn of 1950 he was naturally made chairman of that. This, however, was not enough for him. He wanted to have his own man as general secretary. For this he nominated Kurt Georg Kiesinger, at that point a young and politically obscure lawyer from Tübingen recently elected to the Bundestag. But Kiesinger's Nazi past was too offensive to some, and the Berlin CDU managed to block him. It was only with the approach of federal elections in 1953 that the post was filled by a nominee of Kiesinger, Bruno Heck. At first Adenauer showed irritation, but soon recognised that Heck was a good organiser of elections and, moreover, wholly loyal to him.

There was thus hardly any part of the Federal Government, administrative, parliamentary or party, into which Adenauer's tentacles did not reach. The Länder governments, of course, were a different matter. In Bonn not only was he aware of what was going on, but he made sure that those in office realised that their jobs were dependent on his good will. An example of how this was achieved is the method he used with ex-Nazis. He was prepared to tolerate them in the administration provided their membership of the party had been inactive or necessary for them to keep their job. After all, his brother August and father-in-law Zinsser had been precisely in that position.

Obviously, if anyone had been associated actively with the crimes committed by the regime he was ruled out; otherwise he was ruled in. It was a policy which attracted criticism, but the fact of the matter was that almost all civil servants and professionals with any experience at all had been members of the Nazi Party, and it would have been folly to deprive the fledgling republic of their services for that reason alone. Nonetheless, it was made clear that if they stepped out of line – Adenauer's line – they could expect a case for de-Nazification to be re-opened. It was psychologically brutal, but it was extremely effective for all that; and Adenauer never shrank from that kind of brutality. Nor, indeed, did he shrink from terrifying displays of anger when things went wrong for him or his officials showed particular incompetence.

Be all that as it may, there is no doubt that the construction of a competent Federal Government effectively from a standing start was one of the greatest of Adenauer's formidable achievements. He may have been autocratic and patriarchal, both with his family and with his civil servants, and he may have been brutal and bad-tempered towards his subordinates, but by the time West Germany achieved full sovereignty in 1955 there were few who claimed that the federal administration was not ready for it.

7

POLITICS IS AN ART – NOT A SCIENCE

'Wer Europa verneint, liefert die Völker Westeuropas, insbesondere unser deutsches Volk, der Knechtschaft durch den Bolschewismus aus'*

TREATIES, AS GENERAL de Gaulle once remarked, are like young girls and roses; they last as long as they last. But, as de Gaulle omitted to mention, treaties also need ratification, and the parliamentary proceedings necessary for ratification can be long and politically complex. The rose, or the young girl, may die or change before maturity. As it turned out, the analogy is close to the mark. The EDC Treaty was never to arrive at the maturity of ratification and the General Treaty, which was to establish West German sovereignty, was substantially modified before it reached the final destination of universal acceptance.

At first, in a burst of self-confidence immediately following the signature of the two treaties in May 1952, Adenauer was confident about a speedy ratification in both the Bundestag and the Bundesrat. He told the press that the Cabinet had authorised him to present the agreements to the Bundestag at

---

* 'He who rejects Europe will deliver up the peoples of Western Europe, in particular the German people, to the slavery of bolshevism': Adenauer, speech to the Bundestag, 3 December 1952, *Stenographische Berichte des Deutschen Bundestages, 2. Lesung vom 3 Dezember,* pp. 11132–44.

an early date, and that ratification would take place before the summer recess. The faster the process, he hinted, the less the opportunity for the SPD and some trade unions to make a fuss. Furthermore, he welcomed the appointment of Antoine Pinay as the new French Prime Minister, conservative and Catholic as he was. Since a large bloc of French Socialists had declared for ratification, Adenauer took this as a sign, in his optimism, that the deed was as good as done.

There were, however, three different time-bombs ticking away underneath him. In his period of self-belief – amounting, some said, to arrogance – Adenauer gave every appearance of ignoring them. But in early June they started to explode. The first explosion was a speech by a prominent member of the FDP in Baden-Württemberg (a Land which had been formed out of three smaller Länder in April 1952), Karl Georg Pfleiderer. Pfleiderer was one of the most knowledgeable members of the Bundestag in foreign affairs, having served in the Foreign Ministry during the Weimar Republic and the Third Reich with several postings abroad, not least to Moscow and Leningrad.

It was on 6 June, the day on which the two treaties were presented to the Bundestag, that Pfleiderer chose to make his speech. The message could not have been plainer: the Soviets should not be lightly brushed aside; possibilities for reunification of Germany should be explored with them as soon as possible; and, moreover, in such discussions due account should be taken of legitimate Soviet security worries. Under those circumstances, of course, ratification of the EDC Treaty must wait until those discussions were finished.

Pfleiderer's view was not shared by a majority of the FDP, largely because it lined up with the SPD view. Under normal circumstances, Adenauer could therefore safely ignore his speech. But in the front row of Pfleiderer's audience had sat Reinhold Maier, the leader of the FDP in Baden-Württemberg. Maier had played a clever hand – indeed, he came to be revered as the only German politician who could outfox Adenauer. He had formed a Land government of the FDP, the SPD, the German Party and the Bund für Heimatvertriebene und Entrechtete (BHE, the 'Federation of those expelled from their homes and robbed of their rights'), which was formed largely by those who had lost their lands on the eastern side of the Oder–Neisse line. That left the CDU in opposition.

This was no accident. Where Maier had been clever was in recognising that the votes of Baden-Württemberg were the swing votes in the Bundesrat.

In short, he had ensured that Adenauer no longer had an automatic majority in the Bundesrat, at least until the next set of Land elections took place. Furthermore, the Bundesrat had already asserted its authority in declaring, contrary to the view of the government, that both treaties had to be approved in full by them, rather than only those subordinate clauses which dealt with strictly domestic affairs. Baden-Württemberg would therefore have the decisive voice on the future of the two treaties, and Baden-Württemberg was, in essence, Reinhold Maier.

Adenauer, when he realised that he had missed a trick, was furious. He took it out on his Cabinet and on the CDU national executive, blaming them for not spotting Maier's gambit and explaining to them yet again, in the most wounding terms, that negotiations with the Soviets could only lead to a Four Power agreement over West Germany's head, that he had noted moves in Britain towards support for a neutralised Germany, that Schuman's position in France was being undermined, and that the United States was again drifting towards isolationism. It was essential to press forward quickly with ratification, no matter what the cost or who stood in the way. He was angry – partly with himself. His mood was not improved when the French High Commissioner, François-Poncet, took the opportunity to remark caustically that Adenauer was being hysterical. 'The Chancellor,' he said, 'is battling with ghosts.'[1]

The second time-bomb was even more dangerous, since it exploded in the Bundestag itself. Bundestag members were by now getting tired of being pushed around. Adenauer could do it with his Cabinet and with his officials, but when, on 10 June, he told his Cabinet that he would only allow committee proceedings to last no more than four weeks, asking 'what could the committees possibly say?', Brentano, the CDU/CSU group leader, responded equally angrily that 'you regard Parliament as wholly superfluous'.[2] Furthermore, those whom Adenauer relied on in the Bundestag, the President Hermann Ehlers, his deputy Eugen Gerstenmaier and Robert Tillmanns, were also starting to grumble. The Protestant wing of the CDU was unhappy; and they were encouraged in their unhappiness by a campaign outside the Bundestag led by the ever troublesome Pastor Niemöller.

The rebels in the Bundestag, contrary to Adenauer's expectations, were also encouraged by the attitude of the French government, which was starting to press for a quick Four Power conference. The grounds for their view were subtle: that it was only by the failure of such a conference – which they regarded as certain – that a majority in the French National Assembly could be mustered in favour of ratification of the two treaties. But whatever the different eddies and cross-currents, the parliamentary situation was succinctly and correctly summed up by von Eckardt, who wrote in a memorandum to Adenauer on 23 June that 'no one wants to be responsible for a wasted opportunity for reunification'.[3]

Nor, for that matter, did Adenauer. There could be no question of his openly objecting to a Four Power conference; it would amount to political suicide. The only politically clever solution was to demand one – but on certain conditions. He therefore told Kirkpatrick on 13 June – 'with emphasis', as Blankenhorn noted – that he was very much in favour of a Four Power conference. On the other hand, he went on, there must be clarity on what precise questions the conference was designed to answer. Furthermore, 'it would be unwise to abandon the Note phase, at least not until after the next six to eight weeks had passed by, weeks that were urgently needed for pushing through ratification'.[4] In other words, Adenauer's tactic was now to accept a Four Power conference, but only after West German ratification of the treaties.

There was, however, the third-time bomb. As long ago as 31 January, the SPD had appealed to the Federal Constitutional Court on the grounds that both treaties were incompatible with the Basic Law. The Court itself, an arcane institution set up under the Basic Law, whose members were in large measure political appointments, had divided itself into what became known as a 'Red Senate' since it was presided over by an appointee of the SPD, and a 'Black Senate' presided over by a CDU/CSU appointee. The 'Red Senate' was delegated to deal with constitutional matters; hence it would hear the SPD case and pass judgement, which would be binding on the whole Court.

While he was expecting an early parliamentary ratification, Adenauer could afford to ignore the threat, although he had remarked, as early as a Cabinet meeting of 22 April, that 'nine to twelve men, not answerable to Parliament, have the fate of the German people in their hands'.[5] By June, however, with the slippage in the timetable, the third bomb was about to explode; the 'Red Senate' was preparing its judgement.

The position had become critical. Now fully conscious of the imminent threat, Adenauer riposted with what can only be described as a highly dubious manoeuvre: he managed to persuade the Federal President, Heuss, to become involved. His argument was that it was a constitutional matter, and

that the Federal President, as guardian of the constitution – and by extension its application – had a legitimate role. However doubtful the argument,
Heuss agreed to Adenauer's proposal that he should formally request the
Federal Constitutional Court for a legal report on the whole issue. This he
did on 10 June. As a tactical manoeuvre, it was certainly a success, since
everybody agreed that, pending such a report, the 'Red Senate' would be prevented from voting on the SPD complaint. Nonetheless, Adenauer had, yet
again, brought the presidency down into the arena of party politics, and neither the press nor Heuss liked it.

In the relative calm which followed, Adenauer was able to secure a first
reading for the treaties in the Bundestag on 10 July. The two-day debate
went well for Adenauer, who opened with a carefully composed speech –
heavily heckled by the SPD opposition – and wound up on the second day
with an effective rhetorical flourish delivered without notes. The debate
was also notable for an intervention by Franz Josef Strauss,* the leader of the
CSU group in the Bundestag. There was a man, it was said, for the future.
But a Bundestag debate was all very well. What was important was the
timetable; and that was still slipping. All that Adenauer could negotiate
with the Bundestag leaders was an assurance that second and third readings
would probably, but only 'probably', take place in September.

Political activity then wound down for the holiday period. There was only
one more event of note: a conference of the foreign ministers of the ECSC
in Paris on 24 and 25 July. As it happened, it was, as Adenauer remarked,
one of the most depressing conferences he had ever attended. The French
government put forward a proposal for the 'Europeanisation' of the Saarland.
Saarbrücken, they considered, should be the capital of the Community.

---

* Strauss, Franz Josef (1915–88): Politician. Born in Munich. 1945: Founding member of
local CSU. 1948: Secretary-General of CSU. 1949: Elected to Bundestag; became deputy
chairman of CDU/CSU parliamentary group. 1952: Deputy chairman of CSU. 1953:
Federal Minister 'for special assignments'. 1953: Minister for Nuclear Affairs. 1956–62:
Minister of Defence. 1966–69: Minister of Finance. 1978: Elected Minister-President of
Bavaria. Certainly had large following in Bavaria but much distrusted in northern Germany,
owing to his periodical spectacular shows of belligerence.

This proposal led to a bad-tempered discussion – tempers aggravated by an intense heatwave – in which each delegation put forward its own proposals for the capital to be in its own country. The argument went on until four o'clock in the morning without any conclusion. All that Adenauer could say, in the middle of the night, was: 'Poor Europe.'[6]

By then, it was time to go on holiday, and the Adenauers and the Pferdmenges family duly went off to the Bürgenstock for a rest. As it turned out, it was to be far from restful. Otto Lenz, knowing that Adenauer used his holidays to reflect on longer-term issues, appeared with a three-page memorandum pointing out in the most forthright terms that the Cabinet was not working as a team and suggesting a wholesale reconstruction. Lenz even implied that Adenauer should give up the Foreign Ministry in favour of Brentano, leaving Krone as chairman and leader of the CDU/CSU group in the Bundestag. So far, so unwise; but, Lenz being Lenz, he had been unable to keep his excitement to himself, and had leaked the contents of his memorandum to Krone, who immediately leaked it on to Strauss and Brentano.

The result was that all of them, Lenz, Krone, Strauss and Brentano, appeared on the Bürgenstock for a joint discussion with Adenauer on 18 August. Each of them, for his own individual reason, wanted changes. But Adenauer was far too clever for them. He regarded this whole performance as a challenge to the Chancellorship. He was well aware of the almost unassailable position the Basic Law had given to a Chancellor once elected, and, together with Pferdmenges, planned his tactic carefully on that position.

At first, all was friendly; he let them have their say during an afternoon walk along the cliff overlooking Lake Lucerne and over dinner with the two holidaying families. He then took them aside after dinner and demolished their arguments one by one. There was not, he said, going to be a Cabinet reshuffle. The most he would envisage was the appointment of additional ministers without portfolio to improve relations with the coalition partners. 'The evening,' it was noted, 'ended with bad temper on all sides.'[7] On the following morning, Adenauer summoned Lenz and told him icily that in future, as a civil servant, he must be loyal to his superior or he would have to go. The quartet then trooped back to Bonn, their tails firmly between their legs.

That matter dealt with, it was only a few days later that Adenauer heard of the death of Kurt Schumacher. Schumacher had been ill for some time – his body had never fully recovered from his treatment at the hands of the

Nazis. Although he was at times petulant almost to the point of hysteria, he had a charisma which Adenauer could never match. The funeral cortège, which travelled slowly from Bonn to Schumacher's home town of Hanover, passed hundreds of thousands of men, women and children, many of whom threw flowers on the hearse as it passed. In the streets of Hanover, 'hundreds of thousands more stood tightly packed and waited from seven o'clock in the evening until midnight to wave a last goodbye . . .'[8] Adenauer himself refused to break his holiday to go to Schumacher's funeral on 24 August. He was clearly unwilling to be a bystander at an emotional celebration of which his dead opponent would be the centre. Vice-Chancellor Franz Blücher was sent in his stead, armed with an appropriate message of condolence from the Chancellor. If the gesture appeared ungenerous, Adenauer was not particularly worried. Generosity to his political opponents had never been part of his character.

On the other hand, he was much more concerned about the direction the SPD would take under the new leadership of Erich Ollenhauer. He had indeed reason to be worried. At the SPD congress in Dortmund in September there was a clear shift towards a policy of neutralism and negotiation with the Soviets. For Adenauer it was an ominous sign; at least, under Schumacher, the SPD had been resolutely anti-Communist. But perhaps Adenauer worried too much. The Soviets themselves were not impressed. Referring to the congress, the Soviet Control Commission in Germany reported to the Soviet Central Committee that 'the anti-Soviet orientation of the "collective security" system advertised by the SPD leaders became quite clear'.[9] As far as they were concerned, the SPD was just as anti-Communist as it had been before Schumacher's death.

On his return to Bonn at the end of August 1952, Adenauer found the ratification timetable slipping yet again. The Bundestag committees were determined not to be hurried, and October was now being talked about as a possible month for second and third readings. Adenauer was almost beside himself. On 18 September he wrote a stinging letter to Brentano, claiming that a combination of sloth on the CDU/CSU side and malice from the SPD were holding things up unnecessarily. Needless to say, Brentano, after the episode on the Bürgenstock the previous month, was not in a hurry to reply. To cap it all, McCloy resigned as US High Commissioner to return to Washington, in the hope of a job if the Republicans won the presidential election in November. Another ally had been lost.

September drifted into October, and still there was no progress. But by this time the Federal Constitutional Court in Karlsruhe was turning its full attention to Heuss's request for a legal report. Their first move was to pronounce that their decision on the report would be binding on the whole Court. In other words, the 'Red Senate' could not consider the SPD complaint in a vacuum. So far, Adenauer's tactic was working. But by early November rumours from Karlsruhe were pointing to a clear majority in the Court for a ruling that both treaties were in breach of the Basic Law. If that turned out to be the final ruling, the Basic Law would have to be amended to allow ratification. That would need a two-thirds majority in the Bundestag – which the government did not have.

Adenauer immediately tried, against the advice of Ehlers, Brentano and Gerstenmaier, to hurry a second reading through the Bundestag, in the hope that the Court would give in to a parliamentary majority. The tactic failed. At the decisive vote, seventeen CDU/CSU members abstained and a group of FDP members voted against the government. The result was a defeat – as it happened, the first serious defeat that Adenauer had experienced in the Bundestag.

Quite undeterred, Adenauer had another shot. On 3 December, he moved the second reading again. The debate started on the Wednesday afternoon and ended in the small hours of Saturday morning. It was, to say the least, a rumbustious affair. Personal insults were traded freely, and towards the end of the debate it looked as though it would come to fist-fights between excitable members. Adenauer took it all quite calmly, although he was reported as saying that he 'regrets that a moderate dictatorship cannot be introduced, for it would save such a lot of time'.[10]

Apart from its timing, the reason the debate became so heated was an adroit manoeuvre that Adenauer's advisers had cooked up to put the Constitutional Court in baulk. Two hundred and one CDU/CSU and FDP members signed a complaint to the Court, on the grounds that the SPD was violating their rights as members of the Bundestag. The CDU/CSU/FDP complaint, because of the nature of its attack on an established organisation, would fall within the remit of the 'Black Senate'. It was all very ingenious – and very effective. But when this ploy became known on the second day of the debate, the Bundestag became almost unmanageable. Behaviour passed the bounds of any reasonably acceptable practice – fisticuffs again. Nevertheless, Adenauer kept cool, made sure that his troops were behind him, and managed to get approval for the second reading of the two treaties in a series of votes early on the Saturday morning, 6 December. Pursuing his advantage, Adenauer made sure that the CDU/CSU/FDP complaint was sent to Karlsruhe on the evening of the same day.

By then, the Court had lost its collective temper at these political tricks. On 8 December they announced that they would regard the decision on the Heuss report as binding on both Red and Black Senates. That was all very well; but reports from Karlsruhe pointed to an overwhelming majority in the Court to advise the President that the two treaties did indeed involve constitutional issues and would therefore require a change in the Basic Law if they were to be ratified. In view of these reports, Adenauer changed tack yet again. His conclusion was that, since the verdict on the report requested by Heuss was likely to be unfavourable, the request itself must be withdrawn.

The Cabinet met on 9 December, and on Adenauer's firm instruction concluded that the Court had overstepped the mark in asserting that what was intended to be a legal opinion had now become a binding decision, and decided 'to request the Federal President to withdraw his application for a legal report'.[11] This Heuss did – gladly, since he had intensely disliked his involvement in the whole shoddy affair in the first place. Relieved of this difficulty, the Court sat down to consider the issue on its merits. There was then a period of deliberation. At long last, on 8 March 1953, the Court produced a dissertation of 150 pages, to the effect that the government was right and the SPD wrong. On 19 March the two treaties were given their third reading and approved by the Bundestag.

It was only then that Adenauer started to cool down. Of course, it never occurred to him that he might have overstepped the limits of constitutional propriety. As it happened, however, his overt lack of scruple – he told Globke that 'he would shrink from nothing to get the treaties ratified'[12] – turned out to have done him no damage at all with the West German public. Quite the contrary: polls recording the government's approval rating moved from 34 per cent in favour in November 1952 to 37 per cent in January 1953, 39 per cent in February, and reached 57 per cent by the time of the federal elections in September.

To be sure, there were other factors at work – the public was not particularly interested in political infighting. The most important point, as always in electoral politics, was the behaviour of the economy. By 1953, gross national product had risen by 56 per cent since 1948; real weekly earnings of manual workers were up 80 per cent; agricultural production had grown by 25 per cent; and unemployment was down to 6 per cent. Furthermore, the Equalisation of Burdens Act of 1952 had to a large extent taken the worst of the political heat out of the problem of refugees from East Germany.

It is hardly surprising that, in the light of his favourable poll ratings, Adenauer was turning his mind to the federal elections. Dissatisfied with the way his government was required to spend a great deal of time cobbling together deals to get its legislation through Parliament, he looked with some envy across the English Channel at the British electoral system, which allowed one party to achieve an absolute majority in the House of Commons. In short, Adenauer considered that German goal-posts of strict proportional representation had to be moved. Moreover, they had to be moved in a way which – in the national interest, of course – would do maximum damage to the electoral chances of the SPD. He himself favoured a system of run-offs in a second ballot held one week after the first. The FDP, however, regarded this as yet another piece of Adenauer chicanery and would have none of it. They simply refused to discuss the matter. But Adenauer was not to be put off by that. He simply postponed the battle for another day.

On 5 February 1953, Adenauer met, for the first time, the new US Secretary of State, John Foster Dulles. Adenauer was initially suspicious of Dulles. To start with, he was a Presbyterian from upstate New York, and was known to be militant in his religion. Georges Bidault,* at that time the French Foreign Minister, told Adenauer that Dulles had an aversion to Catholics. Everything with Dulles, he went on, was either black or white;

---

* Bidault, Georges (1899–1983): Academic, journalist and politician. Born near Bayonne. Jesuit-educated, then Sorbonne. 1932: Founded newspaper *L'Aube*, writing on foreign affairs until 1939. 1941: Resistance. 1943: Head of National Council of Resistance. 1944: Foreign Minister in de Gaulle's provisional government. 1946 and 1949–50: Prime Minister. 1947, 1951–52 and 1953–54: Foreign Minister, Defence Minister and Foreign Minister again. 1958: Fell out with de Gaulle over Algeria, founded movement to assassinate him. 1962: Charged with treason, fled to Brazil. 1968: Returned to France on amnesty. Strange, lost man.

there was no subtlety in the man. Moreover, Adenauer had hoped that his ally McCloy would get the job. The new President, Dwight Eisenhower, had almost given the job to McCloy, but, on the advice of General Clay, who thought that McCloy leaned too much in favour of appeasement of the Soviets, had hesitated on the brink. Dulles himself, once appointed, refused to have McCloy anywhere near him.

Up to a point, Bidault was right. Dulles can reasonably be described as something of a prig. But he at least had had the benefit of a wide-ranging education – Princeton, but then the Sorbonne and Madrid. At their first meeting Adenauer was relieved to be 'pleasantly disappointed that [Dulles] was not a narrow Puritan'.[13] In fact, Dulles turned out to have much the same views as Adenauer about the underlying morality of government: there was good and evil, and that was that. To be sure, neither realised that their view was the mirror image of the view of the Soviet ideologues, nor did either admit to any contradiction of their views. With Dulles in charge of the international policy of the world's most powerful nation, and with no apparent relaxation in the Soviet hard line, the stage was set for stalemate in what by then had become known as the Cold War.

With the death of Stalin on 5 March 1953, the equation changed yet again. Perhaps Adenauer was slightly less enthusiastic than Dulles, who, at a press conference four days later, announced that 'the Eisenhower era begins as the Stalin era ends',[14] but he had been relieved by Dulles' support for the EDC. In fact, Dulles had been so emphatic that Reinhold Maier came to the conclusion that, after all, the vote of Baden-Württemberg should be cast in favour of ratification when the matter came before the Bundesrat.

Nevertheless, what Adenauer had not yet appreciated was that Dulles' support for the EDC Treaty was due in large measure to a shift in US defence policy. With their superiority in nuclear technology over the Soviets, they felt able strategically to move away from a large conventional force in Germany to a reduced conventional force able to defend Europe until they were ready to unsheathe the 'nuclear sword', the Strategic Air Command. In their view, the reduced conventional force should largely be provided by the Europeans through the EDC. The shift in strategy was known, in the jargon of the day, as the 'New Look'.

Adenauer found all this out in April, when he went to the United States for his first visit. Before he went, however, he made time to meet the Italian Prime Minister, de Gasperi, to discuss a new project. It was nothing less than a plan for a European Political Community, based on the principles of the ECSC. De Gasperi wished to recruit Adenauer in support of the project, and brought with him a draft constitution for such a Community which the Belgian president of the Common Assembly of the ECSC, Paul-Henri Spaak, had presented to the ECSC Council of Ministers. Adenauer found himself in a something of a dilemma. In principle, he supported the initiative; after all, it was what he had had in mind for a long time. On the other hand, his main purpose was to secure general ratification for the EDC and General treaties. After that, he thought, the caravan could move on. With the ECSC and the EDC achieved, it would be natural to progress to a political community – but not yet.

With all these thoughts in mind, on 2 April 1953 Adenauer left Le Havre for New York on the liner *United States*. The crossing was rough. 'Nearly all the members of my entourage,' he later reported, carefully excluding himself, 'were seasick.'[15] Their arrival in America was greeted with the customary blast of sirens, and even before he disembarked Adenauer had to face a barrage of reporters. That set the tone for his visit: constant media attention mixed with intense curiosity about this new specimen of a friendly German. The following day, 7 April, Adenauer flew to Washington, to be greeted on the tarmac by Vice-President Richard Nixon, Dulles and other members of Eisenhower's Cabinet. It was all somewhat bemusing, and Adenauer was suitably bemused: America, for the first-time visitor, can be a powerful drug.

In reality, the visit was little more than ceremonial. To be sure, there were lengthy discussions on all the issues of the day, but the Americans avoided making any commitments other than to assure Adenauer that he was, in Eisenhower's words, 'among friends who had the good of a free Germany at heart'.[16] For instance, for Adenauer one of the highlights of his visit was the award of a Doctorate of Law at Georgetown University in a ceremony which he described as 'very impressive'.[17]

It was on 8 April, at a lunch given by the National Press Club, that Adenauer showed that de Gasperi had not argued in vain. By then, of course, he was tired, and when he was tired he always spoke for too long. On this occasion he spoke to the assembled journalists, in German, for nearly two hours. They must have been bored to a degree they had never previously known – in Washington nobody ever spoke for two hours, let alone in German. At the end, Adenauer could only note that the applause showed that the audience had listened 'attentively'.

Nonetheless, in the course of his long discourse, he made one significant point. 'Every historical epoch,' he said, 'has its own tasks. In Europe every single rational argument points towards a united advance at the end of which there will one day be the United States of Europe. No one has better understood this than the young people of our continent.'[18] None of the Washington journalists picked up the point; they had by that time perhaps been reduced to slumber. But it was certainly not missed in the chancelleries of Europe.

In terms of ceremony, the most moving moment came on 8 April at the Arlington national cemetery in Virginia. Adenauer was greeted by an American general. Three officers walked behind them, the officer in the centre carrying the German flag. There was a twenty-one-gun salute as Adenauer walked forward, laid a wreath with a ribbon of black, red and gold for the dead of both nations, and stood in silence. The band of the US Marine Corps played first 'The Star-Spangled Banner' and then the 'Deutschlandlied'. The Germans present were in tears. 'It had been a long and hard road,' Adenauer later wrote, 'from the total catastrophe of the year 1945 to this moment of the year 1953 when the German national anthem was heard in the national cemetery of the United States.'[19]

Needless to say, Adenauer's staff made sure that the event was reported in detail by the German media. There was, after all, an election to be won later in the year; Adenauer's reception in the United States was an important card to play. Moreover, by the end of April the Bundesrat had approved the ratification of the two treaties. Apart from the difficulty over electoral reform, all seemed set fair.

At this point Churchill threw a heavy spanner into the smooth-running works. He had taken it into his head that Stalin's death offered new possibilities for peace, and proposed an early summit conference of the United States, Britain and the Soviet Union. It was all, no doubt, heady stuff, and Churchill's oratory in the House of Commons on 11 May was superlative. Yet Churchill had acted against the advice of senior Foreign Office officials, Pierson Dixon, William Strang and Frank Roberts, had ignored American objections, and had not informed the French – who were not offered a place at the conference anyway. Furthermore, the deed was done while

Anthony Eden, Churchill's Foreign Secretary, was undergoing a series of operations for gallstones.

Certainly, Churchill was cautious enough to reassure West Germany that it would in no way be sacrificed or 'cease to be master of its own fortunes within the agreements we and other NATO countries have made with them'.[20] Nevertheless, the message was clear: regardless of the French, regardless of the West German elections or the ratification of the treaties, and regardless of the view of his civil servants, Churchill still saw himself as the promoter of what Pierson Dixon referred to as a reunited and neutralised Germany.

It so happened that Adenauer was in London on 14 and 15 May. He made no reference to what he thought about Churchill's speech; that was Blankenhorn's job behind the scenes. Blankenhorn did his job with his customary diligence, but, with Eden away ill, nobody knew what Churchill was up to. To try to defuse the political bomb, Eisenhower proposed a conference of Western heads of government in Bermuda. It was a good try, but by then the damage had been done. Churchill, it was generally believed, was trying to sabotage ratification of the EDC Treaty. On 15 June, Blankenhorn told Con O'Neill, a brilliant senior official in the British Foreign Office, that Adenauer was horrified at Churchill's ideas. Others felt the same. De Gasperi even went so far as to claim that Churchill's intervention had cost him his majority in Italy.

In the end, it all came out in the wash. On 16, 17 and 18 June 1953, there were riots in Berlin and in other towns in East Germany, provoked by the combination of a literal 'New Programme', which carried a threat to the personal reign of the Communist leader Walter Ulbricht,* and Ulbricht's

---

* Ulbricht, Walter (1893–1973): Politician. Born in Leipzig. Only had eight years' education. 1912: Joined SPD. 1918: Joined German Communist Party (KPD). 1929: District secretary of KPD in Berlin. 1929–33: Member of Reichstag. 1933–45: Fled the Nazis, first to Paris and then to Moscow, where he worked for Soviet military intelligence. 1945: Returned to Germany to organise Communists in Soviet Zone. 1950–73: General Secretary of the newly formed SED. 1960–73: Chairman of Council of State of the GDR. Hardline Communist. A former colleague described his face as 'stiff with a malice that was conscious of its own ugliness'.

response in raising production norms without adjusting wages. The workers' revolt – since that is what it quickly became – was unceremoniously and brutally suppressed by the Red Army. At first, Adenauer was anxious to steer clear even of what was without doubt a popular rebellion, apart from a solemn speech in the Bundestag. Certainly, the Western Allies made no effort to intervene, and Adenauer, as always, was inclined to follow their lead. But Lenz persuaded him that it would be electorally disastrous if he did not go to Berlin and appear in person. Accordingly, he stood with a hundred thousand others in front of the Schöneberg Town Hall in an act of mourning for those who had died. It was the least he could do.

In fact, the East German uprisings, as Adenauer quickly appreciated, strengthened his electoral hand. Strong allies were needed to counter the power of the Soviet Union. This was not a time for preaching neutrality. It was all indeed quite promising. Furthermore, on 24 June Churchill had a massive stroke, which put an end to his ambitious project of a Big Three conference. Lastly, the FDP leadership finally agreed to a compromise on electoral reform, not accepting Adenauer's formula but accepting the need to exclude from representation in the Bundestag any party which failed to win 5 per cent of the total vote. It was certainly not what Adenauer had wanted, and the formula would never supply a secure majority for one party, but it would have to do – at least for the moment. In spite of protests from the smaller parties, the change was forced through the Bundestag.

The decks were now clear, and on 30 June the date for the federal elections was announced: 6 September 1953. It was clearly going to be a bruising campaign, and Adenauer decided to take a three-week holiday at his favourite hotel at the Bühlerhöhe to get himself into shape. His doctors were there to make sure that he was in peak physical condition, and he himself made sure that mentally he was ready for the fight. In fact, although now seventy-seven years old, he seemed to Harold Nicolson, who had met him previously in Cologne in 1928, 'a good twenty years younger'.[21]

Just before going on holiday, Adenauer had made his first electoral move. To general astonishment he renewed his demand of the previous year for a Four Power conference on German reunification. His demand was, of course, supported by all parties in the Bundestag; but, as before, it set out objectives which he knew the Soviets could not possibly accept. Adenauer even went to Washington to present the proposal to a foreign ministers' conference of the three Western Allies. All of them had been taken aback by this sudden shift in Adenauer's position, and it was not until they realised that one of his conditions was that any such conference should take place after the federal elections that they concluded – helped by heavy hints from Blankenhorn – that Adenauer's proposal was no more than a clever election manoeuvre to dish the SPD.

The election campaign itself followed a now familiar pattern. Adenauer changed his clothes; the lofty international statesman became the vulgar political street-fighter. His personal attacks on SPD leaders were ferocious. For instance, he stated quite categorically that two senior figures in the Solingen SPD, whom he named, had received DM 10,000 from the GDR for their campaign. His formal apology for this manifest lie came in front of a court – well after the election. SPD leaders were accused repeatedly, again by name, of selling out to the Soviets, lack of patriotism, effeteness, and any other defect or sin which Adenauer could dream up.

But it was not enough just to hit below whatever belt Adenauer could find. The CDU organisation had to be superb – and it was. Their poster campaign was crisp and effective: 'Moscow orders; bring down Adenauer. So vote CDU.' 'A Yes for Adenauer and prosperity will continue.' Furthermore, the party had rented a special train which previously had been used only by Göring. Adenauer and his staff had their own coach, done up in the greatest of comfort, while behind them was a dining car and sleeping berths for journalists. It was all very professional compared with the ramshackle arrangements of the SPD.

The crowning moment of the campaign came on 3 September. In an aberrant moment, Dulles intervened – against all the established conventions. At a press conference he said that a defeat for Adenauer 'would have catastrophic consequences for the prospects for German unification and the restoration of sovereignty'. Not content with that, he went on to say that Adenauer's defeat could 'trigger off such confusion in Germany that further delays in German efforts for reunification and freedom would be unavoidable'.[22]

After that, the result was a foregone conclusion. When polling day came, the weather was bright and sunny, and nearly 86 per cent of those entitled to vote turned out. As soon as counting started it was clear that Adenauer had won a decisive victory. When the final result was declared, the CDU/CSU had scored 45.2 per cent of the vote as against 31 per cent in

1949. The SPD just about held its vote at 28.8 per cent. The losers were the smaller parties who failed to cross the 5 per cent threshold; the Bavarian Party, for instance, was wiped out by the CSU. In terms of seats in the Bundestag, now expanded from 402 to 487 to accommodate additional members to reflect the proportions of the total vote for each party, the CDU/CSU came out with 243 (just short of an overall majority), the SPD with 151, the FDP with 48, the BHE (for the first time ever) 27, the German Party with 15, and the Centre Party with 3. As Carlo Schmid subsequently reflected, 'the behaviour of the voters . . . made it clear that in times of uncertainty no slogan is more powerful than the call "No Experiments"'.[23]

In terms of forming his new government, Adenauer found two flies in what was otherwise a very agreeable ointment. The first was the striking performance of the BHE. The refugees and expellees had come out in force against him. The second was the success of the CSU in Bavaria; by knocking out the Bavarian Party they had increased their numbers from 24 to 52. Adenauer drew two conclusions: first, that the BHE should be drawn into a new coalition with the CDU/CSU, FDP and the German Party; second, that he would do well not to ride roughshod over his Bavarian colleagues.

Adenauer talked all this over with Pferdmenges and Globke. From the CSU, Schäffer had to stay, although Adenauer would have liked to be rid of him, and Strauss was brought in as Minister Without Portfolio. From the CDU, he brought in Gerhard Schröder and Robert Tillmanns, both from the Protestant wing of the party and Heinrich Lübke as Minister of Agriculture. Out went Dehler of the FDP. The two real surprises were Waldemar Kraft* and Theodor Oberländer,† both from the BHE. They

---

* Kraft, Waldemar (1898–1977): Farmer and politician. Born in Brustow in eastern Prussia. 1923–29: Director of German agricultural organisation in eastern Prussia. 1925: Became chairman of German agricultural trade association. 1940–45: Manager of 'Reich-Society for Agriculture' in Berlin. 1945–47: Interned in British Zone, until de-Nazification certificate issued. 1950: Founded union of BHP in Schleswig-Holstein. 1950–53: Member of Schleswig-Holstein Landtag, holding various ministerial positions in the Land. 1953–56: Member of Bundestag (1955: joined CDU). 1953: Minister Without Portfolio. Never escaped Nazi past, and was dropped as soon as was convenient.

were surprises not because Adenauer wished to have representatives from the refugee movement in his Cabinet but because both of them had openly avowed Nazi pasts. Kraft had been an active member of the Nazi Party and a company commander in the SS, and Oberländer had joined the Nazi Party as early as 1933 and had become a senior company commander in the SA and a Nazi district office leader. As Adenauer admitted, Oberländer was 'brown, even dark brown'.[24]

But the main advantage to Adenauer in all his appointments was that Lenz had stood as a candidate in the elections and had won a constituency seat. He had done so in the belief that Adenauer would offer him a ministerial post. Adenauer might even have encouraged him in this idea, but, as Reinhold Maier remarked, 'anyone discussing affairs with [Adenauer] would do well to keep in mind the relativity of his mode of expression'.[25] Certainly, Adenauer was quite happy to see Lenz out of the Chancellery, since it made room as state secretary for Globke; and the appointment was duly made.

Adenauer was now secure. The election victory behind him, a new Cabinet in place, and with the assurance of a convincing majority for the coalition in the Bundestag, he could move forward along the path which he had set himself. He could again put on the mantle of the international statesman, and play the big game with the big players. But as 1953 drew to a close, it became clear to him that the game was changing. The delays and procrastinations of the previous two years had slowed the momentum that had been carrying the two treaties along. He had seriously to consider his alternatives if the treaties, like two young girls or two roses, failed to reach maturity.

[†] Oberländer, Theodor (1905–98): Academic and politician. Born in Meiningen. Studied agriculture and economics. 1933: Joined Nazi Party. 1934: Professor of agricultural economics in Danzig. 1940: Similar job in Prague. 1940–44: Adviser to government on eastern affairs. 1944: Interned. 1946: Released. 1950: Joined BHP. 1953: Appointed Minister for Expellees. 1956: Joined CDU. 1960: Resigned as minister to fight legal action against him for murder of Jews in the Second World War, which he lost. Thereafter, he worked for the European Conference on Human Rights. A sad figure.

8

WHERE DOES GERMANY STAND?

*'Ich versicherte Dulles dass ich keiner Kompromisslösung zustimmen
würde. Deutschland stehe fest zum Westen'**

'WE MUST HAVE a German army . . . [it is] no use . . . talking of the defence
of Europe against Russia without Germany. [It is] not possible to allow this
immense no-man's-land of Germany to remain utterly undefended.'[1] Thus a
now recovered Churchill at the Bermuda conference of December 1953. He
went on to lecture the French Prime Minister Joseph Laniel and Foreign
Minister Bidault: if the French would not accept the EDC Treaty, he said, he
would recommend the extension of NATO to include West Germany and a
German army. 'He was sorry to have to speak in this way,' he went on, '. . . he
knew well the fearful losses they had sustained . . . he understood the brilliant
and valiant efforts of the Resistance.' At this point, as so often when speaking of past French heroisms, Churchill's voice choked and tears came to his
eyes; but he 'must beg his French friends to understand that we must go on
with EDC, or have in NATO a German army with a minimum of delay'.[2]

Adenauer had thus acquired an unexpected ally. Churchill, after all, had
taken a quite different view in his speech to the House of Commons on

---

* 'I assured Dulles that I would not approve any compromise solution. Germany is standing firmly with the West': Adenauer, *Erinnerungen*, Vol. II, p. 310.

11 May. Nevertheless, whatever the circumstance, Churchill's change of heart was all the more welcome, not least because his view as expressed in Bermuda coincided with Adenauer's view. Not that Adenauer wanted a free-standing German army – he had had enough trouble with German public opinion over the ratification of the EDC Treaty; but if the EDC Treaty failed in the French National Assembly he had no other option. But there was no doubt that he would be in for another bruising row.

Indeed, he had had further trouble in November 1953 after his announcement to the Bundestag that he regarded the US deployment of nuclear weapons in West Germany as essential to its defence. Only a few days later, 280mm nuclear-capable cannon had 'made their journey down the Rhine amidst a fanfare of publicity . . . a curious sight, massive and cumbersome'.[3] There had not only been much publicity. There had been a major political row, exacerbated when the Americans were sensibly vague about the cannons' capability and their deployment. To suggest a free-standing German army at this moment would be to provoke an even fiercer row.

But Adenauer's new ally was not wholly on his side. At Bermuda Churchill had also taken the view that the West should make some move towards the Soviets; at least to agree to another Four Power meeting. The Soviets had indeed suggested this again in August. Dulles, too, had accepted the idea of a conference 'on the assumption that it could be held in the near future and that we would be able to extricate ourselves from it quickly'.[4] In other words, he thought it would be a waste of time.

The upshot was that a message was sent to the Soviets on 15 July 1953 that there should be a foreign ministers' conference to settle the mechanism for free elections throughout Germany with a view to establishing a – reunited – German government. But by then the Soviet attitude had changed. The workers' revolt in June 1953 had convinced them that they should hold on to their position in eastern Germany. The compromise solution was for a foreign ministers' conference to explore ways of 'reducing international tension'. The meeting duly took place, in Berlin in late January 1954.

Adenauer was at one with Dulles in believing that the whole thing would be a waste of time; but he went to great lengths to consult the other major political parties to see if a common West German position could be presented to the three Western Allies. The discussions proved fruitless. Adenauer considered that a freely elected all-German assembly should only have power to develop a constitution. The others, as well as a majority in the

CDU group in the Bundestag, took a different view. They considered that such an assembly should have complete governmental authority. Adenauer was left isolated – not for the first or the last time. In consequence, it was only Adenauer's view which was conveyed to the Western Allies.

Immediately after the Bermuda conference had come, on 14 December, a NATO Council meeting in Paris. There Dulles piled on the pressure by stating that if the EDC failed, the United States would face an 'agonizing reappraisal' of its foreign policy.[5] This pronouncement was meant to terrify the French, implying as it did that the US would turn its back on Europe and retreat into isolationism. In fact, it was a clumsy effort, which only served to provoke an angry storm in the French press. Dulles, as a British observer remarked, was again showing himself to be 'the wrong man in the wrong place at the wrong time'.[6]

By then, there is no doubt that Adenauer was coming to the view that the EDC Treaty would fail in the French National Assembly – whatever concessions were made. Accordingly, he turned to his new ally, the British. He had a long discussion with Eden, also in Paris for the meeting of the NATO Council. The two agreed that they had a common task: not to seem reluctant to negotiate with the Soviets but at the same time not to mislead either the British or the West German public about the chances of success. Eden explained the British difficulties in joining the EDC, while wishing for its success. Adenauer replied that he understood the difficulties, but that 'it was Germany's urgent wish that the United Kingdom should come as close as possible to the EDC and Europe . . . First, Europe could not do without Great Britain's experience, character and way of life, and secondly, the French must not be allowed to think that Germany was striving for hegemony through the EDC.'[7] Whether he meant it, of course, is another matter; but, failing France, Adenauer badly needed a heavyweight ally other than Dulles.

The Berlin conference of foreign ministers duly opened on 25 January 1954. Molotov, Eden, Bidault and Dulles, together with their supporting troops of officials, argued for some five weeks – without any obvious conclusion. The German problem was discussed at thirteen meetings of the conference. Much of the time, however, was taken up with Molotov's long and repetitive expositions of the Soviet point of view, that all possibility of a revival of German militarism should be firmly prohibited. His expositions were backed up by a detailed explanation of the draft peace treaty which he had tabled. Eden, in his turn, tabled a reunification plan based on free elections throughout the whole of Germany. To say the least, there was no meeting of minds.

There was, however, some movement, however minuscule it seemed at the time. The Soviets had adopted the phrase, much favoured by the West German SPD, 'collective security'. Furthermore, their new line, 'Europe for the Europeans', had immediate attraction for those who had been offended by Dulles' aggressive talk of 'agonizing reappraisal' of US commitment to the defence of Europe. In short, 'a more flexible position taken by the Soviet side is hard to deny'.[8] More flexibility, indeed, was to come as the decade moved on.

In truth, the only positive result of the Berlin conference was the convening of yet another conference – this time in Geneva – to try to resolve the problems of Indo-China. As far as Germany was concerned, there was no perceptible shift in the basic Soviet position. Molotov was particularly critical of Adenauer, whom he described more than once as 'an enemy of the Soviet Union'. Furthermore, Adenauer's successors, he thought, would be even more aggressive and dangerous. Finally, he refused even to jump the first fence: free elections. He kept on saying that 'Hitler had come to power as the result of elections which were free'.[9]

In a moment of candour, Molotov showed his true hand in a remark he made to Eden in one of their many dinners together during the conference – Eden noting, in passing, that Molotov was a charming and thoughtful host. 'He agreed,' he said, 'that there should be free elections in Germany, but that the four occupying powers should surely agree beforehand upon the kind of government they wished to result from free elections.'[10] Eden did his best to explain that it was the purpose of free elections to allow the electorate to choose the government they wanted, but by then Molotov was hardly listening. Indeed, he changed the subject to ask why the band of the Royal Irish Fusiliers had provided the after-dinner entertainment at a British dinner earlier in the week when Ireland was neutral, and its soldiers could not belong to the British Army. Eden tried laboriously to explain about Irish volunteers, but it was no good. At that point, and finally, Eden realised that the conference was as good as dead.

The failure of the Berlin conference undoubtedly pleased Adenauer. If the Soviets were not prepared even to accept the principle of free elections in a reunited Germany, there was obviously no point in continuing discussions in any form. But he also had the perfect rejoinder to his domestic opponents who were continually urging him to persevere. All he had to do was to point to the reason for the failure of the Berlin conference. Privately, his conclusion was that the Soviets might not wish to go to war in Europe, but neither did they want to concede any political ground. Their main objective, in his view, was to push the Americans out of Europe and back to America. This, of course, he would resist by whatever means were available to him.

But there was yet another difficulty. When Adenauer met Dulles at Cologne airport on 18 February on his way back from Berlin, Dulles raised another irritating problem – the Saar. Adenauer had done his best to play the whole matter down; it was a minor diversion, he claimed, from the major objective of securing French ratification of the EDC Treaty. To be sure, he was prepared to make minor concessions to the French for that purpose, but any more would have given substance to his opponents' claim that he was prepared to 'give away' part of Germany. Dulles, however, reminded him that he had given an undertaking to President Eisenhower that the Saar problem would be out of the way by the time ratification came before the French National Assembly. With that somewhat menacing remark, he left Adenauer standing on the tarmac and loped heavily up the steps into his aircraft for his journey home.

It was certainly with a sense of weariness that Adenauer embarked on yet another series of negotiations over the Saarland. But he had given the undertaking that Dulles had mentioned, and if agreement on the Saar was one of the elements of the price to be paid for French support for the EDC, so it had to be. As a matter of fact, the matter suddenly became more urgent with the Soviet announcement in March 1954 that their occupation of East Germany was at an end, and that the German Democratic Republic from then on had full sovereignty. The Western Allies, needless to say, responded with a declaration that the GDR in their view was not a legitimate state. The EDC, for Adenauer, thereby became doubly important.

To set the scene for the negotiations, the French government at the beginning of March produced a Saar Memorandum, which Blankenhorn described tersely as 'a straightforward exposition of the French status quo in the Saar thinly disguised as Europeanisation. Wholly unacceptable to us.'[11] But 'Europeanisation', in another version, was the main feature of a more promising plan, put forward by the Dutch diplomat, Goes van Naters. It was around this that Adenauer was prepared to negotiate. He therefore went to Strasbourg in early April, accompanied by Hallstein and Gerstenmaier. He was under no illusions. The process was going to be long, difficult and tiring; and so it turned out.

The whole Saar matter was complicated by the views of the political leaders in the Saarland itself. For a start, all the West German political parties had been banned by the French. Worse than that, from Adenauer's point of view, was that even those who might be sympathetic to Germany were nursing their own particular careers. Johannes Hoffmann, for instance, was 'Prime Minister' of the Saar; it was not a position that he was going to surrender easily. Heinrich Schneider, on the other hand, led the opposing pro-German party. But they were both, in Adenauer's view, weak and self-serving. There could be no prospect of help from them to him, or of him to them.

This being so, the preliminary negotiation with the French on the future status of the Saar quickly ran into the ground. Adenauer insisted that a precondition of the 'Europeanisation' of the Saar was a guarantee from the French government to deliver ratification of the EDC Treaty. The French rejected the precondition. Adenauer further insisted that any settlement should be open to review if and when Germany was reunited. The French rejected that precondition as well. For the moment, therefore, the whole Saar negotiation was put into suspense. It was just as well, since on 12 June 1954 the Laniel government was voted out of office after the French Army's defeat in Indo-China at Dien Bien Phu.

Laniel, whatever his record in the wartime French resistance, was, at least in one British view, a 'small, squat, and weak man'.[12] His successor as Prime Minister, Pierre Mendès-France,* on the other hand, was from a quite different mould. A Jew from a family of cloth merchants, radical, anti-Catholic,

---

* Mendès-France, Pierre (1907–82): Lawyer and politician. Born into a strongly Jewish family (and throughout his life suffered from anti-Semitism). 1932: Elected to the National Assembly. 1938: Under-Secretary of State for finance in the Popular Front government. 1939–41: Served in French air force. 1941: Captured and imprisoned by Vichy government; escaped. 1942: Reached London and joined Free French air force. 1943–45: Served under de Gaulle first as commissioner for finance and then minister of national economy. 1946: Re-elected to National Assembly. 1954: Became Prime Minister; successfully ended France's involvement in Indo-China. 1955: Defeated as PM. 1956: Deputy prime minister in another short-lived government. 1958: Opposed de Gaulle's return to power. Generally regarded as the most able and successful Prime Minister of the French Fourth Republic.

tough and extremely clever, he had been made a minister by Léon Blum in the pre-war Popular Front government at the age of thirty-one. For all this, he was despised, feared and hated by the anti-Semitic French political right. Nonetheless, Mendès-France's government, although it only lasted seven months, was one of the few successes of the Fourth Republic. He achieved a relatively painless, if humiliating, French exit from Indo-China, gave limited autonomy to Tunisia, and went a long way towards fulfilling his ambition of modernising the archaic French economy.

Surprising as it may seem, neither Adenauer himself nor any of his advisers had made contact with Mendès-France prior to his appointment as Prime Minister. They were therefore forced to rely solely on reports from his opponents. As a result, Adenauer's first reaction was one of blank hostility. He told his Cabinet on 7 July 1954 that in his view Mendès-France was recruiting into his government socially acceptable Bolsheviks, that he intended to form another Popular Front government, and that he had promised the Communists that France would sabotage the two treaties. All in all, the least that can be said is that the relationship got off to a bad start.

Mendès-France, of course, had his own priorities, and ratification of the two treaties was well down the list. The settlement over Indo-China was reached at Geneva at the end of June and was ratified by the National Assembly on 20 July 1954. On 31 July, France recognised the internal self-government of Tunisia. It was only then that Mendès-France was prepared to turn his mind to the EDC and the General Treaties. But he had a problem, as he well knew. Both the Communists and the Gaullist Rassemblement du Peuple Français (RPF) were opposed root and branch to the EDC, and the Socialists were split. There was no majority in the National Assembly for ratification, nor was it easy to see how one could be constructed. It was not even certain that his government would hold together. On 13 August, for instance, three RPF ministers, Jacques Chaban-Delmas, Pierre Koenig and Jean Lemaire, resigned even at the mere thought that the government might recommend the treaties to the Assembly.

Adenauer in the meanwhile had his own domestic crisis – the defection to East Berlin of Otto John, the head of West German internal intelligence. It was the first serious defection from the West German government, and the press were duly outraged. Adenauer first played the whole thing down, trying to put the blame on the British, saying that John had held his post under their protection. That did not work, since the press then wanted to know how it was that someone of apparently persistent incompetence, also apparently an alcoholic and a homosexual, was allowed by the government to stay so long in his job. 'Chancellor, clean yourself up!' shouted *Die Zeit*.[13] Adenauer's response was contemptuous – to go on his annual holiday, leaving the press more infuriated than ever.

But his holiday plans were to be rudely interrupted. Mendès-France produced a series of protocols to the EDC Treaty which he thought might get him off his parliamentary hook. One of these, for instance, required the right of veto by any member state on military action by EDC forces; another that integration of EDC forces would only apply to troops stationed in Germany. It was immediately clear that any proposals of that nature would require a fresh ratification in all the countries involved – including West Germany. To Adenauer, that was unthinkable. Indeed, by now he had lost all patience with the French government, and it was in the grumpiest of moods that he left the Bühlerhöhe for an emergency meeting in Brussels on 19 August to try to sort the whole thing out.

The omens were certainly far from good, and they were made worse by the announcement, on the day before the Brussels conference opened, of the death of another of Adenauer's allies, Alcide de Gasperi. Spaak, since March 1954 the Belgian Foreign Minister, chaired the meeting, but a chairman was hardly necessary since the discussion was wholly one-sided – the five versus France, with the US and British ambassadors hovering on the fringes of the conference egging the five on. The conference went through the French proposals one by one. Such was the opposition to them that Adenauer found it almost unnecessary for him to speak at all. The others were doing his work for him. But it became clear that Mendès-France could not, or would not, budge. After three days of discussion the conference broke up. There was nothing more to be done.

It was on the last day of the Brussels conference that Adenauer and Mendès-France finally met face to face – at the latter's request. The meeting took place in Spaak's study, with only Hallstein by Adenauer's side. Mendès-France turned on all his charm. He was, he said, a friend of Germany; his mother come originally from Luxembourg but had lived in Alsace; his first language had been German; he was a convinced supporter of Franco-German understanding; 'he thought of his two sons, aged eighteen and twenty, and he did not want to see their lives sacrificed in a Franco-German war'.[14]

Adenauer wondered where all this was leading. Finally, Mendès-France came to the point. There was no majority, he said, either in the National Assembly or in the Senate, for ratification of the EDC Treaty. When Adenauer asked him whether a majority might somehow be fashioned, Mendès-France replied that it would only be possible if each country had the right to withdraw at any time. Obviously, this was quite contrary to the whole spirit of the project, and Adenauer said so. The meeting then ended, with both sides reasserting their belief that the two countries should continue to search out common ground. Adenauer immediately went back to his hotel to send a telegram to Churchill. The only way the EDC could be saved, he wrote, was for Mendès-France to support it with all his authority as the Prime Minister who had achieved so much for France during the previous few weeks. He hoped that Churchill would be able to bring his influence to bear.

It was all to no avail. Adenauer withdrew again to the Bühlerhöhe to await events. They were to be as he feared. After two days of bad-tempered debate, the French National Assembly on 30 August 1954 voted by 319 to 264, with 43 abstentions, not to allow the motion ratifying the EDC Treaty on to its agenda. At that point, the European Defence Community was effectively dead.

Shortly after 9pm that evening, the West German ambassador in Paris relayed the news to the Bühlerhöhe. Although expected, it came nevertheless as a shock. In fact, although he was usually quite calm when events turned against him, in this case Adenauer was almost broken. When the ambassador's message was handed to him, he read it – and immediately went to his room without saying a word. The next morning Hallstein, Globke, Blankenhorn and Eckardt turned up at his hotel. 'Never before or since,' Eckardt wrote later, 'have I seen him so bitter, so depressed.'[15] He let fly about the French in general and Mendès-France in particular. The French Prime Minister, he said, was untrustworthy. He had sold out to Molotov over Indo-China, agreeing to sabotage the EDC Treaty in return for Soviet support; he was trying to suppress economic growth in West Germany, which was by then rivalling France, with the help of the Soviets. All these views were then expressed to the US and British High Commissioners, Professor James Conant and Sir Frederick Hoyer Millar, who called on him at his hotel to express their sympathy, and, in particular, to John Freeman, the special correspondent of the London *Times*, who reproduced most of them in an article in the edition of 4 September.

It was now a question of picking up the pieces. In this the British government showed unaccustomed energy. Churchill sent a message of encouragement to Adenauer, saying that 'after so many years of war his strongest wish was to see the German people take their proper place in the world-wide family of free nations'.[16] On 11 September Eden set off on a hurried round of European capitals to see whether there was common ground for an extension of the 1948 Brussels Treaty of mutual defence between Britain, France and the Benelux countries to include West Germany and Italy if French opposition to German membership of NATO was insurmountable. Moreover, the whole matter of German membership was, in any event, to be on the table.

At first, Adenauer was uncertain about Eden's proposal – particularly the idea of an unprepared Nine Power conference in London to include not only the original signatories to the 1948 Brussels Treaty but the candidates as well, and, as an additional bonus, the other members of NATO, Canada and the United States. It seemed to him to be a recipe for shambles; and, before agreeing to attend, he wanted to know what Dulles thought of the whole idea. Furthermore, he had come round to the view that the removal of the Occupation Statute and the acknowledgement of German sovereignty should be separated from the problem of European defence. On this, as on other matters, he relied on Dulles' opinion.

But Dulles' view, when it came, was unhelpful. For what it was worth, Dulles weakly told Adenauer that he was content that the British should take the initiative, and that they should go, if at all, together. By then it was all too late, since by 23 September Eden had the London conference set up, and both Dulles and Adenauer had no option but to attend.

In fact, when it came, the London Nine Power Conference of the autumn of 1954 was a spectacular success. Adenauer, after a few acerbic comments about Mendès-France, let others do the talking. Eden's chairmanship showed him at his most elegant and persuasive. Churchill showed where his sympathies lay by giving a grand dinner for Adenauer in 10 Downing Street on 27 September, on the eve of the first day of the conference. Instead of getting submerged in the technicalities, Eden steered the conference to a resolution of the fundamental issues. On European defence, Adenauer undertook, on behalf of the Federal Republic, not to produce atomic weapons, and to agree to controls on its production of warships, bombers and missiles. Eden, in turn, gave an assurance that Britain would maintain four divisions and a

419

tactical air force on the continent of Europe, and that they would not be removed against the wishes of a majority of the signatories of the 1948 Brussels Treaty. After these reassuring commitments, the way was clear for all outstanding matters to be agreed in principle, subject to detailed negotiation in Paris three weeks later.

There were, in practice, no fewer than four Paris conferences at the same time. There was the negotiation between the three Western Powers and West Germany about the winding up of the Occupation Statute in the General Treaty; there was the negotiation between the original signatories of the 1948 Brussels Treaty – Britain, France, the Netherlands, Belgium and Luxembourg – with West Germany and Italy for the extension of the treaty to create what was to become the Western European Union; there was the negotiation between the thirteen members of NATO over the admission of the Federal Republic as a member of the alliance – another treaty extension; and there were negotiations between France and West Germany about the Saar.

In all these negotiations Adenauer shuffled to and fro, returning on each day to his base at the Hotel Bristol in the rue St-Honoré, strategically placed, as it was, close to the official residences of the French President in the Palais de l'Elysée and the French Prime Minister in the Matignon. Moreover, apart from his own personal preference – Adenauer, at his age, liked to stay at hotels where he knew he would be comfortable – it was convenient for his most difficult negotiation: with Mendès-France about the Saar. Insignificant as it might be in the larger context of the future of Europe, Adenauer knew that the Saar was the key to success or failure of his government in terms of West German domestic politics. Indeed, it is not too much to say that his coalition with the FDP might break on it.

Mendès-France had done his best to soften Adenauer up by inviting him to spend an afternoon and evening at the elegant Château La-Celle-St-Cloud, the former residence of the royal mistresses Mme de Maintenon and Mme de Pompadour. Everything was as it should be: the château itself had been restored, the park overlooking the Seine, and Paris beyond, was at its autumnal best. Adenauer had always enjoyed the ceremonial of diplomacy, and this occasion was no exception. In the course of the discussion, he agreed to the separation of the Saarland from the Federal Republic until a final peace treaty should be signed. He also conceded that the Saar should be subject to a statute to be supervised by a commissioner appointed by the Council of Europe.

But at this point Adenauer realised he might already have gone too far. He had made as many concessions as he could. Indeed, his only difference with Mendès-France was on whether there should be two plebiscites, one to confirm (or reject) the statute and the other to determine the Saar's future after the signature of a peace treaty, or whether, as Adenauer argued, the statute should be approved by an assembly including pro-German parties (hitherto illegal) and a single plebiscite after the peace treaty. Either solution, he well knew, would cause uproar in the Bundestag, and, quite possibly, the collapse of his government.

It was one of the few occasions on which Adenauer felt it wise to consult other West German politicians. (His normal procedure, of course, was to negotiate everything himself and to present the result as a *fait accompli* to his colleagues and to the Bundestag.) The Saar, however, was too delicate a matter for that. He therefore invited not only the chairmen of the coalition parties but also the leaders of the SPD to Paris to explain his position. He even had lunch with Ollenhauer and Schmid. The tactic worked. Adenauer explained how all the different issues were interwoven, and how stupid it would be to prevent the signature of the other treaties by digging heels in over the Saar. Most of the others, even Brentano and Dehler, but not, of course, Ollenhauer and Schmid, ended up by agreeing with him. By the time they all left to return to Bonn, Adenauer knew that he could carry a Saar agreement through the Bundestag.

It was just as well. On Friday, 22 October 1954, the day before the full conference was to begin, Mendès-France announced that he would only agree to the treaties if he signed at the same time an agreed Saar Statute. It so happened that on that evening Eden was giving a dinner for the participants at the British Embassy, where he was staying. Before the meal was even finished, Eden took Adenauer and Mendès-France aside and ushered them into the library, along with Hallstein, Blankenhorn and Roland de Margerie. They were to stay there, he implied, until they had settled the Saar question.

'After they had been there some hours,' Eden wrote, 'I became troubled at the delay and asked that discreet enquiries should be made as to how they were getting on. I learned that they had finished some time before and had tip-toed from the Embassy, thinking that we had already gone to bed.'[17] In fact, it had all been over quite quickly. Adenauer accepted a second plebiscite and a 'commissioner' from the Western European Union. Mendès-France accepted modifications to the statute which would allow the Saar to join the Federal Republic if a majority so wished.

In the event, it was on the following morning that the Saar Statute was finally agreed, with the resolution of previous difficulties over German firms' access to Saar markets. Consequently, the signing of the various treaties proceeded as planned, with an appropriate fanfare of trumpets, in the afternoon. Adenauer announced in his press release that 23 October 1954 was the 'day of reconciliation with France'.[18] No more was heard about the villainies of Mendès-France.

On his return to Bonn, instead of being hailed as the Chancellor who had regained sovereignty for Germany and secured the defence of Europe, he was vilified for the concessions he had made over the Saar. He was therefore quite happy to escape on his second trip to the United States, where his states-manlike ability had been fully appreciated and where, for good measure, he collected another doctorate at Columbia University.

In the event, it turned out to be a short trip. The President of the Bundestag, Hermann Ehlers, unexpectedly died during what should have been a routine operation on his tonsils. Adenauer had to fly back – as it happened, bad weather forcing his aircraft to stop at Bermuda, the Azores, and Paris – to arrive in Bremen for Ehlers' funeral. It was as well that he had come back, however sad the reason. There had to be a new President of the Bundestag. Adenauer wanted Gerstenmaier, but the CDU/CSU group nominated a competitor – Ernst Lemmer. Adenauer had to use all his powers of threats mixed with charm to achieve Gerstenmaier's election, not least because Gerstenmaier himself was unenthusiastic about the job. In the event, Adenauer was successful: Gerstenmaier was elected – on the third ballot.

With Gerstenmaier safely in the chair, Adenauer was able to postpone ratification of the Paris treaties until they had been ratified by the French – a wise manoeuvre in the light of his experience over the EDC Treaty. It was therefore not until February 1955 that the treaties were presented to the Bundestag. In spite of SPD opposition and public protest that reunification should precede joining a military alliance, they passed easily enough. That done, the Saar Statute was taken and, in spite of Cabinet abstentions from Schäffer and Kaiser, was passed with a safe majority. During the course of the debate, however, Adenauer treated a backbencher from the FDP to a furious tirade, and then wrote to Dehler, now chairman of the FDP parliamentary group, even more rudely in justification. In truth, Adenauer was tired and easily irritated. But the episode was to sour relations with the FDP almost – but not yet quite – to breaking point.

In fact, Adenauer was convinced that Dehler was leading the FDP towards the SPD position and that, whether intentionally or in folly, the SPD were moving towards the Soviets. As it turned out, his conviction about the SDP was not entirely without foundation. On 9 March 1955, the Soviet ambassador in the GDR was instructed to 'ascertain the opportunity for [a] meeting between . . . SPD representatives and Soviet public figures . . . for the exchange of opinions on the issue of the activation of the struggle for the reunification of Germany, against the restoration of the Wehrmacht'.[19] Furthermore, the Soviet Foreign Ministry was preparing the ground for such a meeting. In a paper dated 11 June, there was a list of questions which 'could be raised by the SPD leaders in the course of a talk with the USSR representatives'.[20]

But by that time it was all too late. At noon on 5 May 1955, the Federal Republic of Germany became a sovereign state. Flags were raised on all official buildings to proclaim the event. Adenauer stood on the steps of the Palais Schaumburg as the flags were raised. The Allied High Commissioners announced the end of the Occupation Statute – not without a few barbed words from François-Poncet. Two days later, Adenauer led a large delegation to the NATO conference in Paris to assume the privileges of full membership for the Federal Republic. On 15 May, the Soviets and the Western Allies signed a treaty for the independence and sovereignty of a neutralised Austria. Within no more than three weeks, on 7 June 1955, the Soviets sent a message through the West German Embassy in Paris that they wished to establish diplomatic relations with the Federal Republic. Adenauer was personally invited to Moscow to discuss the matter. At that point, it seemed that what became known as 'détente' had begun.

9

CAN ANYONE BE TRUSTED?

'Ich werde die Wahlen gewinnen, wenn die Amerikaner keinen Fehler machen'*

IT WAS ONLY ten days after Adenauer had triumphantly proclaimed the sovereignty of the Federal Republic from the steps of the Palais Schaumburg that President Eisenhower lobbed another large pebble into the international pool. In the course of a press conference in Washington on 18 May 1955, Eisenhower answered a question put by a correspondent of *Le Monde*. There was merit, he said, in the idea of a neutral zone consisting of countries in Central Europe. There would not, he insisted, be a military vacuum as a result. Austria, although neutral, would under the terms of its State Treaty be allowed to maintain armed forces appropriate to its needs. Switzerland, too, was both armed and neutral. 'This kind of neutrality,' he pronounced, 'is quite different from a military vacuum.'[1] To those who were listening, it was obvious that he was also thinking of a reunited Germany as part of the neutral Central European zone which he suggested.

Adenauer, when he heard about Eisenhower's intervention, was badly

---

* 'I will win the elections if the Americans make no mistakes': Adenauer to General Lauris Norstad; Blankenhorn, diary entry, 21 May 1957.

shaken. Quite clearly, in his view, Eisenhower had not grasped the reality of 'Central Europe'. That reality was quite simple. Any Germany which was reunited on the basis that it would remain neutral between the two power blocs would inevitably fall under Soviet domination, and – whatever the time scale – eventually be incorporated in some fashion into the Soviet empire. Not to put too fine a point on it, it was simply opening the door, as any good Catholic would realise, to the Antichrist.

It was, after all, that view which had moved Adenauer to pursue the EDC Treaty with such determination. In spite of its obvious military absurdity, the EDC would have locked West Germany permanently into a Western European political system. It would have ruled out neutrality. The NATO solution had only been second best, since it relied on the United States, a country which, for most of its history, had had a strong isolationist streak, not to mention an imperfect understanding of European affairs. Nevertheless, at the time, it had been better than nothing.

Eisenhower's pronouncement revived all the old fears. Immediately, Adenauer recalled the West German ambassadors in Washington, London and Paris, and, along with Hallstein, Blankenhorn and General Adolf Heusinger, met them on 25 May at the Bühlerhöhe. He was uncharacteristically and visibly angry. He was angry at Eisenhower; he was angry at Dulles for allowing such nonsense in the first place; and he was angry at Eden for having put forward a similar idea at the Berlin conference of the previous year. In short, he felt badly let down by those he had previously thought to be reliable allies. In his anger, he gave all present a long lecture on the stupidity and general treachery of Americans.

In the end, they managed to cool him down. They persuaded him gently that his negotiating position was weak. Of course, what he referred to as the 'nightmare of Potsdam' – the Four Powers reaching agreement on the future of Germany over his head – was still a serious possibility; but until a peace treaty was finally signed he would be in no position to cavil. Furthermore, he should know that there was to be a Four Power conference at Geneva in July, the agenda for which was under discussion by an Allied planning group in London. After Adenauer's temper had cooled, they then set themselves to devise a tactic to bring the Allies back into line.

It was no good just being negative. They therefore worked out a new submission for Adenauer to put to the London planning group. The argument was that reunification of Germany could indeed be achieved, but only if there was a general and worldwide agreement on arms control and, moreover, if there was a demilitarised (but not necessarily neutral) zone, 200 kilometres wide, 'from the Baltic to the Adriatic . . . including a large part of the Soviet occupied zone'.[2] It was a clever try, not least because, apart from looking constructive, it was not far from the plan which Eden had put forward at Berlin the year before. In fact, their ideas were to be subsumed into the subsequent and more developed British alternative, to be discussed later at Geneva.

But Adenauer put them forward not just as a blocking manoeuvre – which, of course, was part of the objective – but because he genuinely thought that the Soviets were prepared to negotiate some sort of deal, and that a general arrangement on arms control was the best place from which to start. In this he was certainly right in principle, although even now it is hard to detect what the Soviets had in mind, or indeed whether there was any clear collective thinking in the context of the post-Stalin leadership struggle. Certainly, opinions in Moscow were divided. The 'politically correct' view was that the prospects for German reunification had 'all but vanished with the Federal Republic's entry into NATO'.[3] But the Soviet Foreign Ministry seemed still to have been thinking in terms of reunification and 'free elections'.

The only thing the Soviet leadership could all agree on was that there was some sense in negotiating with the Western Allies, whatever the outcome might be. In June, therefore, the German ambassador in Paris received a note from the Soviet ambassador inviting the Federal Government to Moscow with a view to establishing diplomatic relations. Besides normalising relations, the note went on, the Soviets thought that such a move would improve European security and contribute to the restoration of German unity. It was difficult for Adenauer to refuse, since a refusal would have been difficult to explain away domestically.

Given this new move, there was uncertainty in both the Allied and the Soviet camps about the true agenda for the Geneva Four Power conference. But there was also movement on two other fronts. The first was European. At a conference of foreign ministers of the ECSC at Messina in Sicily on 1 June 1955 there was discussion of a plan to pool the civil nuclear industries of its members into a new organisation along the lines of the ECSC, to be known as the European Atomic Energy Community (Euratom).

True, Adenauer was at first not particularly enthusiastic – Erhard's background brief claimed that the Germans were better off buying technology from the US or Britain. But when Spaak produced in a memorandum the idea of a more general European Economic Community (EEC), he became much more positive. Indeed, he actively promoted this new project, which both he and Spaak saw as 'the best way to solve the German problem'.[4] In other words, if there was to be no permanently reliable defence integration, German security was to be found in European economic integration. With this backing, the conference agreed to set up a committee, under Spaak's chairmanship, to examine ways of broadening the scope of the ECSC by dismantling tariffs and other trade barriers between the member countries. As it turned out, of course, although the decision was modest, it was to be the start of a great adventure, to be put in treaty form in Rome two years later.

The second area of movement was domestic. With the ratification of the Paris treaties, Adenauer felt that he must now relinquish the portfolio of Foreign Minister. It needs hardly to be said that he did so with reluctance, but with the general recognition of the sovereignty of the Federal Republic when the Paris treaties came into effect, it was no longer sensible for him to be both Chancellor and Foreign Minister. The obvious replacement was Brentano – although Adenauer did not think much of him – and the deed was duly done. But that in turn upset Blankenhorn and, to some extent, Hallstein. In the end, Hallstein stayed on in the Foreign Ministry under Brentano, but Blankenhorn preferred to leave to be ambassador to NATO. Defence was also a problem. What had up to then been an office in the Chancellery clearly had to become a department in its own right. Strauss patently wanted the job as minister, and was not slow to let it be known; but Adenauer did not trust him. He therefore promoted Blank to the post of minister, with Strauss moved to take charge of nuclear affairs.

In truth, none of those whose jobs were affected was particularly happy about the new arrangements. Even Brentano was unhappy about the limitations imposed on his authority. 'I keep in my hands,' Adenauer wrote, 'the leadership in European affairs, affairs with the United States and the Soviet Union . . .'[5] But there it was; and, if they wanted the jobs, they had to accept the decision of the Chancellor. Adenauer himself was not at all displeased. He liked his ministers to be uncomfortable; it made it easier for him to play one off against another.

The scene then shifted to Geneva, where the participants at the Four Power conference were assembling in time for its opening on 18 July. Eden, who had by then finally succeeded Churchill as British Prime Minister, came from London; Edgar Faure, the French Prime Minister of the day, came from Paris; and President Eisenhower came in Air Force One from Washington. All of them were accompanied by their respective foreign ministers, the newly appointed British Foreign Secretary Harold Macmillan, Pinay and, of course, Dulles. The Soviets, in their turn, were represented by Marshal Nikolai Bulganin* – 'looks like a Radical-Socialist mayor of a French industrial town . . . he might be *un bon papa*', Macmillan noted; Nikita Khrushchev – 'how can this fat, vulgar man, with his pig eyes and his ceaseless flow of talk, really be the head, the aspirant Tsar, of all those millions of people'; and Molotov – 'already a sick man'.[6] All in all, it was a motley group to try to settle the world's affairs.

The heads of government had their own villas on the outskirts of Geneva, at a suitable distance from one another and agreeably cool, while others sweltered in the town in the summer heat. Conveniently, it was in the library of Eisenhower's villa that the three Western heads met the day before the conference was due to open, to try to bring their respective views into some sort of harmony. Faure spoke first. He produced an elaborate plan under which an international body should be set up, to which all savings from disarmament would be paid and then distributed to 'backward areas'. Nobody quite understood what he was talking about or how it would work. Eisenhower then stuck to his idea of a neutral belt in Central Europe, but with diminishing enthusiasm as his audience started to fidget. Eden's view was well known: that there

---

* Bulganin, Nikolai (1895–1975): Politician. Son of an office worker. Early career in the Cheka (the Soviet Secret Police in the 1920s) combatting 'counter-revolution' in Turkestan. Elected in 1931 as Chairman of the Moscow City Soviet. Survived Stalin's purges and in 1937 became Chairman of the Council of People's Commissars of the Russian Federation. Political Commissar on the Western, Moscow, Baltic and Belorussian fronts in the Second World War, with rank of lieutenant general. 1944: Deputy Defence Minister. 1947–49: Minister of the Armed Forces and Marshal of the Soviet Union. 1948: Became full member of the Politburo. 1953–55: Minister of Defence. 1955: Prime Minister. 1957: Denounced in camera as a member of the 'Anti-Party Group'; confessed to 'political errors'; sent to Stavropol region as chairman of local Economic Council. 1960: Forced into retirement and rewarded with a comfortable pension and a house on the outskirts of Moscow. Charming, but no match for Khrushchev.

should be a demilitarised strip, limitation of armaments in specified areas of Europe, and a European security pact. In the end, failing anything better, they all agreed to start with Eden's proposal. Then 'we all lunched with the President – a disgusting meal, of large meat slices, hacked out . . . and served . . . with marmalade and jam. The French were appalled.'[7]

Adenauer in the meantime had gone on holiday. This time it was his elder daughter Ria who was 'invited' to accompany him, to the Swiss mountain village of Mürren. The choice of Mürren was deliberate. It was not too far from Geneva, so that the German observers at the conference could report from time to time, even though there were no roads to the village and the last stage was a difficult struggle up the hill on a sluggish mountain railway. But there were beautiful views of the Jungfrau, the Eiger and the Mönch, the air was invigorating and the weather tolerable, although Adenauer, as usual, grumbled about the rain.

Down in the heat of Geneva, the conference achieved little. The Soviets were friendly in informal receptions, saying 'with glee that since [Stalin's death in] 1953 they worked a normal day, instead of all night',[8] but stuck to their long-winded written submissions during the plenary sessions. Eisenhower was not at all clear on the details of what was going on, and Dulles, when the British invited him to breakfast at Eden's villa, 'ate boiled eggs one after another . . . he ate and talked so slowly that we got little out of him'.[9] Faure, at least, had one advantage: he was the only one of them who spoke Russian – much resented by the others. But even he could make no great headway. In the end, Bulganin declared that ratification of the Paris treaties had made discussion of German reunification pointless, as there were now clearly two German states, each with its own economic and social order. There was only one result worth mentioning. Foreign ministers were instructed to draft for themselves a directive for a further conference to be held between them, also in Geneva, in the autumn.

The brief which the heads of government accepted was couched in suitably pompous diplomatic language. 'The Heads of Government,' it read, 'recognising their common responsibility for the settlement of the German question and the reunification of Germany, have agreed that the settlement of the German question and the reunification of Germany by means of free elections shall be carried out in conformity with the national interests of the German people and the interests of European security.'[10] It was, of course, a fudge. But by then it was obvious that there was no conceivable meeting of minds. The Soviets would not countenance the reunification of Germany if Germany remained in NATO; the Western Allies would not countenance any solution to the German problem which forced Germany, as a precondition, out of NATO.

As the predictable failure of the October conference of foreign ministers was later to show, Adenauer's Potsdam nightmare was vanishing in the light of the Geneva day. There was no longer any question of the Four Powers imposing a solution of the 'German question' over his head. In the heights of the Bernese Oberland, now relieved of his major worry, the Chancellor of the Federal Republic of Germany could devote his mind to his future visit to Moscow.

There was, indeed, much to think about. Adenauer knew very little about the Soviet Union, let alone its leaders. Nor was it at all clear what the discussions were to be about. He was aware, of course, of the historical baggage, of two world wars and the record of savagery of both nations in the second of the two. He was also aware of the surviving German prisoners of war in the Soviet Union, and that one of the main Soviet objectives was the establishment of diplomatic relations.

One of the reasons for his acceptance of the invitation was to try to negotiate the release of German prisoners of war still held by the Soviets. What he did not know was that the prisoners of war had in fact become a something of an embarrassment for the Soviet leadership. Up until the end of 1949 some two million had returned to Germany. So far, so reasonable; but the remaining 10,000 or so had been adjudged criminals, either on the basis of war crimes or, probably more frequently, on the basis of 'anti-Soviet activities' – in other words, loose talk about their grievances in the prisoner-of-war camps.

It was the remainder that were giving rise to the embarrassment. From 1953 on, after Stalin's death, the new Soviet leadership had given thought to the problem. Some of the prisoners were sent to the GDR. In early 1955 there were attempts to discuss the matter with SPD politicians, but Adenauer got wind of this approach and persuaded the Allied High Commissioners to prohibit any such contact – which they did. In short, Adenauer knew about the problem, and the numbers involved, but not about the Soviet difficulties. Nor, indeed, did he know that the Central Committee of the Communist Party had decided in July to 'set the "criminals" free' as a goodwill gesture during his Moscow visit.[11]

If Adenauer knew little about the Soviets, the Soviets knew equally little about him. Their view, indeed, had been changing over the years. At first they had been trying, without much success, to woo the SPD, and had only gradually come to realise that if they wanted to do business with West Germany it would have to be with Adenauer. It was not an easy process. The earlier attempts to describe Adenauer had been couched in the language of Stalinist cliché. For instance, a report from the Soviet Control Commission in Germany of 24 April 1953 quotes Adenauer as being 'closely connected with West German monopolistic circles'.[12] A further report of 17 August 1953 points out that 'through the threats and blackmail, through the bribes handed out to some opposition-minded [CDU/CSU] members . . . through the use of his own personal prestige, Adenauer and the CDU/CSU leadership are instrumental in suppressing . . . the growth of opposition sentiments'.[13]

The tone had started to change by the summer of 1954. On 6 July a further paper was sent to Moscow, noting that Adenauer had spoken 'on the possible establishment of diplomatic relations between the USSR and West Germany . . . but a week later . . . under direct pressure from the Americans . . . was compelled to declare that no changes in the foreign policy position of the Bonn government towards the Soviet Union took place'.[14] By December 1954, the reports were even more friendly: 'The words by V. M. Molotov in his Berlin address of 6 October on the ample reasons for the relations between the Soviet Union and the German Federal Republic to start developing on a sounder basis have been influencing the broad segments of West German society. After the signing of the Paris agreements, Adenauer declared in Munich that, with the agreements implemented, there would certainly again be a German ambassador in Moscow . . .'[15] The final accolade came in a paper of 22 January 1955. 'It is worth noting,' it read, 'that Adenauer, for whom, with the help of the media, the reputation of the "greatest German politician since Bismarck" was created, enjoys considerable personal prestige among the members and supporters of the CDU.'[16]

In the light of these changing views, the Politburo had commissioned a German expert in the Foreign Ministry, Valentin Falin, to write for them a biographical paper on Adenauer in preparation for his visit. When it appeared it was long and very detailed. By the time it had passed through several hands, it had been reduced to a mere hundred pages; and it read, according to Anastas Mikoyan, 'just like a thriller'.[17] Furthermore, a delegation of West German journalists, which included Hans Zehrer of *Die Welt*, Karl Herold of the *Frankfurter Rundschau* and Hans-Ulrich Kempski of the *Süddeutsche Zeitung*, all of them at the top of their profession, pointed out to their Russian counterparts the great importance of Adenauer's visit to West German public opinion. It was a full briefing – recorded faithfully by the Soviets and passed on to the Kremlin. 'The German side,' the report went, 'presented – with vigour and strength – their point of view on the necessity to normalise relations between the Federal Republic and the East.'[18]

If there was excitement in Moscow – and corresponding disapproval both in Western capitals and in the GDR – it was nothing to the excitement in Bonn. When the moment came, on 8 September 1955, two Lockheed Super-Constellations were needed for the official party to fly to Moscow, and a special train for over seventy journalists. On arrival at Vnukovo airport, the visitors were greeted by Bulganin and Molotov with half the Politburo lined up alongside them in order of precedence. The guard of honour, for some obscure reason, was wearing parade uniforms which were replicas of those worn by the Tsar's personal guard before 1917 – thus looking for all the world like a chorus in an old Russian comic opera. As Eckardt rightly but only half-humorously remarked later, it certainly was 'a journey into the unknown'.[19]

Adenauer had taken great care in assembling his delegation. He had invited not just his own ministers and advisers but the chairman of the foreign relations committee of the Bundestag, Kurt Georg Kiesinger; its vice-chairman, Carlo Schmid; and Karl Arnold, now chairman of the foreign relations committee of the Bundesrat, with their respective advisers. He certainly did not want, on such a hazardous enterprise, to be accused of acting solely on his own initiative. When the party arrived, they were carefully shepherded to the Hotel Sovietskaia, by Moscow standards a luxury hotel, but by German standards, as Wilhelm Grewe, head of the political department of the Foreign Office, caustically wrote, 'a middle-class hotel with old-fashioned comfort and the taste of the petty *bourgeoisie*'.[20] The train, on the other hand, which had rumbled across half a continent, was parked in a siding just outside Moscow's Kursk railway station. It was to be an uncomfortable home for the journalists, but it also had another use: it became an office for the German delegation, with a 'special bug-proof wagon, dining car, radio and telephone equipment, typing facilities and so on'.[21]

The negotiations lasted the best part of six days. They started with a grand gala banquet on the evening of the Germans' arrival. As if that was not enough, the West German delegation was provided with a huge breakfast in their hotel, with large bowls of caviar, on the following morning. There was a reception every night, usually as a prelude to another dinner or, on one evening, a visit to the ballet at the Bolshoi Theatre. As might be imagined, much alcohol was consumed – indeed, one of Globke's main duties was to give each member of the delegation a large dose of olive oil in the early evening to prevent subsequent and possibly embarrassing intoxication. Adenauer, for his part, noticed that many of the Soviets were drinking toasts in water – and promptly insisted on doing the same.

In the event, the formal negotiations ended with only one positive result: an agreement to establish formal diplomatic relations and to exchange ambassadors. To be sure, there were many long and rambling speeches about the past, and one or two histrionic scenes, particularly between Adenauer and Khrushchev. On one occasion, for instance, Khrushchev shook his fist at Adenauer, whereupon Adenauer got up 'and shook my fist back at him'.[22] But, somewhat surprisingly as it seemed at the time, one of the main objectives of Adenauer's visit, the repatriation of the German prisoners of war, was hardly mentioned at all; and, when it was, Bulganin insisted that they were no more than common criminals who had been properly sentenced by the Soviet courts. It was only on the last day, during a gala reception in the Kremlin, that Bulganin 'without warning and very impulsively' came up to Adenauer with a deal: if Adenauer would write him a letter requesting full diplomatic relations 'we'll give them all to you – all! One week later! We are giving you our word of honour!'[23] It was certainly an odd scene, and there were many who concluded that Bulganin had not been subjected earlier to one of Globke's doses of olive oil. What they did not know was that the tactic had been determined well beforehand.

On his return to Bonn, Adenauer found himself caught in intense media cross-fire. The assurance that the German prisoners of war would be released was greeted with jubilation. On the other hand, he was much criticised for relying on Bulganin's 'word of honour'. He was also the object of profound disapproval from the Western Allies, who were furious that he had unilaterally established diplomatic relations with the Soviets – thus accepting as irreversible for the foreseeable future the division of Germany into two states; in other words, as the German press put it, selling out the East Germans.

In fact, the Allied reaction was not unexpected. Indeed, on the return flight from Moscow the policy which later became known as the 'Hallstein Doctrine' was drafted, emphasising that the Soviet Union had a special status as one of the victors of the war. The fact that West Germany was establishing diplomatic relations with the Soviet Union was no more than a recognition of that status. Furthermore, the Soviet Union's relations with the GDR were neither here nor there. The Federal Republic, the policy claimed, alone represented all Germans. There was therefore no question of the Federal Republic establishing diplomatic relations with any other state which had already recognised the GDR. Moreover, any state which in the future sought to establish diplomatic relations with the GDR was threatened with 'serious consequences'.

That was all very well. But nobody was in the least surprised when, only a week after Adenauer left Moscow, the Soviet Union concluded a treaty on full diplomatic relations with the GDR. Nor, for that matter, was Adenauer. Indeed, he was probably pleased that he had caused such a fuss; at least he was being noticed, which was much better than being ignored.

In early October 1955 the first trainloads of German prisoners started to arrive at the transit camp set up for them near Kassel. But at the end of October the flow unaccountably dried up. So much, the West German press sneered, for Bulganin's 'word of honour' – and for Adenauer's naïveté. In fact, it was not until December that it appeared that the Kremlin was linking the return of the rest with the repatriation of Soviet citizens allegedly detained in West Germany. It was all very embarrassing. As a gesture, Adenauer decided to release thirty-one Russians who were serving prison sentences in West Germany; but he made it clear that all the others were under the protection of the United Nations and could come or go as they pleased. Luckily for him, the Soviets unaccountably changed tack yet again. During the Christmas period the trains resumed their journeys. By the end of January 1956 all the remaining prisoners had come home.

By that time there had been two setbacks for Adenauer, one personal and the other political. The first was a breakdown in his health. Obviously exhausted from his expedition to Moscow, he went down with a severe cold which unexpectedly but quickly turned into double pneumonia. From 7 October to 23 November he was out of action, lying miserably in his bed at Rhöndorf, under constant supervision by his doctors, and not allowed to move. Only a few visitors were permitted, of whom, needless to say, Globke was the most frequent. Cabinet ministers, and even the Vice-Chancellor, Franz Blücher, were discouraged – not least by Adenauer himself.

But not only was he seriously ill. As might be imagined, the mutterings started almost immediately. The Federal Republic, it was widely said, was run by a very sick and very old man; obviously he could not go on. There were long discussions in the press and on the radio about the date of his retirement – or death – and the identity of his successor. Even ministers were drawn into the discussions. Indeed, it was not until mid-November, when he was on the way to recovery, that the mutterings began to let up. Adenauer, it needs hardly to be said, was not one to forget them, or the ministers who had been dragged into the discussions.

The second setback had been political, and yet again it was in the Saar. In spite of official encouragement from Bonn to the Saarlanders to vote in the October plebiscite in favour of the Saar Statute, two-thirds of them had voted against it and in favour of joining the Federal Republic. The result was precisely the opposite of what Adenauer had wished and intended. At the very least, it meant more tedious negotiation with the French over the future of the Saarland; at worst, it meant a breakdown in relations between the two countries and the consequent abandonment of the projects for Euratom and the EEC.

The effect of his pneumonia and the consequent speculation about his future made Adenauer in his convalescence even less trusting than ever, and very much more tetchy. With the FDP chairman Thomas Dehler, for instance, he was hardly on speaking terms; he was even more suspicious of Strauss; thought that Brentano was weak and ineffective; that Schäffer was obstructive; that Erhard's economic measures smacked too much of unthinking liberalism; and that Blank was no longer any good. Furthermore, he did not hesitate to let his views be known.

To be fair, although it generally took the form of unpleasant and semi-public backbiting, there was some justification for Adenauer's criticism of his own ministers. Brentano was indeed weak and ineffective, and Schäffer was indeed a troublemaker. Blank, too, was not performing well. The rearmament programme, for example, which he was supervising, was falling a long way behind schedule. By January 1956 there were only 1,000 troops under arms, instead of a scheduled 100,000. Moreover, there was only one French tank with which to teach them. Their clothes were shoddy and their pay well below civilian standards. When Adenauer visited the first training battalion at Andernach two weeks after the lavish celebration of his eightieth birthday – an event which itself left him exhausted – he found the place in dense Rhineland fog, made darker by the dirt-grey uniforms of the troops, with the flag 'hanging like a damp cloth against the flagpole . . . the guests seemed dejected as though attending a funeral rather than a baptism'.[24] It was a far cry from the Wehrmacht – Adenauer insisted on using the old word – which he had hoped for.

February 1956 brought its own troubles, which further interrupted Adenauer's convalescence. A Socialist government came to power in France, under Guy Mollet, and started preaching the virtues of disarmament. The British joined in, and elaborate plans were laid in Paris and London for the control of arms levels. 'In France, in Britain,' Adenauer wrote, 'everyone was pressing for disarmament while we in the Federal Republic stood for rearming.'[25] The British in particular came in for a heavy dose of scorn. Not only had they the effrontery to ask West Germany for a financial contribution to the costs of the British Army of the Rhine, but they were proposing to restrict the number of their own forces to 650,000 men and allow all other European countries, including West Germany, an overall total of 150,000 to 200,000 men. The Federal Republic would become 'ultimately a third-class power'.[26] Nor were individual foreign statesmen spared. Christian Pineau, Mollet's Foreign Minister, was hopelessly unreliable – he wanted to be 'the mediator between East and West';[27] Eden was unstable; even Dulles was too soft, and prepared to sell out West Germany at any moment.

By then, Adenauer's doctors had concluded that his convalescence was too slow and that he should take an immediate holiday, and this he prepared to do. But his preparations were disrupted by a sudden coup in the government of North Rhine-Westphalia. On 21 February a group of young FDP Landtag members engineered a vote of no confidence, which removed the CDU-dominated coalition government – led by Karl Arnold – and put in its place an FDP/SPD coalition. The event was startling enough in itself. In the context of coalition politics it was shocking.

There were immediate repercussions in the FDP group in the Bundestag. On 23 February, the four FDP ministers in Adenauer's Cabinet resigned from their party, only to find on the following day that thirty-six of the fifty-two FDP Bundestag members voted to leave the government coalition and to go into opposition. The ministers were forced to form their own party, the Freie Volkspartei (FVP). Nonetheless, their position was impossibly weak: they were simply accused of hanging on to their jobs after the CDU/CSU/FDP coalition had irrevocably fallen apart.

To be sure, Adenauer's own personal position was unaffected by these ructions, since he had a Bundestag majority behind him without the FDP. But the federal elections were only eighteen months away, and it was not difficult to see how the Düsseldorf coup might be repeated at national level. The answer to that threat was – at least to Adenauer – self-evident: the electoral goalposts had to be moved, yet again, to the advantage of the CDU and CSU. As Krone remarked: '[Adenauer] was never very discriminating in his choice of means to his ends.'[28] In fact, Adenauer had had this in mind even before the Düsseldorf coup. He had already had a row with Dehler about a change in the electoral law to something he described as a 'semi-proportional representation system', by which the straight wins in constituencies would no longer count against the state lists, which would be strictly proportional. Of course, Dehler had been no fool. He could work out the result of such a system as well as Adenauer, and regarded it as yet another example of Adenauer's deviousness. Dehler certainly had a point.

For the moment the matter had to be left there, since even the CDU executive were becoming suspicious of Adenauer's motives, and without their support there was no obvious majority in the Bundestag for change. Although Adenauer made an attempt at the end of February to patch things up with Dehler and to reassemble the coalition, it did not work. His bad temper after his illness, his attempted fiddling with the electoral law, the breakdown of the coalition and the split in the FDP had led to hostility and even hatred, directed personally at Adenauer himself. Voices were loud that the old man had to go.

And go he did, but only on holiday. Even when it came, however, at the end of March 1956, the holiday was not a success. Adenauer's doctors had advised him to avoid the heights of Switzerland – his lungs were still too weak. Instead, he went to a villa in the Ticino and from there to nearby Ascona. But it rained constantly, and, apart from Pferdmenges, he had few visitors who were not considered annoying (for instance, officials of the Ticino government). Everywhere he went, two detectives stayed irritatingly by his side. Even Libet, whose turn it was to accompany him, seemed unable to cheer him up.

It was almost a relief to get back to Bonn towards the end of April. At least the public mood had calmed down, and one good thing had happened in his absence. The Spaak committee set up at Messina had recommended that the six members of the ECSC start immediate and direct negotiations with a view to setting up the proposed European Economic Community. Although there was a row in France, and Erhard was still conducting a rearguard action against the spread of European bureaucracy, the suggestion was accepted quite peacefully by the Bundestag in a debate of only two hours. The SPD had accepted Monnet's arguments that European integration was necessary for stability and security, and Adenauer was able to get away with what was for him a short speech.

Yet he was still irritated and depressed. In the middle of May, Krone noted that 'for the first time he said he was often tired and fed up with office and work'.[29] Besides, his approval ratings were slipping badly in the polls. To increase the intake of the Bundeswehr, the government had had to introduce conscription. Needless to say, it was deeply resented, and, although the period of military service was reduced from eighteen to twelve months in the face of resistance to the whole project from the SPD in the Bundestag and public opinion outside, it was obvious that it would be tiresome to implement and permanently unpopular. Moreover, Blank, who had had to carry the burden of its introduction, was already ill, and by the end of the conscription debate in the Bundestag was on the point of collapse.

It was by then clear that a reconstruction of the Cabinet had become urgent. But on 10 July Strauss came to see him to point out in the most graphic terms that the planning for the Bundeswehr had been faulty, and that the target of 500,000 men deployed under arms was unrealistic. They would be lucky to be able to assemble 100,000 in the medium term. There were simply not enough uniforms, weapons, barracks or training areas to achieve more than that. Blank, he said, was washed out. The inference was clear: he, Strauss, should become Defence Minister.

That in itself was enough to put Adenauer's back up. His response to his Cabinet colleague was venomous. 'Herr Strauss,' he replied, 'I have listened to you. Take note: as long as I am Chancellor you will never be Minister for Defence.'[30] The sombre truth was that Adenauer disliked and distrusted Strauss as much as Strauss disliked and distrusted Adenauer. If anything, Strauss was even ruder about Adenauer – behind his back, of course – than Adenauer was about Strauss, but it was a close contest. The overall effect, however, of Strauss's intervention was that the Cabinet reconstruction was yet again put off.

Events, however, led Adenauer to the inevitable. On 13 July he read of a plan devised by the American Admiral Arthur Radford, then chairman of the joint chiefs of staff, to reduce US conventional forces by 800,000 men and to make up the difference in overall military strength by increased atomic fire-power. The timing was, to say the least, unfortunate, since Adenauer had only recently achieved a victory in the Bundestag for conscription to precisely the kind of army that the US was now apparently considering out of date. Furthermore, it was obvious to the West German press – and if it was not obvious the Soviets were quick to point it out – that if the Radford plan were adopted then German civilians would be the first to be incinerated in the event of a European war.

On 22 July, just before going to the Bühlerhöhe on yet another holiday, Adenauer wrote a long letter to Dulles complaining about Radford's proposals. The letter, apart from its litany of complaints, appealed to Dulles' Christianity. 'I repeat,' the letter ended, 'that this policy is incompatible with the principles of Christianity and humankind . . . I beseech God to lead and guide you.'[31] Dulles' reply was meant to be reassuring; indeed it was written 'as a friend to a friend'. But Adenauer was not to be so easily mollified; when he arrived back in Rhöndorf in late August he was still in his most suspicious mood. Two weeks later, when Donald Quarles, US Secretary of the Air Force, arrived in Bonn to offer the explanation that the US wanted to use German conventional forces to counter attacks 'by guerrilla armed forces from the Eastern Zone', Adenauer simply told him that 'NATO is finished'.[32]

It was this mistrust of the twists and turns of American policy which led Adenauer to his enthusiastic support for Euratom. He was, as always, preoccupied with West German security, and the associated fear that the US would eventually withdraw from Europe. Given this, the way forward was to persuade Erhard – and the majority of the Cabinet which supported him – that Euratom was necessary for the defence of the Federal Republic. But to do that he had to make a tactical concession to Erhard. There was only one concession which was convincing: a retreat from his former stated views on the 'United States of Europe', which Erhard, while supporting the principle of a free trading area, disapproved of as yet more institutionalised cartelisation and consequential bureaucratic interference.

Adenauer's retreat from the concept of the 'United States of Europe' began with a speech to the Grandes Conférences Catholiques in Brussels on 25 September 1956, during his state visit to Belgium. He claimed that the first period of European integration had been successful in its objective of excluding for ever the possibility of another war between West Europeans.

From then on, integration should 'not be rigid, but should be as flexible and elastic as possible'. Supranational institutions should be avoided, since they became 'strangulation barriers'. He went on to claim that they deterred future candidates for entry: 'once a start has been made then one should not be hesitant about [Europe's] expansion and enlargement'.[33] In short, it was a speech which delighted Erhard and the 'free marketeers', but which duly dismayed Monnet, Hallstein and the other 'integrationists'.

But it served its purpose. At a Cabinet meeting on his return from Brussels, Adenauer was able easily to deflect criticism of Euratom, on the grounds that 'Germany cannot remain a nuclear protectorate'. He gracefully accepted that sovereignty could not have been achieved in the London Nine Power Conference of 1954 unless he had renounced all future German production of nuclear weapons. But, he pointed out, 'as Dulles said to me at the time, everything is regarded as *rebus sic stantibus* [things being as they are]'.[34] (The fact that none of the other participants had heard Dulles make the remark was, for Adenauer, neither here nor there.) On 5 October, at another Cabinet meeting, he went much further. He explained that Euratom would allow access to the technology which would permit West Germany to produce atomic warheads as quickly as possible. 'In the long term,' he is recorded as saying, 'the conclusion of Euratom will give us the chance to develop atomic weapons in the normal way. The others, particularly the French, are ahead of us.'[35]

In all these manoeuvres, Adenauer's intentions were quite simple. He wanted atomic weapons for the West German armed forces. The only way to get at the necessary technology was through Euratom. The only way to set up Euratom was to agree in parallel to set up the EEC. Therefore, the EEC had to be set up, even on Erhard's terms.

At this point Adenauer had a piece of luck. In October, there was a revolution in Hungary, which for a time promised to give the country the freedom it desperately wanted. Flowers appeared on the previously drab streets, and Hungarians were able to talk to each other openly without fear. But, much to the dismay of governments – and ordinary people – in the West, the movement to freedom was brutally suppressed by Soviet tanks on 2 November. There was even talk of Western intervention to save Hungary, and there were many who volunteered to help Hungarians evade arrest by the Soviets by manning the frontier with Austria and giving all the aid they could.

At the same time, the Egyptian government nationalised the Suez Canal, and the British and French, in collusion with the Israelis, were preparing to use force to get it back. There was therefore, on two fronts, an international crisis of major proportions. Erhard's economic arguments looked increasingly thin against the overriding political argument for European unity. On 3 November 1956, Adenauer won approval from the Cabinet to go to Paris to negotiate, on his own terms, a conclusion to both Euratom and the EEC.

By then the long-delayed Cabinet reconstruction had been announced. Throughout the early part of October Adenauer had been putting together the pieces. The four FVP ministers were dispensable. To be sure, he would have liked to be rid of Schäffer, but was too worried about offending the CSU; and he would have sacked Anton Storch as Minister for Employment and Social Affairs if his trade union support had not been so vocal. In short, the options had been limited. But there was one ministerial post which had to change – defence. Finally, Adenauer made up his mind. On 10 October he sent for Strauss and offered him the job. Strauss did not immediately accept; he was still smarting from Adenauer's treatment of him in the previous July. Seeing this, Adenauer assumed his most disarming manner. 'Herr Strauss,' he said, 'are you worried that an old man is still in a position to change his mind?'[36] The capitulation was complete. Strauss, with as much grace as was in his character, accepted the portfolio.

On the evening of 5 November Adenauer left Bonn for Paris for the final negotiations with the Mollet government over Euratom and the EEC. As it turned out, it was an unfortunate day to choose. Only that morning British and French paratroops had landed in the Canal Zone ahead of a full-scale assault from the sea and an Israeli attack from the east. As the train made its way across the northern French plain a message came in that the Soviets had threatened an immediate missile attack on London and Paris unless the invasion was stopped immediately. At that point, the train was brought to a juddering halt. Adenauer, now fully awake, telephoned the West German ambassador in Paris to find out whether his visit was still welcome. Indeed it was, came the response.

The train spent the rest of the night in a siding just outside Paris. Nobody managed to get much sleep. In the early hours of 6 November it set off again, finally to arrive at the Gare de l'Est at 8am. To Adenauer's surprise, half the French Council of Ministers was there to meet him — even more tired than he was, since the Council had been in continuous session overnight. Nevertheless, the greeting was dignified and moving. The French badly needed friends, particularly since Eden had signalled that the British, under heavy American pressure, were preparing to accept the UN armistice resolution. For the first time, as the 'Deutschlandlied' and the 'Marseillaise' rang out, the two old enemies were standing firmly together at a time of greatest danger.

The good will thus generated allowed the negotiations on remaining points on Euratom and the EEC to proceed quickly and smoothly. Adenauer's relations with Mollet, which had already improved after the French government (encouraged by a German offer of large capital investment) had kept its word and agreed the new status of the Saar as the eleventh state of the Federal Republic, were now almost idyllic. By the time he returned to Bonn, Adenauer was confident that Euratom – and the EEC – would be successfully achieved. Moreover, his nuclear ambitions were to be confirmed and reinforced in December by a NATO Military Committee which stipulated twelve West German divisions on the front to the east, all equipped for nuclear warfare. Although the directive left aside the matter of who would provide West Germany's atomic fire-power – it was assumed that it would be the US – in Adenauer's view the door to West German use of atomic weapons had by then been satisfactorily unlocked.

That done, it was time for Adenauer to turn his thoughts to the federal elections due in September 1957. Certainly, he had no worries about the West German economy. It was performing well. In the years since the 1953 elections it had grown at an average of over 7 per cent a year; in 1955, the balance of payments surplus had been DM 3.07 billion; the migration from the GDR to the Federal Republic of young, skilled and highly educated workers was keeping productivity high and earnings growth low. All in all, the picture was remarkably rosy. Yet Adenauer still felt that more was needed if the 1957 elections were to be won convincingly. The opportunities for foreign policy initiatives were limited. Much as he might have liked to, he could not reshuffle his Cabinet or change the electoral law so close to an election. There was, in fact, only one conclusion: what was needed was a thoroughgoing and effective electoral bribe.

It so happened that there was one immediately to hand. After the 1953 elections Adenauer had announced a major review of social policy. Those who had benefited from the economic recovery had largely been those in work. It was consistent with Adenauer's political philosophy – and with the Papal Encyclicals he had read twenty years earlier at Maria Laach – that the new wealth should be spread to the less well off. The years 1953 to 1956 had been taken up with the review. At the end of it, the conclusion was that the first priority was the reform of old-age pensions. The SPD and the German Trade Union Federation had their own ideas, for a pension fund into which all in the active workforce would pay a proportion of their income each year and which would be distributed in full to pensioners. This, they argued, would ensure that the pension kept pace with the cost of living.

The CDU accepted that pensions should be indexed to the same extent, but preferred to ensure as well that pensions should be linked to gross income. Needless to say, the measure implementing this reform, the Law on Pensions Insurance, was enormously popular when it was passed in the spring of 1957. Cleverly, Adenauer had also made sure that the new system was backdated to 1 January, which made it even more popular. The only dissenting voice was that of Schäffer, who correctly saw that under the system an ageing population would play havoc with public finances. Adenauer's response was a comment to the CDU executive that 'Herr Schäffer did not feel like a political minister'.[37]

From that point on, the CDU's electoral prospects – and Adenauer's approval rating – improved dramatically. It seemed that all was now set fair for the September elections. In April, however, it all nearly went wrong. At a press conference on 5 April, when asked whether he planned to equip the Bundeswehr with atomic weapons, Adenauer replied that 'tactical atomic weapons are basically nothing but the further development of artillery . . . it goes without saying that . . . we cannot dispense with having them for our troops . . . we must follow suit and have these new types – they are, after all, practically normal weapons'.[38]

Up to that point, in all his public statements, Adenauer had insisted that his objective was to confine the Bundeswehr to conventional weapons. Furthermore, the NATO directive had been kept strictly secret. Now he had well and truly let the cat out of the bag; not only that, but he had tried to play down atomic weapons as merely being a 'development' of conventional artillery.

There was a spectacular political row. Most damaging for Adenauer was not the attacks of the SPD but a powerful missile launched from Göttingen

University. On 12 April 1957, a week after what became known as the 'artillery statement', a group of eighteen eminent physicists, including four Nobel prize-winners, all of whom worked at the Max Planck Institute for Theoretical Physics in Göttingen, issued a document which became known as the 'Göttingen Manifesto'. Its chief author was Professor Carl Friedrich von Weizsäcker, a nuclear physicist, and its message was quite simple. 'We believe,' it said, 'that a small country like the Federal Republic best guarantees its own safety and contributes to world peace by expressly and voluntarily renouncing the possession of nuclear weapons of any sort. Under no circumstances would the undersigned be willing to participate in the production, testing or use of atomic weapons in any way.'[39]

At first, Adenauer tried to brush the whole thing aside. But the press would not let it go. The row developed into a direct assault on Adenauer himself, on the grounds that he had no conception of the effects of a nuclear attack. The row became so loud and intense that it threatened to derail his carefully prepared election strategy. Under fire, Adenauer changed tack. He invited five of the eighteen to Bonn to discuss the matter. Their meeting lasted seven hours, at the end of which a joint communiqué was issued with the statement that 'the Federal Republic will not produce its own nuclear weapons, and consequently the Federal Government has no reason to approach German nuclear scientists about their participation in the development of nuclear weapons'.[40] They were, of course, weasel words, but Adenauer had bought time, and time was what he needed. Nonetheless, the row rumbled on, fuelled by an aggressive note from the Soviets at the end of April, and reached a climax with the NATO spring conference in May. Gradually, however, the personal campaign against Adenauer lost momentum. As he himself remarked, in terms of the elections 'the bomb' had been released too soon.

The stage was thus set for a long election campaign. After his holiday, Adenauer turned again into the uncompromising party politician. His main line of attack on the SPD was that an SPD victory would lead to the decline of Germany. 'The elections,' he said in speech after speech, 'revolve around the question [of] whether Germany and Europe remain Christian or become Communist.'[41] His main defence was the achievements of his government, particularly in pensions reform and – yet again – that there should be 'no experiments'. Erich Ollenhauer, the SPD leader, was brushed aside. All the public saw were almost endless replicas of a huge poster of a lightly tanned and healthy Chancellor – the photograph carefully touched up to make him look some twenty years younger than his true age – gazing purposefully into the middle distance of what was clearly a hopeful future.

When asked how it was that his health was so good and his energy so abundant, Adenauer replied that it was all due to the fitness and long lives of his parents and an equally healthy upbringing. That, however, was for public consumption. What he did not admit was that he had undergone, on the recommendation of his doctor, treatment at a clinic in the suburbs of Montreux in Switzerland known then, as now, as 'fresh cell therapy'. 'We know,' reports the Chief Physician of the clinic, 'that [Adenauer] stayed several times at the clinic.'[42]

The treatment itself is shrouded in secrecy, and is even today a source of controversy. The most that can be said is that it involves injections of foetal cells from a ewe or a cow. The cells are taken from the donor animal and, within half an hour, injected into the recipient human. The whole process involves no more than a short stay in the clinic, and up to four injections. That done, the patient is free to leave – with the assurance that the treatment has rejuvenated the body's immune system and served to counter the outward effects of ageing.

Whatever the truth of the matter, there is no doubt that Adenauer was surprisingly healthy for a man of his age and medical history. The campaign posters reflected this, and helped him win yet another election. In a turn-out of 87 per cent the CDU/CSU won nearly 55 per cent of constituencies and 50.2 per cent of the total vote – the first time that a single party had won an outright majority in German electoral history. By way of some, although minimal, compensation the SPD improved their position with 31.8 per cent – the first time they had broken through the 30 per cent barrier. The chief sufferers were the FDP, down to 7.7 per cent. No other party had managed to achieve the necessary 5 per cent for representation in the Bundestag.

Adenauer had won, and won as convincingly as he had wished. His personal position could no longer be seriously challenged. At the age of eighty-one, he was almost the uncrowned king of Germany. Moreover, 1957 had brought him something else – something which would give him in his last years perhaps more pleasure than anything else. On his spring holiday, in his wanderings in the Italian lakes towards which his doctors, in their concern for his lungs, had steered him, he had discovered Lake Como; and, in particular, he had discovered the little hamlet of Cadenabbia.

10

ENTER THE GENERAL

*'Ich war sicher, dass de Gaulle und ich eine gute und vertrauensvolle
Zusammenarbeit haben würden'**

CADENABBIA IS NOWADAYS little more than a crowded summer holiday resort on
the western shore of a badly polluted Lake Como, merging almost without
knowing it into its neighbour, Tremezzo. Although in official terms it is a
hamlet in the parish of Griante, it has lost whatever character the original
designation gave it. There are expensive hotels; motor launches come by, fer-
rying sightseers from one point to another; sunbathers occupy the lake shore
in carefully organised battalions. Moving, as it were, upmarket (and into the
hills above), those who wish to remain more discreet have at their disposal
handsome villas with expansive gardens, many owned or rented as a weekend
refuge or summer escape by stressed businessmen from Milan. In short, it is
like many other places in the tourist Italy of today.

Nevertheless, even as it is, Cadenabbia retains its own particular beauty. It
looks to the east towards the rising sun, which illuminates the dawn over the

---

* 'I was sure that de Gaulle and I would have a good and trustworthy working partnership':
Adenauer, *Erinnerungen*, Vol. III, p. 434.

small town of Bellagio on the pinnacle of the peninsula dividing the lake into its two southern legs. The sun sets early behind the Sasso di San Martino, but that in turn serves to cast gentle evening shadows across the lake and to cool the summer heat.

It was this gentle beauty that had attracted Adenauer in the spring of 1957. At first, it had been the 'Villa Rosa', which he rented for three weeks at the end of February, in the middle of what was then little more than a village. The accommodation itself was comfortable enough, and on his walks he had come across the game of *boccia* – the Italian version of bowls. But the house was in the middle of the village, and for that reason not entirely to his satisfaction. Attracted as he was to Cadenabbia itself, he thought that he could perhaps do better in the future.

By then, spring holidays had become a fact of life. His doctors told him that he should not imagine that he was still young – he should rest; moreover, his lungs could no longer support the thin oxygen of the mountain air. Adenauer took their advice with his usual care. Nevertheless, whatever the medical advice, and wherever he took his holiday, the pattern set after Gussi's death in 1948 was never changed. One or other of his daughters was 'invited' to accompany him, to cushion what was, without doubt, a sense of loneliness. Furthermore, ministers and officials were summoned to discuss matters of topical interest – which were, in truth, anything which happened to have caught his attention.

In fact, Adenauer's holidays were something of a burden to his subordinates, whether ministers or officials. Apart from the journeys to and fro, while he was away no decisions of any importance could be made in Bonn. Ministers, if they were unwise enough to make any public statement without authority, were duly admonished. Government was run from wherever Adenauer was at the time, either by letter or telephone or by extensive instruction to those he most trusted – Globke, Hallstein, Krone or Blankenhorn. Furthermore, to the dismay of his Cabinet colleagues, holidays were a good time to see journalists for off-the-record briefings. As a result of all this movement, the calendar of visits was formidable. In his three weeks at the Villa Rosa in the spring of 1957, for example, Adenauer, supposedly resting on holiday, had long talks with no fewer than eighteen different people – only one of whom, significantly, was a minister in his Cabinet.

But, as always, the main business of government was conducted in Bonn, and it was there that a new Cabinet had to be formed in September 1957. The emphatic result of the federal elections had left Adenauer with the strongest possible hand, and it comes as something of a surprise to find that the formation of a Cabinet caused him more difficulty than his previous efforts in 1949 and 1953. The CDU/CSU had achieved an overall majority in the Bundestag, but Adenauer felt unable to build on it. He thought it wise to invite the small German Party into a new coalition, since it was suitably right-wing and had its power base in the important Land of Lower Saxony, where the CDU was relatively weak. It was, of course, a carefully thought-out move; it allowed him to construct a government which was very clearly slanted to the political right. The old heavyweights from the trade union wing of the CDU could be, and were, conveniently discarded.

For all that, Adenauer did not find it easy. Satisfactorily right-wing as his new Cabinet might be, he also wanted a strong Rhineland presence; but, given the increased electoral strength of the Bavarian CSU, he had to concede to Strauss and Schäffer the posts of Defence Minister and Minister of Justice (and Vice-Chancellor) respectively. It was only gradually that the other pieces fell into place. In the end, the main surprises were that there was no government job for Gerstenmaier, who remained as President of the Bundestag, and that Franz Etzel,* the former vice-president of the ECSC, was promoted to Minister of Finance. Nevertheless, whatever the intricacy of the allocation of jobs, the Bonn political world was quite clear that, towering over the whole government structure, was an ever more autocratic Chancellor, determined to have his way whatever the personal casualties. As Krone, leader of the CDU parliamentary group in the Bundestag, later confided to the privacy of his diary, 'the Chancellor is becoming tougher and more abrupt, biased and unfair'.[1]

Once sworn in, the new government got off to a rocky start. On 4

---

* Etzel, Franz (1902–70): Lawyer, banker and politician. Born in Wesel. Studied law at Frankfurt, Munich and Münster. 1930–33: Leader of German National People's Party youth section. 1939–45: Served in Second World War. 1945: Joined fledgling CDU. 1949–65: CDU member of Bundestag. 1952–57: Vice-president of High Authority of ECSC. 1957–61: Federal Minister of Finance. Trusted by Adenauer, who thought of him as a future Chancellor.

October 1957 the Soviets launched the first satellite into space – the 'Sputnik'. The Sputnik launch caused consternation in the Western world. Put simply, it was a demonstration that the Soviets were ahead of the United States in missile technology. Nevertheless, in contrast to other Western leaders, Adenauer was delighted by the event. 'I regarded this Sputnik,' he wrote in his memoirs, 'almost as a gift from Heaven, since otherwise the free world would have sunk even further into its twilight sleep.'[2] But, as always, he saw a catch. On 17 October he told his Cabinet that the Soviets were using the 'Sputnik shock' to force the United States into a bilateral agreement, as the two superpowers, to run the world together, without regard for the interests of other countries. This, he went on, must be prevented at all cost.

Adenauer's suspicions were not without some foundation. Even as far back as February 1954, there had been secret conversations between Dulles and Molotov on the fringes of the Four Power conference in Berlin. As Molotov had reported in his otherwise long and tedious account of the Berlin conference to the Central Committee of the Soviet Union Communist Party, 'I had two talks with . . . Dulles on the atomic issue. In accordance with a proposal by the US Government, it has been agreed that . . . discussions would be held in Washington between . . . the USA and the USSR, with Dulles having laid special emphasis [on the point] that this period of bilateral negotiations should be as long as possible . . . [and] confidential.'[3] In plain language, that meant that Dulles and Molotov – the United States and the Soviet Union – wanted to come to some arrangement on how, as the two nuclear superpowers, they could run the world.

That, of course, was in 1954, but there was no reason for Adenauer to believe that the waters in 1957 were any less murky. Indeed, in early October 1957 after the Sputnik launch there was much coming and going. Adenauer had his suspicions, right or wrong, that a similar deal was being hatched. For all that, however, there was little that he himself could do about it. Besides, his attention was soon diverted to the decision of the Yugoslav government on 15 October to establish diplomatic relations with the GDR. On this occasion Adenauer's concern was fully justified. The Yugoslav decision struck at the heart of his claim that the Federal Republic was the only legitimate Germany and that the GDR was no more than German territory temporarily occupied by the Soviets. It could not be allowed to pass unnoticed.

In the event, it was not Adenauer but Brentano who led the attack against Yugoslavia in the subsequent Cabinet discussion, although there is no doubt that Adenauer pushed him to do it. Brentano argued that if the Federal Republic allowed the matter to rest where it was, any number of neutral states – India, Pakistan, Egypt, Syria, many in Latin America and Africa – would follow Yugoslavia's example. A line had to be drawn. The Cabinet took the point, and decided unanimously to break off diplomatic relations with Yugoslavia. To be sure, there were doubters on the fringes – among them Gerstenmaier, Blankenhorn and Eckardt. But they were not in the Cabinet. In fact, the decision was merely putting flesh on the bones of a government statement in the Bundestag on 22 September 1955 following Adenauer's return from Moscow, which had pronounced the establishment of diplomatic relations by third states with the GDR to be 'an unfriendly act' – without specifying the consequences.

Although Hallstein was not in the Cabinet which took the decision, the general principle had become known in the press as the 'Hallstein Doctrine'. Hallstein himself claimed that his name was tacked on to the so-called 'Doctrine' by 'personal enemies'.[4] Be that as it may, there is no doubt that it had his full support, even though the immediate consequence was to wreck the tentative approach which the West German Foreign Office was making towards some form of reconciliation with Poland.

Poland, however, was not at all in Adenauer's favour at that moment, thanks to a plan put forward by the Polish Foreign Minister, Adam Rapacki,* for a zone of limited armaments in Central Europe, to include both German states, Poland, and Czechoslovakia. Adenauer immediately consigned the Rapacki plan to the diplomatic wastepaper basket, on the familiar grounds that it would lead to a vacuum in the centre of Europe into which Communism would eventually force its way. His opinion was, to say

---

* Rapacki, Adam (1909–70): Economist and politician. Born in Lwow in Austria-Hungary (now Lviv in Ukraine). Educated in France and Italy. 1939: Fought in Polish Army. 1939–45: In German prisoner-of-war camps. 1948: Joined Polish United Workers' Party (i.e., Communist). 1950–56: Minister for Higher Education. 1956–68: Minister of Foreign Affairs. Dismissed in 1968 for refusing to support anti-Semitic measures against allegedly unruly students.

the least, unwelcome to the Western Allies, all of whom had agreed that the Rapacki plan might well be a sensible starting-point for a settlement of the general problem of Central European instability, the more so since they believed that the true authors of the plan were the Soviets. But Adenauer was firm; he wanted none of it. His alternative was what it had always been – to reinforce West German defence by arming the Bundeswehr with nuclear weapons.

Much to his surprise, the French seemed to be coming round to his point of view. On 16 November 1957 he received a visit, arranged at short notice, from the junior Foreign Office Minister, Maurice Faure, and the French ambassador to Bonn, Maurice Couve de Murville. It was a Saturday afternoon, and the two were duly invited to Rhöndorf. Adenauer, for his part, instructed Brentano and Hallstein to be in attendance.

The French proposal was indeed startling. Their government, now led by Félix Gaillard, had concluded that sooner or later the United States would pull out of Europe. Since Western Europe at that point would need its own nuclear capability, they suggested that France, West Germany and Italy should jointly develop and produce nuclear weapons and the necessary delivery systems. Needless to say, the suggestion fell on fertile ground. Adenauer saw immediately that 'production' could take place outside German territory – thus obviating the need for a change in the Paris treaties forbidding it in Germany itself. Furthermore, he knew perfectly well that the French were only asking the others to participate because their financial resources were being stretched to the limit by the war in Algeria. In other words, they needed German money. This gave Adenauer what he wanted – a dominant position in the project.

It was quickly agreed that the two defence ministers, Strauss and Jacques Chaban-Delmas, should meet to discuss the technical details, on the assumption that the Italians would agree as well. The whole plan would then be presented to the NATO conference due to take place in Paris in December. At that point, Adenauer delivered his usual lecture on the fickleness of Americans. That done, the meeting then broke up.

When the Soviets heard about the project, they moved quickly to try to defeat it. Ambassador Andrei Smirnov was sent along to remonstrate with Adenauer. This was followed by a letter to Adenauer from Bulganin, pointing out that 'West Germany lies immediately at the point of contact of two military powers, in which each can hit targets in the other's region with modern weapons even of limited range . . . What do they care about the fate of Hamburg, Düsseldorf, Cologne or Munich?'[5]

To some extent, the Soviet protests had their effect. When Adenauer arrived in Paris for the NATO meeting on 14 December 1957, he went to see the British Prime Minister, Harold Macmillan, at the British Embassy. He said emphatically that he did not want to see medium-range missiles sited on West German territory, but, as Macmillan noted, 'they don't want to have to say this openly'.[6] Given his doubts about US policy in the future, Adenauer was obviously cooling towards his NATO commitment, and told Macmillan about his worries. 'He knows,' Macmillan noted, 'how his people (ever since Bismarck) hanker after Eastern dreams . . . When he is dead, he fears that people will fall for the bait . . . With all this in mind, Adenauer is not saying much – especially to his colleagues.'[7]

Apart from his general mistrust of his compatriots, Adenauer was by then without two of the three officials on whom he had relied. Globke, of course, was still there – a Rasputin to Adenauer's Tsar, some said; but Blankenhorn had gone as ambassador to NATO; and Hallstein had been appointed as the senior German Commissioner in the new authority for the European Economic Community, to become its president when the Commission took formal office under the Treaty of Rome on 1 January 1958. Apart from Globke, it was difficult for him to know who to confide in.

The NATO conference of December 1957 came and went, without much definite conclusion. Publicly, Adenauer argued in favour of arms control and disarmament negotiations. Privately, he was intent on securing nuclear weapons for the Bundeswehr. The Rapacki plan was again discussed in meetings outside the main conference, and seemed to be gaining momentum, at least with some of the Western Allies. Adenauer tried to kill it with each ally in turn. In particular, the series of Reith lectures on the BBC during December given by a former US ambassador in Moscow, George Kennan, in which he advocated negotiation with the Soviets on the basis of 'disengagement', focused his suspicions on the British. The lectures were, he considered, 'directed and inspired by the British government'.[8] The British must be brought back into line. Macmillan was therefore treated to another dressing-down.

Absurd as it may now seem, the Kennan lectures gave rise to the first serious row for many years between Adenauer and Heuss. Until then, their relations had been of surprising harmony, given their different backgrounds and political affiliations. But when President Heuss in his New Year address of I January 1958 described Kennan as a 'cautious, profound man', it was too much for Adenauer. He wrote a blistering letter to Heuss. 'Herr Kennan,' the letter went, 'is the man who has contributed in a most embarrassing manner to German softness, owing to his unrealistic observations. [He] will be the chief witness for the SPD.'[9] Heuss wrote back equally firmly that the Chancellor was talking nonsense.

It was a bad row. But, bad as it was, the row was in the end duly patched up, although relations between the two never quite regained their former cordiality. In fact, as 1957 moved into 1958, Adenauer seemed to be in the mood for picking rows. At the celebration of his eighty-second birthday on 5 January 1958, he had a row with Smirnov, who used the occasion to press on Adenauer the unwisdom of acquiring nuclear weapons for the Bundeswehr. Adenauer regarded this as no more than impertinence. On 20 January he had a row with Gerstenmaier at the CDU/CSU parliamentary group executive. Gerstenmaier was tactless enough to say that he no longer agreed with Adenauer's way of conducting foreign policy. He was subjected to a long tirade on the virtues of loyalty. All this, of course, was no more than preliminary sparring before the major foreign policy debate in the Bundestag, due to start on 23 January 1958.

Two days before the debate began there was a further meeting between Strauss, Chaban-Delmas and the Italian Defence Minister, Paolo Emilio Taviani, on the joint project for a nuclear weapons system. During the ensuing two days, Adenauer was acutely nervous that news of the project might leak out. In the event, that did not happen. But the debate was by no means trouble-free. It started in the afternoon of the 23rd and went on until after midnight on the 24th. At first, it seemed to run true to normal form; Erich Mende, the FDP defence spokesman, accused Adenauer of by-passing the parliamentary process; Reinhold Maier asked about the status of former Nazis – looking straight at Globke in the official gallery; Ollenhauer accused Adenauer of failing the nation by ignoring the possibilities of reunification; and a number of CDU members shuffled awkwardly in their seats, and failed conspicuously to support their Chancellor when they spoke.

The debate suddenly came to life when Thomas Dehler rose. He went through the history of the six years from 1949 to 1955, a period during which he had been intimately involved in government, first as Minister of

Justice and then as leader of the main coalition partner, the FDP. Shaking with excitement, he shouted at Adenauer that the Chancellor had never wanted reunification, that he had dismissed the Stalin Note of 1952 with contempt, that he had never been prepared to discuss matters with anybody other than his obedient flunkeys, and that he was incompetent and wholly unqualified to lead the Federal Republic. His speech was not only offensive in content; it was savage in its personal attack on Adenauer.

Dehler was followed by another dissident, Gustav Heinemann. He had moved across the political spectrum to the SPD, and was determined to make his mark there. He, too, launched into Adenauer's failure to take reunification seriously, listing a whole series of missed opportunities. Personally, he said, Adenauer was unctuous one moment, tough the next, and then volcanic. After Dehler's violent attack and Heinemann's scornful analysis, Krone did his best to reply, and Brentano gave a few insults back. But the one person who sat in silence, wearing dark glasses to protect his eyes from the flashbulbs of the photographers, was Adenauer. It looked to everybody like the most obvious and gross contempt for the Bundestag itself. Unsurprisingly, the government went down to defeat.

It might not have mattered so much had not the whole debate been broadcast on the radio and commented on extensively by the press. The press, in particular, were quick to follow up Adenauer's perceived weakness on the issue of 'missed opportunities'. He had remained silent during the debate, they said, because he had no answer. Stung by this attack, Adenauer made an attempt to claw back lost ground. He made a statement on the radio, and got Grewe to give a press conference. But it was no good. The initiative had been lost, and lost badly.

Adenauer did what he had done in previous circumstances when his political back was dangerously close to the wall. He went on holiday. On 31 January 1958 he left, not this time for Cadenabbia but for a hotel just above Vence in the foothills of the Alpes-Maritimes. There he found a light which was clear and weather which was good. It was a place in which he could reflect in peace. This time, as well, there were few visitors. As he wrote to Globke, 'it is warm in the sun; but I feel how tired I have been'.[10]

Nevertheless, he had not forgotten the mauling he had received in the January Bundestag debate. He summoned Globke to Vence for a post-mortem. But in fact there was not much to say except that, to repair the damage, there should be another foreign affairs debate as soon as possible.

Globke was accordingly instructed to make the necessary arrangements. On his long walks in the Provençal countryside, looking closely at the wild flowers, Adenauer also thought hard about his position on reunification, but even after the most intense and introspective analysis he found himself unable to move from the view that it could only safely take place in the context of a general agreement on disarmament and European security. It was not just a German problem; it was a problem for the whole world.

Fortified by this analysis, Adenauer returned on 5 March. He was met off the train at Ludwigshafen by Krone and Globke. They briefed him on what had been going on in his absence. It was a melancholy story: there was a general view that Adenauer was losing his grip, and would soon retire. Erhard, Brentano, Schröder and even Gerstenmaier were jockeying for the succession. Furthermore, the second foreign affairs debate, scheduled for 13 March on Adenauer's instruction, had been postponed. In short, as he reported to Heuss, he had found on his return 'nothing but rows, nothing but rows'.[11]

Adenauer realised that he still had to make up political ground on reunification but, equally clearly, he did not know which way to move. On 7 March he had a long talk with Soviet ambassador Smirnov to see if there was any reasonable way forward. But it was not a success. Smirnov pointed out that the Soviets had proposed a summit conference and bilateral talks between the two German states. Adenauer was unreceptive. Smirnov wanted to know why, but the answer was obvious. Bilateral talks would imply *de facto* recognition of the GDR. This, Adenauer asserted, would in turn lead to the Soviets signing separate peace treaties with both states – thus entrenching the division of Germany.

There, for the moment, the matter rested. Adenauer, indeed, then engaged in what he thought would be a mild diversion. On 10 March, in the Andreaskirche in Cologne, he was invested as an honorary knight of the German Order. He showed an almost childish delight in the ceremony, and went quickly afterwards to show Heuss the photographs of himself dressed in the robes of the order, a white cloak with a black collar and a black cross as a pendant, looking suitably grave – as though at a slightly sinister fancy-dress party. The fact that the whole episode caused great offence in Poland, since the Order was not a decoration of the new Germany but a relic of the old, celebrating the medieval colonisation of lands in the east, did not seem to bother him in the least. If the Poles took offence, he was simply paying them back for the Rapacki plan.

Smirnov returned to the charge a few days later with a note from the Soviet government which, 'to put it mildly, was very unfriendly'.[12] Adenauer countered with the suggestion that the Soviets should give the GDR the same status of neutrality as Austria after the 1955 settlement. Whether the suggestion was made seriously or not is difficult to know. As Adenauer himself wrote, he risked 'being stoned by my own people' for making this 'Austrian offer'.[13] At all events, he must have known that there was no conceivable prospect of persuading either his Cabinet or the Bundestag of its merits. On balance, it seems that the suggestion was made simply in order to shut Smirnov up. In that, it certainly succeeded. Smirnov could only mumble that the GDR was sovereign and that the Soviet Union could not interfere in its internal affairs. After that, no more was heard from him for several months.

When it came, on 21 March 1958, the second Bundestag foreign affairs debate was, unlike the January debate, successfully controlled by the government. Strauss was aggressive and effective – Fritz Erler compared his speech with those of Goebbels in the 1930s, whereupon the CDU/CSU members marched theatrically out of the chamber. It was all good parliamentary fun, and in the end, after four days of long-winded speech-making, Adenauer won the day. The Bundestag voted for a resolution to equip the Bundeswehr with 'the most modern weapons' unless there was general agreement on controlled disarmament. Everybody understood that 'the most modern weapons' meant 'nuclear'.

But there was some annoying fall-out. The SPD had finally joined the *Kampf dem Atomtod* campaign, modelled on the British Campaign for Nuclear Disarmament. Then, on 27 March, Bulganin was deposed, and Khrushchev took his place. There was now only one Soviet leader that mattered. Adenauer, like others, was dismayed. He had, on the whole, liked Bulganin; Khrushchev, who had roughed him up in Moscow in 1955, was another matter. The Western world, he knew, would in the future have to deal with quite a different character.

During April 1958, there was a pause while the events in the Soviet Union were analysed and digested. But there were, as always, a few surprises. The least of those was that the nuclear weapons agreement between France, West Germany and Italy was signed on the 7th; the greatest was that only nine days after the signature the Gaillard government, which had signed the agreement, collapsed. Indeed, under the burden of the Algerian war, and with de Gaulle waiting ominously in the wings, it looked as though the French Fourth Republic was on the point of disintegration. It was perhaps time for Adenauer to cultivate other friends.

By now, it was a familiar pattern. When one ally turned out to be unreliable, Adenauer made overtures to another. Consequently, on 16 April he went to London. The British made him welcome, not least because they were leading a move to create a European Free Trade Area outside the new six-country European Economic Community and needed Adenauer's endorsement of the venture. They also took advantage of the fact that France was without a government to press their claims as a stable and reliable ally.

In London Adenauer was at his most charming and conciliatory. The first event of the visit was a ceremonial dinner in Windsor Castle hosted by Queen Elizabeth. It was the sort of event which Adenauer most enjoyed – full and colourful ceremonial – with no less a person than the Queen of England as his hostess. Not only that, but he was seated between the Queen and the Queen Mother. 'The Germans,' it was noted, 'thoroughly enjoyed themselves. The old Chancellor sat between the two Queens, and flirted with both.'[14] The three days of talks with Macmillan also went well. Adenauer promised to help with the French, and they agreed that there should be a summit, and possibly a series of summits, once the new Soviet government had settled down. All in all, both sides considered the visit a success, and 'the Chancellor was in a merry mood'[15] at a dinner at the West German Embassy on the eve of his departure.

On his return to Bonn, Adenauer reported to Heuss on his visit to London. For the first time since the early 1950s he was, he told Heuss, coming round to the view that Britain would consider joining the EEC and that Europe had to be built with Britain. Heuss was surprised at this sudden conversion, and judged – correctly – that the mood would soon pass.

Leaving aside relations with Britain and France, Adenauer had another item on his immediate agenda: the arrival in Bonn of the Soviet Deputy Prime Minister, Anastas Mikoyan. Mikoyan had come to try to persuade Adenauer not to arm the Bundeswehr with nuclear weapons. In fact, Adenauer rather took to Mikoyan, who, although tough, had a certain Armenian charm. But, whatever the good personal relationship, the talks between the two were peppered with sharp exchanges. Mikoyan claimed that it was not in the Federal Republic's interest to equip its armed forces with nuclear weapons, since they would be the first targets in the event of war. Adenauer, however, held his ground. Once convinced of the deadlock, Mikoyan changed tack, said that the Soviets were ready for a measure of conventional disarmament and invited Adenauer to support them. Adenauer in turn took this suggestion for what it was worth – which in practice was not very much.

Mikoyan's visit to Bonn at least had one advantage. The fact that he had come at all allowed Adenauer to counter the claim of the SPD and a section of the press that he was determined not even to talk to the Soviets, so intent was he on confrontation and, if necessary, war. This was particularly important in the face of the growing strength of the anti-nuclear movement. In Hamburg, for instance, 150,000 people marched in the streets at the time of Mikoyan's visit in a demonstration against nuclear armaments, and there was a rash of well-organised strikes. That was just an overture; there was to be a steady build-up of pressure during the run-up to the Land elections in North Rhine-Westphalia, due on 6 July, which the SPD had decided to fight primarily on the anti-nuclear issue.

Before that happened, however, France had finally fallen into political confusion. On 13 May the generals in Algiers had formed a 'committee of public safety' and were calling on de Gaulle to return to power and restore order in Algeria. In the ensuing chaos, de Gaulle played his hand with the greatest skill. He so pulled all the available strings that at the end of May he was approved as Prime Minister by the French National Assembly. But it was not just the endorsement of yet another Fourth Republic Prime Minister. De Gaulle had made it quite clear that, once the immediate crisis was over, he would propose a new constitution. In short, the Fourth Republic was, for all practical purposes, already dead.

Adenauer waited to see what the new French government would produce. He did not have long to wait. De Gaulle instructed his new Minister for Defence, Pierre Guillaumat, to put the agreement reached with the Federal Republic and Italy for the joint production of nuclear weapons on permanent ice. France was to be the only nuclear power on the continent of Europe – other than the country de Gaulle persisted in referring to as 'Russia' – and that was that. Adenauer's carefully laid plans to control, or at least jointly to control, the production of nuclear weapons by means of the agreement with Gaillard were thus consigned to the dustbin of French national pride.

None of this, of course, was known to the West German public. It was just as well, since the North Rhine-Westphalian election was generally regarded as an unofficial test of the popularity of the anti-nuclear movement. Although it was only a Land election, Adenauer himself campaigned as vigorously as though it were a federal election. He denounced the SPD and the FDP as pacifists and weaklings, ready to roll over on their backs with their paws in air waiting for their stomachs to be tickled by the Soviets. Not only that, but they were economic wreckers who would bring the Rhineland to its knees. No insult was too crude to be thrown at his opponents.

However distasteful its tone, his campaign was successful. The CDU was perhaps helped by a feeling of sympathy after the death of Karl Arnold shortly before polling day, but, whatever the reason, their victory was decisive. They achieved 50.4 per cent of the vote, a clear majority in what was, after all, the most industrialised Land in the Federal Republic. The chief losers were the FDP, who could score no more than 7 per cent. Adenauer, never one to forget a slight, thought that that was a fair reward for their treachery in switching their support from the CDU to the SDP in 1956.

The result of the elections in North Rhine-Westphalia allowed Adenauer political breathing space. In particular, he no longer found it necessary to be seen to be striving for a formula for reunification. He therefore stopped even trying. As he told the next meeting of the CDU executive committee, 'we have to realise that we have been deceiving ourselves . . . in 1948 and 1949 . . . we were all of the view that the Basic Law . . . would be valid only for a limited period of time . . . That was almost ten years ago . . . We now see – and we must be quite clear about this – that it was quite unrealistic to believe that the question of reunification could be solved without a general relaxation of tensions in the world.'[16] With that one speech Adenauer pronounced the funeral rites over nearly ten years of fruitless effort. For the foreseeable future there would be two German states, and in his view they would have to learn to live together.

Having dropped that bombshell, admittedly to the consternation of his colleagues, Adenauer left on 8 August for five weeks' holiday in Cadenabbia – accompanied this time by two daughters, Ria and Lotte – in the Villa Arminio, a handsome villa set in an expanse of parkland above the village itself. But before he left he had received an invitation from Paris. Even during the North Rhine-Westphalian election campaign a special message had been brought to him in Bonn by de Gaulle's chosen emissary, Maurice

Picard, hinting at a meeting between the two heads of government. On 29 July Couve de Murville, now Foreign Minister, issued a firm invitation. Adenauer could not possibly ignore it, and it was agreed that he would meet de Gaulle at his home in Colombey-les-Deux-Eglises on the way back from Cadenabbia. The date was fixed for 14 September 1958. It was, as the French pointed out, a signal honour to be invited to the General's home.

Although the invitation was no doubt an honour, Adenauer was far from enthusiastic. De Gaulle had already withdrawn from the Franco-Italo-German nuclear agreement; in the light of his previous, somewhat lofty, announcements, Adenauer suspected that de Gaulle would try to forge a Franco-Soviet alliance, that he might leave NATO, and that he might block further French integration with her European neighbours. Even when Antoine Pinay, de Gaulle's Finance Minister, called on Adenauer in Cadenabbia on 16 August to explain that de Gaulle's talk of grandeur and *gloire* could be discounted and that at heart the General was a realist, he was not reassured. As he wrote to Pferdmenges, it was, in his view, 'a necessary if not very pleasant visit'.[17]

Nevertheless, it had to be done, and Adenauer duly took the train from Como to Baden-Baden, where he met Brentano and the rest of his small party – ambassadors, one from each country, an interpreter and, of course, his bodyguards. They stayed the night in Baden-Baden and left the following morning for France. As it happened, it was a glorious late summer day, highlighting the near autumnal colours of the Champagne Ardenne. But as they passed through the villages of the northern French plain, each with its carefully tended war cemetery of Frenchmen killed by Germans, Adenauer's nervousness understandably increased. Germans, he thought, could not possibly be welcome.

The three lumbering Mercedes-Benz limousines drove past straggling and mostly silent groups of onlookers, astonished to see, for once, Germans coming to France in peace. When they arrived at Colombey after a journey of a little less than three hours, the two front cars turned into the drive of La Boisserie, de Gaulle's home, leaving the third outside the heavily guarded gates. The leading car drew up in front of the house, and no sooner had Adenauer got out of the car than a tall figure emerged to shake him warmly with both hands, speaking volubly in German. It was General de Gaulle.

After Adenauer had introduced Brentano and his interpreter, de Gaulle hurried them towards the house. In fact, such was the speed of the event that the old Chancellor stumbled on the second step leading up to the doorway and had to put out a steadying hand to stop himself falling over. Once safely inside, with Brentano trailing along behind him, he was introduced to de Gaulle's wife, Yvonne. In truth, Madame de Gaulle was not in the best of tempers. She had refused all help from Paris for the event – no cooks or waiters, no official silver or china, and certainly no flowers, which, she insisted, she was quite capable of providing from her own garden. The fact was that she had not particularly wanted Germans in her house in the first place. Besides, they were late, and she was worried that the lunch would be spoiled.

After lunch, Brentano, the ambassadors and the bodyguards were all sent off to Chaumont, where they were to spend the night at the *préfecture* – there being no room for them at La Boisserie. De Gaulle was anxious to show his guest the garden and, in particular, the view over the valley of the river Aube. 'He made an expansive movement,' Adenauer later reported; 'wherever you looked, there was no single human settlement in this solitude . . . it was this landscape which attracted him.'[18]

Adenauer was bowled over. He had 'to discard all his prejudices . . . [de Gaulle] was neither deaf nor half blind . . . [and] spoke a little German'.[19] In short, the subsequent conversations were wholly open, and revealed many areas of agreement between the two. Both agreed that NATO was in bad shape, that Britain was pursuing impossible policies ('England is like a rich man who has lost all his property but does not realise it'[20]), and that the moment of final Franco-German reconciliation had come. When the party from Chaumont was brought back for dinner, the show was almost over. Adenauer told his colleagues then and on his return to Bonn how much the General had changed during his eleven years of peace in the quiet countryside. He was 'no nationalist . . . very serene when he speaks'.[21]

It was, no doubt, a honeymoon. But, as it happened, the honeymoon lasted no more than three days. On 17 September 1958 de Gaulle sent a memorandum to President Eisenhower and Prime Minister Macmillan proposing a 'Triple Directorate' of the non-Communist world by the US, Britain and France, NATO being the European arm of the 'Directorate'. France, it went without saying, would have a veto over the deployment and use of US nuclear weapons on French territory. West Germany was ignored. The memorandum was copied to Spaak in his capacity as Secretary-General of NATO, who in turn showed it to Blankenhorn.

By the beginning of October de Gaulle's memorandum was common currency in Bonn. Adenauer was furious. Again on the principle that if one ally failed him he should turn to another, he immediately invited Macmillan to Bonn to discuss the matter; and on 8 October Macmillan duly arrived. He found 'the Chancellor very concerned. In the afternoon, with various officials present, he tried to control himself – after dinner he showed his disgust and resentment. He had trusted de Gaulle. They had met for confidential talks only a few weeks before. De Gaulle had seemed to be loyal and open. Now he had struck this cruel blow at Germany and at [his] policy of Franco-German friendship etc., etc. I tried to calm him down as much as I could.'[22]

Their meeting lasted through the afternoon and into dinner. Adenauer did his best to re-create the atmosphere of his visit to London of the previous April. If de Gaulle was going to let him down, he needed Macmillan. The dinner was, apparently, both agreeable and merry. 'The Chancellor, who is a great expert on wine, produced one bottle after another of Rhine wine, and made me take a glass from each, explaining at the same time the different qualities.'[23] Macmillan, who had known de Gaulle well in Algiers during the Second World War, was quick to point out, with his particular brand of delicate malice, that de Gaulle's behaviour 'was proof of clumsiness but also of innocence'.[24]

Only three weeks later the worm turned yet again. On 27 October Walter Ulbricht, the deputy Prime Minister but in practice leader of the GDR, made a speech claiming that the whole of Berlin was within the territory of the GDR. On 10 November Khrushchev announced that all Soviet rights and duties in Berlin would be turned over to the GDR, and that all Allied troops should be withdrawn from Berlin. In a subsequent interview, he compared the recent meeting of Adenauer and de Gaulle with that of Hitler and Mussolini in 1934. Then, on 20 November, Smirnov called on Adenauer to read out a missive which declared that the 1945 Potsdam agreement was null and void. The pace was certainly hotting up.

It was a dramatic turn of events. But the main question in Adenauer's mind was whether Macmillan or de Gaulle could be of the greater use to him in what was obviously becoming a crisis. At least he could find out quickly about de Gaulle, since, as previously planned, he was about to make his first visit to Germany since the war. Britain could, for the moment, wait.

On 26 November 1958 the two heads of government, French and German, met at the Kurhaus in Bad Kreuznach, which officials had calculated was a convenient halfway house between their two homes. In their meeting the damage caused by de Gaulle's 'Triple Directorate' proposal was, at least to some extent, repaired. Adenauer greeted de Gaulle in his almost incomprehensible French, while de Gaulle spoke in German. The upshot of the meeting was that the two leaders declared themselves firmly (and predictably) in favour of the maintenance of the status quo in Berlin. Nevertheless, de Gaulle, according to the British ambassador, Steel, took the opportunity to win Adenauer over to opposition of the British-sponsored European Free Trade Area and to sow 'seeds of distrust in Adenauer's mind over Britain's position on the Berlin question'.[25] Whatever the truth, de Gaulle did not offer anything other than rhetoric. The rhetoric, of course, was most striking. On the steps of the Kurhaus before his departure, de Gaulle clasped Adenauer by both shoulders and pronounced him 'a great man, a great statesman, a great European and a great German'.[26] Adenauer was left standing in bewilderment at this surprisingly Latin gesture.

After that, he quite obviously did not know which way to turn. Immediately after Smirnov's visit on 20 November, he had written to Macmillan in almost desperate terms. 'This letter, dear Mr Macmillan,' he wrote, 'is dictated by serious anxiety about a development the consequences of which we cannot foresee.'[27] He appealed to Macmillan to write to Khrushchev to try to head him off. This Macmillan did, but to no effect.

The day after the rapturous meeting at Bad Kreuznach, events took a new and dangerous course. Khrushchev sent a long note to Washington, London and Paris, informing them that Berlin's Four Power status had run its course and that a new status for the city would have to be worked out within the next six months. If this did not happen, the note went on, the Soviet Union would conclude a separate peace treaty with the GDR.

When Khrushchev's note arrived in the Western capitals, Adenauer was in something of a panic. Obviously, whatever the fine words at Bad Kreuznach, it was no good relying on de Gaulle. To put it bluntly, the French had too many problems in Algeria, and no stomach for a confrontation with the Soviets. On the other hand, he did not want to upset de Gaulle and the new Franco-German entente. On 7 December he therefore went to London to bolster Macmillan in his view that there should be no concessions to the

Soviets, and that the meeting of the Western foreign ministers, called for 14 December in Paris, should be steadfast in maintaining the existing status of Berlin. This, in fact, they were, and Adenauer straightaway wrote to Macmillan that 'the unequivocal "no" of the British government to the Soviet demands has filled the German people and myself with deep gratitude'.[28]

So far, so good. But although the immediate threat from the Soviets had been met with resolution, the situation was still tense. One thing, however, was clear. In such a time of crisis, Adenauer felt that he did not have the authority to conduct his country's affairs in the way he would have liked. It was always a matter of appealing to one ally or another. He could not do business either like Macmillan – who had a sizeable majority in the House of Commons behind him – or like de Gaulle – the apparent saviour of France and the author of a new constitution promising strong presidential government. In this company Adenauer felt that he was still, as it were, in the second rank.

When Heuss wrote to him in mid-December that there was no provision for the Federal President to serve a third term, and that consequently Adenauer might wish to give his mind to the succession, a window suddenly opened. With some manoeuvring, the office of the President of the Federal Republic could become the kind of office which de Gaulle had in mind for France. Adenauer therefore started carefully to prepare his ground.

There is no doubt that Heuss had been a dignified and, in its own terms, successful Federal President. He had kept himself scrupulously clear of party politics. Moreover, he had been able to find the right word at the right time on ceremonial occasions. A Swabian, soft-spoken, intellectual and with a sense of irony which escaped the robust sarcasm of the Rhineland or Berlin, he had quietly appealed to Germans of the west to follow the lead of their much more abrasive Chancellor.

That was all very well. But, given de Gaulle's lead, it seemed to Adenauer that the office of President could become an office of much greater importance, speaking for the Federal Republic in a loftier vein while leaving the mundane management of domestic affairs to a Chancellor responsible to his higher authority. Accordingly, over the Christmas and New Year break, as 1958 moved into 1959, Adenauer developed a plan. It was no less than he should become President of the Federal Republic, with the plenipotentiary powers de Gaulle was about to acquire as President of France. As it happened, in this endeavour – to put it crudely – he was to fall flat on his face.

11

KHRUSHCHEV'S CHALLENGE

'Entschuldigen Sie, Herr von Eckardt, wenn ich jetzt kölnischen Dialekt spreche. Wir haben nochmals fies Jlück jehabt!'*

THERE WAS NOT going to be a war. Khrushchev was quite confident about that in a meeting with the Polish leader Wladyslaw Gomulka in November 1958, which touched on the Berlin ultimatum. 'War will not result from it,' he said. 'There will be tensions, of course; there will be a blockade. They might test [us] to see our reaction. In any case, we will have to show a great deal of cold blood . . .'[1] Apart from wishing to show himself more robust than his recently deposed Soviet opponents, Khrushchev's main aim, he told Gomulka, was to achieve international recognition of the GDR. This, he said, he was determined to do.

It was precisely that aim which Adenauer was determined to block. He was as firm as Khrushchev. He knew that if the access routes to Berlin were to be handed over unilaterally to the GDR as demanded in Khrushchev's ultimatum, the consequence would be that all concerned, including the

---

* 'Excuse me, Herr von Eckardt, if I now speak in Cologne dialect. Yet again we have had a stroke of luck': Adenauer to Eckardt, on the failure of the May 1960 Summit; von Eckardt, *Ein unordentliches Leben*, p. 614.

Federal Republic, would have to deal directly with the East Germans. In other words, the GDR would achieve *de facto* recognition. That done, it would inexorably lead, in Adenauer's view, to *de jure* recognition. But if that happened, the strict application of the 'Hallstein Doctrine' would mean the rupture of diplomatic relations between the Federal Republic and the Western Allies – an outcome which, as Adenauer recognised, would be patently absurd.

The NATO council meeting in Paris in December 1958 had understood Adenauer's argument, and had endorsed his hard line on the Berlin ultimatum. But the otherwise satisfactory communiqué had ended with the proviso that 'they are, as ever, prepared to discuss the question'.[2] This gave Khrushchev the opening he wanted. On 10 January 1959, the Soviets sent another note to the three Western Allies and to all other countries which had fought Germany in the Second World War. The note proposed a conference, at the level of heads of government or – as a fall-back – foreign ministers, to discuss the German problem in its entirety. The Soviet note, moreover, was accompanied by a draft peace treaty, which could be signed either by two German states or a German 'confederation'. Finally, it suggested that Germany could thereafter be reunited as a country – neutral between the two blocs.

This new note put Adenauer in a difficult position. He could not be seen to stand out against negotiations between the Soviets and the Western Allies. On the other hand, he did not want them to arrive at any definite conclusion – at least not along the lines of the Soviet note. It was therefore time for him to look to those he believed to be his friends. But it was not altogether easy. He suspected that the British were the least reliable, and indeed he was right. The British thought, in Ambassador Steel's words, that 'Adenauer is in a bad way and ageing rapidly . . . at one moment [he] is violently pro-French and pro-de Gaulle, at another, highly critical'.[3]

Macmillan seemed still to think that Adenauer had a soft spot for him personally. But that soft spot, if indeed there ever was one, was to vanish without trace when, on 3 February, Steel brought Adenauer a letter from Macmillan proudly announcing the British Prime Minister's forthcoming visit to Moscow. What Macmillan's letter failed to mention, of course, was that there had been no prior consultation with the other Allies, and therefore no agreed position for Macmillan to take in his discussions with Khrushchev.

On hearing the news, Adenauer was both dismayed and scornful. He was dismayed because he suspected that Macmillan was preparing a British *de facto* recognition of the GDR, even though the visit, according to Macmillan's letter, was no more than 'fact-finding'. He was scornful because he regarded the whole venture as no more than an effort to improve Conservative support for the British General Election due later in the year. He grumpily complained about this to Heuss. Understandably enough, Heuss could not resist the reply that Adenauer was the last person to preach about electoral manoeuvres. At Heuss's sally, Adenauer at least had the grace to laugh.

The next supposed friend to approach was the United States. It so happened that, while Macmillan was preparing for his first visit to Moscow as Prime Minister, Dulles was on his last visit to Europe as Secretary of State. When Dulles arrived in Bonn, he looked what he was – a man in the final stages of terminal illness. Indeed, an operation for hernia on his subsequent return to Washington revealed what many had suspected: an earlier cancer, thought to have been under control, had returned. Adenauer was shocked by Dulles' appearance, and quickly realised that this might well be their last meeting.

In the event, it was not to be an easy one. Far from Macmillan's soft approach to the Soviets, Dulles was at his most belligerent. He even talked of the possibility of nuclear war if the Soviets refused to withdraw their Berlin ultimatum. Adenauer did his best to calm Dulles down, pointing out, reasonably enough, that neither Britain nor France would take such a dreadful risk and, for all its power, the United States could not act alone. But, as Krone wrote, 'Dulles was for ultimate toughness'.[4] It looked very much as though Khrushchev's assurance to Gomulka might prove to be badly wide of the mark.

These were certainly dangerous moments. Nuclear war was, for the first time, seriously threatened. Adenauer's position was thus made doubly difficult. He knew perfectly well that, if there was a nuclear war, Germany would again be destroyed and all his lifetime's efforts laid to waste. On the other hand, the only possible negotiating position, from his point of view – as a Catholic and a virulent anti-Communist – was to resist the Soviets in their demands.

It was difficult to know on whom to rely. The British were suspect. Moreover, Adenauer had to sit and watch while Macmillan strutted about Moscow – in a ridiculous white fur hat – claiming to be the world's peacemaker. The Americans, too, were suspect, on the grounds that the obviously dying Dulles appeared to be prepared to blow up the whole world. The third friend, who seemed to be the most reliable, was General de Gaulle.

It was with these thoughts in mind that Adenauer went to see de Gaulle, by then the newly elected President of the French Fifth Republic. It was no coincidence that the meeting was arranged for the day that Macmillan returned from Moscow. Moreover, it was to be held at the royal hunting lodge at Marly-le-Roi, which de Gaulle had seemingly appropriated as one of his official residences as the French Head of State.

Adenauer arrived at Marly on 4 March in a complaining mood. He complained about the Americans, which was a customary theme, but his chief complaint was about the communiqué which Macmillan and Khrushchev had issued on the day before his arrival. It referred yet again to the limitation of armed forces 'in an agreed area or Europe'.[5] Nothing could be more irritating than the revival of what was, in essence, the Rapacki plan, which Adenauer had thought was dead and buried. De Gaulle listened carefully to Adenauer's complaints, quite obviously pleased that Macmillan was out of Adenauer's favour. So far, so encouraging. But the pleasantries did not long survive their meeting. Only ten days later, de Gaulle announced at a press conference that Germany could only be reunited within its existing frontiers – including the Oder–Neisse line. On hearing that, Adenauer classified de Gaulle as yet another unreliable friend.

There was nowhere left to turn. All three Western Allies had shown themselves, in one form or another, to be unreliable. But it so happened that there were other matters on Adenauer's mind, and, for the moment, the Berlin ultimatum, and the response to it, was left to one side. While at Marly, he had been able to tell de Gaulle about Heuss's impending retirement. There is little doubt, as well, that he did so while impressed by the perquisites of his office which de Gaulle seemed to have acquired.

Nevertheless, and however impressed he was, Adenauer had already decided to nominate Erhard for the presidency of the Federal Republic. Apart from the convenience, Erhard would be a strong candidate against the SPD nominee, Carlo Schmid. On 24 February he had therefore convened a CDU/CSU committee to nominate him; and it was duly done. Whether there was any proper communication between Adenauer and Erhard before the nomination is uncertain even today; but what is certain is that Erhard himself did not want the job. 'I never showed any interest in standing,' he is reported as saying. 'The truth is that Adenauer wanted to kick me upstairs.'[6] After that, the Erhard nomination was, with much embarrassment, removed. During March, there was a good deal of bad-tempered wrangling within the

CDU. Some thought that the Basic Law should be amended to allow Heuss to continue. Other names were bandied about – Krone, Etzel, even Gerstenmaier; but there was no consensus.

Adenauer himself kept aloof. He was, he said, fully occupied, as Chancellor, with the international problems of the Federal Republic. Whatever the motive for the excuse, Adenauer had good reason. On 12 March, Macmillan arrived in Bonn to report on his Moscow trip. 'He seemed to cherish some resentment,' Macmillan wrote. 'I was pretty sharp with him.'[7] Adenauer was also pretty sharp with Macmillan. The discussions were both dry and unpleasant.

Nevertheless, Adenauer agreed that there should be meetings with the Soviets on the Berlin ultimatum. He insisted, however, that the meetings should embrace not just Berlin but the whole German problem. In return, he was forced to concede to Macmillan the point he was least willing to concede. The GDR would have the same status as the Federal Republic, as observers at the conference of foreign ministers now scheduled to begin in May. There it was. Khrushchev, after all, had achieved part of the aim which he had explained to Gomulka. In his eyes, the mere presence of a GDR delegation constituted *de facto* recognition. Adenauer, on that count at least, had to admit defeat.

Adenauer's concession to Macmillan in turn prompted him to reflect on his own authority as the head of government of a major European state. He clearly did not carry enough political weight. His new objective was therefore simple: to lever himself into an equal position on the top table of Western heads of government. The problem was how to achieve that objective. It was not until 2 April, in their customary afternoon walk around the gardens of the Palais Schaumburg, that Globke told Adenauer that some senior members of the CDU thought that he should put himself forward as a candidate for the presidency. The more Adenauer thought about it, the more he was attracted to the idea. Furthermore, his family, when consulted, was unanimously in favour. He was, after all, eighty-three, and on his own admission was tired of party politics. Pferdmenges, at his golden wedding anniversary, also advised him to stand.

In the days that followed, Adenauer studied in detail the duties and rights of the Federal President. He noted that the President had the right to propose the new Chancellor, and to be kept informed about all decisions of policy. Furthermore, he concluded that the President was not necessarily bound by the Chancellor's nominations for ministerial office. Finally, the President was not in any way obliged to keep his pronouncements non-political, and that he need not follow advice on foreign policy 'blindly'.[8] When Globke told Krone about the way Adenauer's mind was moving, the note in Krone's diary was straight to the point: 'My first thought: following de Gaulle?'[9]

By 7 April 1959, the CDU/CSU executive council, in order to avoid a repeat of the fiasco of Erhard's nomination, had formed a more widely based committee of selection. Adenauer appeared before it, gave a long lecture on his interpretation of the rights of the Federal President, and announced that he was prepared to put his name forward. Needless to say, his announcement was greeted with rapturous applause, not least by those who wished to see him out of the Chancellorship and into what they believed amounted to semi-retirement. Adenauer then went to see Heuss to tell him of the decision and, on the following day, went on television to reassure his compatriots that he intended 'to safeguard the continuity of our policy for years to come'.[10] That done, he boarded the train at Bonn railway station for a holiday of the best part of four weeks in Cadenabbia.

Almost before the train left the station, the plot had started to unravel. The four most obvious candidates for the succession to the Chancellorship, Erhard, Etzel, Strauss and Schröder, met at Strauss's home and agreed not to campaign against one another. They all acknowledged, however, that Erhard was the front runner – the one outcome that Adenauer was determined to avoid. Adenauer, of course, did not know about this meeting, and passed the first few days of his holiday, again at the Villa Arminio, fully satisfied at the stir he had caused by his announcement.

But he was far from idle. He used the time to review the preparations for the conference of foreign ministers, soon to open in Geneva. As a result of his review, the first of many telegrams from Cadenabbia arrived on the desk of Hilger van Scherpenberg, the State Secretary at the Foreign Office, on 11 April. Adenauer had by then read through a draft instruction for the West German delegation and had found it objectionable both in tone and in content. Above all, it seemed to him to give support to a 'security zone' in central Europe, which in his view was no more than a disguised version of the Rapacki plan. Globke and van Scherpenberg immediately set off for Cadenabbia to mollify him; but he was not to be mollified. He told them that he suspected there were officials in the Foreign Office who were in league with the SPD, and that they should look to it – without delay.

Adenauer then sat down and wrote what must be one of the most offensive letters ever written by a head of government to his foreign secretary. Brentano had asked, through Globke, whether he still had Adenauer's confidence, and offered to resign. Adenauer's reply filled no fewer than ten pages. He did not want Brentano's resignation, he wrote, but Brentano had to correct the weakness of leadership in his department. 'You are ill,' the letter went. 'Half the time during the preparation for the [Geneva] conference you were absent from Bonn . . . You regularly leave Bonn . . . you speak in your constituency . . . quite pointlessly . . .'[11] Furthermore, Brentano was told that he was relieved of his position as leader of the Federal Republic's delegation at Geneva, and was to hand over the position to Grewe. The simple, but unstated, reason was that Adenauer did not want his foreign minister to sit at the same table as his GDR counterpart, Lothar Bolz. To do so, in his eyes, would have given at least the impression of recognition of the GDR. In truth, it is something of a mystery why Brentano did not resign on the spot. But it comes as even more of a mystery to find that Brentano himself, together with Globke and Grewe, actually visited the obviously offended old man in Cadenabbia on 26 April.

Adenauer's main surprise, however, had come on 20 April with the arrival in Cadenabbia of his old friend Pferdmenges, together with his wife, to spend a few relaxing days at the Villa Arminio. As it turned out, the days were far from relaxing. Pferdmenges brought with him a message from Erhard, pledging his loyalty to Adenauer but claiming that, in the event of Adenauer becoming President, there could be no objection to him becoming Chancellor. Moreover, Pferdmenges reported that he had taken soundings with senior members of both the CDU and the CSU, and that they were favourably inclined to Erhard's candidature. Worst of all, Pferdmenges himself supported their point of view.

This was the last thing that Adenauer wanted to hear. His favoured candidate to succeed him as Chancellor was Etzel, who, he assumed, would be satisfactorily docile. Erhard, he told Pferdmenges, was politically naïf; he would sabotage Adenauer's carefully constructed Franco-German reconciliation; he would not last a moment in the hard world of international politics. After a few hours of this assault, Pferdmenges buckled, and agreed to go back to Bonn to talk to Erhard and persuade him not to pursue his candidature.

But the game was far from over. On 2 May there was another visit: Globke and Krone arrived in Cadenabbia. They emphasised to Adenauer that a large majority of the CDU parliamentary group wanted Erhard as Chancellor. Adenauer, by then in a state of extreme irritation, told them that he would reconsider his own decision to stand for the presidency if the parliamentary group pressed him to accept Erhard as Chancellor. Things only got worse, however, when Adenauer took the train back to Bonn on 4 May. He was met at Baden-Baden by Hermann Höcherl, the most influential member of the CSU after Strauss. Höcherl told Adenauer that the CSU were definitely in favour of Erhard as Chancellor. If it had not been clear before, it certainly was now. The Erhard bandwagon was gathering serious momentum.

This in itself was bad enough, but the timing made it worse. On 11 May 1959 the conference of foreign ministers opened in Geneva. As it happened, it was immediately bogged down by a dispute over the shape of the table, to the point where the first session had to be cancelled, since the carpenters responsible for constructing the table were still awaiting their instructions. After much negotiation, however, it was agreed that the table should be round, and that to the side of it there would be a further two tables, each seating German delegations – one from the Federal Republic and one from the GDR. The argument, however frivolous it now seems, had an important underlying point – the recognition to be granted to the delegations of both West and East Germany. In this, Khrushchev felt again that he had won a victory. As he told Ulbricht at a meeting on 9 June, 'they came to the conference in Geneva [and] agreed to the invitation of the GDR to the conference, which signifies *de facto* recognition of the GDR'.[12] Khrushchev had a point. The outcome which Adenauer had always feared – *de jure* recognition of the GDR – had moved a step closer.

Although nothing much came of the conference in its early days, it was certainly not the time for a changing of the guard in Bonn, particularly since Dulles had resigned on 15 April – to be replaced by the little-known Christian Herter. Realising he was in deep political trouble at home, and sensing an opportunity, Adenauer accordingly started to prepare his retreat. On 13 May he had a meeting of an hour and a half with Erhard, who, as he expected, refused to withdraw his candidature for the Chancellorship if Adenauer became President. On 14 May Adenauer told the Cabinet that the international situation might oblige him to reconsider his decision to stand down as Chancellor. On 15 May he had a further talk with Pferdmenges, who had been converted back to the Erhard camp, and succeeded in talking him round yet again. On 19 May he wrote to Krone outlining his objections to Erhard's candidature, inviting him to use the letter as he saw fit – in other words to distribute copies around the CDU parliamentary group.

But there was a setback. Adenauer was, to put it at its mildest, badly put out when Krone came to see him on the following day, not to agree with the contents of his letter but to ask him to change his mind about Erhard. This was almost too much. Nevertheless, it gave him further territory towards which he could retreat. He wrote again to Krone to say that if Erhard was to be the CDU's candidate for Chancellor then he, Adenauer, would not relinquish the office. He also wrote to Erhard, smoothly inviting him to consider the national rather than his own personal interest – and to remain at the Ministry of Economic Affairs. Erhard's riposte was to call on Adenauer again and to reaffirm his wish to become Chancellor.

On 25 May 1959 Dulles died. The political geography immediately changed. Adenauer could now see a way out of his corner. He had gained some much-needed political time, since he would, quite properly, be expected to go to Dulles' funeral in Washington. In fact, the foreign ministers' conference in Geneva was adjourned for the same reason. Before he went, however, he presided over a stormy meeting of the CDU/CSU parliamentary group. Gerstenmaier demanded a statement from Adenauer that he would 'under all circumstances' be ready to stand for the presidency. 'Certainly not,' he replied;[13] and on the next day took the plane to Washington.

After his return on 30 May, Adenauer kept everybody waiting for a few days until, on 4 June, he wrote formally to Krone and Höcherl that he was withdrawing his candidature for the presidency. In his letter, conveniently forgetting that he had started the whole affair in the first place, he deplored the fact that the matter had been conducted in public, thus inflicting 'grave damage to our party and our cause'. At the same time he wrote to Erhard with a copy of his letter to Krone and Höcherl. 'I certainly count,' the letter went on, 'on your remaining loyal to me and that we shall win the next election battle together. I wish you well. Do not strain yourself. Please treat this message as strictly confidential. With all best wishes.'[14] The letter, unctuous and unpleasant as it was, was sent to Erhard at his address in Germany. Adenauer, of course, knew perfectly well that Erhard was in the United States himself, collecting two more doctorates.

The story of the presidency did not quite finish there. There remained two questions: first, who was to be the CDU candidate for the presidency and, second, how Adenauer could finally manoeuvre himself out of his political corner. As for a candidate, Adenauer had lost interest in the outcome. He agreed with the proposal that the Minister of Agriculture, Heinrich Lübke, should be put up. To be sure, his view of Lübke was contemptuous. At a dinner party he is quoted as saying to a Western journalist: 'Do you know who that is, two along from you? That is my Minister of Agriculture, and he is even stupider than the last one.'[15] It was by then clear that Adenauer had no interest in who was to be President – provided he behaved in the pattern set by Heuss.

Adenauer's escape from his corner was to be more difficult. The press onslaught had been unanimous. Adenauer, the public was told, was wholly undemocratic; furthermore, he was playing irresponsible games with the highest offices of state; his desire to hold on to power was blatant and cynical, and due entirely to senile stubbornness. Certainly, the onslaught was all the more effective in that it was largely true. Senior politicians were furious as well: Heuss, for instance, considered that Adenauer had 'lied to him'.[16]

The reaction outside Germany was no better. 'Adenauer seems to have had a bad press,' Macmillan wrote, 'all over the world. Even the French seem rather shocked. The Americans – whose darling Adenauer has always been – seem taken aback.'[17] Of course, Macmillan had some reason to be pleased at Adenauer's discomfiture. Since his visit to Moscow in March relations between the two men had been almost at freezing point. Macmillan wrote about Adenauer that 'he has become – like very many old men – vain, suspicious, and grasping'. Adenauer was not slow to respond in kind, claiming that the British were 'carrying on a great campaign of vilification . . . especially of me' and even hinting darkly that his decision to remain as Chancellor was 'all due to British weakness towards Russia . . .'[18]

Whatever the merits of the case, Macmillan had a point. Adenauer's preferred method of damage limitation, as it is with so many politicians, was to blame someone else. But it was not just Macmillan who was deemed to be at fault. In particular, Adenauer blamed Krone and Höcherl for their handling of the CDU/CSU parliamentary group. Yet, in spite of Adenauer's strictures, it was the long-suffering Krone who, during the period up until the parliamentary recess in early July, stopped the group from making too noisy a row. In fact, so successful was he that the affair dropped out of the press after two or three weeks, although he received 'not a word of thanks'.[19]

Adenauer wriggled out of it. Indeed, he was particularly pleased with the turn of events. At official lunches he was lofty, and talked 'lovingly and with delight of rose-growing, of former, scented roses that have now disappeared, Maréchal Niel, Gloire de Dijon, in a light, pleasing and even voice'. When anybody referred to the presidency, he simply said that 'in two weeks it is all over'.[20] As far as he was concerned, his whole presidential venture could now be regarded as no more than a minor incident.

That done, and with Lübke safely elected as President, Adenauer was able to focus his full attention on the reconvened foreign ministers' conference in Geneva. By then, Khrushchev thought that he had already scored enough. 'If you have thrown the enemy to the ground,' he had told Ulbricht on 9 June, 'you don't need then to kneel on his chest.' Besides, he had never expected the conference to 'have any tangible results . . . Geneva – it's a test of strength; it's a sounding-out of positions'. His victory, he considered, had been to force the Western Allies both to *de facto* recognition of the GDR and to negotiation with the Soviets over Berlin and the future of Germany. Having achieved that, he was now preparing, in his words, to 'create a safety valve'.[21]

The period of the Berlin ultimatum had expired on 27 May 1959, but the Soviets in Geneva did not press the matter of the precise date. Rather surprisingly, they turned down a conciliatory Allied proposal to treat the East Germans as 'agents' of the Soviet Union in Berlin. Instead, they produced the idea of an all-German committee, to report within one year. That was then extended to one and a half years. But Khrushchev insisted on keeping open the threat of a separate peace treaty if that failed. 'I don't know whether we will bring this issue of a peace treaty with the GDR to realisation,' Khrushchev told Ulbricht at a further meeting on 19 June. 'However, such a prospect acts in a sobering way on the Western powers and West Germany. This, if you will, is pressure on them, Damocles' sword, which we must hold over them.'[22] With that, the foreign ministers' conference petered out in early July. Adenauer was duly relieved that it had reached no conclusion.

At that point, he was preparing to leave for his summer holiday. But his plans were badly put out by Eisenhower's European tour in August, which had been set up unexpectedly – but necessarily, to explain the reasons for his sudden invitation to Khrushchev to visit the United States. At first, his tour had not included Bonn. To be sure, Macmillan had invited Adenauer to London when Eisenhower was to be there, but that was obviously not good enough. Adenauer was obliged, however offensive it was to his dignity, to request Eisenhower to pass through Bonn on his way. In truth, it was only a matter of dignity; there was little that the two had to say to one another. Nevertheless, dignity was satisfied, and Eisenhower duly turned up in Bonn. Moreover, his visit was accomplished, thanks to Eckardt's stage management, with some success.

Adenauer was therefore late in leaving Rhöndorf for Cadenabbia. It was not until 28 August 1959 that he was able to take a flight to Milan's Malpensa airport. But although he was late for his holiday, the consolation was that, for the first time, he was able to rent a house that met all his requirements of an ideal holiday home.

La Villa Collina was to be Adenauer's second home for the rest of his life. Its French owners were quite happy to let him rent the place whenever he wished. It was, and still is, situated on a hill above Cadenabbia, with a glorious view over Lake Como and beyond. The house itself, built at the end of the nineteenth century, is large – indeed, large enough to be described as a palazzo. It has, too, the elegance of its period – wrought-iron railings on the balconies of the upper storeys, carefully constructed arches on the ground floor leading to the gardens below, terraces tumbling down the hill to the walls which protect it from undesirable intruders, in the almost rococo Italian style of the time. True, the house itself was not 'comfortable', to use the word of Anneliese Poppinga, Adenauer's official secretary from 1958 onwards.[23] But Adenauer was not accustomed to comfort – least of all at his home in Rhöndorf.

The gardens were entirely to Adenauer's satisfaction. The outside of the house itself was surrounded by palm trees, cedars and cypresses. Wisteria and bougainvillea climbed up the walls. Rosebushes were there in abundance. Moreover, on the terraces protected from the wind there were cherry, lemon and apple blossoms in the spring – and their fruit in the autumn. Lastly, there was also a playing area for *boccia*, on which, in the late afternoon, Adenauer would stage competitions with his visitors.

In the summer of 1959 it was only a trial visit, although it was to be the first of many. On 12 September, after only a fortnight's holiday, Adenauer returned to Bonn. During late September and October, however, everything was surprisingly calm. There were constant and long discussions between the Western Allies about the proposed summit meeting, but in those discussions Adenauer was relegated to the sidelines. For instance, on 29 October de Gaulle proposed a 'Western Summit' of the three Western Allies – the United States, France and Britain – for December, 'with Adenauer to come along later'.[24] In short, he was to be left out.

Under all the circumstances, Adenauer thought it sensible to try to repair his damaged relations with Britain – and with Macmillan. It was therefore agreed that he should pay yet another visit to London in November. He accordingly arrived, accompanied by Brentano and a full retinue, on 17 November 1959. But so compressed was the timetable that the first conversation with Macmillan took place on the same day – in the old Treasury building, which, as Macmillan was at pains to point out, was the room in which Queen Anne had presided, for the last time for a British monarch, over meetings of her ministers. He thought that Adenauer would be amused by the fact that her successor, George I, came from Hanover, could speak only German and could not be bothered to learn English.

The British had indeed prepared carefully for Adenauer's arrival. The message from their representatives in Germany had been quite simple. 'Adenauer . . . is a very bad listener,' wrote a British industrialist after seeing Siegfried Balke, a member of Adenauer's Cabinet, oddly enough at Balke's own request. 'He belongs to the old school of purely political politicians and that is why he admires de Gaulle . . . The Rome Treaty is for him a Catholic alliance reviving the Carolingian Empire in the form of a "third force", a bulwark against the Communists on the one hand, and against foreign heretics on the other. The British, as Protestants, belong to the latter category, and, since the Prime Minister's visit to Moscow, he is deeply suspicious of our supper with the devil, regardless how long the spoon may be.'[25] The view was perhaps overdone, since Adenauer was firm in his support for NATO, but it was nonetheless widely held.

In the event, the visit did not go as badly as might have been expected. Macmillan, on his own admission, was struck by the vitality which Adenauer showed – for a man of eighty-three. All talk of his senility was immediately rejected as nonsense. This being so, Macmillan was forthright in reproaching Adenauer for his sniping at the British. 'He seemed,' Macmillan wrote, 'startled and angry. But his staff, and especially von Brentano, were clearly pleased that there was plain speaking.'[26] On the following day, discussions continued, and seemed to go well, but Macmillan remarked, percipiently, that 'the trouble is that they are all afraid of him'.[27]

The visit to London did at least heal some wounds, although relations never returned to the cordiality of 1958. On Adenauer's return to Bonn, however, other wounds were opened. De Gaulle's proposed 'Western Summit' of himself, Eisenhower and Macmillan, was to take place on

19 December. Since the meeting was called to fix a common position and a date for a Summit Conference with Khrushchev, and was to be mainly about Germany, Adenauer had every right to be insulted that he was not part of the group. But the truth was that both de Gaulle and Macmillan wanted to encourage tripartite discussions with the United States on a wide range of policy issues – one of which, of course, was the future of Germany. Indeed, de Gaulle was particularly enthusiastic, since he had not finally abandoned his idea of a 'triple directorate' as the effective governing body of NATO. The Federal Republic, of course, was not to be included in any of those discussions.

At their December meeting the three Western Allies agreed to invite Khrushchev to a summit in Paris for May 1960. On hearing this – de Gaulle told him on his arrival that the tripartite discussions had gone very well – Adenauer argued that there should be no movement on the Berlin question; in other words that the Western Allies should revert to the position as it was before the foreign ministers' meeting at Geneva. The Americans, however, had, after Dulles' death, become much more ready to consider a whole variety of plans for the future of Berlin. Besides, Eisenhower was by then thoroughly bored by Adenauer's tedious lectures on the evils of atheistic Communism. In a meeting in Paris on 19 December to discuss the agenda for the summit of the following May, '. . . the President was very firm and almost rude. He was thoroughly exasperated. As a result of being "bullied" a bit, the German Chancellor collapsed and did not speak again.'[28] Yet again, the 'German Chancellor' felt that he was being treated as though he only belonged to the second rank.

Nineteen fifty-nine thus ended, for Adenauer, on something of a sour note. It was also made much worse by an outbreak of neo-Nazism in Germany. On Christmas Eve two young men, Arnold Strunk, a baker's assistant, and Paul Schönen, a clerk, daubed swastikas on the newly built Cologne synagogue and on the memorial to the men of the German resistance to Hitler. There was then a series of copy-cat events. Intelligence reports went so far as to suggest that the East Germans were behind them. Whether or not that was true, there was indignation throughout Europe and the United States. Adenauer reacted by broadcasting his view that the 'healthy' way to react was to give racialists 'a good hiding'.[29] That, in turn, brought on him a shower of criticism from the press for encouraging Germans to hit one another. All in all, it was not in the happiest of moods that Adenauer saw the New Year in with his family – and with the usual rituals – at Rhöndorf.

There is no doubt that, with the new decade, the world was starting to change. A generation was growing up which had not fought in the war. Even the memories of the war in the older generations were beginning to fade. Europe, and particularly West Germany, was prosperous and peaceful. The youth of the 1960s felt able to enjoy itself, to take up causes again, to demonstrate, to dance and, above all, to be idealistic. The old men who ran the Western world, de Gaulle, Macmillan, Eisenhower and, of course, Adenauer, were perceived as belonging to the past – as anachronisms, however noble they might have been in their day.

Such movements, of course, take time to gather momentum before they are fully reflected in the realities of day-to-day politics. Moreover, they can frequently only be detected in retrospect. With the benefit of retrospection, however, it is possible to mark down 1960 as the year in which the political tectonic plates started to move. There were, suddenly, new actors on the stage; for instance in West Germany, there were Willy Brandt* and Helmut Schmidt – with a new SPD which had sloughed off the remnants of Marxism at Bad Godesberg in 1959; and there was Mende in the FDP. The caravan, without a doubt, was moving on.

The change came in several forms. The political left in Germany started to stir itself. Students even barracked Adenauer at a rowdy meeting of some 3,000 at Cologne University on 15 February, chanting in unison that Oberländer and Globke, both of whom had admitted Nazi pasts, should go. *Der Spiegel* launched a concentrated attack on Oberländer – after supporting him in 1954. Oberländer was forced to resign – and Adenauer did nothing to protect him. All those events had been unthinkable only a few years earlier. Indeed, the most significant

---

* Brandt, Willy (born Herbert Frahm) (1913–92): Journalist and politician. Born in Lübeck. Studied history in Oslo. Joined SPD in 1922. 1933: Went to Denmark, subsequently living in Sweden and Norway. Returned to Germany in 1947. 1949–57: Member of Bundestag. 1951: Elected member of Berlin Chamber of Deputies. 1957–66: Mayor of Berlin. 1958–62: Chairman of Berlin SPD. 1962–87: Chairman of national SPD. 1966–69: Foreign Minister. 1969–74: Chancellor. 1976: Elected president of Socialist International. 1979–82: Member of European Parliament. Real charisma, but judgement from time to time believed to be questionable.

demonstration of the political change was not that the venerable Chancellor had been subjected to fierce heckling by students in the very university which he had founded, but that one of his ministers had been forced out of office by the press.

Adenauer, in truth, did not know how to deal with this new phenomenon. It was beyond all his experience. He had been brought up in the Prussian tradition of discipline and unquestioning obedience to superiors. To be sure, in 1960 he still had the support of the large majority of the West German electorate, as a leader who had brought the Federal Republic back from the abyss to respectability and prosperity. Nevertheless, it was obvious that there was movement in the political undergrowth. It was certainly something for him to think about; and think he did.

His conclusion was that he could overcome these domestic difficulties not by confronting them directly but by raising his international profile – to convince the younger generation that they could look up to a leader who was respected and admired by other world leaders. It was in this spirit that Adenauer planned his visit to the United States and Japan for March and April 1960. Together with his son Konrad and his daughter Lotte, his two secretaries Anneliese Poppinga and Hannelore Siegel, Brentano, Eckardt and another thirty or so officials and journalists, and diplomats from the embassies in Washington and Tokyo, he set off from Bonn-Wahn airport on 12 March. Sixteen hours later his Lockheed Super-Constellation landed at New York's Idlewild airport in bitter cold. Adenauer, in fact, had spent a large part of the time in the pilot's cockpit. Just as in his youth he had been exhilarated by being driven in fast cars, he now was fascinated by the complexities of flying a large aircraft. Besides, he found the whole business of travel, with all the public attention – not to mention the stays in expensive hotels – thoroughly invigorating.

His trip was largely taken up with ceremonial events and public appearances, all of them, needless to say, extensively covered in the West German press. But there was one meeting at the Waldorf Astoria in New York of particular significance – with the Israeli Prime Minister, David Ben-Gurion. Quite apart from the symbolic importance of the meeting itself, and the consequent political benefit for Adenauer in West Germany, there was one matter which Ben-Gurion was specially interested in discussing: the further supply of German arms to Israel.

Since 1957, the Federal Republic had been engaged in sending military equipment to Israel. Strauss had handled negotiations on the German side, with Adenauer's acquiescence. In truth, the whole thing had been illegal. The Bundeswehr had paid for the arms out of its own budget, and had reported the deficits to the police as theft. The arms themselves had been shipped to Israel out of Marseilles, with the connivance of successive French governments. Ben-Gurion now wanted more: submarines suitable for the Mediterranean and Red Sea, 'similar to those built in Germany for use in the Baltic',[30] anti-tank guided rockets and helicopters. Adenauer, after consulting with Strauss, gave his approval. The dubious deal was done.

Adenauer's Super-Constellation then took the party on, first to Washington and then to San Francisco. Still heading west, they landed in Hawaii ('I cannot remember when I had seen so many American four-star generals together'[31]) for a two-day rest before resuming the long and tiring flight, with a stopover at Wake Island, across the Pacific to Tokyo.

Adenauer's stay in Japan was admittedly little more than an extended piece of tourism. There were, of course, discussions with the Japanese Prime Minister, Nobosuke Kishi, but they were mainly about trade, in which Adenauer had no interest, and about China, in which he was fascinated. But the highlight of his stay was a visit to the former Prime Minister, Shigeru Yoshida, who showed him a dark red rose – named 'Konrad Adenauer'.

The Super-Constellation then made its laborious way back to Bonn, stopping at Anchorage in Alaska and Keflavik in Iceland. The journey took two days. On his return to Bonn, tired but exhilarated as he was, Adenauer had to grapple with another problem. While he had been in Washington Herter had shown him yet another plan, originating this time from the headquarters of NATO in Paris, for German reunification on the basis of a 'control zone' in Central Europe, this time including the Benelux countries, Denmark, Norway, Poland and Czechoslovakia. Adenauer had told Herter that the plan was ridiculous. It did not include control of movements in the air; there would be no protection from missile attack; of the 3,000 'controllers' envisaged half would be Soviets, allowed to roam at will over the territory of the Federal Republic; and the GDR would have achieved treaty recognition. In short, it represented almost everything that Adenauer had fought against in the previous ten years.

On 5 May 1960 General Norstad arrived in Bonn to explain the plan in detail, hinting that Eisenhower would put it forward at the Paris Summit due to convene only eleven days later, in the belief that the formula would at least lead to a satisfactory compromise on Berlin. Adenauer gave him only ninety minutes of his time, and immediately wrote to de Gaulle asking for his support in rejecting the plan root and branch. De Gaulle assured Adenauer that he was on his side. Neither of them knew, of course, what concessions the Americans were prepared to make. But both realised that Khrushchev's 'sword of Damocles' was still hovering over Western heads.

In the event, the summit of 15 May 1960 never took place. On 1 May the Soviets shot down an American U2 reconnaissance plane. Khrushchev made much of it in a speech to a joint session of the Supreme Soviet on 5 May. The pilot fell into Soviet hands, and admitted that he was on a spying mission over Soviet territory. The news could hardly have been worse. Eisenhower, Herter and the Pentagon all told separate and conflicting stories, and 'Khrushchev has made two very amusing and effective speeches, attacking the Americans for spying incompetently and lying incompetently too'.[32]

Even at that point the summit was still due to go ahead. Eisenhower, however, instead of saying nothing, admitted on 11 May at a press conference that the U2 flights were indeed made over Soviet territory, that they were designed to take photographs of ground installations, and that the flights were made with his express knowledge and approval. This announcement put Khrushchev in an impossible situation. He could not now just pass over the matter with a joke or two; his position in the Kremlin was not that secure. On 15 May, therefore, he made a speech at the first session of what was to be the summit which was 'a mixture of abuse, vitriolic and offensive, and legal argument . . . It was a most unpleasant performance.' He demanded that the summit be postponed 'for six or eight months – i.e. till the presidency of Eisenhower had ended'.[33] For good measure, he called the Western Powers 'Adenauer's valets' and the Western press 'Adenauer's riff-raff'.

So ended, before it had even begun, the Summit Conference of May 1960. Needless to say, Adenauer was delighted. It meant, in practice, that nothing could be done, or even proposed, on the German problem until Eisenhower left office at the end of 1960. In fact, there was a succession of Cold War crises in the summer of 1960: the arrival of Castro's government in Cuba, shambles in the Congo, revolution in Laos. But none of these bothered Adenauer. It was in a mood of good cheer that he set off on 25 May for a holiday in the Villa Collina at Cadenabbia.

By Adenauer standards it was a relatively calm holiday. True, Jean Monnet came twice, to discuss the matter of relations between the European Common Market and the European Free Trade Area, and whether or not Britain would in the end wish to join the Common Market; there was an expedition to have tea with the Dutch diplomat Dirk Stikker at his house in nearby Menaggio; Antonio Segni, the Italian Foreign Minister, called in; but, apart from those events and the exertions of competitive *boccia*, it was a tranquil and much-needed rest with his family and close associates. It was therefore with a benign view of the world that Adenauer returned to Bonn on 18 June.

The benign view did not last long. At the end of June Michel Debré, de Gaulle's Prime Minister, made a speech to the French National Assembly in which he expounded yet again the Gaullist theory of the 'triple directorate' for NATO. In the course of his speech he was unwise enough to say that 'states without atom bombs are satellite states'.[34] Adenauer regarded this as yet another attempt to downgrade the Federal Republic, and protested to de Gaulle. De Gaulle's soothing answer was to write on 7 July inviting Adenauer to meet him at Rambouillet.

On 29 July 1960 Adenauer set off again for Paris. At Rambouillet he was welcomed by de Gaulle on the steps of the château with the same charm as he had shown in their first meeting in September 1958. But this time Adenauer was more wary. He was not to be put off, and chided de Gaulle on Debré's speech and the attitudes which underlay it. De Gaulle tried to reassure Adenauer that Debré had been aiming at the Americans and British in advancing the interests of France; but it was only when de Gaulle told him that he saw no reason why the Federal Republic should not acquire nuclear weapons that Adenauer was mollified.

Adenauer reported some of that conversation to Macmillan when he made his next visit to Bonn on 10 August. Adenauer told Macmillan that both he and de Gaulle had agreed that the Brussels bureaucracy which Hallstein was busy creating was arrogating to itself too much power. The Council of Ministers should become much more active; they were both against a federal assembly; any assembly of the six members of the Community should consist of delegates from national parliaments. What he did not tell Macmillan, on the other hand, was that he had secured de Gaulle's agreement that the Federal Republic should in time become a nuclear power, or that he had had great trouble with almost all his colleagues and senior officials – Krone, Brentano, Strauss, Gerstenmaier, Erhard and

Schröder, let alone Blankenhorn and even Globke – when he tried to persuade them of the virtues of the Gaullist view of Europe's future.

The truth was that Adenauer had very little support on the European issue in the places where he most needed it – his government and in the CDU/CSU parliamentary group. Furthermore, when Blankenhorn reported from Paris that the French intended to propose changes to the Treaty of Rome and to withdraw from NATO's supreme command in times of peace, alarm bells were ringing loudly even within the West German Cabinet. Faced with what amounted almost to a revolt, Adenauer was forced to backtrack. He accordingly instructed his officials to delay any French initiatives on either EEC or NATO.

He was then faced with an unpleasant choice. Either he regarded his relations with de Gaulle as his most important political priority – in which case he would have to accept de Gaulle's view of the future of Europe and of the world; or he regarded NATO membership, with its American nuclear shield, as paramount – in which case he would have to reject de Gaulle's ideas and follow the path advocated by the 'Anglo-Saxons'. In short, he could not have it both ways. It was this difficult conundrum that he set out to consider when he left on 27 August for another holiday at the Villa Collina.

Answer to the conundrum, in fact, came there none – largely because there was no sensible answer. Before his return on 19 September, Adenauer had long conversations in Cadenabbia with Amintore Fanfani, the Italian Prime Minister, with Blankenhorn, Spaak and Norstad, and a further ten days of reflection after those conversations. He had written to de Gaulle on 15 August, before his departure for Cadenabbia, asking him to moderate his ambitions for a change in the command structure of NATO. The response had come in de Gaulle's press conference of 5 September. De Gaulle said publicly exactly what he had said to Adenauer at their meeting at Rambouillet in July: the role of the European Commission must be subject to the authority of national governments and NATO must be reconstructed to allow for differences in national character – in other words, in the interests of France. Adenauer might just as well saved himself the trouble of writing.

On 5 October 1960 Debré, accompanied by Couve de Murville and a number of French officials, turned up in Bonn. By that time, Adenauer had received a letter from Eisenhower stating quite plainly that if there were any interference with the NATO integrated command structure the United

States would withdraw its armed forces from Europe. On the other hand, during Debré's visit de Gaulle made a speech in Grenoble claiming that the only reality in Europe was that of the nation state. The two points of view were quite clearly in direct conflict.

Adenauer then made his decision. He told Debré that the Federal Republic would not follow de Gaulle down the road of nationalism, and that, as far as he was concerned, the structure of NATO would remain as it was. The dispute was now out in the open. The formal dinner at the Palais Schaumburg had to be postponed for an hour while the wrangling went on, and during the dinner the French and the Germans were hardly on speaking terms.

Adenauer thought that perhaps he had gone too far. The following morning he made it his business to be particularly friendly to Debré when he said goodbye, even going so far as to present him with a signed photograph – apparently the ultimate compliment. But he was careful to send a letter to de Gaulle reiterating his view that the Cold War was in a most dangerous phase, and in such a situation it was vital to maintain the integrity of NATO. In compensation, he agreed to a French proposal for the heads of government of the Six to meet in Paris in December to discuss ways in which they could and should co-operate. But the breach was far from healed. De Gaulle simply said cuttingly to Debré that Adenauer had opted for the 'Anglo-Saxons'.

In the event, the meeting of European heads of government could not take place until February 1961. The reason was that Adenauer was ill throughout the last half of December and most of January. It had started with a bad cough in November, which refused all treatment. Adenauer kept on working, but the cough turned into bronchitis, and he had yet again to take to his bed. His Name Day, Christmas and the New Year all passed in an atmosphere of gloom. His family, and the few visitors who came to see him noted that his face was thinner and that 'there were new lines on it, particularly on the forehead'.[35]

Nineteen sixty-one thus started badly. Adenauer was ill. Questions were asked about his age, whether he could continue in office, let alone stand the strain of the federal elections due in September. Last, but by no means least, a leader from the new generation, John Fitzgerald Kennedy, had been elected President of the United States. In truth, the general conclusion in political circles in West Germany – and elsewhere – was that the Adenauer era was finally drifting towards its end.

12

THREATS AND COUNTER-THREATS

*'Wie alle seine Vorgänger im Weissen Haus und das gesamte amerikanische
Volk, so versicherte er mir, hätte auch er eine grosse Hochachtung vor
Deutschland und vor mir'*

'BERLIN,' KHRUSHCHEV EXPLAINED, 'is the testicles of the West. Every time I
want to make the West scream, I squeeze on Berlin.'[1] The metaphor was apt.
So, indeed, was the use of the first person singular, since there is no doubt
that the Berlin crisis was launched on Khrushchev's own initiative. 'He personally participated in the preparation of the documents,' wrote the GDR
ambassador to Moscow, Johannes König. 'He submitted to the comrades of
the Third European Department his thoughts on the entire problem on several typewritten pages which he had personally dictated and asked the
comrades to observe this point of view in the composition of documents
and the determination of particular measures.'[2]

The crisis launched by Khrushchev, and the squeezing, dominated the
international agenda throughout 1961 and into 1962. Some of the effects
of the squeezing, however, were perhaps not what Khrushchev intended. If

---

* 'Like all his predecessors in the White House and the entire American people, he assured
me, he too had a high esteem of Germany and of me': Adenauer's account of Kennedy's
remark at their first meeting on 12 April 1961; *Erinnerungen*, Vol. IV, p. 91.

there was one matter on which the Western Allies were united it was Berlin. To be sure, there were differences in each response, and these differences were to become acute; but everybody agreed that the West should not abandon their rights in Berlin – even if it meant going to war to protect them. In other words, Khrushchev, in his squeezing, seemed to have succeeded in uniting the West. The old Soviet policy of 'driving wedges' between the Western Allies was, on the face of it, lost in the dash of Khrushchev's impetuosity. But, as it turned out, the loss was only temporary.

In January 1961 Adenauer still had his usual worries. He was fearful that the new American President would take the softest of all possible lines. Whatever the difficulties of their relationship from time to time, he was missing Dulles badly. Nonetheless, there was nothing he could do but worry – and wait for Kennedy. It was obvious to all the world that there would at some point be a confrontation with Khrushchev. The problem was to know which of the two would blink first. Adenauer, pessimist as he was, thought that it would be Kennedy.

In the meantime, however delicate his health, he was determined to celebrate his eighty-fifth birthday in style. The celebrations were, as might be expected, a suitably spectacular event. They lasted two days, with elaborate rituals – and, for onlookers with a sense of humour, moments of rich, if unconscious, comedy. Starting at 9.30am on 5 January, visitors appeared in a carefully selected order to congratulate him. His family were allowed twenty minutes of his time, members of his Cabinet and of the CDU/CSU were allowed ten, and all others, from President Lübke downwards, were rationed to five. Seven orphans were wheeled in to offer their humble congratulations. Many of the visitors brought presents – not least the four stone cherubs for his garden in Rhöndorf given to him by the Cabinet. The SPD in turn gave him eighty-five tea roses, brought in portentously by Carlo Schmid.

All that took up the morning of 5 January, after which Adenauer lunched with his family and had coffee with Pferdmenges and his wife. There were then more visitors, and a large reception, before he went home. On the following day there was a long and tedious parade, and the customary performances by teams from all over West Germany wearing traditional – even if slightly absurd – costumes. Adenauer, of course, loved every minute of it. As a matter of fact, in this orgy of adulation, his health noticeably improved.

But of all the people who came to pay their respects to Adenauer by far the most interesting was the Mayor of Berlin, and newly elected SPD candidate for the Chancellorship, Willy Brandt. Brandt himself was almost the opposite of Adenauer. He was the illegitimate son of a Lübeck shop assistant, born with the name of Herbert Frahm; he had joined first a left-wing splinter group and then in 1932, when he was only nineteen the SPD. On the Gestapo list of suspects only a year later, he thought it prudent to escape to Norway, where he took Norwegian citizenship under his new name of Brandt. When the Germans invaded Norway he joined the Norwegian Army, was captured and then released by the invaders. He then escaped to Sweden, where he remained for the rest of the war. After the war he returned to Germany as a Norwegian citizen, and for a time was press attaché at the Norwegian mission in Berlin. He then, in 1948, went back to German citizenship, and to SPD politics, under his new name.

Adenauer's personal dislike of Brandt, his origins, his atheism, his illegitimacy and, above all, his youth, was notable – and vitriolic. When he heard of Brandt's election in November 1960 as the SPD candidate for the Chancellorship, Adenauer remarked to the CDU executive council, in his most menacing tones: 'Consideration must now be given to what can be said about Brandt's background.'[3] Consideration was indeed given, and the results subsequently used without scruple.

The fact that Brandt turned up to congratulate Adenauer on his birthday was itself, at least indirectly, an unintended result of Khrushchev's squeezing. In their conference at Bad Godesberg in 1959, and subsequently in November 1960 when they elected Brandt as their leader, the SPD had come to the conclusion that on their existing policy platform they were unelectable. They therefore accepted, not just a revision of their domestic programme, but West German membership of NATO. Neutrality was no longer a viable option.

Adenauer, of course, did not believe a word of the SPD conversion. When he heard of the speech made on 30 June 1960 by Herbert Wehner, the SPD's chief idealogue, accepting – and, indeed, embracing – his government's foreign policies, he simply said: 'The whole thing was very poor theatre.'[4] As far as he was concerned, the SPD were still sunk in the depths of Marxist ideology.

With all this in mind, and with all his doubts about President Kennedy, Adenauer set off on 9 February 1961 to mend fences with de Gaulle, and to discuss the new Kennedy administration and what it might mean for Europe. At meetings over the next two days, both agreed that Kennedy was an unknown figure without international experience – and they both lamented that Kennedy was surrounded by 'many prima donnas'.[5] De Gaulle also told Adenauer about his earlier meeting with Macmillan, at which the British Prime Minister seemed to be taking more interest in the EEC; but the British, de Gaulle pointed out, were in the pocket of the Americans. None of this came as a surprise to Adenauer. He already knew of the shift in the British position towards the EEC. In fact, it was only a few days after the meeting that Macmillan announced to the House of Commons that the British government wished to consult the 'Six' on the whole matter of the future of the European Community.

Adenauer's next stop was, indeed, London. On 22 February, with Brentano in tow, he went to talk to Macmillan. It was not the happiest of their meetings. Macmillan tried to persuade Adenauer of the British case for 'restoring the economic unity of Europe'. What he did not tell Adenauer was that he had 'detected a distinct change in [Kennedy's] attitude towards the Germans and [Kennedy] was quite frank that his enthusiasm for the Common Market was largely caused by his desire to fence the Germans in . . .'[6] But Adenauer was cautious in his reply. He was already aware from de Gaulle that Macmillan saw himself as a benevolent uncle to Kennedy, and that the Anglo-American axis was stronger than it had been since Dulles' death. He was therefore at his most guarded in their discussions. Nothing, at that point, was settled.

On his return to Bonn, Adenauer found that a clever political trick he had tried to play had been trumped by the Federal Constitutional Court. In his admiration of de Gaulle's television technique – de Gaulle was perhaps the first political master of the new medium – Adenauer had tried in 1960 to set up a new television station, to be owned by the Länder governments and the Federal Government. He had been particularly pleased when the Länder governments failed to take up their shares; that only meant that the Federal Government would control the station. There were, however, complaints, and the whole matter went to the Court. On 28 February the Court delivered its judgement: the Federal Government could not own a controlling share in a television station unless it removed itself from any form of operation of the station. The press thought the Court judgement both amusing and humiliating.

For Adenauer, it was certainly annoying. But even more annoying was the publication in a number of German newspapers of an article by Erhard appealing for European unity, not just of the six countries of the Common Market and the seven of the European Free Trade Area but also of the other countries which belonged to NATO, Greece and Turkey. Adenauer thought this ridiculous. Besides, Erhard had no right to trespass on territory which Adenauer claimed to be strictly his own. Matters were not improved when Erhard took the credit for the successful revaluation of the Deutschmark on 6 March. 'I am told that I ought to nail Erhard down,' Adenauer said to his interpreter, Heinz Weber; 'but how do you nail down a pudding?'[7]

It was holiday time again; and, on 13 March Adenauer flew to Milan, to be driven up to Cadenabbia and the Villa Collina. Before he left, however, he had received Kennedy's special envoy, Averell Harriman, who brought with him a letter from Kennedy proposing a visit to Washington. Then, on 9 April, the day after his return from what had been a quiet three and a half weeks in Cadenabbia, Adenauer had a long talk with Dean Acheson in Rhöndorf to prepare for the visit, fixed for the following week. But Acheson made one crucial point. There was no doubt, he said, that in the event of war the United States would, from the outset, be prepared to defend the Federal Republic.

Adenauer was duly comforted by Acheson's message; and, on 11 April, he set off again for America in a good mood with the usual accompanying party (including his daughter Libet). When he arrived, however, he found that there was little that he and Kennedy could usefully say to one another. The President was still in the process of formulating policy. Admittedly, Kennedy came out strongly against nuclear proliferation – thus killing all hopes of nuclear weapons for the Bundeswehr – and, in the wings, McCloy, the Special Assistant to the President on Disarmament, tried to persuade Adenauer, without success, that the Oder–Neisse line should be regarded as definitive. But beyond that, and a rather limp communiqué, the Washington talks produced nothing of substance.

It was therefore with something of a sense of relief that Adenauer left Washington to stay with Vice-President Lyndon Johnson on his Texan ranch. In truth, they made an odd couple. Both were rough and frequently unscrupulous politicians – Johnson had earned for himself the nickname 'Landslide Lyndon' after he had won election to the Senate for the first time by the margin of a handful of dubious votes stuffed into the ballot box in a remote small town in southern Texas. But Johnson was given to striding about in boots and a ten-gallon Stetson, while Adenauer walked about in his usual disciplined manner – in his usual austere dark grey suit. Furthermore, neither spoke a word of the other's language. It was far from a meeting of obvious soulmates.

During the visit, Johnson, for once forswearing his Texan vernacular, did his best to make Adenauer feel at home. But his main task was to explain to Adenauer, amid many compliments about the Federal Republic as a 'major power' which should participate in important questions of international policy, that the invasion of Cuba by exiles based in Florida – and sponsored by the American Central Intelligence Agency – had turned into what can only be described as the lamentable fiasco of the Bay of Pigs. At that point, Adenauer could only look glum. But he still took part with enthusiasm in the great Texan barbecues which Johnson had laid on, even to the point of appearing before the television cameras in something which looked like a twenty-gallon hat.

But enough was enough. It was time to go home. 'Home' in this case meant not just a return to Rhöndorf but a further retreat to Cadenabbia. After a brief report to the CDU executive, in which he praised Lyndon Johnson as 'almost a European',[8] Adenauer took off again on 29 April for another fortnight's holiday at the Villa Collina. *Boccia* was to be the main entertainment. Nevertheless, there was business to be done; and Adenauer's thoughts were now turning to the federal elections due to take place in the following September. They were not going to be easy. Brandt was a formidable opponent, not least because he came from the Kennedy generation. Adenauer explained all this to de Gaulle, who arrived for his first visit to Bonn on 20 May – six days after Adenauer had come back from Cadenabbia. The two then went to Rhöndorf, with their private interpreters. The talk there was all of Kennedy, his forthcoming meeting with Khrushchev in Vienna – and of the SPD threat in the autumn. They agreed that Khrushchev should be resisted, but de Gaulle slipped in the question whether Britain was ready for 'political co-operation' within the EEC.[9]

De Gaulle had indeed started to weave his web, in which Adenauer would in the end be caught. But, for the moment, his whole attention was devoted to the federal elections. Kennedy's talks with Khrushchev in Vienna came and went. Khrushchev announced yet another ultimatum. Yet again, he said that the Soviets would sign a peace treaty with the GDR if there was no agreement on Berlin before the end of 1961. Yet again, Kennedy stated the American position, announcing furthermore, on 25 July, that there was to be a quick build-up of US forces in Germany to support that position. 'To sum it all up,' he said, 'we seek peace, but we shall not surrender.'[10]

By then the world was becoming very dangerous, but, as always, Adenauer was not to be put off from his summer holiday in Cadenabbia. He left on 26 July for a further two weeks holiday at the Villa Collina. Macmillan's announcement on 31 July that Britain was formally applying for membership of the EEC passed almost unnoticed among the competitive games of *boccia*, to which Adenauer was giving his full attention.

Campaigning for the federal elections of September 1961 started in earnest when Adenauer returned from Italy on 10 August. By then Khrushchev had stopped his squeezing; his attempt to gain West Berlin had clearly failed. But the situation was far from calm. Throughout July there were rumours in Berlin that the east would be sealed off; in that one month alone 30,000 refugees poured from East Berlin into West Berlin, and the flow continued. In early August Kennedy was able to say that 'Khrushchev is losing East Germany. He cannot let that happen. If East Germany goes, so will Poland and all of Eastern Europe. He will do something to stop the flow of refugees. Perhaps a wall.'[11]

A wall it was to be. In the early hours of Sunday, 13 August 1961, East German workers, under the protection of the GDR police, sealed off with barbed-wire barricades the border between the Soviet sector of Berlin and the three Western sectors, and West Berlin's border with the GDR. The speed of the event took the Western Allies by surprise. Kennedy was at his country home in Hyannisport, Massachusetts, and Macmillan was shooting grouse in Scotland. For two whole days nothing was done.

Adenauer's reaction was equally lame. At 4.30am, two hours before he was due to be called for Mass, he was telephoned by Globke to be told the news. Undeterred, he went, as he always had, to his customary Mass in Rhöndorf church. Ernst Lemmer, Minister for All-German Affairs, rang to plead with him to go to Berlin at once. Adenauer refused. The best he could do was a television appearance with Brentano on 14 August, in which he told the German people that there was no cause for alarm. By then the barbed-wire barricades were being replaced by a wall.

Brandt showed much more energy – and political awareness. He flew to Berlin immediately, demanded an immediate protest from the Western Allies and wrote to Kennedy reminding him of his promise to defend West Berlin and the access routes. He also called a special meeting of the Berlin Senate and denounced 'before all the world the illegal and inhuman measures taken by those who divide Germany, oppress East Berlin and threaten West Berlin . . .'[12]

Regardless of Berlin, Adenauer resumed his election campaign. He spoke at mass rallies in Regensburg on 14 August, Bonn on 16 August and Essen on 18 August. But not only did he continue his election campaign while Brandt was in Berlin; he went into the gutter yet again. In a clear reference to Brandt's illegitimate birth he called him 'Herr Brandt, alias Frahm'.[13] This was too much even for the normally pro-CDU press. The *Stuttgarter Zeitung*, for instance, castigated Adenauer, calling him 'the election orator, alias Federal Chancellor'.[14] But Adenauer was unrepentant, and two days later, at a demonstration at the Bonn bus station, he repeated the words, and went on to assert that Khrushchev had built the wall only to help the SDP in the elections.

It was not only offensive. It was politically disastrous. The poll ratings for electoral support for the CDU/CSU told the story: from 49 per cent at the end of July, the figure tumbled to 35 per cent in late August. Furthermore, Adenauer was held personally to blame. The situation deteriorated further when Kennedy sent Johnson and General Lucius Clay, the former US Military Governor, to Berlin with a force of 1,500 American armoured troops, crossing the border at Helmstedt, driving through the corridor to Berlin in an assertion of American determination. Humbly enough, Adenauer asked Johnson if he could come with him. The answer – after a quick consultation with the US ambassador, Walter Dowling, in a lavatory in the Palais Schaumburg – was a brusque 'no'. Finally, Adenauer went on his own to Berlin on 22 August. As might be imagined, his reception was chilly. All in all, it confirmed Gerhard Schröder's verdict: 'Adenauer had now lost his once instinctive, ultra-swift powers of judgement . . . He ought to have gone to Berlin.'[15]

The elections took place on 17 September 1961. As the polls had predicted, the CDU/CSU vote fell and the overall majority was lost. The CDU/CSU vote slipped almost 5 percentage points to 45.3% per cent giving them, after adjustment in their favour for the failure of minor parties to pass the 5 per cent threshold, 242 Bundestag seats; the SPD gained ground, with 36.2 per cent of the vote, to end with 190 seats; and the FDP, now led with considerable panache by Erich Mende (under the slogan 'CDU yes, Adenauer no'), put on just over 5 percentage points to end with 12.8 per cent of the overall vote and 67 seats.

It was certainly a blow. But, even so, Adenauer was still the leader of the largest group in the Bundestag and had to set about forming a government. It was far from easy. Mende had gone on record during the campaign that the FDP would only join in coalition with the CDU/CSU if Erhard were to be Chancellor. Mende had also ruled out a coalition with the SPD (not least because much of the FDP's funding came from the Confederation of German Industry, which was far from convinced by the SPD's recent Bad Godesberg conversion). Adenauer knew, of course, that if their funds dried up the FDP would be in mortal danger. Indeed, it was to be one of the cards which he would play in the political poker game of bringing Mende round to a CDU/CSU/FDP coalition.

There were other cards in the game, which, in the event, Adenauer played with the greatest skill. On 21 September he openly invited the SPD to negotiations about forming a 'grand coalition'. The negotiations were, of course, no more than a bluff. But, for a week, Adenauer dribbled out the news that they were going successfully. Mende knew perfectly well that the FDP had not the strength to form a viable opposition against a 'grand coalition' – let alone face the prospect of four more years without a place in government. On 28 September, therefore, he requested a meeting with Adenauer to discuss a CDU/CSU/FDP coalition – with the matter of the Chancellorship left open.

The negotiations opened on 2 October. Mende was almost immediately outmanoeuvred on the matter of the Chancellorship. Adenauer started off by telling him, as he had learned from Averell Harriman, that the United States were expecting trouble from Khrushchev over Cuba. This was not the time, he went on, to allow Erhard to be the master of West Germany. It was, indeed, a telling point, which Mende accepted. But Adenauer was forced to make two major concessions. In order to arrive at a document which would set out the basis for a CDU/CSU/FDP coalition, he agreed, on Mende's insistence, that he would step down as Chancellor in two years' time – or at least before the federal elections due in 1965. Furthermore, Mende insisted that Adenauer live up to the assurances that he had given to the CDU national executive before the September elections, that 'in the middle of these four years . . . I would resign to make place for another'.[16] The commitment was to write to Krone re-affirming his intention, in a form which could be placed 'in the parliamentary group's archives'.[17] This was duly done.

The other concession Adenauer was forced to make was in the matter of who would become Foreign Minister in the proposed coalition. Brentano, in the FDP's view, was far too subservient to the Chancellor. He must therefore go. In the course of the long negotiations, various names were put forward – Hallstein, Kiesinger, Schröder, even Gerstenmaier or Krone. But Hallstein was too much of a European federalist, Kiesinger too soft towards the Soviets, Gerstenmaier too bad-tempered and Krone too valuable to Adenauer where he was, as chairman of the CDU parliamentary group. In the end, the choice fell on Schröder. Realising what was in the wind, Brentano dutifully wrote an elegant letter to Adenauer with his resignation. 'I not only heard what was said, but understood what was not said.'[18] Privately, of course, Brentano was less reticent. He had, as everybody knew, been thrown by Adenauer to the FDP wolves.

In the end, the laborious deal was done. A document was signed; Mende was widely accused of 'capitulation' and 'U-turn'; Schröder became Foreign Minister; and Adenauer was duly elected as Chancellor – for the fourth time – by the Bundestag on 7 November 1961. But the election itself was far from easy. There were those who grumbled about Adenauer's age, and there were those who grumbled about Mende's 'capitulation'. Seventeen members of the CDU/CSU/FDP coalition voted against him, and another twenty-six abstained. It was not, by any means, a happy event. Nonetheless, it was done, and Adenauer could again take up his suite of offices in the Palais Schaumburg. But he was under notice to vacate them in two years or so, and to slip into what all regarded as a well-earned retirement.

None of this meant that Adenauer was content with his new government, or that he was prepared to be thought of as the lamest of lame ducks. On the contrary, he was as energetic as ever. But he now devoted almost all his time to international affairs. On 19 November, for instance, he set off again to Washington to try to persuade Kennedy not to give away too much over Berlin. He had heard that Kennedy's Secretary of

State, Dean Rusk,* was starting a series of talks with his Soviet counter-part, Andrei Gromyko.† The mere fact had in itself aroused his suspicions.

When they met, Kennedy told Adenauer that US policy was now con-centrated on Berlin, and that there could be no general solution to the German problem until the Wall was dismantled. That was reassuring enough. But it was only a few days later, on 25 November, that Kennedy gave an interview to Khrushchev's son-in-law and editor of *Izvestia*, Alexei Adzubei, in which he recognised that the Soviets were not prepared to con-cede reunification of Germany, that the United States were opposed to any German finger on any nuclear trigger, and that peace in Central Europe would be possible if an agreement was reached on Berlin.

On reading this, Adenauer was, understandably, angry and confused; it seemed to him impossible to know where the core of American policy lay. As if this was not worrying enough, there was an even more serious prob-lem: his own health. Those who were waiting for him on his return from Washington were shocked at the sight of him. As he stepped off the air-

---

* Rusk, Dean (1909–94): Lawyer, academic and politician. Born in Cherokee County, Georgia, USA, of a poor family. Educated locally, graduating from Davidson College in 1931. 1931–32: Rhodes Scholar at Oxford. 1934–40: Taught political science at Mills College in Oakland, California. 1940–45: Adviser to US Army on Far East. 1945–50: Various positions in US State Department and US Department of Defense. 1950: Assistant Secretary of State for Far Eastern affairs. 1952–60: President of the Rockefeller Foundation. 1961–69: US Secretary of State. Known as one of the most adamant Cold War warriors, but prepared to do deals if they suited the US.

† Gromyko, Andrei (1909–89): Diplomat. Born son of a peasant in Belarus. Studied agri-cultural economics in Minsk. 1936–39: Senior research assistant in Russian Academy of Sciences. 1939: Appointed head of US division of the People's Commissariat of Foreign Affairs. 1943: Appointed Soviet ambassador in Washington. 1946: Deputy foreign minis-ter. 1949: Promoted to first deputy foreign minister. 1952: Ambassador to London. 1954: Again first deputy foreign minister. 1957–85: Foreign minister of USSR; member of Politburo (1973) and first deputy chairman of the Council of Ministers (1983). 1985–88: President of Supreme Soviet. Very clever, and respected as a hard negotiator for whichever master he was serving.

craft at Wahn airport, after an overnight flight, he was quite obviously very ill. In fact, he had been ill throughout his stay in Washington, and had been running a temperature even before he left Bonn. So worried were his doctors that one of them, Dr Ella Bebber-Buch, flew to Washington (without Adenauer knowing) and stayed in a hotel under an assumed name. Her task was to brief the doctor at the German Embassy on the correct medication for Adenauer's condition, which had been diagnosed as pneumonia.

It was given out that he had his usual bout of autumnal influenza, but that was a convenient fiction. The truth was much worse. Adenauer was confined to his bed in Rhöndorf for a fortnight; and it was noted, by many with wry amusement, that the first major statement of the new government to the Bundestag on 29 November 1961 was read out by the Vice-Chancellor, who was none other than Ludwig Erhard.

But it was not long before Adenauer was up and travelling again. On 9 December he was in Paris to see General de Gaulle. Though de Gaulle gave him a friendly enough reception at Orly airport, their subsequent talk was not altogether to Adenauer's satisfaction. True, de Gaulle thought it too soon for any substantive agreement with the Soviets over Berlin. Also, when de Gaulle reported on a conversation he had recently had with Macmillan about the progress of negotiations, both agreed that Britain could not bring the Commonwealth with her if she were to join the EEC. As de Gaulle said, 'it would no longer be Europe'.[19] But there was a dispute between the two over Berlin. When Adenauer asked de Gaulle not to 'stand aside' on the matter, he received a sharp rebuke. De Gaulle said that if the United States, Britain and West Germany wanted to give up Berlin then France would not stand in their way. That ended the meeting. 'I was,' Adenauer noted, 'most dissatisfied . . . I was very angry.'[20]

The meeting was followed by a conference of Western foreign ministers in Paris on 11 December to discuss Berlin, and by a further conference of EEC foreign ministers to review the results of a commission chaired by Christian Fouchet, the French ambassador to Denmark, on proposals for European political union. Neither of these conferences came to very much. There was no agreed view on Berlin, and Fouchet was told by the French government to go away and think again.

Much of this, however, passed Adenauer by. He was still in uncertain health. His eighty-sixth birthday on 5 January 1962, and the accompanying celebrations, of course, cheered him up. He was, apparently, in sparkling form, in the best of moods, and as quick-witted as ever. Indeed, his best sally was to Erhard, his Vice-Chancellor, who, on behalf of the Cabinet, presented him with an elaborately carved stone seat for his Rhöndorf garden. 'Success in politics,' he said, 'is achieved by the ability to keep your seat for a long time.'[21] Everybody present, understandably in the context, seemed to consider that to be the most amusing remark they had ever heard.

But all was not well. Macmillan noted this on his visit to Bonn on 9 January. Adenauer's face had lost all its previous authority. The wrinkles were deeper, the face looked more depressed, more 'Mongolian'. Even Globke, himself suffering from high blood pressure and cardiac arrhythmia, confided to Krone that 'over the past few days he had seen the Chancellor in a mood the like of which he had never seen him before seen him in. He prefers to withdraw from everyone.'[22]

That was on 21 January. But Globke was right. On that day Adenauer had a heart attack. Admittedly, it was, in medical terms, a relatively minor attack, but it was an attack nonetheless. Once properly diagnosed, it was clear that Adenauer would need proper rest and a period of proper recovery. He insisted, however, that he would not go into hospital, and that it should be given out that he was only suffering from influenza. So was it done; but, as Krone wrote on hearing the news, 'perhaps death is casting his shadow over him'.[23]

Adenauer stayed at home in Rhöndorf for two weeks of total isolation. On 4 February he emerged. But he was still frail, as well as 'tetchy and bad-tempered. He has also become erratic and disinclined to listen to reason.'[24] Nevertheless, he showed the same determination and courage as he had in his motor accident in 1917. He would not admit, or allow anybody else to admit, that he had been seriously ill. Furthermore, only five days after he resumed official duties, on 9 February, he received a request from de Gaulle for an urgent meeting. De Gaulle, of course, was quite unaware that Adenauer had had a heart attack. The secret had been well kept.

De Gaulle himself had only recently evaded an attempt to assassinate him, at Petit-Clamart on his regular journey back from Paris to Colombey; and the French security services were taking no risks. It was therefore agreed that they should meet on 15 February in the annexe to a hotel in Baden-Baden. Adenauer travelled by train; de Gaulle flew to the French air base at Lahr, and drove there at speed, with a heavy police escort.

Their meeting covered the whole spectrum of Franco-German relations. The two leaders met alone in the morning and with their foreign ministers in the afternoon. De Gaulle wanted to convince Adenauer of the merits of the second plan for European political union which had been produced by the Fouchet commission in January.

This he failed to do, not least because Adenauer could easily see that the new plan was for a somewhat loose organisation, separate from the EEC, which would be dominated by France. Besides, Adenauer knew perfectly well that the smaller countries – the Dutch in particular – would insist that the whole matter should rest in abeyance until the negotiations for British entry into the EEC were successfully concluded. Moreover, there was no mention of the overriding importance of NATO. Adenauer, however, did agree to discuss further Fouchet's central idea of a political umbrella over the three European treaties – provided that the EEC was not thereby stopped in its tracks. In the event, it was to no avail, since the smaller countries, the Dutch in particular, insisted that the negotiations with Britain had to take priority before any agreement on political co-operation could even be considered.

Nevertheless, whatever their disagreements on details, there is no doubt that the meeting at Baden-Baden marked a change in the previously uncertain relationship between the two men. They found that they were in complete agreement on two major points – mistrust of American and British attitudes towards the Soviets and the absolute necessity of avoiding another Franco-German armed conflict. De Gaulle had clearly changed his view on Berlin which had so angered Adenauer in Paris two months earlier.

It was by now clear that the Berlin Wall was by then starting to have its effect on the policies of all the major Western participants. There was no longer any prospect of early German reunification. It was equally clear that the Adenauer strategy – of building up Western strength until the Soviets would either collapse or negotiate on the West's terms – was no longer tenable. In response to this new situation, the Americans and the British seemed prepared to offer concessions to the Soviets to placate Khrushchev. That view was supported by both Erhard and Schröder – much to Adenauer's irritation. They were both convinced 'Atlanticists' and, at least in Schröder's case, anglophile. Given all these developments, Adenauer felt that there was only one way for him to turn – to cement an alliance with a leader who shared his robust view that all negotiation with the Soviets was a waste of time.

On his holiday at the Villa Collina in Cadenabbia, from 19 March to

9 April 1962, Adenauer thought it all through. True, there had been a minor upset before his departure: he had conceded to the CDU executive – who had for some time been considering how Adenauer could be levered out of office – that there should be an 'executive chairman', the post being given to Josef Hermann Dufhues, a lightweight former Interior Minister of North-Rhine Westphalia. But in the grand scheme of things – provided Dufhues did not cause trouble – that was neither here nor there.

Having given due thought, between the games of *boccia*, to the problems which faced the Federal Republic, Adenauer came to one firm conclusion, which was to provide the theme for the last eighteen months of his Chancellorship. The Berlin Wall had changed the political landscape. The United States and Britain were unreliable allies. France was the only possible alternative. France and Germany must stand together against the atheistic, ideological offensive of Communism; and France, for those purposes, meant General de Gaulle.

Adenauer flew back to Bonn on 9 April precisely because he had news of another American initiative. Dean Rusk on that day sent his proposals to Wilhelm Grewe, by then West Germany's ambassador in Washington. The proposals were precisely what Adenauer feared. Rusk wished to continue his negotiations with the Soviets, but on new basis. The United States offered to accept the Oder–Neisse line as permanent, international control of the access routes to Berlin (which would involve dealing with the GDR), and an international agreement on non-proliferation of nuclear weaponry. The Germans were given forty-eight hours to comment on the proposals before they were put to the Soviets.

Adenauer refused to accept the deadline. Suspecting that Schröder had been aware of Rusk's proposal – he had met Rusk in Lausanne on 13 March – Adenauer called a meeting of the chairmen of all parliamentary groups in the Bundestag, to be held in Brentano's room in the Bundeshaus on the evening of 12 April. At the meeting, when it came, of the three chairman Ollenhauer of the SPD was cautious, fearful of being led into yet another Adenauer trap; Mende was equally cautious, since the FDP had recently discussed proposals to recognise the GDR in the context of a nuclear-free Central Europe, and was also afraid of being outflanked by Adenauer; Brentano, needless to say, was hostile.

Adenauer was thus able to claim that all three parties were opposed to Rusk's proposals. Furthermore, news of the meeting – and Adenauer's summary of its conclusions – were widely reported on West German radio and television on the same evening. Adenauer then reported the 'unambiguous'[25] conclusion of the party chairmen to Paul Nitze, the US Deputy Secretary for Defense, who was on a visit to Bonn at the time. He then went on to write to Kennedy reminding him of the American obligations which Kennedy himself had accepted in their meeting of November 1961. De Gaulle, too, was asked to join in, and duly instructed Couve de Murville to lodge with the Americans the complete French rejection of the Rusk initiative.

The temperature was rising almost by the day. Adenauer returned on 14 April to Cadenabbia, where he composed a searing memorandum on the Rusk initiative. 'I am worried,' he wrote, 'by both the method and the content of American foreign policy . . . We have no idea what is being negotiated.'[26] Rusk's reply was equally forthright. At a press conference on 26 April, Rusk repudiated Adenauer's view, claiming that the 'factual situation'[27] of a divided Germany had now to be recognised – and might continue for a long time. Both sides should recognise the status quo on that basis. Behind the scenes, he accused Adenauer of a breach of confidence in leaking the contents of his proposals to the German media.

The upshot was that after his return from Cadenabbia on 3 May Adenauer decided to launch a verbal war against the United States. In Berlin on 7 May he gave a public speech which Grewe described as the sharpest criticism ever heard from any German head of government of United States foreign policy. Kennedy replied in kind – again in public – criticising Adenauer in equally unprecedented language and emphasising that the United States would continue to negotiate with the Soviets.

The split between Adenauer and Kennedy was complete. Kennedy remarked that 'the real trouble is that he is too old and I am too young to understand one another', while Adenauer considered Kennedy to be 'a cross between a junior naval person and a Roman Catholic boy scout'.[28] Macmillan was also useless – Adenauer later described him as 'stupid'.[29]

Khrushchev's attempts at compromise after his failure to take West Berlin had worked where his squeezing had failed. The West was again deeply divided on the Berlin issue, and the division was accentuated by personal bitterness. Khrushchev could hardly have been more pleased, particularly when Adenauer sent him a letter on 6 June suggesting that 'serious thought be given to concluding between the two countries – that is the Soviet Union and the Federal Republic of Germany – a kind of armistice, in a figurative sense, lasting ten years'.[30]

Khrushchev was not the only one to be pleased. De Gaulle had taken careful note of the war of words between Kennedy and Adenauer. It was time for him to strike. He therefore sent an invitation to Adenauer to make a State Visit to France in July. The Carolingian Empire was to be re-created – and in the greatest possible style.

13

FROM TRIUMPH TO DISMISSAL

'Die dritte Entlassung war die schlimmste'*

THE CATHEDRAL OF Notre-Dame in Rheims is one of the greatest of France's architectural glories. So majestic was the original plan that it took over a hundred years to build the main structure – almost the whole of the thirteenth century and a large part of the fourteenth. Building continued over the following decades, albeit with numerous disruptions; indeed, the twin towers at the west end were not finally completed until 1475. The cathedral was fortunate in escaping the assaults of the Revolution, but, having survived those, was badly damaged by gunfire during the First World War. As it happened, the restoration was carefully accomplished, with the added bonus, in the apse, of three stained-glass windows designed by the artist Marc Chagall. Dominating the city and the flat countryside around, it even now stands proudly as a monument to the high point of medieval Western Christendom.

But it is not in its architecture that Rheims cathedral can claim to stand

---

* 'The third dismissal was the worst': Adenauer to Gerstenmaier in early May 1963 (the first two 'dismissals' being by the Nazis in 1933 and the British in 1945); Koerfer, Kampf ums Kanzleramt, p. 745.

alone. Chartres, Bourges, Beauvais, Notre-Dame in Paris and Autun are all honourable competitors. Rheims has other claims. For any visitor, there is in the place an unmistakable sense of the continuity of French history. Lying as it does in the Champagne, the territory over which French and Germans had fought many bitter wars, it seems in itself a symbol of the French nation. It is no accident that the Archbishops of Rheims had the prerogative of crowning and anointing the kings of France from the tenth century onward. In short, in July 1962 there could be no more suitable place for the new Franco-German friendship to be celebrated; and celebrated in Rheims it duly was.

On 8 July Adenauer and de Gaulle went together to High Mass in the cathedral. They had first taken the salute at a parade of French and German troops on the plain of Mourmelon just outside the city. It was the first time, it was noted, that French and German troops had been on the same side since the battle of Leipzig in 1813 (although others whispered that that did not count, since the Germans – from Saxony and Württemberg – had deserted before the battle started).

The parade ended, the two leaders, both in reverentially dark suits, arrived at the steps of the cathedral, to be greeted by the Archbishop of Rheims, Monsignor Marty, and a large group of attendant minor clergy. A silver cru-cifix led the grand procession into the church and along the great nave. The General and the Chancellor were ushered to their places – two pries-dieu, their kneelers and the seats behind them covered in red velvet, set in the sanc-tuary to the right of a high altar sumptuously decorated with banks of white roses and lilies. The Mass then proceeded with the greatest solemnity. Immediately after the Gospel, Monsignor Marty welcomed the two men to the cathedral which 'remained the sign of joyous and lasting hope'.[1] At the elevation of the Host, de Gaulle and Adenauer both knelt. Adenauer was reported as staying for a long time on his knees.

A crowd of several thousand listened to the service outside in the Place du Parvis in the bright July sunlight. When the leaders emerged from the cathe-dral, there was much cheering and waving of flags. There is no doubt that Adenauer was very moved. Indeed, the only cloud in an otherwise clear sky was that relations between French and Germans in the crowd were not at all as cordial as the relations between the two leaders. There were reports of scuffles, and of some unpleasant punch-ups; the police, apparently, were required to intervene with some force.

The Mass in Rheims Cathedral was the climax of Adenauer's state visit to France in early July 1962. The visit had lasted six days, and, apart from a trip to Bordeaux during which Adenauer had sampled – at surprising length, given his predilection for the wines of the Rhine and the Mosel – the wines of Château Margaux, there was plenty of time for private discussions with the General. De Gaulle reported on his recent meeting with Macmillan, at which it had become clear to him that Britain was not prepared to make the necessary sacrifices to allow her to join the EEC. Adenauer did not disagree. In fact, he added fuel to de Gaulle's fire by alleging that Macmillan had offered economic union to the United States and had been turned down by Kennedy. British entry, he went on, should be judged on whether it would be to the economic advantage of existing members. Besides, the structure of the EEC was not sufficiently developed to accommodate the other applicants – Norway, Denmark and Ireland – who would follow in Britain's train. 'No three cheers for British entry' was his conclusion.[2] Moreover, Adenauer agreed that France and the Federal Republic should work more closely together. Even at this early stage an arrangement to formalise their co-operation was hinted at.

That was enough for de Gaulle. Realising that he had Adenauer's backing, he instructed French negotiators to take a much harder line with the British applicants. Indeed, so hard was their line that negotiations were suspended on 5 August. But, on his return to Bonn, Adenauer found that he was unable to carry his party with him. In truth, in August 1962 there opened up a split in the CDU which was to last until Adenauer's final resignation in the following year: the 'Atlanticists', led by Erhard and Schröder, were, and would be, at continuing odds with the 'Francophiles', led by Adenauer. The press joined in the row. On 22 August *Die Welt*, staunch supporter of the CDU as it was, came out with the headline 'CDU supports London's accession to the EEC'. The next day it followed up with an article entitled 'England must join – Adenauer's defeat – no longer King of the Hill?'[3] France, it appeared, had few friends in the West German newspapers.

It was not the happiest augury for de Gaulle's return visit to the Federal Republic on 5 September. But de Gaulle rose to the occasion. Refusing to wear spectacles for his very short sight, he memorised his speeches – in German. As he went around the cities of West Germany, he roused his audience to peaks of enthusiasm. 'Long live Germany!' he shouted, raising his arms towards heaven. 'Long live German–French friendship!' he went on.

'You are a great people!' All that went down as well as Adenauer had hoped. De Gaulle, for his part, was in private much more down to earth. 'If they really were still a great people,' he said in an aside, 'they would not be cheering me so much.'[4]

By then, Adenauer was inextricably caught in de Gaulle's web. 'He may have been blinded,' Hallstein was later to remark, 'by the supposed affinity with de Gaulle; old age, too, was a factor.'[5] Be that as it may, during de Gaulle's triumphal visit in September Adenauer produced more arguments against British entry into the EEC. The British Labour Party, he said, might soon come to power, and 'one does not want those people in Europe'.[6] Furthermore, he went on, if Britain wanted to join the EEC, it was up to her to make concessions – not to demand concessions from the six existing members.

De Gaulle duly left; and, for Adenauer, it was holiday time again. On 13 September 1962, he flew to Milan for a three-week stay at the Villa Collina. In the event, the holiday was to be far from peaceful. Even while de Gaulle was in Germany there had been renewed speculation about the date of Adenauer's retirement and the question of a successor. Soon after he arrived in Cadenabbia, he read of an interview Dufhues had given to the *Kölnische Rundschau* in which he commented at length on both points. Adenauer immediately sent Dufhues a petulant telegram. 'I earnestly request you,' it went, 'to refrain from making any comment on my personal decisions in future. I regard your statement as an inadmissible infringement of my privacy. I see in it a severe injury to our party . . .'[7] Adenauer clearly suspected a plot; he had the text of the telegram sent to all members of the CDU national party executive.

There was more pressing business a few days later. De Gaulle sent him a memorandum of six pages, suggesting an agreement between their two governments to co-ordinate foreign and defence policies. De Gaulle stressed that the most important point was that no decision should be taken by either side without prior consultation with the other. Adenauer replied from Cadenabbia: 'I regard [the agreement] as the first priority of my policy.'[8] To emphasise his point, he wrote in similar vein to Krone and Globke.

The holiday itself was then interrupted by a return to Cologne on 2 October for the funeral of his old friend Robert Pferdmenges, who had died of pneumonia a few days before. Adenauer was, naturally enough, much affected by Pferdmenges' death. He had, after all, been a long-standing and loyal friend who had helped Adenauer in many ways, personal, financial and political. Furthermore, it was another ally lost, and Adenauer was by then running short of allies. He spoke at the funeral service in Cologne, and went on to the burial in Mönchengladbach. It was then straight back to Cadenabbia, to enjoy what remained of the fine autumn weather.

There was, however, little time to mourn his old friend. On 8 October it was back yet again to Bonn, to face, as it happened, two new and sudden crises. On 10 October the magazine *Der Spiegel*, always a thorn in the side of the CDU, published an article under the title 'Conditionally prepared for defence', in which it described in accurate detail the NATO September staff exercise – top secret, of course, under the code name Fallex 62. The article claimed that the exercise showed that civil defence and communications in the Federal Republic were wholly inadequate, and that the Bundeswehr itself could only be mobilised if there were a long delay after the outset of a European war – hence the 'condition', which could not possibly be met. Furthermore, it claimed that Strauss had been trying for years to arm the Bundeswehr with tactical nuclear weapons. The article was very damaging – largely, indeed, because it was true.

The second crisis broke only four days after the publication of the *Spiegel* article. On Sunday, 14 October, an American U2 reconnaissance aircraft, flying over San Cristóbal in western Cuba, photographed what was clearly a missile complex under construction. Thus the 'Cuban missile crisis' and the early stages of the '*Spiegel* affair' ran concurrently. The first almost landed the world in a nuclear war; the second was to bring down Adenauer's government.

In fact, the two crises were only related in their timing; but the timing is important in its illustration of Adenauer's reactions in moments of intense nervousness on two fronts. To be sure, the *Spiegel* article was part of a long-running campaign by the magazine and its editor, Rudolf Augstein, against Strauss. To that extent, it might have been expected – and discounted. As far back as April 1961, for instance, the magazine had asserted that Strauss was a threat to democracy, that he was planning a nuclear war, and that his lust for power was inexhaustible. Strauss had sued for libel then, and was to do so again when the magazine accused him of profiting personally from a contract let by the 7th US Army to a German construction company. Although he won both cases, his victories were no better than Pyrrhic. Augstein gained valuable publicity, and continued on his campaign. Above all, he had managed to sow all manner of doubt about Strauss in the minds of the FDP members of the Cabinet.

What Adenauer had not expected – and what provoked the crisis – was that *Der Spiegel* had unearthed state secrets. This threw him on to the defensive. Admittedly, he had already had a row with Strauss in July about Strauss's nuclear ambitions – although in truth they were very close to his own. But now that Strauss was under what Adenauer regarded as a treasonable attack he had to be defended. An initial investigation was therefore launched into the whole matter; and, at the same time, Adenauer assured Strauss on 12 October that he was preparing legislation to prohibit 'press slander and so on'.[9]

It soon appeared, however, that there was a problem with the initial investigation. The Minister for Justice, Wolfgang Stammberger, one of the FDP ministers, who would normally have carried ministerial responsibility for the matter, had apparently been convicted during his military service by court-martial for making false reports, falsifying documents and embezzling military assets. Why Adenauer had not known this at the time of Stammberger's appointment is something of a mystery, but he certainly knew it now. Furthermore, he knew that the information was in the hands of the enemy – *Der Spiegel*. They would without any doubt not hesitate to use it if they thought it would serve their purpose. Stammberger therefore had to be kept in the dark.

At that point, Strauss made his first bad mistake. On 17 October, without consulting Adenauer, he decided to tell the Secret Service that the Public Prosecutor was initiating an investigation against Augstein and his deputy editor, Conrad Ahlers, for no less an offence than treason – on the basis of a report from officials in the Ministry of Defence. What Strauss did not suspect was that there were officials in the Secret Service who were friends of Augstein and who would immediately leak the news to him. Augstein in turn promptly made sure that much of the incriminating material was safely hidden. Ahlers, for his part, took the opportunity to fly to Spain – out of harm's way.

On 22 October Krone had word that the Public Prosecutor was to 'charge Augstein with treason'[10] Strauss also told Adenauer that criminal prosecutions were imminent. Adenauer, according to Strauss, gave his assent. But Adenauer's attention had been diverted. It was on that very evening that the US Ambassador Walter Dowling and an official from the CIA called at the

Palais Schaumburg to deliver a letter from Kennedy. Schröder, Globke, and Adenauer's chief foreign policy adviser, Horst Osterheld, were present. The letter's message was stark. Kennedy would be making a broadcast later that evening announcing a naval blockade of Cuba, and explaining the reasons for it. Dowling produced the U2 photographs, which he showed privately to Adenauer after the others had been asked to leave.

On the following day, 23 October, Adenauer sent a message to Kennedy supporting the American naval blockade unconditionally. He suspected, as did Kennedy's advisers, that 'the Cuban missiles might be designed to gain concessions over Berlin'.[11] By coincidence, almost while he was sending the message, the investigating magistrate at the Federal High Court in Karlsruhe issued an arrest and search warrant against Augstein and Ahlers. At a dinner for the Irish Prime Minister that evening, Strauss took Adenauer aside and told him that he had entrusted the matter to his state secretary. Moreover, he told Adenauer that the matter was also being handled inside the Ministry of Justice by the state secretary. Stammberger, the Minister, was not to be informed. Adenauer, apparently, nodded his assent.

On Friday, 26 October, Strauss telephoned Rhöndorf to tell Adenauer that the police had raided *Der Spiegel*'s office in Hamburg and its branch office in Bonn. The Hamburg office was now occupied by the police and sealed off; no member of the staff was allowed in. Various members of the magazine's staff, including Augstein, were under arrest. Adenauer, however, was in the middle of recording a broadcast to be made later, on radio and television, to explain to the German people the gravity of the Cuban crisis. Understandably enough, he was hardly paying attention to what Strauss was saying. He simply muttered that he wished to be kept informed, but that Strauss should do everything he believed to be possible, necessary and responsible.

Strauss then made his second bad mistake. He had heard that Ahlers was planning to cross from Spain to the safe haven of Tangiers. At 1.25am on 27 October, he called the German military attaché in Madrid and told him to make sure that the Spanish police detained Ahlers before he left the country. This he, and they, did, catching up with Ahlers at Malaga. Ahlers was then put on a plane to Frankfurt and arrested by West German police as soon as he landed there. That done, Strauss reported the arrest in a private meeting with Adenauer in Rhöndorf on the same evening.

By any standards, Ahler's arrest was outrageous. In Germany, particularly, it was all too reminiscent of Hitler's understanding with Franco during the Spanish Civil War. Hermann Höcherl, the bewildered Minister of the Interior, was forced to admit, in the face of an intense media barrage, that he had no knowledge of the circumstances of the case. Stammberger was equally bemused. In the press there was general and sustained uproar. The point that was made, time and time again, was that the new face of German democracy and rule of law had been irrevocably tarnished. Moreover, the blame was universally heaped on Strauss.

By the end of October 1962 the crisis in Cuba had passed its danger point. The Soviets had agreed to remove their missiles; in return, the United States would remove their out-of-date Jupiter missiles from Turkey. The Cold War was brought back to what might be called its normal level of confrontation; and a nuclear war had been – albeit narrowly – avoided. Adenauer was therefore able to give his full attention to the *Spiegel* affair.

Later, Strauss was to claim that Adenauer knew all about the telephone call to Madrid before the event. 'Know of it!' Strauss said. 'He demanded that I call!'[12] Whatever the accuracy of Strauss's recollection, he certainly had a point. Adenauer had been kept fully informed. Indeed, it is highly unlikely that Strauss would have taken the action he did, or that state secretary Walter Strauss would have failed to tell his minister what was happening, without at least tacit support from the Chancellor. But Adenauer's mind, he himself later claimed, had been concentrating on Cuba.

On 31 October, Adenauer invited Mende and other senior members of the FDP to the Palais Schaumburg to discuss the *Spiegel* article, and to show them the evidence which the police had found in Augstein's safe. There were photographs of military property, and documents clearly marked 'secret'. But he did not tell them about Stammberger's earlier conviction, or why Stammberger had not been informed about the police action. Mende and his colleagues were far from satisfied. On 2 November there was an eight-hour meeting of the FDP national executive council. The upshot was that Mende wrote to Adenauer on their behalf demanding that the two state secretaries involved, Volkmar Hopf at Defence and Walter Strauss at Justice, be summarily sacked. If they were not, all the FDP ministers would resign from the government.

It took Krone and Globke several hours to persuade Adenauer to dismiss the two blameless senior officials. Adenauer was tempted to call Mende's bluff, but in the end he recognised that it was the only way to save the coalition. Even so, the event was enough to provoke vociferous complaints at a meeting of the CDU/CSU parliamentary group on 6 November. Adenauer tried to calm them down by a bellicose performance in the Bundestag the next day – claiming that Augstein had 'profited from treason'.[13] It was a certainly a bold performance in front of an unruly Bundestag; but it was left to one of the younger members of the FDP, Wolfgang Döring, to point out that the Chancellor had, in his interventions, violated the fundamental rule that a matter could not be prejudged under parliamentary privilege while it was still *sub judice*. He was, of course, right: but the Chancellor did not seem to care very much.

Nevertheless, Adenauer was very careful to distance himself from the conduct of the police in the affair. 'If I had involved myself wholeheartedly,' he said, 'although I had no time for that – then I would have had to devote myself to the affair day and night. But I could not do that, because I have other things to do.'[14] In other words, his excuse was Cuba. Strauss, of course, knew the full truth.

Matters took a turn for the worse when an official in the Secret Service, Colonel Adolf Wicht, was arrested for tipping Augstein off about the initial investigation on the previous 18 October, the day after it was launched. Alerted to this latest development, on 12 November Adenauer summoned Reinhard Gehlen, the head of the Secret Service, and interrogated him at length about the role of the Service in the whole affair. He even had Stammberger and the chief Public Prosecutor, Albin Kuhn, dragged out of a meeting in Karlsruhe and brought at speed to Bonn, where he told them to arrest Gehlen on the spot. Stammberger replied that it could not be done without a warrant, but volunteered to continue the interrogation of Gehlen himself. Both he and Kuhn came to the conclusion that Gehlen was innocent of any involvement. Adenauer had yet again smelled a conspiracy where there was none.

By then, Stammberger had had enough. When Adenauer left on 13 November for what was to be his last visit to Washington, Stammberger consulted his FDP colleagues. Fortified by multiple and open protests from academics at Bonn, Tübingen and Cologne that the rule of law had been flouted and would continue to be flouted, they made up their mind. They all agreed that Strauss had been dishonest, not only with them but with the Bundestag and the German public, about the whole *Spiegel* affair. On 19 November, after Adenauer had returned from America, Stammberger submitted his resignation. His four FDP ministerial colleagues followed suit.

The CDU/CSU ministers, in reply to the FDP and after a meeting of the CDU parliamentary group, resigned as well. The coalition, and with it Adenauer's government, lay in ruins.

Adenauer, however, appeared unmoved by this spate of resignations. He pointed out to a meeting of the CDU national executive that, under the Basic Law, the resignation letters could not take effect until they were approved by the Federal President, who was on a visit to India, and not due back in Germany until 5 December. In the meantime, there were the Bavarian elections on 22 November. Things, he said, would no doubt take their course.

The fervent hope of the CDU/CSU parliamentary group, demoralised as it was, was that after the Bavarian elections Strauss would take the opportunity to leave national politics to become Bavaria's Minister-President, thus leaving the way open for another CDU/CSU/FDP coalition. Strauss, however, was not going to be levered out so easily. In spite of a resounding success for the CSU in the elections, and the attractions of residence in Munich, Strauss still saw himself as a candidate for the Federal Chancellorship after Erhard. He was, after all, a relatively young man.

To everybody's surprise, Adenauer then opened up a new political front. He decided to start negotiations with the SPD with a view to forming a 'grand coalition'. Of course, Adenauer was up to no more than his usual tricks. In fact, through the Housing Minister, Paul Lücke, and a conservative ally from the CSU (and no friend of Strauss), Karl Theodor Freiherr von und zu Guttenberg, he had been for some time conducting long-range discussions with the SPD. The discussions became more intense on 23 November. In the course of them, Wehner, speaking for the SPD, agreed that Adenauer should remain Chancellor for the time being, but said that 'the Chancellor should not exploit negotiations with the SPD about a coalition to buy the FDP on the cheap'.[15] That, needless to say, was precisely what Adenauer intended to do. Furthermore, he planned to bring further pressure on the FDP by suggesting that a CDU/CSU/SPD coalition would introduce a first-past-the-post electoral system, which would have the practical effect of knocking the FDP out of national politics for good.

Although Strauss knew that there were discussions with the SPD, he did not know any of the details. But he knew for certain that the SPD would never have him as a minister in a 'grand coalition'. He also knew that he was unacceptable to the FDP as the result of the *Spiegel* affair. He was indeed out on an exceptionally fragile limb. When, on 29 November, Guttenberg took a letter from Adenauer with him to Wehner in Berlin authorising the opening of formal coalition talks and when, on the same evening, Mende and his FDP colleagues arrived at the Palais Schaumburg to negotiate a new CDU/CSU/FDP coalition, Strauss realised that his chances of staying in the government had all but vanished. In fact, the FDP refused to sit down to dinner with him. They preferred to eat their dinner in a separate room. Adenauer, of course, was, in the circumstances, and as the arbiter of events, thoroughly enjoying himself.

On the next day, 30 November, Strauss told the CSU executive that he was resigned to surrendering office. In the privacy of the meeting, he was venomous about Adenauer, who, he thought, had betrayed him; as, indeed, he had. But he refrained from the one step which would have brought Adenauer himself down – making public the Chancellor's part in the *Spiegel* affair.

If Strauss was outmanoeuvred, so were the SPD, who had grabbed too easily at the possibility of office. On 4 December, in a state of high expectation, the SPD leaders presented themselves at the Palais Schaumburg for formal coalition negotiations. Needless to say, the press and public were almost dumb with astonishment. After all, here was the Chancellor, who had spent all his political life trying to dish the SPD, suddenly inviting them to join his government. What they did not know, of course, was that this was all part of Adenauer's political trickery. After a day of negotiation about a programme for government, it was obvious to all concerned that there could be no 'grand coalition'. Defeat of the project in the SPD parliamentary group on the following day was no more than a formality.

The way was then open for a somewhat chastened FDP. Although he had played a winning hand thus far, Adenauer was nevertheless forced to make concessions, above all to secure the full support of his own party. In a meeting of the CDU parliamentary group executive he conceded a definite time for his retirement – at the beginning of the new parliamentary session in the autumn of 1963. Whether he meant to stick to it or not is, of course, another matter. There was also the matter of his new Cabinet. On the whole, the negotiations went fairly easily – with one exception. The Defence Ministry was to go to Kai-Uwe von Hassel, the Minister-President of Schleswig-Holstein. Since Hassel could not leave his post for another month, Adenauer agreed with Strauss, after a long – and apparently fierce –

wrangle, that Strauss should stay as Defence Minister until Hassel was free to take over.

On 11 December 1962, Adenauer presented his new Cabinet to President Lübke. On 19 December there was a gathering of senior generals and officials from the Ministry of Defence in honour of the departing Strauss. Adenauer praised Strauss's record, and went on to prophesy that 'he will play a great and decisive role in the political life of the German people in the future'.[16] It is hard to imagine that Adenauer believed a word of what he was saying. All he knew was that he had yet again come out on top. The *Spiegel* affair was dragging on, and would do so until legal proceedings were finally dropped. On 24 December, Khrushchev threatened again a separate peace treaty with the GDR, but his threat was not followed up. After a short Christmas holiday and the celebration in the usual manner of Adenauer's eighty-seventh birthday, Krone could confide to his diary: 'The Old Man is eighty-seven. Fresh, elegant, full of humour, without any sign of weakness. It is not surprising that he does not want to go.'[17]

At the beginning of 1963 Adenauer had three priorities: the first was to try to reorganise NATO to provide for a greater West German presence; the second was to cement relations with de Gaulle and France; the third – by a long way the most important – was to prevent, by fair means or foul, Erhard's succession to the Chancellorship. He no longer seemed to care about the morale of the CDU/CSU, or that he had had rows with all his previously trusted advisers apart from the obsequious Krone and the self-effacing Globke. Nor did he seem to care about the Bundestag. When he attended, it was usually only to sit in brooding silence, his eyes shrouded by thick dark glasses. Under the circumstances, it was little wonder that the move to get rid of him gathered momentum – until it finally exploded in April.

Of Adenauer's three priorities for 1963 the NATO matter came up first. On 14 January the US Under-Secretary of State, George Ball, arrived in Bonn to explain to Adenauer the latest scheme that the Kennedy administration had hatched. It was an obscure plan to assemble a group of naval surface vessels from all NATO countries, to be armed with nuclear weapons and to be crewed by a mixture of sailors from all the participating countries. In truth, it is difficult to imagine a scheme more fraught with operational difficulties; but it was at least an attempt by the Kennedy administration to reassure other NATO allies of the US commitment to them.

Adenauer immediately accepted West German participation in this unlikely venture. De Gaulle, on the other hand, would have none of it. Indeed, it was on the very day that Adenauer gave his agreement to Ball that de Gaulle announced, in the most dramatic fashion, that France would veto Britain's application to join the EEC. The announcement, of course, provoked another, and greater, uproar – not only in Britain and the United States but in West Germany as well. The 'Atlanticists', by now defined also as anglophiles, led by Erhard and Schröder, were fierce in their condemnation of de Gaulle. Adenauer, on the other hand, was unabashed; he was single-minded in his determination to continue with the Franco-German agreement.

It was thus with a chorus of dissent ringing in his ears that Adenauer left for Paris on 20 January – with his daughter Ria – for the final stages of negotiation with de Gaulle. There had, however, been a hitch. Osterheld had found out that a governmental agreement between the two countries might well be unconstitutional under the Basic Law, and might be successfully challenged in the Federal Constitutional Court in Karlsruhe. The only way round the problem was to convert the governmental agreement into a treaty. But the difficulty with that was that the treaty, if there was to be one, would require the approval of the Bundestag and the Bundesrat.

Adenauer then took his decision. A treaty it would be. Nevertheless, the row over de Gaulle's veto on Britain had followed him to Paris. On 20 January, Adenauer and Ria were dining with Blankenhorn and his wife at the German Embassy when Jean Monnet burst in, quickly followed by Hallstein. All three, Blankenhorn, Hallstein and Monnet, almost went on their knees to Adenauer with the request that the Franco-German treaty should be linked with an assurance that negotiations with Britain would continue. Adenauer refused their request. All he would undertake to do was to ask de Gaulle to agree that the EEC Commission should compile a report on the matter.

The signature of the Franco-German Treaty took place on 22 January 1963. To be sure, there were some minor panics. When the two leaders decided that it should be a treaty rather than an inter-governmental agreement, there was confusion in the German delegation. Proper paper had to be found, and a proper folder. In the event, nobody could find the blue-edged paper on which West German treaties were inscribed; French red-edged paper was used instead. There was no proper folder until one was found at the Hermès shop in the Faubourg St-Honoré. It was not perfect, but it would just have to do.

The scenes at the signature itself were reminiscent of a different, and older, world. There was much speech-making, and de Gaulle kissed Adenauer on both cheeks. Adenauer, it was reported, shed a tear or two. But what Adenauer had not realised was that his aims in the treaty were quite different from those of de Gaulle. He was still, in his old age, intent on the grand reconciliation. De Gaulle wanted to pull West Germany out of NATO to be the subservient partner in a French-dominated Europe. If there was a meeting of old men, there was certainly no meeting of minds.

Adenauer returned to Bonn to another critical broadside. Blankenhorn, formerly one of his closest and most admiring advisers, reflected the general feeling when he wrote that the treaty was 'the inadequate achievement of a man who, simply because of his age, is no longer able to see clearly a complex, subtle appropriate place for the Federal Republic in foreign affairs . . .'[18] Ambassador Dowling was recalled to Washington by a furious Dean Rusk. George Ball regarded the treaty as no less than a Franco-German conspiracy. Macmillan never wrote again to Adenauer during the time he was still in office. Kennedy sent a threatening letter with the returning Ambassador Dowling, saying that the mood in the United States was moving in favour of withdrawal from Europe.

At that point, Erhard thought that it was time for him to put his head above what seemed to be a disintegrating political parapet. He gave two press interviews, one to the *Düsseldorf Mittag* and the other to the *Süddeutsche Zeitung*. In the first, he criticised France for not honouring previous agreements with the Federal Republic, and urged careful consideration before the Franco-German Treaty was ratified; in the second, he said that he was prepared to take on the burden of the Chancellorship whenever his party asked him to do so. The interviews were published in both newspapers on 5 February. The next day, Adenauer ostentatiously turned his back to Erhard as they sat side by side on the Cabinet bench in the Bundestag, and walked out without saying a word to him.

Adenauer then wrote a carefully considered letter to Erhard – not despatched until 26 February. Erhard replied on the 27th. But Adenauer made the mistake of leaking the text of the two letters to the *Frankfurter Allgemeine Zeitung*. The texts, needless to say, were seized on by the British ambassador, Sir Frank Roberts, and sent to London as evidence of the serious rift between the two men. Adenauer's letter was, by his standards, reasonably temperate. 'Should the Minister of Economics,' he wrote, 'count it necessary to act in any political capacity, he must reach agreement with the Foreign Office; under certain circumstances my decision must also be sought as I determine the direction of policy.' What was remarkable was Erhard's reply. 'The criticism you have expressed must be rejected,' went his letter; '. . . in a final discussion with Minister Schröder, before the beginning of his holiday, I entirely agreed with him in his judgement of policy affecting European unity.' Then came the final insult: 'You will understand that under these circumstances I will not be attending the Cabinet meeting on 28 February.'[19]

From that day on it was open warfare. Erhard, with Schröder's support, led the charge to incorporate a preamble into the Franco-German Treaty which would support NATO, partnership with the United States, British accession to the EEC and liberal international trade policies – in other words, all the things which the treaty was designed to oppose. Adenauer, for his part, drip-fed journalists with comments on Erhard's inadequacies. The process continued during his spring holiday in the Villa Collina. Apart from a brief return to Bonn to take part in a Bundestag debate on a motion to embargo sales of pipeline to the Soviet bloc, he spent from 16 March to 19 April 1963 in Cadenabbia, with his daughters Ria (for a few days) and Lotte. Libet was to arrive later. Journalists followed in their tracks, eager to hear the latest poison about Erhard.

Depressingly, it poured with rain most of the time. Even a game of *boccia* put on for a visiting television crew was almost washed out. Nevertheless, the bad weather did not discourage those who came to call on him. There were journalists in plenty at the end of March and the beginning of April. Apart from listening to Adenauer's complaints about Erhard, they were able to tell him that the CDU results in the elections on 31 March in the Rhineland-Palatinate had been a disaster, that the polls were showing an equal drop in CDU popularity nationwide, and that Erhard was in fact the popular choice for the succession.

As for official business, although Adenauer was meant to be on holiday, a major event took place on 4 April. On that day, a delegation from all three coalition parties, including Schröder, Mende and, most important, Ernst Majonica, the chairman of the CDU/CSU parliamentary group's foreign policy committee, came to discuss the Franco-German Treaty. There were three hours of discussion before lunch. The visitors were unanimous in advising Adenauer to accept a preamble along the lines Erhard and Schröder were proposing. At the end of the discussion Adenauer took Majonica aside and asked him what were the chances of ratification of the treaty without the preamble. Majonica said that he thought that it would fail. Obviously stunned, at that point Adenauer conceded. 'Why not?' he said gloomily. 'Better a treaty with a preamble than no treaty at all.'[20] Adenauer knew perfectly well what view de Gaulle would take of the preamble; he realised that he had been defeated.

As if that was not enough, there was further bad news. On 6 April Krone and Will Rasner, the manager of the CDU parliamentary group, arrived at the Villa Collina. Krone had the melancholy task of telling Adenauer that the majority of the group now not only wanted him to abide by his commitment to retire; they also wanted him to be replaced by Erhard. Brentano, as chairman of the CDU/CSU parliamentary group, had already taken the initiative in discussions with the group's executive council, inviting them to make a recommendation to the full group on the nomination of a candidate for the Chancellorship. If, after this process, Krone went on, they decided on Erhard, there was every chance of a vote of no confidence in Adenauer himself unless he accepted their decision. Rasner agreed with Krone, and added that the only way to stop Erhard was for Adenauer to come out firmly in favour of Schröder.

On 14 April 1963, Easter Sunday, Brentano himself arrived in Cadenabbia – in his official capacity as chairman of the parliamentary group. He told Adenauer that the group wanted a quick solution. Adenauer, following Rasner's advice, replied that he now favoured Schröder. But Brentano saw this as no more than a delaying tactic, and returned to Bonn to hurry up the procedure. By the time Adenauer came back from his holiday, on Friday 19 April, Brentano had already arranged for a meeting of the executive council for the following Monday.

The twenty-second of April was the decisive day. In the morning, Adenauer summoned the diminished band of his loyalists to the Palais Schaumburg in a last attempt to stop Erhard. But the band was few in number and weak in influence. Furthermore, they told him that Schröder had refused to stand. There was now only one hat in the ring. At the afternoon meeting of the CDU/CSU executive, there was no contest. Erhard's candidature was the recommendation of the executive to a meeting of the full group on the next day.

The CDU/CSU parliamentary group met at 3pm on 23 April. There was only one name put forward by their executive as candidate for the Chancellorship – Erhard. Brentano reported the executive's decision. Dufhues spoke in support – for the rank and file of the party. Schröder also spoke in support, as did Strauss. But Adenauer was not going to go out easily. 'I am sad to say,' he told his colleagues, 'that I do not regard this man, with whom I have worked for fourteen years, and whose achievements are outstanding, suitable for the . . . position which he wants . . . I regarded as my duty . . . to say this to you.'[21]

The group proceeded unceremoniously to ignore Adenauer's advice. In a secret ballot, of 225 votes cast, 159 were for the Erhard nomination, 47 against, with 19 spoilt ballots. Erhard had won; Adenauer had lost. Adenauer conceded with a grudging speech. Erhard commented later that he regarded Adenauer's behaviour towards him as 'not very Christian'.[22] It was, as outsiders remarked, fair comment. In truth, the old man had by then – and by his own behaviour – lost the support of his former friends and colleagues. He had been dismissed by the Nazis in 1933; he had been dismissed by the British in 1945; he had now been dismissed by his own party – the party which he had built into the dominant force in the post-war politics of the Federal Republic. But there it was. The deed had been done.

The Franco-German Treaty was given its first reading in the Bundestag two days later. It was finally agreed – with its preamble – on 16 May. In the intervening period, however, there had been further developments with the Soviets. Ambassador Smirnov had indicated to the former German ambassador in Moscow, Hans Kroll, that Khrushchev wished to come to some sort of settlement over Berlin. Kroll relayed the message to Adenauer, who invited Smirnov to Rhöndorf for a private discussion. Once there, Smirnov told Adenauer the real news: Khrushchev was prepared to make a visit to Bonn to discuss the whole German question face to face with the Chancellor.

It was difficult to know whether or not Khrushchev was serious. Furthermore, now that Adenauer was committed to retirement, there was an obvious limit to his negotiating authority. Schröder, Krone and Brentano, when consulted, all thought that the matter should wait for Erhard. In view of this, Adenauer waited until Kennedy arrived on 23 June for a visit to Bonn and Berlin. As it happened, Kennedy's visit was little less than spectacular. He received a tumultuous welcome wherever he went – most particularly when he made one of his most forthright and eloquent speeches to several hundred thousand West Berliners in front of the Schöneberg Rathaus. If it had not been clear before, it was by then obvious to Adenauer, who stood silent by Kennedy's side in Berlin, where the Germans of the west looked for their security. France was a poor substitute for the most powerful nation on earth led by the young President.

In their private conversations, Kennedy did his best to be friendly. He said that Adenauer was one of the three great statesmen of 'this era', the others being de Gaulle and (perhaps less to Adenauer's liking) Harry Truman.[23] But he was not optimistic about the prospects for direct German–Soviet talks and, although he could not stop them if Adenauer was determined, he was as discouraging as he could be. There was, however, one impression that Kennedy took away from their discussions: that Adenauer was now reconciled to the existence of the GDR, and consequently to some form of *de facto* recognition.

Two weeks later, de Gaulle arrived in Bonn for the first of the twice-yearly Franco-German summit meetings envisaged in the Treaty. He, too, warned Adenauer against further contacts with Khrushchev. But, more important, he let Adenauer know that the preamble to the treaty, the enthusiastic welcome given to Kennedy and the election of Erhard had badly weakened the alliance of the two countries. Even before he left Paris, he had quoted to a group of National Assembly members a line from Victor Hugo: 'Alas! How many young ladies have I seen die!'[24]

Adenauer told de Gaulle on 4 July that he hoped France would continue with her independent nuclear weapons programme. The reason for his remark was that the three existing nuclear powers, the United States, the Soviet Union and Britain, were doing their best to get France to sign a treaty prohibiting nuclear tests in the atmosphere, underwater or in space. The treaty was at that moment high on the US–Soviet agenda – as another step in their joint efforts to control nuclear proliferation, efforts which had intensified after the Cuban missile crisis had brought home to both sides the horrific consequences of a nuclear war. In fact, the negotiations went swiftly in late July, and after only ten days of discussion the treaty was signed by the three powers in Moscow on 5 August 1963. Thereafter, nearly one hundred governments quickly signed up to the treaty, excluding, of course, France and China – but including the GDR.

It was this that provoked the last eruption of Adenauer's Chancellorship. It meant that the West was prepared to recognise the GDR as a nation –

something which Adenauer had resolutely opposed throughout his long years as Chancellor. At the end of July and into early August he summoned no fewer than eight Cabinet meetings, and berated, in turn, William Tyler, a US Deputy Secretary of State, Robert McNamara, the US Secretary of Defense, and any American or British diplomat who was unlucky enough to cross his path. He was even prepared, he told Krone, to resign on the issue immediately.

It required the visit of the US Secretary of State, Dean Rusk, to resolve it. On 10 August, Rusk arrived in Bonn to assure Adenauer that there would be an official statement from Washington and London that the signature by the GDR did not imply any form of recognition. Furthermore, the United States and the United Kingdom would again confirm the right of the Federal Republic to represent Germany (a right, Rusk pointed out, that had already been acknowledged on no fewer than three occasions).

Suitably mollified, on 19 August Adenauer left for Cadenabbia on his last holiday as Chancellor. Ria, again, accompanied him. On the whole, the four-week stay at the Villa Collina was relatively tranquil. True, there were extended sessions with the English painter Graham Sutherland, and there were odd events such as a concert by a local wind-band in the garden. Erhard visited him on 30 August and spent the day – no doubt to be told a few home truths. Lotte came and went, and Anneliese Poppinga stayed through-out. Libet turned up in early September. All in all, it was a holiday of farewells, and reflections about the past.

The farewells had by then started in earnest. On 16 September Adenauer flew to Rome, for an audience with the new Pope, Paul VI. He had always disapproved of John XXIII – and of the Second Vatican Council which had introduced the vernacular into the Mass. Adenauer had been brought up in the tradition of the Tridentine Latin Mass. The change had been unwel-come. Furthermore, he considered that John XXIII had been responsible for a regrettable slide, particularly in Italy, towards accommodation with Communism. All in all, he had hopes for a better future for the Catholic Church under the guidance of the new Pope.

The visit to Rome was hardly an undiluted success. Adenauer was listened to with respect, but it was hot and the Roman scirocco was blowing. He had difficulty in breathing and was unable to express himself in the forceful manner which he would have liked. The Pope listened respectfully, blessed him – and bid him goodbye.

On Adenauer's return on 20 September, the farewells started in earnest. First, there were the visits abroad. There was talk of Washington, but that was ruled out. London was also off the list. The Netherlands were tainted with continued anti-German feeling, and could be ignored. There remained Belgium, France and Italy. Italy had been dealt with, with his visit to the Pope and a four-day stay in Rome. A perfunctory visit to Belgium allowed Adenauer to collect another order of Belgian chivalry. Of course, farewells to France were more earnest. There was a last, autumnal visit to Rambouillet. Adenauer and Ria – with Osterheld and Anneliese Poppinga – landed at Villacoublay airport on 21 September. De Gaulle was there to greet them. The ceremonies were there in good measure; but both men knew that their own special project, the Franco-German Treaty, was as good as dead. The rest was no more than fine words.

It was now time for the farewell tour of the Federal Republic. It was not far short, in many ways, of a truly royal tour. Of course, everybody was glad to be rid of him, but the ceremonies had to be conducted in due style and dignity. There were, in fact, three full weeks of them. He said farewell to Hamburg, at a dinner in his honour given by the German Farmers' Union. He said farewell to Berlin, where he was made an honorary citizen – whatever that meant – and where Brandt made an equivocal speech, saying that the city had missed him in the early days of the Berlin Wall. He said farewell to Bavaria, where the CSU put on a show of admiration. He said farewell to Hanover and the Bundeswehr, in a march-past – and a fly-past – at Wunstorf, watched, it is said, by one hundred thousand spectators.

The grandest ceremonies were, of course, reserved for the Rhineland. First, there was a celebratory festival in the Exhibition Centre in Deutz. Choirs were assembled to sing pieces from Haydn's 'Creation'. Flags and bunting were in order – all paid for by the CDU. In the midst of it all, Adenauer could not refrain from making a somewhat caustic speech about the dangers of détente, the underlying theme, it need hardly be said, being criticism of his successor to the Chancellorship.

On 14 October, the Papal Nuncio celebrated a Pontifical Mass in Bonn in Adenauer's honour. In the evening, he went on to a reception given by President Lübke, to which three thousand guests had been invited. That done, he gave a private dinner for the faithful Globke, worn-out and ill as he was. Adenauer wrote to Globke's family: 'We thank God that He has given you to us.'[25]

The stage was then set for his final appearance in the Bundestag on 15 October 1963. It was a suitably reverential event, with the appropriate speeches. Gerstenmaier spoke for nearly an hour, saying that Adenauer 'in a hundred years of eventful German history, [was] the only one who, after a long period in government, is leaving office undefeated and in peace'.[26] But whatever the courtesies, the truth was that Adenauer had been dismissed by his own party – and all the world knew it. Gerstenmaier, however, was right on one point. Adenauer had never been defeated in a popular election, and the change in the Chancellorship, however bitter the war within the political classes in Bonn, had been accomplished in peace.

14

FINALE

'Unser Hauptleitsatz war der Anschluss an die freien Völker des Westens'*

THE VALEDICTIONS COMPLETED, Adenauer had to set about picking up the threads of a life without political office. For his official work, as a former Chancellor and chairman of the national CDU, he was allocated a small room in the Parliament building. Next to it was an even smaller room with a sofa and a little kitchen, in which the faithful Miss Poppinga would prepare a light lunch for him before he lay down on the sofa for his customary afternoon siesta. In his new office was the desk which he had brought with him from the Palais Schaumburg, a globe, and a painting by Churchill of a classical temple – presumed to be the Parthenon, but in fact the remains of a Roman temple in the Libyan ruins of Leptis Magna. Compared with his expansive quarters in the Palais Schaumburg it was, to say the least, very much more than modest.

Adenauer had announced in the spring of 1963 that his main task in retirement would be to write his memoirs. Indeed, Miss Poppinga had

---

* 'Our basic principle was incorporation among the free peoples of the West': Adenauer, in his last speech to the CDU Party Conference, 23 March 1966; *Reden, 1917–1967*, p. 481.

started to collect the necessary material, and during his last holiday as Chancellor at the Villa Collina Adenauer had himself sketched a plan for a small pavilion to be constructed next to his house in Rhöndorf, a plan which he had given to his daughter Lotte's husband, Herbert Multhaupt – a qualified structural engineer – to be turned into professional architect's drawings. It was to go, he said, next to the strip of sand on which *boccia* was to be played.

In the autumn of 1963 the signs were all pointing to a graceful and elegant retirement. Relations with Erhard were cordial. They appeared together in November at a CDU rally at which Adenauer proclaimed: 'I stand by my successor's government and, as a true friend, I shall help him fulfil his difficult tasks.'[1] Furthermore, the timing of his retirement seemed to be confirmed by Heuss's death on 12 December, Ollenhauer's on 14 December, and the diagnosis of Brentano's seemingly harmless illness as cancer. The torch was clearly passing to a new generation. Indeed, the new generation was quite happy to honour the old. On 5 January 1964, for instance, Erhard broke his holiday to attend Adenauer's eighty-eighth birthday celebrations – and presented him with a four-volume eighteenth-century encyclopaedia on gardens.

Adenauer, however, had not given up his chairmanship of the national CDU. Whatever his resolve may have been at the beginning of Erhard's Chancellorship not to interfere, he started to feel that Erhard was taking a number of wrong directions, particularly in relations with France and de Gaulle. He was particularly displeased with Schröder, whom he now regarded as obsessively pro-American and pro-British and therefore anti-French. As a result, he started to follow the politics of the day with much closer scrutiny than he had originally intended.

In mid-January, he let it be known that he was prepared to continue as chairman of his party for another two years. As former Chancellor and the party's senior statesman his re-election was assured – there was merely some mild grumbling from those who had expected him to subside into honourable and honoured retirement. But the chairmanship of the CDU, as Adenauer well knew, was far from a sinecure. The chairman led delegations when there were negotiations with other parties, for instance about possible coalitions or candidates for the presidency. He was also free to make speeches on the party's behalf, and to give press interviews. In that role he was entitled to request, and receive, any information from government which he considered to be necessary for the discharge of his duties. Needless to say, once embarked on the course, Adenauer intended to use these powers to the full.

Of course, the chief casualty of Adenauer's decision to continue as CDU chairman was the project of writing his memoirs. Although he had signed a contract with the French publisher La Librairie Hachette in November 1963, and in February 1964 was to sign a second contract with the Stuttgart publisher Deutsche Verlags-Anstalt, his renewed political activity made it very difficult to get started. Preparations for the CDU annual conference in Hanover in March 1964 took up a good deal of his time, as, indeed, did the conference itself; and by the time he left for his spring holiday at the Villa Collina on 12 April there was not even the plan of a book, in spite of the fact that he had – most unwisely – agreed with Hachette a delivery date of 31 December 1964.

Certainly, the main event in Cadenabbia the spring of 1964, rainy, grey and cold as it was, was a reception given by the publishers Hachette at the nearby villa of Dirk Stikker, the Secretary-General of NATO, to which the lions of the literary world were invited. Adenauer set out to impress the assembled company, and impress them he did. They went away charmed by Libet and Anneliese Poppinga – and fully convinced that work on the memoirs was proceeding at pace. But in fact, as Adenauer wrote to his son Paul about the occasion, 'I am only making progress with my work in my thoughts.'[2] In truth, he preferred to play *boccia* and worry about the iniquities of Erhard's and Schröder's foreign policies.

While still in the rainy spring of Cadenabbia, Adenauer also heard that he was to be made an associate member of the Académie des Sciences Morales et Politiques, one of the constituent Learned Societies of the Institut de France (as is the better-known Académie Française), at a ceremony to take place in Paris in November. De Gaulle had obviously been at work behind the scenes. This made Adenauer all the more determined to use every opportunity, on his return to Bonn, to bring the Erhard government's foreign policy back on track – and in particular to forestall the wrecking of the Franco-German Treaty, which by then he firmly believed to be Schröder's intention.

His first step was a speech at the Industry Club in Düsseldorf, at which he resurrected the second Fouchet plan for a political union of European states, which had to begin, he said, 'with joint consultations between

Germany and France'.[3] Then there were interviews with the *Rheinische Merkur* and *France Soir* in which he pressed the same line. Moreover, he announced his support for a further term of Lübke's presidency, not because Adenauer thought much of Lübke himself but because he was assured that Lübke would never accept Schröder's appointment as Foreign Minister after the federal elections of September 1965.

On 3 July 1964 General de Gaulle arrived in Bonn, with his customary entourage, for his first face-to-face meeting with Chancellor Erhard. In the morning, de Gaulle called on Adenauer at his home in Rhöndorf. The two old men found so much to talk about that, in spite of the prompting of his aides, de Gaulle was twenty minutes late for his appointment with Erhard. It was, to say the least, discourteous, but it is hard to believe that Adenauer did not take a sly pleasure at the discourtesy. Erhard, if he had not been such a pleasant man, would – reasonably enough – have been furious.

In the event, the discussions were something of a fiasco. De Gaulle gave a rambling exposition of the future of Europe, on German reunification and on relations between Europe and the United States. It went on for a very long time. Erhard made no reply, and Schröder, who was chairing the discussion, moved quickly on to the next item on the agenda. There was thus no German response to de Gaulle's long speech. De Gaulle was deeply affronted. Adenauer, who was obviously not present at the meeting, heard about it from an angry de Gaulle at a subsequent dinner. He too was affronted. Indeed, he subsequently wrote in his memoirs that 'Franco-German relations were wrecked in the summer of 1964 during de Gaulle's first visit to Bonn after my departure from the Chancellery'.[4]

That was the point at which Adenauer determined to launch his first offensive against Erhard. On 8 July 1964 he met Strauss, Krone and Dufhoes. Strauss, as chairman of the CSU, was to make a speech at the CSU annual Party Conference in a few days time. Adenauer encouraged him to insist on a revival of the relationship with France. This Strauss duly did. But Erhard responded immediately. 'A Europe that is made up of only two,' he said, 'is not the Europe that the Federal Government had in mind.'[5]

But the offensive was far from over. Adenauer had discovered a young politician who he thought would, in the course of time, inherit his mantle – Rainer Barzel. Barzel was only forty years old in 1964, and came from the

Catholic wing of the CDU. He was young, deeply Catholic, and very conservative. Adenauer was very much taken with Barzel, and applauded the way in which Barzel, by then deputy chairman of the CDU/CSU parliamentary group, took the reins firmly in hand during Brentano's long battle with cancer. Here, Adenauer thought, was a Chancellor of the future. He lost no time in promoting Barzel's cause to all who would listen.

Erhard was not to be intimidated. He made sure that the CDU press was on his side – particularly the *Frankfurter Allgemeine Zeitung* and *Die Welt*, and promptly denounced the 'black Gaullists'.[6] The offensive, and the counter-attack, rumbled on until Adenauer left for his holiday in Cadenabbia on 17 August. Erhard, however, with the power of the Chancellorship and a large majority of the CDU/CSU parliamentary group behind him, showed that he was not to be removed so easily.

After that first and unsuccessful effort, Adenauer's holiday was to be for nearly two months, again at the Villa Collina. By then Anneliese Poppinga had persuaded him that his first priority was his memoirs. Indeed, she had assembled documents and diaries in due order. There was nothing for it but for Adenauer to sit down and dictate the history of his life in his own words.

But there was an immediate difficulty. 'An authorised biography' of Adenauer had been written and published in 1955. The author had been an unknown journalist, Paul Weymar, who had been introduced to Adenauer at the time by one of his Rhöndorf neighbours, Maria Schlüter-Hermkes. Adenauer had in turn introduced Weymar to his daughters, to his old friend Ella Schmittmann and, not least, to his gardener from the Max-Bruch-Strasse in Cologne, Josef Giesen. Not content with that, he had dictated to Weymar large sections of the book.

That in itself had given rise to a problem. Weymar's book had been, to put it mildly, a flop. It had been regarded by both the publishing world and the public at large as no more than a poorly written hagiography. Adenauer had then done his best to dissociate himself from the whole venture. On publication of the book, he had sent a telegram to the editor. The telegram was terse: 'In *Kölnische Rundschau* of today there appears an advertisement that "Dr Adenauer's personal support opened the safe for the biographer". Ask you immediately to correct that, otherwise I will oppose in public.'[7] The editor had objected. 'For Herrn Weymar,' he wrote, 'it is understandably difficult to put his name to chapters and episodes, versions of which you, disregarding his opinion, have decided alone. As you know, Herr Weymar did not want to be mentioned by his own name. I asked him to do so to counter rumours that you, in reality, are the author.'[8]

To that, of course, there was no answer. But the consequence was clear. Enough people knew the truth behind the Weymar 'authorised biography' to realise that it was in effect the first part of Adenauer's own memoirs. This being so, and Adenauer having disowned the book, it was better for him in his formal, and openly avowed, memoirs to pass over his early life and record only the period of his Chancellorship; and this, apart from a few glancing references to his life prior to 1945, he proceeded to do.

Serious work started in Cadenabbia during his long late summer holiday of 1964. Miss Poppinga had collected a mass of material: letters and notes, extracts from speeches, official documents, diaries, parliamentary agendas, and so on. Throughout the second half of August, the whole of September and the first half of October Adenauer studied the material and dictated to her his comments. The drafts were then corrected and typed again.

This laborious process had two results. The first was that the book was ponderous and difficult to read. As Adenauer said himself, 'I am not writing an exercise in stylistic composition.'[9] The first volume starts well enough but soon becomes a set of seemingly unconnected memoranda. Indeed, this is what Adenauer seems to have intended. He believed that the content of his book should stand on its own without embellishment. As such there is none of the compelling elegance of a de Gaulle or a Churchill. The second consequence was that his memoirs concentrated heavily on foreign policy. There is little coverage of domestic affairs (which, happily, allowed him almost to ignore Erhard).

By the end of his Cadenabbia holiday Adenauer had completed three out of the thirteen chapters of the first volume. He had worked with diligence and discipline, as had Miss Poppinga, although neither of them was in the best of health – Adenauer, in fact, had slipped when getting out of the bath and had broken three ribs. But they were well enough to return to Bonn on 17 October 1964, and he was able to send the first chapter to his publishers as evidence that he was making progress.

Once back in Bonn, however, Adenauer proceeded to launch a second offensive against the Erhard government. In an interview given to the weekly *Bild am Sonntag* and published on 1 November, he accused the government of ruining relations with France and of treating de Gaulle with discourtesy.

Furthermore, he warned that a future French government might well turn away from Germany and towards the Soviet Union. Germany would again be encircled. Having delivered that broadside, he then set off for Paris for his investiture at the Institut de France. In his speech of thanks for the honour bestowed on him, he reiterated the main lines of his policy towards France, citing by name two Frenchmen who had been his allies in the process of Franco-German reconciliation – Robert Schuman and Charles de Gaulle. For this occasion, however, since it was a formal speech to be delivered to a foreign audience, he had taken the trouble to clear the text with Erhard. In fact, he had asked Erhard whether there was any way he could help with de Gaulle. Erhard, who was always anxious to avoid disputes with his party chairman, responded generously, and Adenauer was given a brief to discuss one of the main points of tension at the time, the agricultural policy of the EEC.

Adenauer, of course, did not stop there. He had two long talks with de Gaulle, in which both agreed that sooner or later the Russians would have to make peace with the rest of Europe by abandoning Soviet-style Communism. But de Gaulle went further. He talked of French export credits to the Soviet Union as a means of giving a helping hand to French industry. At that point Adenauer became worried. It seemed, as he said to Krone on his return to Bonn, that de Gaulle 'would one day get involved with Moscow. His most important motive for concluding the Franco-German Treaty was to prevent that and to block the road through Germany to Moscow.'[10] Erhard and Schröder were, in his view, wrecking his whole strategy.

Political manoeuvring was all very well; and, if the truth be told, Adenauer always enjoyed it. But his publishers were not slow to remind him that he still had a contract to produce his memoirs, and time was running short. There was work to be done. In December 1964 the small pavilion, reserved exclusively for his writing, was complete; Miss Poppinga had moved into the guest room in Rhöndorf; and work began in earnest. In truth, it was a dreadful chore – he referred to his book as 'my frightful task' or 'my duty exercise'.[11] On the other hand, he set about his task with the same discipline and attention to detail as with everything else. Admittedly, Miss Poppinga had from time to time to remind him of the grindstone to which his nose had to be applied, and that caused irritation. But the work was done, even if it was done under the greatest pressure. Adenauer was forced to set aside half of every weekday and all weekends for the task. His labours even stretched into his spring holiday in Cadenabbia. In the event, the first volume was completed there in what turned out to be the beautiful weather of late April 1965, and, after revision, was sent to his publishers in mid-June.

It is in itself remarkable that a man aged eighty-nine, who had, after all, led a full and often hectic life, had the energy for such a burdensome task. But what is even more remarkable is that Adenauer was at the same time planning a third offensive against Erhard and Schröder. The trigger for the offensive was a press conference which de Gaulle gave on 5 February 1965. The General's key theme was the 'Europeanisation of the German Question'. In other words, the Soviets should abandon their totalitarian regime, a free Europe would stretch 'from the Atlantic to the Urals', and Germany would be reunited, with the Oder–Neisse line as its eastern frontier, as a nuclear-free territory in friendship with all its neighbours. De Gaulle even went as far as to drink a toast, at a dinner to a departing Soviet ambassador, to the traditional friendship between France and Russia.

That was enough for Adenauer. At the thirteenth CDU Party Conference in Düsseldorf in March, he made an outspoken attack on both the Bonn and the Paris governments. He criticised the Bonn government for failing to establish a sensible relationship with Paris, and he warned de Gaulle that 'our fate is France's fate. If we are swallowed up by the Russians, they will also devour the French.'[12] At the conference, he ostentatiously avoided Erhard. The press, indeed, took a number of revealing photographs of the two men – sitting side by side but looking in opposite directions.

The main conspiracy finally to dislodge Erhard was hatched when Krone visited the Villa Collina from 30 April to 2 May 1965. Erhard's poll ratings had fallen very badly, and the group in Cadenabbia was unanimous in the belief that he would lose the September federal elections. Adenauer wanted Krone to replace him, but Krone was reluctant, pleading advancing years. Rasner, when consulted, thought that the parliamentary group would do nothing to bring Erhard down but that if he resigned they would elect Barzel in his place. The one conspirator who had no chance was the one who was most anxious for the job, Gerstenmaier.

The plot lost momentum for a while after Adenauer's return on 7 May. His train, the 'Rheingold Express', collided with a tractor which had stalled on a level crossing just north of Koblenz. Fortunately, the train had not been travelling at speed and the accident was not serious. It was enough, however, to put Adenauer out of action for three weeks, confined to his bed in Rhöndorf. Once recovered, however, he returned to the fray. He soon discovered that President Lübke would be unwilling to accept Erhard as Chancellor after the elections, assuming that the current coalition stayed in office. Adenauer promptly invited Lübke to Rhöndorf, where they had a long discussion about the alternatives. The Federal President was thus cleverly lured into deep involvement in the conspiracy against Erhard.

At the beginning of June there were further conversations between Guttenberg and Wehner about a 'grand coalition'. Adenauer was aware of the discussions, and did nothing to discourage them. As Krone noted, Adenauer remarked that there was no question of saying 'not with the Social Democrats at any price'.[13] But by then time for the conspiracy was running out. By July, the election campaign had as good as begun, and it was certainly not the moment for a leadership struggle. Besides, Erhard's poll ratings had turned upwards. He was no longer a soft target.

Adenauer came to the view that an SPD victory would be even worse than an Erhard victory, and resigned himself to the task of demonstrating party unity. Even at the age of eighty-nine, he took an active part in the campaign. True, he no longer criss-crossed the whole country. He concentrated on meetings in the Rhineland – although Strauss did manage to persuade him to speak at a mass rally in Nuremberg. His theme, of course, was the usual one. The worst that could befall the country would be an SPD government; it would lead inexorably to Germany becoming a Soviet satellite. Nor had he lost his ability to please a crowd – particularly with his own special brand of withering sarcasm. In fact, only Erhard was able to draw larger crowds at his rallies.

The results of the elections of 19 September 1965 were, in the event, a triumph for Erhard. The CDU/CSU came out with 47.6 per cent of the vote – against 45.3 per cent in 1961 – and only three seats short of an absolute majority in the Bundestag. All talk – indeed all planning of talk – about getting rid of Erhard was no longer in the realm of political reality. The conspiracy had failed. Adenauer found himself reduced to an unsavoury campaign to prevent the reappointment of Schröder as Foreign Minister. He claimed, in an interview with *Welt am Sonntag* on 10 October, that the Federal President had the right to reject the appointment of a minister even if the grounds for refusal were political. He then wrote to Lübke on 19 October urging him to reject Schröder's re-appointment. Lübke was tempted, but was sensible enough to take advice from the Federal Constitutional Court. The advice, when it came was clear. If the Federal President refused to appoint a minister on purely political grounds he would lose the ensuing constitutional battle, and that the only proper course of action then would be for him to resign.

Adenauer left again for Cadenabbia on 25 October. On the following day Schröder's re-appointment was confirmed. When Adenauer was seen off at Bonn railway station by his old allies, Krone and Globke, he told them that he had by now had enough, and wished to relinquish the post of chairman of the CDU when it came up for election in March 1966. In giving up political life, he said, his only consolation was that the first volume of his memoirs, published two weeks earlier, was selling well. He had at last achieved financial success.

But there was, after all, to be one last political campaign. In August 1965, the United States, after extensive discussions with the Soviets, had proposed a nuclear weapons non-proliferation treaty. Its intentions were clear. 'Every state that is a party to this treaty,' went Article I, '. . . commits itself not to give support to a non-nuclear state for the production of nuclear weapons.'[14] If adopted, it would put an end to Adenauer's ambitions for Germany as a political force of the first rank backed by access, direct or indirect through alliance, to a nuclear arsenal. During his election speeches in September he denounced the proposed treaty as a betrayal – as the end of NATO. The campaign lasted beyond the elections and into the late autumn, with further speeches and a flurry of letters. The truth was, however, that nobody was any longer listening. His interventions were disregarded.

On 5 January 1966 Adenauer celebrated his ninetieth birthday. The public and private celebrations took two days. Deputations came to Bonn from all over West Germany on the first day, with the customary array of gifts. On the second day there was a Pontifical Mass with all his family in attendance, a reception for more than a thousand guests in the parliamentary building, a dinner given in his honour by President Lübke, and a ceremonial parade in the Hofgarten. It was nearly midnight when Adenauer and Lübke appeared side by side on the balcony of Bonn University to accept the applause from the large crowd which had waited for them.

It seemed then as though Adenauer had achieved the dignity of old age and was above the normal run of political intrigue. Nevertheless, there was to be one final – and ultimately futile – effort: to prevent Erhard from taking over as CDU national party chairman. Adenauer did all he could to promote Barzel for the post. But everybody knew that Barzel was Adenauer's man. Furthermore, it was clear that Barzel had ambitions beyond the CDU chairmanship, and there were other ambitious young men, including Helmut Kohl, Minister-President of the Rhineland-Palatinate, who were prepared to lead the move to block the appointment of a contemporary. Besides, at the crucial moment, in February 1966, Barzel went off on a skiing holiday.

In the end, the cause was lost. Erhard was duly elected party chairman, with Barzel as his deputy. On 25 March, two days after Erhard's election, Adenauer left for a month's holiday at the Villa Collina in Cadenabbia. He was obviously irritated, and needed the mild spring air of Lake Como to restore his temper. As it happened, it was the time fixed for the Austrian painter, Oskar Kokoschka, to paint a portrait of Adenauer which was later to hang in the Bundestag. The days were long and friendly. The two old men got on well together; the conversations ranged over all the problems of mankind. The spirits were duly restored.

After Cadenabbia, there were two last journeys to make. In May 1966, Adenauer was invited to Israel. The former Prime Minister and Adenauer's old friend, Ben-Gurion, had prompted the invitation from the Israeli government. It was a difficult task, but the visit was, on the whole, a success. Adenauer, as might be expected, did all the right things. On arrival at Lod airport he announced that 'this is one of the most solemn and beautiful moments of my life . . . never did I believe, when I became Chancellor, that I would one day be invited to visit Israel.'[15] Of course there were anti-German demonstrations, and there was a deliberate act of discourtesy from Ben-Gurion's successor as Prime Minister, Levi Eshkol, who refused to go to a party given in Adenauer's honour – and let it be known that the slight was intended. Adenauer went on to visit the western sector of Jerusalem, Mount Tabor, Nazareth and, finally, Ben-Gurion's own kibbutz. But, as he left – being Adenauer – he could not help lecturing his hosts. Sooner or later, he said, they would have to get on with their neighbours – 'you can't go on running around with weapons'.[16]

Once home, there were three things which occupied his attention: his memoirs (thanks to the persistence of Miss Poppinga); his family, particularly his grandchildren; and *boccia* with his son Paul, by then a permanent resident in Rhöndorf. Even the Landtag elections of North Rhine–Westphalia of 10 July 1966 failed to rouse his enthusiasm – and were anyway a disaster for the CDU. Furthermore, when Erhard was finally brought down by the collapse of his government in November 1966, Adenauer had little influence in the appointment of Kiesinger as Chancellor – at the head of a 'grand coalition', with, of all people, Willy Brandt as Foreign Minister. In fact, in those turbulent weeks, Adenauer was much more intent on the successful marketing of the second volume of his memoirs, which had been published on 27 October.

All in all, it was time at long last to accept the inevitable. Events were passing him by. He spent more time sitting in his garden, particularly when the sun was setting over the Eifel on the far side of the Rhine. He was as happy as he had ever been with the visits of his grandchildren, with his walks in his garden, and with the daily inspection of his roses. It was as though, now that political office – and influence – had gone for good, he reverted to the kindly old man of the period during the Second World War, showing the generous, and even gentle, side of his character – rather than the brutal side which stamped his political career. There was more time, too, for Cadenabbia and the Villa Collina – a further holiday, for instance, from 5 September to 12 October.

As it happened, that holiday was to be his last. The old man was feeling tired, and his heart was giving him more trouble. The last stay at the Villa Collina took on an elegiac quality, as did the autumnal weather – and Adenauer's own reflections on the frailty of human life. Furthermore, on his return to Rhöndorf, a further bout of influenza in November kept him in bed for nearly three weeks. He was by then not only feeling but looking tired – and all of his ninety years.

There was, in fact, to be one more journey – to Spain, in February 1967. The Spanish government organised the event and gave Adenauer almost a hero's welcome. He was much taken with Generalissimo Franco, whom he found modest and thoughtful. Franco, of course, was delighted to see him, since Spain at the time was in almost total diplomatic isolation. The carefully controlled Spanish press described him as 'the Grand Old Man of Europe' and his reception in Spain as his 'apotheosis'. Everywhere he went, he was attentively looked after – at the Prado, the Escorial, the Valle de los Caïdos, and Toledo cathedral. He was entertained by Prince Juan Carlos and Princess Sophia. It was all done in the grandest manner.

The highlight of his Spanish visit was a speech he gave on 16 February to an invited audience of more than a thousand at the Ateneo club in Madrid.

He warned his listeners that the Soviet Union was not, and could never be, part of Europe. But Europe, he argued, needed to be united in order to counter the nuclear duopoly of the Soviets and the Americans – 'the greatest danger to the nations of the rest of the world'.[17] Furthermore, Spain could not remain for ever outside the European Community. Adenauer was at his majestic best; and his audience could not have been more pleased.

Nevertheless, there is a footnote to his speech in Madrid. In private, and in spite of the public rhetoric, there is some – admittedly sketchy – evidence that Adenauer was finally coming round to the view that some sort of deal with the Soviet Union had to be struck. Oddly enough, in view of past antagonisms, it was Willy Brandt who is quoted as saying, in Wiesbaden on 2 June 1969, 'I saw Adenauer in the last years more frequently than Kiesinger did. Adenauer told me in one of our last talks that "we should talk to the Russians. We should deal with the Soviets in some other way, different to what my successors were doing. Herr Brandt, they were doing it all wrong."'[18] Brandt, of course, was in the middle of an election campaign, but it is difficult to believe that he would tell an outright lie which could easily be detected. If Brandt was right, however, he had a formidable authority for what was to become the new Ostpolitik.

Be that as it may, once back in Rhöndorf, after stopping on the way in Paris to call on de Gaulle, Adenauer went on making notes for his last volume of memoirs and playing *boccia* with Paul. There were few visitors apart, of course, from his family. Life took on a slower rhythm – with long conversations with Paul and long evenings listening to his favourite music – Haydn, Mozart and, above all, Schubert.

On 29 March 1967 Adenauer had his second heart attack. As in the spring of 1962 it was relatively mild, but it was complicated by his by now almost chronic bronchitis. His doctors ordered absolute rest, but he was determined to keep going. He had written a long letter to the new Chancellor Kiesinger, and invited him to Rhöndorf to discuss it. Kiesinger came on 3 April. In the event, it was the last official visit of the old man's life. On 4 April there was a third heart attack, and what had been bronchitis had developed into pneumonia. His family was summoned. A team of seven doctors moved in to look after him. But there was little they could do. He gradually weakened, and on 12 April suffered a fourth heart attack which pushed him into a coma. He regained consciousness from time to time during the next two days, during which Paul administered the last rites of the Catholic Church. In his last few days, however, he was in a deep coma. The medical bulletin announced that he lay 'in deep peace' as his life slipped away.[19] He died, the bulletin announced, at 1.21pm on Wednesday 19 April 1967.

It was almost inevitable that Globke, who had served Adenauer so faithfully during his life, should take charge of the funeral arrangements. It was, of course, to be a state funeral, only much grander than the funerals of Heuss and Ollenhauer. Globke studied carefully the film of Churchill's funeral two years earlier, and saw in it a suitable precedent for Adenauer – particularly the ceremonial passage along a great river and the final burial in a modest country cemetery.

The organisation was meticulous, and the whole event went without a hitch. On the morning of Saturday 22 April, six officers of the Federal Frontier Police carried Adenauer's coffin out of the home where he had spent more than thirty years, and escorted it across the Rhine to Bonn. It lay in State in the cabinet room of the Palais Schaumburg until the evening of the following day. Tens of thousands passed by to pay their last respects.

From Bonn the coffin was taken to Cologne cathedral, where it lay during the Monday, so that the citizens of Adenauer's home town could say their farewells to their own fellow citizen. During the day, heads of state, heads of government and ambassadors started to arrive in the Rhineland. De Gaulle came, as did President Johnson, and, forgetting the past acrimony, Harold Macmillan. Most surprising of all, perhaps, was the arrival of the founder of the state of Israel, David Ben-Gurion. All in all, at the Pontifical Requiem on 25 April, celebrated – in Latin – in Cologne cathedral by Adenauer's old ally Cardinal Frings, there were twenty-five heads of state and more than one hundred ambassadors. It was, without a doubt, the greatest event that Cologne cathedral had ever witnessed.

It was late in the afternoon that the service finished. The coffin was carried down to the banks of the Rhine. Draped in the flag of the Bundeswehr, it was loaded on to a motor launch and, accompanied by three naval patrol boats, moved slowly upstream past the thousands who stood in silence on both banks of the river. As it left Cologne, four guns fired a salute and twelve fighter aircraft flew low over the cortège. It was said that four hundred million people watched the ceremony on television.

It was almost dark by the time the river procession reached Bad Honnef. There the coffin was unloaded. By the time it reached Rhöndorf, the crowd still numbered many thousands. It was carried to the small cemetery, by now floodlit and under heavy guard. Only Adenauer's family and close friends were allowed in. A choir sang a farewell; Paul said a few final prayers. Adenauer was then laid in his grave beside his two wives, Emma and Gussi. The ceremony was simple – and, to all those present and to those watching, profoundly moving. The father of the new Germany had come home to his rest.

ACKNOWLEDGEMENTS

My first thanks must go to Dr Max Adenauer (Adenauer's son) and Dr Konrad Adenauer (Adenauer's grandson), both of whom were very open in answering even those questions which they might reasonably have regarded as intrusive. The light they shed on Adenauer's life, and that of his two wives, greatly illuminated the path I was following. My next thanks must go to those who followed the project from the beginning, and who volunteered for the penance of reading, chapter by chapter, the book as it progressed: Ralf Dahrendorf, John Grenville and Max Beloff (until his death). Their comments on each chapter were both encouraging and, where necessary, incisively critical. Dr Lothar Kettenacker of the German Historical Institute has also been most generous with his time and his extensive knowledge of German history, as has Dr Alexei Filitov of the Institute of General History, Russian Academy of Sciences. Dr Filitov, in particular, has spared no effort in his researches into the archives of the former Soviet Union, and has generously shared with me his new discoveries on the Soviet side of the Adenauer story.

I have had expert help from those who have undertaken research on my behalf. Agnes Ooms in Düsseldorf has been indefatigable throughout the whole book. She has been almost the perfect researcher, with imagination, tact, ingenuity and, above all, thoroughness – pursuing even the smallest point to the end. I am truly grateful to her. Judith Greenfield, Alexander Jolliffe, Sylke Skär and Bernard Smith have all contributed on specific matters or specific periods. All our collective efforts, however, would have been to no avail without the constant and courteous help which has been provided by the Stiftung Bundeskanzler-Adenauer-Haus in Rhöndorf, in particular by Englebert Hommel and Hans Peter Mensing. They have given me great support, and I am deeply grateful.

Libraries have naturally played an important role. Pride of place must go to the House of Lords library, and in particular to David Jones, Isolde Victory, Parthenope Ward and Caroline Auty. They have met all impetuous demands with the greatest courtesy and understanding. I am also grateful to the House of Commons library; the British Library; the London Library; the German Historical Institute; the Historical Institute of Düsseldorf University; the library of Düsseldorf University; the Central Municipal Library of Düsseldorf; and the Bodleian Library in Oxford. The records of the Industrie und Handelskammer in Cologne were particularly productive.

Of those who have helped with information, either written or oral, Lord Longford has been a constant source of encouragement as well as a mine of knowledge, as was Lord Annan until his death; Lord Robertson of Oakbridge was kind enough to provide me with copies of correspondence between Adenauer and his father; Dr Jonathan Haslam of Corpus Christi College, Cambridge, Mr Anthony Nicholls of St Antony's College, Oxford and Sir Christopher Mallaby have been most helpful in steering me to the right sources; Sir Ronald Grierson filled out my knowledge of the events of October 1945 with a vital piece of information; Dr Mark Pottle of Wolfson College, Oxford has kindly provided me with material from the Lady Asquith of Yarnbury Research Project, and Mrs Mary Clapinson of the Bodleian Library, Oxford has been most helpful about the Macmillan diaries; Derry and Alison Irvine spotted for me the Sutherland lithograph which forms the cover of this book; Dr Angus Blair has given me most accurate advice on medical matters; and Mr Frank Burbach, Head of the Cultural Department of the London Embassy of the Federal Republic of Germany, has done all that he could possibly have done to facilitate my approaches to German institutions. My thanks to all of them. My thanks, too, it almost goes without saying, to Alan Samson and Andrew Gordon of Little, Brown, who have successfully guided a rather erratic ship into a safe port.

I must, however, acknowledge a special debt to Dr Mensing for reading through my final draft, and making life-saving corrections. It should, of course, be clearly understood that any errors which have slipped through the fine mesh of his net are my responsibility and mine alone, as are the opinions expressed.

The book is dedicated to my wife, who is by far my best and most truthful critic. She has had to put up with the tantrums of a husband (and author) for twenty-five years, and has always done so with the greatest wisdom and tact. I owe her more than she will ever guess.

SELECT BIBLIOGRAPHY

There are many thousands of books and articles relevant to Adenauer's life and times. Comprehensive bibliographies can be found in the two major German biographies, by Hans-Peter Schwarz and Henning Köhler, but even they are far from complete or up to date. Bibliographies are also to be found in the books under the category I have labelled 'General'. It would, however, be pointless for me to recite lists just for the sake of it. Such lists can be found through the normal processes of data retrieval. For what it is worth, therefore, the following bibliography, incomplete as it is, only includes works which have been most useful to me in researches for this book. Where direct quotations have been made, they are acknowledged in the Notes, as are references to some other specialist works, as well as magazines and newspapers, not listed here.

The archives which I and those who have helped me have used are also listed, but, where specifically referred to, they are acknowledged in the Notes. As always, there is the problem of translation from any other language into English. In general, the translations I have used in quotations from biographies follow the versions cited in this bibliography, but on some occasions I have adopted a slightly different version, derived from the original German text. Place names are a matter of judgement. It would be wrong – in English – to refer to Cologne always as Köln, to Nuremberg always as Nürnberg and to Hanover always as Hannover. They are too well known in their English version. On the other hand, it seems sensible to refer to Koblenz in its German spelling. The same is true of the names of people. In general German spellings have been used, the one exception being the shortened name of Adenauer's second wife. In English, 'Gussie' (the correct German spelling) is the nickname for Angus, and is pronounced with a short 'u'. Following the English version of the Weymar biography, I have used the spelling 'Gussi'. Similarly, the German letter ß, although officially approved, causes problems for the English reader, and I have used 'ss' throughout.

1. Works by Adenauer

Erinnerungen, Vol. I, 1945–1953; Stuttgart, Deutsche Verlags-Anstalt, 1965

Erinnerungen, Vol. II, 1953–1955; Stuttgart, Deutsche Verlags-Anstalt, 1966

Erinnerungen, Vol. III, 1955–1959; Stuttgart, Deutsche Verlags-Anstalt, 1967

Erinnerungen, Vol. IV, 1959–1963 (Fragmente); Stuttgart, Deutsche Verlags-Anstalt, 1968

Memoirs, 1945–1953 (trs. Beate Ruhm von Oppen); London, Weidenfeld & Nicolson, 1966

2. Related Adenauer Publications

Reden, 1917–1967: Eine Auswahl (ed. Hans-Peter Schwarz); Stuttgart, Deutsche Verlags-Anstalt, 1975

Briefe, 1945–1947 (ed. Rudolf Morsey and Hans-Peter Schwarz, with Hans Peter Mensing); Berlin, Siedler Verlag, 1983

Briefe, 1947–1949 (ed. Rudolf Morsey and Hans-Peter Schwarz, with Hans Peter Mensing); Berlin, Siedler Verlag, 1984

Briefe, 1949–1951 (ed. Rudolf Morsey and Hans-Peter Schwarz, with Hans Peter Mensing); Berlin, Siedler Verlag, 1985

Briefe, 1951–1953 (ed. Hans Peter Mensing); Berlin, Siedler Verlag, 1987

Briefe, 1953–1955 (ed. Hans Peter Mensing); Berlin, Siedler Verlag, 1995

Briefe, 1955–1957 (ed. Hans Peter Mensing); Berlin, Siedler Verlag, 1998

Briefe, 1957–1959 (ed. Hans Peter Mensing); Berlin, Siedler Verlag, 2000

Teegespräche, 1950–1954 (ed. Rudolf Morsey and Hans-Peter Schwarz, with Hanns Jürgen Küsters); Berlin, Siedler Verlag, 1984

Teegespräche, 1955–1958 (ed. Rudolf Morsey and Hans-Peter Schwarz, with Hanns Jürgen Küsters); Berlin, Siedler Verlag, 1986

Teegespräche, 1959–1961 (ed. Rudolf Morsey and Hans-Peter Schwarz, with Hanns Jürgen Küsters); Berlin, Siedler Verlag, 1988

Teegespräche, 1961–1963 (ed. Rudolf Morsey and Hans-Peter Schwarz, with Hans Peter Mensing); Berlin, Siedler Verlag, 1992

Adenauer im Dritten Reich (ed. Rudolf Morsey and Hans-Peter Schwarz, with Hans Peter Mensing); Berlin, Siedler Verlag, 1991

Plus numerous *Rhöndorfer Gespräche* (reports of seminars on various aspects of Adenauer's life).

3. Major Biographies

Köhler, Henning: *Adenauer: Eine Politische Biographie*; Berlin, Propyläen, 1994

Prittie, Terence: *Adenauer: A Study in Fortitude*; London, Tom Stacey Ltd, 1972

Schwarz, Hans-Peter: *Adenauer: Der Aufstieg, 1876–1952*; Stuttgart, Deutsche Verlags-Anstalt, 1986 (trs. Louise Wilmot; Oxford, Berghahn Books, 1995)

—— *Adenauer: Der Staatsmann, 1952–1967*: Stuttgart, Deutsche Verlags-Anstalt, 1991 (trs. Geoffrey Penny; Oxford, Berghahn Books, 1997)

Weymar, Paul: *Konrad Adenauer: Die autorisierte Biographie*; Munich, Kindler Verlag, 1955 (adapted and translated by Peter de Mendelssohn; London, André Deutsch, 1957; revised, and in many ways doctored, by Adenauer himself)

4. General

Agulhon, Maurice (trs. Antonia Nevill): *The French Republic, 1879–1992*: Oxford, Blackwell, 1993

Bariéty, Jacques: *Les Relations Franco-Allemandes Après La Première Guerre Mondiale*; Paris, Pédone, 1977

Annan, Noel: *Changing Enemies: The Defeat and Regeneration of Germany*; London, HarperCollins, 1995

Bange, Oliver: *The EEC Crisis of 1963*; London, Macmillan, 2000

Bark, Dennis, and Gress, David: *A History of West Germany: From Shadow to Substance, 1945–1963* (2nd edition); Oxford, Blackwell, 1993

Cary, Noel: *The Path to Christian Democracy*; Cambridge, MA, Harvard University Press, 1996

Childs, David, and Popplewell, Richard: *The Stasi: The East German Intelligence and Security Service*; London, Macmillan, 1996

Cioc, Mark: *Pax Atomica: The Nuclear Defense Debate in West Germany During the Adenauer Era*; New York, Columbia University Press, 1988

City of Cologne, collection of articles (ed. Hugo Stehkämper): *Konrad Adenauer: Oberbürgermeister von Köln*; Cologne, Historisches Archiv, 1976

Clay, Lucius D.: *Decision in Germany*; New York, Doubleday, 1950

Cloake, John: *Templer, Tiger of Malaya*; London, Harrap, 1985

Craig, Gordon A.: *Germany, 1866–1945*; Oxford, Clarendon Press, 1978

Dahrendorf, Ralf: *Society and Democracy in Germany*; New York, Doubleday, 1967

Eden, Anthony: *Full Circle*; London, Cassell, 1960

Eyck, Erich (trs. H. P. Hanson and R. G. L. Waite): *A History of the Weimar Republic*; Cambridge, MA, Harvard University Press, 1962

Fest, Joachim (trs. Richard and Clara Winston): *Hitler*; New York, Harcourt Brace Jovanovich, 1974

Grenville, J. A. S.: *The Collins History of the World in the Twentieth Century*; London, HarperCollins, 1994

Kirkpatrick, Ivone: *The Inner Circle*; London, Macmillan, 1959

Large, David: *Germans to the Front: West German Rearmament in the Adenauer Era*; University of North Carolina Press, 1996

Küntzel, Matthias: *Bonn and the Bomb*; London, Pluto Press, 1995

Moeller, Robert (ed.): *West Germany Under Construction: Politics, Society and Culture in the Adenauer Era*; Michigan, University of Michigan Press, 1997

Macmillan, Harold: *Tides of Fortune, 1945–1955*; London, Macmillan, 1969

—— *Riding the Storm, 1956–1959*; London, Macmillan, 1971

—— *Pointing the Way, 1959–1961*; London, Macmillan, 1972

Monnet, Jean (trs. Richard Mayne): *Memoirs*; London, Collins, 1978

Nicholls, A. J.: *The Bonn Republic: West German Democracy, 1945–1990*: London, Longman, 1997

Osterheld, Horst: *Konrad Adenauer in Die Bundeskanzler*; Berlin, 1993

Samuel, R. H., and Hinton Thomas, R.: *Education and Society in Modern Germany*; London, Routledge & Kegan Paul, 1949

Poppinga, Anneliese: *Meine Erinnerungen an Konrad Adenauer*; Stuttgart, Deutsche Verlags-Anstalt, 1970

Rusk, Dean: *As I Saw It*; London, I. B. Tauris, 1991

Schwarz, Hans-Peter: *Die Ära Adenauer, 1949–1957* and *Die Ära Adenauer, 1957–1963*; Vols II and III of *Geschichte der Bundesrepublik Deutschland*; Stuttgart, Deutsche Verlags-Anstalt, 1981 and 1983

Spierenburg, Dirk, and Poidevin, Raymond: *The History of the High Authority of the European Coal and Steel Community*; London, Weidenfeld & Nicolson, 1994

Thomas, Michael: *Deutschland, England über alles*; Berlin, Siedler Verlag, 1987

Stern, Fritz: *The Failure of Illiberalism*; London, George Allen & Unwin, 1972

Strauss, Franz Josef: *Erinnerungen* (2nd edition); Berlin, Siedler Verlag, 1989

Williamson, David: *The British in Germany, 1918–1930: The Reluctant Occupiers*; Oxford, Berg, 1991

—— *A Most Diplomatic General*: London, Brassey's, 1996

5. Archival Sources

Stiftung Bundeskanzler-Adenauer-Haus, Rhöndorf (StBKAH)

Archiv für Christlich-Democratische Politik, Sankt Augustin (ACDP)

Bundesarchiv, Koblenz

Historisches Archiv der Stadt Köln (HAStK)

Hauptstaatsarchiv, Düsseldorf (HAStD)

Industrie und Handelskammer, Köln

Archive of the Foreign Policy of the Russian Federation (AVP RF)

Public Record Office, London (PRO)

Russian State Archive for Contempory History (RGANI), formerly Storage Centre for Contempory Documents, Moscow

United States National Archives, Washington

Archives Politiques du Quai d'Orsay, Paris

Notes

Further publication details can be found in the Select Bibliography.

Part One: The Kaiser's Germany

Chapter 1 (pages 3–14)

1 P. Weymar, *Adenauer*, p. 16.
2 Ibid., p. 17.
3 Adenauer to Konrad Adenauer (son), 2 April 1962; quoted in H.-P. Schwarz, *Adenauer*, Vol. I, p. 59.
4 Johann Konrad's discharge papers; quoted in Schwarz, op. cit., p. 60.
5 B. Falk; quoted in Schwarz, ibid., p. 63.
6 Weymar, op. cit., p. 18.
7 Ibid., p. 16.
8 Ibid., p. 14.
9 Ibid.
10 Ibid., p. 16.
11 Dr Max Adenauer, letter to author, 4 April 1997.
12 Weymar, op. cit., p. 16.
13 Ibid., p. 20.
14 Ibid., p. 21.
15 Ibid.
16 *Neue Preussische Zeitung*; quoted in Schwarz, op. cit., p. 27.
17 Dr Max Adenauer, letter to author, 4 April 1997.
18 Adenauer in radio interview (tape from the Goethe Institut, London).
19 Weymar, op. cit., p. 17.

Chapter 2 (pages 15–30)

1 G. Giese, *Quellen zur deutschen Schulgeschichte seit 1800* (Göttingen, 1961), p. 194.
2 A. Poppinga, *Meine Erinnerungen an Konrad Adenauer*, p. 184.

546

3   *Gebetbuch für die Erzdiözese Köln, Ausgabe III* (Cologne, *c.* 1890).

4   R. Amelunxen, *Ehrenmänner und Hexenmeister: Erlebnisse und Betrachtungen* (Munich, 1960), p. 17; quoted in H.-P. Schwarz, *Adenauer,* Vol. I, p. 80.

5   Poppinga; quoted in Schwarz, op. cit., p. 78.

6   P. Weymar, *Adenauer,* p. 27.

7   Ibid., p. 29.

8   Ibid., p. 30.

9   Ibid., p. 31.

10 Apostelngymnasium report, 6 March 1894; quoted in Schwarz, op. cit., p. 92.

11 Adenauer, *Erinnerungen,* Vol. I, p. 13.

12 A student at Freiburg; quoted in Schwarz, op. cit., p. 95.

13 Another student; quoted in Weymar, op. cit., p. 33.

14 Ibid., p. 35.

15 Poppinga; quoted in Schwarz, op. cit., p. 76.

16 Quoted in Schwarz, op. cit., p. 97.

17 Weymar, op. cit., p. 37.

Chapter 3 (pages 31–44)

1   P. Weymar, *Adenauer,* p. 38.

2   C. Hilty, *Glück* (Leipzig-Frauenfeld, 1899); quoted in H.-P. Schwarz, *Adenauer,* Vol. I, p. 112.

3   Ibid.

4   Weymar, op. cit., p. 116.

5   *Hauptstaatsarchiv Düsseldorf;* quoted in Schwarz, op. cit., p. 101.

6   Ibid.; quoted in Schwarz, op. cit., p. 103.

7   Schwarz, op. cit., pp. 103–5.

8   Ibid., p. 105.

9   Weymar, op. cit., p. 40.

10 L. Braun, *Memoiren einer Sozialistin* (Berlin, no date, but probably around 1890); quoted in G. A. Craig, *Germany, 1866–1945,* p. 208.

11 Weymar, op. cit., p. 41.

12 Quoted in Schwarz, op. cit., p. 124.

13 Ibid.

14 Weymar, op. cit., p. 41.

Chapter 4 (pages 45–59)

1   A. Poppinga, *Meine Erinnerungen an Konrad Adenauer,* p. 248.

2   See the *Oxford Medical Dictionary.*

3   P. Weymar, *Adenauer,* p. 57.

4   Ibid., p. 58.

5   *Bonner Rundschau,* 4 May 1873; quoted in H.-P. Schwarz, *Adenauer,* Vol. I, p. 133.

6   Weymar, op. cit., p. 47.

7 Quoted in Schwarz, op. cit., p. 142.

8 Weymar, op. cit., p. 51.

9 Reported in Schwarz, op. cit., p. 139.

10 *Kölner Stadtverordnetenversammlung*, 22 July 1909, p. 302.

11 Sir F. Ponsonby (ed.), *Letters of the Empress Frederick* (London, 1929), p. 20.

12 Bernhard, Fürst von Bülow: *Denkwürdigkeiten* (Berlin, 1930), Vol. II, p. 512; quoted in G. A. Craig, *Germany, 1866–1945*, p. 287.

13 Quoted in Schwarz, op. cit., p. 148.

14 Ibid., p. 149.

15 Weymar, op. cit., p. 51.

16 Ibid., p. 51.

Chapter 5 (pages 60–74)

1 F. Meinecke, *Ausgewählter Briefwechsel*, ed. Ludwig Dehio and Peter Classen (Stuttgart, 1962), p. 326; quoted in G. A. Craig, *Germany, 1866–1945*, p. 339, n2.

2 Quoted in Niall Ferguson, *The Pity of War* (London: Allen Lane/The Penguin Press, 1998), p. 179.

3 'Red sky in the morning' and 'There is no more beautiful death in the world' etc.: Craig, op. cit., p. 340, n4.

4 *Kölnische Volkszeitung*, 2 October 1914.

5 Ibid., 9 October 1914.

6 Ibid., 24 November 1914.

7 Ibid., 1 October 1914.

8 Ibid., 30 November 1914.

9 Konrad Adenauer (son); quoted in P. Weymar, *Adenauer*, p. 55.

10 Ibid. See also E. Hommel, *Der Edison von Rhöndorf* (StBKAH).

11 A. Brecht, *Aus nächster Nähe: Lebenserinnerungen, 1884–1927* (Stuttgart, 1966), p. 409; quoted in H.-P. Schwarz, *Adenauer*, Vol. I, p. 156.

12 Wilhelm Marx; quoted in Schwarz, ibid.

13 Quoted in Schwarz, ibid., p. 163.

14 Max Weyer; quoted in Weymar, op. cit., p. 51.

15 Konrad Adenauer (son); quoted in Weymar, op. cit., p. 57.

16 Quoted in Weymar, ibid., p. 59.

17 Konrad Adenauer (son); quoted in Weymar, ibid.

18 Adenauer diary; quoted in Schwarz, op. cit., p. 169.

19 Ibid.

20 Quoted in Weymar, op. cit., p. 60.

21 Bundesarchiv, Koblenz: Falk papers, No. 385; quoted in Schwarz, op. cit., p. 171.

22 *Kölner Stadtverordnetenversammlung*, Vol. 1917, 18 October 1917, pp. 236–7.

Chapter 6 (pages 75–91)

1 Adenauer diary entry, 13 December 1917; quoted in H.-P. Schwarz, *Adenauer*, Vol. I, p. 169.

2 *Kölnische Volkszeitung*, 15 November 1917.
3 P. Weymar, *Adenauer*, p. 62.
4 *Kölner Stadtverordnetenversammlung*, Vol. 1918, 10 January 1918, p. 2.
5 Ibid., 6 March 1918, p. 67.
6 Weymar, op. cit., p. 62.
7 *Kölner Stadtverordnetenversammlung*, Vol. 1918, 6 March 1918, p. 72.
8 H. Fürstenberg, *Erinnerungen* (Wiesbaden, 1965), p. 264; quoted in Schwarz, op. cit., p. 183.
9 Adenauer to Hamspohn, 11 December 1917; HAStK 902/103/1.
10 Weymar, op. cit., p. 63.
11 Haig diary entry, 24 October 1918; quoted in D. G. Williamson, *The British in Germany, 1918–1930* (Oxford, Berg, 1991), p. 13.
12 Quoted in Williamson, op. cit., p. 14.
13 Ibid.
14 Ibid., p. 16.
15 Quoted in Schwarz, op. cit., p. 187.
16 Ibid.

PART TWO: WEIMAR GERMANY

Chapter I (pages 95–110)
1 Quoted in P. Weymar, *Adenauer*, p. 65.
2 *Kölner Stadtverordnetenversammlung*, Vol. 1918, 21 November 1918, p. 399.
3 Ibid.
4 Quoted in Weymar, op. cit., p. 66.
5 Adenauer interview with Lucien Chassaigne; quoted in H.-P. Schwarz, *Adenauer*, Vol. I, p. 199.
6 Historisches Archiv der Stadt Köln (HAStK), 902/24/1.
7 Haking to CGS, GHQ, 4 December 1918, WO 144/4; quoted in D. G. Williamson, *The British in Germany, 1918–1930*, p. 17.
8 Kilmarnock to Curzon, 24 April 1922, PRO FO 371/7520.
9 Weymar, op. cit., p. 68.
10 *Verhandlung mit General Lawson*, 6 December 1918; HAStK, 902/241/1.
11 'Minutes of a Conference Between the Military Governor and the Oberbürgermeister, Cologne, at the Monopol Hotel, 12 December 1918'; HAStK, 902/241/1.
12 *The Times*, 14 December 1918; quoted in Williamson, op. cit., p. 20.
13 Adenauer memorandum of 12 December 1918; HAStK, 902/241/1.
14 Fergusson to Adenauer; HAStK, 902/241/1.
15 'Notes of a Conversation in Downing Street, 1 December 1918'; CAB 28/5; quoted in Williamson, op. cit., p. 25.
16 PRO CAB 23/15; quoted in Williamson, op. cit., p. 26.

17 Quoted in Williamson, op. cit., p. 27.

18 *Bundesarchiv Koblenz*; Falk Papers, No. 385, p. 50; quoted in Schwarz, op. cit., p. 217.

19 Piggott to Robertson, 12 May 1921; PRO FO 371/5970.

20 Quoted in Weymar, op. cit., p. 79.

21 'Minutes of the First Meeting of the Thirteenth Session of the Supreme War Council, 7 February 1919'; quoted in Williamson, op. cit., p. 22.

22 *The Bystander*, 13 August 1919; quoted in Williamson, op. cit., p. 48.

23 Ibid.

24 Clive; quoted in Williamson, op. cit., p. 50.

25 Ibid.

26 Adenauer; quoted in Weymar, op. cit., p. 81.

Chapter 2 (pages 111–125)

1 Weymar, *Adenauer*, p. 82.

2 Ibid., p. 84.

3 Ibid., p. 85.

4 Ibid.

5 Ibid., p. 86.

6 Ibid., p. 87.

7 Ibid.

8 Ibid., p. 88.

9 Author interview with Konrad Adenauer (grandson), 3 February 1998.

10 Weymar, op. cit., pp. 88–9.

11 Ryan to Curzon, 24 March 1922; PRO FO 371/7520.

12 'Draft Reply to the German Note Regarding the Occupation of the Left Bank of the Rhine'; PRO FO 608/142; quoted in Williamson, *The British in Germany*, p. 65.

13 Daily Press Summary No. 45, 24 March 1920; PRO FO 371/4350.

14 F. Schumacher, *Stufen des Lebens: Erinnerungen eines Baumeisters* (Stuttgart/Berlin, 1935), p. 345; quoted in H.-P. Schwarz, *Adenauer*, Vol. I, p. 238.

15 Hamspohn to Adenauer, 26 July 1921; quoted in Schwarz, op. cit., p. 242.

16 Quoted in Schwarz, ibid.

17 Schumacher, *Erinnerungen*, p. 369; quoted in Schwarz, ibid., p. 243.

18 Weymar, op. cit., p. 90.

Chapter 3 (pages 126–139)

1 Robertson to Curzon, 18 May 1921; PRO FO 371/5970.

2 Minutes of the IARhHC, 28 October 1920, PRO FO 894/7 and Williamson, *The British in Germany*, p. 131.

3 Annotation on Robertson to Curzon, 18 May 1921, PRO FO 371/5970.

4 Norman H. Davis; quoted in G. A. Craig, *Germany, 1866–1945*, p. 436.

5 H. Nicolson, *Curzon: The Last Phase* (London, Constable, 1934), p. 58.

6 D. Gilmour, *Curzon* (London, John Murray, 1994), p. 528.

7 J. Bariéty, *Relations Franco-Allemandes après la Première Guerre Mondiale* (Paris, Editions Pédone, 1977), p. 65.

8 R. Morsey and K. Ruppert (eds), *Die Protokolle der Reichstagsfraktion der Deutschen Zentrumspartei, 1920–1925*, p. 196; quoted in H.-P. Schwarz, *Adenauer*, Vol. I, p. 253.

9 Robertson to Curzon, 18 May 1921; PRO FO 371/5970.

10 H. Stehkämper (ed.), *Konrad Adenauer, Oberbürgermeister von Köln* (Cologne, 1976), p. 356.

11 PRO FO 371/5970.

12 Annual report of Colonel Ryan, Deputy British High Commissioner in Koblenz; PRO FO 371/7520.

13 Mrs Corbett Ashby; quoted in Williamson, op. cit., p. 212.

14 PRO FO 371/5970.

15 Reported in Schwarz, op. cit., p. 254.

16 *Kölner Stadtverordnetenversammlung*, 2 June 1921.

17 PRO FO 371/7520.

18 Kilmarnock to Curzon, 24 April 1922, PRO FO 371/7520.

19 Central European Summary No. 945, 2 November 1922; PRO FO 371/7522.

20 Piggott to Kilmarnock, 12 December 1922; PRO FO 371/7490.

21 Ibid.

22 Ibid.

23 Ibid.

24 Ibid.

Chapter 4 (pages 140–156)

1 E. Eyck, *Geschichte der Weimarer Republik* (Zürich, 1956; trs Hanson and White, Harvard, HUP, 1962), Vol. I, p. 233.

2 'Summary of Events Arising Out of the French and Belgian Occupation of the Ruhr, 1 May 1923'; s5, Ch. 1; PRO FO 371/8731.

3 Ibid.

4 Kilmarnock to Curzon, 12 March 1923; PRO FO 371/8723.

5 H. T. Allen, *Mein Rheinland-Tagebuch* (Berlin, 1923), p. 336; quoted in H.-P. Schwarz, *Adenauer*, Vol. I, p. 261.

6 Eyck, op. cit., p. 243.

7 Curzon to Crewe, 28 April 1923; Crewe Papers, C/12; quoted in D. Gilmour, *Curzon*, p. 587.

8 G. von Klass, *Stinnes* (Tübingen, 1958); quoted in G. A. Craig, *Germany 1866–1945*, p. 452.

9 Kilmarnock to Curzon, 11 August 1923; PRO FO 371/8683.

10 High Commission Minute, 25 August 1923; PRO FO 371/8683.

11 GOC Rhine Army, Cologne to War Office, 23 October 1923; PRO FO 371/8685.

12 K. D. Erdman and M. Vogt (eds), *Akten der Reichskanzlei: Die Kabinette Stresemann I und II* (Boppard, 1978), p. 766; quoted in Schwarz, op. cit., p. 269.

13 *Bundesarchiv Koblenz*, 3491/D 757, pp. 358–61.

14 Adenauer to Hamspohn, 2.xi.23; HAStK, 902/253/4.

15   J. Bariéty, *Relations Franco-Allemandes*, p. 280.
16   Piggott to Curzon, 17 November 1923; PRO FO 371/8689.
17   Silverberg to Adenauer, 18 October 1923, *Bundesarchiv Koblenz (Nachlass Silverberg)*.
18   K. D. Erdman, *Rheinlandpolitik*; quoted in Schwarz, op. cit., p. 276.
19   Adenauer, note of 6 December 1923; HAStK, 902/253/4.

Chapter 5 (pages 157–171)

1   Stresemann to Marx, 16 January 1924; quoted in K. D. Erdman, *Rheinlandpolitik*, p. 361.
2   *Besuch des Herrn Reichsbankpräsidenten Dr Schacht*, 2 January 1924; report by German Embassy in London; quoted in Williamson, *The British in Germany, 1918–1930*, p. 243.
3   Saint-Aulaire to Quai d'Orsay, 11 February 1924; quoted in J. Bariéty, *Relations Franco-Allemandes*, p. 295.
4   Knox to Ramsay MacDonald, 14 May 1924; PRO FO 371/9745.
5   Kilmarnock to Ramsay MacDonald, 19 May 1924; PRO FO 371/9745.
6   Ibid.
7   Ibid.
8   Annual Report of the Inter-Allied High Commission for 1924; PRO FO 371/9738.
9   German Embassy (in London) to German Foreign Office (*Auswärtiges Amt*), 8 January 1925; quoted in Williamson, op. cit., p. 284.
10   Ryan to Chamberlain, 13 February 1925; PRO FO 371/10703.
11   *Auswärtiges Amt* to German Embassy in London, 16 May 1925; quoted in Williamson, op. cit., p. 287.
12   Williamson, op. cit., p. 286.
13   Memorandum Respecting German Disarmament, 29 September 1925; PRO FO 371/10711.
14   Minute by Nollet, 15 January 1925, Vincennes 7N3577-2; quoted in Williamson, op. cit., p. 296.
15   Birch to Kilmarnock, 1 February 1926; PRO FO 371/11307.
16   Weekly Report, GS Intelligence; quoted in Williamson, *Cologne and the British*, p. 702.
17   *Kölnische Volkszeitung*, 1 February 1926.
18   R. Amelunxen, *Ehrenmänner und Hexenmeister, Erlebnisse und Betrachtungen*, p. 81; quoted in Schwarz, op. cit., p. 293.
19   Ibid.
20   Quoted in M. Pottle (ed.), *Champion Redoubtable: The Diaries and Letters of Violet Bonham Carter, 1914–1945* (London, Weidenfeld & Nicolson, 1998), p. 153.
21   Adenauer to Hamspohn, 1 April 1926; HAStK 902/302/1.
22   Kilmarnock to Chamberlain, 23 March 1926; PRO FO 371/11307.
23   Ibid.
24   E. Eyck (trs. Hanson and White), *Geschichte der Weimarer Republik*, Vol. II, p. 68.
25   Ibid.
26   W. Stresemann, *Mein Vater Gustav Stresemann* (Munich, 1979), p. 416; quoted in Schwarz, op. cit., p. 306.

27 Weymar, *Adenauer*, p. 132.

28 Ibid., p. 133.

Chapter 6 (pages 172–185)

1 Herodotus, *Histories*, i.32 (OUP, 1951); trs author.

2 Author interview with Dr Max Adenauer, 19 March 1998.

3 Ibid.

4 Ibid.

5 Quoted in P. Weymar, *Adenauer*, p. 100.

6 Ibid., p. 101.

7 Zapf to Adenauer, 27 January 1927; HAStK 902/101/5.

8 Albers to Adenauer, 6 April 1927; ibid.

9 Quoted in H. Köhler, *Adenauer* (Berlin, Proplyläen, 1994), pp. 205–6.

10 Görlinger to Adenauer, 14 December 1927; HAStK, 902/101/5.

11 Rings to Adenauer, 26 February 1928; HAStK, 902/101/4.

12 Adenauer to Cologne Centre Party caucus, 7 March 1928; ibid.

13 *Kölner Stadtsverordnetenversammlung*, 3 March 1927, Vol. 1927, p. 69.

14 Quoted in H.-P. Schwarz, *Adenauer*, Vol. I, pp. 297–8.

15 Weymar, op. cit., p. 113.

16 Ibid., p. 112.

17 Ibid.

18 *Rheinische Tageszeitung*, 17 December 1929.

Chapter 7 (pages 186–202)

1 P. Weymar, *Adenauer*, p. 115.

2 Adenauer to Ahn, 31 July 1924; HAStK, 902/103/1.

3 *Der Spiegel*, 27 February 1961.

4 G. A. Craig, *Germany, 1866–1945*, p. 535.

5 Ibid., p. 537.

6 Ibid.

7 H. Brüning, *Memoiren, 1918–1934* (Stuttgart, 1970), p. 161.

8 Adenauer to Brüning, 9 July 1930; HAStK, 902/2/1.

9 Weymar, op. cit., p. 147.

10 Brüning, op. cit., p. 182.

11 H. Kessler, *Tagebücher*, p. 646; quoted in Craig, op. cit., pp. 542–3.

12 Adenauer to Heineman, 17 September 1930; Heineman Papers, Vol. I.

13 J. von Leer, *Juden sehen Dich an*; quoted in H.-P. Schwarz, *Adenauer*, Vol. I, p. 327.

14 Brüning, op. cit., p. 214.

15 Adenauer to Brüning, 28 September 1931; HAStK, 902/2/1.

16 Adenauer to Countess Fürstenberg-Herdringen, 22 October 1946; Adenauer, *Briefe, 1945–1947*, p. 350.

17 R. Morsey, 'Adenauer und der Nationalsozialismus' in H. Stehkämper (ed.), *Oberbürgermeister von Köln*, p. 455.

18 Ibid., p. 456.

19 Joachim Fest, *Hitler: Eine Biographie* (Frankfurt, 1973), p. 484; quoted in Craig, op. cit., p. 563.

20 F. von Papen (trs. B. Connell), *Memoirs* (London, 1972), p. 216; quoted in Craig, op. cit., p. 564.

21 Adenauer to Kaas, 12 December 1932; HAStK, 902/11/1.

22 Schwarz, op. cit., p. 339.

Chapter 8 (pages 203–212)

1 A. Speer, *Spandauer Tagebücher* (Berlin, 1975), pp. 212–13.

2 *Neue Zürcher Zeitung (Internationale Ausgabe)*, 8 April 1998.

3 T. Düsterberg, *Der Stahlhelm und Hitler* (Wolfenbüttel, 1949), p. 38.

4 M. C. Domarus, *Hitler, Reden und Proklamationen, 1932–1945, kommentiert von einem deutschen Zeitgenossen* (Neustadt a.d. Aisch, 1962–63), Vol. I, p. 191–4.

5 Ibid., p. 198.

6 Quoted in G. A. Craig, *Germany, 1866–1945*, p. 572.

7 Ibid.

8 R. Morsey, 'Adenauer und der Nationalsozialismus', p. 459.

9 *Westdeutscher Beobachter*, 21 February 1933.

10 Adenauer to Papen, 1 March 1933; H. P. Mensing with R. Morsey and H.-P. Schwarz, *Adenauer im Dritten Reich* (Berlin, Siedler Verlag, 1991), p. 72 (AiDR); also HAStK 902/11/1.

11 *Westdeutscher Beobachter*, 9 March 1933.

12 P. Weymar, *Adenauer*, p. 150.

13 Ibid.

14 Ibid., p. 152.

15 Ibid., p. 154.

16 Adenauer to Heineman, 11 April 1933; StBKAH Bestand Heineman, Band I.

PART THREE: HITLER'S GERMANY

Chapter 1 (pages 215–228)

1 Adenauer to Ella Schmittmann, 1 April 1933; AiDR, p. 101.

2 Riesen to Adenauer, 21 March 1933; quoted in R. Morsey, 'Adenauer und der Nationalsozialismus' in H. Stehkämper (ed.), *Oberbürgermeister von Köln*, pp. 467–8.

3 Adenauer, *Erinnerungen, 1953–1955*, p. 157.

4 Adenauer to Heineman, 12 April 1933; AiDR, p. 109.

5 Adenauer, op. cit., p. 157.

6 Adenauer to Herwegen, 17 April 1933; AiDR, p. 111.

7   *Westdeutscher Beobachter*, 30 May 1933.
8   Author interview with Dr Max Adenauer, 16 March 1998.
9   *Rerum Novarum*, Acta Apostolicae Sedis 1891 (trs Kirwan; Catholic Truth Society, 1983).
10 Ibid., p. 2.
11 Ibid., p. 4–5.
12 Ibid., p. 2.
13 Ibid., p. 10.
14 Ibid., p. 16.
15 Ibid., p. 21.
16 Ibid., p. 29.
17 *Quadragesimo Anno, on Reconstruction of the Social Order*, Acta Apostolicae Sedis 1931, (trs Haas and McGuire; NCWC, 1942).
18 Ibid., p. 421.
19 Ibid.
20 Ibid., p. 422.
21 Ibid.
22 Ibid., p. 428.
23 Ibid., p. 435.
24 Ibid., p. 434.
25 Adenauer to Dora Pferdmenges, 6 May 1933; AiDR, p. 128.
26 Adenauer to Dora Pferdmenges, 29 June 1933; AiDR, p. 151.
27 Gussi Adenauer to Adenauer, 4 June 1933; AiDR, p. 136.
28 *Westdeutscher Beobachter*, 28 June 1933.
29 Ibid., 20 August 1933.
30 Adenauer, Christmas address in 1951; AiDR, p. 194.
31 Ibid.
32 Ibid.
33 Adenauer to Heineman, 14 October 1933; AiDR, p. 182.

Chapter 2 (pages 229–240)

1   R Amelunxen, *Ehrenmänner und Hexenmeister*; AiDR, pp. 194–5.
2   Bonsen to Prussian Minister of Interior, 19 January 1934; AiDR, p. 197.
3   Adenauer to Dora Pferdmenges, 4 March 1934; quoted in H.-P. Schwarz, *Adenauer*, Vol. I, p. 383.
4   Adenauer to Dora Pferdmenges, 4 March 1934; AiDR, p. 205.
5   P. Weymar, *Adenauer*, p. 169.
6   H. Rauschning, *Gespräche mit Hitler* (Vienna, Lizenzausgabe Europa Verlag, 1973), pp. 143–4.
7   Ibid.
8   Quoted in G. A. Craig, *Germany, 1866–1945*, p. 589.
9   Weymar, op. cit., pp. 172–3.
10 Ibid.
11 Ibid.

12 Ibid., p. 175.
13 Ibid., p. 173.
14 Adenauer to Frick, 10 August 1934; AiDR, pp. 220ff.
15 Weymar, op. cit., p. 175.
16 Adenauer to Heineman, 4 September 1934; AiDR, p. 229.
17 *Berliner Tageblatt*, 24 November 1934.
18 Adenauer to *Kölnische Zeitung*, 6 December 1934; AiDR, p. 236.
19 Statement by J. Piggott, 3 April 1934; AiDR, p. 208.
20 Zinsser to Gussi Adenauer, 8 March 1935; AiDR, p. 244.
21 Adenauer to Heineman, 30 March 1935; AiDR, p. 247.
22 Adenauer to Dora Pferdmenges, 5 May 1935; quoted in Schwarz, op. cit., pp. 388–90.

Chapter 3 (pages 241–252)

1 *Die Staatspolizeistelle für den Regierungsbezirk Köln an den Landrat in Siegburg*, 21 May 1935; AiDR, pp. 250–2.
2 *Der NSDAP-Kreisleiter für den Siegkreis an den Landrat in Siegburg*, 23 July 1935; AiDR, p. 256.
3 *Bericht des Polizei-Hauptwachtmeisters Butt über die Vorkommnisse vom 8 Juli 1935*, 29 July 1935; AiDR, pp. 256–7.
4 Undated Adenauer memorandum on the events of 8 July 1935; AiDR, pp. 258–9.
5 *Ausweisung aus dem Regierungsbezirk Köln durch den Regierungspräsidenten in Köln*, 10 August 1935; AiDR, pp. 257–8.
6 Undated Adenauer memorandum, op. cit.
7 Adenauer to Gussi, 23 August 1935; AiDR, pp. 262–3.
8 Adenauer to Gussi, 22 August 1935; AiDR, pp. 260–1.
9 *Aufzeichnung von Justizrat Professor Dr August Adenauer über ein Gespräch mit dem Regierungspräsidenten in Köln Dr Rudolf Diels*, 29 August 1935; AiDR, pp. 264–5.
10 Adenauer to Dr Ernst Schwering, 31 August 1935; AiDR, pp. 266–7.
11 Adenauer to Wilhelmine and Ferdinand Zinsser, 31 August 1935; AiDR, pp. 266–7.
12 Adenauer to Generaldirektor Dr Ing. Franz Lange, 4 October 1935; AiDR, p. 268.
13 P. Weymar, *Adenauer*, p. 184.
14 Author interview with Dr Max Adenauer, 16 March 1998.
15 Adenauer to *Reichspatentamt* (Berlin), 26 October 1936; AiDR, pp. 299–301.
16 Undated memorandum; StBKAH VI-B 68.9.
17 Adenauer to Heineman, 12 February 1936; AiDR, p. 285.
18 Adenauer in interview with CBS correspondent Daniel Schorr, 21 August 1962; AiDR, pp. 291–2.
19 Ibid.
20 Adenauer to Herwegen, 11 April 1936; AiDR, p. 293.
21 W. Conze, E. Kosthorst and E. Nebgen, *Jacob Kaiser, Der Widerstandskämpfer* (Stuttgart, 1967), p. 60.
22 K. Dreher, *Der Weg zum Kanzler* (Düsseldorf, 1972), p. 73.
23 Weymar, op. cit., p. 185.
24 Report of Swiss Consul Dr Franz-Rudolph von Weiss, 12 March 1937; AiDR, p. 308.

Chapter 4 (pages 253–265)

1   Adenauer to Heineman, 6 August 1937; AiDR, p. 315.
2   Ibid.
3   Building specification in building police authorisation (Honnef, 10 April 1937).
4   Adenauer to Walter Braunfels, 22 December 1937; AiDR, p. 322.
5   Ibid.
6   Adenauer to Heineman, 20 November 1937; AiDR, p. 321.
7   P. Weymar, *Adenauer*, p. 187.
8   Busley diary entry, 13 January 1938; AiDR, p. 324.
9   Adenauer to Herwegen, 19 August 1938; AiDR, p. 337.
10 Busley diary entry, 23 April 1938; AiDR, p. 326.
11 Busley diary entry, 20 March 1938; AiDR, p. 325.
12 Adenauer in interview with Ludwig von Danwitz, 4 January 1961; AiDR, p. 339.
13 Busley diary entry, 9 November 1938; AiDR, p. 340.
14 *Teegespräche, 1959–1961* (Rhöndorfer Ausgabe) (Berlin, Siedler Verlag, 1988), p. 103.
15 L. Dawidowicz, *The War against the Jews, 1933–1945* (New York, 1975), p. 96; quoted in G. A. Craig, *Germany, 1866–1945*, p. 635.
16 R. Morsey, 'Adenauer und der Nationalsozialismus', p. 492.
17 C. Burckhardt, *Meine Danziger Mission, 1937–1939* (Munich, Callwey Verlag, 1980), p. 348.
18 Quoted in Craig, op. cit., p. 712.
19 Adenauer to Heineman, 15 August 1939; AiDR, p. 349.
20 Weymar, op. cit., p. 192.
21 Ibid.

Chapter 5 (pages 266–275)

1   Adenauer to Braunfels, 21 March 1940; AiDR, p. 355.
2   L. Adenauer, 'Mein Schwiegervater, der Kanzler' in *Kölnische Rundschau*, 22 December 1975, p. 5.
3   Adenauer to Ria Reiners, 6 June 1940; quoted in H.-P. Schwarz, *Adenauer*, Vol. I, pp. 410–11.
4   Adenauer to Braunfels, 21 March 1940; AiDR, p. 355.
5   Adenauer to Braunfels, 22 December 1940; AiDR, p. 363.
6   Adenauer to Dora Pferdmenges, 11 January 1941; AiDR, pp. 365–6.
7   Adenauer to Dr Wim Schmitz, 9 December 1941; AiDR, p. 371.
8   Adenauer to Braunfels, 1 July 1942; AiDR, p. 379.
9   Father Laurentius Siemer: manuscript account of meeting at Kettelerhaus in Cologne (dated 'Autumn 1942'); AiDR, pp. 381–2.
10 Dr P. Franken, '20 Jahre später' in *Akademische Monatsblätter*, January 1956; AiDR, pp. 384–6.
11 Report of Swiss Consul-General Franz-Rudolph von Weiss to the Swiss Legation in Berlin, 30 June 1943; AiDR, pp. 390–1.
12 F. von der Leyen, *Leben und Freiheit der Hochschule: Erinnerungen* (Cologne, 1960), p. 244.

13 P. Weymar, *Adenauer*, p. 195.

14 L. Adenauer, op. cit.

15 Weymar, op. cit., p. 195.

Chapter 6 (pages 276–290)

1 P. Weymar, *Adenauer*, p. 197.

2 Ibid.

3 Ibid.

4 L. Adenauer, 'Mein Schwiegervater' in *Kölnische Rundschau*, 22 December 1975, p. 5.

5 Weymar, op. cit., p. 198.

6 Adenauer to Ria and Walter Reiners, 27 July 1944; AiDR, p. 407.

7 Ibid.

8 Weymar, op. cit., p. 200.

9 Ibid., p. 206.

10 Ibid., p. 207.

11 Adenauer to Ria and Walter Reiners, early September 1944; AiDR, p. 417.

12 Ibid.

13 Weymar, op. cit., p. 215.

14 Ibid., p. 216.

15 Ibid., p. 233.

16 Ibid., p. 247.

17 Adenauer, *Erinnerungen, 1945–1953*, p. 15.

18 Weymar, op. cit., p. 227.

19 Ibid., p. 247.

20 Adenauer to Max Adenauer, 29 November 1944; AiDR, pp. 427–8.

21 Adenauer, *Erinnerungen, 1945–1953*; AiDR, p. 431.

22 Weymar, op. cit., p. 264.

23 Ibid., p. 265.

24 Report of Lt Just Lunning on interviews with Adenauer, 27/28 March 1945, dated 4 April 1945; AiDR, pp. 440–1.

25 L. Adenauer, op. cit., p. 11.

PART FOUR: ADENAUER'S GERMANY

Chapter 1 (pages 293–306)

1 Fergusson memorandum of 10 July 1945; PRO FO 1013/701.

2 O. Schumacher-Hellmold, 'Konrad Adenauer: Ein Portrait' in C. H. Casdorff (ed.), *Demokraten-Profile unserer Republik* (Königstein, 1983), p. 13.

3 *Kriegsende und Neuanfang am Rhein; Konrad Adenauer in den Berichten des Schweizer Generalkonsuls von Weiss, 1944–1945*, eds H. J. Kusters and H. P. Mensing (Munich, Oldenbourg Verlag, 1986); Doc. 27 of 18 May 1945, p. 247 (Weiss).

4   Schumacher-Hellmold, op. cit., p. 13.
5   Barraclough to Smith, 2 November 1945; PRO FO 1013/701.
6   Weiss, Doc. of 22 September 1945.
7   Political Department in Berne to Weiss, 5 October 1945; quoted in Schwarz, op. cit., p. 462.
8   Author interview with Lord Annan, 6 October 1998.
9   M. Thomas, *Deutschland, England über alles* (Munich, Piper, 1987), p. 136.
10 Lord Pakenham, *Born to Believe* (London, Jonathan Cape, 1953), p. 175.
11 Barraclough to Ingrams, 1 October 1945; PRO FO 1013/701.
12 Ibid.
13 Barraclough to Hamilton, 1 October 1945; PRO FO 1013/701.
14 Adenauer, *Erinnerungen, 1945–53*, p. 36.
15 Barraclough to Adenauer, 6 October 1945; PRO FO 1013/701.
16 Weiss, Doc. of 13 October 1945.
17 Barraclough to Adenauer, 6 October 1945; PRO FO 1013/701.
18 Adenauer to Military Government, North Rhine Province, 8 October 1945; PRO FO 1013/701.
19 Barraclough to Hamilton, 10 October 1945; PRO FO 1013/701.
20 Barraclough to Adenauer, 6 October 1945; PRO FO 1013/701.
21 Ibid.
22 Adenauer, op. cit., p. 34.
23 Quoted in J. Cloake, *Templer: Tiger of Malaya* (London, Harrap, 1985), p. 159.
24 Ibid., p. 158.
25 N. Annan, *Changing Enemies* (London, HarperCollins, 1995), p. 167.
26 Barraclough to Adenauer, 11 October 1945; PRO FO 1013/701.
27 Hamilton to Barraclough, 15 October 1945; PRO FO 1013/701.
28 Thomas, op. cit., p. 136.
29 Barraclough to Mil. Gov. 1 Corps District, 8 October 1945; PRO FO 1013/701.
30 Annan, op. cit., p. 171.
31 Author interview with Lord Annan, 6 October 1998.
32 Annan, op. cit., p. 172.
33 Ibid.
34 Ibid.
35 Col. i/c Co-ordination, Military Government, North Rhine Province to 808 L/R Mil. Gov. Det., 17 December 1945, PRO FO 1013/701.
36 Author interview with Sir Ronald Grierson, 5 January 1999.

Chapter 2 (pages 307–322)

1   CBS interview, 23 October 1962.
2   Adenauer, *Briefe, 1945–1947*, eds R. Morsey and H.-P. Schwarz, pp. 150–4.
3   Strang to Bevin, 21 October 1945: Political Summary No. 2; PRO FO 371/46969.
4   Author interview with Dr Lothar Kettenacker, 17 September 1998.
5   Adenauer in Herford: text taken from ZDF video.

6   Adenauer, *Briefe, 1945–1947*, pp. 145–6.

7   Quoted in H.-P. Schwarz, *Adenauer*, Vol. I, p. 508.

8   Adenauer, *Erinnerungen, 1945–53*, p. 61.

9   Ibid.

10   Ibid.

11   Adenauer, *Reden, 1917–1967*, p. 83.

12   Ibid.

13   Ibid., pp. 85–6.

14   M. Thomas, *Deutschland, England über alles*, p. 149.

15   N. Annan, *Changing Enemies*, p. 219.

16   Ibid., pp. 223–4.

17   Adenauer, *Briefe, 1945-1947*, p. 206.

18   Albers to Kaiser, 15 August 1946; quoted in Schwarz, op. cit., p. 530.

19   *Die Welt*, 30 November 1946.

20   James F. Byrnes, Stuttgart speech, 6 September 1946: *In aller Offenheit* (Verlag der Frankfurter Hefte, 1949), p. 255.

21   Adenauer to Ria and Walter Reiners, 3 July 1947; Adenauer, *Briefe, 1945-1947*, pp. 517–18.

22   Ibid.

23   L. Adenauer, *Kölnische Rundschau*, 13 January 1976, p. 7.

Chapter 3 (pages 323–343)

1   Adenauer, *Erinnerungen, 1945–53*, p. 51.

2   L. Adenauer, *Kölnische Rundschau*, 18 January 1976, p. 7.

3   Ibid.

4   D. L. Bark and D. R. Gress, *A History of West Germany*, Vol. I (Cambridge, MA, Blackwell, 1989), p. 180.

5   D. Childs and R. Popplewell, *The Stasi, the East German Intelligence and Security Service* (London, Macmillan, 1996), p. 39.

6   F. Pakenham, *Born to Believe* (London, Jonathan Cape, 1953), p. 185.

7   PRO FO 3049/1474.

8   Adenauer, *Erinnerungen, 1945–53*, p. 136.

9   *Geschichte der Bundesrepublik Deutschland*, Vol. I, p. 404; quoted in Bark and Gress, op. cit., p. 190.

10   E. Hartrich, *The Fourth and Richest Reich* (New York, Macmillan, 1983), p. 4.

11   Quoted in M. Gilbert, *Never Despair: Winston Churchill, 1945–1965* (London, Heinemann, 1988), p. 407.

12   Pakenham, op. cit., p. 198.

13   Adenauer to Silverberg, 24 May 1948; *Briefe, 1947–1949*, p. 237.

14   Adenauer, op. cit., p. 137.

15   H. Putz (ed.), *Konrad Adenauer und die CDU der britischen Besatzungszone 1946–1949: Dokumente zur Gründungsgeschichte der CDU Deutschlands* (Bonn, Eichholz Verlag, 1975), p. 499.

16   Adenauer to Mozer, 5 July 1948; *Briefe, 1947–1949*, p. 272.

17 Adenauer, op. cit., p. 141.
18 PRO FO 371/70595.
19 Adenauer, op. cit., p. 145.
20 P. Weymar, *Adenauer*, p. 361.
21 Ibid., p. 364.
22 T. White; quoted in H.-P. Schwarz, *Adenauer*, Vol. I, p. 591.
23 H. Macmillan, diary entry, 20 November 1950.
24 Adenauer to Schuman, 4 November 1948; *Briefe, 1947–1949*, p. 339.
25 Adenauer, op. cit., p. 174.
26 Adenauer to Frings, 11 May 1949; *Briefe, 1947–1949*, p. 452.
27 Adenauer, op. cit., p. 176.
28 N. Annan, *Changing Enemies*, p. 224.
29 Quoted in Schwarz, op. cit., p. 606.
30 Adenauer speech, 21 July 1949; *Reden*, p. 147.
31 Adenauer to Heineman, 12 June 1949; *Briefe, 1949–1951*, pp. 33–4.
32 W. Benz, *Gründung der Bundesrepublik: Von der Bizone zum souveränen Staat* (Munich, Deutsche Taschenbuch Verlag, 1984), p. 133.
33 G. Bucerius, *Der Adenauer* (Hamburg, Hoffmann und Campe Verlag, 1976), p. 54.

Chapter 4 (pages 344–361)

1 Adenauer, *Erinnerungen, 1945–53*, p. 227.
2 Ibid.
3 Ibid., p. 228.
4 G. Müller in *Auftakt der Ära Adenauer 1949* (Düsseldorf, 1985), p. 40.
5 Adenauer, op. cit., p. 229.
6 Ibid.
7 Robertson to Attlee: 'Formation of the First Government of the Federal Republic of Germany', 6 October 1949; PRO FO 371/76761.
8 Ibid., p. 5.
9 *Pravda*, 16 October 1949.
10 *Pravda 'International Review'*, 19 October 1949.
11 Office of the Political Adviser (British), BAOR 21, to Foreign Office, 26 October 1949; PRO FO 371/76793.
12 Ibid.
13 Bonn to Foreign Office, 20 October 1949; PRO FO 371/76791.
14 Quoted in D. Kearns Goodwin, *No Ordinary Time* (New York, Simon & Schuster, 1994), p. 516.
15 Bonn to Foreign Office, 21 October 1949; PRO FO 371/76759.
16 *Réalités Allemandes*, September/October 1949, p. 38.
17 Adenauer, op. cit., p. 234.
18 Bonn to Foreign Office, 28 October 1949; PRO FO 371/767663.
19 P. Weymar, *Adenauer*, pp. 475–6.
20 Ibid., p. 485.

21 US State Department, *Documents on Germany, 1944–1985*, Publication No. 9446, p. 311.

22 First source unknown: oral report from Prof. Vyacheslav Dashichev, based on information from former senior officers of the Stalin period while working on the 'Journal of Military History' in the 1960s.

23 M. Narinski, 'The Soviet Union and the Berlin Crisis' in F. Gori and S. Pons (eds), *The Soviet Union and Europe in the Cold War, 1943–53* (London, Macmillan, 1996), pp. 63–5.

24 Adenauer, op. cit., p. 341.

25 Statement of Information Bureau of Soviet Military Administration in Germany (SMAD), 18 October 1949, in *Vneshnyaya politika Sovetskogo Soyusa: 1949 god* (Moscow, 1953), pp. 220–1.

26 *Neuer Zürcher Zeitung*, 11 December 1949.

27 Adenauer, op. cit., p. 320.

28 Schuman to Adenauer, 7 May 1950; *Briefe, 1949–1951*, pp. 210–11.

29 Adenauer to Schuman, 8 May 1950; ibid., p. 208.

30 J. Monnet, *Memoirs*, trs Richard Mayne (London, Collins, 1978), p. 309.

31 Ibid., p. 311.

Chapter 5 (pages 362–379)

1 N. Annan, *Changing Enemies*, p. 225.

2 P. Weymar, *Konrad Adenauer*, p. 551.

3 Author interview with the Earl of Longford, 15 January 1999.

4 Quoted in A. J. Nicholls, *The Bonn Republic* (London, Longman, 1997), p. 88.

5 C. W. Thayer, *Unquiet Germans*, p. 224; quoted in Bark and Gress, *A History of Western Germany, 1945–1963*, p. 281.

6 *Voyenno-istoricheskiy zhurnal* (Journal of Military History), 1989, No. 2, pp. 16–31.

7 I. I. Orlik in *Sovetskaya vneshnyaya politika v retrospective* (Soviet Foreign Policy in Retrospect); ed. A. O. Chubarian *et al.* (Moscow, 1993), pp. 106–7.

8 Archive of the Foreign Policy of the Russian Federation (AVP) 082/37/74/211.

9 Ibid.

10 Monnet, *Memoirs*, p. 347.

11 S. Bjornstad, *Soviet German Policy and the Stalin Note of 10 March 1952* (unpublished research paper, University of Oslo, 1996), p. 6.

12 G. Sheffer, *Moshe Sharett* (Oxford, Clarendon Press, 1996), p. 586.

13 Adenauer, *Teegespräche, 1950–1954*, p. 173.

14 J. Faulder in 'Christ Church Matters', Michaelmas Term, 1998.

15 Blankenhorn, diary entry, 4 December 1951.

16 W. Loth, *Stalins ungeliebtes Kind: Warum Moskau die DDR nicht wollte* (Berlin, Rowohlt Verlag, 1994), p. 228.

17 AVP 082/38/239/108.

18 US State Department, *Documents on Germany*, p. 361.

19 K. Ghotto, H. G. Hockerts, R. Morsey and H.-P. Schwarz (eds), *Im Zentrum der Macht: Das Tagebuch von Otto Lenz, 1951–53* (Düsseldorf, Droste Verlag, 1989), p. 273.

20 A. Filitov, *Germany in Europe from Adenauer to Brandt in Moscow's view* (unpublished paper), p. 5.
21 Transcript from the Archive of the President, published by M. Narinski in *Cold War International History Project Bulletin*, Issue 4, Autumn 1994, p. 48.
22 Transcript published by A. M. Ledowski, *Novaya i noveyshaya istoriya* (Modern and Contemporary History), 1997, No. 2, p. 84.

Chapter 6 (pages 380–391)

1   I. Kirkpatrick, *The Inner Circle* (London, Macmillan, 1959), pp. 230–1.
2   G. Adenauer in *Flensburger Tageblatt*, 5 January 1954.
3   Lotte Adenauer in *Mein Vater*, published in *Deutsche Tagespost*, 1 May 1957.
4   Adenauer to Blücher, 12 July 1950; *Briefe, 1949–1951*, pp. 247–8.
5   H.-P. Schwarz, *Adenauer*, Vol. I, p. 810.
6   Bundeskanzleramt Press Office, *Information über das Palais Schaumburg und zum Ablauf der Vertragsunterzeichnungen*, Bonn, 9 November 1990.
7   Felix von Eckardt in interview with T. Prittie; quoted in Prittie, *Adenauer*, p. 221.
8   W. Henkels, *Gar nicht so pingelig* (Düsseldorf, Econ Verlag, 1965), p. 121.
9   Curt Garner, 'Public Service Personnel in West Germany in the 1950s' in R. G. Moeller (ed.), *West Germany Under Construction* (University of Michigan, 1997), p. 150.
10 C. Emmet and N. Mühlen, *The Vanishing Swastika* (Chicago, Henry Regnery & Co., 1961), p. 33.
11 *Manchester Guardian*, 17 June 1960.

Chapter 7 (pages 392–409)

1   Report of Allied High Commission, 3 July 1952; quoted in H.-P. Schwarz, *Adenauer*, Vol. II, p. 13.
2   K. Ghotto, H. G. Hockerts, R. Morsey and H.-P. Schwarz (eds), *Im Zentrum der Macht*, p. 361.
3   Von Eckardt memorandum to Adenauer, BA Koblenz; Blankenhorn Papers 351/10.
4   Blankenhorn, diary entry, 13 June 1952.
5   Quoted in Schwarz, op. cit., p. 34.
6   Schwarz interview with H. von Groeben; Schwarz, op. cit., p. 25.
7   Ghotto *et al.*, op. cit., p. 413.
8   C. Schmid, *Erinnerungen* (Munich, Scherz Verlag, 1979), p. 529.
9   Kiyatkin to Smirnov, 20 June 1953; Russian State Archive for Contempory History (RGANI), Moscow, 5/28/65.
10 Ghotto *et al.*, op. cit., p. 490.
11 Blankenhorn, diary entry, 9 December 1952.
12 Ghotto *et al.*, op. cit., p. 500.
13 Adenauer in discussion with Heuss, 6 February 1953, as reported in Schwarz, op. cit., p. 52.
14 US State Department press release, 9 March 1953.

15 Adenauer, *Erinnerungen*, Vol. I, p. 565.

16 Ibid., p. 569.

17 Ibid., p. 580.

18 Ibid., p. 585.

19 Ibid., p. 589.

20 Quoted in M. Gilbert, *Never Despair: Winston Churchill, 1945–1965*, p. 830.

21 Blankenhorn, diary entry, 15 May 1953.

22 US State Department press conference, 5 September 1953.

23 Schmid, op. cit., p. 546.

24 Adenauer on 4 May 1960; quoted in Schwarz, op. cit., p. 117.

25 R. Maier, *Erinnerungen, 1948–1953* (Tübingen, 1966), p. 492.

Chapter 8 (pages 410–423)

1 Quoted in M. Gilbert, *Never Despair: Winston Churchill, 1945–1963*, p. 926.

2 Ibid., p. 928.

3 M. Cioc, *Pax Atomica: The Nuclear Defense Debate in West Germany During the Adenauer Era* (New York, Columbia University Press, 1988), p. 21.

4 A. Eden, *Memoirs: The Full Circle* (London, Cassell, 1960), p. 55.

5 A. Baring, *Sehr Verehrter Herr Bundeskanzler!* (Hamburg, Hoffmann und Campe Verlag, 1974), p. 151.

6 J. Colville, *The Fringes of Power* (London, Hodder & Stoughton, 1985), p. 742.

7 Eden, op. cit., p. 56.

8 A. Filitov, *Germany in Europe from Adenauer to Brandt in Moscow's view*, p. 8.

9 Eden, op. cit., p. 66.

10 Ibid.

11 Blankenhorn, diary entry, 8 March 1954.

12 Author interview with Churchill's personal secretary, 20 March 1999.

13 Quoted in H. Köhler, *Adenauer*, p. 841.

14 Adenauer, *Erinnerungen*, Vol. II, p. 287.

15 F. von Eckardt, *Ein unordentliches Leben* (Düsseldorf, Econ Verlag, 1968), p. 301.

16 Adenauer, op. cit., p. 305.

17 Eden, op. cit., p. 170.

18 F. von Eckardt, op. cit., p. 326.

19 Quoted in Filitov, op. cit., p. 9.

20 AVP RF 082/43/303/14.

Chapter 9 (pages 424–445)

1 Adenauer, *Erinnerungen*, Vol. II, p. 444.

2 Blankenhorn memorandum, 11 June 1955; quoted in H.-P. Schwarz, *Adenauer*, Vol. II, p. 186.

3 A. Filitov, *Germany in Europe from Adenauer to Brandt in Moscow's view*, p. 10.

4 Spaak; quoted in Bark and Gress, *A History of Western Germany*, p. 357.

5 Adenauer to von Brentano, 23 May 1955; *Briefe, 1953–1955*.

6 H. Macmillan, diary entries, 19 and 22 July 1955.

7 Ibid., 17 July 1955.

8 Ibid., 19 July 1955.

9 Ibid., 22 July 1955.

10 US State Department, *Documents on Germany*, p. 455; quoted in Bark and Gress, op. cit., p. 354.

11 J. Foschepoth, *Aus Politik und Zeitgeschichte*, 3 May 1986.

12 Kiyatkin to Smirnov, 24 April 1953; RGANI 5/28/65, p. 77.

13 Korkeshkin to Smirnov, 17 August 1953; RGANI 5/28/65, p. 176.

14 Miroshnichenko to Central Committee of the Communist Party of the Soviet Union, 6 July 1954; RGANI 5/28/216, p. 123.

15 Pushkin to Central Committee of the Communist Party of the Soviet Union, 27 December 1954; RGANI 5/28/328, p. 15.

16 Report by Deputy Director of 'Information Committee', N. Solodovnik; RGANI 5/28/327, p. 66.

17 V. Falin, *Politische Erinnerungen* (Munich, Droemer Verlag, 1993), p. 328.

18 Report by Ms T Solov'eva, Department Head of the 'All-Union Society for Cultural Ties with Foreign Countries', 15 July 1955; RGANI 5/28/328, pp. 122–9.

19 Von Eckardt, *Ein unordentliches Leben*, p. 384.

20 W. G. Grewe, *Rückblenden, 1976–1951* (Frankfurt, Ullstein Verlag, 1979), p. 235.

21 Ibid., p. 236.

22 Adenauer, op. cit., p. 512.

23 Ibid., p. 545.

24 G. Schmückle, *Ohne Pauken und Trompeten: Erinnerungen an Krieg und Frieden* (Stuttgart, Deutsche Verlags-Anstalt, 1982), p. 105.

25 Adenauer, *Erinnerungen*, Vol. III, p. 119.

26 Blankenhorn memorandum, 27 April 1956; quoted in Schwarz, op. cit., p. 241.

27 G. Buchstab (ed.), *Minutes of the CDU National Executive Council, 1953–1957* (Düsseldorf, Droste Verlag, 1990), p. 848.

28 Krone, diary entry, 21 February 1956.

29 Ibid., 14 May 1956.

30 Strauss, *Erinnerungen*, p. 272.

31 Adenauer to Dulles, 22 July 1956; *Briefe, 1955–1957*, p. 216.

32 Quoted in Schwarz, op. cit., p. 295.

33 Adenauer, *Reden, 1917–1967*, pp. 328–31.

34 Memorandum from Hans-Joachim von Merkatz, 19 September 1956; quoted in Schwarz, op. cit., p. 299.

35 Ibid.

36 Strauss, op. cit., p. 274.

37 Buchstab, op. cit., p. 1127.

38 Quoted in M. Cioc, *Pax Atomica*, pp. 42–3.

39 Ibid., p. 75.

40 Quoted in Schwarz, op. cit., p. 336.
41 Quoted in Cioc, op. cit., p. 45.
42 Fax to the author from Thierry Waelli, Chief Physician, Clinique La Prairie, Clarens-Montreux, 16 December 1999.

Chapter 10 (pages 446–464)

1 Krone, diary entry, 8 October 1960.
2 Adenauer, *Erinnerungen*, Vol. III, p. 319.
3 RGANI 5/28/65.
4 Hallstein; quoted in T. Prittie, *Adenauer*, p. 259.
5 Bulganin to Adenauer, 10 December 1957; quoted in B. Meissner (ed), *Moskau–Bonn: Die Beziehungen zwischen der Sowjetunion und der Bundesrepublik Deutschland, 1955-1973* (Cologne, 1973), p. 314.
6 Macmillan, diary entry, 15 December 1957.
7 Ibid.
8 Discussion Heuss–Adenauer, 9 January 1958, as reported in H.-P. Schwarz, *Adenauer*, Vol. II, p. 384.
9 Adenauer to Heuss, 2 January 1958; quoted in Schwarz, op. cit., p. 385.
10 Adenauer to Globke, 5 February 1958; ibid., p. 410.
11 Discussion Heuss–Adenauer, 11 March 1958, as reported in Schwarz, op. cit., p. 418.
12 Adenauer, *Erinnerungen*, Vol. III, p. 376.
13 Ibid., p. 378.
14 Macmillan, diary entry, 16 April 1958.
15 Macmillan, *Riding the Storm* (London, Macmillan, 1971), p. 442.
16 G. Buchstab (ed.), *Minutes of CDU National Executive Council, 1957–1961* (Düsseldorf, Droste Verlag, 1994), p. 182.
17 Adenauer to Pferdmenges, 5 September 1958; StBAKH 10/11.
18 Adenauer, *Erinnerungen*, Vol. III, p. 434.
19 Discussion Heuss–Adenauer, 16 September 1958, as reported in Schwarz, op. cit., p. 452.
20 Adenauer, *Erinnerungen*, Vol. III, p. 428.
21 Von Merkatz report to Federal Cabinet, 16 September 1958; quoted in Schwarz, op. cit., p. 457.
22 Macmillan, diary entry, 8 October 1958.
23 Ibid.
24 Ibid.
25 Sir Christopher Steel; quoted in Prittie, op. cit., p. 265.
26 *Manchester Guardian*, 27 November 1958.
27 Adenauer to Macmillan, 21 November 1958; quoted in Macmillan, op. cit., p. 571.
28 Adenauer to Macmillan (undated but 'just before' Christmas 1958); quoted in ibid., p. 578.

Chapter 11 (pages 465–485)

1 Archive for Contemporary Documents, Warsaw (AAN) KC PZPR, p. 113; trs D. Selvage in *Cold War International History Project* (CWIHP), Bulletin 11, pp. 200–3.
2 US State Department, *Documents on Germany*, p. 560.
3 Macmillan, diary entry, 16 January 1959.
4 Krone, diary entry, 11 February 1959.
5 Press Association release, 3 March 1959.
6 Erhard; quoted in T. Prittie, *Adenauer*, p. 272.
7 Macmillan, diary entry, 12 March 1959.
8 Adenauer, *Erinnerungen*, Vol. III, p. 504.
9 Krone, diary entry, 4 April 59.
10 Adenauer TV broadcast, 8 April 1959; quoted in Prittie, op. cit., p. 273.
11 Adenauer to Brentano, 14 April 1959; *Briefe, 1957–1959*, p. 199.
12 AVP RF 4/33/31, trs Hope Harrison, CWIHP Bulletin 11, p. 207.
13 Adenauer, *Erinnerungen*, Vol. III, p. 540.
14 Ibid., p. 545.
15 Quoted in Prittie, op. cit., p. 78.
16 Heuss, *Tagebuchbriefe, 1955–63*, letter of 17 June 1959.
17 Macmillan, diary entry, 8 June 1959.
18 Ibid., 28 May 1959 and 6 June 1959.
19 Burckhardt to Zuckmayer, 18 June 1959; quoted in Schwarz, op. cit., p. 524.
20 Ibid., p. 526.
21 AVP RF 4/33/31, trs Hope Harrison, CWIHP Bulletin 11, p. 208.
22 Ibid., p. 213.
23 A. Poppinga, *Meine Erinnerungen an Konrad Adenauer*, p. 130.
24 Macmillan, diary entry, 29 November 1959.
25 Tennant to Maudling, 29 November 1959; PRO FO 371/145780.
26 Macmillan, diary entry, 18 November 1959.
27 Ibid., 19 November 1959.
28 Ibid., 19 December 1959.
29 Adenauer broadcast; quoted in Prittie, op. cit., p. 279.
30 Globke note on Adenauer/Ben Gurion meeting, 14 March 1960; quoted in Schwarz, op. cit., p. 544.
31 Quoted in Schwarz, op. cit., p. 548.
32 Macmillan, diary entry, 7 May 1960.
33 Ibid., 16 May 1960.
34 Adenauer, *Erinnerungen*, Vol. IV, p. 59.
35 G. Schröder of *Die Welt*; quoted in Prittie, op. cit., p. 282.

Chapter 12 (pages 486–502)

1 Quoted in D. Rusk, *As I Saw It* (London, I. B. Tauris, 1991), p. 199.
2 Political Archive of the Foreign Ministry of the GDR; Files of the State Secretary A 177723 (trs Hope Harrison); CWIHP Bulletin 4, p. 37.

3 G. Buchstab (ed.), *Minutes of the CDU National Executive, 1957–1961*, p. 710.

4 Ibid., p. 737.

5 Adenauer, *Erinnerungen*, Vol. IV, p. 80.

6 Macmillan, diary entry, 23 February 1961.

7 Quoted in T. Prittie, *Adenauer*, p. 282.

8 Note on Adenauer conversation with de Gaulle, 20 June 61; quoted in H.-P. Schwarz, *Adenauer*, Vol. II, p. 638.

9 Adenauer, *Erinnerungen*, Vol. IV, p. 109.

10 Kennedy Papers; quoted in M. Beschloss, *The Crisis Years: Kennedy and Khrushchev, 1960–1963* (London, HarperCollins, 1991), p. 260.

11 Ibid., p. 265.

12 Quoted in P. Brandt and H. Ammon, *Die Linke und die nationale Frage* (Reinbeck, Rohwolt, 1981), p. 199.

13 Quoted in Prittie, op. cit., p. 286.

14 *Stuttgarter Zeitung*, 16 August 1961.

15 Adelbert Schröder, *Mein Bruder Gerhard Schröder*; quoted in Schwarz, op. cit., p. 668.

16 Quoted in Schwarz, op. cit., p. 696.

17 G. Buchstab (ed.), *Minutes of CDU National Executive Council, 1961–1965* (Düsseldorf, Droste Verlag, 1998), p. 43.

18 Brentano to Adenauer, 28 September 1961; quoted in Baring, op. cit., p. 348.

19 Adenauer, *Erinnerungen*, Vol. IV, p. 130.

20 Ibid., p. 125.

21 Quoted in Schwarz, op. cit., p. 710.

22 Krone, diary entry, 21 January 1962.

23 Ibid.

24 Ibid., 8 March 1962.

25 Quoted in Schwarz, op. cit., p. 744.

26 Quoted in D. Koerfer, *Kampf ums Kanzleramt: Erhard und Adenauer* (Stuttgart, Deutsche Verlags-Anstalt, 1987), p. 640.

27 US State Department, *Documents on Germany*, p. 810.

28 Quoted in Prittie, op. cit., p. 283.

29 Adenauer in conversation with Dehler, 28 January 1965; quoted in Schwarz, op. cit., p. 489.

30 Adenauer interview with Smirnov, 6 June 1962; quoted in Schwarz, op. cit., p. 750.

Chapter 13 (pages 503–523)

1 *Le Figaro*, 9 July 1962.

2 Adenauer, *Erinnerungen*, Vol. IV, p. 165.

3 *Die Welt*, 22 and 23 August 1962.

4 J. Lacouture, *De Gaulle*, Vol. III (Paris, Seuil, 1986), p. 305.

5 Quoted in T. Prittie, *Adenauer*, p. 297.

6 Schröder; quoted in ibid., p. 295.

7   Adenauer to Dufhues, 17 September 1962; quoted in H.-P. Schwarz, *Adenauer*, Vol. II, pp. 717–18.

8   Adenauer to de Gaulle, 28 September 1962; quoted in ibid., p. 768.

9   Adenauer to Strauss, 16 October 1962; quoted in ibid., p. 778.

10 Krone, diary entry, 22 October 1962, quoted in Schwarz, op. cit., p. 781.

11 Quoted in F. A. Meyer, *Adenauer and Kennedy: A Study in German–American Relations, 1961–1963* (New York, St Martin's Press, 1996), p. 74.

12 Hermann Abs, *Rhöndorfer Gespräche*, Vol. XI, p. 212.

13 Bundestag official report, 7 November 1962, p. 1994.

14 Ibid., p. 1998.

15 Lücke; quoted in Schwarz, op. cit., p. 794.

16 Ibid., p. 810.

17 Krone, diary entry, 5 January 1963, quoted in Schwarz, op. cit., p. 810.

18 Blankenhorn, diary entry, 28 January 1963, quoted in Schwarz, op. cit., pp. 822–3.

19 Roberts to Foreign Office, 5 March 1963; PRO FO 371/169161.

20 Majonica interview with Schwarz; quoted in Schwarz, op. cit., p. 834.

21 Minutes of CDU/CSU parliamentary group, 23 April 1963.

22 Quoted in E. Mende, *Von Wende zu Wende, 1962–1982* (Munich, 1986), p. 87.

23 Adenauer, *Erinnerungen*, Vol. IV, p. 222.

24 Quoted in Lacouture, op. cit., p. 308.

25 Adenauer to Globke, 8 August 1963; quoted in Schwarz, op. cit., p. 861.

Chapter 14 (pages 524–538)

1   *Frankfurter Allgemeine Zeitung*, 13 November 1963.

2   Adenauer to Paul Adenauer, 27 April 1964; quoted in H.-P. Schwarz, *Adenauer*, Vol. II, p. 952.

3   *Frankfurter Allgemeine Zeitung*, 24 June 1964.

4   Adenauer in outline of Vol. II of *Erinnerungen*; quoted in Schwarz, op. cit., p. 890.

5   *Frankfurter Allgemeine Zeitung*, 10 July 1964.

6   Krone, diary entry, 13 July 1964, quoted in Schwarz, op. cit., p. 892.

7   Adenauer to Kindler, 27 October 1955; *Briefe, 1955–1957*, p. 418.

8   Kindler to Adenauer, 28 October 1955; ibid.

9   A. Poppinga, *Meine Erinnerungen an Adenauer*, p. 156.

10 Krone, diary entry, 4 June 1965, quoted in Schwarz, op. cit., p. 895.

11 Quoted in T. Prittie, *Adenauer*, pp. 305–6.

12 *Neue Zürcher Zeitung*, 29 March 1965.

13 Krone, diary entry, 4 June 1965, quoted in Schwarz, op. cit., p. 906.

14 Draft NNP Treaty: US State Department documents.

15 *Neue Zürcher Zeitung*, 7 May 1966.

16 Quoted in Schwarz, op. cit., p. 970.

17 Adenauer, *Erinnerungen*, Vol. IV, p. 240.

18 *Der Spiegel*, 1969, No. 38, p. 34.

19 Press Association release, 19 April 1967.

Index